BRAINWASHING, DRUNKS & MADNESS

MEMOIRS OF A MEDICAL ICON

By

William E. Mayer, M.D.

Winterwolf Publishing

© 2004 William E. Mayer

All rights reserved. Without limiting the rights under the copyright reserved above, no part of this publication may be reproduced, stored in or introduced into a retrieval system, or transmitted, in any form, or by any means (electronic, mechanical, photocopying, recording, or otherwise), without the prior written permission of both the copyright owner and the above publisher of this book. Brief passages may be quoted by reviewers to be printed in a newspaper, magazine, or online review site.

This is a story of fact. However, some of the names and details may have been changed or omitted in order to protect the integrity and privacy of the individuals involved, or in cases where the national security of the United States may be compromised.

First Printing

Library Of Congress Control Number: 2004107071

Editing by Paula Mangino

Cover art by Kevin P. Grover

ISBN: 0-97527-119-9
PUBLISHED BY WINTERWOLF PUBLISHING
www.winterwolfpublishing.com
Westerville
Printed in the United States of America

Brainwashing, Drunks & Madness

William E. Mayer, M.D.

On Dr. William E. Mayer...

Bud Mayer was an exceptional Assistant Secretary of Defense for Health Affairs. Unlike his predecessors, he came to the Pentagon with "boots on the ground" military medical experience. As a result, Bud had a comprehensive understanding of the complexities and needs of the vast military healthcare system, delicately balanced between peacetime health care in garrison and the urgent need to be prepared to support troops in the field on the first day of the next war. He is a man of high energy and clear vision who starts his day by cleaning out the "Too Tough to Handle" box. Conflict was inevitable in a bureaucracy that is inherently slow to accept change, but Bud was genetically incapable of choosing the safer, easier path. There were few battles that Bud didn't win. As one who was privileged to be a member of his team during those years, reading his book brings back a flood of memories - the urgent need - too much to do and too few hands to do it - too many obstacles - too little time. But somehow, under Bud's leadership, it was accomplished and millions of servicemembers and their families were the beneficiaries.

William P. Winkler, MD

Major General (retired), US Army

"A Washington insider during the Reagan years, Bud Mayer, knowing he has lived through an astonishing, altogether wondrous time, in the history of the medical profession and his beloved country, writes with insight and integrity. Bud Mayer is a true patriot, who served his' country well; I know because I was there for the best part of it."

C. Everett Koop, MD, ScD Surgeon General 1981-89

Doctor Bud Mayer knows all there is to know about the medical programs the Department of Defense uses to provide the best healthcare in the world for our servicemen and their families. It's not often that you find a single person who is a skilled physician, a patriotic public servant and a good writer all at the same time. But that's what Bud Mayer is. Read this book.

William H. Taft IV

Brainwashing, Drunks & Madness

This extraordinary book about an extraordinary man takes the reader seamlessly from childhood through medical school; the mud and cold of Korea to the highest offices of the Pentagon; from psychiatry to the mysterious world of the mentally ill; through an impressive list of characters from the daughter of Alexander Graham Bell to Caspar Weinberger to President Ronald Reagan. The incredible list of accomplishments in this incredible life makes the reader wonder if it is indeed fiction! It is a riveting and important book, one not to be missed. In many ways Doctor Mayer's book IS America.

Stephen Miller
High School English Teacher
Eureka, California

I had the privilege of working for Dr. Mayer during his tenure as the Assistant Secretary of Defense for Health Affairs. I experienced first hand the depth of his commitment to providing the best possible care to our military forces and their families. When allegations arose calling into question the quality of military medicine, Bud Mayer assembled a team of experts in medical quality improvement and implemented sweeping changes throughout the military health care system that restored it to one of the finest in the world. He was equally effective in strengthening the medical readiness of our forces. He convinced Secretary Weinberger that medical planning had to occur at the highest levels of military operations. Due to his efforts, the Secretary established a medical flag position on the Joint Staff. Time has validated Bud Mayer's insight and effectiveness. Our military forces today receive the quality of health care they deserve and our soldiers, sailors, airmen and marines are given the highest level of medical protection possible largely due to the policies put into place by Dr. Mayer. His reflections on his career hold invaluable lessons for the future.

John Mazzuchi, Ph.D.
Former Deputy Assistant Secretary of Defense for Clinical Services

---

This is the insightful record of a great public servant - one who effectively engaged significant challenges to the nation with tenacity and vision. The experience generated is important today and it has implications useful for our future.

Alfred S. Buck, M.D., F.A.C.S.
Partner
Edward Martin & Associates, Inc.

William E. Mayer, M.D.

I have known Bud Mayer for almost 25 years and served with him in the Public Health Service as well as worked closely with him when he was in the Department of Defense. Bud is not only extremely knowledgeable about federal medicine but is an acknowledged expert in military medicine. He was intimately involved in many of the most important military medical policy issues throughout the 80's and was a valuable consultant for those of us who ran the Military Health System in the 90's.

There is no question of his dedication to his country and desire to do the very best for service members and their families.

Edward D. Martin, M.D.
Sector Vice President
Enterprise & Health Solutions Sector

My uniqueness in reviewing this book is as a physician, and as a former assistant surgeon general and chief psychiatrist of the U. S. Public Health Service. From this perspective I was pleased when Dr. Mayer was made Director of the Alcohol, Drug Abuse, and Mental Health Administration in the late 1970's. After I retired from the Public Health Service and became President of Hahnemann University in Philadelphia I was impressed and pleased when President Reagan who knew Dr Mayer both professionally and personally appointed him as the top physician in the United States Department of Defense. I knew all of Dr. Mayer's predecessors and successors. His combined emphasis on readiness for war on the one hand and improvement in the quality of the care of men and women in active service, their families and millions of retirees influenced the quality of care for all American citizens. In my judgement this emphasis and improvement in quality of health care is of historic significance.

Everyone who reads this book will be both entertained and educated. It is the work of a man of courage, wisdom and a delightful sense of humor.

Bertram S. Brown
Ass't Surgeon of the US PHS retired
Medical Executive Vice President, US Health Care
President of Hahnemann University
Regent of Potomac Institute of Policy Studies

I had the privilege of working with Bud Mayer on a daily basis for more than three years. He is a prince of a man, and was one of the most dedicated executives in the Pentagon when it came to such vital issues as combat medical readiness. Bud and I had a shared sense of combat history — I had been wounded in combat as a Marine, and he had treated wounded Marines in combat. One of my proudest accomplishments was working with Bud for several years in order to ensure that the Defense Department developed and funded the DEPMEDS system which enabled our military to deploy quickly-usable deployable medical hospital systems that had great utility in Southwest Asia. The senior military heads of DOD were not anxious to take money from areas such as "quality of life" programs in order to fund this program, but they were quite glad it was in place once the nation went to war.

James Webb
A 1968 graduate of the U.S. Naval Academy, James Webb is one of the most highly decorated marines of the Vietnam era. He served as Secretary of the Navy from 1987 to 1988 and Assistant Secretary of Defense as well as full committee counsel to the U.S. Congress. Webb is also the bestselling author of Fields of Fire, A Country Such as This, Lost Soldiers and The Emperor's General.

I've been privileged to read drafts of both of Admiral Mayer's books. I found myself mesmerized by the sheer breathe of this man's experiences in the half century just past. Not a single living human has so much to teach us about psychiatry, alcoholism, military medicine and the human condition.

Admiral Mayer's selfless display and unyielding devotion to bettering the quality of life stands alone on a global scale. We as Americans are truly blessed to have had leaders of such caliber. Dr. Mayer's works are a testimony to what is possible when one has an impeccable value system and a true desire to strengthen the human condition.

His book makes for a wonderful, inspiring read.

Paul G. Ancich
Commercial Fishing Captain (ret)
Washington Department of Fish and Wildlife
Regional Fisheries Advisory Board
Lakes High school Tennis & Golf Coach

In a lifetime of public service, Dr. William (Bud) Mayer served at the highest levels of medical authority and responsibility, both in the nation's largest state and in two massive federal agencies. Throughout his lifetime, Dr. Mayer played a major role in revolutionizing three distinct areas of our changing society. The first area he influenced was the care of the mentally ill in California while serving with then Governor Ronald Reagan. While serving with the Health and Human Services Agency (HHS) during President Reagan's administration, Bud was able to begin the process of changing society's perceptions regarding the understanding and treatment of alcoholism.

Finally, and most important to those of us who have served in the military and seen combat in the past thirty years, was Dr. Mayer's personal efforts toward vastly improving the medical readiness of our Armed Forces. As with all of his life's efforts, this particular focus has enabled our men and women of the Armed Forces to survive and prevail in combat anywhere in the world while prosecuting our current war on terrorism.

His battles and triumphs in these fields make for an inspiring tale of the life of a great American.

Christopher William ("C.W.") Gilluly

(Dr. Gilluly is a graduate engineer with degrees in Management and Educational Administration, and a former Navy carrier pilot who flew 150 combat missions in two tours in Vietnam, and is a Lifetime Member of both the Naval War College Foundation and the Tailhook Association. During the last twenty years he has served as Chairman, CEO and/or President of three publicly traded companies and three privately held companies in industries providing support to federal agencies involved in defense, global intelligence, intelligent weapons systems and biological weapons defense as well as electronic news and business information and automation systems for the U.S. House of Representatives.)

Brainwashing, Drunks & Madness

William E. Mayer, M.D.

DEDICATION

Dedicated to the legions of honorable men and women who have served our Nation in its uniforms, and to their wives and husbands and children, and their widows, whom I have been honored to serve for most of my professional life.

And to Heidi

TABLE OF CONTENTS

FOREWARD	i
A SOLDIER'S POINT OF VIEW	iii
INTRODUCTION	v
CHAPTER 1: REVOLUTIONS	23
CHAPTER 2: MEDICAL SCHOOL	31
CHAPTER 3: INTERNSHIP	81
CHAPTER 4: LEARNING TO BE A PSYCHIATRIST	127
CHAPTER 5: JAPAN	187
CHAPTER 6: HOSPITAL SHIP REPOSE	213
CHAPTER 7: MARINES IN KOREA	229
CHAPTER 8: JAPAN REDUX AND BRAINWASHING	255

CHAPTER 9: EXPLORING THE PEACETIME ARMY	301
CHAPTER 10: REVOLUTIONIZING MENTAL HEALTH	341
CHAPTER 11: BIG GOVERNMENT 101 – CALIFORNIA	383
CHAPTER 12: REVELATIONS IN ALCOHOLISM	419
CHAPTER 13: ALCOHOL, DRUGS, AND INSANITY	433
CHAPTER 14: THE PENTAGON: CITADEL OF POWER	471
CHAPTER 15: BATTLEPLAN	491
CHAPTER 16: JOUSTING WITH THE JOINT CHIEFS	511
CHAPTER 17: CRISIS RESPONSE	525
CHAPTER 18: MEDICAL EXPEDITIONS ABROAD	535
CHAPTER 19: FINAL BATTLES	553
POSTSCRIPT	579

Brainwashing, Drunks & Madness

William E. Mayer, M.D.

FOREWARD

I first met Major Bud Mayer as a classmate in the Army's Command and General Staff College in 1960. Bud had already established a very enviable reputation on the subject of *brainwashing* by the Chinese and North Koreans on our captured personnel. My next contact with Bud Mayer was in the 1978 - 1980 in Stuttgart, Germany. He was the Director of the Army's Alcohol Treatment Facility (ATF) in Bad Cannstatt and I was the commander of the VII US Corps located in Moreighen. I was so impressed with the ATF that I required all of my major commanders to attend either an orientation or a graduation. During the period 1984 – 1989, as the Director of the Office of US Foreign Disaster Assistance and later as the Director of the Federal Emergency Management Agency I routinely worked with Bud, then the Assistant Secretary of Defense for Health Affairs, on such matters as the National Disaster Medical System (NDMS) and other national emergency matters from a health point of view. Always the professional, always willing to help and not reluctant to *tilt at windmills*, Bud did whatever it took to get the job done. Over the years I have seen many ASD(HA) come and go, but Dr William Mayer remains in that small group of professional medical folks who literally put the well being of the service members and their facilities above all else.

Julius W. Becton, Jr.
Lt Gen, USA-Retired
Former Director, AID/OFDA and FEMA
President Emeritus, Prairie View A&M University
Former CEO/Superintendent, District of Columbia Public Schools

Brainwashing, Drunks & Madness

A Soldier's Point Of View

As a trooper on the ground here in Baghdad, the contributions of Dr. Mayer's service are readily apparent in the success our doctors, nurses, medics, and combat lifesavers have had in saving the lives of wounded soldiers. When leaving our compound none of my fellow soldiers doubt that we will receive excellent medical treatment if they are injured, an immense psychological boost in a challenging environment. This lasting legacy of his work directly reflects upon Dr. Mayer's tireless efforts at the highest levels of government, motivated by his own battlefield experience, to ensure that the warrior on the ground receives the best medical support possible, both physical and psychological. Dr. Mayer's book relates the efforts made to bring military medicine to the state it is today, and more importantly, serves as an inspiration to keep up the fight regardless of the odds and obstacles, for anyone in any profession.

SGT Christopher Alexander
Cavalry Scout
Baghdad

Brainwashing, Drunks & Madness

William E. Mayer, M.D.

INTRODUCTION

The Twentieth Century was quite possibly the most revolutionary period in recorded history. Its first half was characterized by unspeakable human disasters during two world wars, along with the establishment of the most intrusive tyranny ever imposed, a system of social and economic controls that by mid-century had enslaved a third of the human race.

That same period, however, began an era of massive progress in both the physical and social sciences, both of which flourished in the Century's second half. From physics came the promise of new sources of power, and robotics able to do much that once only skilled workers could do. Along with those things came previously undreamed-of destructive forces so terrible that no one, so far, has dared unleash them, except for two small devices used over Japanese cities to end World War II. Chemistry has bestowed blessings in the form of plastics and other new materials, with myriad benefits. The biological sciences have begun to reveal the innermost secrets of the smallest living units, the cells, and the genes that determine their nature and functions. Those genes may well be the key to medical miracles far beyond the magic of antibiotics, CAT scans and PET scans.

The social sciences unraveled much of the mystery surrounding the development of human personality, character, and intellect. What emerged were multitudes of ways to manipulate those aspects of humans, both for good purposes and evil ones. As understanding of thought and behavior grew, older beliefs and certainties about the nature of man were examined and many were abandoned. Doctrinaire beliefs, particularly about matters of religion, sexual activity, ethics and traditional morality were questioned and many were abandoned. Some noted philosophers and social scientists have suggested that such trends may be incompatible with the preservation of a free society.

Not all of the world's peoples – in fact only a minority – have participated in or benefited from the advances in science and technology touched on above. A large percentage of the world's population adheres to beliefs and practices that are centuries old, and views those who do not share their ideas as infidels, purveyors of decadence who threaten the purity of their world. The more fundamentalist among them advocate 'holy war' to cleanse the earth of those destructive forces. It is currently fashionable to assert that only a tiny fraction of those with ancient beliefs actually feel that way, but that may not be true.

Whatever the size and durability of the threat to modern man and his largely new convictions about individual freedom, the limited role of the state and its police forces, the importance of unfettered speech, unregulated news media, due process, gender equality, and such rights as we assert to life, liberty and the pursuit of happiness (undefined in statute,) questions must be asked about the survivability of our relatively free society when faced with an implacable adversary. This is particularly important when adversaries with ideas our forefathers long ago put aside, cling to those ancient beliefs while adopting the modern technology of destruction that free men have contrived.

It may be possible to understand and evaluate the vulnerability of our society, as it exists today, by examining some of the history of the medical world of the century just past, looking at how medicine and psychiatry are taught and practiced, and their impact on the social and economic systems now in place. It is also possible to look at ourselves in connection with two of the great challenges that went unsolved throughout that century, and remain so into the new millennium: the use, abuse, and consequences of alcohol and other mind-altering substances; and our abject failure to treat insanity humanely.

The principle of war and other kinds of competition that assigns importance to knowing one's enemy/adversary/competitor applies equally to knowing oneself. Looking at what has transpired in medicine and in dealing with madness and with supposed character deviations like drunkenness and addiction is one way of examining ourselves. In military education and training, a further principle involves the use of 'practical exercises.' There was, during one of the wars of the Twentieth Century, just such an 'exercise' that can be useful in learning what we must know about ourselves. That was the experience, over several years, of nearly five thousand healthy, average, young American men who lived and died in Communist prisoner of war camps in Korea.

A larger percentage of those young men died there than in any POW camps since Andersonville, during the Civil War. Not a single one of them ever escaped. The great majority informed on their fellow prisoners. Most signed petitions damning their own country. Many confessed falsely to spreading germ warfare. They were not threatened or abused physically, although the food and housing were pretty poor; no one was executed; and the camps were not fenced off or heavily guarded, so how could this have happened? They were exhaustively studied when they came home, and much was learned about Communist so-called 'Brainwashing' techniques. Much more was learned about ourselves.

If those men, even allowing for their harsh living conditions, could acquiesce so completely to relatively benign external forces, can the rest of us be expected to resist vigorously the terrorists and tyrants of the world who now denounce us, and may one day attack us on a far larger scale than the Twin Towers? Can we survive that? The questions need to be asked.

William E. Mayer, M.D.

    This book was written in the belief that a free people, properly informed about the threat, about their adversaries, and about themselves, can come up with the means to preserve this Republic, this 'last great hope' for freedom and justice among the peoples of the earth, this shining example of the triumphs – and the hazards – of freedom. It is a description of the experiences and lessons learned by a physician who went to war with the Marines, served in the Navy, the Army, and the Public Health Service, and at one time or another directed the Nation's largest systems dealing with alcoholism, drug abuse, mental health, and military health care.

Brainwashing, Drunks & Madness

William E. Mayer, M.D.

Chapter 1

REVOLUTIONS

rev-o-lu-tion, n. 2. a complete or radical
change in something (Webster's)

The early years of the twentieth century were a time of revolutions around the world. Several of them marked and shaped my life. The bloody Bolshevik conquest of Eastern Europe was to go on in one form or another for nearly seventy years. The dissolution of most colonial empires was to take fifty of those; that took a whole set of revolutions.

America was having a social revolution, what with women finally being allowed to vote, social welfare programs becoming official government policy, and consumer credit available to all, as the production of labor-saving consumer goods exploded.

Medicine was experiencing a variety of revolutions, beginning with an Army doctor's brilliant move to add chlorine to water – the most important and revolutionary public health measure in twenty centuries. Doctors generally were beginning to accept Louis Pasteur's insistence that tiny, invisible "organisms" actually caused disease, but could be washed off. Ether and chloroform were beginning to supplant whiskey as general anesthetics, so people could sleep blissfully while being hacked at by surgeons who, only a century earlier, had generally been barbers.

The weapons of war, at least in highly civilized countries, were increasing exponentially in lethality. Mass destruction was becoming practicable with the use of poisonous gasses, massive explosive devices, and wonderful transport systems in the air and under the sea to deliver them to their terrified and unwilling consumers. Land transport shifted from beasts of burden to wheeled mechanical contraptions that could go almost anywhere. Communications systems were liberated from wires and signal flags, greatly enhancing command and control. Killing more and more people, more and more quickly, became the guiding principle of war-making.

Forced by the horrific imperatives of modern warfare, military physicians became the front-line soldiers in a huge revolution in medicine. Grasping at the new findings in bacteriology and infectious disease control, they insisted on immunizing the battlefield troops, and advanced the cause of preventive medicine immeasurably. Impressed by the old military adage that an army travels on its stomach, they promoted studies of nutrition and the use of newly discovered vitamins. As it became evident that hemorrhage and shock were what killed most soldiers not instantly done in by direct hits from artillery, grenades and bullets, they went to work on ways to replace whole blood and blood fluids, as well as ways to collect, store, and safeguard those precious human products.

Military medicine, therefore, was undergoing revolutionary changes during the whole of the 1900's. Uniformed physicians didn't themselves invent many of the new things in their trade, but they were quick to discern the potential benefits in new things, like sulfonamides and penicillin and vascular surgery, typhoid and typhus and diphtheria vaccines, skin grafting, organ transplants, reattachment of severed limbs, unimaginable elaborations of the X-Ray and the laboratory, and the use of whole blood and blood products.

Physicians, as a species, tend to be conservative in their thinking, cautious about new nostrums and procedures, wary of miracle cures and loathe to experiment on helpless patients in their care. The overwhelming needs of the thousands of people damaged in the insanities of the two 'great' wars, followed by those in Korea and Viet Nam, and the records of the carnage visited on the Nation during the Civil War not long before, all drove many doctors in uniform to try the new things sooner than they might otherwise have done so. Newer techniques and remedies were applied early after they were developed, and to large numbers of people. From this, millions have benefited immeasurably.

Like most Americans, the sheer accident of my birth on this continent at this time made me, automatically, a beneficiary of all the revolutions listed above, and many more. But the equally accidental lineage and parentage bestowed by a beneficent Supreme Being made it inevitable, as well, that I should become a revolutionist myself, if somewhat inadvertently.

My mother, a gentle, passive-seeming, traditionally lady-like Victorian female, was in reality herself a revolutionist. Her ancestors came over with William Penn, one signed the Declaration of Independence, and others rejected slavery and left the Deep South to start an iron works in Cincinnati. In adolescence she bound her breasts flat to minimize her overt feminism, but busied herself in marches and demonstrations in support of women's suffrage. She also broke with genteel tradition and went to dental college, learned to smoke cigarettes, presided over the PTA with steely determination and initiated an outstanding program of free dental care for poor children in the Cincinnati public schools. She admired Oliver Wendell Holmes and his son, and fretted over the 'starving Armenians.'

Thus armed by her with the conviction that those of us materially and socially blessed must know what is right, and must always do that, I set out to emulate Great Uncle Charlie, an eminent surgeon who helped develop and promote the revolutionary vaginal hysterectomy, and I determined to work toward the eradication of disease and the saving of lives.

The beginnings of my medical education, thanks to a scholarship from the Northwestern University School of Medicine in Chicago, occurred as the Second World War was getting underway. My dentist father had served in 1918 as a cavalry officer in the Army, but I had long believed that the Navy was the superior service, and so signed on in the Naval Reserve as an ensign in the Medical Administrative Corps.

The Great War ended just before I finished medical school, and I felt a bit left out of things and decided to stay on in the Navy. Thus began a long career spent partly in each of four uniformed medical services, with some interspersed civilian practice periods along the way. That half century of 'saving lives and stamping out disease' did not leave me a wealthy man, but one possessed with a richness of spirit and a priceless remembrance of some of the finest men and women among the untold thousands who have served.

Through it all, I was a revolutionist. Once characterized by the faculty of a great American medical school as a "stormy petrel" of our profession, and with a military personnel record that frequently used the career-killing descriptor of "controversial" in my proficiency reports, I did not consciously set out to upset things. Just to do, as my mother insisted, "what was right."

It is true that I successively abandoned my goal of becoming surgeon general of the Navy, senior medical officer of the Marine Corps, and surgeon general of the Army, but somehow ended up being the boss – the direct professional superior – of all of them. Strange things happen.

The decision to study medicine and become a physician is far from a simple one, and never to be taken lightly. The cost in time, money and effort is substantial, often taking twelve to fifteen years following high school and requiring enormous sums of money. After expending all that effort and treasure, the pay is generally pretty good and the prestige is nice (although less than it used to be), but by the time it's over, many of the initial motivations have undergone change or been largely forgotten.

Most of us who go through this most expensive of all trade school courses begin with a certain level of idealism, a desire to do good, to help people, to justify our existence, earn the love and respect of our fellows and, quite naturally, make a decent if not luxurious living while doing so. An M.D. degree generally assures most of those things. This was probably more true in the early 20th Century than it is today. We were – doctors and patients alike – more naïve and trusting then. Some healers seemed almost god-like.

The past three quarters of a century has been a time of medical miracles largely unimaginable before that time. There is promise of much more to come, but at the moment there is some chaos and increasing controversy surrounding the science and the practice of medicine, the relationship between doctor and patient, the "rights" of both groups, and how to manage the delivery of care and the exploding costs of it. Some like to call it a crisis, but that might be too strong a term for right now.

For the doctor, it can be hard to cling to youthful idealism about the calling. There is too much to know, too much 'outside' interference by money managers and attorneys, too many demands by government, too much exposure to liability surrounding even the simplest contact with a sick or injured person. There are also powerful pressures to be able to live a 'normal' life, work reasonable hours, and have time for wife and children.

For the patient, there is too much information and misinformation afoot. Reading the papers – especially the tabloids at supermarket counters – and listening to the news can and often does generate wholly unrealistic expectations about what doctors can do. We are told about stupendous monetary awards attendant upon medical mistakes and misdeeds (beats winning the lottery!) We see displays of wondrous drugs whose advertising seems to dominate television shows. They promise relief from heartburn, irritable bowel, excessive gas, pain of every variety, arthritis, unspecified but universal deadly vitamin deficiencies, allergy, headaches, insomnia, clinical depression, genital herpes, vaginal dryness, and progressive memory loss.

To hear all this, one must conclude we are a sick people, desperately in need of nostrums and care that are implicitly not available to us.

The truth is quite different. As a people we are healthier than ever before, living longer, losing fewer infants, surviving injuries once certain to be fatal, reducing heart disease, conquering at least some cancers, keeping thousands of people alive who a short while ago would have died from infectious diseases, epidemics, kidney failure, brain tumors and a host of other ills. True, not all of us get to go to the Mayo Clinic, but most of us don't need to; we get just as good care without traveling all the way to Minnesota or Boston or San Francisco.

Still, there are those progressive do-gooders who insist we need universal, government-provided health care, that people don't have immediate, unrestricted medical attention whenever they think they need it, that there are millions of medically uninsured children, and only a national health system can save us. That is a really bad idea: check with the Brits, the Canadians, and with our own federal health systems like Medicaid!

My own dedication to the healing arts probably was genetic. Mother and father were both successful dental surgeons. Uncle Charlie was a renowned gynecological surgeon. Uncle Otie, a judge, sparked a tiny interest in malpractice litigation.

William E. Mayer, M.D.

All of this by the time I was five years old. After sampling other careers, like hoboing, dog kennel cleaning, stevedoring, motorcycle policing, fire fighting, hotel clerking, car and dish washing, bookkeeping, shoe selling and a host of other less glamorous things like undertaking and farm labor, it was clear to me by the ripe old age of 16 that there was no possible alternative to becoming a physician.

The fact that I had no parents or other relatives to support me after the age of 12, made it seem a little hard. Thanks, however, to a total (room, board, tuition and cast-off clothes) scholarship to a wonderfully creative boarding school for rich boys including Orson Welles, the Schwinn bicycle kids, Seeburg nicolodeon kids, and the sons of admirals and diplomats, where I scored an 'impossible' perfect score on an early version of the Stanford Binet intelligence test, I decided that, just maybe, it could be done. The absence of money was dealt with in college by various jobs, and in medical school by a scholarship followed by the support of the Navy.

Wholly unexpectedly, I discovered early in life that I was really quite rebellious regarding the status quo in important aspects of our society and its institutions. While a hobo, riding freight trains around the country, I worked with migrant farm workers in the Imperial Valley, where some entire families were being paid one dollar a day. That, I thought, was wrong. They had no medical care whatever. I saw similar things in lumber camps, used car lots, miserable little lunch counters, and endless rural slums in the south and urban slums in the north. I read Dos Passos, Steinbeck and Hemingway and Richard Wright and came up with ideas for social improvement that were probably to the left of Lenin and to the right of Attila, all mixed together.

But I also learned, early on, that to rebel openly, as has become so popular with our youth today as they damn globalization, the WHO, capitalism, industrialization, agricultural research, animal experimentation, the wealthy, white males, and conventional marriage, is not only ineffective but counter-productive. It seemed far more sensible to avoid looking or behaving differently from those who were successful in life, to learn their ways, follow their rules, get inside the system, work my way up to where I had some real power or influence, and then work to make changes in that system. Some might call this a kind of hypocrisy, but it did not require abandoning principle; it merely necessitated banking the fires of my flaming liberalism until such time as I could engage in battles that I had a chance of winning.

It worked for me, by and large, for the next half century. Some of the battles that I engaged in before the time was right, I lost. The first, revising the medical educational system, was doomed from the outset, and while it has gotten better, it was not due to my efforts.

My next major battle, involving the Freudian ethic and its controlling influence over psychiatry, was initially unsuccessful and generated a host of lifelong enemies, but ultimately was largely won, with the help of unnumbered allies, mostly unknown to me.

Yet another involved grappling with the bureaucracy in the sixth largest government on earth – the state of California – and while successful, had dramatic, unintended and unforeseen consequences that are as yet unresolved. We did, however, close most of the ancient state mental hospitals and liberate thousands of people from a kind of bondage.

Yet another engaged me in combat with much of society and the great bulk of the medical profession with respect to the disease of alcoholism. Another – over more than thirty years – had to do with the real, physical nature of major mental disease.

Then came the battle with my colleagues (again) over the care of soldiers wounded in combat, and with the medical-industrial-political complex that prefers to spend billions on glossy new hospitals instead of on people bleeding to death on battlefields, and finally with still other colleagues who fought against quality assurance and risk management in health care facilities, and the automation of medical data.

All of these contests, and many more, some smaller, some larger, inevitably identified me as combative and controversial (but always a nice enough guy on the surface.) I came to appreciate the political theory that the measure of a man and his achievements lies in the numbers and character of his enemies. I also became, along the way, a fervent admirer of Teddy Roosevelt, who offended many, fought often, didn't always win but always tried his damnedest to do what he thought was right. I tried to do the same, and had one helluva great time in the process.

What follows is my tale. All is prelude, leading up to the day when John Kennedy was shot, for that was the day Ronald Reagan and I became friends on a movie set in Hollywood. Out of that friendship based on shared beliefs about mankind and our beloved country, came a path leading to the highest levels of government, serving first the people of California, and then the ten million men, women and children for whom the Armed Forces provide medical care and treatment, all over the world, in peace and in war. All the rest was to prepare me for that immense responsibility – and boundless privilege.

William E. Mayer, M.D.

Brainwashing, Drunks & Madness

William E. Mayer, M.D.

Chapter 2

Medical School

The medical school at Northwestern University, far from the undergraduate campus in Evanston, was situated on the Lake Michigan shorefront close to Chicago's downtown area in a tall, impressive Gothic-style tower across the street from a National Guard armory, occupying the first seven or eight floors. Abbott Hall, the student dormitory and cafeteria, was nearby, even closer to the waterfront, and was quite new. The rooms were small and bare of furnishings except for a bed, desk and chair, and a wardrobe. I remember it as rather bleak and cold.

Our introduction to formal medical education began with short introductory speeches by the Dean, one Roscoe Miller, M.D., who seemed surprisingly young for such a prestigious position, who emphasized how lucky we were to be there instead of fighting in Europe or on some remote jungle island in the Pacific, and how that fact imposed upon us all the requirement that we devote ourselves with total dedication, effort and sincerity to the task at hand, namely to learning to be the finest, most skillful and competent physicians, for that is what our country needed. We were being excused, he told us, from the horrors and terrible dangers of war because we were all outstanding college achievers, highly recommended as superb future physicians, potentially of inestimable value to our fellow citizens and fully expected to bring credit upon ourselves and our school - one of the finest in existence.

We were also told, almost as an afterthought like "Oh, by the way..." that failure in any course could not be tolerated. The pressing need for doctors did not permit the luxury of repeating any course and thus prolonging the educational process, and would result in prompt expulsion from school, cancellation of our temporary exemption from military service, and immediate induction into the armed forces as a private soldier.

We were then treated to a similarly inspiring introductory lecture by the chairman of the Department of Anatomy, a world-renowned embryologist named Leslie Brainerd Arey, whose weighty textbook on that subject we had been required to acquire that very day. Dr. Arey was a distinguished, graying fellow in a long white coat who looked exactly like a great and revered professor of medical students should look. He had a marked New England accent and a notably authoritarian manner that proved to be well deserved. He too emphasized our great good fortune in having been allowed into those hallowed halls to which only one (each of us) out of every thirty fully qualified applicants had been accepted.

As I recall, the overwhelming impression created by these two enormously important and powerful men was a curious combination of relief that we'd made it, a secret element of prideful satisfaction that we'd beaten out all those other guys, a determination to show these people just what we were capable of, and eagerness to get out there and start giving the world the benefit of our superior intelligence and education. Plus, importantly, an element of absolute terror. This latter resulted in a remarkably widespread tendency to loose bowels, which I thought was mine alone but turned out to be nearly universal throughout the class during the entire first two academic years while we all lived in dread of failure or even mediocrity.

Professor Arey also laid down a few simple rules. One was that tardiness to any class or laboratory session was absolutely forbidden. Another was that a spotlessly clean anatomy lab uniform was to be worn at all times in the lab. This consisted of a white short coat and white trousers and was to be turned in to the laundry on the seventh floor each day and retrieved the same day the following week after payment of a small fee. The laundry was a privately owned concession, as was the small snack bar adjacent to it, in neither of which was loitering permitted. It wasn't for many months until I discovered, quite by accident, that Dr. Arey owned and operated both - a closely guarded secret - and derived a handsome income therefrom.

We were also admonished, with some severity, that our behavior in the anatomy lab must follow rules of utter decorum: there was to be no levity, no joking, no naming of the cadavers, no disrespect of any kind shown to these dead persons, no removal of parts from the lab for any purpose whatever, no visiting of other dissection rooms, no outside visitors at any time, no eating or drinking or smoking while dissecting, and, in general, no fun at all; this was serious business.

The introductory ceremonies having concluded, we made our way to the anatomy lecture hall for our first formal class. It was conducted by an erect, carefully groomed, handsome man of about sixty, who without any special preliminaries, jokes, or attempts to connect with his audience of eager students, proceeded in carefully modulated, highly cultured tones to deliver a perfectly organized, exceedingly fact-filled lecture filling the entire hour without pause. Not once did he consult his notes.

Later we were to discover that this man, Doctor Barry Anson, had been a professor of English before turning to Anatomy. He was a superb if slightly dull lecturer, never hesitating, repeating himself or searching for the precise word or phrase he needed. Several of the students who were adept at shorthand and thus took down every word of every lecture, noted with awe and reported to the rest of us that alone among the faculty, Dr. Anson invariably spoke with perfect grammar, sometimes constructing complex sentences that filled half a typewritten page with never a grammatical or syntactical error.

Following this sobering experience, unlike anything any of us had heard in college, we were dismissed to reassemble in the anatomy lab. The lab was divided into separate rooms, each containing three or four coffin-sized metal cases on legs, and about a dozen connected standing lockers along the wall. We had been instructed to pick a locker, put our name on it, and use it from then on to hang our clothes while we donned our anatomy uniforms, giving the place a certain resemblance to a locker room in a high school gym, although there were not the usual benches to sit down on.

A list outside the door bore the names of those students assigned to that room, and another list inside assigned us in teams of four to one of the "tables." When the metal lids atop the coffin-style 'tables' were opened, one could see down inside a naked corpse on a kind of tray, partially submerged in strongly smelling liquid. A crank on the end of the box operated a mechanism that lifted the tray and its body out of the fluid to a point near the top of the box where it reposed at a convenient height for the dissectors.

Each of us had a brand new dissection kit in a shiny black folding case. It contained a couple of scalpels with detachable blades, tweezers, a couple of hemostat-type clamps, a pair of curved dissecting scissors, and several slender metal probes. We had been instructed to turn our cadaver over, onto its belly, and then to make an incision down the middle of the back from the shoulders to the waist with a connecting incision crosswise at each end. This would permit freeing up two large skin flaps by cutting the connecting tissues under the skin and folding each flap outward from the midline, and that would expose the underlying muscle masses. Those we were to free up sufficiently to identify each separate muscle mass. We were then to examine, sketch, and name each such muscle group.

Once our cadaver had been cranked up out of the noisome juice in which it had lain for who knew how long, the four of us gathered close around. Each of us selected one of the scalpels from our kit and held it in hand, like any experienced surgeon, ready to begin. Each made a small motion in the direction of the prescribed incision area, and then turned to his neighbor and said something like, "You go ahead." We were all total strangers to one another and very polite about this as the deferrals made their way around the table to the last man.

There being no one left to whom he could defer for the honor of making the first, dramatic, somehow violent assault upon the integrity of this unfortunate dead person, our designated hitter, so to speak, reached out with his scalpel, but held it motionless, suspended over the defenseless body for what seemed like an eternity. At length, without a word or a look at any of the rest of us, he withdrew the gleaming blade. He picked up his dissecting kit, unsnapped it, carefully replaced the scalpel in its place inside, snapped it closed, and turned away from the table. He went directly to his locker, took out his street clothes and draped them over his arm, and without further ceremony walked out of the room, closing the door behind him.

We three remaining members of the dissection team, finally able to breathe once more, found nothing to say at all, and one of us did the necessary incision. All of us ultimately took part in this single, simple cut because we discovered to our shocked surprise that the skin of the back was so thick - fully a quarter of an inch - that it took repeated slices to get through it. After that, things got progressively easier and we actually started cleaning off and identifying muscles by the time the day ended.

No one ever saw our departed comrade again. Presumably, he was somewhere far away, enjoying basic training as a foot soldier, before leaving for the war zone.

One of the first things we learned in anatomy had to do with the value of mnemonics in memorizing the endless lists of things like the twelve cranial nerves: On (olfactory) Old (Ophthalmic) Olympus' (optic) Towering (trochlear) Top (trigeminal) - etc.; the small bones of the wrist: Never (naviculate) Lower (lunate) Tizzie's (triquetal) Pants (pisiform) - etc.; the branches of the Lingual Duct or the Carotid artery and a host of other branching and crossing and adjoining things you are certain to be asked about on an exam. We were strongly advised never to use such despicable devices, so naturally we all did so regularly.

Many of these mnemonics were mildly to wildly obscene, and were of course the easiest to remember and therefore our favorites. One such, in the mild category, declared, "As Suzie Lay Extended, Sir Oliver's Penis Slipped In." Each first letter coincides with a branch of a very important artery, and it is considered essential, if one is to practice medicine, that one knows, in proper order, the names of all those branches.

Immediately following the first anatomy exam, we forgot the names of the artery's branches, but Suzie and Sir Oliver lived on in the form of our male cadaver, Sir Oliver, and Suzie, who slept in the adjoining metal box. You will recall, as did we, the strict prohibition against naming the cadavers, but these names just seemed to fit. This did not mean that we treated either of those instructive human frames with anything less than solemn respect; we just felt they deserved to be named.

Serious trouble did erupt from time to time in one or the other of the dissection rooms. The lab was on the seventh floor of the tower, and the windows faced out on the open parade ground of the Armory across the street. Assuming, therefore, that no one outside the building could see in, one student humorist decided, at one point, to attach his cadaver's hand to the shade pull over one window, leaving the shade partway up after each lab session and taking it down when each new period began, so no instructor would see it.

What that wag had failed to contemplate, however, was that some occupant of the tall, expensive apartment buildings on the far side of the parade ground might possess an adequate pair of binoculars. That, in fact, turned out to be the case, and the owner had apparently developed a little hobby of peering across the distance to see what he/she could see through the school's seventh floor windows. After coming upon the human hand hanging gaily from the shade pull on the third window from the corner, or some such, that civic minded citizen promptly called the Dean's office to complain, igniting a massive man hunt on the seventh floor.

The offending cadaver team was promptly identified, since their instructional buddy was missing his right hand, but the authorities never could pin down who, exactly, pinned the missing member up there on the pull cord. Eventually the turmoil died down, but only after the entire student body had been summoned to a solemn meeting promising the direst consequences, meaning expulsion, loss of draft-exempt status, immediate induction and deployment to someplace like Guadalcanal, and almost certain death at the hands of some sniper, to anyone brash enough to commit a further similar offense against humanity.

Some time later, I told my mother of this little spirit-lifting episode that gave us a small break from what was otherwise an overly serious, intense, anxiety laden schooling that most days started at about 8 in the morning and often found us still in class or lab at 5 or 6 PM. As was not unusual, she topped it. It seems that when she was in the gross anatomy course during dental college, probably about 1915, she was the only female in the class. It was most unusual for women to attend medical or dental school in those days, and she not only stood out, but also served as the object of considerable attention, not all of it tasteful.

One day, as she and her team members removed the shroud draping their cadaver, they discovered that overnight he had developed a huge erection. This created great excitement and turmoil in the class and, similar to our experience thirty years later, aroused the ire of the faculty. Also, like our situation, the authorities never could identify the culprit, who, though anonymous, earned widespread admiration for his imagination and undeniable anatomic skill at injecting the offending member so outstandingly. It was an experience not unlike a mnemonic - never to be forgotten but of uncertain specific significance.

At the end of the first week of classes, we were given a one-hour written examination intended to cover everything we had covered that week, including the first hundred or so pages in the enormous anatomy textbook. Like nearly everyone in the class, I had gotten close to straight A grades in college and was good at taking exams. I avoided over-confidence, though, and studied hard and then wrote my answers completely and clearly, abundantly, I thought, revealing my complete mastery of the subject so far. I couldn't help but feel, in fact, as I turned in my test blue book, that they might one day want to use it as an example of how a really well-written exam should look, sort of an idealized goal for future students to shoot at.

The test was on Friday. On Monday, our graded test books were returned to us. Eager to see how splendidly the instructors thought I had done, which would doubtless show up in the high grade awarded and the laudatory comments sure to be jotted inside the cover, I opened it up to see staring right at me a large, red "72." No jotted comments. Just "72." That, I knew, represented 72 out of a possible 100 points. In my entire academic career, starting in kindergarten and extending through college, I had never gotten any exam back with a score less than 90. Ever.

There had to be some mistake. Was this MY book? I hurriedly closed it, found my own name on the outside, folded it in half, shoved it in a pocket, and left. What I didn't notice was that everyone else did the same thing. Nobody asked anyone else what kind of a grade he'd gotten. We were all in a state of shock. Hardly anyone showed up for the evening meal. What little camaraderie had begun to develop that first week instantly took flight. From that day on, we were all adversaries. Each competing with one another in dead seriousness for the good grades we were all used to in college. No one ever shared grades with anyone else; it was every man for himself.

It was many months later that I discovered, when I went to work for the anatomy department as a student instructor, that everyone gets a 72 on that first test. Major lesson in humility. The faculty, it was explained to me, knew full well we were all top students and very smart. It was important we didn't get the idea we were too smart to have to work. Hard. I'm not sure the faculty was fully aware of the profound emotional impact this had. I am sure that for many of us this began to implant a level of competitiveness, estrangement from one another, even overt mutual distrust that extended well beyond school years, and does not serve this ostensibly 'helping' profession at all well.

Few friendships formed in that class, especially in the first two years. Those 18 months of instruction, completed almost without breaks except for a few days between 3-month quarters and a single two week pause after the first academic year of 9 months was completed, were filled with a multitude of difficult subjects requiring the memorization of enormous amounts of information. There was little time for rest, let alone recreation, and attendance at a movie was usually contaminated by lingering suspicions that one should really be studying, so it wasn't much fun.

There was a serious problem of relevance, or the lack of it, as the months went by, some of the novelty wore off, and one began to have the temerity to question, at least to oneself, the rationale for learning to do chemical laboratory procedures, pharmacological formulations, tissue preparations, bacterial cultures and blood counting and examination procedures that no physician outside of an Albert Schweitzer hospital in the African jungle ever actually did himself. Yet these were the hardest things to learn to do, and to remember. I found myself becoming increasingly skeptical of the whole medical educational enterprise, and ultimately came to the belief that much of it was simply a sort of initiation and indoctrination process unrelated to the content of what was being taught. Evidently, I was not alone in these feelings, and medical education has significantly changed in recent years, though not always for the better.

Our class of 165 souls had a small amount of what I concluded was a self-conscious diversity, of whose purpose I was never sure. We had, for example, two women in the class, evidently felt to be a nice balance to the 163 men. Those women had clearly been selected with great care. Both were PhD's in some science. That had been true of the two women in the previous class, and the class before that. They were singularly unattractive ladies: a little stocky, plain faces, not attractive or well-tended hair, flat shoes, shapeless clothes, no interest in males, few evident social skills. Both of them undressed and donned their anatomy togs with no show of - or indeed need for - any sort of modesty, in a room full of young males who paid no attention whatever. They were never teased or joked with, seeming somehow to be encapsulated and apart from the rest of us.

In addition to that small gender minority group, there was a small number of Jewish students, who never recognizably functioned as a group, in any sense, and did not wear clothes or ornaments proclaiming their faith. There were possibly ten of them. There was one person of Asian extraction among us, a Korean boy with whom I became as close to friends as anyone did with anyone at that time in that school. His name was Dick Hahn, later to become a surgeon in the Kaiser system, who was large for an Oriental, casual in his movements and given to a kind of All-American boy vernacular speech typical of the lower middle class Chicago neighborhood where his parents operated and lived in a tiny apartment above a small laundry.

We shared the status of scholarship students, but the origin of his imposed a heavier burden of obligation and responsibility. His parents had emigrated from Korea as adults, and took up residence in Chicago after learning that it had a large Oriental population, at that time one of the largest outside the Orient itself. That population, in that city at that time, was almost totally Chinese; there were few if any other Korean families at all. The Hahn laundry was not in Chinatown, but over the years they had made friends with many Chinese in the city, and it was through the combined meager savings of the Hahns, with help from members of the Chinese community that got son Dick into Northwestern. The fact that he had been a straight-A student in high school and college was also an important factor.

We became acquainted during our first year, after meeting in the Embryology Museum on a high floor in the medical school near the laundry. Dr. Arey, chairman of the Department of Anatomy, was an authority known throughout the world for his studies and books on the subject. He proudly proclaimed that his museum contained the most outstanding collection anywhere of 'monster' embryos, so distorted and grotesquely deformed that they could not live, but collected and preserved for posterity in his jars of formaldehyde.

Dick and I had both noted an important fact about Dr. Arey's teachings and especially his examinations, which were frequent. The lab part of his course consisted of recreating the embryo of a pig by reconstructing it from serially cut sections of these creatures. It was a useful and instructive exercise for erstwhile physicians, since the pig embryo closely resembles that of a human, which at that stage it resembles. It was also tedious and difficult, and we were commiserating over this before moving on to his exams.

We had both discovered a great truth about the exams, but because of the competitiveness that had developed, didn't tell anyone else. For some reason, we did talk about it with each other. It was a simple thing that for some strange reason most students missed: Arey drew most of his questions from the extensive footnotes in his book, a huge heavy tome, rather than from the text itself, knowing that most people don't really pay a lot of attention to the footnotes. His little joke, presumably. Since we had both discovered this and began concentrating on the small print at the bottoms of nearly every page, we were shining brightly on tests.

We further discovered, in our little talk in the monster museum, that Dick had the ability to concentrate on what a lecturer was saying and retain it without notes. I, on the other hand, made extensive, meticulous notes - not quite true shorthand, but almost. In college I had gotten so good at note-making and organizing, which I did each day to fix the material firmly in my mind, that I was able to supplement my earnings quite dramatically by selling copies of my lecture notes to less dedicated but better-heeled classmates.

When we put these facts together, we decided we could form a really effective examination-passing team. We would get together at exam time, and using my detailed notes as a framework, engage in an intense review of the subject, whatever it was, formulating possible test questions, bolstered by his detailed recollection of how the professor delivered the material, what he seemed most to emphasize and think important. We would do this, almost without a break, for 16 to 18 hours before the actual exam, and then go take it. When the exam results were returned, we had maxed it. We would then sleep for a few hours, get a good meal, wipe from memory that whole subject, and start on another one.

It worked. We immediately became outstanding performers, always in the upper ten percent of the class, eventually winning election to the national medical honor society, Alpha Omega Alpha. I worried a little, both then and in subsequent years when I became acutely aware of my ignorance, that about all I really learned in medical school was how to take exams. My comforting rationalization, not always successful, was that you don't really learn much during examinations anyway, so that didn't matter all that much, but I always suspected that we'd gotten away with something.

The Hahn family's close connections in Chinatown led to some special adventures, when Dick and I were taken by his family to banquets and events commemorating important religious and political occasions. Often he and I were the only people present speaking English, but we were always welcomed warmly and fed extravagantly. These banquets were unlike anything I subsequently experienced anywhere until more than thirty years had gone by and I found myself conducting an official US Military medical visit to the Republic of China that involved 11 major banquets in as many days, culminating in a special one in the Great Hall of the People in Tiananmen Square. The host was an ancient general, who had been second in command to Mao Tse Tung, made the great march, and led the Chinese army that had invaded North Korea and surrounded the Marine Division I was in.

After one of our banquets in Chicago's Chinatown, Dick and I were asked to remain to meet with a small group of the oldest, most dignified and clearly most important of the people present. We had no idea what to expect.

The leader of this elderly group, dressed in a splendid Mandarin robe and sporting a wispy beard, greeted us graciously and asked about our progress in our medical training and our future plans. This was interesting, because by then Dick had donned the uniform of an Army medical cadet in a program called ASTP as I had in the Navy V-12 program, both designed for medical students who were to become Army and Navy doctors. We responded politely, if somewhat vaguely when it came to our future since we didn't know how the war was going to turn out, or what the military services had in mind for us.

The elderly gentleman then told us that he was authorized to give us - Dick and me - a message directly from "the Generalissimo," Chiang Kai Shek! Astounded, we couldn't wait to hear more.

The Kuomintang, he explained, foresaw the end of the war and the triumph of the Western powers over the hated Japanese and the liberation of all of China. Recognizing the immense need for improved health services - indeed for any health services at all - in the whole of China, and the impossibility of creating the huge body of physicians and nurses that would be needed to deliver such services, they had in mind a workable compromise. They would establish a huge school, ultimately with branches throughout China, to train people with approximately a high school education, in the most important, basic principles of patient care as well as simple public health measures dealing with water and waste disposal and food.

Would we, he asked, be willing to design a program of training, to last not more than two years, to prepare an army of 'barefoot' health workers to spread out throughout their vast country and start it on the road to modern medicine?

Speaking almost in unison, Dick and I enthusiastically agreed that we could and would do that, the minute our education was complete and arrangements were made with our government to release us from our military commitments. After a brief conference in Chinese with his fellows, the ancient gentleman assured us that his government would deal directly with ours, and said he felt sure that whatever needed to be accomplished would be.

We left in a state of sheer exultation, talking animatedly all the way home about what a great idea this was, and how we would go about planning and doing it. For a while it seemed like it might happen, but by the time we were completing school there was growing turmoil in China, the Communists were opposing Chiang, our own State Department was backing away from Chiang and the Kuomintang, and we didn't get to do it. Subsequently, after the Communists took over, they did something like what we had planned. The only real difference was that they used Russians.

The first two years in medical school, dubbed "academic" as opposed to "clinical," were a period of intense concentration on a wide variety of subjects, beginning with gross anatomy, microscopic anatomy, embryology, and moving on into bacteriology, pharmacology, pathology, physiology and, curiously, basic psychiatry. Most of these subjects came with massive textbooks, workbooks and laboratory manuals, and involved long periods of time in various laboratories.

A personal microscope was required for many of the lab courses, and this presented a special problem to me. All my classmates had arrived equipped with gleaming silver and black binocular scopes in fine cases, but I discovered that such scientific instruments cost many hundreds of dollars and I was dismayed to discover that my scholarship did not cover this and the school didn't have any old used ones lying around that I could have. Each doctor leaving Northwestern was expected to own a fine microscope, presumably so he could take it with him into practice and put it to good use in his office, where he would surely be doing innumerable microscopic examinations of blood and tissue and bacteria and parasites.

Desperate, I sought out one of the physicians I had known in childhood, Dr. Ed Tatge, an allergist practicing in Evanston, who had been one of the 'references' who had recommended me for admission to the school. He reported that he still had the very microscope he had used in medical school and would be glad to let me borrow it for as long as necessary. Much relieved, I raced out to his office in Evanston on the Elevated, and collected the precious object. It turned out to be a genuine antique, made all of brass - a bit tarnished with age - cradled in a fine-varnished wooden box with brass fittings and felt-lined cradles inside. It had not two eyepieces, like everyone else's, but one, and stood out in marked contrast to the gleaming chrome and black instruments all my fellow students proudly possessed.

However, it was a genuine microscope with fine German lenses, and while it seemed clumsy and primitive, it worked well enough to get me through. Over time, it gave me a kind of perverse satisfaction and became an item of reverse snobbery that conferred a special elite status, or so I rationalized at the time. At first, it generated a few superioristic sniggles from my competitors as we searched for scientific truths, but they soon died out.

Toward the end of the sophomore year we were treated to a course in physical diagnosis, which began with medical history taking. This was a matter of great excitement, for finally we were to be using our shiny new stethoscopes, head mirrors to focus lights into each other's noses, tongue depressors, ear and nose specula to help us examine those orifices, and little hammers with chrome handles and rubber heads for tapping on knees and elsewhere to elicit reflexes. At last, we were beginning to be real doctors! These wonderful gadgets were not only essential to the medical process; they were tangible symbols of our practitioner status, the very tools of our art. We were entranced, and exultant.

So much so, it soon appeared that we tended to focus on the hardware rather than the process. I remembered reading in a book by Sir William Osler, a great physician and teacher of an earlier era, that the medical history was far more important to arriving at the correct diagnosis and assessment of a patient than was any physical examination, no matter how mysterious and even magical were the manipulations and probings of the learned healer as he explored his patient's frame and its appendages and various openings. That idea did not really catch on among us, surrounded as we were by these marvelous implements and secure in our ignorant pridefulness, believing in our visual acuity and manual skills to lead us to brilliant diagnostic formulations leading to wonderful cures for our suffering patients' ills.

We were, moreover, entering into what we believed was a truly modern, scientific era in medicine, utilizing increasing numbers of laboratory tests, X-Rays, and chemical analyses to arrive at truths only guessed at by our predecessors. Little did we dream of what technologic marvels were to come! Already, though, some of our older and wiser teachers were noting with alarm their students' increasing reliance on laboratory findings and radiologic techniques, along with diminishing interest in taking detailed medical histories and listening carefully to what patients were saying. We were told that medicine was in danger of becoming overly mechanical and dehumanized, that the patient - the person - was being forgotten. We were warned that this would cause trouble.

The old men were right, of course. While the medical developments of this century, many of them happening literally in front of my eyes, were truly miracles piled upon miracles, saving many lives and reducing untold suffering while steadily putting off the death that awaits us all, sooner or later, the patient got increasingly lost in the confusion. We have admonished - nay, implored - class after class and generation after generation of new doctors, armed with technical knowledge heretofore undreamed of, not to forget the patient - the person - who is the reason for it all and yet is curiously ignored while the lab numbers and scans and resonant images are worshipfully attended to.

What they were warning us about is what has happened steadily since then, with dire results in the category of unintended - and largely unanticipated - consequences. First among these consequences, as physicians became more preoccupied with procedures and 'findings' from sophisticated machines and less attentive to the person, once thought of as the 'patient' but turning into the 'client' and even the 'consumer' or the 'customer,' was a kind of estrangement between him and his care-giver. That steadily progressed to alienation, and coupled with growing and often wildly unrealistic expectations as to the ability of medicine to cure all ills up to and maybe even including death itself, led to the explosion in lawsuits charging malpractice.

It is notable that the dramatic increase in the legalistic consequences of this combination of doctor-patient estrangement and unmet (if unrealistic) expectations has occurred mainly in America, where medical science and practice are eons ahead of most of the rest of the world. While it is easy to blame the phenomenon on the existence of a huge number of lawyers in this country, many of them avaricious, the problem goes far deeper than that and is far from being solved.

As in most problems, be they social or economic or political or all of those, the media play a major role in this one. The most widely printed periodical of any kind in the U.S. today is a tabloid sold largely in supermarket checkout counters, The National Enquirer. That little weekly 'newspaper' devotes as much as 30% or more of its printed content to articles or reports directly concerning matters of health, illness, and health care of all varieties. Not only does this reveal how widespread is the public interest in the subject, but this massive attention figures importantly in the public's expectations - and disappointments when those expectations are not realized.

Such media attention is not restricted to that particular publication and its imitators; it is evident to a lesser degree in much that is printed in more respected publications as well, and in the burgeoning health magazine industry. Offshoots of this appear in the proliferation of stores selling "health foods" and vitamins and herbal 'remedies' and concoctions from the far corners of the earth, many of which are finding their way into television 'infomercials' whose promises put the snake oil salesman of yesteryear to shame. This explosion of interest in unproven, untested, often costly and almost always ineffective chemicals and biologicals, all beyond the scrutiny of the Food and Drug Administration, is bound to create increasing problems as time goes by.

Not all of this, naturally, can be blamed on the 'dehumanization' of medicine predicted and deplored by my old teachers, but they were right to worry. Some of them had been in medicine not long after Louis Pasteur had focused attention on those little invisible creatures called bacteria that could make people sick and kill them.

Some of their contemporaries and teachers actually refused to believe in such nonsense. There were surgeons on our faculty, for example, who never wore gloves during surgery because they didn't believe the little buggers could really do anything.

There were others who remained unconvinced that X-Rays would ever be very useful - after all, the images were blurry and indistinct! Some of the older faculty in the Radiology Department had been such early pioneers in the field that they had lost parts of fingers and hands exposed to radiation as they probed abdomens during early attempts to develop the techniques of fluoroscopy.

These people, my teachers in medicine, were understandably skeptical of the newer developments in our field, but it was their fear that we younger people would forget about the human beings we were supposed to care for that proved to be most prescient.

Along with our exciting explorations into physical diagnosis, we were soon introduced into the realm of actual contact with live human beings. This took place in the clinics operated in the medical schools where we and our counterparts in sister institutions throughout the country were first allowed to listen to hearts thumping in people's chests, feel for glands in their necks, palpate abdomens for both the usual and the unexpected masses hidden therein, peer into eyeballs with little lights and special lenses, look down gagging throats at purulent tonsils, solemnly and nervously explore testicles and penises and vaginas and rectums with clumsy, often trembling fingers, and even insert - or try to insert - hypodermic needles into blood vessels and soft masses of unknown composition and contents.

One looks back on those experiences with wonder and a clear recollection of the enormously intense emotions that accompanied them and had to be so carefully hidden. No one talked about "stress" in those days; it was yet to become popular and an excuse for just about everything. However, stressful it most certainly was. Who could ever forget his first venipuncture? We had all been stuck with needles, surely, but here was a real, frightened human being into which we were the ones assigned to plunge a sharpened steel tube which was sure to hurt and much less sure to hit what it was supposed to! My first such victim was a fat eleven year old girl who entered the room screaming, pulled along by an exasperated mother. The child had to be an incubus or succubus sent directly by the devil to torment this poor, innocent medical student. She was there to have a blood sample drawn, but there was no sign of a vein in that fat, thrashing arm, and it was clearly a contest between the two of us as to who would suffer the most from my probing. Finally, blessedly, the blood showed at the bottom of the syringe, and the deed was done. And so, almost, was I.

We students had practiced drawing blood on each other's arms in an earlier class, and I had achieved unprecedented popularity as a target thanks to my large veins, probably the result of my hard labor years before on Jimmy Swan's farm, but the squeamishness of that drill didn't remotely compare to the terrors of sticking a helpless actual patient in the clinic. It was a never-to-be-forgotten experience in major stress. Over the years, it got easier, but never did I master the casual insensitivity that seemed required of true professionals. The needles we used at that time were always washed, re-sharpened on a stone but not always very well, cooked in a small metal sterilizer box with a tray inside that moved up and down with a lever, and those needles seemed much larger than those in common use today. Modern ones are used only once, and then disposed of in a special container to guard handlers from AIDS and hepatitis, about which we knew nothing then. The new ones are almost always extremely sharp, and much easier to use. It was another rarely recognized medical miracle.

We spent increasing amounts of time in the clinics, gradually being exposed to all the usual medical and surgical specialty areas of that period. There was never a shortage of patients. They came from the large numbers of poor people from the slums, who never had family doctors of their own to turn to, and for whom there were few available resources. While some free clinics existed, there was no large government program like Medicaid, and Social Security and Medicare had yet to be invented. Both the working poor and the indigent sought help for their ailments at the huge Cook County Hospital and in the free clinics operated by Chicago's four medical schools, and they tended to seek help late in the course of their illnesses.

The people coming to our clinics were, as a result, quite often seriously sick. The two most common chronic diseases of the day, tuberculosis and syphilis, were common accompaniments to the more acute ailments that drove people to seek care. There was little attention in the media, then limited to newspapers, the early radio stations, and the few widely-published magazines like the Readers Digest, the Saturday Evening Post, the Ladies Home Journal, Liberty, Life, and a few others, to health matters and medical developments.

Once in a while the Readers Digest published an article by one of the few 'medical' authors, a man named Paul de Kruif (spelling uncertain), describing a new and always wondrous drug or procedure. This invariably caused a sudden increase in demands for the new discovery by patients who did have regular doctors, to the immense irritation of the profession. It was not thought to be desirable that people learn about such things from other than legitimate medical sources, which the Readers Digest most assuredly was not.

An even more revealing illustration of the media's - and the public's - detachment from health matters relates to those two commonest of chronic illnesses of that time, syphilis and tuberculosis. Neither of those infections was considered quite proper, which is to say that decent folks were not expected to catch them, or if they did, to do so secretly.

Both were declared by law to be "reportable" diseases, meaning that physicians were required to notify the Health Department when they diagnosed them. There were other reportable infectious diseases, including Scarlet Fever, Smallpox, Chicken Pox, Mumps, Meningitis, Encephalitis, and a few others. Laws and regulations dealing with these conditions, along with those governing water supplies and sewage treatment, reflected the truly monumental discoveries and government measures that had occurred, only in the twentieth century, advancing public health and preventive medicine farther, in a few years, than in the entire previous history of mankind.

None of the reportable diseases had a predictably successful curative agent available. Most laws simply required the confinement, usually at home, of any patient so afflicted until he recovered as most did fairly quickly, or died, eliminating the risk to others. This system of quarantine dated back many years, or generations, to a time when ships arriving in port with sick, contagious people aboard were forbidden to let anyone off until the disease was no longer present. Most of the reportable diseases were acute and readily spread from person to person, but of short duration, and conferred immunity from a further attack, if the patient survived.

Three diseases: tuberculosis, syphilis and leprosy, differed markedly from the others but shared certain characteristics. They were not contagious in the sense of being rapidly transmitted among contacts. They developed gradually, and progressed relatively slowly over a period of months or years during which time the infected person might continue to function fairly normally. They were ultimately fatal.

Leprosy was never much of a problem in this country, but tuberculosis was widespread and particularly so among the poorly housed and poorly fed. It was thus mostly a disease of the lowest classes and especially among slum- and tenement-dwellers in large northern cities. Because it developed and disabled slowly, it was often far advanced among the poor people who came to our county hospital and free clinics. In consequence, people showed up with chronic bloody coughs, general wasting of muscles, and great dark spots on the chest X-Rays representing cavities in their lungs. Sometimes they had large, encapsulated abscesses, called "cold" abscesses because they were not hot from acute inflammation, and didn't hurt, on their necks, or attached to their brain or kidney.

These unfortunate people were hospitalized on special "TB" wards, and were not allowed to leave. Treatment staff wore surgical masks when there. A special treatment was devised to put the most seriously damaged lung at rest, in the common, pulmonary form of the disease. The treatment consisted of introducing a needle into the chest on the affected side, allowing air at normal atmospheric pressure to enter, causing that lung to collapse. That condition was called a pneumothorax (meaning air in the chest) and prevented the lung on that side from taking part in respiration. This left the patient a little short of breath, but we kept him quiet anyway, so it wasn't a problem.

Little by little, the collapsed lung would start to re-expand, so it was periodically necessary to get another big needle, stick it in and get it to collapse again. After sometimes many months of this, and after repeated microscopic examinations of whatever the patient coughed up failed to reveal the characteristic tubercle bacilli, he was set free. He then returned to the same miserable, dirty, cold, dark, contaminated environment that helped him get the disease in the first place.

Rich folks much less commonly got the disease. When they did, they got pretty much the same pneumothorax treatment combined with lots of rest, fresh air, and nourishing food, usually in pleasant sanitariums in warm places like Arizona. The abundant sunshine was believed to be a big part of the cure, too. The Swiss Alps were popular, too.

Syphilis was a different story. While everyone suspected that TB was an ailment mostly of poor people, and therefore not quite respectable for the middle and upper classes, everyone knew absolutely that syphilis had to do with sex and was therefore bad. Totally bad. So much so, in fact, that in the 1940s, in Chicago (hardly a city known for its virtue) no daily newspaper would print the word "syphilis," which ranked right up there with the four letter decorations on the walls of public toilets.

At that time, over half of all the hospital beds in America were occupied by mentally ill persons. Nearly half or more of those were there, not so much as a result of sin, as had been thought for centuries, but as a result of the spirochetal accompaniments of sin, which is at least a little different. Specifically, they were classically insane, posing as Napoleon or Jesus Christ, gesturing, lecturing, proclaiming, screaming and in every way exemplifying the most florid caricatures of crazy people as depicted in cartoons and pulp fiction, and they were that way because of syphilis of the brain.

The condition went by various names: tertiary lues, general paresis, and the generalized paralysis of the insane. Whatever its name, it reflected the invasion of brain tissue by the spirochete that caused syphilis, and represented the third stage of the disease. That stage was reached, inexorably, if the sickness was untreated or inadequately treated. Before it arrived, in some cases, the organism struck the spinal cord, a condition called tabes dorsalis, resulting in a peculiar, foot slapping gait and mental deterioration.

Sometime in the 1920s or 30's a man named Wassermann devised a blood test that detected infection with syphilis. Another physician named Ehrlichman soon determined that the spirochete, a microscopic curlicue worm-like organism determined to be the cause of the disease, could be killed with arsenic, and weakened with the chemical bismuth. A combination of bismuth and arsenic was this researcher's 6 hundred and 6th attempt to find an effective anti-spirochetal agent. It became known as "Dr. Ehrlichman's Magic Bullet," or just "606."

Despite this being a truly stupendous development in the chemotherapy of a disease, and equally world-shaking in that it was the first ever treatment shown to be effective against the world-wide scourge of this terrible disease, the press had a hard time writing about it, and eventually even the number 606 took on a rather risqué, not altogether decent meaning. The treatment was not effective once the third stage of the disease had become established, but worked reasonably well during the primary stage, a secondary stage affecting skin and gums, or a quiescent period called the latent stage in between the others. If lesions resembling semi-solidified abscesses called "gumma" appeared in the liver or brain, the disease was not reversible by arsenic and bismuth, as was true when the victim became wildly crazy.

The trouble with the Magic Bullet was that it was so hard, took so long, and hurt so much. The routine involved a weekly injection, directly into a vein, of an arsenic mixture that first made the patient dizzy, then nauseous, then horribly weak and hot, all this lasting from a half to several hours. Also, if the injected material leaked outside the wall of the vein, which it sometimes did, a horrible looking, painful ulcer developed at the injection site. The weekly injections were given in alternate arms, leaving both quite sore after the course of seven shots.

For the next seven weeks, the hapless victim was given, in alternate buttocks, an immense shot from a huge syringe through a monstrously big needle, of a thick white gooey substance called milk of bismuth, resembling a thick milk of magnesia. The general effects of this were more gentle than those of the arsenic shots, but the buttocks grew increasingly sore, sensitive, and hardened, making sitting nearly impossible.

Following the seven weeks of bismuth, there were seven more weeks of intravenous arsenic, followed by another seven weeks of bismuth in the buttocks, back to the arsenic, back again to the bismuth - continuing for exactly two years. This agonizing, seemingly interminable course of treatment somehow struck many patients as excessive repentance for the single sin of catching syphilis, which could result from a single copulatory adventure.

Knowing that compliance with such an onerous treatment program would be a problem, the authorities provided an incentive. Each patient who was found to have a positive Wasserman test was required to report to an approved doctor for treatment. The patient's name, description, address, etc. and the doctor's name and address were kept on file by the police. The physician was required by law to report to the police any such patient's failure to appear for a scheduled shot, and a warrant was issued for the offender's immediate apprehension and delivery to his healer, or his incarceration if he refused to take any more of this diabolical abuse. Mostly that worked, although a certain number of patients, after failing to appear, simply disappeared altogether and were never found by the police.

The unhappy thing about that was that insufficient, uncompleted treatment with these compounds seemed to hasten the onset of third stage infection, and treatment fugitives were likely to develop general paresis with its florid insanity rather sooner than if they had received no treatment at all, locked up in some mental hospital somewhere else.

Within a few years, as the miracle of penicillin burst on the medical scene and that antibiotic was found effective against the spirochete after only a few (and later just one) shots, the days of sickening shots, ulcerated arms and sore buttocks were ended, and syphilis dramatically receded as a public health problem, though it is still with us.

Penicillin, and before it a chemical named sulfanilamide, were two true medical miracles whose development, hastened by the needs of wounded soldiers during WWII, made their appearance while we were struggling through the free clinics at school. We knew of these developments but they didn't play a dramatic part in our efforts. As we rotated through the various specialty clinics we were far more preoccupied with learning to manage cases of congestive heart failure, gynecological problems, deformities in children, epilepsy, infections - especially the four principal venereal diseases, visual problems and ailments involving the ears, nose and throat.

The single most dramatic clinic event for me, once I had recovered from my first blood drawing from the screaming child, took place in the ENT (ear, nose and throat) clinic. Several of us students were crowded around a man lying on an examination table, undergoing some procedure that required the instructor, a young specialist, to probe deeply into his throat. Suddenly the man stiffened and then began to thrash around. The instructor, startled, backed off with his instrument, but the thrashing continued and the patient grabbed frantically at his throat with both hands, kicking his feet up and down on the table. From the rapidly darkening color of his face and the heaving of his chest, it was clear that he was unable to breathe and was, before our very eyes, suffocating.

No one seemed to know what to do, least of all our instructor who backed away from the table, mouth agape and eyes wide, seemingly unable to do anything at all to help the frantic, heaving body before him. At length the thrashing movements diminished and then stopped altogether, and it was clear that the man had lost consciousness, and would soon enter that state permanently unless he started breathing again, which he failed to do.

The very night before, after a long period of studying the textbook otorhinolaryngological (ear, nose and throat again) surgery, I had read a description of a rather uncommon but simple procedure to open up an obstructed airway, called a tracheotomy. This involved cutting through the skin at the front of the throat below what ordinary humans called the "Adams Apple," finding rings of cartilage that give the trachea, or windpipe, its circular tube-like shape as it heads for the lungs, which lie close to the skin, and cutting through a couple of them. This would permit air to go in and out freely, bypassing any blockage that occurred higher up, in the larynx. It looked to me like just about anyone could do that.

This was my first experience watching someone who was clearly in the process of dying, and it seemed totally unacceptable. Wondering vaguely but briefly why our instructor wasn't doing something about it, I went to the instrument sterilizer near the table, and found in it a scalpel, surgical scissors, hemostats, and some small metal tubes about twice the diameter of a large pencil, with a lip at one end. I seized the scalpel and a hemostat, turned to the man on the table, and pulled his chin up. When I looked at the instructor for some help, he merely gave a short nod, which I took to mean "yes," but neither blinked nor moved. Pulling one of my classmates by the arm, I pushed his hand under the back of the patient's neck, spread the skin below the hapless creature's Adams Apple with my fingers, and sliced. What flashed through my mind at that moment was the time beside Sir Oliver, our corpse, to make that first long-ago cut, and how thick the skin was on his back.

Armed with this memory and the patient's imminent demise, I cut down much harder, apparently, than was quite necessary, piercing both skin and underlying tracheal rings on the first try. I was rewarded with a mighty "whoosh!" of air rushing out, and when I spread the incision with one of the hemostat clamps, air continued to move in and out of the poor man's oxygen-starved lungs.

By this time, the word of the near disaster had spread outside the ENT clinic and any number of more senior people appeared. They shoved us students aside, quickly assessed the situation, placed one of the little hollow tubes in the hole I had so cunningly created, mopped up the surprisingly small amount of blood on the man's throat, and called for an oxygen tank, which any fool could see was no longer necessary. The patient's eyes blinked a few times and then opened wide, signifying survival. At that point, all students were banished from the room.

I fully expected, if not a medal and a generous cash award for my heroic deed, at least some lavish praise from the faculty, but none was ever forthcoming. The few students who were there, however, pounded me on the back and told everybody who would listen about our thrilling brush with a death from laryngospasm. I was, briefly, a celebrity. Even though my grades on exams were high, I always suspected, later, when I was elected by the faculty to membership in the medical honor society, that this event played a part, since I saved the school from the embarrassment of a death in the ENT clinic. Deaths were not acceptable in clinics!

There were other great adventures from time to time in the clinics. Once, during a session in the Venereal Disease clinic when the mandatory 'contact' history was being taken from a robust young man, so that people he had exposed and possibly infected could be identified, hunted down, and offered treatment by the Health Department officials, the patient listed no fewer than twenty separate sexual intercourse episodes in just the previous week! This caused an immediate, excited uproar, and we all gathered around to view this magnificent performer. In reality, he looked quite ordinary, and more than a little amused. When asked where he did all this he laughed, a bit shyly, and said, "Well, mostly in doorways." We loved it. He didn't know the full names of a single one of his partners.

After the sophomore year with its many examinations and then our sessions in the clinics, we started on our clerkships. These were periods of several weeks each, spent on a single separate 'service' in one of the many hospitals affiliated with the University for such training. Some of these, in general medicine, general surgery, obstetrics and gynecology, and pediatrics, were required of everyone, with optional election of various medical and surgical sub-specialties filling out the school year. A modest number of classes were sprinkled throughout the year, and a new academic experience was added: military training.

As the great world war progressed, most of the students had formally joined the Army or Navy Reserve. The requirements for joining the Navy were stricter than those of the Army, so it was considered somehow to be preferable. There was also a long tradition, probably inherited from the British practice of sending its noblemen's sons and the scions of upper class families into the Navy. Those of us with the good sense and the right qualifications to seek Navy commissions, knowing that ships were more comfortable and probably safer (wrong) than foxholes and trenches, therefore felt that we were superior to the poor creatures forced to join the Army and become mud-sloggers. We also, when the time came, had much more attractive uniforms.

The time came, and sooner than we thought. During our second year at school, the Army and Navy both established special programs for medical students, all of whom were expected to enter active duty immediately upon finishing their training. The Army program was called ASTP, the initials standing for "Army Specialized Training Program," although we liked to say it stood for "Absolutely Safe Till Peace," since that also fit the letters and reflected most students' dearest hopes.

The Navy came up with "V-12" for those superior people lucky enough to get in. No one ever was able to figure out what that meant - we hoped it didn't mean "Victory - 12 years" - and no one ever told us. We were required to resign our Naval Reserve Medical Administrative Corps Commissions in the rank of Ensign, and assume our V-12 duties as Apprentice Seamen: lowest of the low. Our Army buddies became Privates.

Following this transition, which we little noticed at first, we were abruptly sent to our respective service's basic training camp. For us aristocrats, this meant the Great Lakes Naval Training Center, a frozen, windswept, bleak set of barracks somewhere up north. It was not very far from Chicago, on the shores of Lake Michigan, despite rumors that it was in reality somewhere just shy of the Arctic Circle. God knows it was cold enough. There, we were to become bona fide apprentice seamen in the U.S. Navy. We despaired of ever seeing our beloved medical school again; much as we actually hated it, we longed to go back.

The few weeks at Great Lakes were a real experience in real life, as it was for millions of our less blessed fellow citizens. It took on the quality of a seriously bad dream, with early morning calisthenics and then marching on a frozen field, classes in drafty makeshift wooden barracks buildings, endless papers to fill out, more marching, a freezing day of nudity in a production-line physical examination process, exhausted sleep alongside thirty-nine other sufferers on hard, narrow cots in another drafty wooden barracks, more marching, more classes, more calisthenics. To make it all more fun, we were doing this over Christmas and New Years, during what should have been a break between quarters.

In addition to the cold and the strain of unaccustomed exercise, however, there were a couple of altogether good and memorable parts to this. The first was the uniform issue. Suddenly, for the first time in my life, I owned six brand new gleaming white tee shirts and six pairs of undershorts. I also had two complete sets of Navy blue coats and trousers, two shiny new pairs of black shoes-plain toe, and several (I forget how many) gleaming white shirts with French cuffs and stiff, detachable collars. Black socks, two black neckties, a hat, a raincoat, and necessary cufflinks and collar buttons. These were midshipmen's uniforms, complete with gold buttons but no insignia. We were henceforth to wear them at all times except, they told us, during sexual congress.

The other good thing was breakfast. The cafeteria line included ham (or bacon) and eggs, potatoes, hotcakes, pork chops, toast, milk, coffee, cereal, fruit juice, and (this really impressed me) peanut butter. You could take all you wanted, they told us, but heaven help you if you left anything uneaten on the tin tray. The quantities and varieties took me right back to the farm in Wisconsin, which was actually not far away, and the admonition about leaving food called up my mother's "starving Armenians," whose plight demanded that we eat everything on our plates, as youngsters.

Somehow, we all survived and headed back to school, resplendent in our new uniforms and feeling very superior to our unfortunate classmates in the Army program, who now wore rough brown wool uniforms just like the ordinary privates that they now were. Some small surprises awaited us.

First, the entire area of the city around the medical school and nearby teaching hospitals and Abbott Hall, about two blocks past these structures in all directions, was declared to be an official Naval Station. This meant that the students, along with the midshipmen in training to be real Navy officers in spite of being called "90-day wonders," whose classes were held a mile or more away on Navy Pier, all had to live in that area, were forbidden to leave it without signing out, were required when moving anywhere in any size group to form up properly and march in step, and were expected to salute any commissioned officer who happened along the street, but especially the Naval Station commander, whether he was in his uniform as a full four-striper captain striding along with his personal aide in tow, or dressed in his favorite knickers, sweater and cap as he whizzed by on his bicycle.

Our Captain was a grizzled, quite elderly (we thought) terribly serious, severe man whose high rank, in those days, put him just below but quite close to God. He was the only full captain any of us had ever seen, equivalent to a "bird" colonel in the Army and just one rank below Rear Admiral or Brigadier General. We were not to see a full bird colonel until sometime later, when our own hated chief of surgery and chairman of the Department of Surgery, donned his new uniform and rank and appeared on our 'station' in full regalia, on his way to Europe to win the war.

The Captain's name was Benyard B. Wygant, and he could have commanded the Bounty in earlier days. He was a graduate of the Naval Academy at Annapolis, and he had a most intriguing and colorful, if tragic, professional history. He was a contemporary of the great Naval commanders who were at that moment conducting the war in the Pacific, with names like Halsey and Nimitz, who had, unlike Captain Wygant, long since become Admirals. He, like those men, had distinguished himself early on, and shortly before the outbreak of World War II was in command of an entire flotilla of destroyers.

While maneuvering off the west coast under Wygant's command, the entire group of vessels ran aground on a reef, and while the Captain was asleep and not in actual operational control of the maneuver, was found by a General Court Martial to have been responsible, since he was the Senior Officer Afloat, and was punished by being "beached," or given a shore assignment and destined never to advance further in rank or command another vessel at sea. The unhappy man was destined therefore to sit idly aside, so to speak, while his comrades went on to glory and he ended up commanding a bunch of medical students and midshipmen in Chicago, far from the sound of battle. This, we were told, accounted for his permanent ill temper, extreme authoritarianism, and general unpleasantness. We were warned never to cross him, and never, never fail to salute him, on his bicycle or off.

A major portion of that final 'pre-clinical' sophomore year was devoted to physiology classes and laboratories, presided over by Professor Andrew C. Ivy, whose son, Andy, was in our class. Dr. Ivy's introductory lecture was an event never to be forgotten. It took place on a dark, stormy day during one of the crashing thunderstorms so common to the Midwest. A small but powerful little man, given to dramatic gestures to emphasize important points in his lectures, he was describing events that could occur during experiments and could affect the outcome of a carefully controlled procedure, distorting the results and leading to an erroneous and misleading conclusion.

He had just reached the place in his lecture where he gave the example of a bolt of lightning striking at a crucial moment during a delicate procedure on an experimental animal, thrusting his arm toward the sky as he described such a startling occurrence, whereupon a brilliant flash of lightning did in fact occur just outside the window of the lecture hall, coupled with an almost simultaneous clap of thunder that shook the windows, rattled the building, and extinguished all the lights. He stopped talking, and we all sat in stunned silence at this proof that the great man could control nature itself and turn it to his purposes to impress his audience and solidify his reputation as one of the giants of medicine.

The power was soon restored, and the professor proceeded with what seemed clearly to be a kind of "See what I mean?" manner, which none of us ever forgot.

Our Dr. Ivy, along with his equally famous antagonist and competitor for fame, Professor Carlson, across town at the University of Chicago, were the principal targets of a wildly active band of rabid anti-vivisectionists under the leadership of a famous professional dancer named Irene Castle MacLaughlin and her husband, who led their band of zealots on periodic invasions of the schools to rescue dogs. They staged these raids accompanied by reporters and photographers from various 'scandal sheets' and sometimes the more conventional press, dramatically bursting into the physiology laboratories and physically grabbing anesthetized animals in various stages of surgical procedures off the operating tables and rushing out into the street carrying the bleeding beasts outside for all to see and be horrified by.

The antivivisectionists ultimately persuaded the City Council to hold hearings on their demands that the medical schools be forbidden by law to use live animals in research and teaching. Drs. Ivy and Carlson were both summoned before the council to defend this barbaric practice, and a large group of us students resolved to show up at the council meeting to lend our support. Accordingly, dressed in our fine new Army and Navy uniforms, we left our Naval Station, without permission from anyone in spite of the fact that we were away during regular school hours, and packed the hearing room.

Our behavior during the hearing was exemplary. Unlike the practices of today, the public behavior of students in the 1940's was quite decorous. We were conscious of our newly established status as members of the Armed Forces, which in itself served as a constraint upon any impulse to be boisterous or confrontational, but our massive presence as serious students at graduate level in the healing arts, we felt, would surely have a positive impact. We listened, enthralled, as two of the world's leading physiologists made a telling case for continuing to use animals (would you have us let students practice on humans? Who? Maybe war prisoners?) That pretty well took care of it, and the antivivisection furor seemed to quiet down after that.

We students, however, were in trouble. Captain Wygant was furious, not just about our truancy from classes to attend this earth-shaking event, but about our unauthorized absence from our "duty station" during regular duty hours. We heard he was considering massive expulsions and immediate transfers to shipboard duty in Pacific combat zones, but evidently that didn't prove feasible, so we were let off with a six week series of Saturday afternoon classes, following drill, naturally, devoted to the subject of 'Rocks and Shoals,' which is an informal name for the Articles Governing the United States Navy, and the Manual for Courts Martial.

When, at long last, the clerkships started, I elected to go first to Children's Hospital. I was seriously considering pursuing a career in pediatrics at that point, having already begun the process of selecting and rejecting various fields of medicine. I had ruled out gynecology, ophthalmology, otorhinolaryngology, internal medicine, urology, dermatology and infectious diseases, along with psychiatry, neurology and nephrology, all of which seemed either to be too dull or too disgusting to devote one's life to. As my choices narrowed down, mostly to surgical specialties, I was beginning to despair. I found myself wondering whether anything in medicine would prove to be attractive enough to do. Taking care of helpless kids seemed to offer hope of a fulfilling mission in life, so I tried that first.

Chicago's Children's Hospital was highly regarded, very large, and the sought-after training spot for clerks, interns, residents and fellows from all the medical schools in the city and many others from elsewhere in the country. The children brought here were of all social and economic classes, and were treated without consideration of their families' ability to pay. They were also, uniformly, quite seriously ill or injured, otherwise they would have been cared for at home or in doctors' offices.

It was here that I witnessed the genuine miracle of chemicals, just now bursting onto the scene in medicine with great impact. The best example, at that time, was sulfanilamide. This was a relatively recent development, a therapeutic agent that directly combated infections of many kinds quite unlike anything known before. At first, it was made available only to military patients, many more of whom had died or became incapacitated due to sickness, mainly infections, than were ever put down by bullets and bombs. Every wound incurred on a battlefield was "dirty," which is to say contaminated not only by soil but by bacteria. Wounds of the arms and legs that didn't do much immediate physical damage frequently gave rise to massive, raging infections that often resulted in amputations and death.

Sulfanilamide and its later variants, sulfathiazol and sulfasuccidine, were often effective in preventing wound infections altogether, or reversing and eliminating the infectious process after it had begun. Nothing comparable had ever existed. Soldiers in combat were given 'sulfa' tablets and packets of sulfa powder to be sprinkled on wounds, and corpsmen and field medical units were given large supplies of it. It was not a panacea; it didn't kill all infectious organisms by any means, and sometimes killed the patient by shutting down his kidneys.

When production of the sulfonamides, as they were generally called, became sufficient to exceed what was needed by soldiers and sailors, the compounds were made available to the civilian community, and Children's Hospital began giving them to the many infected children who came there.

A common, serious infection problem involved the ears. When the inner ear became infected for any reason, the infection many times spread into a bony knob situated just behind the ear, called the mastoid process, on the skull. That bony protrusion was not hard, solid bone but had a kind of beehive internal structure, and infections could spread rapidly through it. When that happened, and the infected area grew in size, it could invade into the cavity of the skull, producing meningitis - infection of the protective coverings of the brain - or encephalitis: infection of the brain itself. Both of these extensions of the infection could result in permanent severe brain damage and death. Moreover, there was no specific treatment for it, once begun. The child survived or didn't, independently of what we did for him.

To slow or stop the infection before it actually invaded inside the skull, an attempt was often made to drain the infected area by means of an operation called a mastoidectomy. That involved opening the scalp behind the ear, and with a hammer and chisel chopping away at the diseased mastoid bone to clean the infected area out mechanically and with antiseptic solutions. Care had to be taken to avoid perforating through the skull and spreading the bacteria into the meninges or the brain itself. The child was left, if he survived, with a pronounced hole, eventually covered with skin but big enough to accommodate a small plum behind his ear. There had been several kids at Lincoln School when I was there who had these pronounced holes in their heads.

The operation seemed brutal and crude, as did so many procedures done in those days, but it was often the only thing that could be done to save a profoundly ill child. Because Children's Hospital was a place of last resort in many cases, it was necessary to do this operation more than a hundred times each year. Until sulfa drugs came along. When they did, the number of mastoidectomies dropped immediately to a handful the very first year, and the number stayed low thereafter.

My weeks at Children's soon convinced me that pediatrics was not to be my chosen path in life. I found myself unable to detach myself sufficiently from the sufferings of little kids to achieve any level of comfort at all. Tiny infants needing fluids had to have needles stuck in the large venous cavity at the top of the skull (the 'soft spot' everyone has felt) because there aren't big enough veins in arms and legs to accommodate needles. I found that hard. Other kids were given fluids through long needles inserted in the soft flesh on the inner sides of their thighs. That seemed barbaric; although the kids who got that were so sick, they possibly didn't really feel much. Once, after I had placed the needles in a particularly ill child, he expired, literally under my hands, as his mother stood by, shrieking.

The children seemed so helpless, so sick, and so sad, and their parents were frequently distraught to an extreme, demanding and irrational as they implored us to deliver their little ones from their awful, often hopeless state, that I found myself wondering how anyone could possibly endure living like that as a pediatrician. At the end of my six weeks, I fled thankfully back to school and other clerkships less destructive of one's soul.

Before starting the clerkships, during our sophomore year, an event occurred that introduced a serious and threatening element in my career. I had taken the opportunity to spend part of a Sunday afternoon ice-skating. Showering afterward, I turned off the hot water faucet firmly, since it tended to leak, and the cruciate porcelain faucet handle broke in my hand. Bright red blood spurted vigorously and pulsated with each heartbeat, revealing that an artery had been severed in my thumb, and it was impossible to shut it off completely even with many layers of bandage.

The skating rink was an outdoor pond in Evanston, so I dressed quickly in the friend's apartment where I had showered, wrapped a towel around the bandaged thumb to catch the leaking blood, and set out to find a bus that would take me to Evanston Hospital, where once I had sterilized mattresses and polished brass kickplates. In about a half hour, with the towel now thoroughly soaked, I made my way to the emergency room where, as it happened, the hospital's senior surgical resident was on duty.

He unwrapped my wound, and stepped back as the blood squirted on the front of his white coat. He was obviously impressed by the seriousness of the wound and the imperative need to stop the blood loss. Grasping a hemostat forceps, he began probing into the open slash, causing me considerable pain, as he tried in vain to grasp the end of the severed artery. After a number of thrusts deeper and deeper into the palm of my hand at the base of the thumb, he finally caught the vessel and clamped it off. By then it was questionable as to which of us was in greater distress, but at last the worst was over.

When he stepped back to gather himself and his equipment, and despite my shocked and tremulous state, I saw that he was pale, sweating profusely, and he was at least as tremulous as I was! Only much later did I learn that he had been up and working for more than 24 hours straight through, common in those times, and moreover was preparing to elope later that very day to marry one of the ER nurses. No wonder he was shaky!

The consequences of that brutal session turned out to be far more serious than he or I suspected. He had successfully stopped the bleeding, a very important first requirement. What he had failed to do was to notice that the tendon, which allowed the thumb to flex, had also been severed by the sharp broken edge of the porcelain faucet, as had the nerve that ran alongside the artery. His repeated and increasingly frantic probings into the wound with his hemostat had doubled over the cut ends of the tendon and nerve, and both had started to retract up into, not only my palm, but also my wrist beyond that.

Within a few days, back in school where I was having great difficulty trying to write because of the bulky bandages, it became clear that all was not well. There was no sensation at all in the thumb, and it would not bend at all. Furthermore my palm and wrist, outwardly intact, were beginning to be seriously painful.

Fortunately, our surgical faculty included one of the world's leading hand surgeons, a man named Sumner Koch, author of one of the definitive texts on this relatively new surgical sub-specialty of the repair and reconstruction of the hand. I caught him in the hall outside a lecture room and thrust my bandaged hand at him, asking if I could possibly come to see him about it. Obviously irritated at the interruption, he agreed somewhat reluctantly and told me to make an appointment. He seemed cold, distant, unfriendly and uninterested.

Nonetheless, I found his office and his equally distant secretary, who signed me up to see the great man a week later at 7 AM, admonishing me to be there at least a half hour early. When the day came, I was steered into his inner office at the appointed hour, and hardly looking up from a chart on the desk before him, he directed me, without preamble, to "take off those bandages!" There had been no greeting, no offer to sit down, and no questions at all. So much for Sir William Osler's medical history taking.

Once that was done, he came around his desk to where I was standing, and took my wounded hand in his with incredible gentleness, delicately feeling along the wound and in my palm and my wrist. All he said was, "Typical porcelain faucet injury. How'd it happen?" I told him, including my ordeal in the emergency room. He merely shook his head disapprovingly, declaring that the tendon was gone, infection had set it, and very complicated surgery would be necessary to repair the "mess." That was hardly reassuring. He then told me to go home and soak the injured hand, up to mid-forearm, in very hot water for two hours, twice a day without fail, and come back in four weeks.

I protested that this would be very difficult with classes all day and multiple exams every week. He scowled, and in evident exasperation said, "You want a workable hand or not?" Properly chastened and apologetic, I withdrew.

A few days later, I was summoned to the Dean's office, feeling exactly like I did when Lincoln School's Principal, Mrs. Cortes, had sent for me. The Dean was far more friendly than my hand surgeon had been, but after greeting me warmly he assumed a far more serious demeanor that I found ominous and disconcerting. He told me that Dr. Koch had reported my visit and his impression of the problem and what had to be done. He then said that it was only fair that he tell me that if the repair and reconstruction of my dominant right hand failed to produce a fully functional result, I could not continue with my class!

That meant, of course, the Navy. As an apprentice seaman, at least at first, for I doubted I could regain my Ensign's commission with a crippled hand, while just about anyone could swab decks.

Severely shaken, I returned to my classes and my hot soaks. I could not write in my accustomed fashion and found it impossible to do so either legibly or speedily enough with my clumsy left hand, so for the next several months took a one-hour oral test every time the class had an hour-long written one, and I did not have usable lecture notes to study. My Korean friend came through during this time of tribulation, frequently sitting with me before tests, whenever that was possible, and firing questions at me that we expected would be asked, earning my everlasting gratitude.

Four weeks after my first visit with Dr. Koch, I returned to his office. He examined my hand, by now beautifully soft and smooth and no longer inflamed, and indicated his approval. I was instructed to check in at Passavant Memorial Hospital, associated with the school and across the street from it, where better-paying private patients were usually sent after being seen privately by members of the faculty.

I checked in on the designated day, after finishing classes, and was placed in a tiny cubicle barely large enough to hold the bed and bedside stand. I remember that I was lying there wondering if the rich private patients were stuck into little cells like this one too, when my reveries were interrupted by the arrival of the anesthesiologist. Finally I was given an inkling of what lay in store.

The operation, I was told, would be a long one, lasting seven or eight hours. My recovery would be a bit slow after such a long period of general anesthesia. The surgeon was planning to take a tendon from my foot (first I'd heard of that!) and transplant it into my thumb and hand, up to my wrist. While that tendon was being dissected out and prepared for the transplantation, which would require two surgeons, Dr. Koch and two other assisting surgeons would be cleaning out the extensively scarred areas in the thumb and palm, using the smallest possible incisions so as to minimize further scarring that could seriously affect function. The doubled-over, badly distorted end of the cut tendon, which had retracted all the way up to the wrist, would have to be freed up, trimmed, cut back to where it was healthy, and then attached to the tendon taken from the foot.

The graft had to lie in a sheath made from other tissues in the foot, threaded through the palm and up the thumb, where it would be attached to the bone. If all went well, the attachments held and the sheath stayed slick and not stuck to the new tendon, and no new infection set in, I'd have a hand that worked, and could once again hold a beer bottle without dropping it! I assumed that would also mean I could stay in school.

Based on my dissection of a hand during anatomy class it seemed to me that what they were setting out to do approached the impossible. I spend the night alternately praying and planning for my new role aboard some ship, and got little rest. When I regained consciousness the following night, I found my right forearm and hand in an extremely uncomfortable plaster cast that held my wrist bent as far as it could possibly go, so as to keep tension off the new tendon attachments that might pull them apart. That was to last for another four weeks of oral examinations and anxiety about the future.

At long last, the cast came off. What emerged was a limp, wasted, pale, useless appendage that looked fresh from a cadaver after lengthy illness, except that the skin was more wrinkled. However, Dr. Koch seemed mightily pleased. He never seemed particularly fond of me personally, but he loved that hand. So much so, in fact, that he periodically, from then on, required my attendance at medical meetings around the entire Chicago area so he could show the results of his work, live, when he reported on it to colleagues. No question was ever again raised about my physical fitness to finish out my education, and the Navy was forced to find its apprentice seamen elsewhere.

Nearly all students, whatever their course, seem forever to feel the need for more money than they usually have, and we were no exception. I had begun medical school on a full scholarship plus a modest stipend for incidental expenses, and while that seemed adequate at the time, I jumped at any opportunity to make a few dollars more. When the Navy program started, things were even better. The taxpayers of the U.S. paid for our room, board, tuition, supplies, laundry, books, instruments and health care, and gave us the handsome sum of $21 a month besides. There was little time or opportunity to spend much more than that handsome sum. In consequence, I leaped at every opportunity to earn more, which usually arose when the call went out for volunteer subjects in medical research projects.

Some of these were memorable. Once, for a couple of weeks at the handsome stipend of a dollar a day, I carried a small rubber tube from my nose down through my throat, esophagus, stomach, and into the small intestine, its upper end clamped off and tucked into my shirt pocket. In spite of the clamp, the upper end of the tube regularly leaked a little green bile into the shirt pocket, permanently disfiguring the otherwise immaculate white shirt with French cuffs and detachable collar that was part of my new uniform.

A blessedly shorter study required an additional tube in the other end of one's anatomy. This one had a small balloon at the nether end, which was periodically inflated. That session paid twice as much, for what we all felt were obvious reasons, and proved to be surprisingly uncomfortable and messy, but was still well worth the money.

Probably the premier study of them all was done in response to a problem that had arisen on the battlefields of North Africa and later in Europe. Soldiers wounded in battle not only bled from their wounds, but also frequently went into shock and often endured severe pain. It became the practice, therefore, to issue to foot soldiers likely to be engaged in fire fights and in danger of being hit by bullets and shell fragments and other projectile objects, two small soft metal tubes looking like miniature toothpaste tubes and containing one half grain (a fairly large dose) of morphine, as the tartrate.

Attached to this little tube was a substantial needle, about an inch and a half long, encased in a cap that covered it. Soldiers were instructed, if wounded - and ONLY if wounded - to pull off the little cap, shove the needle into any handy spot, right through the uniform, and squeeze the tube, injecting the morphine. Unused syrettes, as these gadgets were called, were to be turned in after the battle, if unused. Corpsmen carried extras.

This was, from both a simple medical as well as a humanitarian standpoint, a fairly good idea. In practice, however, there were the inevitable unintended consequences leading to the universal military phenomenon called "SNAFU," meaning 'situation normal, all fucked up." Too often, after a soldier was wounded and down, something like the following scenario would play out. First, he would grab a syrette and give himself his shot. Soon after that, particularly if he began to feel some pain and see more blood, he would give himself the other shot. Before long, one of his buddies would see him lying there. Saying something like, "Jesus, George, you've been hit! I'll get a corpsman; you just stay there quiet-like. Here's one of my shots to help pass the time." In would go the third big dose of morphine. Then, to make matters worse, another buddy might show up, see that George was pretty well out of things and maybe in danger of dying, and give him his fourth dose.

Physical damage to the body and severe pain can be thought of as physiological, as opposed to chemical, antidotes to morphine, counteracting at least some of the narcotizing effects of the drug. Therefore, while the dose received by our wounded soldier might be enough to put a normal, unwounded person who was not in pain completely out, it might not have that pronounced effect on the injured soldier. Even if he stayed awake, though, he was likely to begin ignoring the chaos surrounding him, blissfully enjoying his repose as he watched the pretty fireworks going off around him and making no effort to protect himself in any way.

Someone decided that it would be a great idea to combine the morphine in the syrettes with some other agent that might diminish the undesirable soporific and hypnotic effects of the narcotic but not interfere with the pain-killing and shock-preventing qualities of this otherwise most effective class of drugs. Such potential chemical antidotes did seem to exist in drugs like Metrazol and Coramine, used to produce convulsions in the treatment of mental disease, and stimulants like benzedrine and dexedrine, as well as ephedrine and caffeine.

From this reasoning arose a research project that always ranked first in our minds, of the many we took part in. The problem and the possible solutions to be tested were not explained to those of us who volunteered; we were merely told that during each upcoming test period we would receive a small injection and undergo a brief battery of tests, all to be done in the free hour or so before dinner.

About a dozen of us were accepted as test subjects, and were assembled in the physiology lab, where Dr. Ivy gave us a short speech about the importance of what we were about to do, and its value to our fighting men around the world, engaged at that very moment in bloody and life-threatening battles from which, he reminded us, we were blessedly free. At least for the moment.

We were then given a series of little tasks, resembling parts of the standard intelligence tests then in use, followed by a number of tests of reaction time, coordination and dexterity. Finally we were seated in what looked like a dental chair. In that position we had a small vice-like piece of machinery attached to a thumb, connected by some wires to a small control panel. When a knob on the control panel was turned, causing a needle on a gauge to rise, the machinery compressed the thumb. When the pressure became intolerable, we were to say so, and it would stop. Finally, a probe not unlike an ordinary dental instrument was placed in our mouth touching a gold or silver filling or inlay, whose exact position was recorded.

When another knob connected to the dental probe was rotated, one felt at first a small momentary shock, little more than a vibration, in the tooth being touched. Succeeding pulses were more clearly electrical, steadily increasing in strength until the tooth became painful at each pulse and more so each time it came back. Again we were told to signal when it became intolerable, and they would stop. The readings during both of these little torture chamber device exercises fresh from Nazi Germany were carefully recorded in our individual charts, along with scores on each of the previous tests.

That done, we were each given an injection of some unknown solutions, each one of us getting a differently labeled concoction, and told to sit down and relax. With no idea of what was to follow, we did so.

Within minutes, we had all rushed to lab sinks, our heads under the gooseneck faucets, and started vomiting. We all noted that, while vomiting was usually an exceedingly unpleasant experience, this time it didn't seem so bad, and didn't last long.

A short time later, we were put through exactly the same routine of tests and torture, again not at all unpleasant, and sent on our way. None of us was very hungry.

The vomiting ceased after the second or third test day, and we figured out that we were being given some kind of opiate. On a subsequent test day, we presented Dr. Ivy with our suspicions, which he confirmed, adding that he could not tell us what else might be in our injected cocktails, so not to ask. Nor could he tell us what kind of opiate we were getting, or in what dosage.

The next half dozen or so test sessions were really quite pleasant. Dr. Ivy showed up most times, and engaged with us in wonderful, searching discussions of science and medicine, ethics and honor and politics and war and the mysteries of life. The vomiting had long since stopped, and we all began showing up earlier and earlier for these pleasant, inspiring sessions with this great man of medicine, until, suddenly, they stopped the whole project. We later heard that concern was growing about how much fun we all seemed to be having. We also learned that nothing very useful emerged from the study, and our soldiers kept on getting syrettes of plain old morphine tartrate.

Clerkships made us feel more like 'real' doctors than anything before. There in a wide variety of hospitals associated with the medical school, we saw sicker patients that we had in the clinics, and began to learn about the politics and power structure of hospitals, each of them a special subculture of its own but surprisingly similar in certain respects. In each one, there was a clear, rigid class system among the medical staff. The top rank in each department was always the chairman or chief of the service. In most teaching hospitals this powerful and exalted man - always, in those days, a man - was also a full professor on the faculty of one or another of Chicago's four medical schools: Northwestern, Chicago, Illinois or Loyola, all parts of major universities. Most of these mostly older, dignified and highly prestigious physicians took care of a few private patients, often limiting their selection to prominent, important members of the community who paid dearly for the privilege of being cared for by one of the medical elite.

Chiefs of Service, and chiefs of the emerging subsections of major departments, rarely conducted the actual diagnosis and treatment of patients on wards or semi-private rooms. When one of their "own" private patients was hospitalized, it was in a private room, sometimes in a wholly private section of the hospital, and aside from a daily visit from the great man in charge, was treated by proxies in the form of lesser, but still important, members of their staffs. The clinical duties of the chiefs generally consisted of once-weekly walking rounds and less frequent "grand rounds," generally conducted in an auditorium or amphitheater.

Walking rounds were a kind of ritualized medical parade, led by the Marshal, in the person of the Chief. One or more senior "attending" physicians from outside the hospital might come next, following close behind. Next came the senior resident physician, followed in strictly held order of seniority by the less senior, down to the most junior, of the residents. Behind them trotted the interns, most senior to most junior, and then the clerkship students from the medical school. The nursing staff followed, again in order of rank and seniority, except for the single most senior nurse of that department, variously called the head or supervising or chief medical (or surgical or orthopedic or pediatric, etc.) nurse, who trotted alongside but always slightly behind, the head doctor. Bringing up the rear of that long line came the student nurses allowed that day to go on rounds with the mighty.

The great man leading this entourage would proceed steadily through the ward and the multi-bedded rooms, nodding benignly at the patient in each bed, pausing from time to time to extend a word of greeting or encouragement, and stopping expectantly at the bedside of particular patients warranting special attention for some reason. The nurse at the front of the line (but a step behind the supreme medical being) would hastily produce the patient's chart, handing it to the leader to peruse while the resident physician most intimately familiar with the case or its treatment would step forward to offer details and answer questions.

While this set of activities was taking place, the following line of people would bunch up to form a respectful crowd close to the principal players in the drama, so as to absorb the important learning points to be gained as the case was discussed among the most learned. The Chief might turn to the patient to elicit further details of his history, or to the resident to review physical and laboratory findings, examine the X-Ray films, holding them up to the nearest light or a bright bedside window, and ultimately deliver a brief lecture on the nature and expected course of the patient's illness or injuries. Finally, turning once again to the patient, he might point to some physical manifestation of whatever it is that's wrong and invite closer observation and perhaps even palpation of the object of all this attention by others on the medical staff.

The entourage then moves on, everyone of its members a bit better educated about that particular kind of medical situation, and properly inspired, hopefully, by this demonstration of medical leadership. This sometimes-stilted process was often a truly effective teaching device. It harked far back to much earlier days, when textbooks were smaller and scarcer, when would-be physicians traveled great distances to follow along behind the real giants of medicine in the 19th and early 20th centuries to watch and learn their techniques, to absorb their acumen and wisdom and often revolutionary ideas. Medicine was still emerging from a long dark period of ignorance and dependence upon untested and uncertain nostrums, arsenic and opium, purgatives and bloodletting, salts and prayers, possibly to the wrong Gods. I realized with a certain shock that I was coming in right at the end of that era, as I walked along in various positions in that parade of learners following their teacher from bed to bed, often learning something important that I hadn't heard in any class.

Those parades have all but disappeared today. There are too many patients, too many staff, too much technical data to collect and review, too little time and too much to know, too short stays in the hospital because there is too much cost to it, and too many other demands to be met and forms to be filled out. And money to be made.

As clerks, we followed along in many such parades, and likewise attended many 'grand rounds.' These larger gatherings in places where one could sit down and even take notes are still widely used, not only in teaching hospitals but in others as well. They usually consist of a detailed recitation of a case, from the presenting complaints through the physical findings, the laboratory and radiological studies, various scans and assays, the procedures performed, drugs used, drugs abandoned, and everything known about the patient up to that very moment. In addition there may be discussions of possible alternate ("differential") diagnoses, additional diagnoses, treatment plans, and prognostications as to course and outcome.

Presiding over such an assembly is usually the chief of the service, possibly his boss if the service involved is a subspecialty, often a visiting expert consultant in the field or one with special knowledge of the malady at hand. The case presentation is generally made by one of the resident physicians and may be augmented by the senior resident and other members of the staff. The pathologist and the radiologist may contribute, and the nursing staff is often asked for their special observations. Questions are invited from the audience of other physicians, nurses, students, allied health professionals or even administrators. Ultimately one of the (designated) senior persons present formulates his conception of the case and ideas about its proper further management. Others are free to dispute this and offer alternatives. Generally the session ends with some level of agreement as to further actions to be taken, and everyone goes back to work.

Once again, this can be a superb teaching and learning device. It survives in spite of having to compete with tumor boards, quality assurance committees, risk reduction boards, infection control committees, utilization review committees, credentialing committees, administrative meetings and a host of others like the journal club, mortality review group, and special presentations by visiting dignitaries.

During my clerkship years, most of those groups didn't even exist, but the walking rounds and grand rounds were major parts of the experience.

My clerkship in Obstetrics and Gynecology, or OB-GYN, I elected to take at the immense Cook County Hospital. There were several reasons for this. First was the large number of babies delivered there every day. Second was the well-known shortage of fully trained staff to do the work, allowing medically low ranked people like interns and students, with little close supervision, to perform many procedures themselves that in smaller, especially private, hospitals they would only be allowed to watch. The clincher was the option to take part of that clerkship under an institution without walls but operated from a small office in the hospital, called the Chicago Maternity Center.

Some years before I arrived on the scene, the Center had been founded by a physician at the University of Chicago named Joseph B. DeLee. Like all obstetricians of the time, he was deeply concerned with puerperal infections, often called Childbed Fever, most common among the poor living in what we now call the 'inner city' slums. It was the cause of much illness and suffering among new mothers, as well as infant mortality.

More interested in bacteriology than most of his contemporaries, he had his own bacteriology laboratory where he cultured and studied bacteria. He had observed, in true medical-detective fashion, that he had never observed bacterial growth, or molds or fungi, for that matter, on newspaper in alleys in the slums of Cicago, even when it had been used to wrap rotting garbage. Intrigued, he gathered pieces of filthy newspaper from those alleys, took them to his lab, and put samples of the paper in Petri dishes and flasks of various culture media commonly used to grown bacterial colonies. Nothing grew at all, no matter how correct the conditions for growing microorganisms, and he concluded that for whatever reasons, newsprint would not support the growth of germs.

DeLee saw in this finding the possibility of successfully reducing the problem of puerperal infection in home deliveries, where the vast majority of poor mothers delivered their new babies. With a few (there were few, in the 20's) social workers, and the reluctant participation of Cook County, he designed the program he called the Maternity Center. The word was spread, especially among the crowded brownstone mansions-turned-tenement houses around Maxwell Street south of Chicago's downtown, that free medical care during delivery was available from the Center. All that was required was that the expectant mother come to the little office in Cook County Hospital and register her name and address and undergo a simple blood test for the "old Joe," or "gleet." as syphilis was commonly called in that neighborhood.

There was one other thing. She had to collect a 2-foot high pile of newspapers, opened to full-page size and packed tightly, along with an ordinary bucket. These two items had to be kept in the room where she planned to have her baby, regardless of how many other people were living in that room. (The record number of validated "other people" living in the expectant mother's single room was 12, but was thought actually to be substantially higher.) If she turned out to have active syphilis, her case was reported to the Health Department and she was required to get treatment, but this didn't happen much.

Then, when the pains came, all she had to do was call or have a friend call the Center, and a doctor would soon appear at her bedside to deliver her baby properly.

The "doctor" who was to appear was one of us medical students who had opted for the Center as part of our Cook County Hospital clerkship. We were outfitted with a small black bag which contained, contrary to myth, not a newborn baby but a small steel pan, a bottle of undiluted Lysol and one of green soap, a safety razor, some curved needles with suture material to repair torn tissues, surgical and bandage scissors, hemostats, cotton ribbon for tying off the umbilical cord, and some gauze pads for mopping up.

The first task was to clear the room. There were always 'helpers,' other women from the tenement eager to lend a hand and give advice. In addition there were usually a number of children, relatives and neighbors, and grown men eager to fill the boring hours of their unemployment by watching the drama of the beginning of a new life. Sometimes there were animals - dogs, cats, pet birds, and on one memorable occasion a noisy, aggressive rooster who sat on the foot of the iron bedstead surveying the colorful scene.

Next, we hung our overcoats on the inevitable nails driven into the wall for that purpose, carefully hanging a couple of opened sheets of newspaper on the nail first, to prevent roaches or ants from seeking the warm recesses of our garments as they hung there. We would then turn to the patient.

The leading actor in this performance, which generally took on the character of a major crisis, was usually far along into labor by the time we got there via the elevated trains and the bus. She would at the very least moan and cry out loudly to both the Lord and the doctor to help her escape from the torment and agonies of her labor pains, meanwhile thrashing about on the bed, clutching at helping hands, weeping copious amounts of tears and sometimes actually shrieking. Inevitably this brought back many of the helpers and spectators we had earlier banished from the room, and chaos was the norm.

We would have our helpers roll her up on her side while we spread a pad of newspapers a good half inch thick over the bed, then roll her back, put a large roll of newspapers under her neck, and form a large funnel from still more newspapers, pinning it to the mattress at the level of her hips and directing the narrow end into the bucket she was required to have handy. Bystander-helpers were then enlisted to pull her knees up toward her shoulders, and we would proceed with our first, and often hardest, actual patient-care procedure.

That first-required medical action was to shave the perineum closely and thoroughly, so that no potentially disease-bearing hairs remained to contaminate the emerging baby. No number of years experience shaving one's own face adequately prepared anyone for that shave job. For one thing, one's face wasn't usually thrashing about the whole time, and the possibility of a great gush of amniotic fluid, as the bag of waters broke, was never an issue. However, it had to be done. It was both horrifying and terrifying the first time, and only got a little better with repetition. We used the little steel pan, some green soap solution (and I always added a little Lysol, just to be safe and also to get the poor woman's attention diverted a little from her uterus to her lower levels), cold water and the safety razor from our black bag of magic tricks.

About half the time, the waters burst during this procedure. If you were really alert and really quick, you could dodge and miss most of it, but usually you got wet. It was comforting, a little, to recall that amniotic fluid is sterile and free from bacteria, and the whole area has just been cleanly shaved with strong soap (and a little Lysol).

From that point on, all that remained was to comfort and calm the mother, and encourage her in the timeless words of the midwife to "bear down, Mother" with the arrival of each pain and to "take a deep breath, Dear," between contractions. It was during these breaks in the action that I learned to do hypnosis, finding it useful indeed in the absence of any other agents for reducing pain, and discovering also that most of these poor, largely ignorant women, mostly recent migrants from the deep South, were highly suggestible and easy to put nearly to sleep during the whole procedure. It also eliminated the thrashing and screaming.

As labor progressed, and the newborn's head began to 'crown' at the vaginal opening, it was the usual practice to place a hand on the top of the head and gently partially arrest its progress just enough to prevent a strong contraction from causing such an explosive expulsion of the head that it tore the mother's tissues or bruised the baby's head or face. Once, while I performed this simple act, a male onlooker not even related to the mother suddenly tackled me from one side, admonishing me to "Stop pushing that baby's head back in there, Man!" The student assisting me was able to pull him off and reassure him as to my intentions, and I resumed my healing stance and eased the little head out without damage.

The rooster at the foot of the bed bothered me seriously, the time he showed up to watch. I believed that he was probably very dirty, living as he did in the tenement, and had no business being there anyway, so I kept interrupting my ministrations to the patient and shooing him off his perch, but in moments he would return. Finally I gave in and just left him alone, and the baby was delivered satisfactorily in spite of him.

It was a favorite practice of medical students delivering the babies of poor, uneducated and usually unwed black mothers, to inquire of the new mother what she was going to name the baby. More often than not, she hadn't even thought about it. The student would then suggest something, usually a medical term, usually outlandish, like "Appendectomy" Brown or "Acne Rosacea" Jones, for a girl, and the new mother was often thrilled and grateful for the wonderful suggestion. That seemed kind of a cruel thing to do, and a far better idea occurred to me, having to do with our much-feared, rather pompous chairman of the Department of Surgery at the medical school.

His name was striking and, in a way, highly appealing to our poor clientele. While his daughter, Nancy, who some of us got to know at school dances and parties, was a lovely, gentle, very sweet and enormously attractive person, our chairman, Dr Loyal Davis, shared none of her better qualities. He was the very model of a major neurosurgeon, a medical type thought of in those days as invariably arrogant, imperious, relentlessly demanding of his assistants, rarely willing even to talk to students except to humiliate them in class, entirely overbearing and insufferable. Even worse, Dr. Davis controlled our entire set of grades in surgical subjects, though he rarely actually conducted a class. He did this, we believed, based on a single, brief personal interview during our third year.

Each student was required to report for the dreaded interview immaculately groomed and clothed. He was ordered to sit facing the great man across a properly immense and magnificent desk, while the Chairman glanced through the student's grades in various exams dealing with all the surgical specialties, as well as faculty reports of classroom as well as clerkship performance. He would then demand to know what specialty the student planned to pursue. If the answer was "General practice," we had heard, the hapless student was instantly dismissed and got a 'C' grade for all the surgical courses and clerkships he had taken, regardless of his actual grades, because the good doctor had often made clear his contempt for all but the most highly trained specialists, and primarily those in surgery.

I naturally reported that I would become a surgeon, hoping to match the magnificence of my Uncle Charlie. He gave me an 'A,' but I always felt a little guilty about it since I really hadn't fully made up my mind. In addition, I resented the whole process, which I considered grossly unfair and arbitrary.

My interview was scheduled, with little advance notice, in the middle of my stint at Cook County while assigned to the Maternity Center, causing me no small amount of inconvenience and resentment. My attitude during the interview no doubt conveyed my anger at this imposition on my valuable time, but if anything, Dr. Davis seemed actually to be favorably impressed by my demeanor, which fell just short of surliness. On my way back to the Center after that little ordeal, I had a sudden inspiration, based on the great man's obvious grandiosity and his hugely inflated self-image.

Surely, I thought, he would be pleased that people would name their offspring after him, he being such a great surgeon and all. While no medical student, just as surely, would dream of naming his own progeny in a way that would remind him of the professor who had, beyond any other, seemed to revel in our worm-like status as the lowest of the low, medically, and the stupidest ever to sneak into that medical school, Loyal Davis would never have imagined any such thing. There was, I realized, a wonderful opportunity here.

Henceforth, when any of my new mothers in the unspeakably filthy, poverty-stricken slums of south Chicago wanted a name for her new baby, I would enthusiastically suggest "Loyal." Boy or girl, it didn't matter, for the name carried no automatic gender connection.

The long-term result of this creative idea, beginning that very year in the free clinics at all of Chicago's medical school free clinics, would be a steady stream of scrawny babies, among the poorest of the poor, all proudly bearing the name Loyal.

The inspiration came to me as I left the man's office, and the whole idea was elaborated as I rode the rattling elevated train back out to the county hospital, becoming steadily more excited and enthusiastic about the plan. I shared that enthusiasm with my fellow clerks at the Maternity Center, and it proved highly contagious. A steady stream of both "Loyals" and "Loyal Davises" began to emerge and show up in our clinics. A cherished tradition had been born; how long it lasted I do not know, but surely as long as the original dominated our surgical education.

Many years later, when she was First Lady, I told Nancy how we had started naming newborns after her father, leaving out any hint as to the irony that lay behind it in the minds of his suffering students. The professor, by that time, was quite old and had long since retired from practice and from teaching. On next seeing him she had told him what I had said. She reported that, upon hearing that numerous newborns had been given his name, and clearly having forgotten what the Chicago Maternity Center was like, he began to weep, saying something like "I knew my students loved and honored me, but I never before realized just how much." That was more accurate than he could have imagined, but needless to say, I never pursued the matter further. In truth, it was pleasing to hear that the old man felt good about it, because my creativity and the practice that it spawned always made me feel a little guilty.

Just before my 22nd birthday, I completed all the required courses in medical school and took the National Board Examinations in medicine and passed. In many states these served in place of and largely supplanted State Board exams, so I could now be considered a fully trained physician, although I had not yet served an internship. Accordingly, it seemed like a good idea to sample the actual general practice of medicine, and make a little extra money in the bargain!

That could be done, as long as a fully licensed physician supervised one who was technically unlicensed, in the state of Indiana, only a few miles south of Chicago. An ad appeared seeking a "G.P.'" as general practitioners were called, in the little steel mill town of Indiana Harbor, about an hour away on an electric interurban train. Many physicians were still away at war, and they readily accepted me when I showed up at a group practice office in the bleak, partially boarded up town near to the much larger and more affluent steel town of Gary, Indiana. Both towns had enormous, active steel mills, and had been the scene of bloody labor wars in the 1930s.

The group was headed by a Dr. Niblick, a disheveled, big-bellied man with an affable, 'good ole boy' air and a tremendous protrusion from his left cheek looking for all the world like a big wad of chewing tobacco. That is exactly what it turned out to be, to my horror, as he interrupted himself in mid-sentence when first we met, to direct an untidy stream of brown fluid into a cuspidor he kept by his desk. He gave me almost no guidance as to what they expected of me, simply showing me to a small vacant office with an examining table, cabinet and gooseneck floor lamp and little else. He also pointed out the pharmacy, a large closet with shelves on all the walls. The top shelf at one side supported very large glass containers of pills of all the same size but different colors. These, he explained, all contained aspirin. In one bottle were white tablets, in the next red ones, then pink ones, blue ones, green ones and finally purple ones. It was important, he told me, always to give a new patient some medication to take with him, even if the diagnosis had not yet become clear, because "That's what they come to the doctor for, and what they expect." He added that since one patient will report no improvement on the pink ones, the blue ones worked wonders, and those facts and what pills were issued must be carefully recorded in the chart.

After showing me to the 'minor surgery' treatment room, with multiple cabinets and two examining tables, one with stirrups, screened from each other by movable screens constructed of steel tubing with cotton sheeting stretched from the top tube to the bottom one, he indicated the additional instruments (blood pressure cuffs, ophthalmoscope, speculums of various kinds for various bodily openings, and large bright lights in reflectors hanging from the ceiling. This, he said, was where they did tonsillectomies (that chair over there), circumcisions, ear and nose irrigations, pelvic exams, removals of small polyps, and minor surgery that did not require general anesthesia. They did, however, have tall tanks of oxygen and nitrous oxide, or 'laughing gas,' that could put a patient 'under' if it became absolutely necessary. Located in a tough steel mill town, he said, the clinic saw many people who had been cut up in beerhall brawls, and we sewed them up in this room.

With that, he said, "Well, let's get busy," and off he went to his office. I went to mine, and in a few minutes my first patient appeared. She had a bad cold but no pneumonia, and I knew a little aspirin would probably help and certainly not hurt, so I gave her some of the blue pills. I had spent perhaps 15 or 20 minutes taking her history, calling in a nurse to stand by while I examined her chest and abdomen, listened carefully to her heart and lungs, and doing what I considered an adequate but fairly rapid and in truth, somewhat superficial medical workup. While I was writing up my findings in her chart, Dr. Niblick appeared in my doorway without bothering to knock, and, shifting his wad of tobacco off to the side, announced that he wanted me in his office the minute I finished.

The door to his office was open, and I stepped in to find him seated in a chair facing a young woman who had just arrived as a new patient. He was talking to her, his tobacco wad firmly in place, while he reached out and palpated first one of her breasts with one hand, and then the other breast with his other hand. She was fully clothed. He was totally unconcerned at my arrival, and finished taking her history, sort of, and then scribbled some illegible notes in a chart, handed her some pills which I assumed were aspirin - green - and told her to come back in 2 days. Same time.

"This," he said, "is how we do things here. This is not Northwestern University. There ain't time to go through a long medical school history and physical, and there's lots more patients waiting outside. Check 'em over quick, order some lab work if you think it's really necessary, and send 'em on their way. If you aren't sure of a diagnosis, have 'em come back next day, give 'em some pills to tide them over and keep 'em happy, and work on it some more next time. Got it?"

I got it. And choking down my scientific and ethical concerns over this seeming contempt for all that I knew was good and proper and right, all that I had learned in those years in medical school, I set out to learn about medicine as it is prac-

practiced in the real world - or at least in a small, tough steel mill town in northern Indiana. In the next few months I saw and treated, not just with aspirin but many other drugs in the surprisingly well-stocked modern pharmacy-in-closet, far more patients than I had seen in several years of training. The approach and the system, for the most part, worked surprisingly well, and only once did I come close to a real problem.

That came in the form of a nicely, carefully dressed little man of about 40, wearing a suit, vest, white shirt and tie, and carrying his gray fedora. His shoes were polished and his fingernails clean, unusual for that town's citizens, as was his costume and his demeanor. When I asked what brought him in (he looked quite healthy, if not robust), he hesitated for a long time, looking everywhere around the room except at me, and finally with great effort and obvious embarrassment pointed down at his crotch and said, "It's what's happening down there." "Down where?" I asked, and he said, "Well, I guess I'd better show you." His discomfort was painful to behold.

Standing up slowly, and with great reluctance, he unfastened his belt, pulled down the zipper on his trousers, and produced his penis. On it were several warty growths, not very large but quite noticeable. He then told me that he was soon to marry a very nice lady from his church, who would surely be shocked and revolted at the sight of his disfigured member when he produced it on their nuptial bed, and might well reject him outright and renounce the marriage. They had, he added, never engaged in 'intimate' behavior so this would be a terrible thing to confront her with on their wedding night. Was it curable?

What he had was something called Venereal Warts. Unlike the major venereal diseases, it was not necessarily related to sexual activity, gaining its name primarily because of its location on and around the genitals. The warts are similar to warts especially common on the hands of young boys. Treatment at that time was quite simple and effective. Each wart was touched with a stick of solidified silver nitrate, allowed to 'cook' a few minutes to let the mild caustic begin, usually painlessly, to attack the growth, and the process is then terminated by pouring on a little saline - ordinary salt in solution - that neutralizes the silver nitrate.

A single treatment is often enough to cause the wart to shrink up and then disappear, but to be sure I instructed him to return in a few days, when we would repeat the application if it seemed necessary. The silver nitrate was kept in the treatment room, and I positioned a nurse behind one of the cloth screens to assist me, handing me the silver nitrate and then the saline neutralizer, while keeping out of sight to preserve this painfully shy man's dignity. Surely no female since his mother had ever looked at him "down there!"

When he returned three days later he was agitated and noticeably distressed, barely able to wait to get in to see me and frantically eager to talk. No sooner had I closed the door to my little office when he pulled down his pants and underwear revealing a swollen, bright red penis with suppurating sores where his warts used to be. Having recently attended a florid lecture on medical malpractice lawsuits, blessedly still uncommon in those days of the public's innocence and almost blind trust in their physicians, I studiously remained calm, rubbing my chin with a concerned, thoughtful expression on my face despite a raging torrent of emotion surging inside my chest and stomach. I nodded gravely, observing that he certainly had had a most emphatic response to my medicine. I added that, while it might be a tad uncomfortable at the moment, it would soon (I secretly and fervently prayed to myself and to the Lord and the gods of medicine) settle down and return to normal. Meanwhile, he should take comfort in knowing he would never, ever, have those warts again.

When the poor man left, somewhat mollified but not altogether happy or convinced of the good outcome I had promised, I headed for the treatment room to see if I could discover the cause of the near tragedy. There I found, side by side in the medication cabinet, identical bottles of boric acid and saline, looking the same except for a small label that I hadn't bothered to read when the nurse handed the bottle through the open side of the cloth screen. It was clear I had "neutralized" the caustic with boric acid. Boric acid in that dilute solution is quite benign, but in any strength does not neutralize silver nitrate.

I have carefully examined every label ever since, no matter how familiar the bottle.

That exciting event with the warts calls to mind an equally exciting, but quite different, day in my life the previous winter at the Maternity Center. During a night of rapidly falling temperatures, the streets had become coated with ice, and making my way to Maxwell Street in response to a call from a woman about to deliver had been difficult. At some length I found the address given, and made my way up three flights of stairs to where the laboring woman lay in bed, well along in the early stages of delivery.

As usual, the coats were hung on the wall, the newspapers spread, and the bucket positioned beneath the newspaper funnel. The delivery went well, producing a healthy infant (named, in accordance with our new tradition, Loyal Davis Jenkins) and with a little help and encouragement to bear down "one more time, Mother!" the placenta was delivered with a wet plop into the bucket. I was busily massaging the uterus to assist in its contraction, when there came a disturbance at my feet, causing the bucket to fall over.

Looking down, I glimpsed a small mongrel dog, earlier banished from the birthing room along with the other uninvited spectators. He had crept in, and while my attention was directed toward the new mother, had put his forefeet on the edge of the bucket, tipping it over. He then seized the warm, bloody placenta and headed for the door and down the stairs, the umbilical cord trailing behind, while the heavy mass of tissue clamped in his teeth, nearly as large as the dog himself, bounced on each step as he made his way down at top speed.

This outrage - a mongrel dog carrying a large blob of human tissue in his mouth and headed for Maxwell Street, three floors below - could not be permitted. With no thought in mind other than the fact that this was an animal attack on something human, albeit something recently expelled, and accompanied by the junior student who was assisting me, I raced from the room in my shirtsleeves in an attempt to catch him. Cheered on by bystanders at each landing, I barely caught sight of the fugitive with his precious burden as he disappeared out the front door, opened for him by a little boy standing there. Racing out into the street, both the dog and I slipping and sliding on the icy pavement, I finally got close enough to slow him down by stepping on the trailing umbilical cord, and we both went down. Ignoring his snarling and snapping, I bravely rescued this symbol of humankind from this 10-pound offshoot of wild wolves who had made off with it, doubtless intending to eat it.

Making my way back up to the abandoned mother and her newborn through the crowd of amused onlookers in the hall and stairwells, I began to wonder whether the cheering I had heard on my way down, during the pursuit, had been for the dog - or the doc. I was never really sure. In any event, the mother was happy, the baby healthy, and our work there, for the day, was done.

One of the last classes given before all instruction was complete was given by the Department of Psychiatry. We were divided into small groups of about twenty students, each with a different instructor. It fell to the lot of my small group to be given over to the same man who had taught us our very first course in the subject, during our freshman year. His name was Clarence Neymann, and like many psychiatrists of that day had come from Vienna, where he had known and associated with Sigmund Freud and other early greats in the emerging field.

None of us in the class had ever forgotten Dr. Neymann. He had won fame for his invention of a method for artificially inducing a fever in patients suffering from tertiary syphilis - general paresis - the florid psychosis with wildly grandiose delusions that ended in death and was resistant to arsenic and mercury and other chemicals that sometimes worked in earlier stages of the infection.

In one of those striking cases of medical detective work coupled with sheer luck, intuition, and sheer brilliance, someone had noticed that patients in advanced stages of syphilitic infection who also suffered severe episodes of recurring high fever during attacks of malaria, rarely, if ever, developed the psychosis that other syphilis patients experienced late in the course of the disease. Perhaps, it was thought, the high fever during malarial episodes kept the spirochetes of syphilis from attacking the brain.

To test this hypothesis, patients with advancing syphilis were deliberately infected with malaria through small injections of blood from malarial patients taken during an episode of high fever. The procedure proved to be too risky, and several of the patients died from the malaria even before they finally succumbed to their syphilis, so that experiment was abandoned.

The researchers turned next to Typhoid Fever, another infection that commonly caused a very high fever, and not uncommonly, death. Not many years before, a vaccine had been developed to protect against typhoid, and in larger that usual doses, the vaccine itself caused an episode of high fever but did not cause the disease. While it looked promising as a way to induce the desired rise in body temperature, this too proved unacceptable as a routine measure because some patients died from the high fever.

Clarence Neymann had come up with a better solution. He devised a large box, inside which a person could sit on a chair with his head sticking out a hole in the top of the box. The container was lined with light bulbs, creating a very hot interior, and the temperature could be managed by controlling the amount of electricity flowing to the light bulbs. A temperature probe was placed in the patient's mouth, and when it showed that his body had warmed up to the desired level, about 104 degrees, it could be held there by turning down the current just the right amount. After the desired amount of time - perhaps an hour - the thing was turned off, the box opened, and the thoroughly baked victim removed, given water, and rested. The whole thing was repeated daily, sometimes for weeks.

It seemed to work! Not only did it prevent early paresis from worsening, it seemed to reverse the psychotic condition considerably in more advanced cases. Clarence became famous. Unfortunately for Clarence's fame, however, penicillin became available for civilian use in serious syphilis cases a short time later, and the hot box was abandoned in favor of the new, miraculous antibiotic. It was a little like the Canal built from the Potomac in Washington, to Harper's Ferry to carry freight on barges. Hardly had it been completed when someone built a railroad, and the Canal was no longer of use.

Dr. Neymann, like Freud, was primarily a neurologist who was drawn to psychiatry because so much serious mental disorder was found to be related to actual physical disorders affecting the brain and central nervous system. Modern psychiatry, employing various kinds of psychotherapy, burst onto the scene largely in the early part of the 20th Century based upon the theories and writings of Freud, followed by Carl Jung, Adler, Horney and others who had studied at the master's feet and gone off on tangents of their own, creating different "schools" and approaches to mental and emotional ills.

Neymann was a brilliant exponent of Freud's basic formulations and his later ideas, and he described these still revolutionary ideas to us with great clarity and spirit. As a person and a lecturer, however, he was nothing short of grotesque. He was short, fat, and whatever the season, sweaty. He had very thick lips and a tongue seemingly too large for its containing mouth, teeth stained yellow from the cigarettes that dangled, one after another from that mouth, and an abundance of saliva, which showered the first few rows of desks in any classroom and grew in volume as his enthusiasm for his subject soared.

He had a deep, guttural voice and a pronounced Viennese accent. His words tumbled out in explosive fashion over the barrier of his thick tongue and lips, accompanied by those sprays of saliva that caused us all to seek seats as far from the front of the small lecture room as possible. He always wore the same disheveled, gravy-splattered Navy blue suit, complete with vest, rumpled shirt whose collar compressed his fat neck like a garrote, and a loosely knotted, tattered tie that had to be older than any of us. His shoes were run down and looked to be in imminent danger of falling apart. The palms of his thick, clumsy-seeming hands were actually fat, and the backs of his short, stubby fingers bore a thick coat of hair.

His overall configuration made it seem unlikely that he could get behind the wheel of the immense black Cadillac, never washed, that he drove, but somehow he did so. He always seemed rushed, and watching him park his car became a popular diversion. Barely able to turn and look over his shoulder, he would nose the great machine into a space at the curb between two other cars, and bump the car ahead, ultimately succeeding in pushing it forward a few feet. He would then pull up along side it, back into the space and bump the car behind until it too moved, in the opposite direction. He would repeat these maneuvers as often as it required until he had enlarged the previously inadequate space sufficiently to accommodate his car, not always neatly, whereupon he would with great effort emerge, slam the door, and hurry off to his class.

For all that, he captured our undivided attention as he described his days with Freud and the other greats of the time in Vienna. He was at his best when describing the struggles between the Id, with its primeval impulses and primitive, animal-like drives warring against the Superego, that introjection of God and father and all authority and goodness and right, struggling to constrain the murderous and rapine impulses of the beast within. In his fat hands and thick words it all seemed so beautifully clear, so right, so absolutely correct and so revealing of the eternal struggle between good and evil, right and wrong, that we felt like we were being given glimpses of ultimate truth, of the bases of religion and faith, human conflict, life and death itself, and our fear of it.

He told us as well of the more famed apostates: Jung with his 'archetypes' and 'collective unconscious,' Adler with his 'inferiority complexes,' Karen Horney with her preoccupation with the 'birth trauma,' and many others. He taught us that all of these people were searching for the same things: understanding ourselves and the human condition, our motivations and conflicts, our fears and joys and exultations. In a way, he said, all these great philosophers, irreligious agnostics all, were trying to understand God. I left his classes believing I had been exposed to a magnificent, great mind, an almost magical spirit, who had hinted that there was hope for mankind - and even for me - yet. He became, before our very eyes, a totally beautiful person, disguised in a cloak of human grotesquerie. And, he sure could park that Cadillac.

At long last, after three years of the most intense anxiety, concentration, effort and fatigue, the great day came when we were to assemble as a whole class, minus the few who had dropped out beside the anatomy dissection table or from raging tuberculosis (but, curiously, not by suicide), and swear to the Oath of Hippocrates. That act committed us to a life of service, purity of thought, exemplary behavior, guardian of secrets, and devotion to our fellow physicians, their wives and children, their assistants and all others who strove to heal man or beast, never violating this sacred covenant.

Some of us thought that was really important; others didn't seem even to pay much attention. To judge from today's attention to privacy and confidentiality laws, outrageous bills from one physician to another (hell, we all have insurance, don't we?), lawsuits for malpractice and neglect and medical malfeasance, and physicians' steady fall from grace and the high esteem once bestowed by their fellow citizens, it seems as if the oath didn't do much. Maybe it needs to be re-worked. Maybe the social status and wealth that have rewarded and blessed so many physicians are, like power, corrupting.

Even those many years ago, however, on the day of our oath-taking, two observations struck me as ominous. The first was that the whole process seemed to be, to many around me, just a ritual to be gotten through as quickly as possible so that we could rush on out, become eminent specialists, make lots of money, and incidentally save lives and stamp out disease. Just like I'd been doing in the dinghy little clinic run by Dr. Niblick in Indiana Harbor.

My second observation was that most of the eager young healers around me, all of us repeating our oath in unison, did not have a clue about how ill-prepared we were for the task ahead, how little we knew, and how dangerous it was to turn us loose, as I've said earlier in this work. Dr. Niblick (who soon died from his diabetes because, he said, he never did believe in insulin) once told me that 99% of patients will get well no matter what you do to them (unless you screw up and hurt them yourself), and the rest will die also no matter what you do. I found that excessively cynical at the time, and still do, but fifty years in medicine taught me that he had a point.

When I see, as I did recently when visiting a friend in a hospital, which the Germans more realistically call a Krankenhaus - sickness house - enduring agonizing, relentless pain and discomfort despite her multitude of helpers and reams of lab reports and X-Rays, I cannot help but wonder how far we've actually emerged from the abysmal ignorance that characterized our healing profession earlier this Century. Not far, I'd guess, despite the medical miracles reported in the National Enquirer.

It was a relief to finish medical school. I was well on the way to that 'ticket.' What had ended, I came to realize, was my training in the trade school. What was about to begin was my education, sadly neglected as I rushed through college and medical school. The Great War was ended, and one of the important realizations of that symbolic day of graduation was that it had mostly passed me by, leaving me unscathed and mightily blessed. It was a measure of our self-centered preoccupation during school that most of us had been so little aware, and so poorly informed, of the maelstrom that raged around us and around the world killing millions more people than we would ever save, working changes in our lives as yet undreamed of.

It was inescapably true that we who stood there taking old Hippocrates' Oath were among the very few supremely lucky ones anywhere. It seemed equally true that this imposed upon us an unspeakably heavy burden, a debt that could never be wholly repaid; we owed the world an incalculable obligation for our incredible good luck - for that is what it was, pure and simple good luck.

Internship was the next step in rounding out my basic qualifications. A prized intern position existed at the enormous Naval hospital in Philadelphia, where at one time there were said to be 9000 patients in the main building and spread throughout nearly a mile of outbuildings extending out on two sides of it. At the graduation ceremony we had also received our commissions as Lieutenants, Junior Grade, in the Medical Department of the Navy. The serial number bestowed upon me that day signified that I had just become the two hundred and twenty-three thousand, two hundred and ninety third citizen to be commissioned by the President of the United States to serve in the U.S. Navy, obeying all lawful orders of my superiors, and defending the Constitution of the United States against all enemies, foreign and domestic. So help me God.

The Navy had, in its wisdom, also assigned me to that prized internship in Philadelphia, to spend a year 'rotating' among the various services and learning at first hand all those things heard about in medical school but not yet necessarily experienced in real life.

The first impression on seeing that great building, built a few years earlier for the princely sum of three million dollars, which would cost a billion today, was that it was very large and very beautiful. Before it flew three flags, one signifying the nation, one the Medical Department, and one the physical presence 'aboard' of the commanding officer.

That person turned out to be a gentle, ineffectual soul well past retirement age, named Montgomery, a long-time career Navy doctor. After a few traditional words of welcome to our incoming group of 24 eager new interns, resplendent in our junior grade lieutenant's uniforms, he handed us over to his executive officer. We soon learned it was this man, not the Captain, as all commanding officers are called in the Navy, whatever their rank, who ran the place and, as it turned out, our lives. From that instant on for the next twelve months, our private lives, for practical purposes, ceased to exist. We "belonged" to the Navy.

Bartholomew W. Hogan, Captain, Medical Corps, U.S. Navy, made no bones about it. He would be for us, for the next year, God.

William E. Mayer, M.D.

Chapter 3

Internship

Working hours, Captain Hogan announced, were from "0800 hours" until the work was done. That could take, sometimes, up to one minute before 0800 the next day. The workweek included Saturdays, when we could leave in mid- to late afternoon if patient care demands had been met. Every Saturday morning the weekly inspection of all 'spaces' would be conducted by the senior officers heading each department in rotation. We were to suspend all work when the inspection party arrived in our space, accompany the powerful officer, complete with white gloves, who was in charge, and be prepared to recite the details about each patient under our care.

Sundays would be free, patients' needs permitting, and we were encouraged to attend church services. The Captain seemed to be a religious person himself, inasmuch as he invariably carried with him, to and from his quarters each day, a very large, heavy, leather-bound Bible in the Roman Catholic, Douet version. This tome he kept prominently on his desk in his office. I was to become more familiar with that very book in short order. We were expected to be in proper 'uniform of the day' at all times, removing the jacket only to replace it with a long white coat while seeing patients, and to be 'under cover,' meaning wearing our hats, whenever out of doors. Fraternization with any of the nurses, and particularly with all enlisted persons, was strictly forbidden, as was the use of first names except among our fellow interns.

Captain Hogan was a singularly impressive naval officer cast in an ancient mold. He sported a neat mustache, whose ends were stiffly waxed and precisely symmetrical. His posture was ramrod straight and his general demeanor radiated his absolute authority. He wore an old-style navy hat, which went straight up from the sides rather than flaring out at the top as did the more modern ones. His uniform looked new every day, and during cold weather he wore, rather than the usual severely tailored 'bridge' coat with its shoulder boards and double row of brass buttons up the front, a traditional garment from the 'old' Navy called a boat cloak. This was a long, sweeping dark blue cloak with a stand-up collar fastened by a gold chain, the whole thing lined in what appeared to be scarlet velvet. He cut an altogether arresting figure as he strode up the hospital's front steps each day, cloak swirling around him, neat hat squarely on his head, and Bible under his left arm, enabling him to return salutes with his right hand.

The captain clearly ran what was called a "tight ship." While he invariably conducted himself in a properly deferential manner when the commander, Captain Montgomery, was present during some official function, there was never the slightest doubt as to who was in charge. When the inspection party that he led, rotating among the different parts of the huge, sprawling hospital spread out under the towering central building, showed up on one's ward or service, the atmosphere was unbelievably tense and deadly serious. Each intern prayed weekly that Captain Hogan's party would not hit his ward that week.

The Captain's performance running that major hospital, the largest in the Navy, obviously pleased the powers that be, and he ultimately rose to be Surgeon General. He was the first Roman Catholic to hold that position in the Navy, and the first psychiatrist to do so. I was not to learn of his psychiatric background until a dramatic, highly emotionally charged day exactly twelve months later, on my final day under his command, when he changed my life. That profound turning point, destined to shape the entire rest of my professional life, will show up later in this tale. It wasn't dreamed of when I started out as a full-fledged Navy doctor.

The twelve months 'rotating' internship was spent almost equally divided among the various branches, now called sub-specialties, of internal medicine, and those of surgery, with four months spent in each broad area. Two months of the twelve were devoted to obstetrics and to psychiatry, a month on each. Those two proved to be my most memorable times of all.

Assigned initially to the Department of Medicine, I would be exposed to cardiology, pulmonary diseases, infectious diseases, renal disorders, and a hodgepodge of ailments less readily categorized, grouped together as 'general medicine.' The supply of clinical material and its diversity were endless. In addition to serving on the ward, each intern served for a month on alternate nights with another intern, running the emergency room. I was one of the unlucky first two designated for this task. It turned out to be monumental.

Unlike the elaborate, well-staffed, multiple-room emergency suites depicted in modern movies and television shows, our emergency room was just that: a room. It was situated in the hospital basement, in reality the ground floor underneath the official 'first' floor of the building. It was of modest size and comfortably accommodated a desk and chair plus two additional straight chairs, all of yellow oak; an examination table suitable for supporting a patient during minor surgery, such as suturing; a medicine cabinet and an instrument cabinet; a large reflector-backed overhead light and a bright stand lamp, also with a reflector behind the bulb; as well as the usual wastecans, wastebaskets, and desk lamp. A portable sterilizer on a small cart, and a stainless steel bucket rounded out the equipment list.

The entire staff consisted of the single intern on duty that night. A small steel washbasin hung from one wall, supplying water for drinking and hand washing.

A single door opened into the room, and one small frosted casement window was situated in the outside wall behind the desk chair, and could be opened for ventilation during hot, humid Philadelphia nights. It was here that I learned, among other things, the real meaning of the word 'fatigue.'

The lucky intern destined to occupy the ER that night, reported right after dinner in the hospital dining hall, and did not leave the room except to go to the toilet in a tiny closet next door until the duty day began again the next morning. In the course of a night, the intern might encounter nearly all the common medical and surgical emergencies known to exist, most of them things he had never before seen. My first encounter came early in the evening.

The man entered the room, with which he was evidently familiar, wheezing noisily and walking slowly, waddling from side to side, while his hands were clasped at the sides of an enormously distorted, protuberant abdomen, in seeming support of the ungainly mass. He told me, between short gasps for air, that it was time for him to get tapped again. I had no idea what he meant. He added that his belly swelled up like this fairly regularly, and he always came here to have it drained when it became hard to get his breath.

A few questions revealed that he was a long-time patient in and out of our hospital, due to his chronic cirrhosis - his hardened liver. Interference with the circulation in that organ caused fluid to accumulate in his abdomen, steadily increasing until it led to the sorry state he was now in.

The man was friendly and quite affable, despite his obvious discomfort, and asked me if I'd ever "tapped a belly" before. When I said no, he told me not to worry - he'd show me everything I needed to know. Pointing at the instrument cart, he instructed me to fetch a scalpel and a cannula, an eight inch long bronze tube a little thicker than a lead pencil, with a pointed end like a small rocket, and multiple holes along its sides. While I obeyed, he pulled the steel bucket over in front of one of the chairs and fell heavily into the seat, with the bucket between his feet.

When I turned back from the instrument cabinet, having found the cannula and a scalpel, I saw that he had pulled down his pants and raised his shirt so it rested atop his enormous naked belly. Pointing to a spot below his belly button and off a bit to the side, he told me to make a little cut through the skin "right here." Satisfied that I was in the hands of a true expert far more knowledgeable than I could ever be, I did so, easily penetrating the tightly stretched skin. It did not bleed, to my surprise, and he did not wince, also to my surprise.

"Now," he said, "Stick the pointy end of that thing (the cannula) into the cut and give a good hard push. When you feel something go 'pop,' jump out of the way 'cause the stuff will come squirting out.." On only the second try, sure enough,

I heard the 'pop' and jumped aside, the gushing yellow stream just missing me on its way into the bucket. After I held the cannula in place, penetrating his abdominal wall for what seemed an interminable period, his protruding abdomen slowly deflated, much like a balloon slowly losing air. His breathing became easier and his voice changed, until finally he said, "Okay, that about does it. Stick a little tape over the hole and I'll be on my way. Thanks a lot. See you next month if you're still here." With that, he ambled out the door with far more grace than when he entered.

With barely time to reflect on this lesson in hydrodynamics and the strength of the human spirit, and to put the cannula and scalpel into the little sterilizer, I looked up to see my second major life-threatening emergency case. This second man entered on the arm of an ambulance driver. He was wide-eyed, pale, sweaty, short of breath, and clutched his chest tightly, his arms crossed in front of him. It took only moments to determine that he was having a major coronary episode, which I was not supposed to try to treat in the ER, but send instead to the cardiac ward where the intern on duty there would see him immediately.

No sooner had I accomplished that, than a stretcher was brought into the room bearing a man with what was obviously a serious fracture to both bones of his lower leg. He had had no pain-killing medicine, so I gave him a shot of some and sent him on to Orthopedics where the lucky intern on duty would reduce the fracture with the help of the portable X-Ray machine and put on a plaster cast, or else put him in traction and wait for help from the senior staff in the morning.

Throughout the night there followed a steady procession of what I was sure were examples of every major medical and surgical emergency known to man, or at any rate, known to me. I was wrong. My second night in the ER, two nights later, brought a comparable stream of cases including many I had not even thought of. That included a wildly psychotic man hauled in forcibly by three police officers, the patient and the officers all bloodied about the face and hands. No sooner had the quartet entered my ER when the shouting, excited man broke away from his captors and headed full speed down the darkened hall, the officers in loud pursuit. The commotion quieted as the runners sped away, and I forgot about it, pretty much, as I faced my new arrivals.

Eventually things quieted down and the procession of new patients came, for the time, to a halt. Grateful for the moment of relief, I put my head down on my arm on the desk, only to be awakened by what I took to be a loud explosion just outside the ER's frosted window. I raced to the nearest entry door, a few feet down the hall, and cautiously opened it to look outside. The lighting was poor, but even with that it was plain to see that the entire area was sprayed with blood…and brains. The psychotic man had eluded his pursuers, made his way to the very top of the tower, many floors up, and jumped. He landed headfirst on a concrete gutter running alongside the building, hitting just outside my ER window, and his head had literally exploded from the impact. The mess was horrifying.

Back in the ER, I saw the remaining few cases to show up in those early morning hours, and once again lowered my head to rest on my arm atop my desk. I had had just two night's sleep out of the last four, and worked all day each day, so I drifted off immediately. Once again my rest was interrupted by a loud bang! This time it seemed quite close to my head, came with a little puff of wind, and shook the desk. Leaping to my feet I found myself face to face with a vengeful God, in the person of Captain Hogan, complete in hat and boat cloak with its scarlet lining showing and his hand on his great Bible, which he had just slammed on my desk next to my somnolent head, causing the noise and the little breeze.

"Dahktah!" he said, his Bostonian accent fully in play, "You can be SHOT for sleeping on watch!" Without another word, he picked up his Bible and strode out. I was certain that I was done for, but nothing ever happened, and after a few weeks I stopped worrying about it.

Somehow or other I made it through that month, but I never did catch up on my sleep. No one actually died in my emergency room while I was on duty, most patients were treated adequately or shipped off to the appropriate part of the hospital expeditiously, and while I believed that I had aged considerably, at least I had survived unscathed.

Service on the internal medicine wards was grinding. Each newly admitted patient had to be exhaustively interviewed to determine his past medical history, carefully and just as exhaustively examined physically, the proper blood and laboratory studies and X-Rays ordered, medication orders written, daily progress notes made, and all of it recorded in detail in the patient's chart. Some of us suspected that none of the senior staff ever really read our detailed past medical histories recorded in the charts, and to test this hypothesis took to inserting long quotations from the Bible, lyrics to popular songs, and other creative writings into their write-ups to expand their length and thus their obvious fine medical workmanship. Sure enough, no one ever seemed to notice, and eventually the wags tired of the game and stopped doing it. I am certain many of those records, with their inserted psalms, songs and nursery rhymes still exist, somewhere, on microfiche or computer disks, and have never been discovered by officialdom.

We were off duty during that year every other night and every other weekend (meaning Sunday), which meant we were at the hospital, on duty but often able to sleep a bit, on all other nights and weekends. Nights on the far-flung medical wards could be hard. It was not unusual to have at least one, and more often two or even three deaths each night on one or the other of the several 40-bed wards each intern was responsible for.

When sleeping, or trying to, on one of the narrow cots in one of the interns' rooms, it was common to be awakened by a corpsman announcing that you were needed on one of your wards. When that call came, you put on your shoes and white coat, if indeed you had taken them off, and raced or at least trotted rapidly out the long, seemingly endless hallways leading from the core of the hospital to the 'out-wards,' for the calls signified an emergency. As often as not, the emergency patient would be found to have already died or was gasping his last, agonal gulps of air, and all that remained was to establish that he had truly expired, death sometimes being a surprisingly difficult diagnosis, and sign the paperwork that made it official.

While it seemed that seriously, chronically ill old people tended to die more often at night than in the daytime, without consideration for the interruptions this caused in interns' sleep, sometimes the end would come during the day, even during visiting hours. One such event occurred that proved highly instructive and not very pleasant. Called to an out-ward far from the main building, I found a man of late middle age, who had long been in the process of dying from multiple organ failure related to kidney and liver disease, lying in bed surrounded by his entire family of perhaps six or seven adults, several of them holding his hands on both sides of the bed as they tried to talk with him and he with them. He was coherent, though barely, and his various relatives were trying to encourage him not to leave them, to stay, to get better, and to try harder.

No sooner had I entered the room, receiving the pathetically hopeful glances of all the sad, tearful death-watchers, than the poor man gave a couple of moaning gasps, gurgled a little, and ceased then to show any signs of life whatever. The entire group of onlookers immediately began to wail and cry out, several of them literally throwing themselves atop the corpse, grasping at his head and shoulders and imploring the dead man not to leave them, not to die. Influenced no doubt by this terrible outpouring of grief from these suffering people, and in the arrogance of youth and awareness of my important role in people's lives, I sent the nurse running for a syringe, a spinal tap (4 inch long) needle, and an ampoule of epinephrine, called adrenalin in those days.

When she returned, as she did with alacrity, I drew up the drug into the syringe, banished the onlookers from atop the victim, but not from the room, and with little hesitation and only the briefest of prayers, plunged the needle through the man's chest wall and directly into his heart, from which I withdrew some blood to establish the needle's arrival in the right place, and then injected the drug. A moment later I felt the needle, still in the heart, move, slightly at first and then in regular little pulses as the man's heart resumed its vital pumping.

Within a few moments the man, so recently dead, opened his eyes and rejoined the living! Seconds later the little audience burst into loud, joyous sounds of relief and pleasure that this miracle had come to pass. I, the miracle worker, retreated modestly to one side. When the resurrected Lazarus actually spoke to his tearful relatives I secretly rejoiced along with them, and honestly believed all those years of study and exams and classes had been in a great cause. And this was it.

As I returned to the interns' room for a short break, I believed in a merciful God, in the glory of my profession, and probably most of all, in my wisdom, my quick thinking, my decisive action and my great skill as a physician, healer, saver of life. This was even a greater triumph than saving the placenta from that little mongrel dog in the Chicago slums!

Then, the call came. He was going bad again. I raced out to the ward, to the same group of desperate, despairing, grief-stricken family members close by the dying man's side. Once again he gasped, gurgled, and breathed his last. As I should have known he was certain to do. I was not Jesus doing miracles, not even much of a doctor, not really considerate of the suffering I only succeeded in prolonging with my arrogance and thoughtlessness. I had done them all a disservice. I did not order up another ampoule of epinephrine and long needle, explaining as gently as I could that it would only prolong his - and their - agony, and add to the suffering. He was gone. It was God's will. Just as it had been the first time.

In a way, that little drama was a microcosm of what is routinely done today, a little slower and with more exotic equipment and many more drugs, as we prolong the lives of hopelessly, terminally ill people often of advanced age and with longstanding diseases, at huge cost in resources and emotional expenditures by relatives. Then the sick person, inevitably, dies anyway, as we knew he surely would.

But I never did that again.

The months on the Internal Medicine service were full of patients and long hours, but there were only a few really exciting events. One such occurred to an outpatient who had come in for the periodic check-up ordered because of his aortic aneurysm. That was a balloon-like enlargement of the great vessel leading directly out of the heart before curving and turning downward to supply fresh blood to most of the body. This patient was famous at the hospital, for his aneurysm had grown inside his chest to enormous size, larger than a navel orange. It had eroded away most of his sternum, or chest bone, and could easily be felt as a tense, fluid-filled sack lying just below the skin over the center of his chest.

Whenever this old, skinny but surprisingly spry fellow showed up for his periodic review, all available interns were paged and gathered around to see him. Both the size of his aneurysm and its erosion of his sternum, in addition to his remarkable survival for so long after, by all rights, he should have expired, made him a genuine medical marvel. Each of us got to listen to his chest for the whooshing sounds of blood churning through the aneurysm, and gently feel it through the skin of his chest. He tolerated this well, clearly enjoying the attention and his celebrity status. There was no special treatment available, so we wished him well and off he went until the next time.

He headed down the corridor leading to the hospital main entrance. Just as he was passing the door to Captain Hogan's office, the wall of the aneurysm and the thin overlying skin, which we had all just palpated, burst open. A torrent of bright red arterial blood flew in all directions, and the man died on the spot. A crowd of medical talent quickly gathered, but nothing could be done, and we all drifted away.

Meanwhile, a different but equally compelling medical drama was unfolding on the next floor above. In a single room on that 'deck' was a Marine Corps patient who also enjoyed a certain medical celebrity status. This young man had miraculously survived an explosion that had torn off all or major parts of all four limbs. His face, quite handsome, was untouched. His torso was also largely intact, well-formed and muscular, and resembled the remnant of a Michelangelo sculpture.

Despite the horrifying damage to this brave young man, he somehow managed always to smile, to greet visitors enthusiastically, even to joke, at times, about his altered physical state and the luck that had kept his "best parts" alive. By that he clearly meant not just his heart and lungs and digestive system, along with his head and its contents, but most importantly of all, his genitals. The fear of damage to the reproductive system is universal among foot soldiers, and the issuance of vests that stopped small arms fire and shell fragments from penetrating the chest and abdomen proved that. At first, soldiers were loath to wear the stiff, heavy, cumbersome garments and often took them off in battle, sometimes dying as a result. After much study and discussion by scientists and logisticians who designed such things but had never themselves been shot at, someone finally came up with a solution to the 'non-use' problem.

A crotch protector was added to the front of the vest. Compliance shot up. Now the thing had a really important use. Almost all combat soldiers believe they will not be killed, even if many of their buddies are, all around them. However, they are less sure about getting wounded. That could happen. As bad as any wound could be, a wound in the crotch was absolutely intolerable.

Our quadruple amputee had been wearing his vest - with crotch protector.

As his convalescence progressed, he became the darling of the hospital. Everybody knew him. He had more visitors than anyone in the place, and a steady stream of staff members took to dropping in to boost his morale during non-visiting hours. Many of these were young women: nurses, students, lab technicians, volunteers, even secretaries. His handsome face, good nature and good spirits made him especially attractive in spite of his grievous loss of all his limbs.

On the day in question, the chief nurse and her assistant had entered his room, thinking to bring him a little good cheer, only to find that a Red Cross 'Gray Lady" volunteer was already doing that, her skirt pulled up to her waist and her panties in her hand, bouncing up and down on top of the poor wounded veteran, who was clearly enjoying himself greatly in spite of his inability to grasp any part of the lady.

The nurses instantly retreated in some disorder and confusion, to be followed soon after by the volunteer lady, skirt pulled back down and pants, presumably, restored to their correct location. I was passing by as the nurses were fleeing, and they paused just long enough to tell me to get right in there and put a stop to this outrage. After watching the volunteer making her way swiftly in the opposite direction from the flustered nurses, I went into the room.

"Wow!" the young man laughingly said to me. "You should have seen the look on those old bags' faces!" He went on to tell me that women somehow seemed unable to resist him and often offered to lend him such comfort. If a visiting female didn't volunteer right away, he would invite her to pull down the sheet so he could show her that his "family jewels" were intact in spite of all the peripheral damage, and things invariably proceeded from there. He added that he was a little surprised at the nurses' reactions because he thought 'everybody knew' what went on here and that we'd given him a rare private room for that very reason.

Also, he added, "All the girls know. Why do you think they always come in alone to see me?"

Mostly, things were more routine than that. An exciting hepatitis epidemic filled a whole ward with yellow faces, and then another before it died out. We began using increasing amounts of penicillin, the new miracle drug, for all kinds of infections. A great medical mystery developed on the Dermatology ward, when a young sailor came in with a badly inflamed foot around a particularly raw ulcer at the base of his great toe. The mystery was, how come it didn't hurt? It looked like it should be terribly painful. It took a while for anyone to suspect what it actually turned out to be: a characteristically painless primary chancre of primary syphilis. The young sailor had come by train from the West Coast and had established an intimate relationship with a young woman sitting facing him in the front seat of the coach. When the lights were dimmed during the night, he had worked his stockinged foot gradually up under her dress and accomplished an unusual form of sexual congress. We all knew that you couldn't catch syphilis on a toilet seat, as some claimed they had, but no one had ever thought of what could happen in a crowded railway coach.

One of my older patients had, among a variety of medical ills, a rather benign form of general paresis. His name, appropriately enough, was Joe, fitting for one who suffered from what a certain segment of the population called "Old Joe" rather than the correct term: syphilis. He was by no means wildly psychotic, but was affable, a bit verbose, and given to jumping to his feet at odd times, performing a few shuffling steps of soft shoe dancing, and then sitting down to resume in midsentence what he'd been saying when his terpsichorean impulse took over. When it came time for me to present a case at the major monthly hospital staff conference, I decided Joe would be a good subject, not nearly as dull as most. He readily agreed and even seemed eager for this chance to meet the whole hospital staff.

The great day came, and Joe and I made our way to the auditorium where a small lectern had been set up in front of the audience, where I was to stand, and a small chair was placed near it for Joe to sit on so everyone could see him. The auditorium was packed with physicians, residents, interns, nurses, and anyone else who could get in.

Joe, clearly pleased to be the center of attention, looked around the room smiling and nodding affably at various members of the audience while his long medical history, the details of his physical exam, his lab tests and his X-Rays were all described. Only once did he leap to his feet, perform his little soft shoe routine for a few seconds, and then return to his seat, while I droned on. One item of mild interest in his personal history was his background on the stage, where for many years he had performed as a song and dance man in vaudeville shows. His description of his skill and fame were clearly examples of his grandiosity and his delusional system.

At the end of my part of the presentation, I invited Joe, if he wished, to tell the audience anything else he thought was important about himself and his current illness. Once again he stood up, did a little routine, and then instead of sitting back down, danced his way up the center aisle. Midway into the audience he stopped. With grand, sweeping gestures he announced that as soon as he got out he was going to buy a new suit for every doctor in this hospital, since we were all such fine men and had treated him so well. Continuing to gesture so as to include everyone in the room, he added that he would also get "a pretty new dress for all you ladies. Anything you want."

As if that hadn't been enough to illustrate his pathological grandiosity, he went on to say that he had been such a great performer that he had actually taught the great Al Jolson, star of stage and screen, "everything he knows about dancing." The audience was both amused and enlightened, and the staff conference ended on a successful note.

Within a week, 'the great' Al Jolson showed up at the hospital to visit Joe. After their exuberant greeting, complete with hugs and backslapping, Jolson turned to me and said, "This old bastard taught me everything I know about dancing!" So much for grandiose delusions. We never did, however, get those new suits that people kept asking me about.

At long last the months on Internal Medicine were over, and I embarked on the 4-month adventure in Surgery- my destiny, I believed.

The first part of it took place divided between Ear Nose and Throat half the time, and Genitourinary Surgery the other half. Both were busy, not only because of the usual steady stream of patients in those subject areas, but because of a kind of fad that had developed in the Navy. Now that the war was over, the restrictions on elective - optional, not absolutely required - procedures were relaxed. With that came an unexpected surge in demands among the sailors for two procedures: circumcisions and tonsillectomies. No one seemed able to explain that, completely, but there it was.

Tonsillectomies were very common at that time before the widespread use (and dangerous over-use) of antibiotics, because of the frequency of throat infections, especially among young people living in close proximity to each other, as on board ship. Many of our young sailors had tremendously enlarged tonsils, many of them chronically inflamed, and frequent sore throats. Most had come from lower social and economic classes and rural communities in which children were rarely operated upon to remove their tonsils, in those days, and there were as a result large numbers of young males seeking the operation.

From my days in Dr. Niblick's clinic, where he did tonsillectomies as an outpatient procedure under local anesthesia with perhaps a little 'laughing gas,' and at Children's Memorial Hospital during my clerkship, where they did them under ether dripped onto a mask removed for brief periods to allow the cutting, I was well acquainted with the procedure. Usually a "snare" was employed to do the deed. The snare was a loop of wire mounted at the end of a long handle, which could be tightened up after being placed around the base, or pedicle, connecting the tonsil to the wall of the pharynx. Unless the tonsil, actually a large lymph gland, was inextricably plastered to the wall of the throat by repeated infections, the procedure could be done quickly and simply.

Our Chief of ENT, unfortunately, did not 'believe' in using the snare. This man, a true martinet in every sense, was an immaculately tailored, tiny little dictator who treated interns and junior staff, both, likes inferior creatures. He strutted, rather than walked, always pursued by a group of anxious, attentive junior officers, was a terror during white glove inspections, acted like nurses existed only to serve him, and treated his patients with a haughty, authoritarian, impatient air. We all hated him. But we also feared him, for his wrath was frequent and monumental and we tried hard to avoid setting it off.

He insisted that we carefully dissect out every tonsil, rather than simply whip it out with the wire loop. "Good training," he called this. It also made it harder to successfully anesthetize the site, and caused it to bleed more, sometimes copiously. He was unmoved by any complaint, and rested so heavily on his very senior 4-stripe full Captain's rank that no one dared actually to argue with him. We sometimes did as many as six or eight tonsillectomies in a morning, silently cursing the captain the whole time. Many of our patients were large, strong, very young black fellows, who tended to salivate profusely, sweat copiously, tremble violently, and roll their eyes in terror during the whole operation. We all feared being attacked during their panic, but it didn't happen.

Perhaps my most dramatic day in ENT surgery came late in the month, when a patient was to have a nasal polyp removed. This was a growth the size of a small grape, attached inside his nasal cavity on a little stem. Like most procedures in that kind of surgery, it was done under local anesthesia. In the nose, we commonly used a solution of cocaine for this. A cotton swab was dipped in a bottle of cocaine solution and then inserted into the nose. Despite the solution's mildly irritating quality, it rapidly produced total numbness of the inside of the nose. It is not uncommon for cocaine addicts who often administer their drug by sniffing up the powdered cocaine to develop an actual hole in the septum separating the two sides of the nose because of the caustic nature of the cocaine powder. Seeing that hole makes the diagnosis instantly.

It was a Saturday morning, and the weekly inspecting party arrived just after I had inserted the cocaine-soaked swab and was waiting for it to take effect. I stood respectfully to one side while the inspectors examined the little operating room minutely, checking all the instruments, looking for traces of dust on their white gloves, checking out the 'deck' for any sign of soil, and seeming to take forever in the process. Finally they left.

I turned to my patient. The swab was still in his nose - and had been for much too long. He was sitting in a chair much like a dental chair, and when I looked at him he was stiffened out, boardlike, trembling noticeably. Only his heels and the back of his head were in contact with the chair; the rest of him was bowed backward, and he was clearly on the verge of a major convulsion. He wore an exaggerated, fixed grin on his face, and seemed perfectly happy in spite of all.

In a panic, I tore the swap out of his nose, and together with the young, wide-eyed corpsman helping me, patted his shoulders and spoke comforting words to him, while he slowly relaxed, little by little, and his body sank back into the chair. I proceeded to dissect out the polyp. When it seemed safe, and he appeared to be back to normal, I told him he could go back to his ward. As he left, he gave me a pat on the shoulder and said, "Doc, you sure do good work! I didn't feel a thing." His grin was gone, but he still seemed happy.

On another Saturday morning during inspection, the party caught me in the middle of doing a circumcision. My patient was a huge youngster, perhaps eighteen years old, who was in an absolutely terrified state as he climbed up on the operating table and bravely lay down. His apprehension and fear of what was going to be done to him had no doubt been building for days and had reached its peak. It was not customary in those days, as it is now, to give the patient scheduled for such 'minor' surgery any pre-medication, designed to calm the quite normal fears that accompany many such procedures, and patients were often extremely tense and anxious.

After anesthetizing the young man's notably large penis using multiple injections of Novocain, I prepared to make the initial incision through the foreskin. The inspecting party arrived just as I was cutting down, and the senior captain conducting the party leaned over the table to look more closely at what I was doing, and probably to admire the youngster's quite remarkably large sexual organ.

As luck would have it, the inspecting officer was none other than Captain Morrison, the immaculately tailored, dictatorial popinjay who chaired the ENT department. He was wearing a beautifully fitted tan wool gabardine uniform, constructed to his precise measure by an expert and doubtless very expensive tailor.

Just as he leaned over to look at my handiwork, I cut through an aberrant, unusually placed small artery that promptly, thanks to the patient's high state of anxiety and doubtlessly markedly elevated blood pressure, sprayed bright red blood on the front of the captain's expensive uniform from the lapels all the way down to his waist. He jerked back, furious, but unable to find an acceptable object for his fury. Making no attempt to wipe off the blood, which in any event would never come off that lovely wool gabardine, he turned on his heel and marched angrily out of my operating room without a word.

Once again I had one of those premonitions of disaster and banishment to the reform school that accompanied my appearances before the faculty at Todd School. However, I had a bleeding patient to take care of (that part was actually quite easy), and as I concentrated on my work a growing sense of perverse satisfaction crept over me.

Thanks to the corpsmen who had witnessed the blood-bath, and the ever-present grapevine for disseminating gossip and juicy tidbits that exists in all hospitals, probably worldwide, the word of my achievement spread with lightning-like rapidity. I was met, when I entered the dining hall for the evening meal, with actual applause and considerable backslapping by my fellow interns, all of whom insisted on believing that I had 'done' the Captain purposely, and with diabolical cleverness. I could never persuade them otherwise, and loved my fifteen minutes of fame.

Orthopedic surgery and neurosurgery followed the next month, and it proved to be a tense time. There can be little doubt that, while many factors play a part in a physician's selection of a specialty area to concentrate on for the bulk of his career, his personality and attitudes play the most important role of all. Dr. Davis, the neurosurgeon at Northwestern, was not at all unlike others in his specialty, many of whom earned reputations for hauteur and arrogance seemingly expected of those so brilliant, and so often poised on the very brink of life and death, or worse - their patients' of course, not their own. They were a lordly group, unfriendly even among themselves. Even skilled surgeons who worked on other parts than the brain seemed in a certain awe of these supreme surgical artists.

Orthopedic surgeons - "orthopods" as they were called - were a different breed. They seemed to be far less refined, and were often husky, strong-seeming fellows with ham-like hands and stubby, strong fingers, and a bluff, often brusque manner.

They were more likely than other surgeons to rap their assistants sharply across the knuckles with a heavy steel retractor or bone chisel if the hapless assistant at the table didn't respond quickly to a grunted order or do things exactly as the great man wished. Almost alone among surgeons, they not infrequently threw a heavy electric saw or drill or other piece of costly surgical equipment clear across the operating room if it failed for whatever reason to perform as they wished.

Not all orthopods, naturally, behave that way, but we as interns all noted this. The work was sometimes physically hard, repositioning fractured bones and manipulating dislocated joints tightly held in place by painful, bruised, spastic muscles, particularly in strong young people. Much of what they did seemed more like carpentry, at times striking in its crudity. This kind of work clearly appealed to a wholly different breed than did the painstaking, delicate work of probing inside a brain, or attempting to reconnect delicate nerve trunks. In both of these specialties, it seemed that the personality of the surgeon was what drove him to choose that kind of work in the first place; the work didn't create the personality.

Both neurosurgeons and orthopedic surgeons have, very often, problems communicating with their patients. The former, because of their remoteness and the complex, mysterious-seeming tissues they work on with equally mysterious, complex techniques that patients have great trouble understanding, particularly when they are described in what seems like abstruse, poorly understood, often very big words. The latter, while they deal with problems of bones and joints, and everybody knows about those in ways they cannot know about neurons and synapses, gray and white matter, and meninges, tend to fail utterly to explain sometimes simple things to their patients, and seem as well to be blissfully unconcerned with the often severe, unrelenting pain that damaged bones and joints can produce.

The result is different in the two specialties. Orthopedic patients more commonly develop fairly severe emotional problems, and are more often than others to be referred to mental health professionals for assistance with them. There has also long been a deeply ingrained fear among physicians, particularly surgeons since they most often have to deal with pain problems among their patients, of over-prescribing pain medication, especially narcotics of all kinds, because of the danger of producing dependency or outright addiction to such substances.

It is interesting that, although medical administration of too much, too strong, or too frequent doses of pain killers can lead to addiction, it is rarely the actual cause of that. This was true even in the early days of the century, when severe and sometimes only moderate, pain was frequently treated with opium and its derivatives, because there was not much choice. Today's superabundance of highly touted remedies for pain, relentlessly advertised on television, usually at dinnertime, is a relatively recent development, and the public's appetite for these things, beginning with aspirin, seems insatiable.

Whatever the reasons, and they are many and complex, many orthopedic patients are severely uncomfortable, and possibly orthopedists have to develop a kind of protective failure to see or appreciate, or to empathize, with the phenomenon. Since pain is almost impossible to measure objectively, it is hard to evaluate accurately as to its severity and can be seriously underestimated. It seems true, as some have said, that the growth of the hospice movement for the treatment of terminally ill patients in special surroundings with generous doses of narcotic drugs, is a reflection of physicians' failure to deal with the often terrible pain that may accompany the final stages of disease, especially cancer.

Unbeknownst to me at the time I was assisting in surgery on orthopedic patients, I was to learn far more about pain-killing drugs during my residency training, and on through my entire medical career, and have come away with some fairly strong beliefs about the whole subject, which will in due time emerge in these notes.

A subsequent month was spent partly in the area of genitourinary surgery and partly in gynecologic surgery. Today, those fields are not ordinarily addressed together, but apparently the physical geography of the two justified this sharing of time and attention in the minds of the designers of our internship program.

Perhaps the commonest problem that was brought to the "G.U." service, as it is still universally called, was that of urethral strictures. The urethra is the little tube, longer in males than in females, leading from the urinary bladder to the outside world. It was – and still is - the commonest site of infection by the gonococcus organism - long prominent on the wages of sin list. Ordinary sailors, like most ordinary folks familiar with the disease thus caused have long called it 'clap' or a 'drip,' that being its commonest manifestation early on.

Gonorrhea, by its nature, is much more readily seen in males because of a discharge from the end of the penis called, in its early stages, a 'morning drop,' since that is the time of day when it is usually first noticed. It may go on to a more abundant production as the days go by, and usually causes some burning on urination, and some itching inside the penis. About this time, at the very latest, the victim seeks help. Before penicillin and other effective antibiotic agents appeared on the scene, treatment often consisted of squirting about an ounce or more of a strong solution of silver, called argyral, directly into the urethral canal in the penis, pinching the end of the affected organ so the stuff didn't drain out, and holding it in place for a few minutes.

In addition to being singularly uncomfortable as well as mortifying, the treatment itself could set up an inflammation in the little tube, and was not always successful, so it had to be repeated. Before that remedy came along, in the nineteenth century, it was even harder to treat the infection. If it quieted down, but didn't completely disappear, the chronic infection that resulted caused scarring inside the urethra, and the scars progressively interfered with the urinary stream, whose complete blockage was a genuine medical emergency as urine backed up, first into the bladder, and then on to the kidneys.

Many horrible-sounding remedies were invented to deal with this problem. The most striking was a thin metal tube that contained a number of tiny, razor-sharp blades within it, which could be erected and made to stick out from the tube when a wire handle was pulled. The tube was inserted into the urethra right up to the bladder, the little blades erected, and the tube was then pulled out. On the way it cut through some of the scar tissue and allowed urine to flow. This was done without anesthesia, except for maybe stiff slug of whiskey before the tube was forced in. This treatment never really caught on.

The British Navy, like our own (we patterned ourselves closely on them in this as in many other ways) had historically also had serious problems with gonorrhea among their sailors.

Officers, of course, were expected never to get the disease, even though they did. Ordinary seamen, particularly after long periods at sea, have since time immemorial sought out sexual release the minute they first go ashore, and a small army of professionals of the ancient "sex trade" generally exists in every saloon in every port, eager to earn an honest living meeting the sailors' needs. These ladies have generally been a rich repository of the gonococcus organism, which has been just as eager to find new hosts.

A major problem with gonorrhea is that it can go undetected in females, and for a long time. The discharge, especially in the days before feminine hygiene became a popular and publicly discussed issue, was almost always mistaken for a 'normal' vaginal discharge, widely believed to be almost universal among females, and when copious was believed, especially by male sexual partners, simply to illustrate the female's intense sexual excitement. Seaport prostitutes around the world thus spread the disease very widely.

At one time, the British Naval authorities, exasperated by their inability to control the sea-going epidemic, decreed that any sailor who contracted this infection on three separate occasions would, for his own future health, if not for the health of his soul, have his penis and testicles surgically removed - a sort of 'three strikes you're off" control measure. This was very poorly received, and soon abandoned. The problem continued.

Our own Navy declared, officially, that gonorrhea was to be considered a "misconduct" diagnosis. This meant that the disease ranked right along with deliberately shooting yourself in the foot to avoid duty, or causing yourself a serious infection from tattooing, and several other unacceptable acts that resulted in the need to be treated. The practical effect of the misconduct label was to deprive the sailor of all pay and allowances for however long it took to get over the infection and return to duty, along with, usually, a substantial period of time confined to the ship or the base so he couldn't readily get it again. None of this worked, and it led to unexpected consequences, as I was to find later in Japan.

Penicillin, and later other antibiotics, were found to be successful in treating the disease, but at the time of my internship were not used. Penicillin, just emerging, very expensive, and both difficult and painful to administer, was beginning to be used for the much more serious syphilis, usually caught the same way as was gonorrhea, but not for plain old 'clap.'

Accordingly, on both the GU and the GYN services, the consequences of gonorrhea took up much of our time and effort. Males not only needed repeated, thorough irrigations with the hated silver solution, but the older cases required dilation of the urethra. We did not use the tube with the little knives, but instead a set of heavy steel rods ranging in diameter from that of a pencil lead up to rods twice as thick as the whole pencil. These rods, about ten inches long, were bent almost to a right angle about 2 inches from the slightly rounded pointed end.

That end was inserted into the penis, which was worked up along the metal shaft as it was pushed inward until it collided with the pubic bone. The bent end was devised to allow the operator to work the end of the 'sound,' as the metal rods were called, under and around the bone so as to reach the bladder. Again, no anesthesia was used. It was painful to watch, and far more so for the patient. Starting with the smallest diameter sound, the idea was to insert progressively larger and larger ones, until the biggest one was successfully inserted. At that point the poor guy could, presumably, urinate freely, since the tract was now stretched open. The comparable procedure with females was much easier, since the urethra is much shorter and the sound doesn't have to be manipulated around the public bones, but goes straight in. It still hurt like blazes.

Some of our old veteran patients, who had been treated many times by this medieval process, had been stretched out so badly that they were incontinent and had to wear diapers. Others had worked out their own system, generally carrying a rather stiff rubber tube, or catheter, traditionally coiled up inside their hatband, which they took out and inserted themselves when their bladders felt full.

Women with gonorrhea risked a further and potentially far more serious complication beyond the simple scarring of the urethra. If the organism worked its way up through the vagina and uterus, it entered the fallopian tubes, leading from the ovaries and intended to carry eggs down to be fertilized and implanted. Generally this led to absolute sterility, as those tubes scarred and sealed down. Sometimes, in the process, an abscess developed in the tube, which could cause it to rupture and result in peritonitis and death. In some cases, before the tube closed completely, the woman became pregnant, and the fertilized egg became stuck in the tube, where it continued to grow as a 'tubal pregnancy.' While those fetuses sometimes reached nearly full size, the end result was more often rupture of the tube, copious bleeding, and again, possibly death.

A single shot of penicillin, today, or a few pills of a different antibiotic, can often stop the disease in its tracks. Ominously, however, strains of the gonococcus are beginning to show up that are resistant to most antibiotics, and the day may well come when the disease assumes, once again, a major, serious public health problem.

We did, thankfully, have many other kinds of things to diagnose and treat in both GU and GYN wards and clinics. Hysterectomies were far less common than they have become. Kidneys had to be removed from time to time - a major procedure. The most complex and difficult operations were often those seeking to remove a cancerous prostate gland or a serious benign enlargement of that gland at the neck of the male bladder causing urinary retention. Operations on the prostate through the urethra were beginning to be done, but usually the surgeon approached the gland directly from the outside, through the skin just behind the testicles. Neither of those surgical specialties captured my attention or my devotion, and I moved on to what they called "General Surgery," meaning, for the most part, operations on the abdomen and, less commonly, the chest. This, I knew, was my destiny.

The department called 'General Surgery' was the jewel in the crown of the institution - the most glamorous, the most exciting, the most 'big league,' where truly major procedures were routine. Every day there were three, four or five operations that involved opening up the chest or the abdomen, and requiring from three to five surgeons. The surgical staff included a number of senior men who had served aboard the great ships of the line in the Pacific sea battles and at other major Navy hospitals. Many of them had held prestigious surgical positions in various university medical schools or in their home cities, and were eager to get back to civilian life, so there was a steady drain of talent to deal with a steady flow of major cases.

The smaller, outlying Navy hospitals were shrinking down or facing closure, so their patients were often sent to the big ones at Philadelphia, Bethesda in Washington, San Diego, Jacksonville and Great Lakes, near Chicago. Senior surgical staff often followed, sometimes coming to a major medical center like ours, or leaving to return to wherever they had come from when the Great War began. Many on our staff, despite their great skill and love for their special part of the profession, were with us only briefly, and carried with them a "short-timer" attitude.

This made it an ideal place for an intern. Not only was the intern needed to 'scrub in' on innumerable, often fascinating cases, but if he earned the regard of the senior staff, was actually allowed to scrub as the principal operator from time to time. I soon discovered that the way to earn the opportunity to be the surgeon in charge in a given case was to have written up an outstanding history and physical examination, ordered all the right tests (there weren't that many in those days,) and make a good presentation at the daily surgical staff meeting where plans were laid for the morrow's O.R. dramas.

In addition, one was required to be a quick, responsive assistant at the table, able to anticipate the surgeon's next major moves, and eager to "close up" - perform the often tedious, painstaking stitching of the various layers of different tissues opened up during the operation. Here my experience in the anatomy lab at school, where I had served for a time as a student-instructor/lab assistant for students in the two classes that followed mine, came in to play and proved valuable. Without a fairly detailed and exact knowledge of the anatomy of the operative site, mistakes could be made as various layers of tissue, or sheaths around muscle masses and tendons were ignored in the sewing up, or mistakenly tacked onto places or structures where they didn't belong. This is a common cause of so-called "adhesions" and prolonged discomfort sometimes years after surgery.

It was desirable, in addition, to be very quick to spot "bleeders," little vessels cut during the major incisions that continued to bleed and at least ooze, complicating and obscuring the surgical field and interfering with wound closure and healing. While some surgeons, especially those in orthopedics, often simply touched bleeders with an electric cautery needle, usually enough to seal them off, the more elegant and certain remedy was to grasp the bleeding vessel in a hemostat forceps, named for its ability to "blood-stop" and thus the name, and then quickly tie a suture just below the tip of the hemostat.

The spotting and tying off of bleeders, sometimes very numerous, in order to produce a 'dry' operative field, was an important if rather mundane, part of the process. At times there were very large numbers of these little red fountains and the main event of the surgery could be badly delayed. Surgeons often became highly irritated when that happened.

Operations during the first few days of the intern's participation in the surgical big leagues became, in a sense, a test of the intern in many dimensions. First, his skill at doing the history and physical; next his performance at staff, and ability to propose the correct surgical procedure; third, his performance as a kind of caddy, ready with the right 'club,' and able to anticipate the golfer's or the surgeon's desired instrument for the next shot; and fourth, during the earliest part of the operation in particular, his sharp vision spotting bleeders, and seizing them on the first try with the hemostat.

Finally, he was closely watched to see how quickly and smoothly he could throw a little loop of suture material around the bleeder and tie a smooth, tiny knot. This examination of his manual dexterity, gained in many hours of knot-tying on scraps of cloth and even fragments of suitable animal tissue left unconsumed in the mess hall, continued as the new boy participated in, and ultimately took over, the final "closing up."

When all those hurdles were successfully navigated, the intern was allowed to perform a whole operation, usually an appendectomy, from "skin to skin." His assistant was one of the senior staff members, observing his every move, offering advice and suggestions, and ready to step in, if need be, to save the blessedly unconscious patient from possible mayhem, or worse, at the often tremulous hands of a surgical novice.

Several factors worked in my favor as I strove to achieve 'skin-to-skin' status. The first was the extra time spent in the anatomy lab. Another was the fact that I had already spent three months serving on other parts of the surgery service where there were ample opportunities to overcome the natural reluctance to cut into - to violate, literally - intact, living flesh until then undisturbed by your sharpened steel, to stitch it up neatly, to tie better and better knots as you made alterations in the designs of God. (Remember the circumcisions!) Still another was my superior ability to write up histories and physicals and present them well at staff.

Most important of all, however, was the fact that I got in to scrub with the Chief of Surgery several times during my first few days, and on patients whose work-ups I had managed to do well, partly by staying up most of the night creating super-complete, coherently written case records. The chief was an outstandingly handsome, Adonis-like man who happened also to be an excellent surgeon and a fine clinical (as opposed to classroom) teacher. His name was Bob Brown. Just as Captain Hogan was to do before long, Dr. Brown eventually became the Surgeon General of the Navy after serving at the same time I did, on the Hospital Ship Repose during the war in Korea.

Captain Brown became an enthusiastic coach and mentor, and let me do innumerable operations in his place but with him at my side. Once he challenged me to "set a new record," with him as my assistant, of course, going "skin-to-skin" performing an appendectomy. We were in and out, with the appendix in our hands and the skin sewed back up, in exactly 3 minutes. It was, we discovered, an actual record, at least for that hospital, and won us one more 15 minutes of fame, along with the antagonistic envy of all the slower guys.

That month flew by. In the course of it, Dr. Brown talked to me at length about my future career as a surgeon, often during the drawn-out, 15 minute hand scrubbing that preceded every operation, or following the completion of one while we rested in preparation for the next case. My excitement and enthusiasm grew steadily, and reached its peak when my teacher-leader-idol announced that he intended to contact friends at Hopkins, up the road in Baltimore, to ensure that I would be welcomed there as a surgical resident, my training and pay supplied by the Navy. "Uncle Charlie," I secretly said to myself, "here I come!"

But first, there were two more months to do on my 'rotating' internship: Obstetrics one month, and Psychiatry the final month.

As part of its exercise of community participation and responsibility, Captain Hogan had committed an intern to work for a month at a civilian hospital down town. This was a voluntary assignment that I eagerly signed up for, thinking it would be fun to get out from under the strict, uniformed authoritarianism of the military for a while. The hospital was St. Joseph's, operated by the Sisters of Mercy, mainly for the poor. Figuring it was going to be a cleaned-up, orderly version of those exciting days at the Chicago Maternity Center, I duly reported to the stern, business-like Mother Superior, who welcomed me briefly to her domain and sent me, the first day, down to see the Archbishop of the Diocese in his office near the downtown area.

There I was interviewed at some length by a kindly Monsignor, who inquired into my religious background. I described for him my childhood attendance at the First Presbyterian Church in Evanston so faithfully that I won a whole string of perfect attendance medals from Sunday School, and my shopping around among various denominations (I didn't tell him why, of course) during my years at Todd School. I also failed to mention that every Sunday as we three children set out for Sunday School, my father instructed us, in great seriousness, to remember to cross to the opposite side of the street when we approached the Catholic Church, and then cross back before reaching the Christian Science Church. Presumably this would protect us from some vague kind of spiritual contamination; we were never quite sure.

The monsignor eventually seemed satisfied that I was at least a genuine Christian, if not quite the altogether proper kind. He took me in to the Archbishop's office, where the eminent old churchman shook my hand and blessed me. He said that I would be doing the Lord's work at St. Joseph's, and bade me do it well. He added that I should not hesitate to baptize, "In the name of the Father, the Son, and the Holy Ghost," any infant I delivered who seemed to have died or was in the process of doing so, and that I had his permission and delegated authority to do so. That, he said, would ensure the child's admission into Paradise.

I saw a certain distant similarity to our naming the slum-dwelling infants of south Chicago after Loyal Davis, ensuring their ready admission into the free clinics of the medical schools, but thought it best not to bring that up. Sounded irreligious.

Back at the hospital, I was met by the OB nurse with the announcement that she had three mothers in labor, two of them 'fully dilated.' That meant the births were imminent, so I scrubbed up and followed the nurse into the delivery room, where two delivery tables were set up, each occupied by an already draped female with her legs up in stirrups, both of them moaning periodically and clearly well along in labor.

As is the case in most normal births, there is really very little for the attending physician to do except ease the baby's head gently when it begins to emerge, catch the slippery little creature to keep it from dropping to the floor, sometimes swat the new fanny a couple of times to stimulate the beautiful birth cry, and hand the new citizen to a waiting nurse. While the nurse holds the newborn, the doctor in charge of this miracle ties off and cuts the umbilical cord between two pieces of stout cotton ribbon. Turning back to the real heroine of the event, he massages her uterus through her now floppy-soft abdomen until the placenta shows up - no dogs to worry about here! Additionally, there were no roosters or other onlookers, either.

Turning then from the mother, the doctor was required to drop a small amount of a state-prescribed solution into each of the baby's eyes to kill any gonorrhea organisms it may have picked up in the birth canal en route to the world.

The ballet just described took place in that delivery room twice in about the first ten minutes of my duty at St. Joseph's. Both mothers and both babies were healthy, giving me no chance to exercise my new authority to baptize anybody. In the delivery room next door, however, another mother, alone this time, was up in stirrups, nearly fully dilated and ready to deliver her child, so I scrubbed up again and went in to join her. This one took far longer, and I lingered in the room for hours, having nowhere else to go and no other engagements for the evening. At last, about 2:30 in the morning, another healthy baby was produced.

I stumbled out of the delivery room exhausted after what had been a full, colorful, and, I thought, fairly productive day. The head night nurse pointed to a closed door just off the ward, telling me that the bed in there was for the doctor. I stumbled in, found the bed's iron foot just inside the door, and flopped down on the bed for a few minutes rest, intending to get up, turn on the lights, maybe shower, and crawl between the sheets for some serious sleep.

Sleep came sooner and more profoundly than I had anticipated, and my next conscious, clear thought was that I had surely died. The room seemed brilliantly lighted, the sun having risen and bathed its stark white enameled walls in a blinding glare, through which, looking past the foot of the iron bedstead, I could see a startlingly realistic statue of Jesus hanging from His cross against the wall, His precious blood making its way down his body from a wound over his liver. A loud, booming voice that seemed to shake the very walls of the room, filled my ears with the command: "JESUS, MARY AND JOSEPH! PRAY FOR US SINNERS!" This, I was later to learn, ushered in 'morning prayers' over the hospital paging system turned up to its loudest volume. At that first moment, however, had it been announced that I was to enter the Kingdom of Heaven, or perhaps already had done so, I could not have been more surprised.

The days that followed passed swiftly, and I was privileged to assist, or at least pretend that I was assisting, in the entry into the postwar world of more than a hundred mostly healthy, intact, squalling infants of many sizes, shapes and colors. Part of the time I was assisted by a senior medical student (seriously junior to an intern, of course) from the Thomas Jefferson University Medical School in Philadelphia, and his exuberant Protestantism and sparkling sense of humor greatly livened up my days. He was particularly irreverent, loudly greeting the statue of St. Joseph, which stood in the underground passage leading from the cafeteria to the main hospital and always full of scurrying student nurses and more sedate nuns.

His loud call of "Good morning, Joe old boy!" bordering as it did on outright sacrilege but not actually violating any church law that we knew of, never failed to stop some of the hurrying angels of mercy dead in their tracks.

My student helper only stayed a couple of weeks, unfortunately, and once again I was saddled with what seemed to be an unending stream of mothers on the brink of delivery. Obstetrics was fun - exciting and stimulating, and rendering the doctor into an almost holy status, adored by patients who did not understand how little he actually had to do with the miracles they were producing, showering him with gratitude and affection that he had hardly earned but happily accepted.

Then, in my last week at St. Joseph's, disaster loomed. A healthy young 'primip,' short for "primiparous female," meaning pregnant for the first time, came in for what we expected would be another routine delivery. Her labor was vigorous and seemed to be progressing routinely enough, when progress suddenly stopped. Her cervix, opening at the bottom of the uterus, had dilated properly and the baby's head was well down into the birth canal, when suddenly all further descent ceased entirely, despite strong uterine contractions and earnest attempts to bear down.

After several hours of this, signs of impending doom began to appear. The baby's heart sounds speeded up, then became irregular and began to slow down too much. The young mother was becoming seriously exhausted, and her own vital signs started becoming erratic. We rarely administered intravenous fluids during labor at that time, but I had her moved from the labor room into the delivery room, put her up in stirrups, started an I.V., and tried to perform a maneuver called "version and extraction," used in similar instances to turn the fetus, inside the uterus, so that its head was upright instead of down, as it usually is. Once that is accomplished, it is sometimes possible to extract the fetus feet first, by pulling on the legs.

It proved to be impossible. I had summoned the anesthetist to help, and even when the patient was put into a fairly deep state of anesthesia, the uterus failed to relax and soften up sufficiently to allow any movement of the baby at all. We deepened the anesthesia to a point that stopped labor altogether, to give the mother a little rest, but when we lightened her and contractions resumed, there was still no progress. The usual signs of fetal life had by now disappeared, and the child was clearly dead. The mother, to make things worse, seemed on her way to death as well.

To further complicate matters, the fetus was wedged so far down into the pelvis that it was not possible to perform a Caesarian section without risking massive, uncontrollable bleeding and almost certain death on the operating table.

A prominent local obstetrician, on the faculty of one of the local medical schools, was listed as our on-call emergency consultant and, if necessary, intervenor in emergencies. I had talked to this man several times on the telephone when confronted with special problems, and he seemed highly intelligent, kindly, and mostly sympathetic to my needs, but he invariably pleaded extremely pressing demands on his time and never once had actually appeared at our hospital. This time, I hoped, it would be different.

It was not to be. He made many suggestions, all of which I had tried, to no avail. Finally he said, "Well, Son, if you want to keep that woman alive, you're going to have to do a craniolithotomy." Searching the recesses of my exhausted brain for what that meant, I finally began to recall seeing something about this rare, radical-sounding procedure. However, I also knew I had never seen it done, or even heard of it being done by anyone I knew.

Patiently, my consultant explained. After putting the patient deeply to sleep, the operator begins to operate upon the impacted fetal head, extracting it piece by piece until what remained of the dead fetus could easily be delivered. In extreme cases of what he called "deep transverse arrest" with the head wedged deep into the pelvis and the infant dead, it was the only "safe" way to save the mother.

Badly shaken, and filled with dread, I ordered that the appropriate sterile surgical set, probably never before used in that hospital, be brought to the delivery room, and told the anesthetist what was in store. I unwrapped the sterile package of instruments, which in addition to the usual hemostats and long forceps contained several long knives, resembling carving knives with metal handles, but smaller. I had no idea exactly how those were to be used.

While I studied the instrument set, there was a sudden disturbance at the door to the delivery room. Looking up, I was astonished to see that the room was now lined along each wall with a row of nurses, all of them nuns, standing there watching me intently but motionless and silent. The noise I had heard turned out to be a short, stocky little man dressed all in black save for a glimpse of white collar, wearing a black hat and carrying a small black satchel. Astonished, I watched him bustle across my sterile delivery room, taking off his hat and placing it atop a tray of now non-sterile instruments, and putting his little black bag on another table, hopelessly contaminating all those instruments as well.

With all eyes fixed on this incredibly shocking, totally incongruous black apparition in the midst of what had, moments before, been a gleaming, white, sterile surgical operating room, the fellow quite energetically snapped open his bag, reached in and withdrew a large glass tube, tapered at one end and inserted into a large rubber bulb at the other. Next he pulled out a squat glass jar full of a clear liquid. Opening it, he inserted the glass tube into the liquid, squeezed and released the rubber bulb, and loaded the tube with the liquid.

After a moment or two of shocked silence, I stepped close to the intruder and demanded to know what the hell he thought he was doing. "I'm going to baptize the baby," he said. "The baby's dead," said I. "Nevertheless," he continued to insist, "I intend to see that the infant is baptized."

I pointed out that the baby, dead or alive, had yet to be delivered, and might not be for some time. He shot back the astounding declaration that he intended to perform an "intrauterine" baptism. By that he obviously meant to insert his glass bulb syringe into the operating field and squirt holy (but non-sterile) water on the partially emerged cranium. That did it. Unable to control my growing rage any longer, I picked up one of the large knives from the sterile pack I had just unwrapped, and held the blade up against the man's throat.

I recall noting, incongruously, that his white collar had a dark ring of soil around the top.

With the knife in place, I moved my face to within inches of his, and said (and I think I meant it,) in my calmest possible voice, "If you touch my patient I'll cut your throat!" Neither this man of God nor I moved for what seemed a long time. At long last, he leaned his upper body backward, removing his seriously endangered neck an inch or so from my blade. Seeing that I did not move, either toward him or away, he took a step backward.

He was clearly distraught, but then so was I. His response to the call of his vocation had clearly been violently thwarted (and by a damned Protestant, no less!) To relieve his terrible frustration, I told him I had been authorized by the Archbishop to baptize any infant in trouble, and would do so as soon as it was out. He totally ignored that, turning to grasp his jar of fluid, squirting his glass syringe back into it, capping the bottle, returning it to the black satchel that he literally slammed shut, and, clutching his hat from the other table, made his way out of the room in the highest possible dudgeon.

Vastly relieved that I had been saved from committing a terrible, bloody murder, that for a moment at least I was fully prepared to do, I turned back to my blessedly unconscious, anesthetized, rapidly failing young mother. Still horrified at the prospect of what I had been instructed to do, I tried one last time to push the head back up into the birth passage, hoping to ease the downward pressure on it enough to let me rotate it out of its locked, side-to-side position and into the normal fore-and-aft position that would let it pass out the portal like it should. It worked! Finally the head moved, I rotated it, it began to descend, and the infant emerged intact, though it had long since expired.

The rest of the delivery proceeded without incident, and in a surprisingly short few days the mother, saddened but very much alive, walked out to go home in a taxi instead of in the grim black-curtained hearse she had been so close to. Nearly the entire group of nurse-nuns who had lined my delivery room during the drama with the determined priest were at the door to the hospital to bid our miraculously saved patient goodbye, promising to be there next year when she came back.

Meanwhile, my friendly devoted cleric had registered his outrage with the Mother Superior. She summoned me to her office, and I stood before her desk expecting the worst, told me that Father John, or whatever his name was, had been in to declare that St. Joseph's was not big enough for both him and "that maniac of a doctor" - meaning me, no doubt - down in the obstetrics section. She would be interested, she said, to hear whatever I had to say on the subject. The opening was irresistible, and I told her that he was absolutely right. I added that if she felt that fellow could safely deliver the next hundred babies, as I had just done, I would gladly give up my place to him. However, I said, if I stayed I would similarly assault anyone, white collar or not, who threatened the very life of one of my patients.

She barely hid a small grin behind a rapidly raised, delicate, ancient wrinkled white hand, and told me that she would like me to continue delivering St. Joseph's newborns, which of course I did. The rest of the month passed peacefully.

Now, at last, I was to begin my last month as an intern. It began on a strange note that had a sort of 'good news - bad news' quality about it, in Captain Hogan's office. His yeoman summoned me into the presence of the mighty one to get 'the word' on my assignment.

The Captain began, to my surprise, by saying that the Mother Superior from St. Joseph's had called to commend my busy month there, apparently without mentioning my little run-in with the baptizing priest, and that her report coincided with each of the monthly evaluations I had received since the internship started, nearly a year before. He had noted especially Captain Brown's glowing assessment and recommendations as to my future, and wished to add his congratulations.

All of which, he said, had led him to conclude that I could handle a special privilege and responsibility that he was going to bestow. For the final month of my internship I would function, not as an intern, but as a full-fledged ward medical officer with total responsibility for a particularly challenging and difficult, sensitive part of the hospital, called the Observation Ward, known informally, if not secretly, among the intern group as the Snake Pit. I would be completely in charge, answering only to him personally just as did only the most senior captains in charge of each of the major services.

Fully understanding that this was intended as a high honor rather than as the terrifying prospect it seemed to me, I thanked him with all due humility and expressed my determination to do my best to justify the award of this signal honor. He assured me that he would keep in close contact (horror of horrors!), ready to lend assistance whenever it was needed. And, I was soon to discover, lots of times when it wasn't needed at all.

I had never actually been on the Observation Ward, located two floors below every other clinical space in the hospital in what I had always considered the basement. I had seen its entrance, a heavy, always locked steel door strengthened with three horizontal steel bands riveted onto its surface, at the far distant end of a poorly lit corridor with various small rooms on both sides housing janitorial supplies and surplus equipment. It was mostly below the level of the ground outside, permitting only small windows just below the ceilings of the rooms, too high up to see out of.

After leaving the Captain's office, I made my way to that great door and rang a button in the wall beside it. Soon there was a variety of clanking, metallic noises as the portal was unlocked with an enormous, heavy, flat steel key larger than any I had ever seen, and the door swung slowly open. Two very large, very young corpsmen evidently expected me and led me promptly to the nurses' station about midway down the corridor. The entire ward staff of corpsmen under the command of a Chief Petty Officer was assembled in the small office, about six men in all, each of them large and robust youngsters who seemed eager to meet the new boss and impress me with their good spirit.

The Chief introduced each of his sailors, and explained that the nurse only came to the ward briefly during each 'watch' - the Navy term for shift - to see to the medications to be given, if any, give any shots needed, and check the census. Otherwise, he said, she could be called at any time I wanted her there, but her regular duty station was on the neurology ward, two decks above. He then led me on a tour of inspection of my new domain.

It consisted of a series of single rooms along each side of the corridor, about ten on each side. The walls were smoothly finished concrete and the rooms were totally bare except for a heavy steel adjustable hospital bed and a large, heavy steel bedside stand. The doors on each side of the corridor, also heavy steel with a small opening for observation, were offset to avoid colliding with the doors on the other side when both were opened at the same time. There was a modest office with a large window opening onto the corridor, and a room, larger than all the rest and with no door, furnished with a sofa, some padded armchairs, and a writing desk. Opposite to the nurse's office was the 'head,' a room just large enough for two showerheads, without stalls, three toilets, a urinal, and half a dozen washbasins, along with a rolling laundry cart for dirty towels.

Several of the patient rooms contained a toilet and washstand; these were for seriously disturbed patients who could not be allowed the freedom to use the group head except alone, escorted by at least two of the corpsmen, to permit them to shower. The entire ward was thoroughly scrubbed down and mopped daily, or oftener if need be, and was spotless.

A separate room near the ward entrance held about a dozen folding chairs, some card tables folded against the wall, and a stand for a movie projector that could be brought in for occasional shows. The chairs were set up in the corridor, for those occasions, with the portable screen set up at the back end of the corridor, which became, then, the theater.

Only the most agitated, disturbed, physically active, assaultive and potentially dangerous patients were admitted to the Observation Ward. They came from outside the hospital, from ships in the Yard nearby, from the city jail if they were sailors and not simply drunk, and occasionally from the Veteran's Hospital at Valley Forge, some miles away. Fortunately the ward was rarely more than half full, but even then it was a major management problem.

Even today, with the abundance of nearly miraculous drugs that burst upon the medical scene in the second half of the twentieth century, it can be difficult in the extreme to control behavior in occasional cases. It is still, moreover, as hard as it was then to predict when a previously docile-seeming patient might suddenly turn loose a torrent of horrendously destructive activity and grievously harm those trying to care for him. While this is rare, it does occur, with sometimes disastrous consequences.

Then, however, my options were exceedingly limited, and little changed from the previous century. We could administer powerful sedative drugs, relying mainly on the barbiturates. Their use was not without danger. In those cases involving a large, physically strong, healthy male - sometimes a female, but less often - it required such large amounts of these drugs to successfully subdue a really wildly excited patient that the cumulative effect put his very survival in danger from collapse of his vital respiratory and circulatory functions. In cases where the dosage got dangerously high, a person who was a violently destructive killing machine one minute could suddenly become a critical life-support emergency case the next.

Another control measure was the camisole, commonly called 'straight jacket.' This device was a long garment, open in the back but closeable with stout straps, bearing greatly elongated arms. Once the violent patient was successfully wrapped in the thing, which was made of extremely heavy, rough, stiff canvas that readily scraped off skin, and his arms started into the jacket's armholes, the long ends of the arms were crossed over his chest and pulled around his sides to be fastened in the back. The back straps were then tightened and secured. The patient's legs were still free to do harm, but his coordination and balance were seriously impaired by the confinement of his arms and upper body, and his kicks were generally ineffectual. His struggles, moreover, soon wore him out, and he usually settled down and ceased to struggle fairly quickly.

It could take a well-trained, coordinated team of five or six strong men to put a camisole on a struggling patient. It also took that many, or more, to apply a somewhat more humane form of similar restraint called a 'wet-pack.' This required wrapping the patient in a whole series of wet sheets - the first being by far the most difficult - until he was encased in six or eight layers of stout cotton sheeting, thoroughly wetted down and tightly wound. He ended up able to move almost nothing but his lips and eyeballs, and usually fell asleep quickly, but sometimes ended up in vascular and respiratory collapse, and could die quite suddenly.

A third technique, equally hard on the attendants and sometimes quite dangerous, involved the 'needle-shower.' This required a special shower stall with a perforated pipe running up each corner from the floor to about five feet above, and a high-pressure water source. When turned on, and the pressure raised, needle-like sprays hit every inch of the patient's body. The water ranged from cruelly cold to dangerously hot, depending on the skill and the sadistic tendencies of the staff, and generally rendered a violently assaultive person helpless and begging for release in short order.

All of these methods made enormous demands on the staff, and endangered them. All were subject to abuse. None solved anything, except for the moment.

During the 1920's and 30's, there was increasing interest in convulsive therapy. Through a combination of chance observation, deduction and imagination, it came to be widely believed that generalized bodily convulsions, as in epilepsy and certain kinds of toxic states, had a beneficial effect on 'insane' persons. Two drugs, coramine and metrazole, both used as stimulants in very small doses, were found to produce convulsions when sufficient quantities were given, and both were tried in the treatment of the most widespread of serious mental diseases, schizophrenia. In one form of the disease, the patient withdrew from normal behavior and human interaction into what was called a catatonic state, or catatonia.

Catatonic schizophrenics departed dramatically from the normal. Often they sat motionless and silent, knees drawn up and tightly encircled by the arms, head bent severely forward and back curved in the classical fetal position, as if in the womb. Indeed, a common and since abandoned explanation of the phenomenon held that the patient's withdrawal from reality had become so profound that she had retreated all the way back into the uterus, psychologically, and thus assumed the position of an unborn child.

These people could also do things impossible for any normal being, even an athlete. They could be positioned standing on one foot with their arms raised above their heads in contorted postures, and remain in that position, utterly motionless, indefinitely - even for several hours. Their limbs evidenced what was called "waxy flexibility" when moved by another person into any position, however unnatural. Sometimes, catatonic patients remained in this strange, totally subdued, nearly motionless and curiously passive state for many months or even years.

Catatonia was convulsive therapy's first and greatest triumph. Patients long since given up as utterly hopeless responded like magic to a few induced convulsions.

The latest development in convulsive therapy was called electroshock. A machine had been devised that delivered a brief, powerful charge of electricity to the brain through a pair of padded electrodes held against the patient's temples. The operator on a control box nearby could set both the intensity of the electric current and its duration in advance. The patient had to be carefully restrained by at least four attendants - preferably strong but gentle young males - positioned at both shoulders and both knees, and the patient's head was tilted back over a sandbag placed under the back of his neck. A padded tongue depressor was on the table so as to be immediately available to insert between the subject's teeth during his convulsion, to prevent him from biting off his tongue.

When the patient was properly positioned, with each attendant's hands gently placed upon him, a button on the control box was pushed, and the current flowed for a brief fraction of a second through the frontal lobes of the person's brain. Instantly, every muscle in the body contracted maximally and simultaneously, and for a moment or two the body on the table became rigid, board-like. Soon a fine tremor started in all the muscles, progressing to strong contractions of entire opposing muscle groups throughout the body, and what is termed a "grand mal" (literally "big bad") convulsive seizure, exactly as in epilepsy, was under way.

By now all the strong young attendants were carefully but firmly holding on to their assigned parts of the convulsing body, the tongue depressor was in place between the teeth as the jaws participated in the convulsive muscular contractions, the head was turned to the side to allow the copious amounts of saliva generated to run out freely from the patient's mouth, and the convulsive movements gradually slowed and diminished, disappearing in less than a minute.

Generally the patient was unconscious for a few minutes, awakening gradually after a period of subdued confusion, and during that time was removed from the treatment table and gently placed in a regular hospital bed. He was blessedly amnesic for the entire treatment episode and even the ten or fifteen minutes preceding it. While the convulsive movements were sometimes violent, no harm or injury resulted in the hands of a well-trained attendant team, but we had heard of fractures and bruises occurring in other institutions.

These shock treatments were generally given in the morning, and it took until mid-afternoon for the patient to get over his physical exhaustion and confusion. The usual course of treatment involved twenty applications of electroshock, generally given on alternate days, and at the end of the course some patients, but not all, had serious memory problems for days or even weeks afterward.

The theory behind the treatment, which looked barbaric but, properly applied, was never painful or frightening, was that the tiny jolt of electricity disrupted the flow of the minute electrical currents generated within the brain and necessary for it to function. Severely psychotic people, and profoundly depressed ones, commonly have developed fixed, repetitive thought patterns that are believed to result in their hallucinations and delusions or suicidal ruminations. These require the free flow of microscopically small electrical charges between brain cells, and these are drastically, if briefly, disrupted by the relatively much more powerful surges of electricity from the shock machine. Fifteen or twenty repetitions of that disruption usually wiped out the troubling thought patterns, and the patient recovered.

In at least of third of the schizophrenic patients so treated, however, the treatment was not successful, or it produced only temporary relief. Sometimes another course of twenty treatments did the trick; other times there was no effect even when several more courses were tried. In the case of seriously depressed, often actively suicidal patients, the results were almost always good, often dramatically so, and the treatment rarely had to be done over.

In the intervening years, during the second half of the century, many modifications to electroconvulsive therapy were developed, driven by occasional instances of botched treatment and patient injury, as well as complaints of persistent memory defects. The South American Indian arrow poison, curare, that produces a general paralytic relaxation of muscles, was introduced in minute doses to diminish the muscular contractions. Various tranquillizing and sedative drugs were added to be given before treatment even started each time, diminishing apprehension and fearfulness shown by some patients. Electrical and biomedical engineers devised newer, gentler forms of electrical current dosages that did not even produce a minor {"petit mal" - "little bad"} convulsion but seemed to produce similar results.

Ironically, as these improvements were being developed to make this form of treatment more humane, more gentle, less dramatic and barbaric seeming, opposition to this demonstrably enormously helpful and, in the case of severe depressions, lifesaving, treatment grew, thanks to horror stories of people brutalized, memories wiped out forever, bones broken and terrible bruises created. Most such tales proved false, but those who make a career out of such "causes" managed to convince a number of state legislatures to pass laws forbidding the treatment altogether, or creating nearly insurmountable 'approval' obstacles to its use. No one has done a study, so far, to determine how many depressed people, denied this treatment by 'liberal' intellectuals and stupid or ignorant politicians, went ahead and killed themselves when they could have been saved.

There is surely a lesson in this with respect to lawmakers who 'know best,' practicing medicine in their statehouses, but it will no doubt be ignored, or sent to committee to die.

We did very little electroshock treatment on my Observation Ward - just enough to teach me how important it was to have a well-trained team. That was to come in handy much sooner than I had any idea.

Some of the people who showed up in that dungeon-like setting in the bowels of the great Naval Hospital were colorful in the extreme. One giant of a man, formerly a member of a storied team of unbelievably brave and deadly Marines under the command of a Colonel Carlson and, appropriately enough, called 'Carlson's Raiders,' nearly tore down our strongest room. He was in a state of great excitement when he first appeared, already in a straight jacket, which he was beginning to tear apart despite the manufacturer's guarantee that it couldn't be done. Shouting at the top of his voice, warning us that we were about to be overrun by the "Slant-eyed bastards" hard on his heels but masquerading as six or seven Shore Patrol officers, he was pushed into one of our rooms.

The steel door was shut and secured while we debated what we might give him to calm him down - and how to give it - when we heard a loud crash and the sound of gushing water. Roaring his outrage and shouting imprecations at the enemy all around him, he had managed to get out of his tough canvas camisole and tear the heavy porcelain toilet out of the floor of the room and hurl it at the door. That was the crash we heard. The gushing water was from the pipes he had broken in the process.

An emergency call to the hospital engineering department got the water shut off, but not before the entire ward corridor was awash. All the other patients were locked in their rooms, and a literal parade of senior officers, Shore Patrolmen, engineers and sightseers collected in the ward, all with wet feet and deep frowns on their faces. A conference of the most senior officers was hurriedly called and they assembled, about eight or ten strong, in the tiny nurse's office to construct a battle plan. I was permitted to be present but was not consulted, since this was an emergency situation far above my pay grade. For that I was duly grateful.

Despite the certainty that our patient was undoubtedly bruising himself throwing his body against the door and walls, it was concluded that the lives of innocent people, like my large corpsmen and the senior medical officers who had assembled, would be jeopardized by any attempt to open the door. It was also agreed that the patient could not break it open, thanks to its heavy steel construction.

The only feasible course of action, therefore, fell into that special category of medical inaction euphemistically termed "watchful expectancy." What that meant was simply that we would do nothing, and certainly not risk opening the door, until the wild man wore himself out, and sheer exhaustion rendered him more malleable, if not completely harmless. My orders were to maintain a 'close watch' on him, difficult at best through the door's small viewing window-hole. When I was convinced that he had collapsed, I was to lead a party of no fewer than four of my largest, strongest young fellows, pushing a mattress in front of us to ward off blows and flying objects, into his room. We were to be armed with large syringes full of sodium amytal and one of a special concoction guaranteed to subdue a wild elephant.

This last was a mixture of a violent emetic, called apomorphine, and scopolamine, a drug used in smaller dosages to produce an altered state of consciousness sometimes used in obstetrics to induce something called "twilight sleep." While it sometimes resulted in a state of wild emotional excitement, in the dose used here it would cause total confusion, disorientation and lack of coordination.

Over the next several hours, the noises diminished in that little room, and eventually loud snores replaced all else. Cautiously holding our mattress before us, my little team of medical commandos eased open the door to find our man had not only ripped out the plumbing but had also dismantled the hospital bed and torn up the bedding and mattress, and was lying blissfully asleep in the midst of the wreckage. He was quickly given about four times the usual dose of the sodium amytal, directly into a vein. Satisfied that he was truly sedated, we dragged him out and put him into another room, this one without a toilet or a bed, and left him, under close watch, naked on a thin waterproof mattress.

For the next 24 hours, he was given a booster dose of barbiturates every time he began to stir, and his vital signs were carefully checked and recorded. We then let him wake up.

When he was fully awake, he seemed almost entirely rational, though a little uncertain about what had happened and how he had gotten where he was. He gave a history of several previous outbursts of panic and agitation that ended with him cut and bruised, especially about the head and neck, usually in some brig or civilian jail, commonly with a terrible headache. Later he told me tales of having been put ashore on enemy-held islands in the Pacific just prior to the landing of a Marine invasion force. He and his team were there to conduct close reconnaissance of the intended beachhead, leave markers for the troops to be landing, and identify strong points to be taken out first thing.

When they finished their reconnoitering, these remarkable men would swim off the beach, get into their rubber rafts, and head out to sea to wait out the pre-invasion naval bombardment and then hit the beach again with the first wave of assault troops. His unit, over time, had lost the great majority of its men. Therefore, we concluded, in addition to having a severe, recurring manic-depressive psychosis, the man had good reason to have highly colorful hallucinations when he lost control. It was impossible to predict his future. There was, at that time, no known treatment for manic-depressive disease. Electroshock was usually successful in terminating both manic episodes and depressed episodes among these people, but it was more than thirty more years before medication (lithium) appeared that held promise of successful long-term management of this serious, often familial, illness.

Like most mental and emotional disorders and diseases, manic-depressive (now called bi-polar) disease can appear in many forms and in many degrees. Many people who are overtly quite normally healthy show distinct evidence of what in a more pronounced form would be readily recognized as a specific mental or emotional illness. Sometimes it shows as merely a personality trait, even a quirk, like a greater than average (average?) suspiciousness of others' motives (paranoid?) or overactivity (manic?) or tendency to get down in the dumps more than most (depressive?) or a penchant for dramatizing ordinary things (hysteric?) or to dwell on minor physical complaints (hypochondriac?) or to be seclusive and prone to dwelling on fantasies (schizophrenic?) Sometimes these departures from our fuzzily defined norms of attitude or behavior flare up noticeably for days or weeks or more at a time and then go away. Most of these we don't label as mental disorders in the sense of things requiring treatment, but times - and definitions of what is unacceptably abnormal - change.

Someone with a readily recognized superabundance of energy and activity, sometimes accompanied by more imaginativeness and creativity than we recognize in ourselves and those around us - our yardstick, in a sense - is closer to the manic-depressive or cyclothymic state than we are, and can justify being called 'hypomanic-' or just below manic. Some such folks don't seem more prone to be 'down' than others, so the 'cyclo-' part of the word doesn't seem to fit. In any event, some of the most productive and creative people really fit this category, and are not sick, but neither are they 'normal.' Many successful politicians seem to belong to this group. So, probably, did Thomas Edison. They wear the rest of us out; it is impossible to keep up with them, but they bear watching.

For reasons never adequately explained, there seem to be trends in psychiatric disorders, and some commonly appearing forms seem to die out, or at least show up far less often than they used to. The catatonic form of schizophrenia, for example, was common in mid-century but is rarely seen today. Another, even more colorful ailment was called "conversion hysteria," later modified to conversion "reaction."

The very word "hysteria" has a colorful history. It comes from the Greek 'hyster,' meaning the uterus or womb, and was said to be coined by Hippocrates, father of medicine himself. He described an affliction of women characterized by the 'lump in the throat' sensation that accompanies emotional turmoil in many people, and attributed this to a wandering uterus, in search of fulfillment, that lodged from time to time in the throat in the course of its wanderings, and attached the term hysteria to this phenomenon.

Later on, it was recognized that hysteria was not confined to women, but the name stuck. On our observation ward, these many centuries later, we saw any number of these "conversion hysterics," whose disturbed emotional states assumed a variety of often colorful forms. The commonest was a kind of dramatic, suddenly appearing paralysis and total loss of sensation, usually in the lower half of the body starting at a sharply defined line around the waist. From that point on to the tips of the toes, all voluntary movement ceased, and all sensation was lost. Along with this, the cornea of the eyeballs, ordinarily highly sensitive and instantly protected by blinking at the slightest touch, became completely insensitive.

Neurologically and anatomically, this set of symptoms is impossible. The nerves from the spinal cord which carry sensation from the lower half of the body and control muscular movements in that area do not leave the cord at the waist; even cutting it at that level results in a vastly different distribution of sensory and motor impairment that never assumes the shape, say, of a pair of tights. Furthermore, there is no connection at all between the sensory nerves in the legs and the cranial nerves in the brain that supply the corneas of the eyes.

Sometimes the paralysis and anesthesia affected one or both hands, in a perfect, glove-like distribution. Also impossible. Sometimes, only vision was affected, and the individual appeared to be blind. Even a bright light suddenly shined at the pupil, or a match lighted in front of the eye and close to it, produced no change in the pupil, no blinking - nothing.

Needless to say, there were in those days no exotic devices like CAT-scans and Magnetic Resonance Imaging machines, for use in diagnosis. We used feathers to stroke the skin lightly to assess the sense of touch, vibrating tuning forks used by piano tuners, pins and even long sharp needles plunged without warning deep into the thigh to test for pain and other sensations. A wisp of cotton was drawn across the front of the eyeball to test for the blinking reflex uncontrollable in normal eyes. Using these, it was possible to map out exactly where the areas of anesthesia were on the patient's body and limbs, and this usually made the diagnosis certain.

Hysteric patients, moreover, revealed a curious lack of concern over what one would expect would be a terrifying disability, particularly since the symptoms, whatever form they took, tended to appear suddenly and all at once. The French, always great at labeling things like this, call it "la belle indifference" - the beautiful unconcern, and that is exactly what it seems to be. The medical staff, on the other hand, generally did not share this casual attitude but often got quite excited, launching exhaustive searches for some exotic infection or hidden tumor or something - anything legitimate and properly medical - to account for these people's massive disabilities.

Hysterics had long fascinated the medical profession, and exasperated its practitioners with their mystery, their failure to respond to conventional treatment, the lingering suspicions that somehow they were faking it - malingering - or something that couldn't quite be pinned down. In addition, there weren't that many psychiatrists around in the mid-forties, many of them were foreigners, most of them were Jewish immigrants who had fled Hitler's depredations in Europe, and the whole field, such as it was, carried with it hints of not-quite-respectable attention to things like sex, perversions, dirty words, and criminality. Remember, if you will, that the Chicago Tribune, in the early 1940's, still wouldn't print the word 'syphilis' because of its connection with sex and sin.

In consequence, hysterics were generally not treated at all. Some persisted in their disabled state permanently, and some probably recovered spontaneously. As has been true in much of medicine in the past, no accurate statistics were ever kept to indicate how many cases of hysterical blindness, paralysis, convulsions or other disabling conditions occurred in any given population during any given period of time, or what happened to them. Today, with the excellent work of the Centers for Disease Control and Prevention, coupled with legal requirements that physicians officially report certain diseases, facts on the incidence and prevalence of some diseases can be ascertained better than they used to be, but the data collected are still approximations at best.

There are many reasons why this is so. Diagnosis is not a precise science; it can in any case be wrong, or not even made. Once made, the doctor may or may not report it, in spite of the legal requirement to do so. Many diseases can only be diagnosed with certainty by performing an autopsy, and autopsies have become increasingly rare. In spite of our heightened attention to death rates from coronary disease or stroke or cancer, those rates are at best statistical deductions drawn from what is often appalling bad, unproven data that cannot be checked.

The problem of sloppy data, sloppy recording, inaccurate diagnoses and unsupported conclusions as to the public's health has recently gotten even worse. Increased concern over matters of privacy and issues labeled 'civil rights' and liability and 'entitlements' has now resulted in the astounding battle across the nation concerning reporting cases of AIDS. Here for the first time is a disease that is communicated from one person to another, that is progressively disabling, and is always fatal, that a large number of vocal citizens claim should be kept utterly secret.

That flies in the face of both common sense and science. While so far it is incurable (like coronary artery disease, diabetes, hypertension, some forms of cancer, many genetic diseases and defects, among other things) it can, like most of those afflictions, be treated and managed so as to delay deterioration and to prevent much suffering, to extend life and improve its quality while it lasts. But not if it is kept secret. Also, and worse, secrecy makes it far harder to do anything to prevent its spread to unwitting victims not yet infected but certain to become so, resulting in their illness and death.

My wildly agitated manic-depressive patient showed up early in my tour of duty on the Observation Ward, and along with a steady stream of admissions that seemed to occur mostly late at night, helped me decide before the first week was up that I must stay on the ward full time. Another compelling reason for this was the "help" I seemed to be getting from Captain Hogan. I ate all my meals and slept each night in my tiny ward office.

Every morning, within minutes of the official start of the duty day, I was called by the Captain's yeoman who announced, "Captain Hogan wants you on the double!" This meant I had to take off my white doctor's coat, put on my uniform jacket, and proceed in haste topside to stand rigidly at attention before his massive desk until he looked up from his stack of papers to be signed and fixed me with his piercing glare. In his broad Boston accent he would then proceed to lecture me severely about the buildup of the ward census, the off-duty behavior of one of my corpsmen, or my management of one of the patients. He seemed to know of every new admission - there were several every night - and he required a complete report on each new case: history, circumstances of admission, physical findings, diagnosis, plan of treatment and prognosis.

He never told me to stand at ease, apparently believing it was good training for me to stand at attention during these sessions, and in some little way seemed always to be angry and disapproving. Sometimes he kept me waiting for many long minutes before looking up from his papers to begin our session, and I kept busy looking at a certificate on the wall behind him proclaiming that he was an Admiral in the Great Navy of Nebraska. Having been to Nebraska, albeit mostly on freight trains, and having been good at geography before that, I had some trouble figuring out just where the Nebraska Navy sailed, but it was diverting from the coming interrogation and lecture to admire the elaborate document until my leader finally looked up and launched his daily training session.

Those morning sessions with the captain added up to an intensive course, didactic and clinical, in the specialty of psychiatry. He often gave me books from his extensive private psychiatric library, often directing my attention to particular chapters or case histories described in them. It was from these readings that I first learned about hysteria, and the attempts that had been made to treat it. I was particularly intrigued by several lengthy discussions of the marked suggestibility that hysteric patients showed, and several accounts of success in treatment using hypnotism. I decided to try it.

My first experimental subject was a young sailor who was a classical case of hysterical paralysis. He was numb from the waist down, a fact I verified by suddenly plunging a large intravenous needle into his thigh, not once but several times, in the course of a discussion with the patient about his past medical history. He showed no evidence whatever that anything had happened. Stimulation of the soles of his feet produced no response. Touching his eyeball with cotton didn't cause him to blink, or his pupils to react, as they should.

No one had ever taught me how to hypnotize someone, and there was little in any book that I could find about how to do it. I had seen a famous magician named Thurston hypnotize a young woman on a Chicago theater stage during a magic show when I was about 10 years old, but I wasn't watching with the idea of learning to do it. Still, it seemed fairly simple and I resolved to try it on my paralyzed sailor.

Somewhere or other I got a small glass marble. I turned off most of the light in the room where the man lay in bed, and held the marble up in front of his eyes, telling him to concentrate on it. In a quiet, calm voice I told him that he was going to relax more and more, feel his eyelids becoming heavy, and become sleepy, but would continue to hear my voice. After repeating this over and over, I told him he was now so relaxed that he could not move his arms or hands unless I told him to do so, and invited him to try. Sure enough, he seemed pinned to the bed.

The next suggestion I made to him was that, on the count of three, he would be able to wiggle his fingers. It worked! When I reached "three," all his fingers started wiggling! Emboldened by my success, I worked up to his elbows, and then his shoulders. Now for the acid test. His toes, motionless now for several weeks. On "three!" they wiggled. Then we moved up to his ankles, knees, hips, and lower trunk.

Finally, while he remained in a sleep-like state with his eyes tightly closed, I announced that he had now recovered from his paralysis. He was to sit up. He did. After getting him to swing his legs over the side of the bed and put his feet on the floor, I told him he was going to walk, and that his legs would feel perfectly normal. We were going to walk together, up and down the ward corridor, and this time when I reached "three" he would wake up and find that everything was back to normal. Trancelike, he took my arm and walked with me out of the room and into the corridor. I counted to three, he woke up, and declared that he felt fine and was ready to go back to his ship.

Needless to say, my elation knew no bounds. I could hardly wait to report this therapeutic triumph to Captain Hogan the next morning, to earn his praise for my miraculous powers. On hearing my recitation, however, he merely grunted, and moved on to another patient.

Undaunted, I resolved to sharpen my skills in hypnosis, and read all I could find about it, which wasn't much. My next chance to try it came soon. This time it was a man who had developed severe, exhausting, repetitive grand mal seizures. A loud noise in the hall, or a hand placed on his bed, caused a convulsion to start. Extensive neurological tests using the new electroencephalograph machine that charted 'brain waves,' the minute electrical currents accompanying brain activity, failed to show the characteristic patterns of epilepsy. Medications commonly used in that disorder had no effect.

The only suggestive findings about this man were his apparent indifference to what looked like a serious, major convulsive disorder that he had suddenly developed, plus the fact that his corneal reflexes were absent. That was enough for me; I decided he was hysteric, and was determined to hypnotize him right out of it.

This man's personal history included an extremely emotionally traumatic experience at sea during the final days of the war. He was a member of a deck gun crew on a large ship operating in the western Pacific at the time the Japanese began to unleash their Kamikaze - the 'divine wind' suicide bombing attacks on our vessels. At the beginning of one such attack, he had been pulled off his gun crew by the boatswain's mate who supervised the crews because he had been 'horsing around,' and his best friend was assigned to his position by the gun, while our patient was told to stand aside.

At that moment, a kamikaze plane crashed across the deck. The wing tip decapitated the best friend, and his head rolled across the deck coming to a stop at the patient's feet. At that instant, our man had his first major convulsion, followed by several more that required strong sedative injections to stop. The man had seemed to recover after that, save for some depression and withdrawal from contact with his fellows. He continued to do his various jobs as a low-ranking ordinary seaman until shortly before admission, when the convulsions began again, seemingly without any precipitating event except for a routine firing practice exercise aboard his ship, at which time the convulsions began again, and continued often enough to warrant his transfer to our hospital.

It seemed wise to have some hypnosis practice sessions with this man before attacking the convulsion problem directly. That done, I waited until one day the movie sent down for the patients' diversion turned out to be a war movie featuring many battle scenes. I had discovered that almost all the patients, including some seriously disturbed schizophrenics and manic depressives, loved war movies, even though many of them had seen considerable combat action. What they didn't like was animated cartoons. Those seemed to disturb the disturbed patients even more, and they usually got up in the middle of the film and hid in their rooms.

For this war movie, I led the convulsive patient out into the corridor where I sat him on my lap in one of the large chairs from the patients' lounge. His hypnotic state had been partially achieved in his room, and his convulsive movements were brief and not very forceful. Once the movie started showing battle scenes with loud explosions, he convulsed much more vigorously. During these scenes I held him tightly, talking quietly and continuously directly into his ear, telling him the fits were going away, and everything was going to be all right again.

Little by little his convulsive jerkings lessened, and finally they disappeared altogether. After the movie ended, I led him back to his bed and spent some minutes repeating my assurances that he was now free from his "spells" and would remain so. Then I brought him out of his hypnotized state, and a week later he returned to duty "fit for same," as the final discharge note was required to state.

Our next colorful hysteric arrived on the ward late at night during the American Legion convention then being held in Philadelphia. He wore his Legionnaire's cap badly skewed to one side and required a burly policeman on each side to hold him up, since he was hopelessly drunk. So, it turned out, was his seeing eye dog that stumbled onto the ward behind him, listing badly to one side and looking seriously toxic.

This, it turned out, was a blinded veteran, retired from service and outfitted by a grateful government with a seeing eye dog, a white cane, and a substantial pension. Patriotism and nostalgia for his former buddies drew him to the Legion bash, and similar sentiments on the part of many of his fellow veterans led to his being given heroic amounts of alcohol - along with his faithful canine companion.

In a few days, both the blind veteran and his dog were back to normal, and no longer showed any ill effects from their drunken episode. The man was adept at walking around the ward, which was, after all, a fairly confined, locked space, and made his way cautiously up and down the corridor without much trouble, even without his dog. What struck me about this performance was the fact that he never bumped into a door that happened to have been left open and sticking out into the corridor on one side or the other, even when several doors were open on both sides, requiring a slightly circuitous route around them.

Examination of his eyes told me little except for the fact that his pupils did not react to light, whether from my trusty little flashlight or from a match flaring close to his open eye. On a hunch, I tested the sensitivity of his cornea to a wisp of cotton drawn across it. No response. He was referred to Ophthalmology. The report came back saying that he was indeed blind, but no pathology could be found in the eye itself, so the defect must exist deep behind it, in the optic nerves or the occipital area of the brain, which must be intact to permit vision.

On a hunch, I decided to try hypnotizing this man, to help him, I said, to better 'adjust' to his handicap. He readily agreed, and we went to his room and proceeded with my magic. The inability to show him my marble did not prove to be a problem, after he was told simply to pretend to be staring straight ahead at a point of distant light. I went through the usual routine of getting him to relax, then to feel sleepy and 'heavy in all his limbs,' and finally to hear nothing but me, think about nothing but what I was saying, and drift off.

After he was sufficiently deep into his hypnotic, trance-like state, his eyes tightly closed, I began telling him that he was going to go through a wonderful, miraculous experience during which, little by little, he would begin to see again. At first, I told him, he would just begin to see light, then fuzzy shapes, then sharper shapes, and finally everything would be clear again, just like it was before he lost his sight. He was then commanded to open his eyes, "Just a little, at first!" and then wider and wider, as lights were turned on next to the bed, then in the ceiling, and corpsmen came into the room to lean over him and look closely at him. And Lo! His vision returned.

He was not exactly overjoyed by this. For one thing, his restored vision would no doubt end his blind pension, and he would have to find a job. For another, there was the dog. He couldn't afford to keep him. Would the doctor take him? Sure I would. And I did.

The following day he left. Whether he went down to the Veterans Administration office to cancel his pension or not, we never knew. The dog made an excellent adjustment on a lovely Pennsylvania farm, living happily for many years.

The incidence of conversion hysteria seemed to drop off dramatically in the late 1940s and I never saw another true hysteric patient after my internship. Some have said it is because our population has become too medically sophisticated for this kind of disorder to be sustained, but that seems a weak explanation. A different form of it does show up in some few patients, but not in the dramatic form it once took.

The month on the Observation Ward was absorbing and highly instructive, but by the time it was over I was eager to leave. It was time to embark on my glorious career in surgery and I was prepared to leave for Baltimore, and Johns Hopkins the next morning, if not before.

The final day at last arrived and my short-timer attitude was in full flower; I didn't even want to think for a minute more about psychiatry. Captain Hogan, however, had different ideas on the subject, and as always I was summoned to his office first thing on that last morning.

It was on that fateful day that he revealed himself to me as never before. After a particularly long wait, at attention, studying the Admiral's appointment certificate in Nebraska's Navy, the Captain looked up from his papers and said, sharply, "Dahktah, do you know what the three most overrated things in the world are?" I said no, wondering what on earth the coming lecture was to be about. "Home cooking," he said, "Home screwing, and Johns Hopkins University!" With that he guffawed, slapped his thigh resoundingly, and added, "That's all."

Taking this to mean I had been dismissed, I turned to leave, a little miffed that not a word had been said about my completion of the most difficult year of my life, capped by its most difficult month. Before I made it to the door he stopped me by calling me by what he assumed my first name was, something he had never done before.

"Bill," he said, "You've done a good job here, and I consider you to have been our best intern. You have demonstrated that you are a fine doctor ('dahktah,' again). We need real doctors in psychiatry instead of a bunch of ass-grabbing psychoanalysts, so I have arranged for you to have the finest psychiatry residencies in the country, at the Navy's expense. I've cancelled your thing at Hopkins" Seeing my shock, he went on to explain, a little.

"You may not know this, but I am a psychiatrist. I trained at Hopkins and spent some years there working under Adolph Meyer, one of the few truly great men in the field. His ideas are not widely recognized as truth these days, thanks to the damned Freudian analysts, but mark my words, they will be!"

Meyer, I knew, had established a theory of mental illness relating it more closely to biology, the brain, and physical illness than was currently thought to be true, and at that point could not be demonstrated with any certainty. His ideas were embodied in a school of thought labeled "Psychobiology." While Sigmund Freud, himself a neurologist, had focused his theories on psychological and emotional processes and largely ignored bodily structure and dysfunction, Meyer and his disciples, including Bartholomew W. Hogan, clung to the idea that underlying mental disorders, at least the serious ones, were structural and functional disruptions, probably of brain tissue, that could and should be addressed by "real" doctors.

Other early 'greats' in the field, notably Adler, with his ideas about 'complexes,' Jung, with his theories of a 'collective unconscious,' Horney and her preoccupation with 'birth trauma,' and a host of lesser disciples built on Freud's seminal concept of 'the unconscious' and the struggles between id and superego. Meyer's more 'medical' approach generally received short shrift for many years, while the psychoanalysts and their offshoots enjoyed great popularity. And, I might add, massive misinterpretation and misapplication, which will eventually be recognized as having had disastrous effects on society, particularly in America and Europe; far less in Asia and the Middle East. Those effects have mainly involved the erosion of character, the abandonment of the idea of personal responsibility and free will, the growth of dependency, the concept of 'entitlement,' and the horrifyingly distorted current ideas about "rights," mixed up as they are with political philosophies.

Captain Hogan was the first to say directly to me that the day would come when Meyer's ideas about mental illness would one day be proven to be right, and the psychoanalysts would fall from favor and credibility. He was dead right, and I was being started that very day on a course that would, decades later, lead to my playing a small but crucial role in proving exactly that. A host of other people in and out of psychiatry, up to and including Ronald Reagan (though unbeknownst to him), helped me, ultimately, to demonstrate for the first time, unmistakably, that the major mental disorders were abnormalities in the substance of the brain itself, not legacies from bad parents and bad experiences, let alone the wages of sin or the power of the Devil. We hadn't given those last ideas up completely, even in the mid-twentieth century, and they persist even today. Even in America.

Standing in front of the Captain's desk on that last day of my internship, I had no idea of the magnitude of the life change that he was imposing upon me, beginning with his little joke about Johns Hopkins. All I could see was the destruction of my future, the desolation of my medical career, my banishment into the arcane surroundings of what seemed to me, at best, to be a dismal - abysmal - non-science. He did not ask if I wanted to do this. He told me. The Navy, he said, had lost more people to psychiatric disorders than to anything else.

Psychiatry, he went on, repeating his earlier thought, needs *real* doctors, and I was to fill that role. It took years for me to understand what a great compliment this powerful, dedicated man was paying me. At the moment I simply thought he had ruined my life.

He said that he had arranged for me to have the finest residency training available anywhere. It was to begin at the U.S. Public Health Service Hospital in Fort Worth, Texas. That institution was one of two large federal hospitals designed as medium custody penitentiaries (but never called that) for the treatment, such as it was, of narcotics addicts. Because it had elaborate security systems built into it, the Navy had arranged to use part of the hospital as a locked psychiatric unit for patients too disturbed to be managed in conventional hospitals.

As if I didn't know! That's exactly where my wildly destructive manic-depressive had been sent. Now I was to follow, but at least not in restraints.

There, the Captain said, I would spend a year of 'total immersion' in a unit housing the most profoundly mentally ill, disturbed people. I was to look for signs that there was physical change - illness - underlying their insanity, and would surely see it. Freudians, he pointed out, never treated really sick, 'crazy' people, focusing instead only on upset, unhappy, maladjusted souls - who could afford to pay for it and spend years in the process.

All the others, the really sick ones - and not just those with syphilis of the brain, but them as well - were condemned to spend their days, and sometimes their lives, locked up in mostly remote state institutions generally called 'insane asylums' or, if they were really rich, in small, more pleasant private prisons called "retreats" or "institutes" or some other acceptable euphemisms. In any setting, they rarely got better, or got out.

After my year there, not an easy one, I would be assigned to further residency training at the brand new Langley Porter Clinic (now "Neuropsychiatric Institute") at the University of California Medical Center in San Francisco. Heading that teaching hospital was Dr. Karl Bowman, also a psychobiologically oriented associate of Adolph Meyer (and Bartholomew Hogan), known and respected around the world for his research and writings as he explored the organic bases for mental disease. He would, I was assured, take "good care" of me.

This, then, was to be the beginning of a new chapter, whose explosive arrival in my life seemed no less monumental than the explosions that gave birth to the universe. I set out the next day for Fort Worth.

That long, hot, dull drive to central Texas gave me ample opportunity to reflect on that last full year of my life, and what I had learned. Apart from the obvious details of various procedures and techniques, the most important lessons were of a more general nature. They had to do with the relative roles of art and science in the practice of medicine, the nature and quality of its practitioners when seen up close, and the immensity and complexity of the whole undertaking. Much of what I had taken away from medical school, often little more than suspicions, became far more clear.

It was increasingly evident to me that as a group of professionals, we actually knew very little indeed about the exact nature of the things we 'treated,' and the procedures and nostrums we used in that treatment. I could also see that the "best" physicians were not necessarily smarter or knew any more than the mediocre ones. What seemed to make them superior was the way they dealt with sick people, how they listened to them, and whether they seemed really to care about them. Art far outweighed most of what we thought of as science. Most of our drugs had never been truly tested and their efficacy validated, except empirically - by frequently uncritical observation coupled with long usage bolstered by habit, tradition, and more than a little superstition, however sophisticated the latter was portrayed.

As the new millennium dawns, this is still true, in spite of the earnest efforts of the Food and Drug Administration to require proof of efficacy and safety of the new drugs.

I had also been struck by the realization that physicians' choice of specialty, let alone the basic decision to enter medicine in the first place, was a complex, largely unconscious product of a host of life experiences: different mentors, expectations both real and altogether fantastic, erotic and other desires, altruism, greed, and impulses from both the Id and the Superego that gladden the hearts of Freudian psychoanalysts.

Personality traits also play a large part. Orthopedists are profoundly different people, basically, than are neurosurgeons. Only certain kinds of people derive joy from cutting into live people. Those who do autopsies are quite different. It takes a special kind of person to spend most of his time looking at X-Ray films, still another to probe an endless stream of ears, noses and throats. Those who concentrate on the medical problems of females seem to have special feelings about women, quite unlike those who love to deal with diseased skin, or children, or constipation.

This is not to say that one can safely generalize about those in each specialty, nor pass judgment on their character, but each group seems to have certain qualities in common. Psychiatrists, for example, tend to avoid physical contact with patients while probing deeply into the emotional and mental processes they exhibit. They are probably more different from other physicians, as a whole, than any other group among them.

These things matter in an undertaking as intimate and important as the relationship of sick persons to those who treat them. They lie at the root of what is both the best and the worst of today's medical scene, from the heart-warming victories in treatment to the alarming courtroom dramas that result from perceived harm or malpractice.

This past year of 'training,' more than the years in medical school, was the beginning of what could more properly be termed a genuine education, destined to go on for another fifty years that were filled with joy and pain, triumph and defeat, reward and punishment. The installment to follow was to be a whole series of new revelations and new questions.

William E. Mayer, M.D.

Brainwashing, Drunks & Madness

William E. Mayer, M.D.

CHAPTER 4

LEARNING TO BE A PSYCHIATRIST

The only other time I had been in Fort Worth was on my sociological experiment hitchhiking trip. The road from Dallas to that dusty small city mostly traversed largely undeveloped land occasionally marked by small, seedy farms and rural grocery cum gasoline stations. Midway between the two cities I had stopped at a farmhouse that had been partially converted into a lunchroom. There, for twenty-five cents, I purchased the most delicious, enormous southern fried chicken dinner, complete with all the trimmings that I have ever had before or since. The sweet lady at the counter, what's more, threw in a piece of wonderful apple pie - no charge. I looked for the old farmhouse as I drove by, heading for my new life, but it was nowhere to be seen.

My destination turned out to be a large, pleasant looking facility of a half dozen large stucco buildings with red tile roofs looking vaguely Spanish in design. Behind a tall flagpole a building smaller than all the others and set apart, appeared to house the headquarters, and I headed for that. A nearby gas station had allowed me to shave and put on a clean uniform so that I would be properly Naval when I reported in. My first duty station!

The Commanding Officer's office was easy to find, since it bore a large sign designating it as such, and I entered, orders in hand, ready for duty. A civilian lady secretary, without hesitation, ushered me in to Captain MacDonald's presence. I announced my name, as protocol required, and put on what I hoped was a pleasing, hopeful expression, awaiting the traditional "Welcome aboard, Lieutenant!"

Instead, the Captain, who was a short, small man with a mustache, a perpetual shadow of beard and a fearfully glowering expression, turned his head toward the door and literally bellowed "Mr. Tipton! This man is AWOL! Prepare charges. That will be all, Lieutenant."

Mr. Tipton, it turned out, was a portly, pleasant, somewhat harassed-seeming administrative officer, who hastily assured me, once we were out of earshot, that he was sure the Captain was mistaken, and he would try to set things right. He did, but it took some days. It turned out that the Captain, much given to snap decisions and a mercurial temper, had mis-read my travel orders and thought I should have arrived a day earlier. He never apologized, and never did welcome me aboard.

The Navy kept about sixty patients at the hospital, in two wards that had barred doors and windows, recessed lights and almost no movable objects around. There were housed the most profoundly psychotic, most hyperactive and most dangerous of all the psychiatric patients from Naval hospitals nationwide, including my wild man from Philadelphia who had ripped up the toilet along with his camisole.

Two Navy psychiatrists, both full commanders with combat experience during sea duty in the Pacific, presided over the Navy patients. They were as unlike as two men could be, and seemed rather distant from one another. These were to be my principal mentors and instructors for the year just beginning. Both seemed excessively glad that another doctor, meaning me, had joined the staff; I found this a little ominous, indicating their clear belief that they were overloaded with work. The Captain was said to be a psychiatrist also, but he never saw any patients, and rarely participated in a medical staff meeting. He did conduct inspections, which tended to be bruising to all the staff, and occasionally met with one or the other of the commanders for a 'chewing out' session, but otherwise his activities were a complete mystery.

To the best of my recollection, I had only one face-to-face meeting with the Captain that entire year, and it was for a royal dressing down. The content of the encounter, and the reason for his rage, have long since disappeared from my memory, in all likelihood as a repressive mechanism designed to protect and preserve my own mental health and tranquility. When I left his office after the blistering denunciation, Mr. Tipton sidled - or, more accurately, waddled - up to me, put a reassuring hand on my shoulder and told me not to worry about it. "The Old Man just has to blow off steam once in a while. No need to take it seriously." I gratefully accepted his reassurance, and went back to work.

On the day of my arrival, Commander Harry Colony took me in hand and showed me the wards and arranged for my keys: two of the flat, heavy, large-toothed steel devices that unlocked the barred doors. These, he said, were to be guarded with my very life. He confirmed the fact that they were badly understaffed, with just three docs, but sometimes one of the regularly assigned Public Health Service medical officers could lend a hand. In return for that, I would be expected to watch over one or another of the addict wards when they were shorthanded. It turned out that they needed help at least once a week, providing me over the year with an exhaustive introduction to drug addiction and the addict population.

Harry also announced that as of now, I would be the EST (meaning electroshock) officer, and would administer all the shock treatments ordered for the entire patient population. To assist in this, I would have six corpsmen, all of whom needed to be trained not only in the administration of electroconvulsive therapy, but also in all the basics of being hospital corpsmen. Their training, following the standard Navy training manuals, would be my sole responsibility. Finally, I would review all the often voluminous medical records that accompanied all new admissions, make adequate and extensive admission notes summarizing those records and proposing a final diagnosis and treatment plan. The rest of the time I was free to do as I wished. I was expected, naturally, to see every patient, at least briefly, every day on the two wards.

Commander Colony - Harry, as he insisted I call him in direct violation of Navy custom and tradition forbidding familiarity or fraternization not only between officers and enlisted men but between junior (me) and senior (commanders and above) officers as well - was a fully trained neurologist as well as a psychiatrist, and he clearly preferred the neurology. This was good for my training, as he carefully coached me in the intricacies of detailed neurologic examinations and diagnosis. At that time, most specialists in 'neuropsychiatry', as it was usually called, were trained in both fields but tended in private practice to concentrate on psychiatry since there were few workable remedies for neurologic disorders of the brain, spinal cord, and peripheral nerves.

The other commander, Bernie Kahn, was what today would be called 'laid back.' He was that. A large, obese man who truly looked roly-poly, he seemed to take nothing seriously, cruising through life as though nothing really mattered. He was, in his own mind and most certainly his heart, primarily a writer of fiction. He seemed particularly aware of life's absurdities, and frequently performed a quick, dismissive gesture with his great fat hand in discussions of problems. Always pleasant, he readily revealed his enormous intelligence and clinical acuity when asked for opinions or assistance, but he rarely volunteered. He did make staff meetings colorful and often amusing, with his joviality and irreverence.

On my first full day of duty at Fort Worth, I went first to the EST treatment room. Seated on benches in the hall were twenty patients awaiting their convulsions. Inside the room were my six eager corpsmen, most of them appallingly young-seeming but gratifyingly large and strong. They had all helped with 'shock' any number of times before, but were a little surprised at my assertion that they were going to be trained as a team, better than any gun crew on any ship in the fleet.

I assigned each of four men a specific position at the sides of the table. The other two, who were the biggest of all, were to be the 'escorts.' It would be their job to lead the patient to the table, swing him aboard, put the sandbag behind his neck, and stand close at each end of the table to capture and contain excessive movements of the head or the feet. The others were to place their hands gently, but ready to grab hold hard, over the shoulders and knees. This was all to be done silently and smoothly - like a good gun crew.

We rehearsed a few times, using one of the 'sideboys' as a patient, and I demonstrated how I would smear on the electrode jelly, grab the electrode headset, put it in place and punch the control button. They were to watch carefully, like the choirboys at Todd with their eyes fixed on Mr. Hendrickson, and the instant that button went down, all hands were to make firm contact with their assigned spots to make certain the patient didn't jerk so hard as to break a bone, or fall off the table.

The youngsters caught the spirit of the thing immediately. After we started the patients coming in, the corpsmen developed a kind of rhythm, their actions smoother and swifter, and it wasn't long before the operation seemed as slick as any gun crew anywhere. Within weeks, we were treating our twenty patients each day in less than an hour, and more importantly, no one - patient or corpsman - was ever injured in the process. In the course of that year we gave at least five thousand treatments, all together, often with great success.

Captain Hogan had been right about my being immersed in a patient population of the most profoundly psychotic, disturbed patients that the Navy, or anyone, had. Our treatment options were still limited to the things earlier described: wet packs, needle showers, sedatives given intravenously when necessary, occasionally apomorphine and scopolomine, calming baths in a big tub of warm water with a canvas cover allowing only the head to be above the water, sometimes physical restraint with camisoles or leather straps holding arms and legs to the bed, and of course electroshock.

One of the wards, smaller than the rest, was used to house female patients. Most were long-term chronic schizophrenics. My introduction to the women's ward was a special event.

No one escorted me to the ward, but Commander Colony called ahead and told them to expect me, and I headed for that special domain little suspecting what lay in store. I opened the barred door with my heavy new dungeon-style key, to find the head nurse waiting for me. She greeted me pleasantly and pointed out the nurse's station, where any physician arriving on any ward usually headed first for a brief report on the patients and any special problems.

The construction of the buildings was massive, incorporating solid concrete walls and floors. Each ward was perhaps 40 feet wide and 60 feet long, and about every twenty feet there was a concrete pillar, square in outline and measuring about two feet in diameter. I headed for the nurses station midway down the ward and had only taken a few steps when, from behind one of the massive pillars, there emerged a stocky female in a shapeless, flour-sack style hospital gown who hurled herself at me, feet first, knocking me completely off my feet and sprawling on the concrete floor with my attacker almost on top of me. She picked herself up quickly, seeming to be experienced at this sort of thing, and stalked off, muttering what sounded like really vulgar obscenities as she headed away with never a backward glance.

The entire ward staff of five or six nurses and attendants instantly appeared, seemingly from nowhere, to help me up, barely concealing their obvious amusement with apologies for this terrible incident and inquiring with great insincerity as to my well-being. It immediately became clear that this was a totally predictable, preventable occurrence allowed to happen to all new medical officers (junior officers, that is) as a kind of introduction to the realities of the female ward.

My welcoming party of one, a former schoolteacher named Ada, was a severely psychotic schizophrenic woman who held the (informal) title as the world's most vigorous misanthrope, specializing in misandry. She was absolutely convinced of the validity of her paranoid delusions, all of which involved men - all men - all of whom wanted and were trying to rape her. She had hit upon her special karate-like skill at sudden attack using both feet after a short run at her target, as her best defense.

Ada had been in the hospital for many months, and seemed to be getting worse every day. If left unsupervised for even a few minutes, she would go to the far end of the ward and crouch down beside a window, opened to its maximum four inches and protected on the outside by a steel grill. There she would lie in wait for a man to pass by outside, be he a patient, a staff person or a visitor, and as he approached would unleash a torrent of obscenities, imprecations and accusations about his obvious intentions to commit violent rape upon her innocent body. While this amused the staff (especially the groundsmen and janitors) it was considered unacceptable by the senior medical officers other than Commanders Colony and Kahn, who found it amusing, and the experience was shocking to visitors.

Many, if not most, people whose schizophrenia had become chronic and fixed, without even brief periods of normalcy, settled over time into a subdued, withdrawn state, seeming to come to terms with their delusions and their hallucinations. If challenged, they readily revealed their delusions, be they of persecution or grandiosity or special destiny, and admitted that their "voices" or, sometimes, their visions, persisted, but they seemed less concerned with them; they were just 'there.' It was a generally accepted belief in psychiatry that about a third of all psychiatric patients progressed steadily to this chronic state. Another third had a single episode, lasting from a few weeks to a few months, most often during adolescence, and never again.

The final third, also usually starting in adolescence, had repeated episodes at irregular intervals, sometimes throughout life. Suicide was common in this group, and most attempts were deadly serious, and deadly, unlike the suicidal 'gestures' of rejected lovers and others who are temporarily depressed or eager to punish family or friends for inflicting real or imagined wounds to the spirit. Such gestures can be dangerous and do real harm, but in the vast majority of cases do not kill.

The frequency with which schizophrenia appears during adolescence accounts for the old-fashioned term for this devastating, commonest of all mental illnesses. That term, in use for generations, was "dementia praecox," meaning, literally the insanity of the young. The more modern term recognizes that it is not solely a disease of the young and can appear much later, though rarely beyond the 20's. "Schiz" means 'split,' and for years this was taken to mean 'split personality,' but it was never intended to signify that.

The "phrenia" part of the current label refers to the mind, not the personality, but even that is not exactly what was intended. What the modern term was supposed to indicate was the often marked lack of connection - splitting off - of the individual's thinking and his emotions. The latter are often inappropriate to the person's thoughts; even thoughts one would expect would be highly emotionally charged, like a parent or child's sudden tragic death, or some other catastrophe. What the patient reveals of his emotional life - how he emotes and expresses feelings - is called "Affect," and can be described as 'colorful,' 'normal' or 'appropriate,' in healthy people, and 'flat,' 'distorted,' or 'inappropriate' in the schizophrenic.

Ada had never drifted into a quieter, more subdued and withdrawn state as her illness, after a sudden onset, progressed. Instead she became, if anything, more excited and disturbed by her paranoid delusions, wilder in her accusations, increasingly assaultive not just toward males but sometimes toward other women as well. Locked in a 'quiet room,' where seriously disturbed patients were usually confined, she would shout, scream, and beat on the door and walls sometimes for hours. She could be quieted with injected drugs, but only in doses so large they threatened her survival.

A new therapeutic procedure had been developed by a world famous neurosurgeon, that had been discussed but never tried at that hospital, and inevitably the procedure was discussed in staff as a possible solution for poor Ada, not to mention protection for her bystanders.

Called "Prefrontal Lobotomy," the procedure consisted of a surgical operation on the frontal lobes of the brain, usually through holes drilled in the skull at about the level of the hairline. The rationale, which is to say the philosophical and logical basis, for the operation was related to a late nineteenth century event that had a special place in the history of medicine.

"The Great American Crowbar Case" occurred when a railroad worker dropped a crowbar into a box of blasting caps, as he was leaning over the box. The caps exploded. The crowbar became a projectile, shooting upward. It penetrated the man's head just above his eye and came out the top of his head, stopping when the pointed end was about six inches above his scalp. The lower, curved end hung down in front of his face.

He fell to the ground, unconscious but not bleeding very much. A small crowd gathered, and someone ascertained that the injured man was still alive. After an excited discussion of what ought to be done and considerable heated argument, and with no doctor available, it was collectively decided that someone should pull the crowbar back out, and someone did.

Nothing much happened. There was still no great bleeding. After a while, he was lifted up and carried to his little company-supplied house, which he rated because he was a senior foreman, and placed gently on his bed. His care was given over to his horrified wife. Some time later that same day he woke up, but his wife kept him in bed.

The following morning, this grievously wounded man arose from his bed and made his way out to his front porch. His men gathered around, and he announced that he had a helluva headache and thought he would take the day off. He sat down in the rocking chair on his little front porch, to wait patiently for the arrival of the company doctor later that day. That worthy found him apparently intact except for the wounds in his forehead and cranium, and told him to take off from work as long as he wanted.

This foreman was a typical "boss" of his time. Authoritarian, moralistic, no-nonsense tough, and well respected for his ability to handle crews of roughnecks and Chinese laborers who were traditionally strong, uneducated and rowdy, he tolerated no shirking, no horseplay, and no profanity. He was known far and wide for his lack of humor and highly proper behavior and general demeanor. He tolerated but did not participate in Saturday night shindigs and disapproved of drunkenness, dancing, and whoring around. His one outside activity was attendance at church on Sunday mornings, dressed in his best suit and tie.

It soon became apparent that a major change was taking place in this man's behavior. He took to talking boisterously from his porch to the men passing by after work. His language became as crude as that of his meanest subordinates, incorporating words and ideas he had never even tolerated in his presence before his accident. Worse, he started making overtly obscene comments to passersby and took evident pleasure in telling crude dirty jokes.

In church, he took to contradicting the preacher, loudly expressing his own views, and was asked to leave unless he could control his outbursts.

Most remarkable of all, he began to take his wife to the local tavern for the Saturday night dances. There he shocked both that proper Victorian lady as well as the bystanders by his boisterous talk and his new habit of vigorously swatting his lady's buttocks in time to the music.

The company doctor made notes about this remarkable change in behavior, and prevailed upon the railroad to retire the man. What ultimately became of him is not known, but by the time he disappeared from the scene, the changes in him were clearly permanent.

Information about this remarkable case made its way, over the years, into writings that came to the attention of a prominent neurosurgeon. He discussed it with his colleagues in neurology and psychiatry, and came to the conclusion that a physical change in the frontal lobes of the brain, such as the foreman had experienced, might prove to be of value in individuals with chronic, life-threatening, violent forms of mental illness that could not be treated successfully any other way.

He devised an operation in which a small hole, less than an inch in diameter, was drilled in the skull at the hairline, above each eye. A long, sharp scalpel was inserted into the front of the brain about an inch and a half, and then swung back and forth from side to side, cutting brain cells and connections in the frontal lobes, which had no very clear function with respect to movement or sensation, vision or hearing or coordination, all of which had by then been quite accurately identified as being controlled by other specific areas of the brain.

Fifty years later, it should be noted, we are still not entirely certain as to the functions of the frontal lobes of the brain. Recent studies do suggest that they play an important part in so-called "higher" brain functions having to do with abstract ideas, including concepts like morality, loyalty, responsibility and honor. One might even suspect we are on the brink of finding the physical site of Freud's superego, but no one dares say that yet. At the very least, it leads one to wonder what the frontal lobes in Bill Clinton's brain are like!

Back in Fort Worth, in the mid-forties, faced with the problems of poor Ada and medical 'science's' inability to do anything about that tormented soul, the idea of doing a lobotomy, already done on many patients elsewhere with reportedly good results, inevitably came up and was debated at length for many weeks, in staff meetings, in the dining hall, on the way to and from work, in the nurses stations - everywhere. Ultimately, inevitably, the conclusion was reached: she should have the operation.

The famed neurosurgeon, Walter Freeman, who was advocating lobotomy, had worked out a method for doing the operation immediately following, within seconds, an electroshock treatment. During the period of unconsciousness following the shock, it was possible to drill the necessary small hole, insert the scalpel and do the cutting well before the patient woke up. When a second hole was to be drilled, to slice up the other side, a second shock was given, and the patient felt and remembered nothing of the entire event.

With the entire Navy and Public Health Service staffs crowded into the operating room to observe this historic medical milestone, Ada was lobotomized.

As an aside, it should be noted that the Egyptians at the time of the Pharaohs were doing something not so different from this, although their rationale was a little different. They believed, as many did for thousands of years, that mental disease was caused by demonic possession. They deduced that demons, in such cases, inhabited the skull, so they drilled holes through the skull to let them out. Statistics on the therapeutic outcome of those operations, then as now called 'trephining' or 'trepanning,' are lost to antiquity, but examination of skulls thus ventilated have shown clear evidence of healing of the hole in the skull, meaning that the patient survived for a considerable period after surgery.

Ada tolerated the operation well. Within a half hour she was up, walking around and cursing the men around her with her usual eloquence. Nothing seemed to have changed. Ada was returned to her ward, and the staff assembled in the conference room for an intense "post-op" conference to examine exactly what had been done and speculate as to Ada's seeming imperviousness to the surgical violation of her brain.

Many days passed, with at least one conference daily about Ada, who had not changed at all. After about a week, someone pointed out, accurately, that the bone of Ada's skull had not yet filled in the holes we drilled, so... Everyone immediately agreed, and Ada was taken back to surgery, shocked again, and lobotomized again through the same holes. The surgeon held up his scalpel to show just how deeply he had penetrated this time (any farther in would have jeopardized her life), and demonstrated how widely he had swept it back and forth, and everyone agreed that should be plenty to do the job.

Once again Ada made a miraculous-seeming, nearly immediate recovery from the operation. Once again Ada changed not at all, and the daily conferences continued, along with calls to other institutions around the country where the operation was being done, to get advice and recommendations. The exasperation and frustration of the staff were palpable, and arguments raged far into the night as to what to do next. Finally, it was decided that we had no choice; it had to be done again.

One more time, Ada entered the operating room, cussing the assembled males as always, but unresisting as she was placed on the table. Once again she was shocked. Once again the scalpel passed through her skull openings and into her brain. Once again she seemed to tolerate the procedure well. Once again she awakened fairly quickly, but this time she did not resume her previous level of loud profanity.

She was taken back to the ward, curiously docile. The post-treatment dullness wore off, but her violence did not return. She still approached any man who entered the ward, but instead of attacking by flying through the air feet first, she would sidle up to the man, put her face to within an inch of his, and with a furious expression would whisper, "You son of a bitch, I know what you're trying to do to me!" With that she would stalk off. No more shouting out the window or pounding the door. Just that enraged whisper.

Success.

Many of the patients at Fort Worth were as sick as Ada, but less violent. Most of the variations of schizophrenia were represented, including giggling, wildly inappropriate hebephrenics, named in honor of Hebes, an ancient Greek goddess of youth. This group was absolutely intractable. There were any number of catatonics, most of whom improved on electroshock. One such proved highly instructive one day on ward rounds.

We had been honored that day by the arrival of a distinguished senior psychiatrist, a civilian consultant, who accepted our invitation to conduct the rounds. He was tall, stately and quite dignified in his manner and appearance, and he led the long, single file parade of eager learners, arranged in strict order of power, importance, seniority, professional qualifications, rank, and overall value to the human race - from the greatest to the least - very much in the manner of the Archbishop in a grand cathedral leading the processional toward the altar. In keeping with long and hallowed tradition, he paused periodically to talk to a patient, examine his chart, and then discourse briefly about the case.

It was customary to conduct such learned discourse in the immediate presence of the patient. While many patients were not in sufficient contact with reality to understand any of it, some were. That had been troubling to me when Captain Hogan, who conducted every single Saturday inspection on the Observation Ward, required that I recite the entire patient's history and both physical and mental status examinations as he stood staring into the poor creature's face only inches away. Following that, he would question me further, ask the details of the treatment plan and prognosis, and then talk to the patient.

Inasmuch as all except agitated and violent cases were required, during the prolonged Inspection-cum-ward rounds, to stand at attention at the doors to their rooms, this meant everyone's highly personal information was heard by everyone else. That didn't ever seem quite proper and right to me, but like so much in medicine, was hallowed by long usage. One of the problems I saw in this ritual was that, in addition to memorializing and advertising the patient's problems, it illustrated to him sometimes that his doctor (in this case me) was mistaken, possibly quite stupid, and altogether on the wrong track. This has a certain erosive effect on the doctor-patient relationship.

During our consultant's procession through the women's ward at Fort Worth, the great man came upon one of our sickest patients. This young woman had developed severe catatonic schizophrenia and had so far not responded to 20 shocks, her first 'course.' She spent her days sitting on the floor, her back against one of the concrete pillars, her legs pulled up to her chest and tightly encircled by her arms, and her head buried between her knees. She never looked up, never spoke, showed classical 'waxy flexibility' of her limbs, and while she could be lifted to a standing position and led to a table to eat, or to bed at lights out, she never actively resisted or responded in any way.

This, the consultant announced, was a classical case of catatonia. He said that the woman's inability to tolerate reality had led her to withdraw completely from it. What we were seeing, he said, was her defense against the real world. To protect herself, she had been going through a process of regression to earlier and earlier phases of her life, all the way back through childhood, infancy, and now, the ultimate regression, into the womb itself, necessitating that she assume this fetal position. It reflected her desire for the absolute comfort and security of *in utero* life, where she was finally safe. This was fairly standard Freudian doctrine, at least as espoused by his disciples, who could (and did) explain everything in terms of their master's writings and speeches.

The consultant moved on, the entourage emerging again in single file from the gathering that had formed about our totally regressed young woman, which uncoiled in the manner of a coiled snake setting out for a new location where there might be prey. As the tail of the procession, formed by the newest and most innocent of the student nurses, was about to follow along as prescribed, our catatonic lady suddenly looked up - something she had never before been seen to do - and said to the last student in the line, "Isn't that the biggest bunch of shit you ever heard?" She then put her head back down between her knees and regressed again, presumably back into the uterus.

A similarly regressed catatonic was also seen during our tour through the men's section. This fellow, a man of middle age, had been quiet and relatively uncommunicative but not mute, and had moved about the ward, sat in on movies, ate, and had not been diagnosed as catatonic until a few days before. At that time he had ceased all activity and became mute, but he did not curl up into a fetal position. Instead, he lay flat on his back in the bed, motionless. Strangely, he kept his head tilted up with his chin nearly touching his chest, stared off into space and refused to be fed.

Our consultant explained this as a late state of regression, probably into infancy but not yet into the womb. His refusal to eat was an expression of his desire to be breast fed, since he was now 'back' to such early infancy that he was not yet on solid food. He had assumed a position of total passivity, waiting for the breast.

The procession moved on, and as I came close to the man lying immobile in the bed with his head tilted forward, it seemed to me that he wore an expression of anguish looking for all the world like an El Greco painting of Christ crucified. That seemed odd, because schizophrenics characteristically have a flat affect, revealing no emotion at all. Stopping by the bed, I lay my hand on the man's abdomen, thinking to give him a little human contact and possibly some small comfort.

He did not move, and I pressed down with my fingers because his abdomen seemed to have a wholly unnatural hardness to it. Sure enough, it was what the textbooks (of surgery, not psychiatry) called "board-like." As the procession moved on without me, I further explored the man's abdomen. The whole thing felt like a board. Pulling my stethoscope out of my coat pocket (psychiatrists never carried one around their necks like almost everyone in a modern hospital from janitor to senior residents now does,) I listened to his belly. Usually there are multiple gurgles, rushes and other odd noises, but here was mostly silence except for an occasional tinkling sound.

There were just two surgeons on the staff of that hospital, and neither had been on rounds since neither was remotely interested in psychiatry. I got to a phone and called one of them, telling him of my findings and asking that he take a look. He came running, literally, arriving breathless at the bedside. He felt the abdomen, listened to the sounds, and said, "Let's get this guy upstairs right now!" Turning to me he said, "I never heard of a psychiatrist diagnosing an acute bowel obstruction before! Damn! Wanta scrub in?"

Within the hour we had the man in surgery, opened up his belly, and found a bowel obstruction so advanced that gangrene was setting in. That required a major procedure called a bowel resection, in which we removed about two feet of intestine, and the placement of drains and a colostomy (meaning 'colon-mouth' construction) opening. Ordinarily an acute bowel obstruction produces excruciating pain, which does not stop until the victim is anesthetized and the obstruction is removed. This man never complained of pain. He just went to bed and lay there, mute, with his head tilted up.

When I looked in on him some hours later, he was in a bed in the surgical ward. His head was on his pillow and his eyes were closed, making me wonder if he was still unconscious or perhaps dead, since I'd never before seen him with his head back on the pillow or his eyes closed. Suddenly, however, his eyes opened and he raised his head from the pillow. Then this man, long mute, always expressionless, made a small but definite smile and said, "Thanks, Doc," and put his head down on the pillow!

While his abdomen recovered from the surgery over the next few weeks, his psyche similarly seemed to recover from its schizophrenia, and he was ultimately discharged from the hospital to go home, a rare occurrence in that place, where most patients were sent to chronic care in a Veterans Hospital to live out their unhappy lives. What made this man's recovery so remarkable was that he had been psychotic for years, and considered quite beyond hope.

There weren't many such triumphs - almost none, in fact, that I can recall. We didn't, after all, get the acute cases of schizophrenia, mostly occurring in young people and often lessening or disappearing entirely after a few months. Those people did not need the close security that our hospital provided. Similarly, we rarely saw manic-depressives, except for the unusual case like the Carlson's Raider who was in a prolonged manic state. Mostly that disorder comes and goes, sometimes cycling back and forth between excitement and depression. Once in a great while we treated someone with a profound, prolonged psychotic depression who harbored the fixed, agonizing delusion that he had caused World War II, or the death of Franklin Roosevelt, or a major epidemic.

Among the varieties of schizophrenia that tended to become chronic and more or less fixed, the commonest was the paranoid form. These people developed deep-seated delusions of demonic possession, influence by radio waves, direct orders from God to perform certain acts, including killing people, conspiracies by foreign agents - some of their neighbors among them - bent on their destruction, and similar demonstrably untrue thoughts about any number of things. Along with these paranoid delusions there were frequently hallucinations: sensory experiences that no one else can hear or see or feel. Commonest among these are voices, whose origin may be known to the afflicted person or may not. When he says he "doesn't know" whose voice it is, the paranoid person is simply refusing to reveal it, because his questioner may be in league with his enemies, or so he believes.

What makes this form of the disease, probably its commonest, most interesting is the fact that there are innumerable people who do not have schizophrenia but who are paranoid to some degree. In truth, nearly all 'normal' people have some paranoid ideas at least some of the time. They are most common in adolescence, when social uncertainty or worries about one's attractiveness and acceptance by peers are most frequent. A small group of kids in a high school hallway that seems to fall silent as one approaches, may be talking about or making fun of the 'normally' paranoid youngster. One whose clothing doesn't conform to whatever the fashion currently is may begin to feel ostracized, which is why certain bizarre costumes tend to appear in adolescent groups.

A little later in life, a boss with poor people management skills arouses in some people the suspicion that he doesn't like them, is against them, may even be scheming to screw up the job situation, or worse. A seemingly poor reception at church or at a party or a PTA meeting can stimulate, even in healthy, relatively well adjusted people, the suspicion that for some reason, some people don't like them or are 'against' them. All normal.

At some ill-defined point, in some people, such feelings begin to loom large and occupy more and more of the individual's attention, and cause considerable distress. If the feelings become strong and persistent, and the person starts actively looking for further evidence of slights and veiled hostility and exclusion, and ruminating often about these things, then at some point, also ill defined, the acceptable boundaries of "normal" may be exceeded. The boundaries and definition of 'normal' are matters of loose social consensus and vary sometimes widely from one society to another, even among small sub-groups of societies.

Adolph Hitler fostered and encouraged widespread paranoid ideas about Jews, with astonishing and tragic consequences. Stalin did it even better, focusing on land-owners and other 'capitalists." The Chinese went much farther, portraying not just owners and bosses but intellectuals, professionals, educators, many minorities and all dissenters as members of a huge conspiratorial group bent on 'exploiting' and thus harming everyone else. Even Hillary Clinton tried the 'huge conspiracy' approach to explain away her husband's despicable behavior - and not just with interns. Fortunately, in her case, it didn't sell.

The reason it didn't sell was that the American People sensed, even though no one - certainly not the press - ever quite labeled the idea what it was, which is paranoid - that the assertion exceeded our societal consensus as to what is 'normal' and what is not. It was a logical thing to try, given the fact that this society appears to be pushing the outer limits of what is acceptable paranoid thinking and what is not. She simply miscalculated how far out the limit has been pushed. A few more years and things may well be different.

A great many people exhibit what might be called a "paranoid personality disorder." Not many years ago the idea that there is a governmental conspiracy to destroy democracy would have attracted far fewer adherents than it does today, as attested by the proliferation of militias, survivalists, and devotees of conspiracy theory having to do with the assassination of John Kennedy, nuclear power, international Jewry.

Some have joked that even paranoids have enemies; this is quite true. It seems, moreover, that paranoid habits of reasoning and thinking are often learned, and do not represent some inherent genetic or biologically determined condition. Hitler and Stalin had valid reasons to be suspicious of plots against them. Richard Nixon seemed to grow more paranoid as the press became more - and more obviously - determined to bring him down. In ancient days conspiracies abounded: pharaohs were slain, kings assassinated, Borgias poisoned their adversaries, a group got together to kill Abraham Lincoln, Stanton supporters tried to impeach Andrew Johnson, and the Old Testament is rife with examples of destructive plans and actions, like murder, that amply demonstrated that some paranoid thinking was almost a prerequisite for survival.

What is happening today, however, is more widespread, more insidious, and more likely to result in the destruction of society's institutions. No longer is it mainly the mighty who have reason to suspect forces at work against them. Now it is the common man, feeling exploited by false advertisers, impoverished by the Internal Revenue Service, defrauded by financial managers, cheated by contractors who fail to deliver, bad debtors who refuse to pay and slink into safe bankruptcy courts, environmentalists who think more of spotted owls and trees and snail darters than they do of people, and a host of others who can be thought of as exploiters, oppressors, and cheaters.

In itself, this may not be much different than in Colonial times. However, something has been added that legitimizes and encourages paranoid thinking by rewarding it in ways never before possible. The first part of that is the growing preoccupation with 'rights' and 'entitlements' always said to be enshrined in the Constitution, or at least in the hearts of its framers. The second part is the concomitant growth of belief in the universality of remedy inherent in litigation. A proliferation of attorneys dedicated to suing alleged wrongdoers with the goal of winning large monetary judgments (read "winning the lottery") helps this along. It is not the attorney's fault, entirely. They are simply doing their jobs, or so they say.

The third part of the new encouragement to be paranoid is the growing concept of victimization. Both Freud and his most influential American disciple, Dr. Spock of child-raising fame, contributed to this. Both, in their discussions of early childhood development and emotional growth tended, perhaps (hopefully) inadvertently, to downplay long-held beliefs in will, self-determination, and personal responsibility. We now find great attention being given to 'unhappy childhoods,' 'abuse,' lack of 'empowerment' and material deprivation as not only causative reasons and explanations for unacceptable, unproductive, even violent criminal behavior, but as exculpatory excuses for such behavior.

Finally, the almost prurient, sometimes gleeful behavior of the press as it sensationalizes the truly obscene excesses of the judicial system in its lavish awards of huge fortunes for often trivial, asinine alleged 'hurts' like hot coffee in a woman's lap, from her own hand, strongly validates the idea that we are all victims, all helpless ('unempowered?'), not responsible for what happens to us and unable to do anything about it without millions from McDonald's or Dow Chemical or some other rich source.

What the ultimate result of this growth in 'acceptable' paranoid thinking might be, no one knows, but it gives great hope to social revolutionaries.

Most schizophrenics are not paranoid, and paranoid personalities, however severe, do not as a rule become schizophrenics. When one with a tendency to paranoid thinking does develop schizophrenia, however, the paranoia is likely to intensify and take on bizarre forms.

There is a further form of paranoia, however, that is uncommon if not rare, that has nothing to do with schizophrenia and does not seem to be simply an outgrowth or result of having a paranoid personality. It is called "true" paranoia. We had one such patient at Fort Worth, and I have seen perhaps one more in fifty years of psychiatry.

Our one 'true' paranoia case was a senior officer in the Navy, who arrived with an 'escort' at the hospital, but without restraints or guards. He was a handsome, exceedingly well-groomed man in his late forties, dressed in an exquisitely tailored officer's uniform with a chest full of medals. He had no history of bizarre behavior, wild delusions or hallucinations, or any of the 'incidents' that often led to psychiatric hospitalization. He stated quite calmly that his admission was a complete mistake that he was certain we would rectify in short order, and pledged his total cooperation and absolute honesty.

He brought with him voluminous documents, all in carefully labeled folders bearing the titles of the contents and the date prepared, revealing that he had worked on them for over a year. During most of that time this officer had been assigned to the Pentagon, and had reportedly performed his duties satisfactorily.

He came to the attention of his colleagues when he began first to hint, and then to insist, that he was being considered for the position of Vice President of the United States, and in fact was certain to be so designated prior to the next election. His massive collection of files and documents had been assembled to support this contention. He insisted that reading them would convince us, and handed them over, whereupon he went through the admission procedure without incident.

His history, both from the man himself and from official records, was of a highly educated man with advanced degrees in engineering who had served devotedly in the Navy since the outset of the Great War in 1941. He was unmarried, a fact he ascribed to the demands of his professional life, in good physical health, and without any signs of mental or emotional problems. The one item that stood out from this description of normalcy and superior performance was his absolute conviction that he was about to become the Vice President.

We read and discussed the extensive documentation he offered. Much of it consisted of quotations from speeches and letters of prominent political figures, with interpretive comments by the patient. Nowhere in the mass of carefully organized papers was there any mention of political office of any kind, but the man had, in his comments, drawn conclusions that, while not wildly illogical did not impress any of us who read them as supporting his firm conviction about his future. When we expressed our doubts as to the meaning of his supporting material he was unfazed, indicating only that we simply were not well enough informed. He patiently pointed out a number of ambiguous and vague comments by important public figures, always asserting that it should be clear that the hidden meaning was validation of his convictions.

Aside from his unflinching but unemotional assertions on this one issue, always central to every interview, there was absolutely nothing out of the ordinary in his behavior or conversations about other subjects. He adjusted well to life in a locked ward with people who were obviously mentally ill, helped the ward staff with their chores, and waited patiently for us to discover the truth. Ultimately he did indicate that there might be some opposition to his inevitable elevation to high office, and that had probably caused him to be admitted here, but he named no conspirators plotting against him. Never did he express any other ideas suggesting suspiciousness, distrust, a feeling that anyone was 'against' him, or any ideas that were clearly abnormally paranoid.

Presented at staff and thoroughly questioned by several of the most experienced psychiatrists, he maintained his calm demeanor and stuck to his matter of fact declaration that he would soon be the Vice President. No other signs of illness could be found. After his long examination in the conference, he was dismissed to return to the ward. The discussion that followed was even more prolonged, and led finally to the conclusion that he indeed had a rare disease called "true" paranoia. The striking thing about this disease is that the individual is entirely 'intact' and healthy seeming, mentally and physically, except for one massive grandiose paranoid idea. The prognosis, based on extensive review of the literature, was hopeless. Other similar cases had never been seen to recover, and the delusions had gradually expanded lifelong, but other signs of mental disease did not show up.

The significance of this case and others like it, including patients who are actually paranoid schizophrenics but only very mildly schizophrenic, is that they may harbor serious delusions for years without anyone noticing. Those delusions are often persecutory, unlike those of our Naval officer, and the person so afflicted may carry on normal activities for a long time until quite suddenly and seemingly without warning, he walks into his office and shoots people, or takes his shotgun and kills kids who run across his lawn.

Paranoid ideas and habits of thinking do not account for all of the instances of sudden violence, especially shootings that have figured so prominently in the press. Whether they have been occurring with increasing frequency or have just received more attention than they used to, no one can say for sure. The retrospective investigations into the past lives of such killers often suggest peculiarities of 'personality,' previous inexplicable eruptions of violent but non-lethal activity, and distortions in the individual's relationships with others. Many times, however, there is nothing very substantial to indicate mental illness, and friends and acquaintances and fellow workers commonly express complete surprise that the person they thought they knew could do such terrible things.

As the century draws to a close following a hundred years of literally miraculous progress in the identification of mental disease and the development, for the first time in history, of effective treatments, this society has not yet figured out a way to cope with several serious problems connected with mental disorders. The sudden, seemingly irrational killings done by doubtlessly severely disordered paranoid people, is the most dramatic of these, but there are others of far greater impact on society as a whole, particularly with respect to the large percentage of homeless people and the possibly even larger percentage of jailed criminals who are without question seriously mentally ill, even grossly psychotic.

In California, in 2001, it has been said with some accuracy that there are more mentally ill people locked up in the Los Angeles County jail than in all the California state mental hospitals combined. Most are getting no treatment. Most will get out, and fairly soon. These two major problems, far worse today than in the first half of the century, have come about for several reasons that need to be examined. Carefully.

The first has to do with the definition of "insanity," a legal, not a medical, concept. There is no generally accepted definition, and thus no national or even community-wide agreement as to what it is, exactly, or when something should be done about it, what is allowable to be done in a 'free' society, and who should do it. This in spite of the fact that everybody "knows" a "crazy" person when he sees one.

Crazy people walk around talking to themselves, proclaim messages from God, accuse the government of persecution, and look crazy in their poor grooming, bizarre clothing, poor hygiene and disorderly behavior. Right? Right, yes, but only for some people with mental disease, not most. The man with "true" paranoia is perhaps the most extreme example of one who is profoundly 'crazy' but who shows no signs of it. The wild-eyed, disheveled, largely incoherent, confused long-haired creature shouting imprecations from atop a soapbox to an audience of only two or three bemused passers-by is the other extreme. There are many gradations between these two, and they are impossible to quantify.

Every society, for generations past, has had problems about this. It plagued this nation from before its inception. One of the most prominent of our founding fathers, Benjamin Rush, who was a hero of the American Revolution involved in declaring our independence and fashioning our Constitution, was a physician who was an early psychiatrist. Like most educated and thoroughly civilized men, he recognized that there were many degrees of mental abnormality, many of which were generally tolerated. Thus each community had its fools, eccentrics, "tetched," oddballs, 'defectives,' and 'feeble-minded,' who might suffer considerable derision and social ostracizing but were tolerated. As long as no one got hurt and no substantial property was damaged. When that happened, steps were taken, ranging from beatings to confinement to execution. The limits of community tolerance varied from time to time and place to place, but were generally similar.

It was hard to shake the traditions of the past when it came to dealing directly with crazy people. Until the great French physician, Pinot, "struck the chains" from the tormented mental patients in Paris's great mental hospital in the eighteenth century, they were quite literally permanently chained to stone walls and logs - for life. While the chains were long gone, we were doing much the same thing with camisoles and leather strap 'restraints' past the middle of this century, when we switched to chemicals, like Thorazine.

Many people throughout the world, including parts of the U.S., have believed mental disorder to be caused by possession by evil spirits. It seemed logical, therefore, to take steps to get the demons out, by drilling holes in the head like they did in Egypt three thousand years ago, or by beating the human vessel they had invaded until the demons decided it was too uncomfortable to stay in there, and left. In the early 1950's I watched as Korean villagers hung schizophrenics, naked and upside down from cattle-butchering racks and whipped them with stout saplings to drive the devils out. There are no good statistics as to the efficacy of this sort of treatment.

What all this illustrates is the limited options open to any society when faced with people whose behavior exceeds the limits of what the community loosely agrees is acceptable. Some such behavior - killing other people, stealing their stuff, kidnapping their women and children, and the like - has for eons been clearly labeled as crimes, and at least since the Code of Hammurabi has had prescribed socially imposed sanctions, mainly execution, corporal punishment, confinement, exile, sterilization, and enforced confinement. The mentally ill population of our jails and prisons attests to the fact that mentally ill people do commit such acts - crimes - and are dealt with like anyone else.

Most people with mental disease, however, do not commit any crime. When their behavior exceeds the limits of what the community will tolerate, the options are even more limited. Corporal punishment is out (officially, at least); execution is unthinkable; exile impractical; enforced compensation ridiculous. That leaves confinement and/or forcible medication. Both of those can run afoul of constitutional guarantees of due process and endless judicial decisions and pronouncements about informed consent, privacy, and individual freedom.

Because of the tremendous overlap between psychiatry and the law, the judicial system has for the entire century tried to define mental illness, clarify its legal implications, and establish clear guidelines about personal legal responsibility. These efforts have largely rested upon something called the McNaughton Rule. That 'rule' holds that a person cannot be held to be legally responsible for a criminal act if, because of "mental disease or defect" he is unable to comprehend the nature of the act, cannot distinguish right from wrong with respect to it, or is subject to an "irresistible impulse" to do it. This in turn rests upon a broad social consensus prohibiting punishment for what is an illness and not just bad acts.

This rule works fine when the accused is incoherent, unresponsive or inappropriately so, or is clearly unable to figure out what the court is about and what the judge is saying. In cases where he is more intact, however, the matter becomes more difficult. Even someone with fairly profound paranoid ideas may know that attacking or killing another person is "wrong," at least in the eyes of the law, but still believes that doing so in a particular situation was justified. When a jury is involved, they may have problems with recognizing this as legal insanity, though strictly speaking, it may be.

This confusion is compounded by many people's deep-seated feelings that criminals should be punished, while the law says that if the defendant meets the 'rule,' he can't be. There have been innumerable instances of heinous crimes committed by people who were without question psychotic but whom the jury has convicted anyway because the act was so violent or barbaric. The "not guilty by reason of insanity" plea is often invoked, but many times is rejected by panels of indignant citizens who chose not to be persuaded by the claim that the perpetrator is so sick that he shouldn't be punished. When the plea does work, the offender is sent off to a mental hospital and in many jurisdictions is free and back on the street when he seems to have recovered.

A serious problem with this course of events occurs because the prisoner-patient's apparent recovery may be the direct result of medication. Naturally he is given a supply of it to take home after his discharge, and usually assigned to a supervising social worker and supportive outpatient treatment to ensure his continued normalcy. The trouble is, particularly among paranoid patients, they often stop taking their medication, lie about it to the social worker, who can hardly monitor them hour by hour, or even disappear from view altogether, while their delusions of persecution grow ever more compelling. Any number of times such people end up killing someone else, sometimes quite soon, and the whole process starts all over again.

Other 'rules,' related to the basic McNaughton one, have been constructed in most if not all states to be used when someone, family member or physician or mental health worker, wants to have someone confined because of mental disorder. These rules generally require that the individual demonstrates - usually by observed actions - that he is a danger to himself or others, or unable to provide for his own basic needs for food, clothing and shelter. While every human being fits these criteria for a long period after birth, the rules don't mean that. They just mean "like" that. Another fuzzy area, especially when it comes to juvenile crime.

Under these rules, because of our constitutional protections, people can usually be held in confinement only briefly, typically 72 hours, whereupon a formal judicial hearing must be held and a court ruling handed down that explicitly confirms or denies the allegations of dangerousness or helplessness and either sends the subject off to involuntary confinement or sets him free. Such judgments are highly subjective and even speculative. Judges, being human, tend to err on the side of caution and confinement after a few school shootings or post office worker blowups, but in today's broadly paranoid, litigious social climate with increasingly fervent attention to individual rights, soon slip back into erring in the other direction.

As this century of miraculous progress in understanding and treating mentally ill people winds down, the quandary about how society and the law are to deal with them has gotten worse, and is far from a solution. The problem will steadily grow worse; of that there can be no doubt. Just watch.

Like so many problems in psychiatry, and in medicine generally, we don't really know very much about paranoid disorders. Surely habitual patterns of thought that include suspiciousness, victimhood, distrust and hostility can be taught and readily learned, and that seems to be happening. Less and less attention is paid to the individual's autonomy with respect to what happens to him and what the outcomes will be. That goes hand in hand with the abandonment of a sense of personal responsibility, without which there can be little hope for the survival of a "free" country.

After all, if one is not responsible for failure in school or on the playground or on the job, because of outside forces working against him (including abusive parents and policemen), then he can hardly be expected to assume responsibility for correcting the misfortunes that have befallen him. The remedies must come from outside, from government through its judicial system and its magisterial and executive powers to intervene and make everything all right after a flood, a hurricane, or other disaster.

When a large enough number of individual disasters - job loss, sickness, marital breakups, mounting debts, and leaky roofs - begin to be grouped with 'natural' disasters warranting government intervention and corrective measures, government will have to grow even faster than it now does. Moreover, with almost all new growths in government, however well intentioned, go losses in personal wealth and personal freedom. Witness the IRS, or the EPA. Look also at the Departments of Agriculture and Labor and Commerce and Energy and Education, all of which make laws that they pretend are not laws, just rules, since the Constitution restricts law-making to the Congress.

There is amongst us a brilliant, living, even flourishing demonstration of the truly disastrous consequences of a kind of societal paranoid thinking coupled with an absolute conviction of victimhood, persecution, injustice and absence of responsibility. The government, attempting to be fair and caring, protective and supporting, has managed to degrade and largely destroy the will and productivity of a whole group of our fellow citizens who seem unable to contribute to the general welfare except by building gambling casinos.

We call this group "Native Americans." It is politically incorrect almost to the point of blasphemy to criticize these people in any way, let alone even mention that many of them were slaughterers of the innocent - both whites as well as other Indians - who have made no effort, over generations, to break out of their almost total dependency on others. Over this remarkable century, during which no law requires them to live in remote reservations, they have largely hunkered down in their hogans and trailers and miserable shacks, unwilling to strike out to take advantage of the abundance of educational and training opportunities and jobs they could have if they simply went after them.

They mostly sat around and made trinkets. Now they operate electronic slot machines.

Far too much time has passed since General Custer, broken treaties and P.T. Barnum's Wild West Shows, to blame it all on cherished, institutionalized paranoid ideas that they have, all this time, been persecuted, have no responsibility for themselves, have 'rights' as 'sovereign nations' that no other Americans have, and are 'entitled' to permanent, total care, provided by the government.

Here we see a whole people who historically produced little of value, rarely worked except to kill the abundant animals and fish around them in this largely uninhabited, incredibly rich continent, made their women do the great bulk of domestic work necessary to maintain life, warred on each other until the whites showed up and were an easier target, and who now assert they are entitled to untold millions of dollars to pay for land they never really owned and certainly never improved.

Unless one believes in a kind of genetically determined, species-specific inferiority, sure to be denounced as horrific racism, then he has to face the fact that it is learned attitudes and cherished beliefs about things demonstrably not now - or for many generations - true, that account for the "plight" of our fellow 'native American' citizens. Such is the nature of the paranoid disorder: it gets worse, and carries with it a special kind of grandiosity.

We may be doing the exact same thing to our whole population.

Abandon idealistic goals, develop a 'healthy' cynicism, be wary of being trusting, watch your back, eschew your responsibility for what's happened and for making things better, concentrate on your rights, be sure you get your entitlements. Some day you may win the lottery or a big malpractice or liability judgment, but meanwhile, demand that 'government' take care of all your needs. You start learning to run a casino. In your abundant leisure you can make nifty beaded bracelets and nice turquoise jewelry. Maybe some baskets.

There are more Indians in North America today than there were when Columbus, now revealed to have been a monstrous criminal exploiter of helpless innocents, discovered this land. How many of them do you know? How many of those are lawyers, dentists, nurses, teachers, journalists, engineers, architects, and successful businessmen? It is wonderfully ironic that our Indian Nations have discovered gambling casinos - temples to the false god of 'something for nothing.' We've taught them - and increasingly ourselves - that that's the way to do it.

All this may seem a far cry from our paranoid patients at Fort Worth, but it isn't, really. We started as a nation made up of people, not all of them good by any means, but people who accepted responsibility, took risks, believed absolutely in the sanctity of one's "word," meaning they were basically trusting and trustworthy, were skeptical of con men and snake oil salesmen but not everyone else, and saved many of their paranoid ideas for King George.

Today, thanks to a multitude of factors including our transiency, our astonishing oversupply of information rife with outrageous advertising claims, false political promises and reports of both wrongdoing and huge, unearned fortunes bestowed on semi-literate athletes, all steadily sensationalized by the media, we are more isolated from one another, understandably suspicious of what we hear and see - in other words far more 'paranoid' than our fore-fathers even dreamed of being. This could be the most serious threat to freedom and the on-going experiment we call democracy than any event in our history.

The drug-addicted patients at Fort Worth fell into two categories: sentenced prisoners and voluntary patients. Nothing distinguished one group from the other except the paperwork. Voluntary patients agreed on admission to stay 90 days, and many did. The prisoners were there for periods of a year or more. Together, they provided a fascinating glimpse into an American subculture that outsiders knew little about.

The drug of choice for most of these people was heroin. Like morphine, it was made from opium, and had been used for medicinal purposes for many years but was felt to be less effective for pain management and more likely to produce addiction. Both of these drugs usually came in powdered form, and were most effective when injected into a vein. Opium itself, usually in the form of a sticky black tarry goo, was usually smoked, usually by Orientals, but existed in every retail drug store, dissolved in alcohol and tainted with a touch of camphor added to discourage over-use by making it taste bad, and in large doses, cause stomach irritation and vomiting.

Paregoric was the name given to this concoction, and it was widely prescribed for diarrhea, a common ailment and common killer of children before the chlorination of water was invented by an Army doctor in the early 1900's. Still widely prescribed it could be found in a large glass container, sometimes holding 5 gallons, on a shelf in every drugstore. My introduction to the addict population came through the agency of this traditional drug.

The occasion was a birthday party on one of the drug wards. The whole staff was invited to visit the ward and take part in a celebration of the 87th birthday of a man who was something of a hospital pet. He was a gentle, spry, white-haired old fellow who had been addicted to Paregoric for more than 50 years, long before there was any law against using opium and its derivatives. He was serving his fourth or fifth sentence at the hospital, where over the years he had gotten to know most of the staff and all of the 'regular' addict patients. He had a warm, friendly manner and was most cooperative, always sweeping or straightening up the ward furniture, or making a new patient feel comfortable.

After the party, he and I sat down together to talk, and he told me his story. He had come from a poor Appalachian farm family who lived without sanitary facilities except for a ramshackle outhouse. Water was drawn from a nearby well, and its polluted state caused frequent bouts of diarrhea, from which several of his infant siblings died. He was fortunate enough to be given paregoric for his many bouts of loose bowels, and developed a real liking for it, considering it a genuine treat. Somehow, his stomach tolerated the camphor well.

In his early teens, he headed for the flatlands, and found work sweeping up in a small drugstore. He had found his career. He discovered the big jug of paregoric whose level of liquid didn't vary dramatically from the sips he took in the evenings, after the shop had closed. Inevitably, the time came when the druggist did notice that he had to re-order his paregoric more often than he expected, and suspicion fell upon our young recreational user. Before he was actually accused, he decided that discretion demanded that he take his sweeping skills and his penchant for paregoric elsewhere, and he left town.

Another town and another drug store were not far away, and he had no difficulty obtaining a job sweeping it up, and nipping at the paregoric. Again, after a while, he knew it was time to move on to another town, another drug store, and the inevitable jug of his favorite elixir.

He did this for more than sixty years, except for the several nine-month enforced treatment periods awarded to him by various courts, when some suspicious druggist caught him at his usual practice and the paregoric supply was dwindling too rapidly. Aside from this, he never committed even a minor offense, never denied his addiction, and never resisted his sentencing to one of the Federal Narcotics Hospitals in Fort Worth or Lexington, Kentucky. Nor, unlike most addicts, did he ever use any other drug, or buy his drug on the street.

From this gentle, harmless old fellow and from contact with a wide variety of addicts, I was to learn much about this affliction. The addict population of the United States at that time was far smaller than it is now, and was surprisingly stable. Many of these people knew many if not most of the others. Overwhelmingly they preferred heroin for its heightened pleasurable effects, but when it was not available would settle for anything. Morphine was usually easier to get, since it was carried in most pharmacies and all hospitals, and could often be stolen quite easily. Cocaine was not much in vogue, and was believed not to be addictive to the same degree as opium, morphine and heroin. Marijuana was not used at all among the 'real' addicts, even as a stopgap when supplies ran out. Alcohol was more commonly the stopgap agent used to try to avoid uncomfortable withdrawal episodes, which every addict had endured from time to time.

Codeine, and recently developed narcotics like dilaudid and demerol were other acceptable substitutes for the traditional opium derivatives, but all were becoming increasingly difficult to get. There were peddlers on the mean streets of large cities, and a few 'distributors' who supplied the often-addicted street corner salesmen, but very few big time importers. It was not unusual for a major drug bust at the wholesale level to create a massive panic among a whole city's addict population, since there were very often no alternative sources of supply.

The cost of illicit drugs was, if anything, relatively higher than it is today. Most addicts, in consequence, engaged more or less constantly in petty thievery, shoplifting, pickpocketing, and less often, robbery. Crimes of violence were avoided, usually, but when an addict went into severe withdrawal, he sometimes became irrationally aggressive, sometimes killing a shopkeeper or robbery victim on the street.

There were few federal or state narcotics agents bent on arresting addicts, concentrating instead on the peddlers and hoping to find the big shots above them - usually without success. The addicts accepted the existence of these agents with a certain resignation, considering them as unavoidable adversaries who were simply part of the cost of maintaining a 'habit,' but not enemies. There was one enemy everyone seemed to agree on: the informer. The traditional and not at all unusual penalty for this supreme treason was a form of crucifixion, in which the offender was literally nailed to a wooden fence to await death and eventual discovery by the police.

There was no record of anyone ever having been caught and punished for administering this unique retribution, and nearly every long-time addict knew of every such execution, often well in advance.

New doctors arriving for duty at Fort Worth were immediately sized up and put to various subtle tests by the addicts. The first was designed to assess the gullibility of inexperienced physicians. Many of the patients were highly skilled malingerers, able to mimic the symptoms and sometimes even the overt signs of a whole array of illnesses. They became masters at this as they traveled from one doctor's office to another, usually complaining of some exceedingly painful recurrence of a previously diagnosed (by a family doctor at home many miles from here) affliction usually calling for a narcotic. Gallstones and kidney stones were favorites. Both can be excruciatingly painful, both can be fired up by the pressure of a routine examination of the abdomen by palpation, and given the right symptoms and (feigned) signs don't require X-Ray or laboratory confirmation.

Since the suffering victim declared that he was on his way back to his family physician, to whom he would instantly report, there was little for the deceived doctor to do other than try to relieve the pain - this always required a narcotic - and give the poor guy a few doses to take along the way as he hurried home. A really good actor-addict could sometimes get enough narcotics this way to last him for several days. Two or three different doctor's office visits later the same day could set him up for a week or more.

Hospitalized addicts in a hospital such as ours could not hope to fake an illness so severely painful as to justify a narcotic. They knew this, but invariably, almost daily, would put on one of their performances designed to convince the doctor - especially the new doctor - that some kind of medicine was needed. Any medicine, from aspirin on up, but preferably something that could be injected. Addicts generally love needles, so much so that some told me they would be happy if I just gave them a small shot of saline solution.

If the doctor failed to fall into the many such traps laid for him during his first few days, the complaints and presumably the excruciating pains fell off abruptly. That was the first test.

The second was designed to determine whether the doctor could be trusted to preserve confidentiality. He would be told, in confidence, of a patient who had secreted some contraband drug somewhere around his bed or nightstand. Would the doctor tell anyone, like the hospital commander, or just quietly find the drug, usually aspirin, and talk it over with the offender without revealing his tipster? My test was a little more serious.

After my first half-dozen rounds on the ward, a patient said he had to see me alone on a matter of great importance. I had already learned that the addict population enjoyed an altogether incredible nationwide communication system, having to do with supplies, busts, informers, and the like. No one knew exactly how they did this, but they did. This patient wanted to talk about an informer. He named the traitor and the city where, that very night, he would be 'nailed to the fence.' That was all.

I realized that I was being tested, and everyone knew it. For several hours I wrestled with my understanding of medical ethics in this situation. Then I considered what, if anything, I could actually accomplish if, for example, I alerted the police in that far distant city that this tidbit of information had come my way. Finally, realizing that these people would know exactly what I did - or didn't - do, I tried to estimate what the consequences would be, both for me personally and for my on-going relationship with these patients. I was sure that no matter what I did, they wouldn't nail me to a fence. I was equally sure that the entire group would learn by morning exactly what I did do. Finally, I was sure (this could have been just a rationalization for cowardice) that no matter what I did or whom I told, it would not affect the outcome in the slightest.

And so, worrying through the whole night about my character and my fitness to pursue this noble profession, when I should have been worrying about the poor sinner on his way to his Maker and how I might possibly help him (the rat!) I did nothing.

The following morning, unable to tolerate the uncertainty of the situation, I put in a call to the police headquarters in the city where it was supposed to happen. Yes, they'd had a couple of homicides last night, and yes, one was a known drug peddler who was found this morning, nailed to a fence. "Must have been a stoolie." Yep.

Things changed after that. A steady stream of addict patients requested 'private, confidential' interviews. I learned about a multitude of sins, small and large, both in and out of the hospital, none of which could I actually do anything about. Mixed in were many seemingly sincere confessions of undiscovered offenses, harm to wives and children, promises broken, contracts violated, cheating, lying and generally behaving badly. This was great practice in non-judgmental - but not excusing, either - counseling that opens the way for some beneficial change to take place.

It was with these sad people that I began to learn that psychiatry need not be the totally passive interaction, or more accurately non-action, then in vogue. I learned also that the therapist could convey to the patient what society's judgments were likely to be about his thinking and behavior, without personally passing judgment. It was daily becoming more clear to me that trying to understand the roots of behavior, no matter how evil or destructive that behavior was, did not equate with trying to excuse it. There is great confusion around this point, especially among the public, but among psychiatrists as well. It shows up in nearly every murder trial, when psychologists and psychiatrists are called (and paid) to testify.

Every social and economic class was represented among the addict patient group. Interestingly, there were few Orientals and almost no blacks or Jews, but otherwise there was no commonality of ethnic background or ancestry. Most were men, and appeared superficially to be lower middle class, educated through high school, and relatively articulate. Some were remarkable.

One such was a well-known movie actor who was instantly recognizable because of his small stature, superficially obsequious manner, and soft, whiny way of talking. Never the leading man in a film, he was often one of the principal characters, and was often paired with a huge, frightening man named Sidney Greenstreet, who was not an addict. This little guy had a quick smile, a lovely sense of humor, and a manner that suggested that he saw in all of this something quite amusing and not really serious. He had been committed by a court, but seemed to bear no resentment for that, and remained in the hospital for most of the year.

Another outstanding member of this curious society was an exceedingly attractive woman of about thirty, who was a voluntary patient. She wore heavy but well designed, rather exotic makeup that made one think of Cleopatra (same heavy eye shadow), and wore at all times a thin, clinging silk robe in a dramatic leopard-skin print, that looked like it was the only thing she had on, which indeed it was. A shapely leg often emerged, quite bare, as she sat down or moved about.

This lady was the mistress of an extremely rich and powerful Texas oil tycoon, who kept her in great luxury and with little or no effort to keep the liaison secret. She explained to me that her heroin habit, characteristically, reduced her sexual impulses drastically, and as her drug intake rose, it became more and more difficult to carry off the pretense of ecstasy that her lover expected, and insisted upon. When she became intolerably unresponsive, he would send her off to Fort Worth. A couple of months of enforced abstinence in our hospital, along with rest, a good diet, and assistance in "coming down" from her highly addictive state would allow her to cut her dose dramatically, and she could then perform far better in bed.

Every time I saw her, to check on her progress and dosage of methadone, which we used to assist in withdrawal, proved to be a real adventure. Invariably she would allow her gown to drift open to reveal a shapely leg right up to mid thigh, lean forward to enable a peek down the top of the gown at her outstanding breasts, and put her hand gently on my arm. In a soft, sensuous voice, she would then begin her campaign for "just an itty-bitty little shot of 'good' stuff" to make her recovery more tolerable. In return for this kindness and compassion, she would be more than willing to bestow abundant physical blessings on her benefactor.

This was the first time that I had ever been so overtly and explicitly solicited by any woman, let alone one so strikingly attractive, to exchange a medical favor for a sexual reward. My shock at this proposal was a measure of my vast naiveté and inexperience, of course, as well as a momentary flash of temptation. The office was secure. No one would dream of intruding during an interview. The woman was hardly an innocent virgin and was free of communicable disease. No one would be hurt, as she insisted, and no one would ever know, so what could be the harm?

Quite suddenly, that damned Hippocratic Oath popped into my mind. There was a sense of a thunderous pronouncement from on high, without words but no less clear in its declaration that to give in to this, even to contemplate it for a moment, was the greatest possible sin and violation of professional honor, that would render me forever a despicable, low creature wholly unworthy of this sacred calling - the physician. It saved me.

That sort of situation was to recur fairly frequently over the coming years of treating psychiatric patients. Usually it was more subtle; rarely was the temptress so strikingly tempting, or the quid pro quo so simple and clear. Often there was no "quo" at all.

The very nature of the psychiatric therapeutic relationship is such that it mimics the behavior of a lover and is commonly interpreted by the patient as such. The therapist is generally kind, attentive, accepting, encouraging in his manner, and genuinely caring. He may, moreover, actually like the patient and be aware of her attractiveness as a person. Female patients who are often unhappy and feeling emotionally deprived, pick up on all this and may respond by developing strong emotional, affectionate feelings, coming to believe that they are in love with this kind person.

The Freudians (and others) label this common phenomenon "transference." It has to be confronted explicitly and fairly early in therapy, for the therapy to progress smoothly. It cannot be ignored for long, nor dismissed brusquely, or labeled ridiculous.

Volumes of learned writings have been devoted to the proper 'analysis' and 'resolution' of the transference and the not infrequent, complicating matter of the "counter-transference," wherein the therapist develops romantic feelings for the patient. Such feelings can make it very difficult to deal realistically and helpfully with the patient's loving impulses. The end result can be disastrous for the patient, can totally disrupt therapy, and incidentally can bring the therapist to untold grief in court. Judges and juries are notoriously unsympathetic in these cases, usually.

My first encounter with this kind of temptation, the one we all pray not to be led into, (whether we mean it or not,) was specially instructive and helpful to me. First, it was very simple and explicit - no ambiguity involved at all. In addition, it wasn't really a matter of transference, for the lady barely knew me and we were not engaged in an intimate psychotherapeutic relationship. My own recognition of her charms, instantly recognizable to anyone not blind and deaf, was hardly countertransference.

Yet in spite of all, many of the elements of the transference situation and the problem of resolving it were present. In that instance it was easy. I simply told her, not unkindly, that while I appreciated the offer, I could not do as she wished. To do so would prolong her recovery, which would be to do harm, and I was sure she wouldn't want that. Also, I said, even though she had made the offer, to accept it would be to take advantage of her, and I could never do that. We parted friends, and remained so for her remaining months at the hospital. Never again did she beg for "a little bitty shot of the good stuff" and before long, began to abandon her sexually provocative dress and behavior. By the time she left, she looked quite normal, and she bade me goodbye with warm thanks. I knew she would be back on heroin, though in much smaller doses, in hours. But for the time, at least, she would be much better in bed.

Even though the hospital was equipped with steel bars over the doors and windows, it was not exactly escape-proof, and was considered a 'medium custody' penal institution. Still, during the year I was there, no one tried to escape. Some voluntary patients signed themselves out prematurely, violating their agreement to stay the full 90 days, but even that was uncommon. A few failed to return from passes, but were not pursued. Never did I witness any violence from the addict population.

Not once did a patient who was addicted to opium derivatives like heroin, morphine, or opium tar, whether voluntarily there trying to "get off" the stuff or sent to us by the courts, promise to stop using drugs. When I questioned many of them about this, they generally said something like "No one ever gets off this stuff, Doc. You should know that by now." Senior staffers, sometimes with many years of experience treating addicts, told me that maybe 2 percent would stay "clean," but even that was maybe too optimistic.

No one, at that time, suspected that there would be an explosion in drug use in coming years. It would not have been believed, at that time, that many young soldiers in Viet Nam would use powerful narcotics for many months, become seriously addicted, and then stop using them altogether, as any number of them apparently did. There was no such thing as 'designer' drugs or 'recreational' drug use. Most professionals believed that cocaine was not addictive; 'crack' had not yet appeared on the national scene. Neither professionals in the field nor the addict population believed marijuana was dangerous, or addictive, or a 'gateway' to more serious drug use, and could hardly be classified as a 'drug.'

It was widely believed that it took only a few doses of narcotics to initiate addiction, characterized as a craving dependency upon them and the appearance of serious, terribly uncomfortable, agonizing withdrawal symptoms when it was not regularly supplied. It was also believed that the development of a certain tolerance to these substances always forced the user to steadily increase his dosage to obtain the same desired results, and it was true that some of our addict patients, on admission, were taking doses that in normal people would be fatal, and taking these doses daily without apparent ill effect. It was that fact that accounted for a substantial number of volunteers entering the program when their costs got too high, in order to reduce their dose requirements and cut their sometimes enormous expenditures.

Many long-term addicts stayed pretty much on a constant dose. While initially they may have used narcotics to obtain a "high" of some sort, they had reached a stage where that was no longer their motivation. Instead, they kept themselves on the smallest regular dose that would keep withdrawal symptoms at bay, as a kind of 'maintenance' system, never stopping completely but never enjoying it very much.

There has been much attention to the so-called 'addictive' personality of late as part of the specious "psychobabble" of mostly untrained and often ignorant proponents of silly theories about drug addiction. Using this concept, many people who should know better draw unwarranted parallels between drug addiction and alcoholism. Both have undoubted physical and sometimes psychological and characterological elements, but this does not make them the same, or even similar. To fail to understand this can cause great confusion and harm to both groups, and to attempts to treat them, however well-intentioned.

Addiction is not the same as habituation. The addict is physically dependent upon some chemical substance to maintain homeostasis - a more or less level physiological and psychological state. His body, with its magnificent adaptive capability, has responded to a steady input of a chemical that alters how his body works, causing real physical changes like diminished bowel activity, alterations in the production of saliva and tears, changes in the pupils of the eyes, regulation of body temperature, muscular contraction and sensitivity to pain, heat and cold, and touch.

This adaptive process, during which the body seeks to resume its normal level of such functions, eventually succeeds in counteracting the changes that the drug produces, as long as the supply of it is fairly regular. When the chemical that has been adapted to is no longer present, yet the adaptive mechanisms are still in place but don't have the chemical to keep them busy, they cause an over-reaction. The bowel becomes overactive, causing diarrhea. Tears and saliva may flow copiously. Body temperature may soar and drop alternately. The pupils dilate widely and won't constrict to keep out excessive light. Muscles contract violently and go into spasm. The slightest touch to the skin becomes painful. The psychological impact of all this can be terror.

This is withdrawal. It is altogether awful. It is almost never fatal.

It starts within hours when someone who uses narcotic drugs regularly stops getting his drug. It does not occur in anything like the same way to alcoholics, despite some superficial similarities. There is quite a different picture in cocaine users who can't get their cocaine. The same is true of steady users of amphetamines and barbiturates and some tranquillizers, which is to say there are some physiological and symptomatic consequences to the sudden cessation of those compounds after steady, heavy use, but the adaptive mechanisms' overactivity is markedly different.

What all this means is that the use of drugs, the abuse of drugs, and addiction to drugs are different things, just as the abuse of alcohol and alcoholism are different things. Being different, they must be understood differently and treated differently. The terribly sad truth is that we know very little about how to do it, although some things seem clear enough at least for now, and should be stated.

The first is that narcotics addiction, possibly including serious cocaine use, is not at this point in history, curable. It may be manageable, but only in limited numbers of cases and probably only with the use of other drugs.

The second is that alcoholism is probably not curable but is definitely manageable.

Neither of these maladies is primarily psychological or emotional in origin.

The year at Fort Worth was a rich learning experience, about chronic severe mental illness, about electroshock therapy, and about prefrontal lobotomy. It left little room for doubt as to why more than half the hospital beds in this country were occupied by such people, for we rarely saw a patient improve enough to go back to living in the community. The richness of the staffing and the excellence of the care and living conditions notwithstanding, we really had little or nothing to offer that held hope for long-term improvement, let alone cure.

The contrasting situation with the addict population also offered a host of insights into what was then a serious problem but was destined to become a catastrophic one that, 50 years later, we were still largely powerless to correct. It outfitted my belief system with the conviction that narcotic addiction for most people was a lifelong, unrelenting affliction with scant hope for escape, and a steady downhill course. Only the apparent abandonment of narcotic use by some young people who started it during military service in Viet Nam and later abandoned it seemed to cast any doubt at all about the hopelessness of this self-inflicted disease, and no study, to my knowledge, has carefully examined that situation and drawn useful conclusions from it as to treatment.

As for the other commonly used chemicals like methamphetamine, marijuana, cocaine, and a host of 'designer' drugs, they seem to have little in common with narcotics derived from opium or with one another, except that they alter brain function and in some users produce intensely pleasurable sensations and illusions followed by a significant, sometimes quite unpleasant or dangerous let-down, yet tend to cause the user to want more.

Additionally, all these substances are associated with criminal activity. It is utterly simplistic to assert, as some do, that only the arbitrary passage of laws forbidding or controlling their use is responsible for this. It is their inherent properties that fosters criminal activity, beginning with their ability to generate a desire for more, a tolerance for increased dosages to produce the same effect, and ultimately both psychological and physical dependency with the promise of severe distress and discomfort - even, rarely, death - when they are withheld.

All this produces a self-perpetuating 'market,' and a steadily expanding one of incomparable "brand loyalty" among users. The potential for profit is irresistible to anyone unconcerned with the disastrous human consequences, which accounts for the steady growth of powerful international drug cartels, corruption of officials to permit illegal traffic, elaborate smuggling and transport systems exceeding the wildest dreams of old-time smugglers, and the generation of unimaginable fortunes for the big producers and distributors.

Nothing we have done to date in the silly, mostly pathetically ineffective "war on drugs," has made much of a difference. The generally compassionate nature of our people, constantly assaulted by the soft-headed advocates of 'legalization' who blame the law and the authorities for the problem, enthusiastically if clandestinely supported and egged on by those who profit from the drug trade, has led to a national policy, both informal and official, of trying to get at the source (impossible) and only deal with the 'demand' side by attempts, equally impossible, mostly, at something called rehabilitation.

States like Texas, who have been relatively hardheaded about illicit drug use, are condemned as inhumane and even cruel when they lock up poor innocent youths who have (as who hasn't, in some way?) been led astray and had a few innocent puffs on a joint, or sniffed a little white powder. After all, we are told, "everyone" makes mistakes.

In spite of horrifying statistics on drug use among younger and younger people, who after all cannot be held responsible for anything including murder, and admissions by successful, powerful people that they 'experimented' (but didn't inhale, naturally) in their youth, the truth is that most people do not make this mistake. Ever. It is still deviant as well as a knowing violation of law to use illicit drugs.

Societies that do not wink at or in any way tolerate drug law violations have far less of a problem with this than we do. Turkey is one example. Turkish prisons are notoriously unpleasant, and stays are very long. Lawyers rarely if ever can make plea agreements or file successful appeals. Singapore is another example. Evidently there is no significant drug 'problem' in that little country. Drug abusers are promptly jailed. Drug importers, even legitimate tourists with a few marijuana cigarettes or a little tiny bit of cocaine powder in their luggage are not only jailed promptly, but are held for very long periods. Peddlers are executed, with equal promptitude, and if not publicly, then with great public attention.

Are those ancient civilizations less civilized than we are? Is it more civilized to do as we do, to make great noise about our concern, endlessly debate the 'rights' of criminals intent on turning a whole generation into a market for addictive, harmful, destructive drugs, and perpetuate the problem by lamenting abusive parents, oppressive government regulators, racial tensions, cruel policemen and DEA and FBI agents, granting blanket forgiveness to erring adolescents, and making plea bargains? And to do all this while the problem grows steadily worse?

So far our national leadership, in this as in so many serious matters, has merely made feeble gestures to rectify the situation (Drug "Czar" indeed! What power? Something like what Nicholas had at Ekaterinberg? Before or after they shot him?) Our former president, who never inhaled, lamented and viewed with alarm, but never proposed anything that had the slightest prospect for success in dealing with what may well be the most serious threat, ever, to the continued viability of this nation. This is worse than AIDS, folks. Moreover, it is not primarily or even importantly a medical problem, or one that can be solved with 'rehabilitation.'

It can be solved with what America has always relied upon and currently totally lacks: committed, realistic, honorable leadership. Give the Czar some power. Advocate for special laws to deal with this special situation. Use the bully pulpit to lead, to change public perceptions and misperceptions, to inform as to the horrendous threat that faces us, and the drastic steps necessary to turn it around, which does not include bombing some poor illiterate peasants in Columbia and Mexico and the Golden Triangle around Myanmar, or even the jungle refineries.

The Fort Worth educational adventure ultimately drew to a close. Great new experiences awaited in far off San Francisco, where life would take another dramatic turn. For now, this is Sunday, and time to watch the news, and rejoice in the day the Lord hath made.

Captain Hogan's plan sent me next to the gleaming new Langley Porter Clinic (later renamed "Neuropsychiatric Institute") on the San Francisco medical campus on the slopes of Mount Parnassus in that fabled city. The director of that institution, situated just beyond the dental school next to the U.C. SF Hospital, was an eminent psychiatrist named Karl Bowman, known and respected world-wide for his research, his writings, and his influence in psychiatric post-graduate education.

Like Hogan, Dr. Bowman had studied with Adolph Meyer at Hopkins and, also like Meyer and Hogan, believed that we would one day prove without doubt that serious mental disease reflected and arose from an organic disorder of the brain itself. He welcomed me warmly and enthusiastically to the resident staff, and told me a little of his philosophy. The human brain, he said, was the most complex structure imaginable. It contained billions of individual cells arranged in six layers in the outer part, or cortex, alone. The deepest of those layers carried on the simplest, routine brain activities, while the outermost layers were involved in increasingly complex, sophisticated functions about which we knew little beyond that.

It was, then as now, next to impossible to do direct research on living brain tissue. Work during surgery on brain tumors and hemorrhages, and careful microscopic examination of brain tissue after autopsy had revealed much about the incredible complexity of the cellular structure and myriad interconnections of the cells themselves as well as the different areas of the brain. Comparative studies of primate brains and those of simpler life forms had also revealed a great deal, as had the new technology of electroencephalography - recording the minute electrical currents generated by brain activity.

In spite of that, however, we knew less about the details of how the brain actually works, in the mid-twentieth century, than our forefathers knew, hundreds of years earlier before autopsies and human dissection were allowed, about the rest of the human body. Neuroanatomy was well explored and details of brain structure were well known. How the various parts of the brain affected functions throughout the body, however, had to be deduced mainly from gentle stimulation during surgery, or removal of tissue along with the carving out of tumors, or observing the effects of injury to specific areas, reflected in alterations of speech, movement, sensation, and even reasoning, to some extent.

We knew for certain that specific parts of the brain were essential for certain functions. The rearmost, occipital lobes received impulses from the eyes that they converted into images, enabling vision. Areas of the side, or parietal, lobes were not only necessary for hearing, but even for the ability to retain memories of sounds of different pitch, and thus the ability to carry a tune. The 'Great American Crowbar Case' had given us an early inkling of the functions of the frontal lobes.

Deep within the brain were easily recognizable structures identical to those found in lower forms of animal life, like a great swirl of cells called the gyrus singulum, identical to that of dogs and tigers and even birds, that receives, remembers, recognizes and retains memories of odors, without which there could be no perfume industry, revulsion at the scent of decay or human waste, and the ability to detect scents of fear that animals instantly perceive. The human species has long spent great effort and treasure attempting to cover up or eliminate unwanted odors, and has allowed the enormous potential of the gyrus singulum largely to languish, but the equipment is still there.

Finally, it was known that the neural tissue of the brain had numerous connections to structures that were more glandular in nature, like the pituitary, that had the power through mysterious chemicals called hormones to affect other glands like the thyroid and the adrenals, lying atop the kidneys, that in turn could affect a multitude of bodily functions like heart action, digestion, and the marvelous set of almost instantaneous reactions necessary for the "fight or flight" reaction to a sudden encounter with a saber-toothed tiger. Alternatively, for that matter, with a mean boss or a policeman bearing down with a flashing red light and screaming siren.

All of this we knew. Nevertheless, Dr. Bowman declared, it was but a minuscule part of what needed to be known about this wondrous organ, floating in fluid, covered with several layers of tissue, and cunningly encased in a hard, protective shell of bone, that controlled everything about every living creature. Our methods, he told me, were too primitive and crude. Our tools were like giant steamshovels trying to pick out individual grains of sand. Our powers of observation and deduction were little better than those of our anthropoid relatives, yet we had to rely chiefly on those as long as we couldn't do direct experiments on living brains, and we could certainly never do that.

The day would come, he told me, when newer methods of non-invasive examination of the brain and its functions would open up vast new vistas and allow us, for example, to prove that brain dysfunction lay at the root of major mental disease. Even as we talked, he went on, he was planning an experiment, in which I was to take part, exploring the possible role of the thyroid gland in schizophrenia. He, and others, had observed that schizophrenic patients could tolerate immense doses of thyroxin, and its important component, iodine, that were impossible for non-schizophrenic people to tolerate. When given to a person, this material was rapidly 'taken up' by the thyroid gland, situated in the lower front of the neck.

A new radioactive isotope of iodine, labeled I-131, had been released by the Food and Drug Administration for limited experimental purposes, and could be obtained from the Lawrence Radiation Laboratory in Berkeley, across the Bay. It was Dr. Bowman's idea to administer the isotope to schizophrenic patients in the laboratory, and with the aid of a Geiger counter, measure the uptake of the material by the thyroid gland, comparing it to the amount and speed of uptake by the glands of non-schizophrenic volunteers. From these studies he hoped to deduce a possible connection between thyroid gland activity and the disease, possibly pointing the way to a new therapeutic approach.

It would be my job to bring the patients to the lab, administer the radioactive material, and then hold a Geiger counter over their thyroid gland and record the readings and the time they were made. This was a far cry from Fort Worth.

Sadly, this imaginative early foray into what has become a valuable medical activity now called Nuclear Medicine, which has come to play a major role in the diagnosis and management of some cancers, including cancer of the thyroid gland, failed to tell us anything usable about schizophrenia, and was abandoned after a few months.

As far as I could tell, none of the faculty led by Dr. Bowman at Langley Porter shared his hopes for the eventual validation of Adolph Meyer's ideas of 'psychobiology.' Most of these men (and a tiny number of women) who practiced and taught us residents were what was called "classical" - meaning Freudian - psychoanalysts. A few were disciples of Carl Jung. One was a Freudian anthropologist, not a physician at all, who was married to a truly great anthropologist, Margaret Mead, whose classical study "Coming of Age in Samoa" was both a psychological and anthropologic milestone. One was a gastroenterologist who refused to be labeled a psychiatrist, and who loved to poke fun at the analysts by asserting: "No matter what you people say, you've got to eat, first!"

Bowman cautioned me not to minimize the importance of what the psychoanalysts were teaching us. Freud and the others had contributed enormously to our understanding of neurosis and emotional disorder, and even to the emerging field of 'psychosomatic' medicine, linking many physical disorders like peptic ulcer and hypertension to psychological and emotional turmoil. Those who studied and practiced this were beginning - but just - to bring psychiatry back into the fold of respectable medical practice, from which it had steadily drifted away.

Psychiatry had never held much interest for most physicians. Partly this arose from ancient traditions and beliefs about the essentially sinful or evil forces thought to play a part in mental disease, society's rejection of the mentally ill and penchant for locking them up and even throwing them into chains, and the absence of any consistently successful approach to their treatment. The common association of late-stage syphilis with insanity contributed to a nihilistic, hopeless view of this form of human ill.

Freud, himself a physician and neurologist, changed all that, but only for a small, select group of troubled people. His explorations and explications of the unconscious part of the mind, of the eternal struggle between impulses toward good and evil, illustrated by the workings of Superego and Id, his explanations of early childhood experiences, sexuality, dreams and obsessions, all brilliantly reasoned and based on exhaustive sessions with patients embodying a process called free association, seemed to open up an understanding of many of life's most profound and troubling mysteries.

The process he used was nothing like Sir William Osler or any other 'legitimate' physician could have imagined. It involved a daily 'hour' (generally precisely 50 minutes) of contact between patient and therapist. The patient had to meet strict requirements for the process to succeed. He could not be crazy. He had to have superior intelligence. He had to be utterly obedient to the rule that he appear every day at the same time, arriving promptly and assuming a relaxed position, lying on his back on the therapy couch, not looking at the therapist but speaking freely about whatever came into his mind.

And, of course, he had to be able to pay the fee, on time, for his daily treatments, which could extend over a period of four to seven years.

There were rules for the therapist as well. He could not take a history or conduct a physical examination, and was never to touch the patient. He did not greet him or engage in any polite social conventions of conversation. He could neither express sympathy or approval or condemnation, limiting himself to such brief verbalizations as, "How did that make you feel?" "Why did you say that?" "Really?" "Tell me more." Never "Hello" or "See you tomorrow." Sometimes he said nothing at all during the session, seated out of the patient's sight at the head of couch. Sometimes the patient didn't say anything either, for the whole 50 minutes, but was expected to come back the next day and talk about that.

The process may well have been designed by Freud as an investigative tool based mainly on his belief that the unconscious, a veritable treasure trove of memories and feelings deeply buried but capable of excavation and examination, could be coaxed out into the open as a person freely associated - jumped from thought to thought until something important came up - in a 'safe' setting, and that doing this would lead to "insight," that would free the patient from unrealistic, 'neurotic' remnants of childhood fears and conflicts that he should have given up long ago and that were causing him trouble.

No psychotic person, his mind filled with delusions and his reality confused by visual and auditory hallucinations, could possibly do this.

'Neurotic' persons, sufficiently motivated and financed and articulate and self-preoccupied, on the other hand, could, and did. Freud wrote brilliantly about them.

His following steadily grew, and formed a kind of cult with strong resemblance to some religions. It was highly exclusive. Institutes were formed, to which applicants for membership in this elite group turned for a lengthy 'training analysis' to cleanse them of their own neurotic hang-ups and for training in the strictly prescribed behavior of the true psychoanalyst. Clinical reports and papers flowed. Psychoanalysis developed a kind of snob appeal, and it became fashionable to refer, offhand, of course, to "my analyst." who supposedly said this or that but probably never said much of anything.

The trend in psychotherapy among the great bulk of psychiatrists was toward something called 'dynamic' or psychodynamic therapy. This was an attempt to utilize as many of Freud's concepts as possible without imposing the strict rules of the analytic couch. This held sway because most people couldn't afford to spend six or seven years looking for insight, and most physicians who went into psychiatry could not tolerate the passivity and exercise the monumental patience seemingly required of the true 'analyst.'

At Langley Porter, the psychoanalytically trained faculty did not, to their credit, attempt to recruit widely among the residents. Many of them had long since adopted modifications in the strict regimen that the classicists in the group prescribed, but they were quiet about it. In addition, they were not eager to have too many 'analysts' running loose and competing for what was already a limited market, though they would have denied this.

Most people - ordinary, middle class folks with fairly traditional attitudes about privacy, and right and wrong, proper and improper, would not voluntarily go to a psychiatrist for treatment at mid-century. If you were crazy, you were locked up in a remote State Hospital somewhere out in the boondocks. If not, but felt you had problems, you should be able to take care of them yourself, sometimes with the help of family, or friends, or bartenders or, in extreme cases, ministers. There was great mystery about what psychiatrists actually *did*, besides just *talk*, and most people were reluctant to spend money on that.

The emergence of psychoanalysis as a kind of fashionable, elitist activity of the upper socio-economic class, helped break down the old barriers. A small number of 'graduates' from the psychoanalytic couch began to boast a little about their experience. Some psychiatric terms began to be heard in movies and even in polite society. The 'Oedipus Complex' was a favorite, as was 'inferiority complex.' 'Repression,' 'sibling rivalry,' even (whispered) 'penis envy' started to show up, and Doctor Benjamin Spock began producing Freudian-inspired handbooks absolutely necessary for the correct raising of children.

Briefly, although it is not quite over, even the Halls of Justice seemed to be littered with psychiatrists testifying about the psychological underpinnings of criminal behavior, too often seeming to be offering excuses for it, and offering abstruse explanations for 'diminished capacity' and 'irresistible impulses.' "Not guilty by reason of insanity" seemed to be giving way to "forgivable by reason of emotional conflict."

Seeking help at a great institution like the University of California Medical Center at San Francisco's Langley Porter Clinic rapidly went from being a little suspect and tentative to being respectable and then even to admirable as mid-century approached. Our outpatient clinic had an abundance of patients. A few people, severely disturbed but not usually psychotic, were actually admitted as inpatients, because of their teaching 'value.'

Every patient contact was followed by a full 50-minute hour with one of the faculty. The Resident's copious notes and prodigious memory were examined in detail as to the meaning and the objective of everything the student-therapist said or did. Criticisms were made, corrections suggested, and little lectures and sermons were given. Such was the learning process, designed not merely to help the Resident understand his patient, but, more importantly, himself. It was not fun, and not intended as such. The goal was to turn out properly trained psychodynamic psychiatrists, properly applying the great truths revealed by the master, Freud, and just possibly able to help some of his patients in some unspecified way.

At some point during my Langley Porter days, it was decided by the powers that be, to conduct a trial of a new development in the treatment of alcoholism, called the 'conditioned reflex' treatment. Based on Pavlov's work with dogs in Russia, the idea was to produce in alcoholics a conditioned response to alcohol that caused intense nausea and vomiting whenever the poor soul had a drink. Presumably, and hopefully, this would so sour him on the stuff that he would not go on drinking.

A large room on the top floor of the clinic was remodeled to resemble quite a nice tavern. It was carpeted, mirrored behind the handsome mahogany bar, lighted softly, and filled with popular tunes, played quietly. There were half a dozen tables with soft leather chairs. A small staff (nurses, actually) were outfitted as serving girls, to their delight, and they circulated among the tables taking orders for any liquor the unsuspecting victim desired, no matter how expensive.

The lucky patients selected for this experimental treatment were taken, two or three at a time, up to the cocktail lounge first thing in the morning. This was agreeable to them, and not at all unusual, since many alcoholics began their drinking as early as possible every day.

Before they left the ward for the lounge upstairs, they were without fanfare given an injection. It was not customary, in those days, for any patient to be so presumptuous as to ask what he was getting as medication, and they never did. In this case they were getting a good-sized dose of a powerful emetic, appropriately called emetine. It did not have any effect until something - anything - was introduced into the stomach. Wholly unaware of what was about to happen, the patient would happily order a shot of Jack Daniels or a fine scotch and soda, and toss it down.

Within minutes, his blood pressure would fall precipitously, sweat would break out on his brow, and he would experience major waves of nausea, followed by copious vomiting. The bar girl/nurses would rush to his side, solicitous and concerned, put a cool wet cloth on his brow and comfort him until the episode passed. No mention was made of the emetine still circulating in his bloodstream.

The episode was soon over, and he was offered another drink with expressions like, "Boy, you could really use a pick-me-up after that! What'll you have?" He would order, drink, and once again have an extremely unhappy vomiting episode. At this point he was told he must have some 'bug' and probably should hold off on further drinking until tomorrow, and he usually agreed.

Back on the ward, there were usually no further ill effects, and the drinker soon forgot about his adventure and looked forward to another morning in our handsome lounge, drinking the finest booze available. Free, at that!

The next morning the same thing took place. Never did one of the patients connect the shot he got in the morning with his nausea and vomiting later, even after half a dozen repetitions. True, he was deeply troubled by what seemed to be a growing tendency to tolerate alcohol badly, often switching drinks or brands in the hope of finding something he could hold down, but always with the same result.

After a week or so, the patient began to drink his drink more tentatively, hesitating before tossing it down, waiting apprehensively to see if it would happen again, as it always did. Not long after that, he would react to alcohol even when his morning shot was nothing but saline solution - no emetine at all. It wasn't long before these long-time alcoholics actually started to decline cocktails and elect fruit juice, without unpleasant consequences.

Everyone believed we had hit on a cure for a disorder previously considered incurable. A score or more of patients were thus "conditioned," and sent back home. On follow-up visits, some of them reported, shaking their heads in wonder, that even the sight of a billboard advertising whiskey or gin made them feel nauseated. Success!

Premature. We hadn't studied our Pavlov closely enough.

Pavlov had pointed out that a conditioned reflex needed to be 'reinforced' periodically to become permanent, and could be reversed by repetition without the usual or expected reward or consequences. Some of our 'successful' patients figured this out for themselves. These were people who seriously wanted to drink, regardless of consequences, and they set out to reverse their 'cure.'

The usual process was to rent a room in a cheap hotel, and take a bottle of cheap whiskey to the room. After locking the door and hanging out the "Do Not Disturb" sign, the graduate of our wonderful new break-through program would strip down, climb into the bathtub, take a drink, and vomit. Then he'd take another drink, and vomit again. This cycle was repeated, over and over, until finally a drink stayed down. Ordinarily that cured him from the cure, and he could resume his normal alcoholic lifestyle.

This happened often enough that the conditioned reflex treatment was judged useless, and could be dangerous for people with liver or kidney or heart disease because of the violent vomiting and retching and alterations in the body's fluids and electrolytes. Other institutions were experimenting with the treatment and uniformly reached the same conclusions.

In spite of this, one of the largest national chains of private psychiatric hospitals was using the same method forty years later, touting it as a medical breakthrough, and trying to charge insurance companies and Medicaid and Medicare for it.

Langley Porter was about as different from the barred-door wards at Fort Worth as one could imagine. The surroundings were pleasant, and while some of the wards were locked, this was not as evident; the keys were ordinary ones instead of the clanking Bastille-type hunks of steel we all carried around in Texas. This institution was designed mainly for outpatient treatment of various forms of neurosis, the training of residents to prepare them for private practice and teaching, and some research.

Some of the outpatients were fascinating. One lady of late middle age, for example, while mildly hypochondriacal, mainly had a problem with farting. She looked for all the world like exactly what she was - a well brought up, well-to-do matron from the highest level of San Francisco society. She was always well dressed, complete with hat and gloves (all 'proper' ladies wore a hat and gloves when in town in the City in those days), held herself very erect with back straight and chin high, and spoke in carefully chosen phrases uttered in a cultured, soft but resonant voice that clearly bespoke her aristocratic background and status.

The one thing marring this otherwise perfect picture of a matriarch of high San Francisco society was her unfortunate tendency to pass gas, loudly, every 60 to 90 seconds. She did this throughout any conversation, whether with another patient in the waiting room or in the doctor's office. If seated, she would lift one buttock majestically, without missing a word of what she was saying, let fly with a loud, brief expulsion of gas, and settle back down as if this were the most natural thing in the world.

Interviewing this lady, especially the first time, was considered the ultimate test of a new resident's composure, self-control and professionalism. Not all passed, but the lady never seemed to mind.

Another of the regular visitors to the Clinic was a squab rancher from Hayward, a small community across the Bay. His ranch supplied most of the finest restaurants in the area with squabs. He came in initially because he had been finding slips of paper tucked away in various places in his house, bearing obscene words and phrases. He had no idea where these came from, and assumed an enemy sneaked into his house while he was out tending his pigeons each day, and secreted these vile notes to disturb him, which they did. He had not involved the police because the whole thing was too embarrassing.

In addition, he said, he had one other little problem. He was required by some mysterious power to count, accurately, all the letters in all the highway signs he encountered on the trip from Hayward across the Bay Bridge to San Francisco, every time he made the trip. Both ways. This took a long time, sometimes over two hours to make the 30-minute drive, and had caused his arrest on numerous occasions for obstructing traffic. It also required that he be given an appointment in mid-day, so as to permit him to come and go when there was no rush hour traffic.

Besides these two classical examples of obsessive-compulsive psychoneurosis, which made for excellent teaching sessions as residents struggled valiantly and always unsuccessfully to free these people from their really weighty burdens, there were many cases of anxiety neuroses characterized by panic attacks; phobias that kept people from venturing out of their houses except with guardians of some sort; people who couldn't sleep and others who slept too much; people with paranoid personalities who suspected nearly everybody; a couple of kleptomaniacs repeatedly brought in by police who had come to know them well; and a few schizophrenics and manic-depressives who were not yet sick enough to be locked away in the State Hospital system.

Some of the schizophrenics were given a newer form of treatment called insulin 'shock' or, more accurately, insulin 'coma' therapy. Insulin, discovered only 15 years earlier, was still being extracted from the pancreas glands of cows and pigs, and had been found to be effective in lowering the excessively high blood sugar levels now considered dangerously low, but the effect could be reversed by giving the person some sugar, preferably the simple form of it, glucose, that the body converts all carbohydrates into to use as fuel.

The dropping blood sugar level resulting from the insulin injection causes weakness, sweating, confusion, falling blood pressure and ultimately coma and death. Someone had discovered, somehow (probably by accident) that some people with schizophrenia seemed to improve after repeated episodes of insulin-induced near-coma, so this was believed to be a promising new treatment for this commonest of the serious mental diseases. While no deaths had been reported, at least in our clinic, there were any number of frightening episodes when patients' comas became too deep, and intravenous injections of glucose to reverse the insulin effect were next to impossible because the patient's veins had collapsed as he went into shock. Some patients did improve, however, even quite dramatically, but eventually the treatment fell into disfavor and was mostly given up.

By the end of that second year of psychiatric residency training, so different from the year spent with the far more seriously, and often hopelessly, sick patients at Fort Worth, I was beginning to have some serious doubts and misgivings about psychiatry and about medicine in general. It was hard to pin down with any precision, but I was increasingly aware that I had been, like most physicians I was encountering, over-trained and under-educated.

Ever since abandoning my career as a homeless person, hitchhiking and riding freight trains, my life had been a headlong rush, not to get truly educated, but rather to get the training prescribed for anyone wanting to get a ticket certifying him as legally able to carry on this trade. Largely gone was the idealistic drive to go out among my fellow humans and relieve their suffering and save lives, disappearing almost unnoticed under an avalanche of mostly irrelevant, often trivial, never to be used details of biology, chemistry, physics, bacteriology, pathology, physiology, and crude techniques for violating the integrity of the human body in the hope, rarely borne out by solid research and consistent results, that some good would result.

This is not to say that the whole effort had been for naught, and the medical miracles that occurred or were refined during the second half of the century prove without question that much good can come from medical education and research into areas hardly yet dreamed of. But as I entered into my third year of postgraduate specialty training in an area of human suffering perhaps more pervasive and crippling than any other, I had an overwhelming sense that physicians, in the main, didn't really know very much, rarely actually knew what they were doing, and ordinarily didn't affect the course of a patient's illness very much at all.

Thirty-five years later, a careful statistical study in California showed that the counties with the smallest number of physicians, per capita, also had the smallest death rates. No one was sure what that meant, if anything.

Despite my growing unease with my hallowed profession, and growing feelings of hopelessness about psychiatry and psychiatrists, it was a matter of great joy when the Navy, in which I continued to serve on active duty as a medical officer though working full-time in a civilian institution, agreed to let me continue on at Langley Porter for my third post-graduate year, in a fellowship status. Since they (the Navy) paid me throughout my training, I was expected to pay them back by serving two years for each year of residency training, once it was completed. This seemed reasonable enough; after all, I had made it all the way through World War II without once being shot at, and surely owed the country something.

The only condition that the Navy attached to this third year was that I put in some time, as needed, at either or both of the two Naval Hospitals in the Bay Area, at Mare Island in Vallejo at the north end of the Bay, and at the newly opened Oak Knoll, in Oakland.

Then, to these three locales - Langley Porter, Mare Island and Oakland - I added a fourth. Because of the growing demand for psychiatrists in private practice, as therapy became more accepted by decent people and we had yet to develop the hordes of "therapists" and "counselors" who have sprung up in the last decade, most poorly trained and wholly unfit as substitutes for psychiatrists and well-trained clinical psychologists, and encouraged by several of the Langley Porter faculty, I decided to start a small private practice in my free evenings.

A half block from the Clinic, I rented the ground floor of a small, old duplex. It had a little room just inside the front door that was perfect for a waiting area for the one patient at a time who would occupy it. That led through a door to the living room, of fair size with vaulted ceiling, a fireplace, and a large bay window. At the back, opposite the bay window, lay a dining room screened off by sliding doors. Behind that were a kitchen, bath, and small bedroom.

On the floor of the living room, destined to be treatment room, I placed a deep green shag rug, and painted the walls a matching, very dark Lincoln green. The vaulted ceiling was left white, and the woodwork and fireplace surround were given a matching coat of white enamel. Against the wall opposite the fireplace sat the couch, to be used optionally by any patient who wished. In front of the bay window, draped to the floor in off-white muslin, were the therapist's chair, a comfortable but modest stuffed red leather chair and ottoman with a fine brass lamp and small side table next to it. At the other end of the room was an off-white leather wingback chair for the patient who preferred sitting up to lying on the armless and backless therapy couch. A highly conventional old English hunting print hung on the wall above the couch, and another above the fireplace.

The 20th Century not yet having reached its halfway point, people still did not simply walk in to psychiatrist's offices off the street requesting treatment. They were referred by other physicians, mostly other psychiatrists, less often by former patients or family members. Those of us new guys lucky enough to be Langley Porter fellows got our patients from faculty members, most of them well-established and well-regarded private practitioners. My particular benefactor, Dr. Gliebe, stood out from most of the traditional psychoanalysts both in his appearance, which was more like that of a friendly, warm old-fashioned general practitioner, and his speech, remarkably free from the special jargon of the Freudians.

Dr. Gliebe received far more referrals than he could possibly accommodate in his schedule, and he referred on to me a steady stream of patients. It wasn't until several years had passed and I was on to far different challenges that I realized that almost every person he referred, with a few notable exceptions, had a significant alcohol dependency problem, along with serious emotional problems. We were being taught, in those days, that alcohol abuse and alcoholism were always symptoms of underlying neurotic disorders, which could be treated with conventional psychodynamic psychiatric methods, or they were manifestations of an underlying character disorder, in which case they couldn't be treated at all.

Established psychiatrists at that time in San Francisco charged twenty dollars an 'hour,' while new, younger ones like me got 15 dollars for our 50 minutes. A few great and famous psychiatric personages sometimes got $25, but that was unusual. Patients in classical analysis were seen five days a week. Most of the rest came in once a week except during periods of crisis when the frequency could be temporarily increased.

It was my plan to employ the techniques of psychodynamic psychiatry, charge fifteen dollars per session, let the patient lie down on the couch if desired, or sit in the wingback chair. I would begin by encouraging a clear, honest description of what was bothering the person who came to me, assuring her (most patients were women) of my impartiality and non-judgmental position, whatever she might tell me, and the absolute secrecy of our shared thoughts and words. That usually took up the first session.

In the next few sessions I would take a thorough, searching but not prying, personal history going as far back in life as the patient could remember. I wanted to know about what she could tell me of the circumstances of her birth, the configuration and relationships within her family, her early development, school history, specially recalled incidents in childhood, sexual development - very hard for most people to talk about then, and still - occupational history, and marital history.

Early on, I would ask the patient to have a complete, thorough physical examination with all results sent to me. We would then discuss the findings.

The personal history could take many sessions, and memories would beget other memories of things long 'forgotten' but sometimes of great significance and importance to the problems at hand. Frequently things would be thought of, or remembered, in between sessions, and eagerly brought in the next time. A little judicious prodding often produced a kind of free association that was not really 'free' but could still effectively contribute to an individual's healthy self-awareness and some level of insight into what was going on, and going wrong, in her current life.

Commonly, the patient would ask at some point for a judgment. That could be given, cautiously, but only in terms of what the therapist believed society's judgment might be, without endorsing or disputing it.

Frequently, patients ask for advice or even instructions as to 'what to do.' It is easier than one might think to fall into the trap of giving this (after all, as the therapist, you are much smarter and free from all possible hang-ups!) but if you have any sense, you never do it.

Sometimes a patient begins to express romantic feelings toward the therapist. When this comes from a reasonably - or maybe extremely - attractive female whose charms you have duly noted and who doesn't seem very sick anyway, it is important to maintain a friendly, accepting, understanding, intelligent, concerned - in a word, psychiatric - demeanor, with no hint of being surprised, flattered, nervous, uncaring, overly caring, unimpressed or overly impressed. The thoughts need to be talked about and gently interpreted. This is the transference situation that the analysts talk about, and can be very tricky, leading to disastrous consequences for the patient if improperly dismissed, and for both the therapist and the patient if improperly pursued.

Hopefully, after perhaps a dozen sessions, more or less, the patient shows signs of some relief from whatever brought her in, and some understanding of herself and the origins and reasons for her feelings. A 'trial period' of a few weeks without sessions, possibly by a follow-up meeting to finalize the relationship or extend it for a time if that seems necessary, may be proposed and accepted. Otherwise, therapy can go on - and on and on - and inordinate amounts of time can be spent to no clear or good end.

Different systems work for different therapists as well as different patients, and there are no hard and fast rules. It became clear to me during this excursion into unsupervised individual psychotherapy that there were unlimited possibilities for abuse of the process. Patients can - and not infrequently are - trained to be perpetual patients, permanently dependent upon "therapy" that is subjective and subject to innumerable transmutations and corruptions.

The process can become the patient's principal or only source of recreation and diversion. What may begin as a valid and legitimate self-examination to root out fears and fantasies that should long since have been abandoned can turn into an even more pathological self-preoccupation and an unhealthy kind of self-absorption and self-love that precludes healthy relationships with others and with the real world.

The psychiatrist's professional ancestors are said to be the witch doctors of yore. But his family tree also contains some snake oil salesmen and gypsy fortune tellers and voodoo practitioners, and his descendants are an even more motley crew.

Therapists abound, with those of no real training or competence far outnumbering the legitimate ones, among whom there are more than a few who are not so hot themselves. Exploitive, greedy, fundamentally ignorant, self-proclaimed "counselors" can do untold damage and harm as they wade heedlessly through the indescribable complexities and vulnerabilities of the mind and spirit, getting rich as they do it.

Sadly, no one has yet come up with a way to control this.

In a culture such as ours still is, wherein work has value, effort is respected if not always rewarded, and being productive is still considered desirable, the role and value of the psychiatrist who may seem to do little more than the friend or pastor or elder once did for those who are troubled, can seem to be of questionable worth. Having worked at many jobs on the way to my private office with its comfortable leather chairs and couch and cozy fireplace, I often felt, uneasily, that I wasn't *doing* anything to justify my $15, at least some of the hours. It may be easier to justify now, with pills to prescribe, but at ten times the old price, I wonder.

One other problem, essentially economic in character, also proved troubling. Even though I had 'earned' my entire way through my education, by working and winning scholarships, I couldn't really claim to have paid for it. Other people paid for it: churches and philanthropists and government, meaning my fellow citizen-taxpayers. They had made, relatively speaking, a huge investment in me. Were I to devote all that investment to just a few new people a year, keeping my patients in therapy six months or so each, it seemed like a poor return on that large investment. And certainly not justified by the outcomes.

Those were the thoughts that were to direct my entire future professional life, although at the time I did not recognize that.

One of my first 'private' patients proved also to be one of the most troubling. Carole was about 19. She had run away, in a sense, from her highly successful, intensely controlling father who owned a large company in Minneapolis. My principal benefactor, Dr. Gliebe, had referred her, cautioning me that she might in fact prove to be psychotic, and that she posed a suicide risk but could not be committed, in her present state.

Carole opted from the first to use the couch, but insisted on lying on it face down. She was tall, slender, and generally well groomed. At first she seemed extremely shy and almost withdrawn, answering questions with monosyllables, and never looking directly at me. Little by little her history came out, describing a materially blessed but sharply restricted adolescence dominated daily by her powerful father. She had made her way to San Francisco, she said, to escape his smothering control.

For the first several sessions, she mostly kept her face buried in the soft cover of the couch, turning only slightly as she made her terse answers. As she grew more comfortable with the situation she began to keep her head turned toward me, and her answers expanded into sentences. After perhaps half a dozen therapy hours, she began lying on her side, with her head propped up on one hand. A few hours later, she actually sat up on the couch, and ultimately moved to the chair.

This little sequence of positional performances, spread out over many weeks, paralleled her progress in therapy. She gradually told a story of having started 'on her own' as a waitress, at first in small restaurants but progressing rapidly to up-scale establishments, where she often made as much as several hundred dollars a week in tips.

She soon tired of this work, and decided to seek office jobs with various major companies. To facilitate her being hired, she had developed an unusual approach involving her explicit offer to the personnel manager, during her job interview, to perform oral sex upon him there in his office. This was startlingly successful, and she obtained several fairly good jobs this way, until she found one she really liked, and stayed with it.

In spite of this bizarre (to me, anyway) approach to a business career, Carole gave every evidence of having shaken off her almost schizoid shyness and withdrawal, developed a circle of friends, moved into a decent apartment, and finally contacted her father to tell him of her success and happiness with her life, which he seemed to accept.

We agreed that she had probably achieved maximum benefit from psychotherapy, and that she could, and should, 'graduate.' She departed after a final session during which she offered, rather off-handedly, to show me how she had persuaded the personnel directors who had given her jobs, which I equally off-handedly declined, and we parted with mutual expressions of admiration and affection.

I was to see her once more, quite unexpectedly, in El Paso, Texas where I had gone to deliver a speech on 'Brainwashing' some six or eight years later, and she came to the hotel where I spoke. She had been transferred to that city as a junior executive in a firm she had been with for that whole time, and looked every bit the part. She was poised, gracious, and warmly friendly during our brief visit, and reported that life was treating her well indeed.

Not all my private patients did so well. Another woman, about 50 years old, came in because of severe marital problems. Her husband still lived at home but had moved to a separate bedroom and was demanding a divorce. She was vague about the reasons for the rift, and described a dull but untroubled marriage of many years. After many sessions, with little apparent progress, she finally, with great effort, was able to tell me the "horrible truth," something so awful that her husband wanted her gone but dared not allow the reason to come forth during divorce court hearings.

She had, she said, decided to try to enliven their increasingly infrequent and unrewarding sexual contacts by attempting to perform fellatio upon this husband of 25 years, father of her three grown children. Her clumsy attempt was not only rebuffed, but her husband flew into a monumental rage, declaring that only "sluts and whores" did such filthy things, and ordering her out of the house, on the spot. He refused to talk to her after that, except to demand that she hire a lawyer and leave permanently.

I offered to talk to her husband, alone or with her present, but he would have none of it. He was absolutely adamant about it. Over the next few sessions we talked about this kind of sexual activity, which was rarely if ever discussed in those days, and I tried to lessen her feelings of guilt and remorse for having had such thoughts. This may have helped her in some small ways, but it did not save her marriage.

Neither of those two women had any kind of alcohol problem, but nearly every other patient who came in, did. Not once, at that time, did I so much as suspect that the use of alcohol was actually the core problem. My efforts at psychotherapy directed at problems that were the result of drinking rather the reason why the person drank, as we'd been taught, were not dramatically successful, and I wondered at that. My conclusion was that Gliebe and other psychiatrists referred, mainly, patients they didn't want, recognizing that their alcohol 'symptoms' indicated that they had character disorders, then called 'psychopathic personalities.' It was widely accepted in psychiatric circles that these "psychopaths" could not be changed, significantly, by any therapeutic process then known.

"Psychopathic personalities" had been recognized for many generations. Their asocial or antisocial behavior and personality traits were sometimes ascribed to possession by evil spirits or inherited "black sheep" tendencies believed to be present at the moment of birth, if not before. It wasn't until the early part of this century that a psychiatrist by the name of Kleckley published an historic book, "The Mask of Sanity," that for the first time outlined a set of characteristics common to such people, whom he believed had a kind of 'moral insanity,' as opposed to the usual kinds of serious mental disease.

The classical psychopath, we had been taught, might resemble 'normal' people to a greater or lesser degree, but actually, down deep, was quite different. He was unable to learn from experience, unable or unwilling to plan for the future, did not consider the consequences of his acts, was heedless of the effect of his actions upon others, was impulsive, self-seeking, and in general did not experience remorse, sympathy, anxiety, guilt or regret the way most people experience these things.

What was deceptive about this condition was that the affected person could be quite bright and possess superior intelligence. To the casual observer he might seem not at all unusual, and often expressed seemingly genuine or even exaggerated feelings, like remorse, especially when caught in some antisocial act.

In place of normal anxiety, he felt impelled to 'do something,' called 'acting out,' sometimes with unhappy consequences for himself as well as others. He was never genuinely depressed, but could make quite of show of seeming to be. He was manipulative in his dealings with others, devoid of genuine loyalties, capable of outrageous, facile lying when that suited his purposes, and capable of the most heartfelt promises to mend his ways and never repeat his transgressions, with no real intention of changing at all. Finally, many with this characterologic disfigurement developed a charming, disarmingly ingenuous manner that was attractive and seductive to others.

Curiously, most psychopaths were not criminals, at least in the usual sense. They were rarely given to violence, but frequently engaged in "minor" crimes like petty thievery, cheating at cards, perpetrating small frauds, failing to repay debts and running various 'con' games. They commonly jumped bail, left town, and disappeared when caught at something serious. Finally, they paid little heed to ordinary social conventions unless that suited their purpose at the moment, clearly believed that the usual 'rules' of behavior did not apply to them, and that laws were made for dummies.

We have all known people like that in some degree, but unless they are close relatives, we don't know them very well, for they don't let us. Also, let's face it: there is a bit of a psychopath in us all, as reflected in the hallowed assertion that every man has his price. We are born psychopaths, all of us, impulsive, thoughtless, unable to plan for the future, willing through our smiles and gurgles to manipulate those around us, and, at least early on, not too good at planning for the future.

Most of us, however, can be trained out of that normal infantile condition, and such is the role and the mission of parents. Almost from earliest infancy, the encouragements, admonitions, prohibitions and consequences administered by parents are not just learned, but are introjected into ourselves and, when we finally grow up, are administered by our selves. Not so with the psychopath; not that he doesn't learn, exactly, but he doesn't learn that the lessons are important for him - only for others. He doesn't seem to experience "feelings" the way the rest of us do. Freud, who didn't spend much time on these folks, might have said that his Superego never got going, but that's just a guess.

It was easy to connect alcoholism with this disorder of character, at least on the surface. The far-gone alcoholic seems unable to profit from experience. When drinking, he is heedless of the consequences of his actions, careless about their effect on others. He swears to do better, to avoid drunkenness or possibly any drinking whatever, but goes ahead and does so. He lies about where he's been, whom he has been with, what he's been doing, when he will come home, how he will save his money and pay his bills, and seems to mean it, but doesn't follow through. He seems not to care about his wife and children, risking their lives and those of others when he drives drunk. Surely this is a character disorder?

Not usually. Maybe not ever. Descriptively it is, when the individual has alcohol in his system. When he does not, however, he may give every evidence of character traits of the highest order. Such traits are necessary for genuine achievement in art, the professions, engineering, the military, even government, and yet many who have succeeded in all of those fields have seemed to develop profound defects of character, when drinking, that are altogether incompatible with making it through West Point, or M.I.T., or medical school or learning to land a jet on an aircraft carrier or command a battalion of nuclear artillery.

Those inconsistencies in the conventional assessment of people with alcohol problems were just beginning to occur to me, in my cozy little traditional psychiatric office on the slopes of San Francisco's Mount Parnassas, but it took a lot more years and a lot more patients before I began to understand. Back then, in the 1940's, when we were being taught that nothing much could ever be done about psychopaths until they did something so bad that they had to be locked up, it was convenient to put hard cases, like alcoholics, into that hopeless category.

It is no longer "correct" or even permissible to use the term "psychopath." We have gentler terms now, like 'sociopath,' and a host of behavior disorders usually ascribed to some sort of 'abuse' in childhood, or 'stress' induced by outside forces, or poor environments, poverty, educational shortcomings, pollution, environmental degradation and probably even global warming and burning off the rainforests. However, be not deceived. Psychopaths - whatever they are called - are still with us. Some even make it to high office.

You can train someone to be a psychopath. A child who tries instinctively and quite naturally to imitate parents who by word and deed exemplify defiance of convention and contempt for traditional values having to do with honesty, loyalty, concern for others, respect for the law, compassion for infants and the disabled and the old and infirm, can hardly be expected to emerge into responsible, public spirited adulthood. However, such a person is not automatically destined to be a psychopath. Many children of horrible parents, brought up in unspeakably poor environments, have emerged as quite ordinary and sometimes entirely admirable people, in spite of all.

What all that shows, once again, is how little we actually know. There may well be genetic and developmental as well as learned aspects to this fascinating departure from what all of us 'good' people accept as normal. Nevertheless, one thing seems certain: alcoholism does not belong in this dismal category.

A famous picture depicts Freud sitting at his desk facing a line of tiny figures depicting many of the patients he studied and wrote about. Sometimes, reflecting on that year of private psychotherapeutic practice, I can almost see my own little lineup. Some of them wear expressions of relative tranquility, others look quizzically, a few glower accusingly. Such was the procession of souls who sought, trustingly or skeptically, my help with problems in their lives. I sometimes wonder how they all turned out.

Even at fifteen dollars an hour, my income from this excursion into the 'real world' of medical practice was better than I had expected, but there were a few dead beats. One of the most outstanding was, like many of the others, primarily an unrecognized alcohol problem.

Margo, my patient, was the wife of a vice-president of the Southern Pacific Railroad. The couple, childless but otherwise vastly blessed, materially, lived in a penthouse that occupied the entire top floor of a six-story building facing Golden Gate Park, with large, floor-to-ceiling windows along both sides. The apartment was so large that the main room contained no fewer than two dozen overstuffed chairs, several sofas, and a grand piano. Access was by a private, key-operated elevator, and a uniformed doorman stood guard.

In response to her husband's urgent pleading, I agreed to accept Margo as my first 'house-call' patient, since she refused to leave the penthouse for any reason and desperately needed help. My twenty dollar per session fee was readily agreed to.

On my first of perhaps twenty visits, I was greeted at the elevator door by a skinny little lady in her mid-fifties, weighing less than a hundred pounds and barely five feet tall. She led me to one of two facing chairs, richly upholstered and softly padded in a dimly-lit corner of the huge room. When asked about what was troubling her, she launched immediately into a description of terrible turmoil, all caused, she said, by her husband.

Several months earlier, she had come to suspect that her husband was involved romantically with a woman in his office. She challenged him and he admitted it, but insisted that it was a passing thing of no importance and now over. She had fled to her bedroom in tears and locked herself in. The next evening, when he stepped out of the elevator after work, she threw herself at him, scratching his face deeply and shrieking her outrage. This time it was he who fled to another room, locked himself in and did not leave until morning.

That night the same thing happened. The following night he came home late, expecting the worst, and despite his enormous advantage in size and strength, was again attacked, and again wounded. Over the next few days, Margo's attacks diminished in frequency and violence and her husband got better at protecting himself, but at least once a week she repeated the performance. In addition, she refused to cook; all food and wine was brought in by a caterer, and her staff of maids took care of all maintenance of both her apartment and her person. She did not converse with her husband except to curse him and his infidelity.

Ultimately, she agreed to 'talk to somebody,' and thanks to Dr. Gliebe, that was me. She was a reluctant patient, but warmed up somewhat when her cats made friends with me. These were two of the largest domestic cats I had ever seen. One was a dull white color, and the other uniformly gray. I had from time to time seen them creeping about the apartment, but paid little attention. One evening, however, the big gray cat leaped up on my chair and settled himself down against my neck, while the big white cat draped itself across my feet.

From that moment on, our therapeutic relationship improved, and every meeting was conducted with the two cats lying atop my shoulders and feet. Margo seemed to take this as verification that I was trustworthy. She talked more freely, but continued fixed on her husband's perfidy and her own suffering. After a few weeks she stopped attacking George, but she made it clear he was far from being forgiven. Therapy ended by mutual consent.

Despite repeated billings, George never paid me a cent. Margo kept on drinking wine, daily.

That third year of post-graduate training in psychiatry and neurology, centered around my fellowship year at Langley Porter, turned out to be a full, sometimes exciting educational experience of many parts. My evening private practice flourished, more than doubling my Navy pay. Work at the clinic put me in the role of an instructor, reviewing junior residents' encounters with patients. Senior staff meetings were open to me, and revealed some wholly new dimensions to the workings both of private psychiatrists and of the University.

The staff decided to put on a two-week 'refresher course' in neurology and psychiatry, designed to prepare those physicians who had completed the required three years of formal residency training as well as the two additional years of practice limited to those fields that qualified them to take the American Board of Psychiatry and Neurology examinations to anoint them, officially, as Diplomates of the Board.

My job, in connection with the course, was to attend all the lectures, scheduled for eight hours each day for the two weeks, make detailed notes of my own and obtain from each lecturer the notes he used for his presentation, and combine them to produce a syllabus. Each participant in the course would be offered the resulting document for one hundred dollars, of which I would be allowed to keep half. Nice easy deal, I figured. More like a nightmare, as it turned out.

Just as I had done during college, making notes and selling them to my classmates to use in preparation for finals, I set about to create a set of notes these people could use to get ready for the 'Boards.' The Clinic Director, Dr. Bowman, had managed to assemble all the most eminent experts from his faculty and several others in the Bay Area, and every one was an experienced teacher, highly articulate and eager to parade his enormous store of knowledge. Many of them were dignitaries who actually took part in administering the board exams.

Each night I would retype my notes, insert major portions of the material the lecturers gave me, type them in final form on the smelly, purple forms used in mimeograph machines, (Xerox having yet to develop copiers, and probably not yet even in business), and run off the fifty or sixty copies needed for all who had signed up for them. That left about three hours completely free for bathing, shaving, and sleep.

The two weeks' effort produced about six hundred pages, put together in two 300-page loose-leaf volumes - a real bargain. They were well-received, and constituted a fully comprehensive review of what was then current in the two fields. Most of it I soon put aside as my life took a wholly unexpected turn.

Before that happened, however, I had become reacquainted with the fact that I was still in the Navy. Two or three days each week the call would come for me to report either to Mare Island or Oak Knoll Naval Hospital to "help out." The Secretary of Defense at that time, a man named Johnson who had headed General Motors before taking that job, had called for a massive economy drive throughout the Armed Forces because of budget cuts. Staffs were getting short in the hospitals, as a direct result, but patient populations had not dropped.

At Mare Island, a long drive from San Francisco, I found a hospital headed by one of those doctors who had entered the service at the very outset of World War II, profited from the relatively rapid promotions that occurred during that war, and found themselves full Captains, one step below Admiral rank but destined never to go higher, and not wanting to do so. Some of these people were thrust into positions of great power and responsibility, and many perks, as more energetic, more ambitious, and often far more competent officers eagerly left the service to pursue more lucrative and prestigious civilian jobs.

The result, unfortunately, was that some grossly incompetent, poorly prepared 'senior' officers, suddenly thrust into command positions for which they were entirely unprepared but usually didn't know it, delighted with the fine quarters, houseboys and other 'perks' that went with command, hunkered down in their newfound luxury and made a real mess of the hospitals they were given to command.

The Captain commanding the hospital at Mare Island was one such. After a wholly lackluster wartime career ashore, he arrived there determined to make the most of his new, exalted status. He moved with his young wife, many years his junior, into the imposing colonnaded brick quarters reserved for the Commanding Officer. It rested atop a small hill behind the hospital and commanded a sweeping view of that structure with the Naval Shipyard and docks, and the upper reaches of San Francisco Bay spread out below.

The Captain was intensely conscious of his importance. He held himself aloof from all others (the loneliness of command), maintained a rigidly military posture at all times, appearing to march, rather than just walk, head held high, uniform impeccable, shoes brilliantly shined, hat perfectly square, eyes straight ahead. Every day at exactly the same moment he marched from his quarters down the paved drive that led in front of the new, all concrete psychiatry ward (locked; 2 stories, barred windows), then described a sharp loop just past that building, changing course 180 degrees as it headed for the hospital's main entrance in an older 4-story brick building.

At the instant he entered, a boatswain's pipe sounded, and the flag was raised on the large pole just in front of the entryway. Our day had begun.

At 5 PM (1700 hours Navy time) the flag was lowered. When it reached the hands of the sailors waiting below, the hospital door opened, the pipe sounded again, and the Captain marched out, briskly. He would retrace his steps of the morning, making the turn in the drive just past the NP (for neuropsychiatric) ward and heading up the hill toward his palatial quarters, his eager young wife, and his newborn son, the pride of his existence. With his departure, the whole hospital seemed to breathe a sigh of relief, and even the structure itself seemed to relax.

The Chief of Psychiatry, Commander Griswold, was a seasoned naval physician who had served with distinction in combat aboard several major vessels during the war. A portly, rather relaxed man in his late forties, he also had a young wife and a son about 3 years old. The Commander genuinely detested the Captain, whom he considered to be an overblown, intolerably arrogant and pompous, insufferably ignorant, stupid man. True to his naval training and discipline, he never openly criticized the Captain, which would have been mutinous, but his feelings were clear.

Commander Griswold had become incensed - truly outraged - when he had been invited, as an obligatory gesture of *noblesse oblige* - to attend one of the Captain's famous formal (dress uniforms for all) dinners at his quarters. The table was draped in an immaculate white tablecloth and set with heavy silver. A crystal chandelier hung overhead. Ten guests, in order of rank, were arranged at the sides. The Captain presided at the head of the table. To his right was seated his most senior guest, Griswold. At the Captain's left, in a high chair, sat the Captain's 9-month-old son.

At one point during the stiff, formal dinner, served by white-coated mess attendants, the infant son of the great man started to fuss, as kids will, and finally to cry. At this the Captain, having ignored this disturbance until now, reached over the tray on the high chair and pulled it forward. He then reached down to the baby's diaper and pulled it loose. When the child's genitals were exposed, the Captain slapped the exposed penis with two fingers, pulled the diaper back up, shoved the tray back into position, and resumed his reign over the diners.

Griswold nearly had a convulsion, he later said, and was barely able to keep from socking his Commanding Officer on the jaw. He was still upset about it the following Monday, and we devoted an entire Psychiatry staff meeting to trying to predict the consequences to the child's psyche. The consensus was that he was a serious suicide risk beginning in about 5 years.

The Commander and the Captain rarely had direct contact with one another, but of late the previously scanty communications from 'the Bridge' as the Captain called his office suite, had increased in number and in critical tone as the 'Old Man' tried to enforce ever tighter cost control measures on the hospital staff. These reached a new height of idiocy, in all our minds, when the Captain ordered that no one under the rank of full Commander would be allowed to use any hospital elevator, thus saving electrical costs. Since the hospital medical staff consisted of eight or nine commanders, and just three Lieutenants, Junior Grade, who did almost all the clinical work of the whole institution and who therefore really *needed* to use the elevators constantly, this new rule seemed particularly outlandish.

It was at about that same time, when the new rule came out, that the Commander began to alter his luncheon menu. Explaining that he was on a diet, he had been in the habit of drinking three dry martinis at the bar in the officers club each noon, rather than joining the rest of us in the dining room for more solid fare. Now, however, he increased his intake to 4 martinis, then 5, and finally six. This had no effect upon him whatever, as far as any of us could see, and naturally no one said anything about it to him. To each his own, so to speak. In addition, all the rest of us working in NP were far junior to him in rank.

About a week after the infamous elevator message, an interesting thing took place. One evening, as the Captain was marching in his customary grand manner up the hill, just as he made the turn at the NP ward building, a loud voice bellowed out from a partially opened window on the upper floor of the ward. Directed at the Captain, it called him a whole series of really obscene terms, reflecting upon his sexual behavior with his mother and various animals, among other things, and thoroughly damning him to Hell or worse.

The Captain could not have missed hearing this performance, but his step never faltered, his posture remained perfect, and his eyes never strayed from his straight and narrow path. Everyone else in the area heard it all, and delight reigned supreme at Mare Island.

A curt formal message from the Bridge the next morning directed the Chief of NP to maintain better control of "the more obstreperous of the patients," and for a day or two thereafter, all was quiet. Then it happened again. This time the message commanded the Service Chief to establish control. A few more days, and the "obstreperous patient" was at it again. By now the Captain had picked up his pace noticeably, and took to glancing sideways at the NP ward as he passed it. It was rumored that certain threats had been made concerning Commander Griswold's future career, and the disturbances finally died out.

Everybody in the hospital, except the Captain, knew long before that who the "obstreperous patient" really was, and the Commander was everyone's hero thereafter.

The situation at Oak Knoll Naval Hospital was quite different. It was mainly in use as a rehabilitation center for amputees still needing care following injuries sustained during the war in the Pacific five years earlier. The hospital was quite new but had been hastily constructed as a series of single-story frame structures perched on the fairly steep hills of east Oakland. The long, low buildings were poorly insulated, if at all, and each one held about forty beds in a large, open space.

The psychiatric ward was a busy one. My old friend, Commander Kahn, whom I had known at Fort Worth, was in charge of the NP Service, and was more than ever absorbed by his science fiction-writing career as his success grew. He did his job well, though, conducting daily ward rounds in traditional fashion, reviewing the work-ups of the younger psychiatrists and paying close attention to the performance of the corpsmen and nurses. Many of the amputees required considerable attention for their emotional problems arising from their amputations, but we had not yet discovered the 'Post-Traumatic Stress Syndrome,' and things like Prozac were far off in the future, so we did things that would later be called "Reality Therapy," along with PT, OT, and RT: physical, occupational, and recreation therapy, and had fairly good results.

Commonly, after loss of a limb, particularly in a young male, there occurs a serious loss of self-confidence, hopelessness, and depression that goes far beyond the realities of the problems that a lost limb undeniably generates. The Freudians, perhaps correctly, talked about this as a reflection of castration anxiety, and sometimes that connection was apparent.

An unanticipated consequence of success in dealing with these feelings was the emergence of an exaggerated form of machismo, although we hadn't heard of that word then. It took the form of racing each other down hill in their wheelchairs, and becoming highly grabby and predatory toward females. Some of the amputees became highly successful at both. Some of them suffered grievous further injuries crashing into each other, or cars or buildings, at the bottom of the hills.

Others became habitués of Oakland's seedier bars, of which there were many, and developed acute venereal infections repeatedly during their months of physical and psychological rehabilitation at our hospital. All of them shared a remarkable, carefree "don't give a damn" attitude toward both the disciplinary as well as the genitourinary consequences of their macho behavior, and we never did deal with it very effectively. I found it easy to identify strongly with these youngsters, convinced, had I lost a limb or two, that I would have done exactly as they were doing. I was reminded of our quadruple amputee at Philadelphia, with his multiple daily sexual adventures. We couldn't really be mad at him either.

My bouncing around from Langley Porter to Mare Island with its martinet Captain to Oak Knoll and over to my neat little private office involved a good bit of driving around (though I never stopped to count the letters in the road signs), and an opportunity, almost daily, to reflect upon my involuntary career in psychiatry, the seeming impossibility of ever seeing a reconciliation between mental and physical medicine, the prospects for making money in private practice and the certainty of not doing so in the Service, and my contractual as well as my ethical responsibilities toward the people of the US, who had paid my way, and toward patients I suspected I couldn't do much for in any case.

I had already been exposed to some of the best and the worst of military medicine, the finest in medical education in both private and public institutions, the practice of medicine and psychiatry among the very rich and the very poor. I had gotten to know, in some degree, a host of physicians ranging from clods and charlatans to inspired researchers and geniuses, and was unsure what position I occupied in that wide spectrum. What was clear was that almost none of it was what I had expected. Uncle Charlie was nowhere to be found. Maybe I should have stuck with being a motorcycle cop, or a fireman, or even an undertaker. Were any of those less fulfilled, less socially valuable, and less useful? My dear, sweet Mother's repeated insistence that people as lucky as we were, owed a great debt that we could never wholly repay but must forever try to settle. Was I doing that? Hell, no.

Those kinds of reflections and doubts, although I had never heard them from my seemingly blissfully fulfilled colleagues, were surely not unique or original, but I felt that they were mine alone. And as was to happen so many times throughout a long and colorful, if not highly checkered, life, Fate or History or perhaps God was about to step in to direct all my energy and thought and effort in a totally new and unexpected direction.

In this case it was the North Koreans.

On a lovely day in late June of 1950, even as I was driving around between San Francisco and Oakland and Vallejo preoccupied with myself, they sent a powerful force of soldiers, tanks, cannons and airplanes south across the 38th Parallel that ran across the Korean peninsula, determined to eliminate the political division of North from South and unify the country under their Communist dictatorship.

The President and his advisors, acting more rapidly than expected, invoked the approval of the United Nations and declared our support, including military forces, for our allies in the South. At that moment, my life changed, absolutely and forever. The Navy summoned me to Naval District Headquarters on Fell Street in San Francisco, and announced that I had the honor to be the first naval doctor to be ordered to the war in Korea.

Two days later, exactly, having given over my office and all my patients to an eager, and as it turns out, rather greedy, colleague, I boarded a four-engined C-54 airplane at Moffet Field, south of the city, and watched as the California coast disappeared behind me and the great, beautiful, blue Pacific stretched out endlessly to the west.

Along with perhaps a dozen other benumbed naval personnel, I was seated on one of a row of canvas stretchers along one side of the aircraft. The entire center space was occupied by a row of large wooden crates, about six feet high and ten feet long, securely strapped down to rings in the floor. Another row of stretchers along the opposite side of the plane was occupied by another dozen or so sailors.

We were headed, they said, for Hawaii.

My dominant sensation was a strange, unexpected sense of release, and relief. I deduced from that an unexpected realization that, good as it had seemed on the surface, what I had been doing in the Bay Area was somehow not 'right.' There had to be more to life than what was being presented there. Perhaps this is what I was meant to do. Maybe this is where the debt would start to get paid off.

Lulled by such thoughts, I ate my box lunch, dozed off and on, watched the sun slowly set as we pursued it to the west, and finally saw the lovely lights of Honolulu. Little was I to know that this was going to be my first crash landing, but it was - in the dark, on the foam, red lights flashing, terrible sparks, screeching - suddenly silence. Holy smokes!

This was my introduction to the Korean War, and an altogether new life.

William E. Mayer, M.D.

William E. Mayer, M.D.

CHAPTER 5

JAPAN

All of us aboard the ill-fated airplane were given the night off, and told to report to the airfield early the next morning. Several of our number stepped forward, clearly shaken, to declare to the officer in charge that they would never, under any circumstances including the threat of court-martial and prison, board another airplane again. We never found out what happened to them, but they were not among us at morning muster.

Five of us 'survivors' decided, as long as we were in this Pacific Paradise, to rent a convertible and try to see as much of it as possible, dark as it was. It was a typical Hawaii night - warm and humid, with soft trade winds blowing and the sweet scent of tropical flowers in the air. We raced around the city of Honolulu, still something of a small town, then up to the Pali, a high ridge above the city with a magnificent view of the lights below, and over to the Punchbowl, where lay the national cemetery with its sobering rows of grave markers. At last, thoroughly exhausted, we fell into bed at quarters on the base, at historic Pearl Harbor. We were also soaked through; it had rained off and on the whole night, and we had stubbornly kept the top down on our convertible.

The next morning was a typical Hawaiian daybreak, clear and warm with gentle breezes that caused the tall emperor palms to sway gently alongside the runway. We boarded an identical but older C-54 airplane reluctantly and a bit apprehensively, and were soon headed once again toward our wartime destiny, seated again on stretchers along the sides of the cargo-laden plane.

Our first stop was a place called Johnson Island, some hours to the west and as different from Hawaii as it was possible to be. There was almost nothing above ground except a small makeshift-looking control tower and a few scruffy palm trees. We all got out and walked around, watching the antics of gooney birds on the runway. That was to be the last break for many hours over the next three days.

Our itinerary took us to a number of the storied islands that American soldiers and sailors and marines, at terrible cost in lives and limbs, had wrested from the Japanese forces in one horribly bloody battle after another. We touched down and refueled at Saipan, Guam, Kwajalein and finally Manila. Each seemed hotter and more humid than the last. For the first time I saw it rain so hard that a mist about a foot deep rose from the ground, obscuring it, as the rain poured down, then stopped abruptly as a raging sun took over.

After one last stop in Okinawa, we flew on to Tokyo and were at last free - exhausted, smelling terrible, hungry, unshaven and a miserable sample of US fighting forces. Tokyo, five years after WWII ended, showed no outward signs of the terrible damage inflicted by our firebombs and explosives, except that much of it looked like a huge, hastily thrown together shantytown. There were hordes of people on the streets, rushing this way and that, many rickety bicycles, almost no cars or trucks or busses. Most people wore what looked to be old clothes; here and there a woman clopped along in wooden geta, a flat sandal raised on two little wooden crosspieces that held the sole an inch or two above the street, wearing a faded kimono, her hair piled in a neat, twisted mound. All in all it was sad, in addition to being unbelievably hot and humid.

My destination was the port city of Yokosuka, some thirty miles or so to the south, past the much larger port of Yokohama. The Japanese Navy's principal base was at Yokosuka, and we had taken it - along with everything else in that country - for our own use and control. This was the Occupation.

As one traveled south past Yokohama and into the countryside dotted with small but crowded towns, everything seemed much more intact. Most of the prewar houses were apparently undamaged and while most houses were tiny, they all seemed to have little fenced yards and gardens, and the larger houses were often impressive. Almost all had peaked roofs with tiles, upturned ends on the long beams, and walls that included traditional shoji, the beautiful, multi-paned panels made of light wood and covered with rice paper. This scene, with the picturesque houses, steep hillsides, winding streets, lush foliage and myriads of tiny, precisely groomed rice paddies, was entrancing.

The whole environment, with its many shrines, its rushing crowds of little people, all shorter than I, (that was a first!) its special smells unlike any I had ever known, its air of industriousness, and its marvelously groomed, tiny fields and gardens and houselots, struck me as so different and so foreign as to be impossible to take in all at once. I determined during that first trip in the Navy jeep, passing the enormous, beautiful statue of the ineffably tranquil DaiButsu - the great Buddha - and past the towering statue of the Goddess of Mercy high on a wooded hill, that I would plunge myself into this strange, exotic place, absorb all I could of it, and learn all that a Westerner possibly could about how it came to be.

The question that struck me most forcefully, was how this collection of quaint, busy little people, in this beautiful, intensely cultivated and cultured place, could have turned into a powerful, deadly, modern military force that nearly wiped out our Pacific Fleet, and nearly defeated giant America in a huge war over half the globe, conquering untold millions of people and a dozen countries in a whole series of often cruel, heartless battles and campaigns. Everything now seemed to lay peaceful and tranquil as it had always been, as if nothing at all had happened.

We passed through the gate to the U.S. Naval base, Yokosuka, and once again I was aware that I had entered a different world. The huge base, with its many drydocks and giant cranes, still retained in the design of its buildings and little cultivated garden plots a distinctly Oriental flavor, and the mixed scent of charcoal fires, sandalwood and flowers that had greeted me as I left the airplane, persisted here, stronger than ever.

My quarters were relatively palatial for a junior officer. They consisted of a two-room suite in the Officers Club building, done in a style that could only have been created for a setting in a Somerset Maugham novel. The rooms were rather dark, with heavy wooden furniture and hand-rubbed mahogany walls. There was a massive head- and footboard on the ample bed, with a draped mosquito netting hanging over the whole thing. There were several large leather chairs, a stout chest and matching desk, and a beaded curtain separated the two rooms. It came complete with a full-time houseboy, a wholly unexpected luxury.

Jiro, my new houseboy, was very shy and retiring, almost standoffish. He spoke some English, hesitantly, and instantly disappeared from sight when there were no chores to be done, but reappeared as if by magic when I spoke his name. I never did find out where he hid. In typical American fashion, I tried to make friends with him right at the start, but it was soon evident that he did not welcome that, and I carefully avoided pushing him. His work was excellent; he kept my uniforms laundered and ironed, my shoes shined, my raincoat handy, and everything in the rooms neat and immaculate. Over the ensuing months his reserve softened a bit, and once he even confessed to me his difficulty in distinguishing one American from another, since we all had red faces and big noses, and therefore we all looked alike!

Jiro, as he called himself, was an orphan from Tokyo, where his parents died during the war. He was, he said, 19 years old, but I later discovered that due to the curious way the Japanese figured age (he was 1 at birth, 2 the first New Year,) he was in reality 17. His ambition was to go to college and become an engineer, and he worked for us to earn enough money to do so. Without doubt, he eventually did just that.

The hospital where I was to work contained 80 beds had a major and a minor surgery, small lab, and a staff of five physicians. It occupied five or six two-story buildings, connected by central hallways on both levels, which led to a dozen or more identical buildings now converted into quarters for married Navy men and their families. The whole set of connected buildings had been built originally as a large Naval hospital, but our forces didn't need anything that big when the Occupation started in 1945.

The medical staff of five doctors was headed by the commanding officer, one of those wholly incompetent carryovers from the big war, with the rank of Captain. He did no medicine whatever, even, as it turned out, during a major medical crisis, as we were to discover. The other four of us, all Lieutenants, Junior Grade, included a general surgeon, an internist, an ob-gyn specialist, and myself - doing the neurology and psychiatry.

One memorable night, very late, the Captain called our surgeon from his bed, ordering him to come immediately to the Captain's quarters with a complete surgical 'kit,' because our leader's pet dog was evidently choking on a bone and needed surgery. He naturally obeyed, there being no real grounds for disobeying a direct order, only to find that the pooch had spontaneously and miraculously recovered. We four 'J.G.'s' had a wonderful indignation session over the incident that surely bordered on the mutinous.

The atmosphere at the base was one of genuine wartime excitement, undoubtedly similar to the early days of WWII. Ships of all descriptions were arriving daily, and left taking along most of the officers and men stationed at Yokosuka, leaving their wives and children suddenly alone. The officers club, nightly, had a kind of anxiously festive air of forced gaiety much like most New Years Eve parties. Officers from the ships putting in after many weeks at sea headed, as seagoing men customarily do, for the club, to dine and dance with the left-alone wives, nurses, Red Cross ladies and unattached female civilian employees who showed up in increasing numbers to lend emotional support to those about to sail off into harm's way.

Food at the club was superb, and ridiculously cheap. A huge, magnificent steak or an enormous broiled lobster dinner cost two dollars. Drinks, including the finest scotch and bourbon, were twenty-five cents. A really big evening could reach four dollars, each. There were a number of Japanese dance orchestras available for a relative pittance, each trying to outdo the others in precise imitation of the great bands then popular in the US, sometimes with hilarious results, and band intermissions were filled with dancing girls, jugglers, magicians and other entertainers.

The Occupation, for most of its participants, provided the best of all possible worlds. The US forces became the owner-landlords of nearly everything in the country that was intact and desirable. Sergeants customarily were given the large homes of rich, prominent Japanese businessmen and government officials to occupy as their quarters, usually equipped with several servants that the departed owners left behind to look after things.

The finest, most modern office building in Tokyo, the Dai Ichi building, just across the moat and the boulevard from the Imperial Palace grounds had become MacArthur's office and headquarters. The grand old Imperial Hotel, designed by Frank Lloyd Wright and put up after Tokyo's disastrous 1923 earthquake and fire, was occupied by senior US officers and visiting dignitaries there to see the American emperor. Another famed downtown hotel, the Sanno, was similarly used for senior US military people. The fine old Kempae Tai building, also across from the Imperial Palace and once occupied by the infamous "thought police," upon whose roof captured American aviators were beheaded after interrogation, was now the headquarters for our own Counter-Intelligence Corps.

Golf had appeared on the upper class social scene in the years just before the war. The courses had all been designed, laid out, and their construction overseen by famous U.S. golf professionals of the day, like Bobby Jones and Gene Sarazen. Only very rich businessmen and noblemen played, and they did so with characteristic Japanese ritualism. The senior executive in a foursome would bring along perhaps a dozen of his highest ranking subordinate executives. The other members of the foursome, depending on their status as determined by an impossibly complex set of criteria, would bring along lesser numbers.

A round of golf on one of the magnificent courses around Tokyo, then, would look for all the world like a major tournament. The large group of onlookers would gather in a crowd around each player as he took his shots, bursting into applause after well-hit balls and into loud laughter - not, in this special situation, considered derogatory or offensive in the slightest - after flubbed shots. Each player had at least two caddies, usually pretty young girls, and a huge bag of clubs. Lost balls were ignored. Most rules were also ignored. The game took hours, with frequent pauses for refreshments, and everyone left feeling happy and exalted.

All that ended with the Occupation. We owned all the golf courses. Those of us who used them also used two caddies, usually the same pretty young girls, but we didn't bring along an audience of rapt subordinates.

We also owned a superb, exquisite hotel nestled among towering pines and cryptomeria the size of giant redwoods, a mile up the slopes of Mount Fuji about sixty miles from Tokyo. That magnificent, nearly perfect cone with its immaculate white crown rising more than two miles above the sea could almost serve as the official logo for all of Japan. Revered as a supernatural Being, it provides a beautiful background for the countless lovely scenes that abound throughout the main island, Honshu.

'Our' hotel on Mt. Fuji, aptly named The Fujiya, had been the special province of the mighty of Japan: hereditary nobles and the Daimyo, powerful industrialists who controlled most of the important business and finance of the entire Japanese empire. It was built into and out from the mountainside, and was literally a fairyland of winding paths, fishponds, beautiful plantings, tame parrots, lovely rooms and suites and an array of wonderful Japanese baths.

The largest of the baths could accommodate a dozen or more people. Like all baths in that cleanliness-obsessed land, it was so hot that it seemed at first impossible to tolerate. A few feet away, in the same large, tiled room, was a swimming pool about sixteen by twenty feet, fed by icy water falling into it over a lovely rock wall as long as the pool itself. Overhead, the entire ceiling was glass. Above it giant koi, the beautiful Japanese carp, swam gracefully about in perhaps two feet of water. Above that was the sky.

The idea was, a bather entered the hot 'tub,' and soaked there for as long as he could stand it and then climbed out to dive into the icy water below the waterfall. When hypothermia started to set in, back he went (this time much faster and more easily) to the hot tub, only to repeat the sequence two or three times until he reached the desired level of exhilaration and exhaustion and returned to his sumptuous quarters high above in the hotel proper.

As with all 'our' Occupation properties, this fine old hotel went back to its owners when the occupation ended, and I am told that today a night at the Fujiya can cost seven or eight hundred dollars and up. We paid two dollars a night. Food was another dollar. Life was good. Some of the mixed parties in the big tub and pool room were said to be historic occasions.

One of the last things I did in the two days the Navy allowed me for closing up my practice and arranging my affairs prior to flying off to war in the Far East, was to buy a small car, arrange to have it modified slightly and then shipped to me at Yokosuka on a commercial freighter. I had been told that with the outbreak of war in Korea, neither families nor private vehicles would be sent at Navy expense to Japan, but no regulation existed preventing me from arranging for the car at my own expense. I had to have a car.

After about six weeks in Yokosuka, the car finally arrived. It was a small, dark red Morris Minor convertible with a tan canvas top. I had had the dealer adjust one of the front seats so that it could be shoved far forward under the steering wheel, while the back could be lowered to form a fairly level platform between the front and rear seats. It was just possible to stretch out on this makeshift bed, and actually sleep. It was my intention to use this miniature camper to explore Japan, and I did exactly that.

Occupation Regulations forbade eating in local restaurants or staying in 'unauthorized' lodgings such as inns and hotels. We were also not to drink any 'local' water or consume any fresh produce that had not been thoroughly washed in an 'authorized' disinfectant.

I equipped that little car with a blanket, a small pillow, a five gallon can for gasoline and another for water, and set out after work each Friday to explore Japan. The hospital was not especially busy, since as yet there were no substantial Navy or Marine forces engaged in combat in Korea, and my war was turning out to be quite a nice little adventure in cultural anthropology.

Before my car arrived, I acquired a bicycle and explored the naval base and the surrounding areas constantly in my free time. The base backed up against some cliffs, perhaps a hundred feet high. At their base were a series of tunnels, each large enough for a small train or a large truck to enter to deposit munitions and other supplies. The tunnels were poorly secured and I managed to penetrate many of them, to explore the treasures therein.

In one such tunnel I found what appeared to be a cache of large bottles reminiscent of our big aspirin bottles in the clinic in Indiana Harbor. These were filled with a slightly oily, pungent yellow liquid that obviously had some medical purpose, judging by the stretchers and aid kits stored in that same space. I found a small empty bottle and took some of the yellow liquid to determine what it was. The hospital pharmacist recognized it immediately as an old-fashioned disinfectant, no longer in use in the US but still effective in cleaning out contaminated wounds. It was soon to prove a Godsend. Little else stored there seemed to have much use for us.

The hospital treated mostly conventional problems - pneumonias, fractures, diarrheal disease, childbirths - but a few exotic things, like hemorrhagic fever and malaria that I had not seen previously. Occasionally there was an exciting case, like the young lieutenant admitted as an emergency after his Japanese lover amputated his penis and testicles following an evening of heavy drinking and heavy sex that he had announced would be their last night together. Both his equipment and his former lover disappeared and were never seen again.

Venereal infections were an ever-present problem. Gonorrhea was still officially declared to be a 'misconduct' diagnosis requiring punishment as well as treatment, so sailors who were found to have developed the infamous 'drip' had their pay docked during treatment and were restricted to the base for some weeks. Second offenses resulted in reduction in rank, and could lead to a "bad conduct" or "undesirable" discharge. While we had some supplies of Penicillin, available only in a thick solution of oil and beeswax that had to be given for several days at 3-hour intervals, and through a very large needle, most cases were treated using a silver solution, argyrol, squirted into the urethra through the end of the penis and held in place for minutes of severe irritation. Those irrigations were repeated daily for several days or longer.

It was widely known that Japanese doctors also had Penicillin, although not much, and that penicillin was far more effective, sometimes in a single shot, than argyrol. It was to be expected, then, that many sailors sought treatment from local physicians to avoid both the discomfort and the disciplinary consequences of bringing their sinful afflictions to official Navy attention. Always with a buddy or two, the "clapped up" "swabbie" (Naval expressions, both) would find a local doctor, usually after a few drinks to bolster his courage, and enter his office to demand a shot of this new miracle drug.

A few unfortunate 'incidents' occurred, when a Japanese doctor declined to treat the diseased, usually drunken, sailor, and the latter broke down some of the shoji walls of the doctor's office to emphasize the seriousness of the request for treatment. This was easy enough to do, because the shoji were constructed of light, beautifully fitted wood strips backed only with rice paper.

Ever quick to learn, and anxious to avoid offending the occupying conquerors, the local doctors quickly devised a solution to avoid both damage to their offices and depletion of their limited, still very expensive, supplies of penicillin. They had discovered that a classical American product called Jergens Lotion looked exactly like penicillin in oil and beeswax when drawn up in a syringe. So they used that, injecting it deeply into the buttock. The sailor left happy, and the office was left intact.

There were several problems with this creative therapeutic approach. The first was that it had no effect on the gonorrheal infection, and the drip continued. The second, worse, was that the non-sterile Jergens Lotion always resulted, within days, in a large, painful abscess in the injected buttock, usually with fever and other symptoms of infection, and the unhappy sailor would show up at the hospital in sad shape indeed.

The remedy required surgery under general anesthesia. It was soon discovered that the excised abscess still carried the scent of Jergens, and a little questioning brought forth the awful truth. For a while we saw a steady stream of infected buttocks, and "the word" was officially passed to all hands and all arriving ships that people were to avoid seeking treatment for anything at all from Japanese doctors because of the great risk of severe infections requiring 'major' surgery, and the epidemic abated.

Word had been received from the Army, who had most of the personnel in Korea, that the incidence of psychiatric disorders was extraordinarily high among the soldiers exposed to combat. This had always been the case when our forces, as well as those of the Israelis, the French, the British and all the other Armies we knew about, had begun to fight. Even though it had always been a huge surprise, it should never have been even a little surprise, to anyone.

This fact has consistently provided the most convincing evidence that our military planners and leaders, who should know better, persist in a disastrous form of denial, coupled with a wholly unfounded, unjustified, almost mystical confidence in our weapons systems and mechanical devices as being somehow invincible, when they never really are. I was to see this over and over again in the Pentagon, when I was privy to the heated discussions of our top military officials about sophisticated weapons, with little attention to the most highly sophisticated - and most vulnerable - weapon of all: the soldier, and his psyche.

Beginning in the First World War, in 1918, the emotional breakdown of soldiers in the field began to get serious attention and concern, but no effective treatment. Large numbers of soldiers became incapacitated by what appeared to be intense reactions of fear and loss of emotional control. This was widely believed to be due to the sometimes-prolonged artillery bombardments, whose explosive blasts were believed to cause damage to the brain. It was called "Shell Shock." It was considered untreatable, and thousands of troops so diagnosed were evacuated to the US. Many were medically retired and placed in Veterans Hospitals. Most of them were still there, filling much of America's largest hospital system, still unable to function normally, when the Second World War broke out more than twenty years later.

The terrible tragedy in all this was that most of those 'shell shocked' veterans need never to have been hospitalized in the first place. There is no such thing as shell shock.

This became evident in the early phases of WWII, when our forces first went into combat in North Africa. So many cases of serious emotional disruption and incapacity showed up in the earliest battles that the personnel replacement system could not keep up. Entire units had to be disbanded, with the few remaining healthy soldiers farmed out to other units with heavy but less disastrous losses. The situation was a complete surprise, a great shock. It raised wholly unacceptable questions about the 'fiber' of our fighting men, and the possible fate of our armies as they faced the tough, disciplined troops of the Third Reich.

Two psychiatrists, fired up by ideas they had developed when they studied the shell shock situation in the first war and the records of the Veterans Administration, sought and finally gained permission to go to the forward battle areas, where they were destined to revolutionize all of psychiatry, civilian as well as military, with far greater effect even than the brilliant insights and works of Sigmund Freud and his disciples.

Joining front-line units, they managed to intercept the acutely mentally disordered soldiers slated for evacuation to the rear, then to the coast, and finally to the continental U.S. for placement in VA hospitals, before they actually left their units. Gathering these men together in a large tent, they sedated them all heavily, putting them to sleep for a full 12 hours.

After this much-needed rest and escape from the turmoil of battle, the men were gotten up, fed well, put into small groups of eight or ten and ordered to tell the details of their most horrifying battle experiences, with their buddies terribly maimed and dying all about them. Many wept inconsolably during their recitations and seemed on the verge of reverting to their helpless, disordered state, but carried on with the encouragement of others in the group who assured them it was okay to be upset, and were eager to tell their own stories.

These sessions took up most of the first day after the first good night's sleep, and most of the second. The men were offered individual sessions with the doctors, but most declined. Late the second day they were dressed in fresh uniforms after showers and shaves and haircuts.

All this was taking place so close to the actual battle area that the sounds of rifle and mortar fire could clearly be heard, and casualties were being carried in, right off the battlefield.

On the third day, these special patients were assigned to help receive and welcome the new batch of psychiatric casualties who continued to pour in, get them settled and fed and ready for their sedatives. That done, they were issued their weapons and combat gear, and sent back, forward, to rejoin the exact same units they had left. Many were genuinely eager to go. They had been under treatment exactly 72 hours.

Miraculously, the men so treated performed adequately when they rejoined their units. None suffered any recurrence of their emotional disability during the months that followed. Not one was evacuated as scheduled to the United States, or entered a VA hospital to spend his life as an emotional cripple like the victims of non-existent "shell shock."

What had happened to those earlier cases of what was now labeled "combat fatigue" and later, "combat exhaustion," was that their emotional disorder, initially transient and treatable, had been endorsed, validated, verified - and made worse, and chronically fixed - by the universal attitude of medical professionals that they suffered from a near-psychotic, essentially hopeless mental disorder that made them helpless dependents of the government that had disabled them - maimed their minds - by sending them off to war.

Most men who go to war - nearly 90% - never hear a nearby shot fired in anger. The bulk of those who do are mostly adolescents, not yet wholly emotionally mature, who are understandably frightened and horrified at what they see, and are often emotionally devastated when they see their close friends torn to pieces and killed. This is true no matter how good their training is. It even happens to Marines, supposedly the toughest and best trained of all, although the Marine Corps leadership pretends that it does not and doesn't want to think about it. In Korea, for example, only the Marine Division, with nearly 20 thousand fighting men, did not have a division psychiatrist. 'Don't need one,' I was told.

Nevertheless, combat exhaustion was here to stay, as it had been all along, and the Army hospitals in Korea and Japan were feeling its impact. The Navy, parent service of the Marine Corps, knew that we would soon have Marines in combat, and we'd better get ready. They had already done their bit by sending me to the Far East Command, where I was the only trained Navy psychiatrist west of Pearl Harbor.

What we didn't have was any place to take care of Marine Corps psychiatric patients, whatever their diagnoses. Our Commanding Officer at Yokosuka was ordered to prepare a psychiatric ward, just in case. He called me into his office, and told me to design such a facility. One more two-story wing of the original Japanese naval hospital was then cleared of the families living in it; the inside was completely gutted from the ground beneath the cellar to the roof above the attic atop the second floor.

The Captain, typically, did not ask me if I knew how to design a building from the ground up, or whether I could. He just told me to do it. So of course I had no choice.

After pacing off the cavernous, newly cleaned-out concrete building and measuring ceiling heights and stairway widths in the other wards already in use, I set to work utilizing my extensive experience as a high school sophomore in a class in mechanical drawing. What I came up with was space for twenty patients, most in open ward spaces upstairs ('topside') with three "strong rooms" with padded walls, canvas covered, and heavy refrigerator doors with small observation holes cut into them, a rather grand, walnut paneled doctor's office and screened (no glass) nursing station on the lower level. There was also a modest ward kitchen, and group 'heads' and showers on each floor.

All windows were to be covered on the outside with cyclone fencing, which was locked to prevent unauthorized absences, and an alarm button was built into the nurses station for use in case of a riot.

I took my plans, drawn smartly to scale on some graph paper I had found, to the base engineering officer. He glanced at them, grunted, scrawled his initials on one corner signifying approval, and said he'd turn them over to "the Japs," meaning some building contractors permanently occupied on the base. The Captain was completely out of the loop, and never consulted.

Not more than three days later, a veritable small army of tiny, skinny brown men, most wearing a variety of loincloth and straw slippers, and sometimes a headband, appeared in the building shell. They carried a variety of what looked like children's play tools, miniature straight saws, little hammers, pry bars, wrenches, screw drivers, and boxes of nuts and bolts, screws and nails - the last of more normal size. Outside the building there appeared as if by magic great piles of lumber along with rolls of cyclone fencing, wiring, hinges and metal angle irons and braces.

Nowhere were there any power tools or machinery of any kind. There were some pulleys and piles of rope for hoisting heavy things, but the power was all human.

This horde of construction workers seemed almost to fill the concrete shell of the building. Stout pillars were rapidly erected, and connected with cross beams and joists. One little group worked outside the building with acetylene torches, angle irons and cyclone fencing to create precisely fitted covers for each window. Subflooring began to appear, and a stairway materialized, linking the two floors. Several men, evidently sailmakers, measured and cut the heavy, stiff canvas and gathered piles of kapok stuffing to be used lining the walls of the strong rooms. A group of what appeared to be electricians began running wires and setting fixtures throughout the building.

After exactly eleven days of frenetic activity, all marvelously coordinated and conducted with only short breaks for lunch, from a little tin box of rice and vegetables carried by each worker, the 'army' disappeared. The man who had obviously been in charge, no bigger than all the others but with a distinct aura of command authority, presented me with the keys to the building, bowing repeatedly and grinning broadly, particularly when he led me into what was to be my office - appropriately large and beautifully paneled in walnut, hand-rubbed the previous night.

What I had witnessed was a miracle of industry and skill. When the Base Engineering office submitted a bill for all labor and materials to the hospital commander, it came to exactly sixty thousand dollars. Every detail was exactly as I had designed it on my little sheets of graph paper. We had a superb, traditional, secure, 20-bed psychiatric treatment facility raising our total hospital bed count to 100 beds.

What no one could possibly have dreamed was that this new ward was to contain 90 acutely ill combat psychiatric casualties and the hospital census would total a thousand sick and wounded Marines, just six weeks later.

They arrived, our thousand new patients, over a single weekend, flown out from the battle zones still swathed in battle dressings, filthy and exhausted after days under fire. The Marines had landed at the Port of Inchon, in a brilliant MacArthur-style assault on the middle of the enemy's forces, cutting them in half. Some of the landing Marines carried hand-printed signs proclaiming, "Relax, Mac - we're back!" as they entered into a furious, successful onslaught that led, ultimately, nearly to the Yalu River on Korea's northernmost border. The North Koreans fought furiously and well, and the price we paid for their resistance was dramatically illustrated by our arriving wounded.

There was no time to think about that. We hurriedly expelled all remaining families from what had originally been the wards of the big Japanese hospital, but were hard put to place sufficient numbers of beds and linens into the newly emptied spaces. At first, the newly arriving wounded men were left on the litters that had borne them in, and placed on the floors of existing wards and the long halls. Kneeling beside them, we four young doctors (the Captain remained in his quarters and didn't participate), aided by every available nurse and corpsman, removed the battle dressings and searched our patients for each of their often multiple penetrating wounds. Sometimes we were able to get portable X-Rays taken to help in the search for shell- and grenade-fragments causing most of the wounds.

Within hours of the first arrivals, we had used up what little blood we had for transfusions, all the available IV fluids, and all the penicillin. Soon we were to be out of bandages. Our little hospital was not ready for this.

War wounds are characteristically dirty, deeply contaminated with ordinary dirt and teeming with bacteria. Each wound, whatever its size, had to be debrided - surgically trimmed and cleaned - and probed for embedded fragments or - much worse - open tracts leading into the chest or abdominal cavities. Those required prompt major surgery to repair pierced intestines, liver, kidneys or lungs in order to preserve life.

While I was busily engaged in debrieding some twenty tiny puncture-wounds in a young Marine's back, a corpsman reported that we were out of penicillin as well as topical disinfectant, and would have to rely solely on soap and water for cleansing wounds. A sudden image of my explorations into Yokosuka's tunnels came to mind, and I sent several men out to find and bring back those big, 5-gallon glass bottles full of the smelly, oily solution that the pharmacist had told me was an 'old fashioned' disinfectant. We used that, and it turned out to be an adequate supply for that time of need, doubtless saving countless men from painful, grievous infections that could have been far more serious without it. Sometimes, I reflected, 'old-fashioned' is plenty good enough.

Wholly unbeknownst to me during those hours of medical crisis, which were to extend over the next several days, I was learning a lesson that was to dominate my entire tour of duty, many years later, in the Pentagon. That lesson had to do with something called Medical Readiness.

Somehow we got through those first few days of combat surgery. Turning my attention, or what was left of it, to my 90 patients crammed into double deck bunks on my brand new 20-bed ward, I was shocked to find that half a dozen or more of my new arrivals actually had a form of encephalitis rather than emotional problems. I strove to treat the others as if we were situated close to the battle lines, employing groups in which men were encouraged to 'ventilate' their experiences and feelings, and expect to return soon to a more normal state and return soon to duty as well. Most of them did.

Most of the wounded men did surprisingly well, and we were soon able to send most of them back to the States by ship, with those more urgently in need of definitive surgery traveling by air. No sooner had we gotten that problem fairly well under control, when a new situation arose that caused me no little concern. It had to do with homosexuals.

At that time, homosexuality, practiced or even 'inclined' toward, was grounds for discharge from active duty. Aggressive homosexual behavior resulted in arrest and, not infrequently, a prison sentence. Psychiatrists and other medical officers were expected and duty-bound to report discovered cases so that prompt administrative or legal action could be taken to remove these 'perverts,' as they were commonly called, from the ranks of 'decent' men.

I was accustomed to having an occasional sailor confess to homosexual leanings and even to overt homosexual behavior, wanting to make a clean breast of things. And, incidentally, get out of the Navy and out of harm's way. These sudden plunges into a self-righteous need to confess past sins and finally turn honest troubled me, especially when the behavior had persisted for years without being troublesome. The temporal association between the need to come clean and the escalating danger of getting shot at always made me feel that the Navy and I were being manipulated by people who, understandably, wanted to avoid the risk of combat.

I was not wholly sympathetic to the Armed Forces' policy of ridding themselves immediately of such people. It was true that most Americans, at that time, were wholly unsympathetic and often openly hostile to homosexuals, and didn't want them around. This deviation was officially declared to be a psychiatric abnormality that was incompatible with honorable membership in the Army Forces and potentially dangerous to young, innocent men entering upon active duty. On occasion, homosexuals had been beaten up, taunted, and at least on one occasion actually thrown overboard to drown by indignant, outraged fellow crewmembers. This was not good for morale and discipline.

Additionally, suicide was more common among homosexual males, and some young sailors developed something called a homosexual panic, which sometimes signaled the onset of schizophrenia, after being approached by a predatory homosexual shipmate or even a stranger in a tavern or at a party. More often, such panics occurred when a youngster, usually in a group shower aboard ship or in a barracks, felt himself becoming even slightly sexually aroused when surrounded by other naked males, and became panic-stricken that he was, or was becoming, similarly 'perverted.' Sometimes this ushered in an acute episode of withdrawal, hallucinations and delusions, and sometimes suicide.

Based on what was then known, the leadership of the military departments were probably well-justified in believing that homosexuals posed a threat to unit cohesion, as well as good order and discipline, critical especially aboard a ship many months at sea. Therefore, the policy stood.

Not by nature a particular rebel, and willing to accept the logic of this as well as many other Naval traditions and regulations that at first glance seemed arbitrary or difficult to understand and accept, I found myself increasingly disturbed about this policy as the morning sick call line grew longer daily, with a steadily increasing number of self-declared homosexuals wanting to "confess" and get sent home. This presented me with a moral and ethical dilemma. On the one hand I was bound to abide by official Navy policy. On the other, I believed that strict adherence to that policy did harm to the Navy.

I decided, therefore, on a kind of rationalized compromise, leaning toward what I believed to be the greatest good, or maybe the least bad. There were many more such dilemmas ahead of me through the years, particularly as I occupied positions of increasing power and more responsibility, and they were never easy to resolve. This one was perhaps the prototype I would follow.

I decided to listen non-judgmentally to each confession, following which I would deliver a little speech, thoughtfully and as matter-of-factly as possible. First came my declaration that I liked girls, a lot, was easily aroused by them and often felt the impulse to make a fairly aggressive approach to a pretty female. I did not ordinarily give in to such impulses because the potential consequences posed a price I was not willing to pay. Most emphatically, there was no way I could trick or force some girl to give in to my uninvited advances, for to do so would constitute at least assault, and quite possibly, rape. Even if she didn't do anything about it, I would forever know what I had done, and felt guilty and unworthy.

You, the repentant sailor would be told, like boys. While your object is different from mine, in a sense, your feelings of arousal and impulse toward making an aggressive approach were doubtless the same as my own. The cost of giving in to such an impulse, in your case, carries consequences whose price is even greater, the danger of retaliation far more immediate, and surely the residual self-loathing and guilt were the same, and inescapable.

In the judgment of this officer, (me), your sexual inclinations, though different from my own, should not be allowed to deny you the honor and privilege of serving your country. Your country needs you, a trained, experienced member of our naval forces. Therefore it would be wrong of me, unjustifiably so, to take any action that would deny you this honor and privilege, so I will not do so. This will remain a confidential matter between you and me.

The final part of my little speech was cautionary. Any aggressive pursuit of sexually provocative behavior or even speech could result in official disciplinary action against me, and the same was true of you, even if your target was another male. In other words, if you make unwanted homosexual advances toward any - repeat any - of your shipmates, I would personally see that you go to prison.

These brave words and impossible threats were uttered fully forty years before the birth and outrageous exploitation of the idea of sexual 'harassment' so popular today, yet they were delivered with seriousness and some intensity, and seemed to hit home.

And so, Sailor, go out from here, go back to your ship, do the duty you were trained to do and have every right to do, as long as our country needs you. Then leave the Navy and pursue any way of living ("lifestyle" hadn't yet been invented) that you want. Then, your behavior will be your business. Right now, your behavior, like mine, is the Navy's business. Brave though it was of you to 'confess,' your confession cannot be permitted to deny you your right, as a citizen, to serve honorably in this uniform!

Rarely did my response to these earnest confessions vary from this, and not once did the penitent object to the decision. They seemed to be saying to themselves, as they left my office, something like, "Oh well. What the hell; it was worth a try." None seemed very upset or seriously downcast. Not a single one committed suicide.

The hospital was very busy, and we all helped one another out, regardless of our specialty or natural inclinations. I started seeing patients at about six every morning, and rarely finished before nine at night. Breakfast and lunch were brought to me in my fine walnut paneled office, but I reserved the right to dinner at the Officers Club, devouring steaks and lobster on alternate nights, following two large dry martinis. The drinks were my first taste of gin for over ten years, since the good Kitty Davis introduced me to this particular poison on that long ago, disastrous evening in her nightclub in Chicago.

My staff of nurses and corpsmen was superb, rising to the occasion without complaints over the twelve to fourteen hour days with no days off. I watched young men and women giving of themselves unstintingly, and filling my heart with feelings of admiration and thankfulness for the privilege of doing, with these splendid young people, something that really mattered. I began to feel that maybe, after all, this was a reason to be proud to be a doctor. That feeling, until now, had been all but absent.

One bright morning, the sick call line included a young officer who waited patiently for his turn to see the only Navy psychiatrist west of Pearl Harbor. He turned out to be a medical officer aboard one of the ships in our port, and he complained of overwhelming depression, despair, and unshakeable thoughts of suicide. What was more, he was a trained psychiatrist fresh from his residency at a famous institution, and knew from his training that he was increasingly incapable of performing his medical duties.

He did tear up repeatedly during the interview and was genuinely depressed, but I saw in him a possible answer to my prayers for assistance with my overwhelming workload, so I made him a proposition. He would be admitted to my service but would remain in uniform, and spend his days helping me with preliminary interviews to screen the steady stream of patients that kept showing up. In return for this small service I would undertake his therapy, giving him a full hour each day, on the couch if he wished, and together we would work through this depressive episode.

With great reluctance, he agreed to try. On about his third 50-minute hour, the underlying problem finally emerged. He was a clandestine homosexual, and was devastated by this separation from his lover, which he could not possibly endure, and survive.

Here was another of those moral-ethical dilemmas. Technically, I was expected and required to report this man's confession of his homosexuality to the Legal Affairs Office, which would initiate instant action to bring him to trial by General Court Martial. That would inevitably lead to his conviction, possible incarceration in a federal prison for up to two years, and a Dishonorable Discharge. That "D.D." was the only discharge that could be given to an officer, whereas enlisted people could be separated for 'unsuitability,' 'undesirability,' or given a 'bad conduct' discharge, or a DD, which was the most severe category. That last very nearly deprived the dischargee of citizenship. He could never hold public office, be bonded, obtain a passport, or, in some instances even vote; it was a modern Mark of Cain.

This man, however, had special value, if not to the Navy, then to society as a whole. He was the product of perhaps 24 years or more of formal education, most of it, like my own, at the expense of his fellow citizens. He had violated no law, as far as I could tell, and was in this terrible jeopardy solely because he said, without corroboration, that he had loving feelings toward another man, who was a civilian. He had not actually 'done' anything "wrong" as a Naval Officer, like seducing or even approaching an innocent young sailor.

The final, and most convincing, element in my resolution of this dilemma was the fact that he was genuinely ill, had a diagnosable disease, depression, that could justify medical disability retirement, and as his physician I had sworn an oath to "do no harm" to him. The problem here was not exactly unique for military doctors. Having been commissioned by the President to serve as an officer of the armed forces, sworn to defend the lawful orders of my superiors, it could be argued that my first responsibility was to the Service of which I was a part, and only then to my patient. Generally I could accept that, for there were times when others' lives depended on it.

Sometimes, though, like now as I faced this genuinely sick man, it wasn't all that clear. Were I to fail to report his deviation, would I be serving his interests at the expense of the Navy's? Was the Navy's good order and discipline endangered if the man were to be dealt with medically, as he would be if the issue of sexual preference were not involved? Would it be different if he had actively pursued sexual contact with his shipmates? I concluded that it would indeed, but that was not the issue here.

Ultimately, well aware that what I was about to do might be seen as failing in my larger duty, and very possibly reflecting an unfair, parochial bias in his favor arising from our shared profession, I wrote him up as having an incapacitating psychiatric disorder, a near-psychotic depression unresponsive to therapy. As such, I ordered that he be evacuated to the US for further treatment and consideration for discharge on medical grounds. I did not mention his acknowledged homosexual tendencies or relationships and did not attempt to identify a 'cause' for the depression, since often this disorder occurred without an identifiable cause.

I cautioned him, however, not to bring it up. Ever. He followed that advice, I was to learn much later, and he was medically discharged, but without a pension, his personal and professional reputation intact. He served satisfactorily and honorably for many years after that, as a medical professional, and ultimately was appointed to a high level position in the California state Department of Mental Hygiene.

The Navy, meanwhile, got along just fine after he left.

While we were having these great medical adventures in Yokosuka, our Marines were fighting their way, alongside major Army units, up and down and across the Korean peninsula against bitter resistance from North Korean Army forces. Smaller contingents of fighters and support troops from other United Nations member countries began to join in. The end of the conflict appeared to be at hand, as the bitterly cold North Korean winter descended upon our forces.

Severe frostbite occurred with increasing frequency, approaching epidemic proportions. We were amputating toes, fingers, and sometimes whole feet, and the situation caused great concern in both medical and command circles. An investigation was launched, and turned up the fact that individual soldiers and marines were sometimes hanging a sweaty, stockinged foot out the side of a moving jeep or truck in below-zero weather, with the deliberate intention of producing enough frostbite to warrant their medical evacuation and thus their escape from the horrors of war.

As a result, frostbite of the lower extremities, at first a 'war wound' earning award of a Purple Heart medal, was officially declared to be a self-inflicted wound, like a rifle shot down through the top of the foot, and as such was considered to be misconduct. Most troops had no idea at all of the massive, permanent destruction of foot structures caused either by a high-velocity rifle round or freezing of a foot hanging out of a jeep. In consequence, many ended up permanently disabled, reduced in rank for their infraction, and given an "other than honorable" discharge on top of everything else.

The Air Force had developed a superb aeromedical evacuation system, flying patients from fields near field evacuation hospitals directly to our hospital and the Army's two Tokyo facilities. We never lacked for patients, but didn't experience any weekend deluge like the one that brought us so many of the wounded some weeks before. Anticipating the worst, however, the entire remainder of the original Japanese hospital was emptied of all the families living in the former ward buildings, beds were brought in, and the equipment and supplies necessary to operate new wards was put in place as it arrived aboard the steady stream of ships coming in from the States.

New corpsmen, nurses, lab techs and physicians also began to arrive, and the hospital staff multiplied dramatically. At long last, a new psychiatrist showed up, to my immense relief. I had been seeing and working up twenty to thirty new patients every day, still had a line of outpatients outside my door each morning, and helped out in surgery and obstetrics.

In spite of all that, I still managed to get away for at least part of most weekends, to continue my explorations in rural Japan in my much loved little car. Even when the pressure of work was great, I managed frequently to run up to Kamakura, to rest and rejuvenate my spirit while gazing upon the lovely, tranquil countenance of the great Buddha. In later years, when things got particularly trying or distressing, I was often to recall those visits, see his face in my mind's eye, and derive comfort and a broader perspective from doing that.

My new psychiatric colleague turned out to be a Reserve Officer recalled to active duty from his job in the Wayne County, Michigan, Health Department. He was a senior commander in rank, a status he had achieved rapidly after entering the Navy late in World War II, and had never served in any foreign country or on a ship.

Harold was a tall, handsome, rather dandified man with a dark mustache and a distinctly unhappy air about him. For a while after he arrived, I feared he would have to be converted to patient status just like my earlier depressed psychiatrist, and I prayed he wouldn't have to be evacuated. He arrived one morning, his well-tailored uniform bearing only two ribbons, the American Defense medal ribbon (meaning he had served in WWII in the US proper,) and the Victory Medal ribbon, a pretty, rainbow-colored device given to everyone on active duty at the end of that war.

He introduced himself by saying that he was there to assume my position as Chief of Neuropsychiatry. But, he hastened to add, he wanted me to continue exactly as I had been doing and continue to use my fine walnut-walled office. He would merely sit quietly in a corner of the office while I saw and disposed of my daily stream of patients, walk around with me on ward rounds, and join me in the Club for dinner and to rehash the day's activities. That way, he said, he could learn how this job was to be done, so as to smooth the transition.

That said, he left for the rest of the day to write letters to his wife and daughters, whom he missed terribly already, and worried about constantly.

That was Monday. True to his word, he showed up every morning at about seven, when I was well into my patient interviews, and quietly took a seat on a small chair in the corner. As always, when time came for lunch it was brought in, and I wrote up charts while I ate at my desk, continuing after the meal to make notes, see patients, conduct ward rounds, write orders, meet with the corpsmen and nurses, sign requisitions for supplies and requests for overnight liberty from my crew.

Friday arrived, and still he sat quietly, watching my every move. About noon he finally announced that he and I had to have a talk. I readily agreed, expecting him to tell me how he planned to operate the service, and what my new role as his subordinate would be.

Instead, he simply said, "Doctor, I can't do this. I can't possibly do what I've seen you doing with all these patients. The thought of even trying is just overwhelming. I'm depressed. I can't stand being away from my wife. I can't sleep after about 3 in the morning (a sure sign of depression) and find myself bursting into tears. You'll have to admit me." He was not making a joke.

While there was a sense of unreality to all of this, I had to agree. The man was a wreck. I weakly offered to take him into therapy, but he would have none of it - he just wanted to go home. I wrote up his case, as best I could, put in an order for his evacuation to the US, and within days he was back in the States, presumably being processed for a medical discharge. I was forced to conclude that psychiatrists were worthless wimps, and was beginning to think I would never get any help.

Within a few weeks, however, two more psychiatrists showed up, thanks to an unexpected visit from none other than my old mentor, Dr. Karl Bowman from Langley Porter, who was a senior civilian consultant to the Surgeon General. One day, without explanation, I was summoned to the Captain's office, told to check out a jeep and find my way to the Imperial Hotel in Tokyo, where I was to meet with some important visitor sent out from Washington.

Ever obedient, I put on my best uniform, got the jeep, and set out. The roads were not well marked, and I had no map, but there were frequent signs pointing the way and conveniently bearing the word "Tokyo" in English letters below the Japanese characters for the city. Little did I realize that getting back to Yokosuka, a much smaller city with almost no recognizable signs pointing the way, was to prove far harder.

Driving itself was easy enough, for there was almost no vehicular traffic except for occasional military trucks, and once inside the borders of central Tokyo, a number of plodding, smoking, ancient sedans bearing Taxi signs. These relics were old gasoline-powered cars that had been modified to run on vaporous gas generated by charcoal burners built into the trunk. They were noisy, slow, smelly, and very hot in the back seat, as I was later to learn.

I reported in at a desk in the charming, low-ceilinged hotel's lobby, manned by military police officers, who made calls, told me to wait, and soon ushered none other than my old surrogate father, Dr. Bowman, to where I sat. He greeted me warmly and enthusiastically, led me in to the bar for martinis, and demanded to know all the details of my great adventure in Japan. I spared him nothing, including the huge number of patients we were seeing, the building of my 20-bed ward and housing nearly a hundred patients in it, sorting out the encephalitis patients commonly mixed up with the psychiatric cases, and the uselessness and hopelessness of psychiatrists as a species, one that I had come to despise.

My old friend and teacher seemed to find all this amusing, but he was very laudatory and supportive of my work, to my great relief. I even confessed to him my "stretching" of the clearly defined policies on homosexuals, and he supported what I had done, to my great relief, but cautioned me not to launch a quixotic campaign to reverse what was a Command, as opposed to a valid Medical, decision. Meanwhile, just go on doing what I thought was right, and best.

After a wonderful dinner at the Imperial, I set out in my jeep to return to Yokosuka. Night fell, there were no readable signs, there were no people about who spoke English to give me directions, and I felt hopelessly lost. At length I decided to look for "Tokyo" signs and follow them backward, away from where they pointed. This seemed to work, but it took nearly five hours to make the 2-hour trip. Exhausted, I finally spotted the huge cranes of the Naval Base, found the gate, and gratefully entered. None of my independent explorations of the Japanese countryside had ever been so difficult.

On one such trip, I had headed up into one of the larger mountain ranges that run up and down the island of Honshu not far from Yokosuka. The road uphill was narrow but was evidently quite new, and was paved with concrete. Just after reaching the crest of a sharp, high mountain ridge, the concrete abruptly ended and the car lurched down with a crash onto gravel about a foot below the level I had been driving on. The crashing sound had an ominous metallic quality, but the car continued to run and I proceeded cautiously down the steep grade through lovely forests. Suddenly the engine began making horrendous, screeching noises, and I turned it off, put the gear in neutral, and coasted for at least a mile until it reached a valley floor, leveled off, and stopped.

I was on the outskirts of a small village, and was immediately surrounded by a crowd of children, soon joined by women, and then by men. They chattered among themselves, many of the children pointing at me and laughing excitedly, until an older man approached, bowed, and indicated by his gestures that I should wait right where I was.

Soon a younger man, dressed in an ill-fitting western suit, complete with shirt and necktie, came running up, coming to an abrupt stop a few feet from my car. He bowed low, repeatedly, and then began a little speech in halting, but understandable English. Addressing me as "Honorable Sir," he told me that I was the first American ever to have honored his village with a visit, and he was the schoolmaster and the only person in town who could speak English, which he proudly said he had learned at the university.

He told me he understood that my car was damaged, and begged to be allowed to show me the way into the center of the village, where he would arrange a room for me at the one hotel, food as I wished, and have my car towed to the little garage across the street from the hotel, where they would be honored to repair it. Naturally I agreed, there being no real alternative, and the school teacher did all that he promised. This was to be my first independent exploration of a rural Japanese inn, and it proved to be utterly delightful and charming.

I left my shoes at the little vestibule of the inn, donned a pair of waiting slippers, and was ushered inside and upstairs to a lovely room empty of any furniture save for a small low table in the center. To one side was an alcove, the tokonoma, with a lovely, simple flower arrangement, called ikebana, placed in it. From behind a shoji hiding a closet next to the tokonoma, the woman who had ushered me in to my room brought forth a cotton kimono, called a yukata. A large character on the back of the garment showed the name of the inn.

My escort placed the robe beside my feet, indicated somehow that I was to put it on, and left the room in a continued low bow as she backed out through the door.

Ever obedient, I stripped down to my shorts and put on the cotton robe. In a few moments the lady reappeared with a small tray bearing a pot of tea and a cup. I squatted down at the little table in the middle of the room where she had placed the tray, and she poured the hot green tea into the cup and motioned me to drink, so of course I did.

Satisfied that I was content with things, she then went to the large shoji screen covering the window to the outside, which led to a little balcony, and she pointed proudly to the garage, right across the street, where my car was being operated upon. Then, bowing and backing up, she left again.

After a few minutes for tea drinking, she appeared again, bowing and extending a thin terrycloth towel, and beckoned me to follow her. She led me to a small room with a tiled floor, different slippers at the door, and a large wooden tub full of steaming hot water sitting in the middle of the floor. Bowing deeply for perhaps the twentieth time, and motioning toward the tub, she backed out the door again.

I had learned from an 'information guide' published by the Navy for new arrivals that I was expected to sit on a tiny stool next to the tub, dip out some of the very hot water using a large wooden cup with a long handle that rested nearby, pour the water over myself and scrub down with a scratchy ball of what I later learned was a kind of dried seaweed. Only then, when thoroughly clean, was it acceptable to enter the tub. Several times during this ritual I was aware that one door leading into the o-furo, or bath, was opened slightly and I could hear rustling - and was that suppressed giggles? Well, just outside, the hotel staff took turns peaking at what was their very first view of a Caucasian male!

The bath itself seemed murderously hot at first, but summoning up my best Bushido - Samurai spirit - I managed to survive and after a few minutes found the experience truly pleasant and rejuvenating. I dried off with some difficulty, using the flimsy towel that the hostess had supplied, donned my robe, and went back to the room for another cup of tea.

This tea-drinking and bathing routine was, like so much else in Japan, a fixed routine that every traveler was expected to go through on arrival at a hostelry. The next step was also expected if the weather was fine, as it was that day. Making my way back to where all the shoes were lined up at the front door, I easily identified my shiny black uniform shoes and put them on, without socks, and stepped outside, wearing only my thin, labeled cotton robe, to stroll the nearby streets. This had the dual purpose of letting me see what shops and souvenirs might be available, and letting the natives get a really good look at this stranger.

It all went extremely well. After returning to my room, another middle-aged woman showed up and bowed her way into my room bearing a tray of delicious, totally strange Japanese dishes that were my supper. That consumed, down to the last grain of rice, I read for a while and went to sleep on the thick, comforter-like futon one of the staff women had extracted from the closet next to the tokonoma and spread out on the tatami-mat floor.

The next morning I was awakened by daylight coming through the rice paper-covered shoji and a polite cough as the door to the room slid open. Still another serving woman appeared with tea. I got up, made my way to the benjo, or toilet, in its own little room with its own set of different slippers at the door, and on my return found the futon folded and stored back in its closet and a delicious breakfast on the table, consisting of a bowl of steamed clams, a bowl of hot red bean soup, and a bowl of rice.

Not long after that, my new friend the school teacher showed up, and we engaged in the extensive pleasantries customary in that country. He then asked if I would kindly accompany him to the garage where my car had spent the night, and we headed out and across the street. There stood the little car, freshly washed, polished, and looking brand new. What appeared to be the entire staff of the garage, about six men in all, was lined up behind the car in immaculate coveralls, standing stiffly at attention.

The man in charge, much older than all the others, stepped forward and handed me the broken connecting rod they had removed from one cylinder of the motor, and motioned for me to look under the car to see the plate they had welded over the hole that had been gouged in the oil pan when I crashed down over the edge of the concrete, high on the mountain. With a ceremonial flourish, he turned back to the car, reached in and turned the key. The engine ran perfectly!

The bill for the work, which took the whole crew all night, involved totally dismantling the engine, fabricating a new connecting rod and bearings, and putting it all back together again: the equivalent of seven US dollars!

On the way back to the base I reflected at some length upon this extraordinary demonstration of the industriousness, the creativity and the skill of these people, as well as their inherent respectful considerateness and kindness. They were certainly not motivated by fear of the victorious conquerors of their country, of whom I was but one tiny piece. It was equally certain that they harbored no traditional hatred of foreigners, but showed me instead a delightful curiosity and evident pleasure in this, their first face-to-face encounter with one of these strange, large creatures with red faces and big noses. Moreover, even here, in this tiny mountain village far from the great industrial cities of Tokyo and Yokohama, there was a fluent, English-speaking teacher, visibly proud of his little city, and a crew of extraordinarily skillful, technically expert mechanics.

Coupled with my witnessing the remarkable army of little men with tiny, toy-like tools who put together my most excellent new ward at Yokosuka, this experience helped me understand at least a little of how these people, only a hundred years beyond a long era of medieval feudalism, had suddenly emerged as a major, threatening world power.

It also was becoming evident to me why there were such deeply-rooted rituals and practices of politeness, profound respect for authority and strict, compelling rules for dealing with others, including strangers, that were so striking about these people. Here was a nation the size of California but largely covered by mountains too rugged for settlements, with a population nearly half as large as that of the whole United States. The population density was far greater than it was even in our larger cities. The tiny houses were crowded together and the streets, even in small towns, were full of people and activity. Without rules, it would have been chaos. There was, moreover, no room for people who were unproductive, so there was an incredible work ethic and intense attention to learning and skill development.

Had Japan had access to sufficient raw materials, especially metals and petroleum products, coupling these with their industriousness and determination and skills, the outcome of the war in the Pacific might have been far different.

This adventure with the car was but one of many excursions that led me to a state of fascination with that ancient Oriental land that persists to this day. It also motivated me to try to learn to speak their language, and to learn to read at least a little of it, which I promptly set out to do. Very soon, though, my life would change again, abruptly and dramatically.

Shortly after the two new psychiatrists arrived, thanks to Dr. Bowman's immediate demand on the Navy Surgeon General after our brief visit in the Imperial Hotel, I got new orders. The message from Washington directed me to proceed directly to the Hospital Ship Repose, at that moment tied up in the Port of Pusan, at the southern tip of Korea. I would be assigned as the Chief of Neurology and Psychiatry, replacing a man who had left abruptly due to family problems.

William E. Mayer, M.D.

William E. Mayer, M.D.

CHAPTER 6

HOSPITAL SHIP REPOSE

Within days, I had been flown to our airfield near Pusan and driven to the dock where lay the gleaming white vessel with large red crosses on its sides. Built during World War II on what was called a "C-4" hull, the great ship measured over 500 feet from stem to stern. The hull, designed for a freighter, had been modified to accommodate a crew of nearly 500 souls, and a total of 900 patients jammed together in double bunks.

About half the crew was there to operate the vessel itself, and had nothing to do with patients. They were under the command of a Reserve Naval officer who, in civilian life, was captain of a real, cargo-hauling freighter. He held the rank of Commander. The "US Naval Hospital Aboard the US Naval Ship Repose" was commanded by a Captain in the Medical Corps. While the Captain held a higher rank than the Commander who ran the vessel, he could not exercise control of the vessel or tell the Commander, officially called the 'Captain' of the ship, what to do or where to go. Oddly enough, this arrangement worked fairly well.

There were about two dozen physicians on the hospital staff, including two full captains, several commanders and lieutenant commanders, about a half dozen full lieutenants, and the remainder lieutenants, junior grade. There were three or four medical administrative officers, twenty-four nurses who were all commissioned officers below the rank of commander, and about two hundred hospital corpsmen, among whom were six or eight Chief Petty Officers.

The ship's crew of about a dozen line officers, that many Chief Petty Officers and several score lesser petty officers, along with over a hundred more enlisted sailors, lived in a separate area toward the stern of the ship. The nurses' quarters, alone, were on the main deck. Medical Officers occupied staterooms, mostly double, on the deck just below, in the forward part of the vessel, and the corpsmen were crowded together in large open spaces below that. Patient wards were spread throughout all decks, along with operating rooms, the lab, pharmacy and X-Ray areas.

On each side of the ship, near the waterline, was a large hatch that could be opened to allow patients to be loaded aboard when brought alongside in smaller craft, and above the stern was a helicopter-landing pad for patients arriving by air. An elevator from the landing pad led to the ward decks below. As with any naval vessel, the 'official' entry to the ship was by way of a set of steep steps that could be lowered along the port (left) side down to the water, and gave access to the main deck high above, guarded by the officer of the deck and a number of "side boys." Ordinarily, one entered the ship, whether from a small boat or from the dock, by climbing the outside steps, or 'ladder,' saluting the ship's US flag flying from the rail at the stern, then saluting the 'O.D.' and saying: "Request permission to come aboard, Sir!"

When you became an Admiral, or 'Flag' Officer, you were greeted at the top of the boarding ladder by a boatswain's mate who blew his bos'n's pipe, a kind of whistle, and a flag was immediately hoisted displaying however many stars your rank called for. You still asked the O.D. for permission to come aboard, though, whatever your rank, after saluting the ensign flying from the stern rail.

I always thought there was a certain splendor to the whole affair. Whether you had just stepped aboard a small submarine or a giant battleship, you knew when permission was granted to come aboard that you had entered into and on a special, powerful thing that represented the whole glorious history of the nation and its sea power.

Conscious of the historical significance of my personal moment as I boarded the great ship, I went through the drill as prescribed, and was escorted to my stateroom. To my relief, it was a single room, possibly because no one wanted to room with a psychiatrist, built 'hard up' into the very bow of the ship at the waterline. The wall curved up and out from the floor, and the ceiling was quite high, there being insufficient space above the room to allow for other useable space to be built there. It had no porthole or means of escape other than the small entry door.

This fact had some importance, since if the ship hit a mine or torpedo, this is where the hole would be blown, but I gave that little thought until we were underway, when the sound of the bow cutting through the water was quite loud and a little ominous.

The room had a bunk bed, bolted to the deck, a steel desk and chair, steel standing locker and fixed footlocker, and a heavy steel armchair. On the desk, as was customary, there was a small safe for valuables, like a bottle or two of booze, strictly forbidden on naval ships. I was soon to learn that every officer's safe on the ship held a supply of fine liquor, available at bargain prices at every military port or base in the "class VI" liquor store. All safes were opened at 5 PM daily for a cherished and hallowed happy hour.

My reception aboard the ship was not unfriendly, but not warm, either. Most of the crew had been aboard when the vessel first sailed from San Francisco, many months earlier, and I was the first outsider to intrude on the special little community that had formed up. As I soon discovered, almost all of the senior officers had paired up with individual nurses and these 'couples' generally spent their evenings in the respective officers' staterooms, and when they went ashore in the evenings or on weekends, did so quite openly as steady couples. No prude, I still saw this as seriously detrimental to the morale of the great bulk of the crew, who were mainly young sailors who spent a great deal of time thinking about sex and having phantasies -sometimes quite accurate - about these 'couples" activities. They were bitterly envious.

Once in a while, some particularly courageous sailor managed to establish a temporary liaison with one of the ladies, usually ending up with a risky coupling in one of the airlocks leading from the inner spaces on the ship out onto the deck. Risky because of the danger of being surprised by the roving patrols of security officers who roamed the ship at night.

One of the officers who was 'unattached' was a urologist named Mo. He was a lieutenant commander who was married and had five children, at home with his wife in Oakland. He and I struck up a friendship, and he related to me that just before the ship sailed, his wife announced that he would have to get himself "fixed" or not to come home. This followed a Sunday drive in the family convertible. His youngest girl, a lovely little creature of about four with golden curls and an angelic face, was riding in the back seat facing aft, with her chin resting on her hands, her elbows on the seat back.

It was a beautiful Sunday afternoon, and the drive took them into the Berkeley Hills toward the new Caldecott tunnel. Traffic was heavy and at one point came to a complete stop. The driver of the car behind Mo's honked his horn, probably accidentally. At that point the angelic-looking child, having learned a new phrase from her urologist-father's characteristically (for urologists) extensive verbal obscenity collection, shouted out in the brilliantly clear tones that only a little girl can produce, "Blow it out your ass, you ugly son of a bitch!"

While it may no longer be true, in those days urologists were notorious for their foul language, and Mo's casually vile outbursts had become a point of serious dispute in his family. He believed his wife was dead serious about her ultimatum.

When the ship sailed from the West Coast, headed for Korea, the staff was required to attend long medical conferences, daily, to prepare for the casualty care that lay ahead. Mo found these tedious and repetitious and hit upon a plan. Complaining of some unspecified illness, he excused himself from one of the meetings and headed for his room. There he injected his pubic area with a local anesthetic, opened the skin and lifted out the vas deferens - the little tube that carries sperm from the testicles - on each side, cut each off and tied the cut ends tightly, ensuring his sterility. He then sewed himself up and took to his bunk for a little rest.

He recovered 'uneventfully,' as they say, but he was to have a much more serious surgical experience some months later. The ship had put in to the great port of Sasebo, in southern Japan, for restocking and repairs. While wandering around the fascinating port city, Mo had been smitten by a beautiful young maiden he met in a nightclub, and ended up going home and to bed with her. He made a regular thing of this, often staying overnight with his new-found lover, and all went well until the girl's "regular" boyfriend, a large, tough Army sergeant, unexpectedly appeared early one morning, fresh from combat in Korea.

Enraged, the sergeant attacked poor Mo, hitting him so hard in the face that he broke the zygomatic arch - the cheekbone - causing Mo's left eye to drop down nearly an inch, with grotesque effect. Somehow my urologist friend made it back to the ship, complaining of a mugging, and was taken to the operating room immediately. Repairing the damage was complex and very difficult, and Mo never looked the same after his surgery. Curiously, he rarely uttered obscenities after that, and never went ashore again, at least in Sasebo.

I was busy with my psychiatric and neurological cases, but not so much so that I couldn't go ashore every evening to explore this new country. It was completely different from Japan. The people looked different and behaved differently. Their ordinary speech tended to sound expostulatory and angry even when it was not so intended, and the people in this terribly crowded, frightened city seemed rough, jostling one another in crowds and wholly lacking in the politeness and deference so common in Japan.

More than a million (some claimed 3 million) refugees had poured into this port city whose normal population numbered perhaps 300 thousand. Makeshift shelters were everywhere. Street vendors who lighted their pathetic little collections of junk with odorous acetylene lamps tried most of each night to sell something - anything - so they could buy food. There were little gangs of up to a dozen or more small boys ranging in age from 8 to 12 or 13, who were vigorous thieves and pickpockets, alternately begging for cigarettes and grabbing for exposed fountain pens and sun glasses.

Recent successful forays by the North Korean forces still operating in the far south of the peninsula, within miles of Pusan, caused a sudden new influx of fleeing refugees into the city shortly after I arrived. Several of us from the ship had independently observed what looked like severe cases of acne among the crowd, and realized with a shock that these were in reality cases of smallpox. None of us had ever seen so much as one case of this dreaded disease, since vaccination against it had long been in effect in the US.

A hurriedly called conference of the medical staff, along with physicians from a newly arrived Danish hospital ship that had tied up astern of us concluded that we were seeing the beginning of a massive epidemic. Frantic radio calls to Japan and the US were made, requesting every available dose of smallpox vaccine, and deliveries of the little glass tubes and the small darning needles used to 'scarify' the skin were soon on the way.

Meanwhile, increasing numbers of people appeared, literally covered with the angry, raised, eroded pimples and sores typical of the disease - sometimes painfully appearing even on the eyeballs, lips and tongue. We were back in the Middle Ages!

Nearly every physician and nurse aboard the two hospital ships, taking along a corpsman or two, loaded up with the tubes of vaccine and the needles and headed out in the port city to set up vaccination stations at busy intersections. We had no real plan, and there had been no way to tell the disorganized crowds of people what we were doing, and why. In spite of this, each of us vaccinators found that a line of people formed immediately when we set up our little tables, obediently exposing a place on their arms where we did our procedure, scratching the skin gently with the needle and then squeezing a drop of vaccine on the same spot.

How many people we vaccinated can never be known for sure, but it was probably several thousand. Among those passing through our hands for their shot of vaccine were innumerable crippled, blind, and seriously ill people with tumors, unrecognizable skin diseases, and all the various forms of leprosy. The latter had all fled from leper colonies as the invaders from the north charged toward Pusan.

The North Korean advance, blessedly, came to a halt just short of the outskirts of the city, now jammed with frightened people. Before the Communist forces started to withdraw, however, I was to have a wholly unexpected brush with them myself.

Just as I was completing my vaccinations on a Pusan street corner, an Army major came up and asked if he could help. He was very friendly and willing, but I told him I was about finished and needed a little break and a good stiff drink. That, he told me, was something he could readily provide, and he led me to his jeep, parked nearby.

We drove for what seemed to me to be quite a distance, ending up in front of a large, sprawling Korean building built in quadrangular style and sited in the middle of a fair-sized field, bordered on two sides by forest land. We were at the outermost edge of the populated area. The major got out of the jeep and walked up to a large double door with a small barred window in it. He called through the little window, and soon the doors swung open and we drove into an open area surrounded on all sides by the structure.

He led me into a large room with a small bar at one side and a number of armchairs, sofas, and small tables. After mixing a large gin and tonic for each of us, he sat down and told me that this was his outfit's 'club.' What outfit is this, I wondered, and looked quizzically at my host. He laughed, and told me he knew I must be wondering what this place was. It was very special, he said, and was not under the command of any local military unit. Instead, it took its orders directly from Washington, and was authorized to act with a degree of independence. How would I like to meet his colonel?

Naturally I agreed, and he led me into a large room outfitted as an office, where sat a somber, well-groomed officer behind a very large desk. I took the chair he indicated directly opposite the colonel, who fixed me for a long silent period with a steady gaze before extending his hand so that I had to get up and lean over the large desk to shake it. His grip was very hard, and he held it longer than usual.

The major introduced us, and told the colonel that I was a medical officer from the Hospital Ship, the Repose. He had found me, he told him, on a downtown street corner in Pusan stopping people and vaccinating them, since the medics feared a smallpox epidemic among the natives. The colonel, his eyes never leaving my face, then launched into a set of questions about where I was born and raised, educated, medically trained, gotten into the Navy, came to Korea and expected to do in the future. He also wanted to know details about my parents, my sisters, my ancestors, my hobbies (as if I had had time for hobbies!) my girlfriends, my feelings about Koreans and about our being in a war out here and many other subjects that I increasingly felt were none of his business.

I was becoming rather uncomfortable with this rapid-fire interrogation, when suddenly the colonel did an extraordinary thing. He reached up, plucked out what appeared to be his eyeball, breathed on it and began polishing it with a handkerchief he pulled from his pocket. The major, whose name was Mike, told me later that the colonel always performed this little maneuver whenever he was examining a 'new guy.' It was a kind of test, and I seemed to have passed with flying colors, since I did not flinch, did not stare at the plucked-out artificial eye, and kept looking steadily into the colonel's one good one that remained fixed on my face.

That exercise over, the colonel urged me to stay for a 'very good dinner,' and the major and I headed for the dining room. The dinner was indeed a very good one, and while we ate, my new friend Mike set out to explain something about the 'unit.'

It did not, he told me, have a formal unit designation, but among themselves the members semi-jokingly called themselves 'the Company." They were here in Pusan to seek out and interrogate enemy agents who had infiltrated the hordes of refugees converging on the southern tip of the country. Since North and South Koreans were really one and the same people, this was proving to be extremely difficult, but they worked closely with the South Korean Army Intelligence agents who usually ferreted out the bad guys and turned them over to 'our people' when they were through interrogating them.

He told me that many of the people turned over to them had been badly abused by their South Korean Army captors, and hard to interrogate because of their unhappy physical condition. The 'unit,' therefore, needed a good solid American doctor to help these poor souls recover enough to permit their questioning, but they had no medics assigned. Would I be willing to help out, in my spare time? After being assured that they would make no demands on my time that would interfere with my ordinary duties, I agreed to try to help.

At about this point in our conversation, the quiet of the compound was shattered by a burst of what sounded like (and was!) a burst of automatic weapons fire. The major grabbed my arm and hastened me down a hall, stopping at an open door through which an Army sergeant handed each of us what looked like one of the large metal pump devices used to force automotive grease into appropriate fittings underneath vehicles. The difference was that these crude-looking devices had, attached to the under side, what was clearly a long metal magazine full of bullets.

"Know how to work one of these grease guns?" the major asked. When I indicated I did not, he worked a lever on the side of the weapon, pushed a button, which he said was the safety, and said okay, I was all set; all I had to do was pull the trigger and point it at whatever moved. He then pushed me down into a crouching position beside a partially opened door to the outside. Through the opening, as dusk was rapidly approaching, I could see the woods a short distance away. He told me to watch that spot carefully, and if I saw any movement out there at all, I was to point the grease gun at it and squeeze the trigger in short bursts. With that he ran to a different spot down the corridor.

Within minutes, I saw shadowy figures darting among the trees and did exactly as I had been instructed during my 30-second training period.

This happened twice more, and some fire was returned but none of it aimed at my particular doorway, and then all was quiet. Not long afterward, the lights inside the building, all of which had been extinguished when the first shots were fired, were turned back on, and the major led me back to the 'club' room where twenty or thirty heavily armed men had gathered. He loudly proclaimed that 'our new doc' had proved himself 'one of us,' firing valiantly at the enemy sneaking in from the woods. The colonel himself, his ophthalmologic prosthesis firmly replaced in his eye socket, shook my hand and actually patted me once on the shoulder - unusual for him, I was told.

There was a little conversation about this most recent attack on their compound, but it seemed awfully casual to me, considering that the dark figures in the woods evidently intended to kill us all, and then everyone went back to whatever he was doing before the minor disturbance. The major announced that he would get me back to my ship, and we boarded his jeep again for the ride back to the docks, which was blessedly uneventful.

Thus began, with a jeep ride, a drink of gin, a glass eyeball and a good dinner, and then a little gun battle, what was to be a special look at our secret intelligence unit, that was to take many forms and present me with more than one moral dilemma before this adventure was over.

A few days later, Major Mike appeared aboard our ship, and searched me out in my crowded 'psych' ward, containing about 30 double-deck bunks, all full of patients who were mostly sedated. He told me that they had a "little job" for me, if I could get away later that day. When I agreed, he said he'd meet me in his jeep at dockside, and true to his word I found him there at the appointed time. He took me back to the compound where I had had my first real taste of a shooting war, and we went to a small, windowless room where lay a Korean man on a canvas litter.

The Korean lay quietly as I examined him and found many bruises and abrasions over most of his body. He moaned and grasped the edges of the litter, however, when I got to his feet. Not only were both feet badly cut and bruised, but also it was evident that both his ankles had been broken. I cleaned and bandaged the worst of his many cuts, positioned his feet as well as possible, and bound them firmly in Ace bandages after learning that there was no plaster of Paris available for casts. There was a fairly adequate medical chest available, and I took some aspirin and barbiturate capsules from it and put them into a small medication envelope with instructions for their use.

That done, I was taken back to the 'club' for another gin and tonic, and then driven back to the ship. The whole episode only took an hour or so, and seemed quite simple, but Mike was highly complimentary of my skills and grateful for the help. When I expressed my concern over the signs that the patient had been severely beaten, and that his ankles had been broken intentionally by blows from a heavy object, he sighed and said that was common among the prisoners delivered to them by the South Koreans, and assured me that his people never used physical force on its prisoners. I almost believed him.

Never, in a whole series of similar 'treatments' they asked me to administer, was I asked to come back for a follow-up visit to the same patient. Some of the people I saw were close to death, and there was little I could do for them except try to relieve their evident pain, but my hosts were always vague about what became of them after my merciful interventions. After many such missions, when I had earned the trust of the 'Company,' I was told quite casually that they generally let their prisoners go, delivering them 'by air' over North Korean units.

With a shock, I realized they meant that these people were pushed out of airplanes, without parachutes and screaming all the way to the ground, as a variety of psychological warfare!

This realization confirmed my growing suspicion that I was, in a sense, party to a cruel, inhumane activity that dramatized the much larger cruel and inhumane reality of war - this one and all others. Could I go on doing this and retain my self-respect as a person and my honor as a physician? Was this ethical? While I never saw any abuse, let alone execution by whatever means, was it right to help prepare these unfortunate souls for what was without doubt going to be a horrible fate?

I expressed these growing concerns to Mike, and he said maybe he could help me resolve them. I had pretty well concluded that it was ethically okay to ease the suffering of people in agony, whatever I suspected their fate might be later on, for if I didn't help them it was possible that no one would. What's more, as a military physician I was committed to repairing wounded warriors so they could go back to battle and kill and maim some more people, although not usually by dropping them out of airplanes, just by firing rifles and artillery pieces and throwing grenades and sticking them with bayonets.

Still, I wasn't really comfortable with my minor role in this great drama, and began to wonder if I were becoming some kind of anti-war, conscientious observer-type nut. I said these things to Mike, who had proven to be a remarkably bright, perceptive, thoughtful man despite what appeared at first to be a sort of bluff, hail-fellow-well-met exterior. He said it might prove instructive for me to sit in on one of his interrogations, and I said I would do so.

A few days passed with no special demands on my medical talents, when one day Mike showed up aboard ship to invite me to an interrogation session. Once again we drove to the compound that had by now become a second home, and entered one of the windowless rooms used for interviews. This prisoner, Mike told me, was 'banged up a little' but not in need of skilled medical attention. Moreover, he spoke fair English and we would not have to use an interpreter.

The prisoner was an unremarkable seeming individual of typically small stature, who appeared neither very frightened nor especially hostile. Mike conducted the questioning along fully conventional military lines, probing for details of the man's military unit, his background and training, his mission in this area and what he had managed to accomplish. We were seated on the ground, facing our prisoner and quite close together. His answers were very brief, often only a word or two, and he sat quite motionless, facing us.

Suddenly, without any warning whatever, the prisoner leapt forward from his squatting position, raised his arm above his head and brought his fist down hard at the base of my neck. Startled, I fell backward and as I did so, glimpsed a long narrow blade protruding from the bottom of his fist. It wasn't for several minutes until I realized he had plunged the blade down into my chest, collapsing my right lung.

Mike, meanwhile, had plunged forward, knocking my assailant over backwards, and proceeded to beat him on the head with a tire iron - a flat heavy metal bar used to mount vehicle tires that he had stuffed into his back pocket for just such emergencies. I could hear the peculiar popping noise of the prisoner's skull actually being crushed by the repeated blows of the iron bar, continuing long after the man had crumpled into a lifeless heap.

At first I thought my shortness of breath was simply an effect of the excitement, but soon realized that I really couldn't get an adequate breath at all, even when the initial excitement was over. Mike scooped me up in his arms, kicked the corpse just to make sure, and rushed me to his jeep and back to the hospital ship where the staff took over. An oxygen mask helped with my breathing problem, a large dose of penicillin was injected to prevent infection, and I was put to bed on the surgical ward.

That pretty well ended my adventure into the interrogation of enemy agents, except for the sudden appearance of huge hives on my hands and feet and inside my trachea, requiring repeated doses of adrenalin to counteract anaphylactic shock due to a heretofore unknown allergy to penicillin that nearly completed my attacker's mission. Following that, I recovered uneventfully, the lung re-expanded, and I went back to work.

There were a few more interesting patients to see at the compound, in my spare time, and on one of my visits the Company members held a special little celebratory dinner, with appropriately copious quantities of alcohol for all hands, during which I was awarded a paper 'Purple Fart' medal, memorializing my wounds in combat, which could not, I was told, ever be recognized officially with the real thing. It was good enough. Meanwhile, my ethical and moral dilemmas, while not settled, (even now) seemed to have moderated somewhat and I was able to go on working with a tolerable conscience.

The massive smallpox epidemic we feared never quite materialized, although there were hundreds of cases during the weeks following our vaccinations. A surprising number of people, mostly children, actually survived the disease, though often with faces that were scarred over every square centimeter. On occasional visits to hospitals that the Koreans had set up to treat both military and civilian war casualties, one could see whole large ward tents full of people with this historic disease that few American doctors had ever seen, many in advanced, terminal stages of the terrible malady.

Another disease that we never saw in medical school was also in abundant evidence in those sad tent hospitals: tetanus. The bacillus that causes tetanus has an unbelievable ability to survive in a dormant state, sometimes for many years. Some of the rare cases seen in the US were believed to have been caused by tetanus spores deposited in the droppings of horses during the Civil War, and only the very widespread administration of tetanus vaccination, since the 1920's, kept it from being a major public health problem, along with prompt injections of tetanus toxoid when people suffered dirty cuts, especially puncture wounds as from rusty nails. All our military people were given tetanus shots.

Not so in the Korean Armed Forces, or in the country generally. As a result, there were hundreds of cases of tetanus infection. Whole wards were occupied by men whose bodies were held rigidly in massive muscular spasm, their faces pulled back into horrific grins in a grotesque expression called 'risus sardonicus:' the sardonic smile, while they slowly died. We also saw typhoid fever, diphtheria, and other infections we had all learned about, but which had largely disappeared from the American medical scene. Along with terrible dysentery, including cholera and all kinds of parasitic infections, the medical scene was a sobering reminder that public health and preventive medicine, neither very popular subjects for US medical students, were without doubt the most important part of medicine.

Unbeknownst to me at the time, I was undergoing conversion to what was to become my true calling and ultimate destiny in medicine, from a focus on treatment to a dedication to public health and preventive medicine.

Pusan, like all Oriental cities, had a street market where people bought most of their food as well as household items and articles of clothing. With the enormous influx of refugees as well as the expansion of the port activities with ships unloading tons of supplies every day, the street market had expanded tremendously. Walking through it revealed that there was a flourishing trade in military clothing and equipment, much of it brand new and obviously stolen from the docks. Many of our troops, in Pusan for a day or two of rest and recuperation from the battle zone, bought new combat boots, field jackets and even bayonets - all new, US Government issue - at the market when their own supply sergeants were unable to provide needed replacement gear.

Many of us from the ship had noted the abundance of US equipment and supplies freely available in this black market, including various pieces of medical equipment and drugs, including penicillin, and reported our observations, indignantly, to our superiors. We were told that nothing could be done, because we were in Korea as "guests" of the Korean government and had no authority to seize back our own, obviously stolen, goods or do anything else that might offend this 'sovereign' nation. Insane!

That, it seemed to me, was not only ludicrous, it was outrageous. Here were our soldiers, fighting to save this country from invaders, dying on the frozen rice paddies and often suffering from lack of supplies because they had been stolen by the very people we were here to help. Moreover, we were powerless because of some idiotic diplomatic niceties to do anything at all about it! Much later I was to learn that huge amounts of the aid this country so generously provides to suffering people around the world after wars, terrorist attacks and natural disasters ends up exactly the same way our supplies did. We still seem to be powerless to do anything about it.

The word was passed, one day, that the ship would be sailing for Yokohama for some refitting and resupply in a few days. The trip would be quick, for the work would not take long, and we would be able to empty the ship of patients who would be transferred to the hospitals in Tokyo and Yokosuka in only a day or two. Great joy reigned aboard. The "couples" planned romantic excursions ashore, and the sailors hatched elaborate schemes for visiting the nightclubs and whorehouses, many quite beautiful, that existed in such abundance in Tokyo's storied entertainment district.

The day before we sailed, after I had treated another badly mauled prisoner at the compound, I was summoned to the Colonel's office. Without any preamble, he asked if I would be willing to participate in a 'little operation' to assist my fellow medics in the Korean Army. I said sure, if I could. He went on to explain that they were terribly short of penicillin. Our own forces did not have sufficient quantities of this new miracle drug for our own needs. Let alone to supply the Koreans. It was available in any desired quantity from pharmaceutical companies in Japan, but current laws in both countries forbade any such purchases, and our government was unwilling to skirt those laws. Officially, that is.

Here was where I (and, unbeknownst to them, the US Navy) came into the picture. The 'Company,' with its own unique set of rules, was going to solve this by giving me a large amount of US currency, having me buy the penicillin in Tokyo, and having the Navy (albeit unknowingly) transport it on the Hospital Ship back to Korea where the Company would get it to the Koreans.

The money, all of it in US currency of the standard green variety as well as large amounts of Military Payment Certificates (the "play money, printed in Japan, that all US personnel were required to be paid in and to use, and never give to the locals) came from the black market, beer halls and bordellos of Pusan - all controlled by the Korean Army.

My role was to let them tape the money comfortably (!) around my chest and abdomen, carry it to a place in Tokyo's Ginza district, and pick up the boxes of penicillin, take them back aboard ship labeled as souvenirs and personal items, and hand them over to my Company friends when the ship got back to Pusan. Sounded simple enough.

I tried not to think about the implications of what I was to do: smuggle unauthorized currency between two mutually hostile countries, buy drugs from an anonymous source in Tokyo and smuggle them out of the country on a US Naval ship, and then smuggle them into another country and turn them over to a quasi-military unit that I really knew nothing about, while strongly suspecting that some of the stuff, at least, would end up on the black market. Talk about moral dilemmas!

The black market thought gave me an idea that helped resolve it. I told my friends at the Company that I would take this terrible risk on one condition. That was that they would arrange for the Korean Army intelligence people to conduct a raid on the black market, seize every boot, jacket, ammo pouch, web belt, bayonet and all other US military items that were there for sale, and deliver them to the Army Quartermaster in Pusan.

We had a deal.

The ensuing several days proved to be extremely uncomfortable, due both to my mounting anxiety and to the bulky, itchy mass of currency taped around my body, which I dared not remove. I stayed mostly in my stateroom, and left the ship the minute it hit the port. A set of directions, written in Japanese, provided my taxi driver with clear instructions, and after a long ride from the Port of Yokohama to an alley between two brightly lighted streets in the Ginza district, he deposited me and pointed down the alley to a doorway with a single incandescent bulb glowing above it.

The alley was quite dark, and I made my way gingerly down it toward the single, dim bulb above the door, which seemed a long way off. I felt farther from Chicago than ever before, even on the streets of Pusan, and sweated profusely under my girdle of currency. About half way to my objective, the light, and indeed the brighter lights of the street beyond, suddenly disappeared as a huge, smelly creature, his chain rattling, rose to his full height of about 7 feet, directly in my path and nearly blocking the narrow alley.

Equally startled, the monstrous creature and I stared at each other for many long moments, until finally it sank down against the wall of the building and kind of curled up. When my breath returned, and my heart slowed down, I was able to determine that what I had just encountered was an enormous, blessedly peaceful, Hokkaido bear, waiting outside the back door of a nightclub where he would later perform with his trainer.

As cautiously and non-threateningly as possible, I made my way around him and made it to the designated doorway without further incident. My knock was promptly answered by a large (for a Japanese) man who opened the door and without a word pointed me toward another door at the top of a narrow stairway. It was opened by another man who motioned me to a seat in what appeared to be a small but richly decorated waiting room containing a brocaded sofa and matching chairs placed around an elegant, richly carved low table. He then left the room, and I sat alone, in silence, for several minutes. Soon another door opened and a woman dressed in a kimono padded in, bringing a pot of tea and a cup. She poured some of the steaming green tea and then left. Again I waited. There were no magazines.

Finally, a small man in an expensive western-style business suit entered and introduced himself. He asked if I were the doctor from the ship in Chosen - the Japanese word for Korea - and when I said I was, he said that he understood that I had something for his company, which I took to mean the money. When I confirmed this, and added that it was taped under my uniform, he apologized profusely for what he said must be most uncomfortable, and added that, with my permission, his assistants would help me remove it, apologizing for the unavoidable indignity that this would entail.

With my immediate assent to this offer, he left the room and promptly returned with three men, all of whom appeared to have weapons under their suitcoats. Two of these set to work helping me off with my clothes, and then the tape holding the money against my body, while the third man stood attentively to one side. When they finished, they promptly left and I got dressed again, whereupon the first man returned. He told me that the merchandise would be carried down the steps

I had entered by, and placed in a taxi that had been summoned to take me wherever I wished.

A small hotel not too far from the dock provided a place to bathe, finally, a good futon to sleep on, and a place to stash my three crates of "souvenirs." I took them aboard the ship the following day during three different watches, so as to encounter a different officer of the deck each time and not attract too much attention to my excessive souvenir buying, and a few days later took the small crates ashore in similar fashion and handed them over to my Company friends back in Pusan.

Some of the penicillin, as I had suspected, ended up on the black market, but it was explained to me that the profit was so enormous from selling just a fraction of the stuff that it paid for all the rest, which went to the army medics. That made me feel a little better, but the whole experience proved to me that one had to be more courageous than I was, or incredibly stupid, or both, to do this sort of thing for a living.

The fighting on the Korean peninsula was going well, for our forces. The brilliant amphibious assault up north, at the port of Inchon, had succeeded in cutting the North Korean forces in half, and our Marine Division was making its way north toward the Yalu River, separating Korea from Manchuria. Several Army divisions were also headed north as well as consolidating US control of the southern half of the country. Rumors abounded that our ship was to be relieved by the only other hospital ship then commissioned, named the Benevolence, allowing ours, the Repose, to head for Pearl Harbor. Increasing resistance by the North Koreans, now getting support from Chinese forces just north of the Yalu, led MacArthur to demand that he be allowed to attack the 'sanctuary' enjoyed by Communist Forces across the Manchurian border. His dispute with his civilian superiors in the Pentagon and with President Truman over this issue led to his dramatic firing.

It also led to intense discussions and disputes among all of us engaged in the Korean 'conflict,' which had never been declared to be a war in spite of all the fighting and dying. Most of us, at the time, while paying lip service to the ascendancy of civilian authority over the military, tended to side with MacArthur, even though nobody liked him very much. We believed he was right in demanding to neutralize the Manchurian sanctuary, for that was a logical and indeed inescapable, sound tactical next step to bring the war to an end and save countless casualties and lost lives.

Morale became very much of a problem, among officers and men alike. It hit a new low when Chinese forces entered the fray, streaming across the Yalu into the frozen northern reaches of the country in overwhelming numbers that far exceeded our own forces. Suddenly the whole picture of the war changed and disaster loomed. MacArthur had been right, we believed, and his replacement, Matthew

Ridgeway, faced a daunting task. What was perhaps the greatest retreat in American military history began, as our forces headed back south, toward the 38th parallel. No simple withdrawal, this. They were forced to fight their way, often surrounded by a sea of fresh Chinese troops sent against them from all sides in human waves seemingly heedless of their own casualties.

At this moment I got new orders. I was to join the First Marine Division, 'in the field,' 'somewhere in North Korea.' My orders indicated that I was to be given transport by any available military means to reach my assigned unit, the First Medical Battalion, 1st MarDiv, Fleet Marine Force, Pacific.

Brainwashing, Drunks & Madness

William E. Mayer, M.D.

CHAPTER 7

MARINES IN KOREA

It was the dead of winter in North Korea, and I had no winter clothing whatsoever, nor was any available on the ship or even in the black market. Dressed in my cotton khaki uniform and thin Navy raincoat, carrying extra tee shirts, shorts, socks and shaving gear in a little canvas bag, and bravely armed with a new Combat Masterpiece Colt Revolver I had managed to buy, I headed north.

It seemed to grow colder by the mile as I hitched rides in trucks and jeeps all the way up the peninsula. En route I managed to talk a number of sympathetic supply sergeants out of a field jacket, warm socks, boots, even a GI sweater and some heavy leather gloves with separate woven woolen inserts, and by the time I found the Marine Division, still fighting its way south and still surrounded by an entire Chinese Army of several Divisions, I looked almost like I belonged. With a great sense of relief, coupled with a huge helping of outright fear, I finally found the Medical Battalion Headquarters Company just in time for the evening meal.

The unit had thrown up a circle of pyramidal 16-foot square tents and 30-man squad tents on a frozen rice paddy. True to their tradition, the fighting force of Marines had positioned themselves, fairly densely concentrated in a much larger circle of trucks, weapons carriers, tanks and men on all sides of their medics.

I found the Command Tent, and was welcomed brusquely by the commanding officer, a Navy Commander named Dick Lawrence, who told me to take his mess kit and head for the line outside if I wanted something to eat. All the men in the unit were indeed standing in a line around the inside of the circle of tents, leading to a field serving station heated by flaming gasoline stoves. In the middle of the open space in the center of the circle of men and tents, a pipe about 18 inches high and 5 inches in diameter protruded from the frozen earth. This was the "piss tube." I desperately needed to use it. Never in my entire life, before or since that memorable moment, has it ever been that hard to perform a simple excretory act. While I struggled, a hundred men looked on, sizing up the new doc, for the word had spread that one had arrived. Finally, blessedly, success. Relief!

I took my place in the chow line, got my tin mess kit filled with stew and potatoes, and headed back to the command tent. A group of half a dozen officers was clustered around the pot-bellied stove, which was actually glowing red as it was fired up as high as possible in honor of the sub-zero cold, and one of them motioned me inside. Another pushed over a small ammunition box for me to sit on. I leaned over to move the box nearer, and at that moment committed the one unforgivable Marine Corps sin.

I dropped my weapon. The snap closing my shoulder holster had come undone when I opened the front of my field jacket, and when I leaned over, my new 'Combat Masterpiece' slid free and fell with a loud clatter onto the ammunition crate and off onto the frozen floor of the tent. It did not fire.

Every man in the tent ducked and sprang outward, away from the tight circle around the glowing stove, emitting little exclamations like "Shit!" "Goddam!" "Son of a bitch!" and others indicating their inhospitable disapproval of my clumsiness, stupidity and manifest unfitness to join their select company. I picked up the unfaithful pistol and secured it in its cradle at my breast while the men whose lives I had just threatened returned to their places around the stove amidst much head shaking and muttering.

The only worse sin a marine can commit, and only just slightly worse, is to fire his weapon accidentally. Thanks to a benevolent God, I had not done that, but almost. It was clear that my introduction to my new combat brethren had not been auspicious. As manfully as I could, I apologized, choked down my dinner, and headed outside to perform the ritual dipping of the mess kit into a garbage can of boiling soapy water over a flaming gasoline burner, followed by another dip into cleaner boiling water to rinse it. Still preoccupied with my stupendous opening gambit, and paying little attention to what I was doing, I plunged my whole hand into the blistering hot rinse water, scalding it seriously. Naturally it was not acceptable to seek any kind of palliation for this. Served me right.

Sometime before dawn, in the intense cold and darkness, the unit gathered itself from an uneasy sleep and moved out. Since I had removed only my boots to climb into my sleeping bag, leaving everything else, including my field jacket and shoulder holster on because of the cold, it was fairly easy to get ready to go. The breakfast consisted of cold C-Rations, so my red, swollen hand was not further endangered by boiling rinse water.

We marched steadily southward in traditional Marine Corps formation. Wounded men were in 'box' ambulances and litter jeeps and ordinary jeeps at the center of the mass of men. Around them were corpsmen and medical officers. Around them, were other vehicles and trailers bearing tents and supplies. Still farther out were whole companies of heavily armed infantrymen, with every conceivable kind of man-carried weapon including bulky mortars. When the terrain forced us into a narrower line, riflemen climbed the bordering hills and formed a protective shield around those in narrower spaces below. At times the ground flattened out, and we moved steadily across frozen rice paddies and through ruinedvillages.

At last, after what seemed like many days and freezing, frightening nights with sporadic weapons fire only at the outer edges of the small army of men surrounding and protecting us, we reached an area near the east port city of Pohang-dong, deemed safe enough to serve as our destination. Still cold and snowy, but far less so than it had been earlier in the mountains to the north, the place designated as our hospital site lay at the foot of some small hills on three sides of a large flat area of frozen paddies. The corpsmen, all Navy sailors but indistinguishable from the Marines, immediately set to work erecting tents and unpacking the surprising amounts of equipment and supplies necessary to put a field hospital together.

Commander Lawrence, the Navy doctor who commanded the Medical Battalion, had introduced me as his new Executive Officer, and announced that he and I would share his command tent, a canvas pyramidal structure 16 feet square, furnished with a potbelly stove, two cots, and a field desk and two foot lockers.

The Marine Corps, set up originally to provide a force of fighting men aboard naval vessels, considered every man in the Corps to be, first and foremost, a fighter. Basic training was extremely hard and rigorous, and on its completion the recruit was required to be an expert rifleman, skilled in the use of his weapon, his bayonet, and hand grenades. Advanced individual training turned out men further able to operate BARs - the long, enormously heavy, fully automatic rifle made by Browning; light or heavy machine guns; light and heavy mortars; armored personnel- and weapons-carriers; tanks; tank recovery vehicles; artillery, from 105-mm to 155-mm howitzers capable of throwing a heavy shell many miles with great accuracy; all kinds of vehicles: jeeps, ambulances, trucks, truck-mounted bridging equipment; self-propelled artillery pieces; recoilless 'rifles' that were actually a kind of rocket launcher, and all the other weapons of war "in the field."

Smaller numbers of Marines, all still primarily riflemen able to fight alongside their comrades in foxholes and bunkers, were trained to cook, repair vehicles, service weapons, manage supplies, fly and maintain airplanes, do heavy engineering work, and do the myriad other tasks necessary to keep a fighting force in the field, but they were all still, basically, riflemen, and proud of that.

The Navy, as the 'parent' organization of the Corps, supplied from its own ranks all the doctors, corpsmen, chaplains, supply officers, legal officers and other professionals that the Marine Corps did not train. I was never to discover what, if any, criteria were used to select Navy doctors, like myself, for service with the Marines. None of us was given any special training (not even an instruction booklet!) to prepare us for this duty in those days, in spite of the fact that it was as different from Navy duty aboard ship as it was from being a ballerina. 'Joining' the Marines at a base in the US during peacetime was hard and jolting at best, but joining them while they were at war was unimaginably challenging.

No amount of experience on overnight hikes with the Boy Scouts or camping in State Parks, and no amount of workouts in health clubs (which didn't exist in those days anyway) or playing on high school teams could prepare one for living with the Marines in their beloved "field." They prided themselves on the care they took of their medics, as evidenced during our 'attack to the rear' marching down from the Yalu. They also prided themselves on how tough they were, surviving in the wilderness - anywhere: jungle or desert, arctic or tropics, France or Korea - with minimal comforts, no frills, basic supplies, skimpy shelter and lousy food. We medics, well cared-for or not, were expected to participate in all this.

There were, however, certain permissible modifications of this spartan, warrior life. For example, if your unit were to stay longer than overnight in the same location, it was okay to make your tent as comfortable as possible. If you needed a jeep and saw one sitting around unused and unattended, it was considered acceptable, under certain conditions, to take it, as long as you were prepared to repaint it in Marine Corps green and give it a new set of numbers. Quickly. It was also quite all right, even desirable, to trade little items you might have found lying around former adversaries recently sent off to a far better place and no longer in need of them, to rear area 'pogues' for prized items like booze, spare cash and assorted personal luxuries rare up forward but common in the safe, luxurious rear areas.

"Pogue" is a cherished Marine term, not entirely definable but applied to all those creatures of a lower life form with limited intelligence and no manly warrior skills whatsoever, who inhabit perfectly safe, posh surroundings well to the rear of any conflict. Their uniforms are different.

The procedure for procuring needed supplies and equipment, luxury items and other necessities not available through normal supply channels is called "Kumshaw." It may involve subterfuge, barter, fraud, misappropriation, midnight requisitioning and even thievery, but it is widespread and widely believed to be entirely justifiable when the perpetrator is a hard-fighting, death-defying US Marine operating in behalf of his buddies, and the victim is that fat, lazy, super-safe, oversupplied and generally useless blob of humanity living in the rear.

Our hospital had lost much of its gear on its trip from the far north, so our kumshaw experts went right to work to repair things. Before long, we had a reasonably well-equipped tent hospital of about a hundred beds, complete with operating rooms, lab, X-Ray, galley, pharmacy and storeroom. While this was going on, I was learning as fast as possible about being a Navy doctor with the Marines.

Commander Lawrence turned out to be a great teacher, as well as something of an unforgettable character himself. He was from a prominent, historic Massachusetts family after whom an old, largely blue-collar town was named. Something of a free spirit, if not an outright rebel, he rejected his family's support and worked his way through a major private New England university. He sold lampshades in Macy's department store, hated it, and took up boxing, for money.

After college, during which he distinguished himself and disgraced his family by taking a Negro dancer to dinner at Boston's finest hotel, a distinct first for that city, he headed for China with the intention of setting up a trucking business.

He put his trucks to work moving people, which the authorities considered to be smuggling, and he was arrested and thrown into jail. His family was able to enlist the help of Joseph Grew, then our ambassador to China, and Dick was freed. Returning to the US, he went to medical school and specialized in internal medicine before joining the Navy where he was assigned to the Marines. He distinguished himself when he parachuted along with a Marine unit, and broke both his legs landing on a small South Pacific island. Undaunted, he mounted the back of a strong young Marine and 'rode' him until the assault ended, directing his troops from his piggyback position. He was decorated for that, for his valor.

All this my new leader told me during our daily cocktail hour every afternoon before we headed for the mess tent. He had managed to appropriate a small refrigerator from some unsuspecting Army unit, and had discovered that it would hold exactly sixteen quart bottles of Gilbey's Gin, with a small bottle of French vermouth lying on top. Each time he filled the refrigerator, he took the cork out of the vermouth bottle and inserted it into each gin bottle in turn, giving it a brief shake before treating the next one. He told me this was the proper way to mix a really dry martini, and we faithfully consumed some of it every day.

During the weeks that I shared the Commander's tent, I discovered that he was a truly spirited man whose boundless energy and high activity level clearly marked him as hypo-manic. He traveled constantly among our five field hospitals, touring the wards, looking in on surgery, giving pep talks to the corpsmen, and sharing a meal with the medical officers and giving them both medical consultation and inspiration.

He always stayed up reading, long after I had gone to sleep, and ordinarily was up before me. I discovered this early on. My first morning in his tent I was awakened by a sharp flat-handed slap on my abdomen and the loud declaration, "C'mon, Willie! Time to hit the deck!" No one else had ever called me Willie, but of course I responded when he did. In an attempt to protect myself from these early morning assaults, I took to getting up before him, and witnessed his extraordinary wake-up routine. With no hint that he was about to arise, he would literally leap from his cot, landing on his feet in a boxer's crouch with his clenched fists in traditional prizefighting position, shake his head vigorously from side to side several times, and then open his eyes. He would then straighten up, shout a greeting, and proceed to dress.

His command style reflected his high level of both mental and physical activity. He was very supportive and encouraging toward people who were performing well, and almost brutally critical and punitive toward those who did not, in his judgment, measure up. He was particularly intolerant of any officer commanding one of the five hospital companies who did not show proper leadership, and over the next year he summarily fired four of the five at different times. Each time he would anoint me, on the spot, as the new Commanding Officer, with the admonition to 'straighten this mess out, Willie!'

The military expressed the alphabet at that time with words like 'able,' 'baker,' 'Charlie,' 'dog,' 'easy,' 'foxtrot,' and so on, rendering the letters USA, for example, as "Uncle Sugar Able." It's been modernized now to alpha, bravo and others that I still haven't learned. My first command, therefore, was "Dog Med," meaning D Medical Company, 1st Medical Battalion, 1st Marine Division.

I found Dog Med in a sad state of disarray. Its equipment was poorly 'policed,' which is to say, maintained in proper order, and its staff was disorganized, disorderly, and discontent - all beginning with their company's designating letter. Like the other hospital companies, except one, this outfit had about 200 men, half of them Navy corpsmen and half Marines. The latter maintained the equipment like tents and trucks, operated the mess and the portable showers, when we had them, and kept their weapons handy since they were responsible for the security of the hospital, its staff, and its patients.

The corpsmen and the marines were at odds, generally ignoring one another unless to make disparaging remarks and bicker over petty disputes. The several chief petty officers were older, bored, disaffected, and unfriendly toward their counterparts, the senior Marine Corps non-commissioned officers. The eight or ten physicians on the medical staff seemed disgruntled and resentful regarding their great misfortune at being assigned 'in the mud' with a bunch of stupid foot-soldiers. The Commanding Officer I was to replace had no idea how to handle men, and his weak, passive persona didn't help.

After visiting the Division Headquarters, and studying the disposition of all the 18,000-plus fighting men, their tank companies and artillery units, motor pools, ammunition dumps and POL (petroleum, oil and lubricants) storage yards, I decided on a strategy that I hoped would help me shape things up - either that or lead to total disaster.

Returning to the Medical Battalion Headquarters, I told Lawrence that Dog Company was poorly located, underutilized, and would be of little help if any serious shooting started. I proposed moving it much father forward, nearer to the units likely to be at the forefront of any combat action if such should start, arguing that it was basically a good bunch of people who should respond to such a challenge. He agreed.

That evening, back in my own 16-square foot pyramidal command tent, blessedly mine alone, all the senior non-commissioned officers and commissioned administrative officers who commanded the two groups, were assembled to 'get the word' from the new 'old man.' I told them I had visited both of our higher headquarters, at Division and Battalion, and that the message from on high was that we would be moving. Tomorrow. Our maps were already marked to show our new location, which got everybody's attention instantly, since we would be nearer than any other medical unit to the line of contact with the enemy. This, I pointed out, was a great tribute to our (potential) excellence, and we would darn well live up to and exceed the brass's expectations.

There followed a busy night of packing, loading trucks, and planning for the next day's move. The preparations took all of 10 hours and required large amounts of inspirational activity by the sergeants and chiefs, mainly in the form of cursing, threats and shouting but, at least as far as I could see, no physical violence. Shortly after noon, our convoy set out for our new destination, taking up nearly a half mile of road when we were under way. We reached our new site in a few hours, and once again the commissioned and non-commissioned leaders gathered around for instructions.

Fully aware that the first order of business was ordinarily (after latrines were dug) erection of tents for the men, and mess halls, I announced that since we were first and foremost, now and always, a hospital, we would set up the surgical tents, the X-Ray and Lab, and some of the ward tents first. When they were up and ready to operate, and not before, we would put up the squad tents to house our own staff, and the mess tent. After all, they were told, we could start getting patients this very night.

And so we did. Not a great many, but enough that the hospital core that we had set up was fully occupied for several hours right after the evening meal, and the sound of firing and occasional flashes of light from artillery fire could clearly be heard and seen. The result of that new experience, for most of the men, was that many worked far into the night digging foxholes, some quite deep, right next to their newly erected squad tents, without even being told!

By noon the next day I thought I could detect the beginnings of a major change. The work of packing, moving, unpacking and setting up again was hard, and had been done reasonably well, thanks mainly to the efforts of the senior sergeants and chief petty officers. I went into the crew's mess tent, got everyone's attention, and told them, accurately, that they had done a hard job and done it well. They could be proud of themselves. They could also - as they well knew - do one helluva lot better, as I was certain they would, next time.

Surely, I said to the Marines, you could see that a lot of these sailors can actually help with the heavy work - sort of like a Marine. They were expected to do that, and you guys can help them learn some things. Also, I added, you've noticed that each corpsman has his own weapon, the same as yours, and they could probably stand a little help learning to maintain those weapons and keep them clean and ready to use, since they don't get much practice like you people do.

In return, I said, these corpsmen can teach you some important things about what they do, and what they teach you can save your life when things get rough. What I want to see, I told them, is a bunch of sailors trying to be as good marines as you marines are, and I want to see at least some of you killers trying to learn enough about what the corpsmen do that you can help us take care of wounded marines, when we need for you to.

The same message was delivered to the senior non-commissioned officers in their separate mess tent, along with the announcement that they were responsible to see that it happened.

Those little speeches, combined with a newly set up, newly scrubbed tent hospital and the sounds of gunfire not very far away, were all that was necessary. The situation that existed previously rapidly disappeared, and a new, positive spirit was everywhere evident. Within a few months, Dog Med was singled out by the Commanding General of the Division himself, for special praise for its outstanding performance. It became a matter of pride when a marine was mistaken by some visitor for a corpsman, and equally satisfying for a corpsman who was thought by some passing soldier to be a "gyrene."

It wasn't long before small groups of corpsmen could be seen gathered around a Marine, acting as their instructor, who taught them the proper way to clean and oil their weapons, sharpen their bayonets, and handle these things like a proper fighting man should. In turn, Marines started showing up on the wards, helping to move patients, learning how to start IV fluids, and being taught about cleanliness and sterility.

One day a young Marine was brought in, and we were surprised to see a young, magnificent German Shepherd dog following close behind his litter. We had to operate on the man for a penetrating abdominal wound, and when he recovered from the anesthesia I told him we were going to have to evacuate him to Japan and probably on to the States. He told me a wild story about having bought the dog, a superb pedigreed creature descended from the excellent shepherds imported by wealthy Japanese from Germany before the war. With the complicity of his friends in the unit, he managed to smuggle the dog with him when they were sent into action in Korea.

For the second time in my career, I was asked if I would consider taking the dog, much like the blind veteran whose blindness I had 'cured' with hypnosis back in Philadelphia, who gave me his Seeing Eye dog. Naturally his request was granted - enthusiastically.

In subsequent weeks the dog, whose name was 'Master,' lived in my tent in a bed of Army blankets beside my cot, and was fed better than he had ever imagined. He rapidly reached full size, much larger than those of his breed usually seen in the US, and we became constant, inseparable companions. He was adoringly attended to by almost everyone in the hospital company, and his presence alongside me everywhere undoubtedly generated warmer feelings of loyalty among my men than I could have earned without him.

After a couple months of steady improvements in Dog Med, the commander came by one afternoon bearing a bottle of his famous super-dry martini mix, and as we shared our cocktail he told me he wanted me to take over another hospital company, Charlie Med. The next morning, having delivered a farewell inspirational speech to the men of my first real command, and feeling like George Washington bidding farewell to his Army, I set out in my jeep, my beautiful dog sitting upright in the other front seat, for Charlie Med.

This company was in far better shape than Dog Med had been, but like that other field hospital, was situated too far from the FEBA - forward edge of the battle area - to be easily reached on foot when our little helicopters couldn't fly (which was often) and the box ambulances and litter jeeps couldn't handle the load. My solution to this perennial field evacuation problem was to move the unit closer to where people were getting wounded, so that their buddies could carry them in on litters. Each combat battalion had an aid station, but these were each manned by one very junior medical officer and a handful of corpsmen, and were equipped only to do initial, hopefully lifesaving procedures like stopping bleeding and starting IV fluids so that the casualty could be moved on back to one of the medical companies.

By siting my hospital only a few hundred meters behind the aid station, we could get to wounded men much more quickly and do fairly elaborate procedures including major surgery and multiple transfusions as well as elaborate splinting and immobilization of mangled limbs.

During my days aboard the hospital ship, in between trips to the 'compound' for company business and my daily struggles to learn to write simple Japanese characters and speak the complex language that often sounded like nonsense syllables, I studied what I could find about field medicine, starting with the Civil War.

One thing that I saw in my studies, repeated many times, was that few men were killed out-right on the battlefield. Many died there, or nearby, but usually not until six or eight hours after they had been hit, sometimes by a bullet but far more often by fragments of bursting artillery rounds, mortars, and grenades. At Yokosuka, I recalled with great clarity, most of the casualties brought to us directly from the combat areas had multiple fragment wounds, and lacerations from flying debris propelled by explosions nearby. They had survived to reach Japan, in many cases, because they had been fairly competently bound up in battle dressings.

If left on the field for more than a few hours, or if their transport took longer than that, men died in substantial numbers due to blood loss and shock - a precipitous drop in blood pressure due both to hemorrhage and to the trauma they experienced - with a failure of vital functions such as respiration and kidney function. Recognizing this, our military services over the years had put great effort into the training and equipping of expert field medics who could initiate the life-saving measures of stopping the bleeding and combating shock. These often heroic men, usually with no real ability to protect themselves, went into battle right alongside the riflemen and mortarmen, and ministered to them where they fell. Many of them died doing this. Fighting units also had the battalion aid stations described above, where young, green, often inexperienced and always terrified physicians operated from a small tent very close to the actual shooting, in terrible danger.

Small field hospitals, like ours, that could be expanded to treat as many as 200 wounded men, were placed somewhere behind the aid stations. Sometimes, in Army divisions, there was an intermediate way station, called a 'clearing company,' between the aid station and the forward field hospital unit, but we did not have those in the Marine Division.

Our medical companies, like Dog and Charlie, as earlier described, had about a hundred Navy corpsmen to care for patients, and a hundred 'regular' Marines to do everything else. The medical staff, mostly surgeons with at least a year, often more, of specialized surgical residency training, usually numbered from ten to a dozen physicians, a dentist, at least one laboratory officer, and sometimes a pharmacist, with a medical administrative officer assigned to manage medical records, requisitions and personnel actions.

Each medical company was equipped with electrical generators, galley equipment, dozens of chests of medical supplies, instruments, operating lights, surgical tables, a dental chair and appropriate equipment, refrigerators, chests of whole blood and crates of intravenous fluids. There were enough powerful '6-bys' - 2 1/2 ton trucks with power to all 6 wheels - to haul all this stuff, along with the enormous quantities of tentage necessary to set up five or six "ward tents" that could hold up to 30 or 40 litter patients, tents for the operating rooms, X-Ray and pharmacy and lab, and squad tents to house all the personnel and mess tents to feed them in. Usually there was also a latrine tent, and sometimes one for showers.

Along with all of this, there were tents for the vast quantities of litters, blankets, cots, uniform items like cold weather coats and special boots, pot-bellied stoves for all the tents, fuel for those and drums of fuel for all the vehicles, water purification equipment, radios and telephones, and everything necessary to maintain a community of several hundred souls and give medical care to hundreds more. It was commonly believed that there was well over a million dollars worth of equipment in one medical company, and many years later I was to learn it was far more than that.

Moving one of these things along the rough, unimproved winding roads, especially in the mountains and even more especially in the winter, was a monstrous undertaking. The column was long, and highly vulnerable to snipers and small patrols while moving. During nighttime stops, and in spite of extensive security patrols and precautions, attempts were frequently made to raid and steal items from the column, as I was to discover when a fifty thousand dollar generator once disappeared en route to a new location as part of an armed and guarded convoy. No trace of it was ever found, and it may still be supplying power to some

South Korean village.

The hospital, when set up, occupied perhaps three acres, although that made for a crowded camp. Five acres was better. Korea does not have a good supply of three-acre open spaces, and we were in competition with ordnance units, motor pools, tank parks, and fuel dumps for available space. When the division was moving frequently, it was often extremely hard to break down the hospital, pack in the trucks, make it to the next location, unload all the gear and set up the new hospital, and get it operating without wiping out the entire crew from exhaustion.

Consultation with the Division Engineers led me to a partial solution, and nearly to the end of my very existence. Whenever we got the word of an impending move, I would go to the Division G-2, the intelligence section, look at the maps of where we were going and where the enemy lines were, and get tentative approval for a new site. Then, while the crew was preparing for the move, and accompanied by my beautiful dog and a husky corpsman, both of us armed with pistols and grease guns, we would head out to look over the terrain. One thing we had plenty of was tent stakes, so we took a stack of them and a dozen rolls of gauze bandage along with us.

When we arrived at a likely site, we'd pace it off, drive stakes and string the gauze to show the outlines of the hospital, usually in the shape of a huge cross, and head for Division headquarters to establish our 'claim.' Usually it worked, and although some of the Ordnance and Transportation Officers groused about the medics always grabbing the best spots, we got away with it.

That first reconnaissance mission almost proved to be my last. The dog, Master, had achieved a certain fame for his ability to smell out mine fields, numerous in the combat zone and never marked, if left by the enemy. If we approached one, even in the jeep, he would become agitated, whining and moving about on the seat of the vehicle and sometimes even putting his forepaws atop the windshield. On this occasion he showed some of that behavior as we neared our new site, but then stopped moving around, so I figured all was well. We dismounted, and the three of us started pacing off the area we had chosen, which was covered with small trees and bushes. Suddenly the dog stopped and the corpsman, who was behind me, grabbed my shoulder and said, "Don't move!" When I stopped, he stepped up beside me and pointed at my feet. Inches ahead, a string was stretched tightly across our path, just inches above the ground. "Bouncing Betty, Doc," he announced.

What this meant was that the string was a crude 'trip wire' set to explode a particularly vicious variety of mine that first jumped straight up to 3 or 4 feet above the ground and then exploded its main charge, sending steel fragments out in all directions, parallel to the surface of the ground and capable of cutting a man in half at the waist. We had just missed it. The dog stood well back, growling, while we searched out the end of the string and disabled the device. We looked carefully, but found no others, set our stakes and gauze outlining our hospital, and returned to Division to file our 'claim.'

The next day we pulled out with Charlie Med fully loaded, and after arriving at the new site the men set an all-time record by setting up the cross-shaped core of the hospital and getting it ready to receive patients in just 2 hours! It took much longer, naturally, to set up the crew quarters, mess, and all the other ward tents, but that record stood until the war ended. It was later matched, but never bettered, and 2 hours became the standard.

Patients usually came in to the hospital in clusters, with as many as twenty being delivered by helicopters, jeeps, and on litters carried by their comrades. The surgical tent was set up with four operating tables, each with a fairly good light, and it was common to have all four going at once. There were no nurses, male or female, serving with our units, so the atmosphere was different from that depicted in movie and TV productions about the Army's MASH (Mobile Army Surgical Hospital) units, but truly remarkable, major surgical feats were commonly performed there.

Between clusters of arriving casualties there were periods of great boredom. These could extend for hours or even days, and I soon learned to devote all available 'down time' to improving everything that contributed to my 'quality of life.' Over a period of time, I managed to improve my tent by using ammunition pallets as a kind of floor, hanging Army blankets from wires strung a foot inside the canvas walls of the tent, and keeping a supply of hot water in a brass artillery shell set atop my potbellied stove. I rapidly learned what all the old hands already knew: it was essential to keep oneself as clean as possible (hard when heating small quantities of water in a steel 'pot' helmet sitting on your stove), to shave every morning, wear clean socks, maintain regular bowel habits, and eat all the food the mess cooks gave you, bad though it and C-Rations (huge gas-producers!) seemed.

All the little details of daily living, so minor and casual at home, are laborious and time-consuming in the field, but absolutely essential to maintaining some level of sanity. In addition, they use up major amounts of the tedious quiet times between those episodes of chilling terror that come with gunshots and explosions, and help keep your mind on normal things.

As the months alternately dragged and raced by, we moved Charlie Med two more times, and became quite expert at packing and unpacking, and our two-hour goal for having an operating hospital core was met. Our last move placed us in the immediate vicinity of a huge, unmarked mine field estimated to contain upward of a million small anti-personnel mines. The field's edge lay about 50 feet away from my command tent, ensuring that no roving enemy patrol could approach from that direction.

In addition, my dog had moved outside the tent as the weather became milder, and took to sleeping right next to my cot, but outside the tent wall. He had an uncanny ability to smell North Korean soldiers, possibly because of their garlic - and pepper-rich diet, and on several occasions raised an alarm signaling an enemy patrol long before our own sentries detected their approach.

There were no stray dogs in Korea, in those days, probably because there were many hungry, displaced people who saw them as a heaven-sent dietary supplement. It was a surprise, therefore, when a skinny, dirty and quite lively little white mongrel showed up one morning. A female, she was evidently in heat, and my guardian-comrade shepherd literally went wild. He chased frantically after her around the many tents that filled our compound, his man's-best-friend role completely forgotten, until she headed out into the minefield. He stopped abruptly at the edge of the field, barking loudly in evident distress. The little dog stopped momentarily and looked back at him, then playfully continued on. The shepherd hesitated, and then began to pick his way carefully into the field behind her.

Suddenly there was a loud explosion, and the little dog disappeared in a cloud of dirt and debris. The shepherd gave a sharp, short bark and collapsed where he stood, obviously wounded by flying fragments from fifteen or twenty feet away. One of our Marines, proceeding with great care, made his way into the field, hoisted the dog into his arms, and brought him out.

The hospital was quiet just then, with no combat casualties coming in, and the explosion of the land mine, so close to us, brought everybody running. The dog was immediately examined by expert trauma surgeons, and found to have many small fragment wounds but only one serious injury, resulting in an open, compound fracture of one femur. Without instructions from anyone, several of the corpsmen lifted the wounded animal onto a stretcher that instantly materialized from the admissions tent, and carried him off to surgery, surrounded by a small crowd of concerned onlookers.

In surgery, after the leg was shaved and disinfected, and loose bone fragments were removed, the consensus was that he needed an intramedullary pin inserted into the marrow cavity of the animal's large femur, or thigh-bone. After some discussion, it was decided that an aluminum alloy rifle cleaning rod could be cut down and used for the pin. A rod was produced, modified, inserted, and seemed to be just right, so the wound was closed, bandages applied, pain-killers administered, and he was laid gently to rest inside my tent.

For a couple of days, the great dog seemed to be doing well, taking water and even bits of food, as he recovered from the injuries and the surgery. Then, without warning, his respiration became labored; he coughed and seemed to choke, and died. He had suffered a fat embolism, wherein a blob of fatty marrow had broken loose, entered his bloodstream, and lodged in his lung.

We buried the magnificent animal with appropriate solemn comments from several of the men who had been his particular friends, and I entered upon a period of serious mourning along with a heightened sense of loneliness and vulnerability with the loss of my wonderful, alert guardian.

My next move was to E Medical Company, affectionately known as "Easy Med." Once again, I found an organization in some disarray, poorly located to allow for easy access when troops were engaged, so once again I sought and obtained permission to move it forward. This time, the site I picked on the map turned out, when I looked it over, to be a classical wartime disaster area.

Situated at the foot of a good-sized hill, I had set my sights on the recent site of what had been the town on Munsan-ni, supposedly totally destroyed in an assault by heavy artillery followed by an airborne attack a few days earlier. When I arrived on the scene, the stench of decaying bodies was horrible, and the destruction was complete except for a single fairly large house that stood, miraculously, almost unscathed in the midst of piles of rubble that had been other houses, shops, streets and gardens.

The Division Engineer, whom I consulted, was undismayed when told I wanted to put a field hospital in the midst of this chaos. No problem, he averred, and within hours had his bulldozers there, energetically carving out the side of the hill and moving tons of rock and earth atop the ruined town until all but the intact house had been covered by at least six feet of fresh 'fill,' and I had an uncluttered several acres on which to place my hospital.

Easy Med moved in the following day, had its admissions tent and operating room up and operational in the mandatory two hours, and set about to put the rest of the facility in place in record time. We were alongside a road leading up into the higher hills to the north, and a location destined to become famous, named Panmunjom. At the moment, however, it was distinguished only by the sounds of rifle and mortar fire, and a steady stream of casualties carried in on litters, litter-jeeps, and an occasional box ambulance or little Bell helicopter with a coffin-like box on each side, above the skids, containing a wounded Marine in particularly bad shape.

Shortly after our arrival at our new position, there was a particularly sharp encounter with the Chinese forces, who had now completely taken over from the North Koreans, and we received a larger influx of casualties than at any time since the debacle near the Chosin Reservoir in the far north. When the battle wound down after days of intense conflict, an entire Marine regiment of nearly five thousand men was dug in atop a sharp ridge that faced another ridge less than a thousand yards distant, with probably twice that number of Chinese dug in on top of that. Between the two forces lay a steep-sided, narrow valley that neither side had been able to cross despite repeated attempts.

With the coming of daylight when the firing had largely died down, it was possible to see that there were a number of Marines on the steep sloping side of the valley below our lines, lying motionless in positions indicating that they were probably dead. But maybe not.

It is an absolute article of faith, among Marines, that no man is ever left on a battlefield - dead or not. No discussion. This, however, was a potentially deadly enterprise.

By noon, word was passed for all senior officers and heads of special staff sections to assemble in Division Headquarters. 'Special staff ' includes medics, engineers, ordnance, transportation, communications and quartermasters, and the senior medic is the Division Surgeon. Next in line is the Medical Battalion Commander, my boss Dick Lawrence, and under him the Medical Company Commanders, of which I was one. I was still, however, also the Battalion Executive Officer, so I was next in line. Both the Division Surgeon and the Medical Battalion Commander were out of the Division, down in Pusan, meaning that for the moment, I was the senior medic.

The Commanding General, a storied hero from WWII named "Chesty" Puller, announced when we all assembled that he intended to "Get those Marines" off the sides of that ridge, no matter what it took. We were all to go back to our respective units and draw up a plan for doing this, returning that evening to brief him on the operation.

Medics do not do casualty estimates; combat intelligence people do that, so I sought them out to see what we could expect. What we could expect was utter disaster. My hospital, closest to the action, was full. Evacuation facilities - ambulances, jeeps, helicopters - were limited. I had about 10 surgeons: not enough.

My entire staff of physicians, administrators, the dentist (who really liked helping out in surgery), the chief petty officers and the senior Marine sergeants were all summoned to our headquarters, the Korean house we had fitted out as Easy Med's command post. They listened, shocked, at what was to happen. We decided that all we could do was send out every patient who could be moved without killing him, using not just the usual vehicles but the trucks as well, erect some of our spare tentage, put another operating table in with the other four in the surgical tent, and pray.

When it came my turn to brief the general that evening, I tried as dispassionately as possible to tell him that if the G-2's casualty estimates were correct, we could still not adequately treat the numbers expected. The operation was not "medically supportable" given our existing available staff and facilities. The general listened without comment, as he did to all the others who briefed him. When every one had finished, he sat in silence for long minutes, his chin resting on his hands, elbows on the table in front of him.

Finally, looking up, he said, "Okay, gentlemen. We kick off at 0500 hours!" With that, his adjutant announced that we were dismissed.

I was thunderstuck. Didn't he hear me? Had I not been clear? Was this maniac going to commit several thousand Marines down a steep hill facing a huge, hostile Chinese force armed to the teeth, knowing a large number of people would be shot or blown up, merely to collect some dead bodies? The answer to that was yes.

It was dark when I got back to Easy Med and told everybody what to expect. There ensued a whirlwind of activity, as patients were packed up into every available vehicle, and spare tents were pulled out of supply and hastily erected. Fortunately the engineers had done a wonderful job of leveling what was the graveyard of the former town, and we had plenty of space.

The attack went off as planned, and every fallen Marine was recovered, all dead. For reasons unknown, the Chinese did not counterattack during the operation, contenting themselves with 'harassing fire,' and the number of casualties was far smaller than had been predicted. Easy Med performed splendidly in spite of having worked all night without a break. Every wounded man we received that day survived. We all agreed it had been a truly worthwhile exercise.

The war steadily quieted down after that, and before long our principal enemy was boredom. There began a steady stream of visiting dignitaries from the States, coming to see the war at first hand so as to advance their personal and political agendas. Once, when a visiting member of Congress was being shown through our hospital by the General, the visitor asked about psychiatric casualties. The General, leaning up against the corner of one of our ward tents, assured the man that we didn't have those in the Marine Corps, made up as it was of tough, disciplined, highly trained volunteer fighters.

Fortunately, that dignitary didn't desire to go into that particular ward tent, which was lucky because it housed at least 30 seriously upset psychiatric patients. Naturally I said nothing.

We had great food in the mess that day. We always had great food the day a visiting politician came through. When asked by our visitors if we always ate this well, we always assured them that we did. This was also a Marine Corps article of faith: everything was invariably just great, no problems, no complaints; we loved it here, serving our country.

No one ever seemed to recognize the fact that not all of us were volunteers - like almost all the Navy people assigned to the Division, not to mention a fair number of citizens who had been conscripted in the regular draft, only to find that they had been assigned to this group of tough, disciplined, highly trained "volunteer" fighters! The vast majority of whom, it should be pointed out, performed very well indeed.

A high point of this prolonged adventure in camping out, for me, came when someone decided to award me a combat Bronze Star medal, 'with V' (meaning valor), for moving my hospitals close to the battle lines. Our ability to intervene medically, so soon after a man was wounded, contributed significantly to one of the most extraordinary medical statistics to emerge from US military medicine, not restricted by any means to my units. That statistic revealed that if a man were wounded in battle, not killed outright, his chance of surviving was better than 97%.

No army in history had ever approached this survival rate. It is a reflection of the fine field medics, the ever-improving evacuation technology, the generous use of whole blood and blood products in the field, antibiotics, vascular surgery, and even sophisticated lab capabilities and communications systems.

In most of the world, even today, few men survive after being wounded. Many bleed to death long before they are tended to, or die from shock. Many who make it past those life-threatening developments face horrible infections, gangrene, loss of limbs and vision, to spend their years in helplessness and hopelessness. No third world country has a veteran's administration. Most industrialized, 'modern' nations don't either, and only a few have a field medical system remotely approaching the one we now take for granted.

Nevertheless, major problems loom and have yet to be adequately addressed. Our military medical system was very adequate for the war in Korea. The fighting and the tactics changed fairly significantly in Viet Nam, and while the medics there adapted as well as possible, there were some serious problems. We were medically over-prepared for the Gulf War, but it was not a "war" in any conventional sense, and there were relatively few casualties. What has been emerging, even in more benign settings like the Balkans, as opposed to steaming jungles and blistering deserts in the Middle East and Southeast Asia, is a set of problems more akin to the traditional public health and preventive medicine challenges of the 19th Century.

Worse, the weaponry is changing, dramatically. There was, for example, some limited use of toxic chemicals in WWI, little or none in WWII, and essentially none since - certainly none affecting our troops. Our safety with regard to these agents used to lie in a fairly reliable set of formal and informal agreements among the few powers capable of making and using poison gases, not to use them. The same with nuclear devices, and biological agents. Today, however, toxic chemicals and infectious agents have been 'rediscovered' by any number of countries, including rogue states and groups of fanatics. Also, the formerly small 'nuclear community' has expanded to neighbors who hate each other like India and Pakistan, and thousands of nuclear devices are beyond the control of at least one of the major powers that created them.

Mark this well: as of this moment, at the dawn of the new millennium, there is absolutely no military or civilian medical capability, in this country or anywhere else, to deal with the effects of these 'weapons' if they are employed against large numbers of people. There exist some antidotes, but only to some chemicals. There is no quick, sure way even to identify many chemicals, even after they have been released. There is next to no way to decontaminate more than a tiny fraction of people exposed to them. There is no feasible system for identifying biological agents until infection is rampant, which is too late to do much good, and no stockpiles of appropriate medications to treat those infected by them.

And finally, there is no one, save perhaps a few aging Japanese doctors who happened to survive near Hiroshima and Nagasaki when the bombs went off, who has any experience at all treating the survivors of a nuclear explosion. The Soviets sickened and killed some people with both biologic and chemical agents that got away from them, but they haven't come up with a body of useful medical information as a result.

I have heard it said that this may all be part of God's plan to deal with the burgeoning over-population of the planet. It could very well prove to be a solution. People used to worry some about a worldwide nuclear holocaust, but nuclear devices tend to be very expensive and difficult to build and even more difficult to deliver. The devices have steadily gotten smaller and lighter and easier to deliver, but both chemicals and biologicals are far cheaper and much easier both to make and to put in place to wipe out even larger numbers of people than any nuke, any size, ever could.

None of this is new, nor should it be startling. Every state has some kind of emergency services organization, and there seems to be some growing interest in terrorism and weapons of mass destruction in Washington, but the leadership there obviously isn't very worried. Known terrorists, especially females who have lived quiet lives as fugitives long enough, are treated gently, while those from Puerto Rico are granted extremely rare presidential clemency and let out of jail. The money dedicated by the government to measures to protect against the terrible threats posed by the new weapons is relatively minute, and has so far failed to stimulate much thoughtful attention, let alone action, toward what must be done. It is as if someone up there has decided *nothing* can be done. Better to invest our time in prosecuting Microsoft.

To get back to Easy Med; it became our best field hospital, treating large volumes of incoming wounded and steadily refining its facilities and systems. By the time the second winter of the war approached, all the tents were well protected against the cold, everyone had an adequate 'foxhole' to dive into should the situation require it, and our headquarters house had its central heating system operating.

That consisted of a fireplace built at one side of the house below the level of the ground floor, and a chimney at the opposite side, with its smoke intake opening also below floor level. All the other spaces between the ground and the wooden first floor were sealed. When a hot fire was built in the fireplace, the smoke and the heat generated passed under the floor and up the chimney on the far side. This kept the whole house comfortably warm, and the floor sometimes quite hot.

Somewhere near the edge of our buried town someone found a large bell nearly buried in the rubble. The bell was cleaned up and mounted on a wooden frame about five feet high, made of logs about six inches in diameter. A large letter "E" with "Med" in smaller letters beneath it, painted in bright white enamel on the front side of the bell announced our presence. Beneath that, in neat, classical Korean characters, our hospital motto was memorialized. All passersby admired our splendid marker, evidently assuming that the Korean characters simply repeated the larger English letters above.

The day after the bell, proudly decorated, was hung just outside the entrance to the hospital, the commander pinned my new decoration on my chest as we both stood in front of the bell beaming widely. Official photographs were made of the occasion by the Public Information Office, and copies were sent to the major cities nearest to our homes of record: Boston for Dick Lawrence, and Chicago for me. We then forgot about it.

A few weeks later, in response to indignant inquiries from the Korean embassy in Washington, who had been sent copies of the picture by newspapers in both those cities, the Pentagon demanded to know what the hell we thought we were doing, offending the Korean government that way? What had happened, we finally learned, was that some Korean dignitary, able to read our motto rendered in his native language, failed to understand that our motto, "The Cat's Ass,' was a flattering, not an insulting, term! We left it on the bell; it was a matter of honor, and unit pride.

The war quieted down in the fall of 1951, and the opposing forces dug in on their respective sides of the 38th parallel. It became difficult to maintain unit alertness when business was slack, so we took to undertaking more elaborate medical and surgical procedures than were feasible during busier times, and I pursued my campaign to turn Navy corpsmen into good Marines, and the latter into serviceable corpsmen. As part of that, I instituted a traditional activity common at bases in the States but largely unheard of in combat zones: the Saturday morning parade.

'Parades' were essentially formations that required every man to assemble on a parade ground with his unit, come to attention when ordered by the officers grouped in front, and submit to a close inspection of each man's uniform, grooming, equipment and weapon. Preparation for this scrutiny involved a flurry of uniform washing, boot polishing, and, most importantly, the disassembly, cleaning, oiling and reassembly of weapons. Marines were particularly good at this meticulous process, well aware that their survival rested upon the smooth operability of their weapons. Corpsmen were notoriously sloppy about it.

The inspections were conducted in a good-sized open field adjoining the hospital tents by a Marine lieutenant, a Navy administrative officer, and senior non-commissioned officers of both services, who tended to be very demanding and totally unsympathetic in their conduct of this hallowed procedure. The complaining and protesting of the men, palpable early on, rapidly converted what had been a rather casual, dirty, sometimes sloppy collection of troops into a quite presentable, well-groomed, respectable assembly of fighting men who could not be distinguished, at first glance, as Marines or sailors, but all with immaculate, gleaming weapons.

The next thing to happen was that other units, both Marine and Army, heard about this bizarre procedure (done by Medics, for God's sake!) and outsiders began to show up on Saturday mornings to watch. At first derisive, the onlookers who hung around after the ceremony were put down by haughty Easy Med guys who pointed out proudly that they were the only troops in the entire combat zone sharp enough to carry this off.

Word finally trickled back to Division Headquarters, some distance to the rear, and the Commanding General was greatly amused. He sent word that the Division band could be made available for our next parade, if we wished, and of course we did. Our next parade was an event none of us could ever forget. The General himself couldn't come, as we had hoped, but he sent a senior deputy to 'observe.'

At about that time, by fortuitous coincidence, I learned that the Japanese government, as one of its measures designed to emulate the democratic procedures practiced in the US, had decided to conduct nation-wide medical licensing examinations. Until that time, any graduate of a Japanese medical school was considered competent to practice without further examination or certification by the government. Henceforth, just like in the US, they would have to pass a test and be granted an official license, regardless of what school they graduated from.

I decided to try to take the exam, and requested a 3-day pass to fly to Tokyo for that purpose, not really believing they would let me do it. Quite possibly due to the General's satisfaction with Easy Med's performance, and to my complete surprise, my request was approved.

My reasons for seeking a license to practice in Japan were a happy combination of the desire to perform a useful service with my personal desire to spend more time in a place I loved and, incidentally of course, make a handsome living. I had learned that the growing numbers of Europeans and Americans arriving in Japan representing large corporations were desperately unhappy with Japanese physicians and medical practices. Most hospitals were not like any in Western countries, but were upstairs rooms in doctors' office buildings. There were usually no nursing personnel to give daily care, since patients' families were expected to provide this - including food.

Moreover, perhaps arising from cultural traditions of stoicism and 'bushido,' the samurai "spirit," attitudes toward pain were quite unlike our own. It was common, for example, to conduct 'minor' surgical operations, like hemorrhoidectomy and even tonsillectomy, without any effective anesthesia. The same with childbirth and many gynecologic procedures. This sort of thing was unacceptable to American and most European patients. These people sought out Westerners who were there as medical missionaries, and paid them handsomely to step in and help, but there were few such missionaries available.

Not wanting to see these few medical missionaries diverted from their assigned

Christian duties, it would be a good, dutiful Christian move to set up a practice of my own, freeing them to do their churchly work. It would also be richly rewarding.

My long hours spent memorizing the Japanese phonetic alphabet, 'kana,' during quiet spells both aboard ship and with the Marines, proved invaluable. I was the only foreigner taking the exam, which was not very difficult, and there were several monitors who translated questions that I couldn't understand completely. Most medical terms are either Greek or Latin in origin, and when rendered in kana could be deciphered quite readily. Much of the exam was rather concrete, requiring the recording of laboratory values in specific diseases, for example, and using diagrams and sketches. In any case, I passed.

It occurred to me at the time that the examiners may have passed me simply on the basis of knowing that because I was a fully qualified, licensed US physician, I must be well enough trained that I would surely pass, no matter how poorly I did on the test, due to the language problems. Despite my doubts, they awarded me an elaborate license to practice in Japan, and a narcotics license as well.

Before the next year's examination, the Japanese authorities discovered that no foreigner could simply come to America and take our exams. In order to make their process more selective, and more like ours, a law was passed requiring that any candidate who wanted to take the test had to have graduated from a Japanese medical school, so there have been no further Americans getting medical licenses in that country.

Back at Easy Med, I prepared for cold weather, kept up the parades and inspections, and settled in quite comfortably. As the New Year approached, our military leaders decided on a special, dramatic celebration. At that time, the US forces had massed a larger array of heavy artillery than had ever before, in our nation's history, been assembled in one place. The decision was made to fire every howitzer - cannon - that we possessed, all at the same time and all aimed at the enemy, at exactly midnight, New Years Eve.

In the early days of my Korean adventure, I had managed to get hold of a bottle of the finest, most costly Napoleon Cognac, and kept it with me for over a year, carefully guarded, to be used to celebrate my orders to go back to civilization, supposedly after the customary year in the field. That year had long since passed, without orders or any hope of them, and the coming artillery celebration seemed a good excuse to open the precious bottle.

December 31st proved to be one of the coldest days of the year, with the temperature well below zero under a cloudless, star-studded sky. Heavy snows over several weeks had left more than a foot of snow everywhere. As the celebratory hour approached, two of my corpsmen, both big farm boys who had informally appointed themselves to watch over and protect their 'old man,' came to my tent to wish me a happy new year.

I sent them back to their tents to get their canteen cups. Mystified but obedient, they ran to get them and came into my tent. I bade them sit down, and brought forth my fine cognac, which neither of these youngsters had ever tasted before. Then, consciously and deliberately violating the strict precept that forbade fraternization between officers and enlisted men, and particularly between a commander and his enlisted subordinates, I poured about an inch of the brandy in each of our canteen cups. To this I added an equal amount of "95," the 190-proof, 95% pure medical alcohol that was stored in a 5-gallon tin in my tent.

"95" was not only too powerful to drink without dilution; it was also extremely valuable, which is why it was stowed in my tent. As an item of trading, for example, a 5-gallon tin of alcohol was worth exactly one jeep. This tin had never been touched, until tonight. Each cup of cognac received an equal amount of the medical alcohol, and we proceeded to sip it. When that cup was finished, we did it again, and finished that dose, along with most of the cognac, just as the great celebration broke out. The dark sky was brilliantly lighted, and the earth shook with the thunderous explosions of the big guns. We were sure the Chinese noticed.

We had gone outside to see the spectacle, and when it was over went back inside to get warm. One of the young men indicated he would be urinating first, outside naturally, and when he failed to follow us, after a few minutes, the other young man and I concluded that he had gone back to his own tent, since we were all getting quite sleepy and dizzy from the powerful alcohol drinks. In minutes, both of us had dozed off.

With the arrival of the New Year's first dawn, we went outside the tent to head for the main camp latrine on a path that led next to one of the grave-like holes, six feet long, two feet wide and six feet deep, constructed for protection in the event of heavy incoming fire. At the bottom of the hole, blissfully asleep in the snow at the bottom, was our companion of the previous night. We woke him, a little frantic as to his possibly desperate physical condition, only to find that he was evidently unaffected, perfectly healthy and only a little hung over. It had been an altogether memorable, earth-shaking New Year celebration.

There continued to be some contact with the enemy during that unbelievably cold winter, but never again did we have a great rush of casualties. Frostbite was again a problem, but had ceased to be a self-inflicted wound. There was time to visit units on both flanks of our division's position, including an Indian (from India) Ambulance Platoon that was part of the British Commonwealth Forces who had joined us under the United Nations Command. The Indians were Sikhs, all with fine beards and turbans and all surprisingly large, tall men. They invited me and my two visiting medics to join them at a meal, which turned out to be an unrecognizable conglomerate dish with the hottest curry spicing imaginable, and we invited them to visit Easy Med and try some of our best rations.

We also visited the Army MASH hospital closest to us, near the northern outskirts of the city of Seoul, by now reduced largely to ruins with hardly a single structure at all intact above the ground floor. The frozen corpses of two enemy dead - spies - still hung from the bridge over the Han River running through the town, and people huddled miserably in the blasted remains of former buildings.

The Mobile Army Surgical Hospital convinced us of how tough, and thus much better, we were in the Marine Division. It was actually housed in Quonset huts, had what seemed to be abundant supplies and equipment, and live, female nurses! There had been MASH units farther forward (though never as close to the battlefield as we were,) sometimes housed in tents like in the movies, but they got into more solid structures as the war wound down. One of the nurses was the wife of a young medical administrative officer in my company, and we began a long process of getting permission for her to visit our hospital.

That absolutely unprecedented invasion of a Marine Division in the field by an American woman was finally arranged, and she arrived one day escorted by no fewer than a dozen heavily armed Marines assigned to assure her safety. A 'private' pyramidal tent had been set aside, with appropriate sentries posted around at a decent interval, so that the young couple could have a bit of privacy. Meanwhile, every other man in Easy Med enjoyed florid fantasies and came once again to a crystal clear understanding of "Why We Fight!" The overnight visit was a high point in all our lives, if only in our imagination.

On one of my exploratory forays into the territory around our hospital, I happened upon a small village where a curious ceremony was in progress. This village had a tall, gate-like log structure in the middle of it, where a freshly killed cow would be suspended by its hind legs for butchering. On this day, however, rather than a cow, a naked man hung from the crossbar by his feet tied together with a long rope that had been used to hoist him up. He was howling. Four or five of the villagers were whipping the suffering man with long, flexible willow sticks. A couple dozen other villagers stood by and watched.

The South Korean soldier I had brought along with me because he spoke some English and knew the area, seeing my consternation, hastened to explain. The hanging man, he told me, was "crazy." Since craziness was caused by demons invading the victim's body, it was necessary to whip him in this way to drive the demons out by making it too uncomfortable for them to stay. In addition, after the beating, if there was electrical power available to the village, they would give him an electric shock with bare wires briefly touched to his temples, causing a convulsion, with the same goal in mind. They had learned about electric shock treatment from an American doctor, who had told them we used this in the US, so of course it must be a good thing. It was a certainty that the friendly American doctor had no idea that these people would try this barbaric adaptation of our technology!

Spring finally came, and the snows receded. At long last, my orders came. I was to return to duty at Yokosuka! Relieved and delighted to have survived, although

although I had never been in much danger, I packed my gear, was driven to the Air Force base near Seoul, and left what we had all come to call "Frozen Chosen."

William E. Mayer, M.D.

Brainwashing, Drunks & Madness

William E. Mayer, M.D.

CHAPTER 8

JAPAN REDUX AND BRAINWASHING

Yokosuka - and Japan generally - had changed dramatically in the two-plus years since my earlier departure for the hospital ship and the Marine division. All signs of the war's damage had utterly disappeared, and evidence of the astounding vigor and enterprise of the Japanese people was everywhere, in their clothing, the sudden abundance of cars and trucks, and the bustle of the repaired and cleaned streets.

The Naval hospital I had left had been permanently expanded to something approaching five hundred beds rather than the 80 we had started with, the grounds were groomed, and the old officers club with my exotic little suite had been redone. Prices in the club had risen to nearly double what they had been, and the excited, anxious partying atmosphere of the early days of the war were gone. True, the war was still on, but it had stabilized as the forces dug in on both sides of the 38th parallel, and the only sense of urgency that survived surrounded the negotiations at Panmunjom about a possible cease-fire.

The principal obstacle to arriving at an agreement was a dispute over the issue of voluntary repatriation of prisoners of war. We had captured a large number of both North Korean and Chinese soldiers, and they were held on two islands off the southern tip of the Korean peninsula, Cheju-do and Koje-do. Although these were escape-proof locations, we had a great deal of difficulty maintaining order in the POW camps there because of the tyrannical internal coercion and control imposed by highly organized, hard-core Communist elements among the prisoners.

Growing numbers of both Chinese and Korean prisoners were becoming openly antagonistic toward the standard Red Army rules, self-criticism meetings, daily indoctrination sessions and demonstrations imposed by the doctrinaire Communists among them. The prisoner-leaders in the camps reacted brutally, with beatings and even executions, and informers among the prisoners reported that massive, open rebellion was brewing and would soon explode.

The usual staff of POW Camp guards had been increasingly unable to maintain order within the camps, and combat troops were drawn from front-line units to help. It was not until the UN Command had committed an entire Regimental Combat Team of five thousand tough, heavily armed troops, that some acceptable level of control was established. By then it was clear that large numbers of the prisoners wished to be allowed, at war's end, to remain in South Korea rather than be sent back home to North Korea and China. Were that to happen, it would constitute a terrible loss of 'face' to their countries. The UN negotiators wanted to make repatriation voluntary; the Communist side vehemently opposed the idea, and the peace talks came to a halt.

Meanwhile, we were enjoying an almost peacetime-style life in Japan. MacArthur's proposed constitution for a new, free, democratic Japanese nation had been accepted by the Diet and endorsed by Emperor Hirohito, all the war criminals had been locked up, and the end of the American Occupation, with its wonderful 'perks,' was approaching rapidly and, for us, sadly. All our low-cost servants, golf courses, resort hotels and confiscated mansions were about to disappear, and we would be remaining in Japan as 'guests' of the people, just like we were in Korea, without special privileges.

Once again, however, suddenly and without any warning whatever, my life and career were about to change, this time in ways no one could have foreseen. It began with a call from the hospital commander's office informing me that the Far East Command Surgeon General, for reasons unknown, had summoned me, by name, to his office in Tokyo.

Once again, recalling my first solo mission to meet with my old mentor, Dr. Karl Bowman, at the Imperial Hotel in Tokyo a lifetime ago, I checked out a jeep and drove to the Surgeon General's office in the Dai Ichi Building in Tokyo, across from the Imperial Palace grounds. The senior American military medical officer turned out to be an Army major general, who was a warm, friendly but no-nonsense gentleman seated behind a large, clean desk flanked by an American flag and his personal flag bearing the two large stars depicting his rank.

He greeted me pleasantly, and for a few minutes we talked about my tour with the Marines in Korea, my medical and psychiatric training, and my current duties. He then said that he was going to share with me some highly classified information that I was absolutely forbidden to pass on to anyone, and wanted my word on that, which I gave.

The North Koreans, (with whom we were technically still fighting even though they had in reality been completely displaced by the Peoples Republic of China Army) had agreed, he said, to the principle of 'voluntary repatriation' of Prisoners of War. This removed the last barrier to a cease-fire, which would be announced in a few days. Great news! But what, I immediately wondered, did this have to do with me?

He explained. We had lost several thousand US troops, and a few other UN soldiers, captured mainly during the massive Chinese incursion across the Yalu River and our retreat from the Chosin Reservoir area and back down to the 38th parallel, where the fighting had ended, more or less, in a stalemate. Thanks to our absolute air superiority, we had been able to identify about a dozen villages along the Yalu, from which the inhabitants had been expelled, and replaced by American POWs. No other prison camps had been found.

Like anyone who had fought in Korea, I had heard numerous broadcasts from the north, featuring American-sounding voices claiming to be captured US soldiers, exhorting us to lay down our arms and join with them in the happy camps of the glorious Peoples Republic of North Korea so that this evil, capitalist-imperialist aggression against the peace-loving North Korean people could come to an end. These messages, repeated almost daily, were universally greeted with amusement, initially, and then contempt and disgust, by our men.

The general told me that the volume of such broadcasts, coming from military personnel that could be identified by name, rank and unit, far exceeded anything comparable in any previous war, and raised serious doubts about what was being done to these men.

Worse, he said, was the fact that while several thousand men had been captured and were being held in small villages that reconnaissance had shown to be without fences, guard towers, dogs, or large numbers of armed guards, not a single one of the thousands of men in those village camps had ever escaped and made it back to our lines. This stood in such marked contrast to our experience in WWII, when some of our men escaped from supposedly escape-proof prison camps and even dungeons in ancient castles in central Europe, that it had generated the most serious concern among our leadership. We needed to know why this had happened, he told me, for it could never be allowed to happen again.

It was therefore planned to conduct the most searching, thorough investigation of the returning POWs that had ever been undertaken. The team being assembled to conduct this special, highly classified research, would mainly be composed of intelligence officers, a legal officer from the Pentagon, and research assistants to assemble and cross-check data. There was to be one psychiatrist on the team.

A review of the records of the several psychiatrists on duty around the Far East Command, and consultation with the chief civilian psychiatric consultant to the Army - my old friend, Dr. Bowman - resulted in my tentative selection for the psychiatrist slot. Would I be interested? Would I! What a fascinating opportunity! I assured him, enthusiastically, that I would indeed be interested.

There was, the general said, just one little detail that needed to be settled. Yes? The 'little detail' turned out to be anything but little. Since this was an Army assignment, made by the highest authority with strict guidelines, it would be necessary for the psychiatrist selected for the project to be a member of the Army. Crushed, and obviously crestfallen to learn this, I pointed out, respectfully, that I was an officer in the Regular (as opposed to the Reserve) US Navy, obligated for several more years as 'pay-back' for my years of residency and fellow-ship training at Navy expense.

Chuckling, the general told me he thought he could take care of that, if I were willing to make the switch. How, I had no idea. What flashed through my mind was the conviction, firmly implanted in my years in the Navy and Marine Corps, that we were vastly superior to the Army, which is why probably no Regular Navy officer in history had ever switched to the Army. It smacked of a kind of treason, far beyond disloyalty. What about my oath of office, on commissioning? How could I face my naval brethren? What would I do with my complete sets of Navy and Marine Corps uniforms, all bought at my own expense?

A decision was needed right then. It was growing dark outside, on this Halloween evening, and the thought flashed through my mind, briefly, that either this was some version of 'trick-or-treat,' or else there really were spirits hovering about. Reason finally won out, and I first nodded, and then in a soft voice verbalized, my assent to this earth-shaking proposition that was to change my life.

Evidently satisfied that we had a deal, the general directed me to go check in at the Sanno Hotel, reserved in those days for officers senior to me. He said that I should stay strictly within the hotel, have one of their famous baths and maybe a massage, follow it with a good dinner, and stay in my room. A little numb, I took my leave without saluting, since the Navy never salutes uncovered (no hat) indoors, while the Army always does in situations of this sort. That was to be my last naval act.

The Sanno was a lovely old hotel, not as grand as the Imperial but eminently lush and comfortable, and I followed the general's instructions to the letter. My numbness began to abate, and I drifted off after a great lobster dinner. My reverie was interrupted by the shrill, persistent ringing of the telephone. A brusque masculine voice announced, when I answered, that I was to report to the general's office immediately; a sedan would be waiting.

When I entered the office, the general looked up from a paper on his desk and without a word of explanation or preamble of any sort told me to raise my right hand. I did so, and he swore me in to the Regular Army. He did this very formally, as we stood on opposite sides of his desk, more or less at attention. Then he relaxed, extended his hand, congratulated me warmly, and assured me that I wouldn't regret this. Then, with a twinkle, he said, "Glad to have you aboard!" I realized much later that this was his little joke.

I returned to the Sanno, had two martinis, and fell into bed, a full-fledged Army officer.

The next few days were not easy. Under what I took to be the disapproving gaze of the hospital commander, I signed the appropriate papers to 'clear' the base and my quarters, gathered up my possessions, and headed to the 8167th US Army

Hospital, Sumida-ku, Tokyo, Japan. This was to be my official duty station, where I would live and work until the special project began.

The hospital, formerly a large civilian hospital, was situated next to a magnificent five-tiered pagoda erected alongside the Sumida River at the exact spot where thousands of terrified Tokyo residents had died in 1923. Both the pagoda and the hospital had been built to honor the souls of the people forced into the river as other thousands of people, fleeing from the devastating fires that raged after the worst earthquake in Japan's history, pushed them into the water.

The Army used this facility for the treatment of medical and psychiatric patients, while surgical and orthopedic cases went to the larger Tokyo Army Hospital several miles away. The hospital commander was a fine, gracious southern gentleman from Alabama, named "Buck", who carried an immense burden in the form of a wildly misbehaving, hopelessly addicted alcoholic remnant of a graceful southern belle, whose antics had kept him, for years, from being promoted to Brigadier General.

My uniforms, the traditional "pinks and greens" worn by Army officers since WWI, had been procured from the Army thrift shop, since I couldn't afford new ones. They looked presentable, despite their humble origin, and I remembered to salute, uncovered and indoors, for the very first time as I entered the Colonel's office to announce my readiness for duty. When he stood to greet me (no "welcome aboard" this time), I saw before me a sad man in his fifties, who had been doodling five-pointed stars on a blank pad of paper - the only paper - on his desk. I wondered why.

My interim duties at the Army hospital, while I waited for a cease-fire to be announced and prisoner repatriation to begin, proved to be interesting. Army traditions and practices seemed to be similar in some respects to those of the Navy, but there were many subtle differences beyond saluting, 'uncovered,' indoors. The atmosphere was far more relaxed and informal; officers and enlisted people, while not exactly given to warm familiarity with one another, were less sharply separated and distant. Similarly, senior officers seemed more relaxed with one another, and friendly in ways I was unaccustomed to. I wasn't at all sure I liked this atmosphere, and suspected that it weakened the military structure.

Naval customs and traditions, most of them adopted directly from the British Navy that established and held together the 'sun never sets upon' British Empire around the globe, had generally evolved for cogent and readily understandable reasons. A ship at sea is literally its own country, indeed its own universe. Even the largest vessel, like our newest carriers and thousand-foot long hospital ships, is a tiny space in which to crowd hundreds or even several thousand men, tons of fuel, massive machinery, all the utilities needed by any community, and tremendous quantities of weapons or all the supplies and equipment of a large general hospital.

Every ship, moreover, exists in an alien, often hostile, environment capable of erupting into unimaginable violence whether due to wind and waves or to enemy fire. Even when all is tranquil, the seas calm and the enemy far away, the ship needs constant, detailed, even loving attention to stay alive, afloat, and headed in the right direction. That requires the constant, collaborative interaction of an impressive collection of talented people able to navigate - by the stars, if necessary - to run and repair and feed the huge, voracious power plant, maintain a livable environment, service and fire the weapons, keep the whole thing clean, and feed the astonishing number of men crowded into the small, cramped spaces.

Once out of sight of land, particularly in the days before radio communication when there was no means of communication at all, the ship was a nation unto itself. The Captain, for good or evil, was its absolute ruler. His lieutenants had to be good at what they did, in a technical sense, and they also had to understand exactly what their leader wanted, ready to carry out his every wish, for in his hands, literally, lay the lives of all aboard. The Captain had to know every nook and cranny of his vessel, how everything aboard worked and what could go wrong with it, what every officer and man in that little universe needed to know and needed to do for it to survive and accomplish its mission.

The rules that evolved over the centuries, designed to hold these little communities together and ensure that they functioned as designed, were not altogether unlike the strict rules of social intercourse and the place of authority that had emerged in Japan, as that tiny nation became increasingly packed with people. Like sailors, the Japanese had very limited privacy or freedom of movement. There were few or no fugitives in Japan, as a result, for there was literally no place to hide and nowhere else to go. Authority at all levels was clearly defined, beginning with the father and extending outward to the policeman assigned to every neighborhood, to his superiors, to the community officials above them, right on up to the Emperor. This maintained a level of order and comfort quite foreign to most Americans, albeit at the price of the individual liberty we cherish, and for the most part, it works for them.

As it does as well in the Navy. The authority structure is powerful and largely inviolable, whether in the hands of the Chief Boatswain's Mate supervising the lowliest sailors swabbing the deck, the Gunnery Officer directing the fire of huge cannons, or the Captain himself. Freedom of dissent, of assembly, of speech are all sharply limited, and when those limits are exceeded then mutiny - otherwise called treason - has occurred and must be put down instantly. Otherwise the whole universe is threatened, and it must stay intact if it is to survive.

Curiously - or not, perhaps - most freedom-loving Americans, once aboard ship sailing forth to do battle, tolerate this situation remarkably well. Mutiny - even mutinous thought - is uncommon, for even the simplest among the 17-year olds who have joined up as part of their adolescent rebellion seem to grasp quickly the logic and the necessity for the restrictions they encounter at sea. Ashore, all bets are off. Sailors in port after long periods at sea tend to behave with some exuberance, in direct proportion to how long they've been afloat.

The Army rarely faces the same kind of situation, in which a mutually dependent group functions in isolation from all others, and in which the majority of those present must have, and must effectively execute, special talents and training essential at all times, day and night, for the group to survive. Distinctions among and between different levels of skill are less clear. Lines of authority tend to become blurred, particularly in the field, where officers and enlisted people share the same living (and dying) situation, the same kinds of foxholes, fight with similar or identical weapons, eat the same unpalatable food, and climb the same hills.

Complaining about one's sergeant or even lieutenant was a far cry from mutiny; second-guessing about tactical decisions and bitching about them openly, forbidden on a ship of war, was almost considered to be a fringe benefit-entitlement of the job.

The Army had failed to learn from the Navy that this could be disastrous if it went too far, as it did more than once in Korea. On more than one occasion, a number of soldiers openly rebelled against an order from their young company commander to advance along a ridge-line, where it was hard to walk, and insisted instead on following the easier road below the hills, only to be devastated by enemy fire from troops emplaced high above them.

The trouble had begun with the return of peace following the Second World War, five years before Korea. Many of the authoritarian practices of at least some Army leaders were thrown aside, with at least tacit approval from on high, and the Army underwent a brave new democratization movement. Junior officers became more personally involved with their men, often acting more like benign big brothers than hard-nosed battle leaders.

Officers and enlisted men in some units became known to one another by their first names. Sometimes they shared a pleasant meal or even an evening away from the post. Money was sometimes loaned - absolutely forbidden in the Navy - and friendships developed.

In that social framework, it was much easier for a corporal to argue with his lieutenant about climbing a miserable hill in what looked like a quiet valley in Korea, and for his buddies to join in, and apparently easier for the lieutenant to acquiesce. With fatal results. So much for collaborative leadership and committee decision-making in war. Or, probably, in any seriously threatening stressful situation.

Once again, there are other lessons to be learned from this. Just as young soldiers yearn for confident, decisive, even authoritarian, leadership at times of great danger or hardship, so also do whole peoples when things get rough, as after a natural disaster, or in Pre-World War II in Germany, when the selected leader was so evil. The Navy seemed to know this, as did the Marine Corps, but the Army was less sure.

My new commander was an Alabama native from a small town famous for its statue erected in honor of the boll weevil, in response to which the town had switched from growing cotton to growing peanuts when the cotton crop failed. He was a product of the "old" Army, pre-WWII, and had served honorably and well as an internist for more than twenty years. He was very senior among colonels, and should long since have been promoted to the rank of Brigadier General but wasn't, because of Mildred.

One of Mildred's pet campaigns involved generating a happy camaraderie among the officers and their wives. To this end, she prevailed upon her husband, Buck, to schedule a gala dinner dance every month at the Officers Club. All officers and their wives or girl friends (the term 'significant other' not yet having been invented) were invited. It was understood that the events were not optional, fun or not. Attendance approached 100%.

During the course of the meal, Mildred invariably consumed large quantities of wine to top off her multiple pre-prandial martinis. Long before after-dinner brandy was served, she was gloriously, loudly, sloppily drunk, to the intense discomfort of the Colonel and the embarrassment of all within hearing. She became profane, expansive, given to bursts of songs popular ten years before, easily offended, and generally obnoxious. Poor Buck! It took him an hour or more to get her to depart from the scene, and we all felt we dared not leave ahead of the happy couple.

Once, during a holiday celebration put on by the Commander-in-Chief, Far East, Buck and his wife were invited, and showed up at a famous 'party house' owned by a rich Japanese industrialist. The house and its beautiful grounds were constructed solely for entertaining. A magnificent, curving staircase, fed by two beautiful sweeping staircases that joined into one as they reached the main floor, dominated the huge foyer. Mildred, seriously drunk and caught up in the holiday spirit, made her entry by sliding down the long, curving banister with her ball gown flying grandly, whooping loudly and capturing the attention of all.

She landed in a heap on the floor at the foot of the stairs. As she struggled to her feet, the wife of a very senior general, standing right there beside her, admonished her severely for her unseemly behavior. As Mildred rose to her full height, and without even a moment's hesitation, she brought up her right fist from down near her knees, and landed a thudding right cross to the senior lady's chin, knocking her down. Buck, mortified, grabbed his happily giddy, drunken bride by the arm and rushed her out the front door. They did not reappear. Buck, unsurprisingly, never got his promotion, and ultimately retired to Alabama.

My duties were about evenly divided between seeing patients at the hospital, and evaluating serious offenders imprisoned at the Nagano Prison, taken over by the Occupation authorities for the incarceration of convicted military criminals from the entire Far East Command. It was there that I met Captain Peter Paul Ungvarski, Medical Service Corps.

Pete, who hailed from Brooklyn, was a jovial, blustery, moderately big-bellied character who ran the prison infirmary and clinic. He met me with the announcement that he was a "Hunky" (meaning Hungarian,) and what was I? Despite his happy exterior, he was a serious man who had literally fought his way up from poverty, and who "took no guff" from the residents of that dark, forbidding fortress, all of whom, he told me, tried to 'work deals' with the medics to get away from their cells. He undertook to teach me about the military justice system, about which I was largely ignorant.

The text from which we studied was the "Uniform Code of Military Justice," always called the "UCMJ." It outlines every conceivable offense that a member of the armed forces can commit, and spells out the guidelines for the appropriate punishment. Also precisely specified are rules for conducting investigations, bringing charges, convening the proper forum for trial, sentencing, appeals, legal counsel, calling witnesses, and all the other details of the judicial process.

Largely unknown to most people, the military justice system incorporates all the best qualities of American jurisprudence. It contains elaborate, effective measures to ensure fairness, freedom from influence from any source, independent psychiatric evaluation when there is the slightest question of the accused's mental health, automatic review and, in serious cases, an automatic appellate process reaching up to a body composed of eminent civilian jurists, comparable to the Supreme Court, and probably less political.

It begins in the individual's basic unit: the Company or the Ship. A Company Commander or ship's Captain can hear charges and decide to impose final punishment, carefully limited and prescribed in detail, or refer a case to the next higher level, called a Summary Court. That court consists of a commissioned officer specially selected for the duty and in no way connected to the accused. Sworn testimony can be taken from the accused, his accusers, and witnesses. All is recorded. Once again, there are strict limits on the punishment such a court can impose, and the outcome is officially placed in the individual's service record.

The next higher level is called a Special Court Martial. This usually is conducted by a group of three officers not connected with the defendant, who administer oaths, take testimony, and pronounce sentence following guilty pleas or verdicts, once again within strict limits imposed by the UCMJ. This court can order an administrative discharge from the Service. The findings are reviewed for approval or lessening of the sentence by the commander of the next higher unit.

The most serious offenses are tried before a General Court Martial. The 'Convening Authority' for a GCM, as this is called in typical military abbreviation, is ordinarily a General Officer (from one to four stars) commanding a major military command, like a Brigade, Division, Corps, or Army. He appoints the six or more 'members' of the court, as well as the law officer, an attorney from the Judge Advocate General's Corps, who presides over the proceedings to assure their correctness. All appointed officers are unrelated to the defendant, who is provided with legal counsel for his defense and can employ civilian attorneys to conduct or assist with that. Any attempt, however subtle, by the Convening Authority, whatever his rank and status, or anyone else, to influence the findings or outcome of a General Court Martial is strictly forbidden and can result in the most severe punishment.

The GCM can impose any sentence, including execution, life imprisonment, or sentences of many years duration. The legal staff of the Convening Authority reviews all serious cases, and the General himself must approve or reduce the sentence. He cannot increase it. In all cases involving long sentences or the death penalty, the entire case is reviewed by the Court of Military Appeals, whose long-serving civilian members are appointed by the President and whose decisions are final.

At any level of court martial, and at any time during the process, either counsel or the court itself can require a complete psychiatric and psychological evaluation of the accused. The psychiatrist, like the members of the court, must be entirely free of any connection with the prisoner, and must render an independent report as a servant of the court, not either side. In the most serious cases, a defendant can bring in his own 'outside' civilian psychiatrists, in addition, to examine him and render an opinion to the court.

My work at the prison involved evaluations prior to trial, during trial, and during the review process, and brought me a fascinating assortment of true miscreants who had committed rape and murder, at least two of them awaiting execution by hanging - the Army's traditional method. Another, a well-regarded senior sergeant who had raped an 8-year old daughter of a fellow soldier, had been sent after he testified at his trial that, as he held the child's head under the water in a little creek behind the family quarters area on a military post, he had ejaculated. The officers of the court, inexperienced with this kind of offender, rapidly concluded that he must be insane, because of the horror of what he had done, and the sexual overtones to the offense.

The sergeant was not insane, of that I was certain after many hours of careful examination. It proved surprisingly hard to convince this jury - this court - of that fact. Surely, they reasoned, someone would have to be mentally ill to do such a terrible thing and get animalistic pleasure out of it. After a long period of testimony, answering questions posed by every one of the six officers on the court, some of them still doubtful, I said in exasperation, "Gentlemen, you don't have to be crazy to be a really mean sonofabitch!" Which is the truth. A truth I was called upon to declare on other occasions, one of them twenty years later in a small town in Oregon.

Among the many prisoners who passed through our hands at the prison, one stood out because he was quite different from most of the others, and his crime caused me to reflect with some seriousness about my own integrity. The man was an Air Force lieutenant, who had been convicted by a General Court Martial for violation of a Far East Command regulation, namely his possession of a ten-dollar bill in ordinary US currency. He was to be sent to Leavenworth Penitentiary in Kansas to serve his one-year sentence - probably only 9 months or less if he behaved - until he left with a 'DD,' a Dishonorable Discharge.

Regulations at that time, almost universally violated, forbade any member of the Armed Forces in the Command to possess or use US currency. We were paid in a form of locally printed paper resembling Monopoly money, called MPC - Military Payment Certificates. These could be spent in PXs and any facility operated by the US government, and could be converted into Japanese Yen at officially authorized currency exchanges. They could not be given to any foreign national for any purpose. There was, unsurprisingly, a large amount of MPC in the hands of foreign nationals, and every soldier and sailor kept at least one piece of cherished 'greenbacks' tucked away in his wallet. MPC could be converted into Yen at a far better than the official rate in dealings with merchants and blackmarketeers on the street.

When a military person arrived in the Command, the first thing he was required to do, the minute he got off the plane, was surrender every bit of US money he carried. A military pay officer would give him the exact amount in MPC. Most people secreted a couple of one dollar bills, a five or a ten, rarely more, to keep as mementos of home. They would have kept more if they had known that you could buy 5 or 10 dollars in MPC for a single dollar in legitimate greenbacks, or get 5 to 10 times the official number of Yen for it.

Our lieutenant was assigned as the 'issuing' paymaster at our largest air base in Japan, where the great bulk of incoming personnel first landed. He had also managed to be assigned as the 'survey' officer for old, worn MPC, which was turned in by the Post Exchanges, Commissaries, liquor stores, hotels and officers' quarters when it began to fray and deteriorate. His job required that he bundle the old MPC in packages, record the face amounts in each package, and burn it, in front of two witnesses.

He had been doing this for more than a year without any problems or special attention being paid to what he was doing. One day, however, the Internal Revenue Service filed an inquiry with the Air Force about this officer's source of income. His pay as a Lieutenant seemed hardly enough to warrant his recent cash purchase of an apartment building in Los Angeles.

Alarmed, the Air Force assigned investigators to watch the lieutenant, even interrupting his currency-burning ritual to assure themselves he wasn't making some kind of a switch and burning something other than old, worn-out money. They found nothing, but continued to watch him, surreptitiously, believing he must have been doing a switch of some kind, and stashing away the greenbacks he was collecting from soldiers to whom he gave at least some of the used MPC he was supposed to destroy.

Undercover criminal investigation agents had seen him go into a large Japanese bank on several occasions, so they posted some Japanese-American agents inside the bank. Sure enough, one day he came in and headed for the safe deposit boxes. After he had signed in and opened a large box, they pounced, arresting him and seizing the box. Inside they found exactly one ten dollar bill, U.S. Currency!

The lieutenant was arrested and submitted peacefully. The investigators knew full well that they had been duped but were helpless to do anything about it. No stash of illicit cash was found anywhere else, and the authorities were forced to go with what they had: a relatively minor, certainly widespread, violation of a Command regulation that carried a maximum sentence of a year and a DD, for an officer. And that is exactly what he got. If all officers' wallets were confiscated, almost everyone would have been found to have some of the green stuff and could have been prosecuted, but no one was. Needless to say, no other young officer had bought any L.A. apartment buildings, either.

Johnnie, the lieutenant, was quite open and forthright about his misdeeds, when I interviewed him. He would not say exactly how much money he had appropriated this way, but did admit he had shipped the currency back to a friend at home in small packages labeled as souvenirs over a period of more than a year. He admitted that he knew that sooner or later he would be found out, and was pleased it had taken as long as it had. Asked if he felt any remorse for his actions, he said his only regret was that it had to stop when it did.

What he said next was what got me to thinking about myself. What actual harm, he asked, had he done? Obviously, if a lot of people did the same thing, it might have some tiny impact on the local economy, but no one else was in a position to do anything like it. Was it any worse than the common trading of MPC for Yen on the street, or selling a bottle of whiskey, bought at the Post liquor store for $2 to a Japanese innkeeper for $15 worth of Japanese yen? He said he could not find that he had hurt anyone in any way, or damaged anyone's property, and that he was perfectly willing to spent eight or nine months locked up in Kansas, in return for his riches - it seemed a reasonable bargain.

The Dishonorable Discharge? He wouldn't be allowed to hold public office, but didn't want to anyway. Could it interfere with getting good jobs? Sure, but he wouldn't be needing a job. Furthermore, he couldn't be drafted or required to pay restitution of any kind. He would get a lot of reading done in coming months, and then head for a comfortable life, probably in Los Angeles. He had socked away far more than the cost of the apartment building.

My problem was, I couldn't find much to counter his reasoning. I didn't think what he did was right, exactly, but it was hard to say why. When he left, quite happily, for his new temporary quarters, I could only wish him well and try not to seem envious at all.

With the end of the Occupation in sight, power was returned to the Japanese authorities to prosecute any American who committed a crime against a Japanese citizen, until then a privilege solely of the US military officials in the offender's unit. This was a highly symbolic indicator of the resumption of Japan's sovereignty, and was widely viewed with some apprehensiveness. The first case, testing this new power, involved a murder. An American soldier had allegedly fought with his Japanese girl friend, beating her until she died. He was to be tried by an all-Japanese court, defended by bi-lingual Japanese lawyers.

Peter Ungvarski and I were appointed to represent the Command, attend the trial to assure that American standards of fairness were applied, and report back to General Mark Clark, the World War II hero, who then headed the Far East Command. The trial was to be held in a rural prefecture in the northern part of the main island of Honshu.

We took along our legal library, in the form of the single volume containing the Uniform Code of Military Justice, and headed north from Tokyo by car. Despite the small size of the country, relatively, it took at least 12 hours of hard driving, much of it along winding mountain roads, to reach our destination. We checked in to a small hotel, the only one in town, found out where the courthouse was, and settled in for the night. We were not authorized to interview the defendant, nor his attorneys.

The court convened early the next morning, and proceeded at glacial pace for the next four days. Every word uttered by anyone in the chamber was promptly translated verbally for our benefit after every sentence. Every word of both languages was recorded and given to us for our review at the end of each day, but we did not participate in any way in the process. The judge, a dignified elderly man, conducted the trial gravely and with great deliberation, and both the prosecutors and the defense lawyers were exceedingly proper and polite in all that they said and did. There was no drama, no histrionics, and no excitement whatever.

At long last, the jury after a fairly short deliberation, returned a verdict of guilty, about which there could be little doubt. The judge promptly passed sentence, sending the soldier to a Japanese prison for something less than ten years, and he was led away. We were elaborately thanked, in typical Japanese fashion, for having done them the honor of our attendance by the judge, the bailiff, the prosecutors and the defense lawyers, a lengthy process. We then set out for Tokyo.

Along the way, we stopped at a family-run (like so many small industries in Japan) pottery, deep in the mountains. The workers were quite taken aback by the unexpected appearance of two American officers in their midst, for the very first time ever. Several of them took off at a run to summon the family patriarch, an ancient, kindly man who greeted us with deep bows and profuse expressions of gratitude for the honor we were bestowing by our presence.

Soon, surrounded by the entire work crew of at least 20 men and women, and a few boys and girls in their teens, we were being conducted on a tour of the entire operation, spread out among four or five buildings, all partly open on at least one side, with a row of kilns lined up at one edge of the property. The setting was lovely, with carefully tended shrubs and trees placed here and there. The buildings used log beams, and huge bamboo 'pipes' carried the considerable amounts of water involved in the process.

The pottery, as far as we could tell, was devoted to just two products, cups and teapots. The cups, more like small mugs without handles, were two shades of moss green, the darker of the two around the lower half, which was a separate outer shell that merged smoothly with the lighter top half and had heart-shaped perforations, edged with gold, so that the heat of the liquid in the inner cup was kept from the hand of the holder. The random superficial surface cracks in the lighter part of the cup, inside and out, were enhanced by being rubbed with charcoal before the final glazing and firing.

Peter and I found these cups pleasingly attractive, and we each bought a half dozen, for a ridiculously small price. Later I took one to the manager of the Tokyo PX, who liked it and began stocking the cups and pots, which sold well, and can be found in specialty chinaware shops in this country to this day, nearly a half century later. One can only speculate as to the effect of this modest economic success on that little family pottery in the mountains.

In a few months the Cease Fire was announced, and repatriation of prisoners on both sides began. A relatively small group of men for the first exchange, called "Operation Little Switch," was formed from among those who were in need of special medical attention. The interrogation agents assigned to our little research group questioned many of these, especially those who seemed perfectly healthy, suspecting that they had somehow gotten favorable treatment from their captors for being specially cooperative, but that did not appear to be the case.

Then began "Operation Big Switch," a steady stream of several thousand men, most of them prisoners of the Chinese for about three years. All were put into the military hospitals in Tokyo for physical examinations and a few days rest and good food to start their readjustment process before being evacuated to those military hospitals closest to their homes in the US, from whence they would be discharged, if they did not want to reenlist.

Physically, the great majority was in surprisingly good condition. There was no physical evidence that they had been badly treated or fed poorly, although there were no fatties in the group. On the whole, they seemed strikingly passive and uncommunicative. While a certain subdued, even a little vague or confused, air is common to men long confined, it ordinarily dissipates rapidly and is often replaced by a kind of euphoric, verbose hyperactivity and joy as the reality of liberation sinks in.

Not so with these men. What was first most striking was their silence and lack of any inter-action with one another as they sat, mainly on their beds on the wards, passively waiting for whatever was to come next. They did not wander around the hospital, or even their own wards, few read any of the books and magazines provided, and no little 'bull session' groups formed. All this was unusual for ambulatory patients, as all of these people were.

The American Red Cross workers were particularly generous, welcoming and attentive to the returned prisoners. The 'gray ladies' were always on the wards, passing out candy, reading matter, letter-writing materials and packages of those personal items notably absent in prison camps: soap and toothpaste, shaving cream, razors, lotions, and anything that a soldier could want. Best of all, they offered the men the opportunity to call home to the US, at no cost, and talk to anyone they wanted, family or friends, to tell them they were safe and free at last.

To everyone's astonishment, most of the returnees declined that offer. They weren't pushed to do it, or questioned about it, but their refusals were noted and reported to us.

Similarly, it was notable that most of the men, all of whom had been given partial pay and could expect far more, soon, passed up the 'passes' they were offered and stuck around their wards, even their own beds, rather than venture out into Tokyo to shop or drink beer or seek friendly girls or other diversions customary among soldiers.

Every returnee was interviewed at some length about his experiences in the months he had been held prisoner. For our research, we decided to subject every third man to far more extensive questioning, giving us a sample of more than a thousand of the repatriated troops. Unbeknownst to them or to anyone else in their group, these men were kept in the hospital several days longer than the others and interviewed in far greater detail.

Every word of the questions and their answers was recorded, transcribed the same day, and delivered to our research group the following morning. The transcriptions were carefully analyzed and cross-checked during the night before we got them, with careful records kept of every reference to a specific person, whether he was a camp guard, a so-called "instructor," or a fellow prisoner. Similarly, all references to specific dates and places were recorded and listed together with identical or similar references from other interviews. Those records were delivered to us along with the verbatim transcripts every morning.

Each transcript was read by at least one member of our team of senior intelligence agents, who passed to me or to our attorney member any case with information that seemed to suggest the possibility of psychiatric or legal implications that needed scrutiny, including face to face interviewing by me or the lawyer, or sometimes both of us. We all made notes on the transcripts and in special notebooks, in every case, to be used in presenting and discussing our findings with the others.

The very existence of the research team and its activities were known only to a few senior officers. We met daily, seven days a week, in a large, unlabeled conference room with long tables arranged in a square, in the Dai Ichi Building, MacArthur's old headquarters, across from the palace moat.

We began each day there about 9:30 in the morning, and rarely left the room before 11 or 12 at night except to go to the toilet. Food was brought in for lunch and dinner. Two sides of the room bore large chalkboards, while a third supported an enormous cork bulletin board for pinning up documents. There was one telephone. Three carefully selected sergeants were placed at small desks to one side to distribute and re-collect the transcripts, post papers on the bulletin board, make entries on the chalk-boards when so directed, and tend to chores like supplying paper and pens, and bringing our food. An armed guard was positioned outside the door to the room, and no outsider ever entered.

The atmosphere, from the beginning, was grave, without the casual banter and friendly exchanges common to groups of military men embarking on an important project, no matter how serious the mission. We had been charged with finding answers to questions that had shaken our whole military structure: why had so many men, known to have been captured, failed to come back; why had no one ever escaped and returned to our hands from almost unguarded village camps in a small, narrow peninsular country; why had so many collaborated with the enemy to make propaganda broadcasts to our units in the field; why hadn't a single one of our air-dropped escape and evasion 'rescue' specialists, sent to help people escape, even survived? Why had some of our splendid young Air Force pilots, in uniform, openly confessed, in front of news cameras, that they had been spreading germ warfare in the bombs they dropped on innocent civilians in North Korea, killing thousands?

And there were new questions. Why were the returned men so subdued; why did they talk so freely about one another; why didn't they want to call home or go on pass downtown? Were they drugged? Did the Chinese have some magical way to "brainwash" these seemingly ordinary young Americans and turn them into passive zombies? Was our military training seriously deficient? Would they get over it?

Never, before or in the many years since, have I worked with as impressive a collection of dedicated, intellectually superior, skilled men as those senior intelligence analysts brought together in that room to try to find answers to those troubling questions. Never before had such a collection of talent been assembled to examine a group of repatriated prisoners of war, beginning at the moment of their return to our hands.

In the evening of each day, each member of the group would briefly present the results of his day's studies to the others. Postings on the walls' boards were reviewed and discussed. Cases of particular interest, particularly those involving men most frequently mentioned by others, were examined carefully. Reports by different prisoners of special 'events' in the camps were compared. Unexplained absences from the camp were carefully charted.

A huge amount of information was gathered from our one thousand research 'subjects.' It was both fascinating and devastatingly dismaying. Many of our comfortable, long-held assumptions were cruelly dismantled and utterly destroyed by masses of evidence. New understandings emerged, of how the Communists had, almost without a shot being fired, imposed their tyranny over nearly a third of the world's population. Any previously-held convictions about the inherent ability of a free country to produce a strong, robust, highly resilient, informed, principled populace dedicated to the preservation of individual freedom, looked foolish and baseless.

In short, the Communists seemed to do better at what they did, than we did with what we believed in. Our fine young men had, it seemed, been conquered - subdued and thoroughly subjugated by a relatively few UCLA- and USC-trained Chinese "instructors" using words alone, while we had had to commit an entire regimental combat team of thousands to maintain order among the prisoners we held on two small islands off South Korea.

The picture of life in the camps, as told by these men who had survived there for three years, was Orwellian, perhaps, though not magic. Nobody's brain was "washed," but many a character was badly eroded.

In the beginning, when the North Korean Army was in charge, the POW experience was a classical example of forced marches, brutality, some summary executions, little food or shelter, widespread sickness - mostly diarrhea - and terror. At length, however, the straggling column of captured, depleted men arrived at the villages along the Yalu River at the northernmost border of Korea. The Chinese were in the process of taking over the war from the Koreans, expelling the villagers from their homes and dismissing the Korean Army troops in the area. The beatings and other brutalities stopped, the prisoners were crowded into the newly vacated huts, guards were posted, and small but regular amounts of food were provided.

It was during those remaining bitterly cold months of the war's first winter, in the interim between the depredations of the Koreans and the beginnings of 'reeducation' by the Chinese, that most of the deaths occurred among our men. So many men died during that period, mainly from infection and cold, coupled with barely life-sustaining food and no medical care at all, that the death rate among the American POWs exceeded the death rate in the infamous Confederate prison, Andersonville, during the Civil War!

The subjects in our study, almost without exception, described that time as a period of "every man for himself." "You take care of yourself, Buddy, and I'll take care of me." When a sergeant or officer in the prisoner group tried to mobilize men to help one another they were universally rebuffed, often threatened, by others who declared they no longer had any authority, but were just "God-damned prisoners, like the rest of us!" There were innumerable accounts of sick men thrown out of huts, their clothes and food seized by others who were stronger. Those men never survived.

There were even more numerous accounts of men who were not overtly sick, but who seemed overwhelmed by their plight, gave up eating, huddled in a corner of the hut, and were found after some hours to have died. So common was this that the prisoners gave the phenomenon a name, calling it "Give-up-itis," and deeming it hopeless. This had never been seen before among American POWs, to any significant extent. The only thing resembling it had sometimes occurred among elderly Jews in extermination camps run by the Nazis. Some of these old people seemed to 'give up' in despair, dying on their own before they could be herded into a gas chamber. This, however, was a new thing in the American Army.

With the return of better weather as spring arrived, conditions in the camps improved and the death rate dwindled. The Chinese introduced a number of 'instructors' into each camp, and they promptly began an indoctrination program. Prisoners were assembled into small groups and told by young Chinese teachers who spoke excellent English that the Army of the People's Republic of China bore them no ill will. The instructors wore no rank, but obviously held positions of authority quite unlike the soldier-guards around the camps, whose numbers steadily diminished.

The first major event in the camps was the distribution of writing materials and some simple questionnaires for each prisoner to fill out, dealing with their personal histories. Questions were asked about their place of birth, their parents, education, work experience, and time in military service. It was explained that their captors needed this information to establish their identities firmly, so as to inform the Red Cross of their well-being and the fact that they were now safely in the hands of the Chinese people, who promised to care for them until this 'capitalist, imperialist aggression' came to an end, and all peace-loving peoples could return to their homes.

Each of the Chinese instructors was evidently assigned permanently to a group of 15 or 20 prisoners. After the questionnaires were collected, the instructors conducted private interviews with each prisoner, during which the man's questionnaire was reviewed in detail and additional notes made from the conversation. This was to be the first of many such individual conferences over the ensuing months, during which the prisoners became more trusting of their captors, and the latter gleaned enormous amounts of information about their wards.

Soon there was established a daily instruction session, with the same familiar instructor addressing the same group of a dozen or more prisoners. At first the content of the lectures dealt with the Chinese view of the world, and the enormous challenges and problems involved in governing China's billion citizens, most of them illiterate peasants who needed education, public health measures, and the skills necessary for their country to survive and flourish in the modern world. None of this was anything like what the captured men had expected, and it was all completely new to most of them. Our schools didn't - and still don't - teach much about Chinese history or the current situation in that huge country.

Following each lecture there was a 'discussion group,' to go over the material that had been taught. Each "student" was required to reiterate the main points of the lesson in his own words, to verify his attention and understanding. 100% participation in this exercise was ensured by the requirement that every man recite before anyone was allowed to go to the next meal. Predictably, the peer pressure to conform was powerful, and all did.

Over time, the content of the lectures and discussion groups turned to a Marxist version of the economic and social history of the United States. Many of the powerful industrialists of the late 18th and early 19th Centuries, like the Rockefellers, Mellons, Carnegies and Hills were described in great detail, both as to their lifestyles and their actions as they amassed their power and their fortunes. Great emphasis was placed on such people's "exploitation" of the working classes. For the first time, for most prisoners, they heard about 'starvation wages,' near-enslavement of immigrants in sweatshops, child labor, payment for work in company script, usurious interest rates, mortgage foreclosures, property seizures by the railroad barons, and every other form of unfairness and abuse of the common man that had taken place as free enterprise flourished in the US. Books by Dos Pasos, Hemingway, Steinbeck, Lincoln Steffens and other legitimate American authors were produced by the instructors and excerpts used to prove the points being made.

All this was new to most of the prisoners. Over and over again the instructors emphasized that these true things, these crimes against humanity, characterized America and all capitalist-imperialist nations, and were hidden from the downtrodden masses by the capitalist-owned and -operated press in a massive conspiracy of silence.

The Chinese people, they were told repeatedly, had nothing at all against the people of America, but loved them and wanted them to know the truth so that they could one day liberate themselves from their oppressors, as the Chinese people had done. These lectures were designed to tell these soldiers what the truth really was, about China and about their own country as well. All they asked was that they listen with an open mind, then make up their own minds about what was true, and then, one day, when the capitalists decided they had made enough profit from this conflict and let the war end, go home and tell their families and friends the things they had never been allowed to learn.

One glorious day, they were told, the oppressed workers of the world would unite, throw off their yokes and enter upon a new era of peace and harmony wherein there would be no rich robber-barons, and no poor, where all would work for the common good, "the people."

This carefully designed and reasonably presented educational program went on, daily, for two years. Every soldier, no matter how poorly educated or inarticulate, learned to recite, each day, the few main points presented, to the satisfaction of his peers and his instructor. Before lunch. Sometimes the discussions went over into the afternoon, or later. Students who seemed resistant or argumentative were granted special interviews with the always-reasonable teacher. Those who rebelled and seemed impervious to persuasion were sent off to one of several "reactionary" camps.

Almost all commissioned and senior non-commissioned officers were apparently considered to be poor candidates for reeducation, and segregated into special, 'reactionary' camps where they could not influence the great bulk of ordinary soldier-prisoners. Far less effort was expended on trying to bring the 'truth' to them, and they were given more physical work to do. They were, however, made to fill out the questionnaires, and were questioned many times about apparent inconsistencies and contradictions in their histories, always with the underlying hints that these were deliberate lies, suggesting that they might be spies who were not entitled to the protections of the Geneva Convention, which in any case the US had never signed.

The "reactionary" prisoners were sometimes subjected to interrogation techniques that were reminiscent of Arthur Koestler's "Darkness at Noon," and other accounts of the questioning and eventual 'confessions' of fallen Communists and suspected enemy agents in the worst days of Stalinist rule in the Soviet Union. Such techniques were not much used by the Chinese Communists, but evidently at least some of the instructors in the reactionary camps had been trained by the Soviets. Physical abuse and open threats of execution were not part of the Reactionaries, nor of the general prisoner population, but an underlying atmosphere of fear was more commonly generated among the older, higher-ranking prisoner group.

The repeated interviews with instructors, and reviews of personal histories with questions about details of prisoners' and their family members' occupations, social standing, daily activities, marriages and religious practices were reported by the majority of returning POWs as having been superficially pleasant but basically threatening. Many reported feeling that the Chinese knew more about them than they knew themselves!

They also, very often, said much the same thing about their fellow prisoners, thanks to a mandatory, hallowed Communist practice called "Self Criticism," widely if not universally practiced in the shops, communes, and villages throughout China. Borrowed from the Soviets, the process required people to gather into groups and individually confess their shortcomings and failures to live up to the rigidly prescribed principles and moralistic practices, and even thoughts, demanded of all members of a people's democracy.

These politically and socially correct principles were taught, and were expected to be learned, in the daily lectures, and applied to one's daily life as well as his past. American soldiers, with their characteristic contempt for what they see as preachy, righteous moralisms at first greeted this requirement as a kind of ridiculous joke. At the risk of offending their serious-minded instructors, many of them made up outrageous tales of how they persecuted their slaves, exploited the poor, stole from the state and otherwise had been evil capitalists, to everyone's amusement.

The instructors generally accepted such exaggerations and absurd fictions without comment, until the next individual interview, when they were reviewed in detail, and suddenly seemed far less funny. The practice soon stopped, and the men began trying hard to come up with examples of their characterological and behavioral shortcomings, when measured by Marxist standards. It wasn't long before they were engaged in a level of self-examination and self-revelation that was wholly unusual for them, along with a growing feeling that they had talked too much and revealed too much that was true about themselves to all the other members of their group. To defend against the anxieties of this over-exposure, they began listening more closely to the confessions of the others.

What developed, over a surprisingly short time, was a general atmosphere of distrust, and uneasiness among the men. Almost universally, our POW-subjects reported that "You couldn't trust anybody" in those camps. It became clear why they had never been able to group together for purposes of resistance or escape, impossible without mutual trust and the assurance of secrecy. Somebody, to protect himself, would surely 'tell.'

What we were seeing, among decent Americans who in all previous wars were notorious among their captors for their rebelliousness, lack of cooperation, attitudes of contempt and pervasive, constant attempts to escape, was a successful effort by these superficially benign Chinese folks to plant such seeds of dissention, such an atmosphere of mutual distrust, that they could be controlled in loose confinement. No barbed wire fences, guard towers or guard dogs, let alone a regimental combat team, were needed.

Americans, it appeared, were no more immune to these gentle methods than the Chinese, Poles, Czechs, Georgians, Ukranians, Uzbekistanis, Kazakhstanis, Russians and millions of others brought into Communist dictatorships without ever mounting a substantial organized rebellion with any chance of success. The early stages of communist takeovers in many countries had been bloody and brutal, as were the early days of our men's captivity in the hands of the North Koreans. What had not been understood, however, was why those millions of people had seemingly acquiesced with surprising docility, to what was arguably the most intrusive, minutely controlling tyranny in all of history.

Obviously, every group has some surviving 'reactionaries,' so tyrannies will always need some special 'camps,' like the Gulags and the barren wastes of the Tibetan plateau for use in really long-term reeducation. They need to be carefully insulated against conflicting information and ideas, as well, and conditions should be hard and sometimes fatal. However, for the great bulk of people, who mainly want only peace and shelter and food, with perhaps a bit of entertainment, it appears that lectures and self-criticism meetings, applied often and regularly enough, work wonders.

The POW experience in Korea was far more complex than what has been described above, of course, since time and space will permit only a rough outline of what took place. There were also athletics, culminating in an inter-camp "Olympics;" visiting lecturers including some world-famous Communist authors; demonstrations of germ warfare bombs (actually casings used for dropping leaflets but fancied up with rats' nests, dead birds and insects;) and 'demonstrations' against the US with all the prisoners marching in formation, waving Red banners and shouting anti-capitalist slogans. The whole thing was like nothing before in our military history.

Research, even an investigation such as ours, based upon the minute, thoughtful review of every word spoken by each of a thousand men about an experience still fresh in their minds, needs for its verification and evidence of validity, a "control" group for comparisons to be made. The control group must have the same 'ailment,' in this case captivity in North Korea in the hands of the Chinese Communist Army. The conditions of treatment must be the same - here the camps, lectures, food, physical treatment, period of confinement - except for at least one significantly different element, in this case the nationality of the subjects. The outcomes of the two groups, the research group and the control group, can then be compared. If different, the difference can with some confidence be ascribed to the one different element, or 'variable.'

Our 'control' group consisted of more than two hundred Turkish soldiers who were all captured at about the same time as our troops and in the same general area. Many of the Turks were sick or wounded at the time of capture. While their number was much smaller than the number of Americans taken prisoner, it was large enough to permit a number of valid comparisons. The outcome for this group was clear: every one of those men survived right up until the Cease Fire, while more than 2 out of every 5 Americans did not.

The Turks were all placed in one camp. Like the Americans, they had been brutalized by the North Koreans, but their custody was then given over to the Chinese. The behavior of these men during the bitterly cold winter months of the first year, when our men were dying n appalling numbers, was dramatically different.

Upon their arrival in the village set aside as their camp, the few officers and sergeants among the Turks immediately gathered together and established who was senior, and thus in command. The relative rank and seniority of all other commissioned and non-commissioned officers was then identified and made known to all, and a traditional hierarchical military structure was put in place.

The remainder of the men, most of them simply Privates, were immediately formed into small groups with definite assignments: wood gathering, fire-tending, searching for edible plants and roots, food preparation and care of those sick and wounded unable to work. Discipline in the Turkish Army is harsh, by American standards. There is no discussion of any decision or order. The slightest misbehavior is instantly punished with blows and can involve periods of standing barefoot in a frozen field, slaps and kicks from other soldiers, and even being spat upon by everyone who passes by. Relationships between superiors and subordinates, even between corporals and privates one rank apart, can never be said to be warm and fuzzy.

In spite of that, every sick or wounded soldier had two healthy soldiers assigned to his care. The caretakers dug for roots and brewed unknown teas for him to drink, helped him eat, lay beside him to keep him warm at night, encouraged him to recover, reminded him of his duty to get well, to survive, to help the others. And every one of them did.

The Chinese, alarmed by this soldierly behavior, removed the commanding officer and sent him off to a reactionary camp. The next most senior man immediately took over his command. When the Chinese found that this had happened, they took that man off as well. And the next, and the next. At length there was nothing but privates left in the camp. The senior - oldest - private took command, and was duly 'segregated,' as were those who stepped forward to follow his example. Ultimately the Chinese gave up, and put the whole group of Turks back together again.

Instructors for this group turned out to be Turkish-speaking Chinese. They delivered the same message given to the US soldiers, and set up the same kinds of lecture groups. Only two Turkish soldiers participated actively in the discussions. Those two men were ostracized by their fellows but remained in the camp, untouched. On the way home following repatriation, these two, alone among all the others, suffered the misfortune of falling overboard from their ship to become the sole Turkish POW casualties.

Turks, despite the harsh qualities of life in the Turkish Army, are not tougher than Americans. Nor are they more dedicated to freedom. Many, it is true, had grown up in a far crueler environment, socially and physically, than existed in the

US. It is possible that, having survived childhood in far less hygienic settings than in most American homes, they had a broader immunity-building exposure to diseases than Americans do. Their survival, however, and their day to day behavior in their years in the camp, stood in such marked contrast to our own that one could not but draw significant conclusions about how we prepare our people for terrible stress, such as military captivity can be.

Two small groups of Americans in the camps, while not held as separate from the bulk of POWs, who were mainly low-ranking Army enlisted people, behaved in significantly different ways from the majority. These were a relatively small number of Marines, and an even smaller group of Air Force officers The Marines were mixed in with the bulk of other prisoners, making valid conclusions about their behavior impossible to assess accurately. One fact was clear: their survival rate was far better than among their Army fellows. There were no reports of "give-up-itis" among the Marines.

In actual fact, the Air Force people were not collected into a group, to be held as such. Most of them were commissioned officer pilots, captured when their planes were shot down or crashed for other reasons. They arrived mostly singly, at various times during the war rather than as a group all at one time, like the Army troops. As would be expected, these officers were highly intelligent, well-trained young men from middle- and upper middle-class families.

Unlike the bulk of prisoners, these men were evidently segregated immediately from the main prisoner groups and held in solitary confinement. Each was assigned one or two Chinese interrogators: English-speaking, US-educated college graduates who came daily to conduct lengthy sessions dealing with the same kind of personal historical information called for in the 'student' questionnaires and interviews, but going into far greater detail concerning political beliefs, family and other personal relationships, and religion.

Some time was given to explaining China's current situation and the rationale behind their intervention in Korea, but little to America's alleged history of rampant capitalist exploitation of the working class. Instead, the interrogators talked at length about the "germ warfare" supposedly being employed by the US, with endlessly repeated questions about the officer's participation, hammering away at the idea that some of the bombs dropped by these men, perhaps unknown to them, had been loaded with disease-producing materials.

This sort of thing went on daily, sometimes for many months. During that time the individual was allowed no contact with fellow prisoners, and the only information he got about the war came from copies of Communist papers and publications from around the world, including the U.S. editions of the "Daily Worker." Supported by this distorted version of the news, and bolstered by a few selected articles and books by Communist authors, the idea was advanced that America was losing the war, unpopular at home anyway, and would soon pull out, abandoning all its prisoners.

Throughout the process, the prisoner was encouraged to engage in dialogue and political discussions with his interrogators. Every officer had been warned, in his training, to avoid to his utmost, doing this with a captor. The rule he was to live by was "Name, Rank and Serial Number;" tell this and nothing else - on any subject.

However, these men later told us, as a result of their long isolation and the daily encouragement of the not-unfriendly young Chinese who talked to them daily, this was a new situation. It was not a standard POW setting, and the old rules probably didn't apply. And so it was that nearly every man put into this special captivity made that first profound mistake.

He began to 'relate' to his captors, and talked more and more freely with them. Most believed that they were smarter than these young Chinese, and could easily mislead and deceive them. In addition, since the interrogators seemed not to be interested in 'military' or technical information, it seemed perfectly safe to talk to them at length.

Perhaps most important, they were encouraged to think that their cooperation would ingratiate them with their keepers, ensuring better care and the chance, broadly hinted at, to get home after all, when the fighting came to its inevitable end. That, instead of simply being abandoned and 'forgotten' by their uncaring, defeated country.

"Cooperation," as it always does in prisoner-captor interactions, becomes a bottomless pit of collaboration sapping the strength to resist, with steadily increasing demands on the prisoner to participate in activities that advance the captor's cause. This was a prime goal of the 'reeducation' and seemingly benign treatment of the great mass of general prisoners. It led to widespread cooperation in the signing of 'peace petitions' addressed to the world's powers, broadcasts to American units extolling the "socialist" People's Republic of China Army, and organized parades and demonstrations by hundreds of prisoners, carefully filmed by Communist 'news' agencies and distributed around the world.

With these men, cooperation took on a more precise, sinister quality. What was wanted from them was a 'confession' that they had participated in spreading germ warfare. Those willing to do this would be dressed up in their regular Air Force Uniforms, fed well and rested, and simply have to read some simple statements, prepared for them, in front of the news cameras of "neutral" (but actually Communist-ruled) countries.

Most of these pilots refused to do this confessing, regardless of their captors' best efforts. Those who did were generally those held the longest, who were the least hopeful about their future freedom. They often rationalized their participation in this most important of the enemy's propaganda campaigns (which they didn't know anything about) by convincing themselves that the whole thing was so ridiculous that nobody would believe it anyway. Some told us they believed that anyone who saw them 'confessing' would know by their voice, inflections and general demeanor that they didn't really mean it.

Top level Air Force officials were understandably terribly disturbed when the filmed 'confessions' of some of their officers began to appear. Later, even after several years had gone by since the fighting stopped and the prisoners came home, they did not want the subject even mentioned, and went to great lengths within the Pentagon to try to prevent me - or anyone who knew of it - to talk about it to anyone.

Partly this was because many people, in and out of the Service, believed that these men had brought discredit upon their uniforms and cast doubt upon the honor of military (or at least Air Force) officers generally. Mainly, however, they were concerned about the impact of such information on recruitment. When the Korean War broke out, many fliers were called back to duty from the Reserves. Five years earlier, at the end of the "big" war, a large number of these men, then young, glamorous heroes who had fought the glorious air battles of World War II, joined the Reserve because they loved to fly and wanted to go on doing so.

By the time, five years later, when they were needed once again to fly into harm's way, with their lives on the line every time they took off, their situations had largely changed. Not only were they five years older. Now they had regular civilian jobs, houses, wives and often children; their situations and their outlooks were quite different.

What was more, this was no grand global campaign against monstrous dictators like Hitler and Mussolini and Hirohito; this was a strictly local conflict between little yellow men in a distant, unknown Oriental land. Not worth risking your life for!

Suddenly a new 'disease' appeared. For the first time in medical history, this was a disease limited to members, of a certain narrow range of rank, in a single military service. Growing numbers of Reserve pilots, recalled to active duty and destined to fight in Korea, reported an incapacitating fear of flying that seriously impaired their ability to perform the many complex acts necessary to operate a complicated fighter plane. They didn't openly refuse to perform their assigned duties - they merely reported that they could not, due to this serious emotional disorder.

A new diagnosis was needed, and duly created. It was called "Fear of Flying," and was bestowed on these otherwise healthy young men. Counseling and psychotherapy were tried and found ineffective. Drugs were out of the question; Prozac had yet to be invented and anyway, pilots on such concoctions are routinely forbidden to operate aircraft. Punishment was not an option, because our society does not (knowingly) punish emotionally disturbed citizens. Fighter pilots who cannot fly are of little use in air combat, and the Air Force was obliged to release these men from their military obligations and let them go home.

In spite of heroic efforts by Air Force public information officers to minimize it, this singular, exotic occupational disease was widely known and commented upon. As had been expected, there was a negative effect upon recruiting. Now, in addition, information coming out of Korea suggested that a shot-down pilot, if he survived, was likely to be singled out by an enemy for 'special' coercive treatment, used for propaganda purposes and forced into a kind of treason. This was just what hard-pressed recruiters needed!

While the entire education and self-criticism program was designed to erode soldiers' convictions about the essential goodness of our country, weaken their loyalties and encourage their participation in ordinarily forbidden activities like signing petitions and taking part in anti-US demonstrations, and large numbers of the prisoners succumbed to Communist manipulations, few of the men were actively collaborators with the Chinese.

Of this small number, even fewer seemed to have accepted the Communist philosophy. It was common for a returnee to say something to the effect that the 'socialist' system, as the instructors called it, was probably a good thing for China, but would never work in the US. Those soldiers who had openly, even eagerly, cooperated with the Chinese appeared to have been motivated more by self-interest than by ideology.

A few of these people, readily identified on our wall charts by the frequency of reports about them from other returnees and duly recorded, were exhaustively examined. They turned out to be men of weak character, no convictions, often cowardly and ready to inform on others or take an active part in lectures and discussions so as to curry favor and gain privileges. The most blatant offenders among them were charged for what were military crimes, and later prosecuted and imprisoned. Theirs was a sorry tale, but not unique in large groups of people in a situation of continuing stress and danger. It was important to identify and punish men like that, but it was more important to identify what had been done to all the others, to make them so seemingly passive and acquiescent to their loss of freedom.

Our research team spent many hours, spread over all the evenings of the several weeks when the data were being collected and sorted out, and then all day every day for more weeks, as we examined hypotheses that might explain what we had seen, and struggled to produce a coherent, workman-like final report to submit to the top military authorities. One topic that received considerable attention had to do with a process recently labeled "brainwashing."

The term was the invention of an author who had done considerable research into Communist indoctrination techniques. As he described it, a rather mystical process incorporating hypnosis, post-hypnotic suggestion and esoteric educational and training techniques could be used to "wash away" long-held convictions and stored memories, allowing new, alien ideas to be implanted in the brain, permanently altering the individual's beliefs, and his behavior.

We found no evidence that anything of the sort had taken place in Korean prison camps.

What we did find was that our men were subjected to a nearly universal practice in all the villages, cities, shops, government offices, factories and farms throughout China. Based on the experiences of Soviet officials as they took over the governments of country after country, and then modified and refined in keeping with ancient cultural traditions of the Chinese peoples, it was essentially a process designed for the control of large groups of people. It did this, as we had been shown, with great success.

The Chinese are noted for their reliance upon ancient principles, such as those espoused centuries ago by the great military philosopher, Sun Tzu. One such, possibly the most important of all, is the principle of 'divide and conquer.' The subjugation of the entire Chinese population, over a billion strong, and the control of the American soldiers held captive in the POW camps of Korea, were both brilliant applications and elaborations of that simple, basic idea. The Chinese use it because it works.

While the techniques applied in China for purposes of fixing Communist rule in place over that vast land and its huge population had their origins in the Soviet Union, there were modifications that were peculiarly Chinese. Early on, in both countries, there was a period of widespread cruelty, imprisonment, exile to remote areas, and executions. In the Soviet state, powerful members of the community were commonly taken away to prison, where they were subjected to harsh conditions and interminable interrogations aimed at getting them to confess crimes against the people, as these things were defined in Communist orthodoxy. Once satisfactory confessions were made, the 'criminals' were either executed or they were banished to Siberian gulags, never to return.

In areas where the entire populace was resistant to the new order, such as the Ukraine, measures were instituted to control food and fuel supplies and deny even simple health care, a process designed to lead to disease and starvation. In this way entire populations, like the Kulaks - peasants who worked the land in the Ukraine - were decimated or destroyed. The best estimates are that 7 million Kulaks died in this prime example of ethnic cleansing, or genocide, long before Hitler began his campaign against the Jewish people.

This legacy, coupled with compulsory public lectures on Marxism and "People's Democracy," and regular self-criticism meetings leading to universal self-exposure and inevitably to feelings of vulnerability and suspiciousness, created a mass of people who felt isolated from one another. Conventional religious practices were forbidden, churches converted to other uses, and religious beliefs denounced. All education and information services were strictly controlled, and used to create around the concept of "The People" an atmosphere of spirituality and mysticism to serve people's needs for these things, now that conventional religious beliefs were shown to be spurious and had to be abandoned.

The Chinese, characteristically, modified the Soviet system to fit more closely into their own cultural traditions. Following the consolidation of Communist rule over all of China in 1949, and lacking an extensive police system, a gulag, or a strong, faith-based spiritual religious setting more common in Russia, they set out to dismantle the social structures and practices that had long held Chinese communities together.

Their first targets were easy: the landowners and operators of mills and factories who for centuries had controlled the very lives of ordinary people, the great bulk of them peasants. A few trained Communist agents - "cadre" - were dispatched to every village throughout the vast landmass of China to arrest the "imperialists" and bring them before "People's Courts" composed of the entire population of a village. There, the accused was first of all publicly humiliated so that he would lose "face," perhaps the most powerful personal quality in the Chinese value system. While the things done to such criminals might seem ludicrous or even silly to Westerners, to Chinese steeped in ancient traditions they were not.

To make certain the accused suffered profound loss of face, he was stripped of his rich clothes and forced to stand on a small platform, barefoot and clad only in his underwear. A foolish hat might be put on his head, and he might be forced to perform an awkward dance on his platform while his tormentors used flexible willow branches to strike his legs and keep him dancing. After a prolonged period of abuse, he was then required to stand with head bowed while his "crimes" against the people were outlined and denounced. The audience was required to join in the denunciations, and cadre kept careful, ominous watch to make sure everyone participated with appropriate enthusiasm.

After that, the onlookers were urged to shout out their recommendations for punishment. Sooner or later a voice would urge that he should die, and the leaders of this little drama would encourage others to support that idea, praising those who did so, until eventually the crowd was demanding execution. A single bullet to the back of the unfortunate offender's head was the customary outcome. It would be announced that henceforth, all would be free at last from capitalist oppression, that all would collectively own the dead man's property and all would work it for the common good.

The same ceremony, with little modification, was performed throughout China, in thousands of villages and hamlets, and in identified neighborhoods in larger cities. Something quite similar was done in large factories, and in a relatively short period of time, nearly the entire Chinese class of landowners and other owners of the means of production simply ceased to exist.

The next group of targets was harder, because there was no comparable reservoir of resentment and hostility toward them, as there had been toward the first group, and the next step struck more pointedly at the most deeply entrenched Chinese loyalty: devotion to the family, with unshakeable fealty to the male head of that family. The Communists accurately foresaw that devotion to "the People" and those who led it required that the traditional family structure, with its inherent authority, must be dissolved.

The same technique was employed, but somewhat more selectively. Patriarchs of large, powerful, socially prominent families were singled out for attention. They were put on public trial in much the same way as the landowners, but if there seemed to be substantial sympathy among the audience, the old man might be sent away for "reeducation" rather than shot. Nevertheless, sufficient numbers of family heads were dispatched to cause severe erosion of the traditional family system in a surprisingly short time.

When it came to managing the US POWs in Korea, the Chinese had far less ambitious goals. They needed to control these men, minimize the expenditure of soldiers and equipment needed to keep them in place, hopefully make some use of them for propaganda purposes, possibly build at least a small core of Americans with positive feelings about the new China alongside feelings of eroded faith in the goodness of their own country, and in the long run advance the cause of what they choose to call - and what may be - their own special version of "socialism."

There was no need, therefore, for the public humiliations and quasi 'trials' used to build a permanently submissive Chinese population. While it was necessary to keep natural leaders, rebels and agitators apart from the main group of prisoners, they didn't have to be held up to scorn or executed; one merely had to denounce them as "reactionary" and put them off by themselves in a separate, more heavily guarded location. The great bulk of POWs were neither powerful landowners nor revered family patriarchs, either, so they posed no threat.

It was, however, necessary to employ those techniques developed and refined in the villages of Russia and especially China to keep people isolated from one another psychologically and emotionally so that they dared not share secrets or conspire to rebel against authority. So it was that they employed their educational process and the self-criticism device, along with multiple interviews, encouragement of informing as a way to help one's comrades achieve a better understanding of real truth, and a certain amount of the sports activities American's love.

What was astonishing, as we studied the stories of our thousand research subjects, was how successful this fairly simple approach to the control of groups of people had proven to be with young Americans. A careful analysis of the backgrounds of our troops did not reveal them to be significantly different from those who had fought in World War II, except that the soldiers fighting in Korea had, on average, slightly more education. Otherwise, all the factors one might expect to be important were not different. Military training was essentially unchanged, equipment was if anything a little better, and there was no great public outcry against the war like there was to be in Viet Nam, so far as the POWs knew, at any rate.

The fact remained that this group of men performed differently as POWs than any previous prisoners in any previous war. The question was why? Surely there was nothing magical about the Chinese process, unique though it was in military annals. There had been no systematic physical abuse in the camps. At least one other identifiable group of more than two hundred men, the Turks, had been subjected to the same process with no evident effect on their behavior.

After several weeks of reviewing records and our notes and transcripts of interviews, we reluctantly came to some unsettling but inescapable conclusions. They had more to do with us than they did with the Chinese.

Several things about the returnees were particularly striking. The first, already noted, was their passivity and docility. A certain amount of this is not unusual among people freshly released from confinement, but it tends not to last as long as it did with these men. Moreover, they had not been strictly confined in small cells, but had a considerable amount of freedom of movement within the confines of their village-camps. Most of the camps were not fenced, and were without guard-towers or armed guards, yet there seemed to have been no problem of men wandering off, let alone making a serious attempt to escape.

The next thing that struck us was these soldiers' willingness - at times eagerness - to talk about the other prisoners, outlining details of incidents of unfairness among the group, and dwelling at some length on individuals who seemed most willing to curry favor with their captors at other prisoners' expense. Nearly every man reported that informing was constant, and it often resulted in long, tedious individual conferences with instructors, trying to explain away some minor misbehavior that a fellow prisoner had described, or that the conferee had himself revealed during a self-criticism meeting.

This seemed to account for the absence of traditional escape plotting. US troops in previous military captivity, both in Europe and Asia, had achieved a well-earned reputation for cooking up escape schemes. Very often these were elaborate and drawn-out, requiring the participation of an 'escape committee' and undertaken at times with the active help of a number of individuals working to prepare just one or two escapees to get away. When such an endeavor succeeded, usually in the face of severe punishment for failure, everyone in the camp was inspired with a certain sense of triumph and hopefulness.

That never happened in Korea. The reason, simply stated by almost every repatriated prisoner, was that "You couldn't trust anybody." Early on, some of the men had talked about trying to escape, only to be told forcefully by their fellows that such behavior could hurt everybody, and to forget about it. Worse, the instructors seemed to learn about such talk almost immediately, and the long, implicitly threatening conferences were sure to follow.

Another striking difference between these soldiers and those captured in earlier wars was the apparent universal rejection of authority among the prisoners. While it is true that the Chinese segregated commissioned officers and many sergeants in 'reactionary' camps after the first few months, they had not done so during the early period when so many of the men died. From the outset, attempts by corporals and sergeants to organize the men for mutual support were met with strong, often profane refusals. These commonly took the form of assertions that "You can't tell me what to do. You're no sergeant here, buddy; you're just a goddamned prisoner like me, so bug off!" We heard this over and over again.

Even in the 'reactionary' camps, attempts to organize, and to assert authority of the most conventional military type, met with resistance and failure.

Our little group of researchers, now officially dubbed the "Japan Joint Intelligence Processing Board," were hardly a collection of starry-eyed idealists. On the contrary, the seven or eight intelligence agents who were the principal members, and the senior Defense Department attorney, were if anything a little cynical about human behavior in dangerous and stressful situations. None was a super-patriot who expected every man to be willing to make any sacrifice, risk any danger, or rush to join any group to resist the oppressive enemy. They entered into the project in a highly professional, rather matter-of-fact manner that appeared to me to be free of any particular preconceptions or bias, determined to find out exactly what it had been like for these returning prisoners, what had been done to them, and what could be learned from them to better prepare future soldiers who might one day themselves face military captivity.

It was fascinating, then, to watch the changes that took place in these officers' attitudes over the weeks we spent interviewing the POWs, charting details of their reports, comparing notes on interviews we ourselves conducted, and discussed, often far into the night, what we were hearing. The initial incredulity over what we were learning soon gave way to indignation, anger, disgust, sadness and a growing sense that our assumptions about the quality and strength of character of the American soldier were faulty - seriously so.

The utter rejection of all authority seemed to be the most ominous finding. We discussed at great length the possible reasons for this. Soldiers in WWII, like those before them, often rebelled in varying degrees toward authority, as Americans always have since colonial times, but this generally takes place early in training, and soon diminishes, though some grumbling persists forever. Not so with the Korea POWs. They instantly rejected every effort by nominal superiors to provide direction of any kind, from the first days in the camps. This appeared to be a deep-seated, long-term attitude that basic military training had evidently not modified. We concluded that it had to have begun in childhood, and been permitted if not encouraged in adolescence.

As part of this, these young men seemed wholly unaware of what we all thought was almost an instinctual impulse to gain strength and effectiveness, in any situation or contest that was too large or powerful to be overcome by individual effort, by joining with others, under at least nominal leadership. That was why we had football teams, Boy Scout troops, and, in the Army, squads, platoons and companies, all with leaders in charge. For some strange and unexpected reason, these people evidently believed that being captured by an armed enemy in battle wiped out all such requirements.

Along with this widespread, open rejection of anyone trying to take charge, there went an equally common belief, often clearly expressed, that each man's problems with getting enough food, staying warm, nursing a bad sprain or dealing with diarrhea were his alone. "It wasn't my problem" was the usual answer to our questions about lending a hand to injured or sick men, and "You take care of yourself, Buddy, and I'll take care of me!" was a frequent declaration among prisoners.

The general relaxation of discipline and a new pattern of 'kinder, gentler' basic training that seemed to emphasize good fellowship rather than obedience and mutual aid and toughness, all of which were reactive sequellae to the terrible hardships of WWII around the globe, no doubt played some part in what happened in Korea. Even in active combat, there had been disturbing reports of infantry companies defying or simply ignoring their leaders' orders and being annihilated as a result.

The problem in the camps, however, seemed to reach much farther back than basic training in a peacetime army camp. It reflected negative attitudes toward authority figures, namely parents and schoolteachers, early in childhood, and without serious consequences. That is, until you were driven through the frozen mountains of North Korea and put into a prison camp. There, men died needlessly, and in horrifyingly large numbers, because other men ignored them and no leader emerged to order that they be cared for. "You take care of yourself, Buddy, and I'll take care of me!"

Another finding that was particularly disturbing had to do with the widespread informing that went on. It happened, often, that a man informed on others during one of his individual sessions with an instructor, in order to divert attention from himself about something some other man had reported about him. In this way an endless circle of informing was set up, and, as many prisoners said, "You couldn't trust anybody." No one reported that he had informed on others' violations of camp rules because of the threat of dire physical harm. It was done, we heard, because 'everybody was doing it.'

The fact that informing on fellow prisoners was the highest form of disloyalty seemed never to have occurred to any of the returnees. Not a single one expressed any regret or guilty feelings whatever for having done so. Evidently, if you couldn't trust anybody, you had no obligation to anybody either. That, in any case, is how it turned out.

Among the Turkish POWs, not a single death occurred from 'give-up-itis,' and no sick soldier was ever left by himself, day or night. In addition, no Turk died in the camps. We were sure there was an important lesson here.

Some weeks after the last prisoner had been processed and sent on to his home, and after endless, searching discussions and arguments over the causes for what we had found, we wrote the "Final Report of the JJIPB," the Japan Joint Intelligence Processing Board. In the report we described in great, accurate detail, the handling of the American POWs by the Chinese, the situation in the camps, and the behavior of our troops. We discussed the content of the 'education' sessions, contrasting what was taught there with what was being taught in US schools.

We described in equal detail the process of student-instructor interviews, self-criticism meetings, and the massive informing and pervasive air of mutual suspicion that resulted from these things. Given that universal lack of trust, we illustrated that it was impossible for the prisoners to group together for purposes of resistance or (especially) escape.

There was much more to the report, of course, but we carefully avoided naming names, even of the most notorious collaborators and turncoats, of which there were a few. We did identify a number of soldiers (by code, rather than by their names) who had admitted during interrogation that they had been recruited by the Chinese to serve as Communist agents after their return to the States, and had even accepted assignments to be carried out when they got home. Neither of these groups was large, and they did not reflect the more serious problems that the study uncovered. Those problems had more to do with how we in America raise and educate (or fail to educate) our children, and worse, how we seem to be abandoning, as a people, our hallowed commitment to moral principles having to do with the place and function of authority, the idea of personal responsibility, and concepts like honor and personal, individual loyalty - all powerful ideas espoused by the founders of the Nation.

Our group of initially cool, detached, highly professional intelligence and legal and medical experts had become, in the process of our work, seriously worried - even alarmed - old fashioned American patriots who believed we were seeing real cracks in our country's moral armor that were portents of serious trouble ahead, particularly in times of stress and danger.

The years since then have been filled with abundant evidence that what we feared may be happening has in fact happened. The continued erosion of the family as the basic societal structure; the 'free speech' movement, demonstrations, rebellions and violent rejections of authority that began in the 1960s and erupted violently during Viet Nam; the "Me" generation's self-preoccupation; the explosion of drug use; the wild growth of legalized lotteries (whatever happened to the 'numbers racket?') and other forms of gambling; the growth of a huge population content to live on Welfare; the exodus from the churches; the exploding prison population; all of these share their roots with those underlying the sad behavior we saw in the POW camps nearly a half century ago.

In my independent, non-partisan best judgment, the horrifying characterological faults so brilliantly displayed by the century's final chief executive and so blithely tolerated and even admired by so much of the electorate, epitomize what William Bennett has called the death of outrage, and a moral decline in America that may prove to be incompatible with our concepts of freedom, and may prove as well to be its nemesis.

Our final report, we decided, needed the widest possible distribution, because it described real problems that had resulted in hundreds of mainly avoidable deaths, unprecedented collaboration with an enemy, a breakdown of military discipline, and the need for some serious reflections about education, training, and the duties of citizenship in a free country. We therefore ordered that several hundred copies of the report be printed, and so they were. Since we had carefully avoided naming anyone or blaming anyone, we anticipated no problems. We were wrong.

A senior officer of the Far East Command, shown an advance copy of the printed report, decided, in his wisdom, that "people aren't ready to hear this kind of thing" and ordered all but two copies of the report destroyed - and they were burned. We in the JJIPB had kept one copy for ourselves, and we sent it by ordinary mail to the Chief of Staff of the Army in the Pentagon. Silence. Nothing happened.

We reconvened the Board to plan our next move. We were determined to get the information out, one way or the other, even though we couldn't lay hands on any more printed copies. Finally a plan emerged. "Doc," someone said, "Couldn't you rewrite the thing as a psychiatric article?" "Sure," I said, dreading what was to come. The Board promptly voted to direct me to do so, and to present it as a paper at a major Far East Command-wide medical conference scheduled in a few weeks. "And don't worry," I was told, "If they try to court martial you for revealing the information, we will all defend you at your trial. We'll get you off." The die was cast.

I laboriously rewrote our report, examining much of the POWs' behavior in psychological terms. Of particular interest were the individual questionnaires and interviews with the Chinese instructors, both designed to heighten the soldier's sense of vulnerability and total loss of personal privacy. These measures were distorted applications of what happens in individual psychotherapy, where individual strengths and weaknesses are examined with the goal of helping the patient to discard old attitudes, behavior and social techniques that are no longer effective or appropriate and interfere with a satisfactory adjustment to life. At the same time, those behaviors that the patient exhibits that do work, and aid in successful adaptations, are identified, examined for their usefulness and reinforced.

In the lectures on 'socialist' philosophy as interpreted by the Chinese, the standards of desirable belief and behavior were clearly set forth. Great emphasis was placed on the evils that men had done in the name of capitalism, and the captains of the industrial revolution were singled out for attention as heartless abusers of the worker class - the people - whom they exploited mercilessly as they amassed fortunes and power. Men such as Rockefeller, Morgan, Ford, Carnegie and many others were castigated as the true "enemies of the people" who caused untold suffering amongst the masses. Political leaders, past and present, were pictured as the 'lackies' and 'running dogs' of these evil men. The unvarying underlying theme of these lessons was that all who were in power were enemies of the people, and that leadership, as Americans thought of it, was an evil that had no place in egalitarian, socialist society.

Self-criticism meetings, held daily in the camps as they were in the factories, offices and farms throughout China, were designed to reveal thoughts and beliefs that violated the spirit of a true people's democracy, so that they could be corrected and eliminated. Most of the prisoners initially viewed the meetings as ridiculous, and even silly. Some contrived tales of their own evil past, exploiting their slaves while living in luxury on their huge plantations; others told of imposing cruel working conditions in women and helpless children in their factories.

The Chinese instructors, graduates of UCLA, Cal, USC and even Harvard, were not deceived, of course, and tolerated such nonsense good humouredly, at first. As time went on, however, they began to pick apart the manufactured tales of capitalist excess, and, armed with masses of information from the questionnaires and personal interviews, began to focus in on actual realities of the soldiers' past lives. This was done in a benign, non-accusatory way while the men were encouraged to describe more and more details of their lives, their families, girlfriends, jobs, schooling and aspirations, all of which were then examined against the standards of behavior deemed desirable in the "people's paradise" such as that being constructed in China.

Over time, the process - itself a distortion of group psychotherapy sessions - had a wholly predictable outcome. The repatriated prisoners described growing feelings that they had somehow exposed too much of themselves, that the other guys knew more about them than they did themselves, that maybe life in the US wasn't as good as they'd always thought, and that they were somehow transparent and at the mercy of others. This had no doubt played a major part in the curious alienation from one another that we had observed when the prisoners were liberated.

The paper I presented also discussed the striking rejection of authority, and the failure to group together, even in the hard early months before any indoctrination had started when mutual aid, essential for survival, was almost non-existent. The death rate, highest in our history for military prisoners as far back as the Civil War, spoke for itself.

The fact that in nearly three years of captivity, not a single prisoner ever successfully escaped and made it back to our lines, and few even tried, was eloquent testimony to the success of this modern version of the ancient 'divide and conquer' approach. So also was the total absence of any kind of collective turmoil or signs of rebellion among the captives, of the sort that caused our people so much trouble on Koje-do and Cheju-do among the Chinese and Korean prisoners.

At the beginning of the large medical conference, it was announced by the chair that we were all honored to have among us the Inspector General of the Far East Command, an unexpected presence never before seen in a medical meeting. This worthy, a dour Brigadier General, was seated in the second or third row of the large auditorium, just a little to one side of the midline so that he could be seen clearly from the podium.

After the customary administrative announcements at the beginning of the meeting, I was to speak. Glancing at the I.G., I noted that he seemed largely uninterested, and even a little lethargic. After only a few minutes into my speech, however, he came alive. He sat up straighter in his seat, and hurriedly pulled out a small notepad that he began to fill with notes. This continued until I finished, and I watched with some dismay as the General got up and made his way briskly to the door. As he disappeared through it, I felt sure he was on his way to influence my future in undesirable ways.

Sure enough, the day the conference ended I received a curt summons to appear at the Surgeon General's office at Camp Zama, on the distant outskirts of Tokyo, "without delay." I left promptly, experiencing a strange combination of defiance and anxiety, and was told by the general's secretary that the senior staff had been in session for several hours, that the Inspector General was in attendance, and that I was expected. Disaster was imminent.

The General's conference room was large, and equipped with long tables in a U-shape. At its head sat the Surgeon, a Major General in the Medical Corps, flanked by his deputy and the I.G. About twenty other senior medical department officers sat around the tables. All wore, I thought, expressions surely learned during earlier incarnations as members of the Spanish Inquisition.

The S.G., without preamble, said "Doctor, the IG tells me you delivered a most provocative paper at the Medical Command Conference the other day. I would like for you to tell us exactly what you said." Only slightly reassured by my memory of my JJIPB colleagues' promise to defend me at my court martial, I proceeded to deliver my paper. When it was over, I was told to step outside for a few moments.

About a half hour later, during which my uniform changed color as I sweated in the humidity of the room and the anxiety of my soul, I was summoned back.

"Doctor," the General said, "I want every officer and enlisted man in the Far East Command to hear that report. My office will make all the arrangements, and you will proceed immediately. You will represent this office. That is all."

Both stunned and exhilarated, I made my way back to Tokyo, called for a meeting of the Board, which assembled with remarkable speed, not knowing what had transpired but fearing the worst. When we were all together, I related my experience in the corridors of the medical mighty (plus the I.G.) The news was greeted with a shout, mutual congratulations and appropriate backslapping, and we all then went out for a visit to the Officers Club.

For the next few weeks, I made my way to the Philippines, Guam, Korea and Japan, giving my lecture to all the troops, usually assembled in movie theaters. My reception was good everywhere, and many officers and men expressed great interest in what we had found. Of particular interest was the subject of "brainwashing," a term coined by a writer who suggested that the Chinese had developed a kind of magical process that wiped out men's memories and convictions, and replaced them with Communist ideology. We had seen no evidence at all of any such thing, but it was certainly true that an attempt was made to cast doubt on American beliefs and principles, and promote the philosophies of Marx and Lenin.

The ensuing months were spent in Tokyo at the Army Hospital, the prison, and the headquarters of the Counter Intelligence Corps, the "CIC," in the Kempei Tai - 'thought police' - building across the street from the imperial palace grounds. The commander, a portly, rather serious man with a well-hidden sense of humor and lurking twinkle that occasionally leaked out unexpectedly, had heard my talk on POWs and invited me to give a special briefing to his assembled agents, and then answer questions.

The session at CIC headquarters lasted many hours. I was impressed by the agents, whose questions were thoughtful and penetrating. After a lively discussion, the Colonel invited me to join him in his office for a drink. He talked for a while about CIC work in Japan, where there were not only some serious Communist cells in operation, but also some deeply committed, fanatical right-wing secret organizations dedicated to restoring the 'old order' in Japan. Then he got to the real reason he wanted to talk privately: his wife.

George, the Colonel, was a classical intelligence agent of many years' experience, who had married a fellow agent, a European woman of great beauty. She had, over a period of ten years, shown increasing signs of mental disorganization, culminating in a series of severe psychotic episodes. These were ushered in by bizarre behavior like having the apartment building they owned painted in bright purple and orange, or issuing eviction notices to all the tenants the same day, without cause or warning.

Totally dedicated to his work, George was utterly at a loss as to how to deal with this floridly disordered woman, whose repeated involuntary commitments to private psychiatric hospitals, arranged by his Los Angeles attorneys, were frightfully costly. A devout Roman Catholic, he would not consider divorce. Recently he had established a relationship with a beautiful Japanese girl, one of his clandestine agents, thinking it was merely a superficial 'outlet,' but found himself deeply in love, and deeply disturbed by that. He needed to talk to someone about this unexpected complication in his life, and in his sensitive and powerful position, had no one to confide in. I had arrived at just the right time; he decided that I could be trusted absolutely, and I was chosen. We never even discussed a 'doctor-patient' relationship, but instead became friends and colleagues, and took to meeting regularly. I couldn't offer him solutions to the problem of his psychotic wife or his Japanese paramour, but it obviously helped him to be able to talk about both.

Most of our time together was spent on other things. George, like all who manage intelligence people, had to watch his agents with care. Not only were they under a special kind of stress, much of the time, but also they operated largely alone and unsupported by close associates, and were sometimes in serious personal danger. The principle underlying much of their work - these were the people who uncovered and caught enemy agents - was suspicion, along with a kind of global distrust. Over time, these qualities influenced the personalities and behavior of the men, sometimes seriously disrupting their personal lives and their professional relationships.

It was important for their commander, my friend George, to be able to detect warning signs of emotional distortions among his men, and take steps to offset them. He sought my help with this, and we worked out ways to evaluate individuals in seemingly benign, mostly social, settings, of which there were many. The CIC interacted widely with what was called the 'foreign trader' population in Tokyo - representatives of foreign companies and foreign diplomats - who entertained lavishly and commonly used parties to recruit Japanese guests, mostly women, to various causes beyond the obvious ones. We would attach ourselves, in friendly fashion, to one of his agents attending a party that we also went to, and spent the evening observing him (or her) for warning signs.

The colonel had a wonderfully colorful history. He became involved in intelligence work at the outset of World War II, and undertook a number of exceedingly daring and dangerous missions in Germany and Occupied France during the war. His most outstanding achievement occurred in Africa, in the Belgian Congo.

Unbeknownst to most people, interest in nuclear fission and the potential for developing and using atomic weapons occurred quite early in the war. Uranium had been identified as the most important element in this work, and it had been established and was well known that the Congo was probably the richest source of this material. Our adversaries in Germany, Italy, Vichy France and Japan, as well as our faithful Soviet allies, all had agents in the Congo, seeking out the most important uranium deposits and setting plans in motion to obtain it for their scientists.

George, equipped with a small airplane and experienced pilot, along with an abundance of personal weapons, was assigned the job of eliminating the threat these enemy operatives presented. He did exactly that, with dispatch. Shortly after he arrived in the Congo, every one of the Axis representatives had disappeared, forever, and their operations were shut down. The Allies retained control of the Congo's rich uranium deposits, some of which eventually found their way to Hiroshima and Nagasaki. The Soviet agents suffered the same fate, and George came away from that experience with a deep, unshakeable distrust, mixed with a certain grudging admiration, for his Soviet counterparts and their leaders.

One day it was announced that the G-2 of the Army, head of all Army intelligence units and activities, was coming out from the Pentagon to visit Tokyo CIC headquarters as well as every CIC field office among the twenty or more positioned around Japan. George suggested that I come along, and I was ordered to report to him for that purpose. What followed was the most remarkable journey I ever took.

The Occupation was still in effect, so the US forces still had control of all of Japan's resources. Among these was the Emperor's private train. George decided that was the ideal vehicle for our trip, and indeed it was. The General from the Pentagon, George, and I were assigned to ride, alone, in the Emperor's private car, complete with a large gold chrysanthemum on each side. The car had four lovely private sleeping rooms, other rooms for luggage, and a large, comfortable lounge that could be set up for formal dining.

I arrived at Tokyo's central railway station at the appointed hour to find that an immaculate bright red carpet had been laid from the sidewalk all the way along a private passageway through the large terminal and right up to the steps of the emperor's car. We were informed that such a carpet was required whenever the car was to be used, whether the emperor himself was to board or not. Accepting this gracefully, we paraded along the crimson path as if it was our due, completing the first of many such red carpet-walks wherever the train stopped. As we traversed the whole length of Japan, we found at each station we passed through, however small, and despite the fact that no stop was planned, not only the inevitable stretch of red carpet, but standing behind it in their best uniforms, the entire station staff standing at attention until our car drew abreast of their formation, when they bowed deeply. This, we concluded, was the only way to travel!

The journey had been carefully planned. Our itinerary started in Japan's southernmost island just as the cherry blossoms reached the height of their glory there, and the blossoms all along the way to our last stop on the northernmost island of Hokkaido came out in time with our slow progress. The CIC units we visited were mainly small, two- or three-man operations, often in villages or parts of cities that had no substantial American presence. They didn't take long, so we had ample time to explore our surroundings, sample the cuisine of the area, and - George's most favorite activity of all - poke around in dozens of antique shops and art galleries. The colonel had become a recognized, world-rank authority on oriental porcelains, and by the time we got back to Tokyo, the fourth bedroom in the emperor's car was piled floor to ceiling with his loot, bought with his considerable private resources but often at ridiculously low prices. He seemed to know every antique dealer personally, and was always greeted warmly when we entered the shops.

Following that wonderful trip in the Emperor's private car and train, life settled down somewhat. Through my contacts (and parties) with the counterintelligence people, I was introduced to a number of high level Japanese government officials, and consulted these dignitaries about my still tentative plans to leave the military and set up a private medical practice in Tokyo, limited largely to the 'foreign trader' population.

What I learned, in short order, was that it was entirely feasible and even desirable, but that between federal and municipal taxes, I would have to pay out nearly 90% of what I took in. When I suggested that I might set up a small company that would take in all the revenues from patient care and simply pay me a salary, own my house and car and pay the servants, and supply my food and other needs, which was the practice of the rich families that owned major businesses, I was told that, regrettably, that was not permitted for foreigners.

In a way, that was a relief. Deep inside, I felt strongly that there was still a huge debt to pay back to my fellow citizens who had paid for my education, and that what we had learned from the unfortunate men, the POWs, who had been the first Americans to live under a Communist tyranny, needed to be told to the public back home. It was certain that my colleagues on the Japan Joint Intelligence Processing Board, now disbanded, were prevented by the nature of their intelligence duties from doing that, and once again I discovered that I'd been elected. I wasn't quite sure how to carry this out, but as always during my life to date, subsequent events were to show me a way that I neither planned nor could avoid.

What had we learned, actually? Certainly we were given a clear view of a simple but incredibly effective way to manage groups of people - not just a few prisoners but whole communities. The methods used by the Chinese were undeniably coercive: people were confined in the POW camps but were equally confined in the villages and neighborhoods throughout China. There was in both the camps and the country at large an initial period of terror, brutality and deaths, although in Korea that was only in the first few months and only in the hands of the Koreans, not the Chinese.

Following that, while living conditions were hardly comfortable, they were tolerable and entirely survivable. A determined, simplistic, repetitive "education" program then began, and never let up, outlining in interminable, tedious detail the personal and group behaviors and thinking required in the new social order. Along with that there was a daily program of individual and group interviews and discussions and confessions that was a corruption of conventional psychotherapeutic techniques, designed to alienate individuals, foster suspicion and distrust, and minimize the possibility of organized resistance.

What was new about all this was its success in producing a degree of passivity and acquiescence to external control, not by some powerful authoritarian figure but by a vague, diffuse, almost mystical, God-like entity called "The People." The power inherent in that huge conglomerate of human beings appeared far more immediate than that of a dictator in a far-off capital, or a God in a far-off heaven, who indeed had been superceded by this new deity that required absolute obedience, daily obeisance and was the source of all blessings, as well as punishments. There is much in this that resembles a cult, and Communist authorities to this day fear and harshly suppress all other, possibly competing cults, like the Chinese are doing in late 1999 with a group within China devoted to exercise and contemplation that seems quite harmless to the rest of the world.

The Soviet/Chinese techniques for social control cannot, however, be considered to be some kind of 'Brainwashing,' originally defined by its inventor as a kind of magical process that washes the brain 'clean' of all previous convictions and values and substitutes new, evil ones. It surely did not convert young American soldiers to Communism. It did allow them to be controlled, as never before.

Our research group concluded that while this study provided fascinating insights into the Communists' success in subjugating - and keeping subjugated - literally dozens of countries and millions of people, it gave us, more importantly, some disturbing suggestions about what might be happening in America to young Americans, and what this might portend for the future.

On an immediate, practical level, we learned that military training was sadly lacking. We have never emphasized, to new soldiers, much about the horrifying negatives of warfare: wounding, dismemberment, death - and capture. It has long been assumed that everybody knows these things, and there is a serious downside to talking about bad things like that. In psychiatry this is called denial, and it works okay until those bad things actually show up. Our soldiers knew, vaguely, that when captured one is supposed to confine his communication with the enemy to "Name, rank, serial number and date of birth." Simple enough, and not discussed much. Also not much help in a mud hut prison camp in the freezing mountains of North Korea. Especially when they are just talking to you about your home and family and church, and not asking you to give away military secrets.

We hadn't taught these kids about the inescapable, profound dangers of trying to compromise with your enemy, no matter how reasonable he sounds. We did not tell them that once you start, you can never stop, and as you continue to talk, you steadily strip away your own defenses, and become more vulnerable. We hadn't mentioned personal questionnaires, and self-criticism meetings, and late-night interviews with friendly, unarmed, unmilitary-seeming young 'instructors.'

The Army had also failed, since WWII ended, to teach much about the importance of authority, the 'chain of command,' the leadership of the squad, platoon and company without which it could not survive when the going got really rough. Following orders had taken on the aura of "blind obedience," unthinkingly "just doing my duty" as illustrated by the excuses of war criminals in the dock at Nuremberg, and had not been given much emphasis in military training during the peaceful years of 1945 to June, 1950, when we were once again at war.

The overt, explicit rejection of authority, however, was new to us. So was the widespread refusal to help one another, to organize little groups for mutual aid and protection, to come up with ways to harass and frustrate the keepers, to keep alive a spirit of rebelliousness and determination not to give in easily, to get away.

Those things could not be blamed entirely or even largely on the military training system. All young soldiers are, after all, mostly civilians, the products of 18 or more years of 'training' by parents, peers, schoolteachers, the media, movies, and the examples of what Mark Twain described as the only genetically predestined criminal class in America, the politicians, who seem to have gotten worse since then, finally reaching the highest levels.

This experiment we call democracy, or a representative republic - what Lincoln called in such charmingly naive terms 'government of the people, by the people and for the people' - and what someone else called the worst government on earth, except for all the others, has now survived for over 200 years, but is not guaranteed to endure forever. More than any previous government scheme, it consciously and explicitly drew its basic principles from Christianity's elaborations and modifications of Judaism, even though it is no longer fashionable or even politically permissible to recite that fact. More denial.

It began with a conspiracy among men who pledged their lives, their fortunes, and their "sacred honor" to achieve a state of freedom that guaranteed the pursuit (not the assured achievement) of happiness, among human beings who were all considered equal in the eyes of a God who endowed them with certain unalienable rights to life and liberty and the aforementioned pursuit. They proclaimed their trust in that God on their coins, asked that He guide their deliberations, enunciated a list of rights - each demanding the exercise by all of certain clear responsibilities - declared special previously unheard-of protections for individuals and their families, and set out to make this last great hope for humanity a reality.

I believe that it is not an exaggeration to assert that the disastrous death rate, the collapse of all resistance and the massive collaboration that took place among the tragically unprepared soldiers who fell into Chinese hands were all clear warnings that the principles of honor, loyalty, willingness to sacrifice, faith in a higher power, and confidence in the perfectibility of man that energized our founding fathers are languishing in modern America, and that their abandonment presages disaster when the going gets rough. Which it hasn't, of course, so far, since no one has delivered a nuclear or chemical or biological weapon to our shores, and "the economy, stupid" is still apparently just fine.

The fundamentally good, brave men who suffered and died in Korea, not from torture and executions and degradation like their comrades later did in the jungle prisons of Indochina, but from the terrible isolation, confusion, and cruel living conditions of North Korea, did by their suffering and deprivation bestow upon us all a priceless gift of insight and learning that we have evidently been unable or unwilling to accept.

There seems, in the latter half of this century, to have been no recognizable revitalization of 'old' ideas about God and duty, honor and personal, individual responsibility, loyalty and honesty that permeated the thinking of the truly great men who designed the system. Many good men and women have marked a moral and characterologic deterioration of our society, and as William Bennett has eloquently noted, even outrage seems to have died. Since the national design was based upon conceptions of morality and solid faith, the question is whether or not "a nation so conceived and so dedicated can long endure" if the belief in such things is abandoned.

Evidently it can, so long as nothing threatens it and folks are comfortable. What is worrisome is whether that can be true in the face of economic collapse, serious social unrest that spreads outside of Los Angeles, terrible natural disasters, or attack by some insane adversary with a weapon of mass destruction. All of which can happen.

Neither I nor my fellow researchers, as you might expect, had any workable ideas about what to do to make things better, except to agree that if our fellow citizens could know what we had found it would set them to thinking and looking for solutions to the problems that may lie ahead.

My days in the exotic Far East soon came to an end. Orders came from Washington directing me to the Medical Officers Advanced Course at the Army's Medical Field Service School at Fort Sam Houston in San Antonio, Texas. With more than a little reluctance I set out for a state I remembered as very large, very hot, but important in my memory as the site of my first year of residency training and earlier, a place where I once had a delicious chicken dinner with all the 'trimmings' for exactly twenty-five cents.

William E. Mayer, M.D.

Brainwashing, Drunks & Madness

William E. Mayer, M.D.

CHAPTER 9

EXPLORING THE PEACETIME ARMY

Fort Sam proved to be an attractive, historic army post built around an enormous parade ground. Dwight and Mamie Eisenhower had once lived in a palatial old house with long covered porches on three sides, fronting on the parade ground. He was an appallingly under-paid lieutenant back then, but at least they had a big house, two military houseboys, and access to the commissary.

The school, across the parade field, was a group of three storied stucco buildings of vaguely Spanish design with red tiled roofs, under which large colonies of bats resided. There were numerous classrooms that held perhaps 40 students, and a small snack bar in the basement of one of the buildings. There were no fans and no air conditioning. I found the 9-month course largely boring and bureaucratic, dwelling as it did on organizational charts and logistics. The few weeks spent in field training at Camp Bullis, some dozen miles to the north in the "hill country" were the one welcome diversion. We spent it learning to read field maps, shooting Army rifles, and crawling under barbed wire barricades, as well as carrying stretchers. We were all physicians and administrative officers who would never be used to carry stretchers, but we needed to know what it was like. It was hard.

I escaped from the school in response to temporary orders sending me to the Pentagon in mid-winter. There I was to report the findings of our research on POWs to a group of very senior, highly-ranked and decorated officers who were in the process of designing a Code of Conduct for men who might one day be POWs. These serious old men listened with great interest to my reports, read what we had written, questioned me closely, and came up with a code that eased the absolute (and unrealistic) requirement that no words except name, rank, etc, ever be uttered. It also required the soldier to care for his fellow soldiers in need, to remember his oath of allegiance and the honor of serving his country, to trust in God and the US Government, and to obey his superiors.

It was a good Code, and proved genuinely useful to the men who were later captured in Viet Nam, according to many of them. Never again would we hear that the captive US soldier had no idea what he was supposed to do, as we had heard over and over again during our studies.

The publication of the Code, which was made mandatory in all training administered by the Armed Forces, also proved to be the vehicle that was to carry me on my mission, assigned by my fellow researchers, to carry the word to the American people.

After my temporary duty in the Pentagon, a strange adventure in itself, the Commandant of the Medical Field Service School, Major General William Shambora, summoned me to his office to report. After I did, he asked to read my notes, and we had several discussions, alone in his office, about the implications of the study. "Big Bill," as we secretly called him, was a genuinely thoughtful, serious man who agreed that our findings indicated serious problems both with military training and with the education of our youngsters. Having learned about my lecture tour of the Far East Command installations, he decided that I should give the same talk to all the 600 or so students at the school.

The lecture was given to the entire student body and faculty in the Post Theater, and was a great success, stimulating all kinds of questions and heated discussions in the snack bar and classrooms afterward. The result was that my classmates voted me most likely to rise to the rank of General, and the General decided I should lecture all the officers on the post; which I obediently did soon after. A number of civilian dignitaries from San Antonio were invited to attend that lecture, and thus began my public speaking career.

The people in positions of power in those days, both in government and in business, were products, in a sense, of the Second World War. Many had served in uniform, and most felt strongly about the importance of serving the country, preserving its values of duty and honor, believing in a Supreme Being, and being individually responsible. For this reason, and because of some public concern over "Brainwashing," which had attracted some attention in the press, I soon began to get invitations from local civic groups in San Antonio to give my talk to them. I also started getting death threats, always anonymous.

The threats were reported by my Army superiors to the local office of the FBI, and from then on they always arranged to have a couple of agents at any talk I gave. Eventually the Agent in Charge had had all his people attend a lecture, and was inviting agents from other offices to come too. Finally, he announced that there were now so many talks that having his men and women there each time was too much of a burden. He suggested that I always carry a pistol when I talked, and in order to do this legally, had me sworn in as a Bexar County deputy sheriff so I could keep it concealed.

Thus equipped, my appearances now spread to Dallas and Fort Worth, then to El Paso and Brownsville, and from there to New Orleans, other cities in the South, then on to Los Angeles and San Francisco, up through the Midwest to Cincinnati and Chicago and Cleveland and then to the National Association of Manufacturers at the Waldorf in New York. I was not permitted, by Army Regulations, to accept honoraria for any of these trips, but the civilian groups paid my transportation and housing, and I lived, for a time, a truly materially blessed, glamorous and exciting life. I loved it, and felt ever more strongly that people both needed and wanted to hear what we had learned. I felt genuinely useful. Nice.

The Medical Officers Advanced Course finally wound down and my new assignment was as a member of the school's faculty. That was accompanied by attendance at the "charm school," a course designed to teach the niceties of lesson-planning, speaking up, joke-telling and the dangers thereof, brevity, summing up: "start by telling them what you're going to tell them, tell them, and then tell them what you told them!" In reality, it was quite a good course whose principles were to serve me well for many years.

General Shambora was succeeded by another medical general named Elbert DeCoursey. Elbert seemed to have been named appropriately, somehow. He was a gentle, soft-spoken scientist-researcher who had won worldwide admiration for his studies of the pathology of the heart. He really loved hearts, especially diseased ones, and was observed on many boring occasions like banquets and retirement ceremonies to have sneaked one of his specimens out of his pocket and focused his attention on it, in his lap, while the speakers droned on.

In those days the government was still drafting doctors - the only group conscripted because of their occupation. It was now nearly ten years since the ceremonies aboard the Missouri, the 'police action' in Korea had drawn to a whimpering close, and we were at peace. There was still a fairly large Army, and few physicians were attracted to the idea of leaving their residency training or their practices to don a khaki suit, so the draft was deemed necessary. This was exceedingly unpopular with the medical profession.

Medical schools tended to finish up their classes in June, so the doctor draft was designed to bring these people in during the summer months. They would arrive in groups of about 600, for six weeks of training that would, hopefully, convert them from slovenly civilians to bright, neatly tailored, proudly erect defenders of democracy ready to plunge into battle to save lives and stamp out disease among the troops. The Army is not very naive about most things, but they were about this.

Many, if not most, of the newly-minted military physicians were disgruntled and often angry at the unkind fate that had delivered them into our hands. Those who had served in WWII or Korea and then went to medical school, only to be drafted as a result, were particularly bitter. The overall disaffection of these new Army doctors showed up in many little ways: striped socks with the uniform, insignia on backward or upside down, sleeping or reading letters, or even typing replies, during class, inattention on the small drill ground and resulting chaos, and continuous complaining. Some of it was wholly understandable. Following the end of WWII there had been an explosion in medical specialty training programs and a great rush toward entering the specialties that outpaced the growth of the training slots.

Complete post-internship training in most specialties took three years, more in the sub-specialties, especially in surgical fields. This meant that the young physician had had, in all, 24 years of formal education by the time his residency was over, and he still faced two years of practice restricted to his specialty area before achieving certification as a specialist. The abrupt intrusion of a two-year period of military service imposed by a stupid, unfeeling draft board was considered by the victims to be nothing short of criminal.

Elbert, our Commandant, felt their pain. He went to great lengths to prepare a welcoming address that he delivered to all incoming classes to show these young people that we in the Army sympathized with them, realized their training and careers were being seriously disrupted if not totally ruined (!) and sincerely hoped they wouldn't blame us! The Army, he explained, didn't draft people. The government did, so the Congress should be blamed. Meanwhile, we'd all just have to live with it. Elbert was not only not born to leadership; he had no inkling of how it should be done.

After hearing my Commandant deliver this incredible 'welcome' to several new classes of unhappy young doctors, and taking part in indignant, incredulous and possibly mutinous coffee shop discussions with other outraged faculty who 'elected' me, since I was the only psychiatrist on the faculty, to go talk to our leader about this, I made an appointment with the General, and prepared myself for the worst.

Dr. DeCoursey received me cordially, and I tried to approach the subject of my visit gently, declaring that I felt honored to be on his faculty and assigned to perform what is traditionally one of the physician's prime duties: to teach his young followers in this hallowed profession. I had learned that he himself was deeply resentful of his assignment to the school, preferring instead to pursue his cardiac pathology work at the Institute of Pathology in Washington, and I hoped this approach would soften what I was about to say.

Explaining that my background in the study of the mind and emotions of people led me to the conclusions I had drawn, I then proceeded to suggest that his welcoming speech was just possibly giving the wrong message - teaching an unintended lesson. That got his attention. Plunging on, I told him that he was telling these young people that being in the Army was a terrible thing (so why was he in it?) rather than a privilege and an exciting new learning experience.

Furthermore, he seemed to be blaming the Congress (our constitutional superiors,) which might be considered a little disloyal, which of course he wouldn't dream of being. All things considered, while it was fine to acknowledge that this brief period of service was of course an interruption, wouldn't it be better to emphasize its positive aspects, the maturity and professional experience they would gain, and the adventures they would have?

We shared what seemed to me to be a very long period of silence. He looked off into the distance, lost in thought, and I consoled myself with the observation that at least he was not studying one of his beloved pickled hearts in his lap. Finally, all traces of cordiality gone, he said he would give serious thought to what I had said, and I withdrew. He barely noticed my salute and smart about face.

To give this good man his due, he drastically revised his welcoming address. It wasn't exactly a potboiler of the George Patton variety, but it was pretty good. Further, he accepted a pet scheme I had proposed. Henceforth, we would start each class with a full week at Camp Bullis with students dressed in fatigues and eating out of mess kits, riding around in trucks, spotting wild animals like armadillos, firing weapons like carbines and caliber .45 automatics, and learning the most important lesson of all - how to stay alive.

The effect was dramatic. The new students still arrived griping loudly about their tragic misfortune of being drafted, but most of them, almost none of whom had ever been camping overnight in their entire lives, seemed to love it and be energized by it.

My lecturing around the country continued to occupy at least half my time, and the invitations became so numerous that my Army superiors decreed that only audiences of at least 500 could be accommodated. An exception was made for special groups, including joint sessions of state legislatures in Nebraska, Texas, and Georgia, and management groups in AT&T, Eastman Kodak, US Steel, Corning Glass, Kaiser Aluminum, and some others. At many colleges and universities, like Florida at Gainesville, Brigham Young in Utah, and Arizona State at Tempe, they assembled nearly the entire student body in the field house or the football stadium on campus, and I faced a sea of young faces.

There were some interesting side effects to all this. One, of course, was the envy-based hostility my glamorous career sideline generated amongst some of my Army colleagues, especially other psychiatrists. Many of them seemed to feel I was corrupting our famously non-judgmental 'science' by talking about moral and even (horrors!) spiritual values - not the stuff of legitimate Freudian psychiatry in those days. Some of that persisted, and more than twenty years later, when I had retired once and was considering a return to active duty, those same psychiatrists, now very senior, actively resisted my return.

Another unexpected consequence of my public success occurred one day when I answered the phone in my office at the school. A stentorian voice with a pronounced Texas twang announced, "Major, this is Lyndon Johnson." Certain that one of my esteemed fellow faculty was needling me, I replied, "Sure it is. What's on your mind?" " Son," came the reply, "This is the President callin'." "So what else is new?" I countered, cleverly. "Damn it, Boy, you listen up!" Somehow, at that, I knew. I leaped to my feet and stood at attention there at my desk, offering some pathetic, trembling apology and excuse that I thought it was one of my buddies being funny, and he forgave me.

What he had on his mind was what in hell I thought I was doing taking potshots at his "Great Society" program. In recent speeches I had inserted some comments about that great program, asserting that it was a further misguided example of government intrusion into people's lives that relieved them of responsibility and increased their dependency, weakening their character and working against the basic principles of self-reliance and hard work that had made our forbears strong and successful. He didn't think much of that, apparently.

I tried to explain that I was most assuredly not trying to criticize the government, or him, which of course I was, but he paid little attention. Instead, he told me that henceforth I was to follow, carefully, a script prepared in advance and submitted through channels to Army Headquarters for approval, before any speech I gave to the public. There was to be nothing in any speech that could be taken to be critical of the Administration. Yes, Sir!

Word of that decree got out, inevitably, and resulted in a front-page political cartoon on Cincinnati's leading newspaper after I spoke there to a large audience. It showed an Army major speaking from behind a lectern, his manuscript unrolling down the front, marked by great black marks throughout the text, where words and sentences had been blacked out. It was not much comfort to realize that the paper was published and owned by the politically powerful Republican family of the former conservative president, William Howard Taft. It was ironic that his great-grandson, William Howard the IVth, was Cap Weinberger's deputy when I was Assistant Secretary of Defense some years later.

Not long after that political adventure, curiously enough, I got orders transferring me to duty at Fort Benning, in Georgia. There was no discernible connection to my recent activities and utterances, of course. The Army was forming a new kind of combat organization named an "Air Assault" Division, and I was to be the Division Surgeon. So, off I went, to the sand hills and scrub pines of the Deep South.

The new division was to be a lightly equipped helicopter borne fighting force that could be rapidly deployed when needed, with highly mobile elements that could get in and out of combat zones quickly. Unlike the much more heavily armed traditional Airborne Divisions, the troops would not jump out of big airplanes, but would be landed by hordes of helicopters. Because of the limitations on what choppers could carry, there was not much in the way of heavy artillery or tracked vehicles, like tanks, but lots of firepower nonetheless.

Life at Fort Benning was not much fun. Someone decided that the Air Assault troops would be given jump training even though they wouldn't be jumping with parachutes, so our days were filled with calisthenics, vigorous jogging, road marches, being hauled up and dropped from tall towers, and firing automatic weapons.

The Air Force, it turned out, was adamantly opposed to the operational concepts being developed for the new organization, because it involved arming the helicopters. When the Air Force was founded, in 1947, by taking the old Army Air Corps out of the Army, it had been agreed that while the Army could have some planes of its own, like troop carriers and a few little choppers, these were not for use in combat and only planes of the newly-born Air Force could have weapons installed. While the larger helicopters of the new Division were mainly to carry troops, they would swoop down into enemy territory and should at least have some firepower to protect the men being discharged onto hostile ground. The Air Force believed - rightly, as it turned out - that this would be the first step in eroding that earlier decision that only their planes could shoot, and they bitterly opposed that. It was bad enough that the Navy and Marine Corps had been allowed to have such planes.

As often happens, this was a turf war with budgetary overlays. Ostensibly a quarrel over tactics, wherein only the Air Force was to give close air support to ground troops and thus the budget to buy more such aircraft, it was actually a battle over that budget. In addition, if the new Division's helicopters were to be fitted out with guns, it implied that the Air Force couldn't (which they often couldn't, actually) do the job of close support, they would lose support in the Congress for their mission, lose face, and lose money.

In this classical inter-service battle, one of the targets they selected, somewhat ridiculously, I thought, was me. Thanks to my public comments about the collaborative behavior of some of the Air Force personnel in POW camps, I was 'known' to be a dedicated antagonist of the Air Force, and part of the plot to usurp their exclusive ground support role (and budget.) They insisted, at the highest levels, that I should go. And go I soon did.

Once again, without warning or any kind of explanation, I received orders from Washington to report to the Communications Zone - "Com-Z" - Europe headquartered in Orleans, France. There I was to serve as the Neurology and Psychiatry Consultant for all Army medical facilities in Com-Z: France, Belgium, Netherlands and Luxembourg. En route, I was to report to the Armed Forces Institute of Pathology in Washington for special training in Neuropathology.

Piling my stuff into my almost new Lincoln Continental, I set out for the Nation's capital. I had gotten the Lincoln, my third, at an outrageous discount from the dealer in San Antonio, who had heard me lecture on two successive days in Amarillo and Brownsville, Texas - hundreds of miles apart - and discovered I was driving a tiny, chartreuse Nash Rambler that he considered inadequate and unsafe. Every year after that, he sold me his wife's demonstrator car, at well below his cost. Those were wonderful cars that I drove more than 75 thousand miles each year, between lectures, and frequently slept in, quite comfortably, in the back seat.

At the Pathology Institute, I was given over to a wonderful, sweet man who was a legend in his field. His name was Webb Haymaker, and he was a man of such awesome stature that I could hardly believe I was meeting him, let alone that he was to be my personal teacher in this difficult field. He had already called the Surgeon General's office and arranged for me to room at the home of the Army's chief neuropsychiatrist, one Don Peterson.

Colonel Peterson was a very senior medical officer who had always seemed to me to be infinitely higher on the command scale than I could ever hope to become. He was tall, with dark, deep-set eyes that he had used to great advantage as he achieved a reputation for skill at doing hypnosis and peering deep into the psyche of anyone he looked at directly. He held himself rigidly upright at all times (I suspected even while sleeping) and moved with a slow grace that was fascinating to watch. He had been known to hypnotize entire classrooms of nurses all at the same time! I fully believed it.

Don and his wife lived in a large suburban house in Silver Spring, Maryland. He invited me to ride in his carpool, sharing space with the Chief Psychology, Internal Medicine, and Orthopedic Consultants from the Surgeon General's office, and I gladly accepted. Every morning I would watch him dump six heaping teaspoons full of powdered Nescafe into a cup of hot water and drink it just before we left. This seemed to have no effect whatever; he always seemed moderately sleepy. He reminded me, somehow, of a sort of benign Rasputin. We had long, fascinating talks about combat psychiatry, agreeing that what we had learned about the rapid successful treatment of combat exhaustion in WWII and Korea could revolutionize conventional psychotherapy, which it later did.

The Psychology Consultant, one of the carpool group, was an affable man who insisted that we all come to his house for Christmas dinner. All accepted, and we gathered in his house, all but me with accompanying wives, and after a civilized drink, sat down at the festive board bearing a huge turkey and innumerable other delicacies. Our host carved the turkey, served everyone, and then, as if remembering something important that he had neglected to do, bade us all eat while he ran "an errand" in the cellar.

Everyone proceeded to eat with great gusto, and only noticed after some considerable time had passed, that our host had not returned. One of the guests volunteered to go to the cellar to see if there was a problem, which indeed there was, as it turned out.

The guest who had gone looking returned to he table, where he stood with a stricken look on his face, immobile and clearly in a state of shock. Several of the others jumped up and headed for the cellar, where they found our host hanging from an overhead beam, quite dead.

As was the Christmas party.

No one had any inkling that this unhappy man was even a little depressed, let alone suicidal. Or that he was so mad at everybody, starting with his wife, that he would inflict this horrible, forever unforgettable act of hostility upon us all. I feel certain that every one of the dinner guests, forever after, remembered that incredible Christmas dinner whenever the turkey is served.

Dr. Haymaker, truly a giant among medical scientists, spared no effort to teach me everything he possibly could in the few short months I was in his hands. I had free run of his extensive laboratories, which contained the largest collection of preserved human brains ever assembled. Each was carefully catalogued and cross-indexed according to the clinical findings before death, each had been sectioned - sliced - systematically, and each had an attached collection of microscopic slides made from each brain's healthy as well as injured or diseased areas.

Throughout my stay at the Institute, I tried mightily to live up to this great man's expectations and emulate his working style. The latter was hard because he was always at his microscope when I arrived in the morning, no matter how early my carpool got me there, and he was loathe to leave the lab's workbenches until late at night. Fortunately the local busses ran until the early morning hours, so I could usually get back to the Peterson house without difficulty. What made the work even more fascinating than it inherently was, was Haymaker's fascination with the history of medicine. He frequently interspersed our tutorial sessions with often obscure references to medical practices of the distant past, obviously viewing many of medical history's milestones with wonder and reverence.

Webb Haymaker was one of the rare people I encountered in a long, half-century of medicine, who was without any doubt truly a great man, and a great physician. Often I have looked back on those months with him with a sense of awe and wonder at my great good fortune in having been touched by him. When I left for my assignment in Europe, he gave me an old, curiously-shaped 'venisection' knife, used for blood-letting, a common medical practice in the days of the early American colonies. He also gave me a copy of his latest textbook of neuropathology, and inscribed a long and affectionate personal dedication inside the cover. When he discovered that he had mistakenly written it inside the back cover, accidentally holding the book upside down, he wrote it all over again inside the front one. I've never been more touched by any gift.

The flight to Europe was long, since jet airplanes were not yet in use, and after landing in Paris I found my way by train from the Gare d'Orleans to the city of Joan of Arc, sixty miles or so to the south. First, though, I spent a couple of nights on the Left Bank in an old but respectable hotel named, appropriately, in honor of a famous 19th Century physician, Claude Bernard. My room, quite a cold and sparse one, nonetheless had its own bidet, a plumbing accoutrement I had never seen before. I finally figured it out, scrubbed it thoroughly, put newspapers on the floor on each side of it, and sat there (it had hot and cold water) while I took invigorating sponge baths.

The toilet was located two floors below my room, on the ground floor in a little 'cabinet' adjoining the hotel's central courtyard. It was little improvement on the "o-benjo" of Japan: a slit in the floor with some kind of receptacle a few feet below. The French version seemed to have water running along the bottom, however, while the Japanese system depended upon a wooden bucket that was periodically collected by the "honey bucket" man with his wooden cart half full of empty buckets and half full of full ones and surrounded by a horrible odor that announced his arrival from afar.

Orleans turned out to be a major provincial city with its largest buildings arranged around a large cobblestone square. In it center, on a tall stone base, was a magnificent statue of Jeanne d'Arc, banner flying as she sat astride her great horse who stood, nostrils flaring, mane and tail flying and one forefoot raised as if in preparation for plunging into battle. All destinations in the city were figured at certain distances in certain directions from that glorious statue.

American soldiers stationed in the area took to calling this splendid statuary "Joannie on the Pony," which infuriated the natives and provided the final proof that Americans, in their green, Nazi-like uniforms, were barbarians.

The GIs didn't like Orleans or the Orleanais much either. The climate tended to be cold and gloomy, the shopkeepers were unfriendly and made no effort, just like the soldiers, to learn the others' language, the food was not very good, and all the pretty girls had long since left to live in Paris. Worst of all, the plumbing didn't work well, there was a huge odorous pile of horse and cow manure in front of every farmhouse, and bartenders thought that a martini was a glass of sweet vermouth that tasted like cough syrup!

These hardships, coupled with the appalling lack of personal hygiene among the French and their seeming inability to understand that we had liberated them from the Fascist dictators and saved their country, made France a notoriously bad duty assignment. Whenever possible, military people traveled to Germany for recreation. Many soldiers never left the post at all during their entire 2-year tour of European duty, and griped the whole time.

The Army hospital that was to be my base of operations was located a few miles north of the city along the Loire River at a place named La Chapelle Ste. Mesmin, while the Com-Z headquarters was in the center of Orleans. Both were situated in former German facilities called caserns. Some dozen miles to the south, across the river, was a large logistical base from which all supplies were sent to the many units dispersed throughout the Com-Z.

Duty at La Chapelle was unexciting, in the main. Everyone was aware that Charles deGaulle, the hero of France, was trying to make a political comeback and a prominent feature of his campaign was the expulsion of hated foreign troops from the country. This, coupled with the unfriendliness of the people generally, had an effect on morale, and I soon discovered that the suicide rate among troops and especially among their dependents was higher than anywhere else in the Army.

When I wrote a paper about this and tried to bring it to the attention of the senior troop commanders, I was told it must be some mistake, and nothing was done.

There was trouble brewing in the Middle East at that time, and the European Command had been instructed, secretly, to prepare for an invasion of any one of a number of countries bordering on the eastern Mediterranean. The Communications Zone, Europe, responsible for the logistical support of all troops stationed anywhere in Europe, was required to develop detailed plans for the logistical support of those troops, should they be sent as an invasion force.

Utter secrecy was deemed necessary to avoid offending any of the Arab countries or Israel if they learned we had war plans involving them, so almost no one was privy to the scheme. Com-Z Headquarters set up a secret planning group involving relatively senior representatives of all the logistical support services: communications, ordnance, medical, engineers, transportation, supply and quartermaster. I was honored to be the medical member of the group. Each of us, in the event that we were to invade, was to be the commander of our special element in the invasion force. We did our planning in the late evenings, under heavy guard, in a special room in the Headquarters Caserne.

On my arrival at my new duty station, I made contact with the local CIA element in the area, as I had been instructed to do by their representatives in Washington; my medical superiors had not been told of this and were not to be. The intelligence people had been functioning in an old, somewhat shoddy but essentially intact Chateau not far from the hospital. I found them packing up to leave for another quite distant location, and they graciously offered to allow me to assume their lease on the chateau, named La Mouche - The Fly. Since the rent was an absurdly low $60 per month, I leaped at the chance, and promptly moved in.

La Mouche, it turned out, was owned by the French branch of the DuPont family, one of perhaps a dozen throughout the country. It was the one that the family had largely abandoned since a young man of the family had decided to honeymoon there and while doing so, accidentally drowned in the River directly below the chateau. Most of the furniture, china, decorations and linens had been deposited in the chateau's main ballroom where they remained undisturbed and gathering dust, for a dozen years.

The Chateau had a tree-lined bridle path, several barns and outbuildings of various kinds, and a set of tunnels built into the riverbank to serve as sites for the cultivation and storage of mushrooms. The main building had a large marbled lobby running nearly the entire width of the building, the ballroom right behind it with all the treasures, and at one end of the structure a grand dining room, hotel-sized kitchen, butler's quarters, pantries, a large, high-ceilinged parlor and several bedrooms. There were more bedrooms on the second floor.

On a lower level of the house, facing the river, were several rooms for servants to live in, a separate kitchen, and some utility rooms. Between the main house and the river, about 75 feet away, were elaborate formal gardens. The guardian - caretaker - of the estate occupied the lower level. He turned out to be a former factory worker from Paris seeking the good life of the countryside. His name, naturally, was Henri. He had converted the entire formal garden into one made entirely of different vegetables, fished in the Loire without a license, and hunted rabbits similarly unofficially. Henri had a sad, silent little wife, who tended to shrink into the shadows when I appeared nearby, and a delicate boy child named Andre.

I did what I could to make the chateau comfortable. It was built in the 1600s out of stone, with walls nearly two feet thick. There was an ornate fireplace in each room, all of them very shallow so as to require frequent resupply of wood - no problem in the days of many servants - and were inadequate to warm the large, high-ceilinged rooms. I bought an oil heater and many feet of chimney pipe to get the outlet above the high roof, and decided to repaint a couple of the rooms.

One day, while I was perched precariously atop a ladder trying to paint the ceiling of the parlor, Henri appeared and watched curiously. We did not talk much, ordinarily, since my French was less than primitive and his English was nonexistent. At that time, DeGaulle was campaigning vigorously and I managed to ask Henri what he thought of the General. He indicated that the great man was indeed great, and that he was for him. He also indicated that he, Henri, had been a Maquis freedom fighter throughout the war. "Sure," I said with some skepticism - "Everybody was a Maquis, now that it's over."

At that, in a classical Gallic explosion of indignation and outrage, Henri literally tore his shirt open, ripping off the buttons, to reveal a line of healed bullet wounds extending completely across his chest from one shoulder down to his waist. I apologized profusely for disbelieving him, and went back to talking politics. Did he have a political party? Yes. Which one? "Anarchist," he replied. "Anarchist?" I asked in astonishment. How can one be an anarchist and still support an authoritarian, dictatorial guy like DeGaulle? "Simple," he replied. "What this country needs is discipline!"

My French did not permit further exploration of this utterly French logic.

At one point in my stay in France, I was invited to attend a medical meeting in Germany, and set out in my long black Lincoln. It earned me unvarying curious and often hostile stares along the road, signifying as it did someone of great power, like a senior Nazi. It was entirely too big for the narrow roads of Europe, and the driver's side front window wouldn't open for want of an 11-cent fuse that would cost $100 to get at, under the driver's seat.

Nonetheless, I headed for the German border in my grand chariot, eagerly anticipating my highly symbolic, victorious return to the land of my forefathers. My grandfather, along with all his heirs and descendants, had been banished forever from Germany many years before by Bismarck, whose scheme for using conscripts Grandfather had opposed, along with all his fellow Prussians who made up the German officer corps.

It was cold and misty during my trip, and the haze and fog thickened as I approached the border. Once there, I opened my door to present my identification to the customs officer, and then proceeded onto the long-forbidden soil of the Fatherland. Suddenly there appeared in the fog before me a Volkswagen. I applied my brakes, but the road was now icy, and the car slid forward and mashed the VW's fender, badly.

The next two hours were spent in a German police station, from which I finally escaped unscathed and unpunished. However, my victorious return to the land of Bismarck and Hitler was badly tarnished. The medical conference, after that adventure, was something of an anticlimax.

On my return to La Mouche, a messenger arrived from the commanding general at Com-Z headquarters with an order to prepare to leave, that very night, to execute the plan we had created in our secret sessions. No hint as to the target country. Just be in the General's office with all field gear at 2400 hours - midnight.

I locked up the Chateau, told Henri I'd be away for a while, and drove to the HQ caserne in Orleans. In the General's conference room, he appeared at the designated stroke of midnight and announced to the dozen of us there assembled that we would be leaving for Lebanon. We were to turn in the keys to our vehicles and our quarters, which would be taken care of in our absence. The married men among us were given a few minutes to say goodbye to their wives, waiting outside, and we were led down to a bus waiting in the courtyard below.

Our bus headed out immediately, crossing the river on Orleans' main bridge heading for an airfield a few miles distant at a place called Chateaureux. The bus raced through the narrow streets of the little town across the river, when suddenly, I was later told, Jesus appeared in the headlights, pulling a small wagon. The bus driver swerved abruptly to avoid the white-robed, bearded figure that was undeniably the Savior, and ran head-on into a large truck loaded with cut-up logs that was coming toward us, also at a high rate of speed.

Both drivers and all six of the officers sitting forward of me perished in the collision, which demolished the bus. People rushed from their beds to see what had caused the terrible noise, and victims were soon extracted from the wreck. The dead were placed to one side, under a tarp, and before long the sirens of police vehicles and ambulances announced the arrival of official help.

Through it all, I was unconscious, and was to remain so for several days.

One of the injured, I was told later, was the senior military police officer who was one of our planning group. His upper arm was broken, with the bone sticking out, but he ran around supervising the rescue, and before collapsing, demanded that the dead all be taken to the hospital rather than the morgue, some miles to the south. That man saved my life. Exactly thirty years later, when he and I were both on duty in the Pentagon, I was able to find him and thank him. He had even saved pictures of the wreckage, which I had never seen before, and showed them to me proudly.

The reason he had done me such a big favor was that he had insisted upon the dead being sent to the hospital. I was one of the dead, under the tarp, because the rescuers had been unable to detect any heart sounds or breath when they first dragged me out. When I arrived at the hospital with the other corpses, they had laid us all out and one of the hospital staff recognized me and announced his discovery.

A second man then stepped forward to save my life. He was an internist named Jim Hansen, at whose home I had been treated to a wonderful meal and too much fine wine just days before. He insisted that they try to resuscitate me with an airway and fresh blood, and called for all hospital staff with type A blood to step forward and give me some of it by direct transfusion. With little or no preparation and no cross-matching, they did numerous transfusions, blessing me with Oriental, Occidental, African, Catholic and Protestant donations that brought me back to reside among the living, eternally grateful for my truly ecumenical heritage.

Several days later I finally woke up in an oxygen tent, with needles at many places, profound shortness of breath, pain everywhere, and the inability to feel my legs or wiggle my toes. Elsewhere in the room I could hear the moans and groans of several of my fellow survivors. Jim Hansen stood beside the bed. "What," I asked him with some difficulty, "Are my chances, Jim?" He did not answer, but I could see tears welling up in his eyes. At that, I was overwhelmed with a feeling of surging rage, whereupon I fell back to sleep. When I awoke some time later he was gone, but the intense anger remained, as it was to do for many weeks.

Those weeks passed swiftly enough, since I was mentally quite dull and probably sedated most of the time. My feelings of anger persisted, and were intensified by my inability to make my legs work, or to take a deep breath. I was to discover that I had sustained 'MSI,' shorthand for "multiple severe injuries" including blessedly non-displaced fractures in four vertebrae that had resulted in what was to be transient paraplegia. My right lung was lacerated from internally-displaced rib fractures and was collapsed and surrounded by blood, making breathing difficult. A severe blow to the left side of my head had caused some bleeding and, for a time, pronounced difficulty remembering things.

My wristwatch, recently purchased at the Paris PX, was smashed into my wrist, and my left knee joint was opened to the air. The latter healed quite well before full feeling returned to my legs. The watch was replaced by the Army, who told me much later to go back to the PX, pick out any watch I wanted, and they would pay for it. I came away with a much better watch, a gold Omega Seamaster that many years later I gave to my son, who still likes it!

When I was deemed well enough to leave my bed, a wheelchair was provided, along with a young soldier to push it. For many weeks thereafter I was to learn, first-hand, what truly disabled persons must endure while trying to do even the simplest daily activities. It was a lesson never to be forgotten. Many of my trips were to the physiotherapy department, where I was first to learn that the physio techs were agents of the Devil, sent to torture helpless, innocent victims, and later to find they were angels incarnate, sent by God to do his miracles. They painfully taught me to breathe, and ultimately to walk again, in spite of my body's reluctance.

When I felt well enough, and bored by inactivity, I had myself wheeled into my office, and started seeing patients again. To my complete astonishment, I found that some of these people, whose charts contained many progress notes written and signed by me, seemed complete strangers whom, I could swear, I'd never seen before. A lesson in head trauma.

When it became clear that my friend Jim Hansen's sad appraisal of my prospects no longer applied, I began to think seriously about my future, my profession, the possible reasons for my survival in the face of considerable odds, and about faith, and God.

My Presbyterian Sunday-school childhood had left me with no doubt that God existed, that Jesus was his Son and that the way to heaven was through Him, but not much more. In my adolescent explorations of various churches, while admittedly at least partly in search of pretty choir girls, I had developed a certain impatience with details of doctrine, and with what seemed to be a degree of artificiality, theatrics and even hypocrisy in organized religion that has largely persisted to this day.

My 'near death' experience, however, which was not momentary but lasted for some time - many days, at least, of uncertainty - made me think long and hard about the existence of a Higher Power, culminating in the certainty that it existed, was sentient, cared, and mattered, more than any other thing. And that we were part of it. There must, I concluded, be a point to all this; not just my recent experience, but all experience, it seemed to me then, as it still does, reflects and determines our relationship with that Higher Power.

God became for me then all that is beautiful, and loving, and determinative of each man's course in life. It ceased to matter whether He was an old, bearded patriarch on a throne 'up there' someplace or not. It also did not matter whether Jesus' birth was exactly as described, whether the saints really performed miracles, or whether non-Christians could ever get in to heaven. All of that, and more, were earnest and maybe totally sincere ideas created by humans in their desperate attempt to understand what God is and wants and does. I have never needed to believe that there was some kind of supernatural creature sitting up there monitoring each human's every act and thought, judging it to determine eligibility to enter paradise.

All of the above, of course, is but a tiny part of what I thought about and felt as

I came back to life. It would hardly qualify for what is called a 'spiritual awakening' or being 'born again,' which is something I feel uneasy and distrustful about at best, but it was a real experience. It guided my life from that time on, in spite of lapses and deviations and failures.

Now, as I grow old - or at least older - I discover feelings of reverence and awe for some of the beautiful things man has created as he searched for ultimate truth. Whether they take the form of magnificent cathedrals or the lovely music of Christmas, or the miracle of flight and electronics, I find comfort and beauty in them and in man's desire to create them to glorify that Higher Power, and assure himself of eternal life. It is not exactly a religion, but it is enough, at least for me.

At long last, after some months of physiotherapy, I was able to walk and breathe normally, drive my car, (and remember where I parked it!) and recognize old patients. My strength, energy and endurance were at an all-time low, and France's unpleasant gray winter was beginning. Accordingly, I resolved to resign from the Army, and seek a new life in a gentler clime where my rehabilitation could proceed more comfortably.

A help-wanted ad in a medical journal seemed to offer the ideal opportunity. The State of Hawaii was seeking a mental health director for the Island of Hawaii - the 'Big Island.' I applied for the job, and they accepted me sight unseen - ominous. In spite of that, I submitted my resignation from the Army and headed west, crossing the US to board the famed old Lurline ocean liner that sailed regularly from Los Angeles to Honolulu.

That trip aboard the fine old luxury liner cured me forever with regard to ocean cruises. Five days at sea with nothing to do but eat, walk the deck, eat, watch shuffleboard performed by jolly old geriatric cases who mistook it for vigorous exercise, eat again, listen to a poor dance band while the old folks shuffled about the dance floor between drinks, eat one last time, and head for a narrow bunk in a tiny stateroom - these made up the highly-touted glamour of a Matson Line cruise to Aloha-land. I shall never do that again.

The good people of Hilo welcomed me warmly to the Big Island with piles of flower leis around my neck, and led me off to a curiously insubstantial old-fashioned hotel facing on a small bay. The principal and most enthusiastic greeter was a tiny Japanese-American lady named Kay Miamura, along with her tall, hearty, overly Americanized, jovial husband, Richard, who turned out to be one of the island's two superior court judges.

Kay and Richard, both born of parents who had immigrated from Japan, were to become dear friends. Kay was the only psychiatric social worker on the island, and as such was my principal assistant. She had been born in Hilo to a wealthy Japanese businessman who had been sent to Hawaii by his government in the 1930s to set up a radio station there for use when, according to plan, the Japanese would invade Hawaii at some distant future time. That impressed me as real long-term planning. And he did it, very successfully, except that the invasion didn't quite come off.

It turned out that they had had great difficulty recruiting both a mental health director and a county health officer, so I was asked to do both jobs. No extra pay came with the extra duty, but the jobs were both easy. There were six or eight qualified public health nurses on the island, who for years had done most of the medical work for the poor (most of the residents) and, more recently, the sugar cane workers. I was to supervise them, see the few seriously mentally ill, and make periodic visits to the three outlying health clinics some distance from Hilo.

Hawaii is in fact a 'big' island, more than sixty miles in length and nearly that wide, in places. On it are situated the extinct 12,000+ foot high volcano, Mauna Kea, and a slightly smaller active volcanic peak named Mauna Loa. Both bear heavy growths of vegetation, fields of lava both old and new, and substantial populations of wild boar and sheep originally brought in by early settlers. A magnificent, remote spot on the island, the Waipio Valley, with sheer walls a thousand feet high, tall waterfalls, abundant fruit lying about on the valley floor, and a fish-laden stream running through it, is the spot where King Kamehmeha "the Great" gathered the other tribal chieftains together to plan and launch the conquest that made him ruler of all the islands.

The northernmost third of the island was entirely taken up by the Parker Ranch, second largest cattle ranch in the world, and had one little town near the tip, named Kohala. We had a health clinic there. The entire western half of the land mass, from the slopes of the mountains down to the sea, was a mass of lava fields, a little pasture, the tiny settlement of Kona, and an ocean of prickly pear cactus. A second clinic was in Kona. Down the coast from Kona, now an expensive resort town, was Kealakekua, site of the "little grass shack" memorialized in song.

The Kona side was very dry, sometimes getting only an inch or so of rain a year. Hilo, on the leeward side of Hawaii, got 165 inches or more every year. Sugar cane is grown up and down the coast from Hilo, but no pineapples were grown anywhere on that island. The southern tip was covered with dense jungle and bore a lovely, palm tree-lined beach of clean, glistening black sand, courtesy of ancient volcanic flows. A third clinic served the sparsely populated southern area.

Prior to my arrival, only one other psychiatrist had ever shown any interest in living and working on the Big Island. That worthy had actually traveled to Hilo to explore the possibilities, but declined the position out of his openly expressed fear of the tigers (there are of course no tigers in all of Hawaii except maybe at the Honolulu Zoo on the distant island of Oahu) and uncertainties about the volcano, whose lava has not approached Hilo for a millennium.

For many years, the great sugar cane plantations had worked their fields with Filipino laborers, who were paid ten cents an hour. These workers, only men, were recruited in their homeland, thousands of miles distant, and came to Hawaii on ships with their fare paid by the plantations. They received five cents cash per hour for their backbreaking work; the owners held the other five cents in trust. At the end of three years, their accumulated held-back pay was given to them, and they got a free shipboard cruise back to the Philippines. Returning to their home villages, where they were joyfully greeted as truly rich men, they partied, impregnated their wives and girlfriends, exhausted their accumulated wealth, and boarded the ship once again to return to Hawaii for another three years.

The plantation owners provided all the workers' food, clothing, shelter, tools and medical care. Until one Harry Bridges came along, got the workers to strike for higher pay, and converted them into the highest-paid unskilled agricultural workers on earth at two dollars an hour. Instantly gone were the free food, clothing, tools and medical care. The savings didn't offset the new labor costs, the workers gambled away much of their pay and couldn't afford the fare back home, and everything went to hell.

The owners responded quite logically, as it turned out. They hired skilled engineers to design and build huge machines that pulled the mature cane out by the roots instead of having little brown guys cut each stalk, built long, water-filled sluices that carried the cane in great clumps, roots and all, to the mills, modified the machinery to wash away the dirt and rocks, and they were back in business. Unfortunately, the Filipinos were out of work. This was a classical example of what has happened over and over again in many industries, and continues to this day. Nevertheless, Mr. Bridges was a great humanitarian hero, at least for a while.

My plan was to work in the Hilo clinic three days a week, travel one day a week to one or the other of the outlying clinics to lend moral support and technical assistance (rarely needed) to the public health nurses there, and spend the next three days each week on my own physical rehabilitation program.

That program involved skin-diving, mountain climbing, boar- and sheep-hunting, exploring Waipio Valley, trimming back the exuberant growth of bougainvillea, cup of gold, wood roses, gardenias and even orchids that threatened to overrun my house a thousand feet up on the side of Mauna Kea, and occasionally playing golf. It worked wonders, and after a year of these exercises I felt well again, at long last.

One day, at the Hilo office, a teenage girl was brought in because she had become mute, withdrawn, and given to strange posturings. She was a classical example of catatonic schizophrenia. Before bringing her to me, her family had taken her for repeated visits to a Kahuna, or Hawaiian witch doctor, of which there were many on our remote, rural island.

The wise old Kahuna, who ultimately referred her to me, correctly diagnosed her as being schizophrenic, although the native word for the disease was different. Hawaiians, like people in the villages of Korea, believed that this disorder was the result of the liver being upside down, and demons having invaded the body. The standard cure, among Kahunas, was to massage the abdomen vigorously, over the liver. This process, hopefully, would turn the inverted liver right side up again, curing the patient.

To facilitate the massage, they first applied a quantity of magical vegetable oil, whose name, Jewel Oil, announced its precious qualities. This common cooking oil, available in grocery stores, was bottled by the Jewel Tea Company, an old-time grocery chain, from whence came the name, but no matter. It still drove out demons.

The most effective treatment for catatonic schizophrenia in those days was still electroshock, and I wanted to try the girl on a course of those treatments. In a closet of the clinic, I was told, was an electroshock machine, lying there unused for some years since no one was trained to work it. I dug it out and opened its fine wooden case expectantly, only to find that the whole thing was covered with mildew and rust. I was dismayed.

After hours of work, the machine appeared, if not new, at least presentable. But would it work? How to tell? It is designed to deliver a small, precisely measured and controlled current of electricity for a similarly measured, very brief instant, without burning or otherwise damaging the skin - let alone the underlying brain. There was no electrician on the island who could possibly make the necessary measurements of current and time with sufficient exactitude to assure me that the machine was safe to use on a human being.

Suddenly, as I pondered this therapeutic dilemma, a brilliant thought occurred. Recently, during the early evenings as I sat on my seaside porch admiring the great pounding waves breaking on the boulders at the water's edge, I had noticed one of Hawaii's grotesque wild dogs skulking around the perimeter of my yard. These animals usually kept to the jungled areas and were very shy. They had serious chronic skin diseases that caused them to lose their fur and develop thick, convoluted skin, giving them a horrible appearance. I had always shouted at this wild, ugly beast to drive her away when I saw her. That was to change.

That evening I brought a small piece of meat and another of cheese to the front porch, and spoke soothingly and as seductively as I could to the awful beast when she appeared. After many minutes of coaxing and cajoling, she crept to the foot of the steps, and I rewarded her with the food. She seemed pathetically grateful, and slunk back into the underbrush. This was repeated over the next several days. I noted that she had had many litters, and her teats actually dragged on the ground when she walked in her half-crouch.

At length I decided that we had made friends, sort of, and she began taking my food offerings from my hand. It was time. I plugged the electroshock machine in to an outlet on the porch, lubricated the earphone-like electrodes with electrode paste, and turned on the power. No sparks or smoke, and when I handled it, I got no shock. So far, so good!

I enticed my sadly disfigured canine friend up onto the porch, that evening, and petted her head, gingerly. After a bit, I began massaging her temples with a little of the paste on my hands, and after a bit, applied the headset, very gently. Not only did she not seem to mind, she seemed in a kind of dreamy state of ecstasy at being petted, probably for the first time in years.

After a few soft words of endearment, I pressed the button. Instantly this decrepit, sagging, helpless-seeming creature leaped straight up into the air, all four legs stiff, eyes wide, tail erect, every muscle tense. On landing, she immediately took off at full speed, disappearing into the protective jungle in a burst of energy and power. Clearly, she had not been injured! My shock machine had passed its test, maybe not good enough for the Food and Drug Administration's medical device division, but good enough for me.

Starting the next morning, I gave my little catatonic teenager a treatment, done for safety's sake in the emergency room at the hospital surrounded by curious nurses and a couple of the local doctors. She tolerated it well, and after saying a silent prayer of thanksgiving to a benevolent God, I sent her home with her family, to return the next day.

After only about six treatments, she appeared entirely normal once again. I instructed her parents to take a message to the Kahuna, thanking him for the referral (there were several more to come in the months following), and thanking him as well for his efforts with the Jewel Oil, which I was certain had played an important role in her recovery.

On one of my trips to the tiny clinic in Kohala, up north, I had been scheduled by the nurse, at the request of the school authorities, to examine an eleven-year-old girl who had recently delivered a baby. What the school people wanted to know was whether that event had so corrupted the child that she must be kept out of school for the protection of the other kids.

The new mother was a chubby, cheerful, typical 11-year old Hawaiian girl. She knew there was a new baby at home, that her mother was caring for, and she was delighted at that. She was totally unaware of any connection between a recent bout of violent abdominal distress and the birth of an infant. She was overjoyed when her mother told her she could name the new baby-plaything, and promptly dubbed it "Alvin," after a squeaky-voiced cartoon character then popular.

In all, the child seemed altogether normal, if not terribly bright, and not at all corrupted or capable of spreading hurtful, sinful harm to her fellow elementary school classmates. I cleared her for full return to academia.

Then I called the sheriff.

He appeared, in due time, huffing a little due to his huge girth, around which was an ammunition-laden pistol belt with a holster and large revolver at one side. He wore a broad-brimmed cowboy hat (this was, after all, cattle country,) and on his bulging breast there dwelt a large, shiny star with little balls at the points and the word "Sheriff" emblazoned across it. His feet were appropriately shod with elaborate cowboy boots that made a loud noise as he crossed the office floor. His face clearly revealed his Hawaiian heritage, and bore a friendly, jovial expression.

"Howdy, Doc!" he said, pleasantly. "What can I do for ya?"

"Sheriff," I replied, you have a major crime on your hands - a felony."

"Oh?" he responded. "What crime? In my town? When?"

I asked him if he was aware that the child I had seen had just had a baby.

"Sure," came the reply. "Everybody in town knows about that!"

"Don't you realize," I asked, "That whoever got her pregnant committed first degree rape, statutory rape, molestation of a child, contributing to the delinquency of a minor, and probably a dozen other crimes?"

He told me he hadn't really thought of it that way. "These things happen, you know."

"Do you know who did it?" I asked. "No idea," he lied.

When I asked if he'd investigated the crimes, he said he hadn't. The reason? "No one made a complaint."

"Look, Sheriff," I tried again, "If you, as the Law here, know a crime has been committed, isn't it your duty to investigate, whether someone complains or not? Surely you could see, when this kid got pregnant and had a baby, that a whole bunch of laws had been violated."

No answer. I pushed on.

"Sheriff, let's say you were patrolling Main Street out here in the middle of a dark night and up ahead, just around the corner, you heard someone smash the window of the jewelry store, sweep out an armful of stuff, and run off. Would you wait for someone to make a complaint before you investigated?"

Long silence, eyes downcast. Finally, his expression brightened as he looked up at me, with a certain curious expression of triumph. Came the answer: "We ain't got no jewelry store, Doc." I gave up.

Some weeks later, on a subsequent visit, the Sheriff appeared unbidden in the clinic. Without preamble, he announced, "It was the kid's uncle, Doc. I investigated and he admitted it was him. Everybody knew it all the time, but it wasn't 'til I investigated, like you said, that it came out."

There was no sentiment in the town for punishing the confessed criminal. He was sorry that he did it and wouldn't do it again, so it was generally agreed that the whole thing should be dropped. The kid, happy with her little plaything, was back in school and everything was okay.

I was to learn that this event was not all that unusual in those days in rural Hawaii. In the all-Hawaiian settlements of a group of houses on stilts even though they were far from the water, it was not uncommon for as many as eight or more adults and twice that number of children to live together in a single structure, often with great uncertainty as to which kid belonged to whom, exactly, and nobody at all concerned about it. This was 1960.

Life for me on the Big Island was exactly what I needed to regain my health and physical strength, and was, overall, peaceful and mostly unexciting. An exception was the great tsunami that arrived one day with minimal warning. An earthquake in Alaska sent a huge, rolling, strangely quiet wave toward Hilo and Hawaii's northeastern shore. Just before it hit, the tide receded much farther from the shore than usual, and a number of children ran out on the newly-exposed ocean bottom, excitedly gathering up the many shells thus revealed. Then the wave came.

At first it seemed only to be the resumption of a high tide, with the water rising quietly but with ominous swiftness, and a number of the children far from the normal shoreline were lost in it. The tide continued to rise, and eventually reached back a quarter mile or more from the normal high tide boundaries, and everything in its path - houses, cars, bridges, tall trees - simply became submerged.

Darkness was near, the twilight in those latitudes being short and the onset of night abrupt, and light faded from the sky as the water first receded even farther from shore than usual, and then returned in greater quantity than before, reaching in some places a mile inland. An illustration of its depth at the usual shoreline was provided by a tourist who had been standing on a bridge, fascinated, watching as the water beneath the bridge rose. Suddenly he found himself lifted high above the bridge, which disappeared in the depths beneath him. The water began to recede, rapidly this time, while he paddled frantically seeking safety.

Suddenly, in the water before him, he saw a curved pair of iron braces sticking up out of the water, that he was approaching with increasing speed as the water pulled him along toward the open sea. He succeeded in grabbing one of these, which seemed solidly anchored, and hung on for dear life. When the wave retreated seaward, he found himself at the top of a fire escape above the four-story high roof of the local movie theater.

My 24-foot sailboat, purchased soon after my arrival in Hilo to legitimize my application for membership in the Hilo Yacht Club, had disappeared. Only after several weeks of clean-up was the mystery of its disappearance solved. A man who lived south of Hilo and about 3/4 mile from the shore, brought in the transom of the boat, which had been deposited in his yard. There was no trace of the rest of it. It was just as well. I'd felt a little foolish about the boat, an old hulking, handmade wooden sloop, ever since I had discovered, on my acceptance into yacht club membership, that it was the only boat in the club, which served mainly as a drinking party bar for the upper middle class Haole population. I did not much like the all-white club group anyway, and resigned from it not long after the tidal wave.

Race relations in this part of the Aloha State were not what I had been led to believe about the great, benign Pacific melting pot paradise described in the tourist literature. True, full-blooded Hawaiians were disappearing on most of the islands, with the largest residual on the Big Island. They enjoyed certain educational and property-right privileges denied to all others, largely through the beneficence of the last queen, Liliokulani.

Whether as a result of the queen's bequest of a special welfare system for native Hawaiians, or the ease of life in this mild semi-tropical land of abundant free fruit and coconuts and fish, or some inherent traits of passive indolence among Polynesian peoples - politically incorrect as a notion even in those far-distant days - this group of mostly relaxed, gentle people were perceived by all other groups to be at the bottom of the social scale.

Speculation among the Caucasians - Haoles, or more commonly, "Goddam-haoles" - and among the Nisei and Sansei - 2nd and 3rd generation Japanese, and the Portugese-descended aristocratic light-skinned Portugese as well as the darker "black Portugees" was endless about the causes of the Hawaiians' low status. All seemed to agree, however, that they were lazy, "shiftless," unreliable, poor and sporadic workers of little skill, uneducated and probably not educable, and interested mainly in eating and copulating, in that order, which is why so many of them were so fat.

These attitudes did not result in open conflict; there was never a 'Wounded Knee' event on the island, but the easily recognizable (slow-moving, off-hand, almost invariably obese) natives were treated with disdain by most other residents, and stayed largely to themselves.

The Japanese-descended were clearly the dominant group, both in numbers and in educational achievement. These were the teachers, nurses, social workers, attorneys, active politicians, our judge, and the like. None of these did farm work; few ran small shops.

The Portuguese, all with similar names, divided themselves into two distinct, mutually exclusive and openly antagonistic cliques. Those whose forbears were upper-class men who were officers aboard the early sailing ships that landed in Hawaii considered themselves true aristocrats. They were given to fancy clothes, elaborate parties, expensive cars and a haughty demeanor.

The 'black' Portugee, on the other hand, descended as they were from ordinary seamen who, frequently, had jumped ship to enjoy this tropical paradise, were far more down-to-earth. They often married Hawaiian women, cared little for the outward signs of affluence, worked in warehouses or as longshoremen or fishermen or construction workers, and openly despised their betters.

The Chinese community on the island was similarly distinct from all the rest, and largely associated only with one another. Many were shopkeepers, but among them were large property owners and managers, financiers, and traders. One such, Chin Ho, after leaving to set up shop in Honolulu, became Hawaii's - and one of the world's - richest men. The Chinese loved to gamble, and their social activities revolved around games of chance, Chinese versions of board games, and the multitude of Chinese holidays.

Surprisingly, the most active seekers after success, in school and in business, were the growing numbers of Filipinos. With the end of the old plantation system, women from the Philippines began arriving in Hawaii, many of them trained nurses and teachers. Their children were strongly encouraged by their parents to excel in school and seek higher education, and they became competitive with the Japanese, with whom, as a residue of the Great War, they never socialized or became friendly.

The Haoles constituted at most 20% of the population. Among them were most of the physicians, supervising nurses, attorneys, accountants, business owners, sugar cane plantation owners and managers, and upper level employees of the five great factoring companies who owned the shipping lines and dominated Hawaii's economy until recently. Like the other groups, they tended to associate mostly with one another. The mixing pot was not much in evidence, but generally people got along.

My job, as an employee of the state, required periodic trips to Oahu, since all major government offices and operations were headquartered in Honolulu, and the state's only mental hospital was on that same island. On one such trip, I was invited to visit the office of General Isaac D. White, who was the Commander in Chief, Pacific, or CINCPAC. "I.D.," as he was universally known, had been a bonafide hero of WWII, serving as George Patton's deputy in that legendary commander's triumphant march, with his tank army, across Europe. I had met I.D. on one of my speaking tours, talking about the Code of Conduct and the POWs in Korea.

General White was a truly splendid soldier whose bearing, commanding presence, chest full of well-earned medals, perfectly tailored uniform and impeccable grooming all proclaimed him to be exactly what he was: the Alpha Wolf, the unquestioned top authority who reigned absolute over every uniformed soldier, sailor, marine and airman throughout the Pacific theater of operations. Every ship, tank, airplane, cannon and rifle in that huge area of the globe was his to command, and he did his job superbly.

He greeted me with great friendliness and recalled in amazing detail what I had said in my speeches about moral values, the importance and place of authority, military training, the 'great society' programs, military discipline, and old-fashioned ideas about honor and loyalty and duty. He had become increasingly concerned about morale and discipline in the armed forces, and the erosion of basic American values and convictions, which he had observed as he traveled throughout his vast area of responsibility.

He had summoned me, he said, to make a proposal. He wanted me to travel throughout the Pacific Theater, as his personal representative with authority to interview any and all military persons regardless of Service, rank or position. I was to assess the morale, commitment to duty, readiness to fight, attitudes towardsuperiors and subordinates, and any other matters that bore upon the ability of our people in uniform to perform their mission. I would travel as a VIP with status equivalent to a general officer, and was to report instantly any obstacles I encountered, or any hint of failure to cooperate by anyone, regardless of rank. What an assignment! My report was to go to him alone, and be delivered personally.

I.D.'s influence with the state officials, not surprisingly, was great, and my superiors instantly agreed to my "loan" for six weeks, when he asked for it. After a quick trip back to Hilo to gather some clothes and tell my staff about my temporary absence, I returned to Oahu, reported to the General, and was soon on my way.

What a journey that turned out to be! I carried a set of orders signed by the CINC himself, directing all personnel under his command to lend me any assistance and accommodations I required, make anyone available to me that I requested to talk to, and in every way consider me to be his personal representative. A message went out separately, to all commands, announcing that I would soon be arriving to conduct a special, highly classified study designed by the CINC himself and that had the highest priority.

The curiosity of the senior officers that I met first at each stop on my long trip across and around the entire Pacific Ocean area was intense; the higher the rank, the more intense it was. In tribute to those people, however, it was notable that not a single one, even those bearing the top rank of generals and admirals and quite used to having things their way, ever questioned me about what I was doing, or why, or what the possible consequences might be for them, or even if there was a problem they should know about.

Each day began with interviews with some of the senior unit commanders, then with their junior officers, senior non-commissioned people, and then with both groups and individuals made up of the rank and file soldiers, sailors and airmen. I worked out a system whereby I could select my subjects, instead of having their superiors pick them out for me, and it worked well. Each person was given my solemn word that their identity would never be revealed or even recorded. This, I told them, was their chance, probably their only chance ever, to tell the Commander in Chief anything - absolutely anything and everything - they thought he should know, and be sure he would hear it.

I devised a set of questions, first about non-threatening things like living conditions, the way they were organized, their usual day-to-day duties, the food, housing, and how they were able to spend their free time. From there, especially with the lower-ranking enlisted troops, I moved on to questions about the way they were being trained (a continuous process in the military) and supervised, their equipment and supplies, and their ideas about anything that was really a pain, or useless, or that needed to be changed for the better.

Two groups of interviewees that were always talked to privately with no one else present, were the officers who commanded small units, and the chaplains. I asked the former about their 'command style,' getting all kinds of answers but almost invariably describing widespread resentment among their men toward all authority, and seeming inability or unwillingness to do their jobs without detailed, minute supervision. Strangely enough, the junior enlisted men I talked to did not express particular resentment toward their officers, but often signified their lack of respect for their competence and reliability as leaders.

The chaplains, also talked to individually, were most eager to ventilate their frustrations and dismay at what they saw among the troops. They reported poor attendance at services, obvious signs of disinterest, many complaints about trivial problems and widespread, griping disaffection. Of greatest concern to most of them, was what they saw as flagrant immorality and sexual promiscuity practiced at every opportunity among the men when they left the post or the ship.

The Chaplains Corps, at service headquarters in Washington, had always been deeply concerned with venereal disease among military personnel. Indeed, along with the AWOL and desertion rates, the incidence of V.D. was always considered a signal indicator of morale among troops, as well as incontrovertible evidence of the lack of moral and religious rectitude.

As so often happens, an institutionalized programmatic "solution" was devised by the senior bureaucracy. In this case, it was something called the "Character Guidance" program. At regular intervals of perhaps 2 weeks, the office of the Chief of Chaplains came forth with a detailed lesson plan to be used by all unit commanders and unit chaplains in mandatory assemblies. Attendance was compulsory for all enlisted personnel. No one was to be excused from attendance and, presumably, rapt attention.

Chaplains were instructed to deliver the entire planned information without allowing their personal or denominational biases to enter in. They were not to deliver it as a sermon; 'required religious instruction' was forbidden. The unit commander was to attend each session to support the chaplain and to engage with him in a stimulating dialogue about the content, unless his 'command responsibilities' required him to be elsewhere (which they almost invariably did.) The talks mostly dealt with sexual behavior, sinfulness and the wages thereof, especially gonorrhea and syphilis.

It was hard to tell whether the chaplains or the enlisted men were most antagonized by the program. Every single young chaplain complained to me about it; none had ever complained through channels to his superiors. The men never brought it up. When questioned, they said they mostly slept through the sessions and everyone agreed it was mostly bullshit. What did chaplains know about sex anyway?

A couple of years later, in testimony before a Congressional committee, I commented on the absurdity and uselessness of such programs as the one entitled

"Character Guidance," which did not guide character very well and had no discernible influence on the incidence of venereal disease, yet persisted to that day. I was promptly attacked, officially and through channels, by an indignant Chief of Chaplains who probably concluded that I was a typical Godless psychiatrist long overdue for excommunication if not for burning. They did, finally, give it up, though.

More serious than that, however, was the evidence that existed everywhere that the problems that seemed to have beset the Korea POWs were far from resolved. Many senior non-commissioned officers, the ones who manage the great bulk of troops from day to day in all their duties, voiced great frustration and disgust over their inability to enforce discipline or build morale and a sense of unit pride, as they had done in earlier days. Many complained that the junior commissioned officers who were their immediate superiors were engaged in 'popularity contests,' and failed to back them up.

A large number of senior sergeants and petty officers told me frankly that they would leave the service, in disgust, when their current enlistments were over, and that in fact proved to be true throughout the services.

My report to the CINC when I got back to Hawaii was not really a happy one. There is a strong tradition in the armed forces that it is wrong and unmanly and unmilitary to complain, especially to "higher-ups." This applies particularly to civilian higher-ups like congressmen and senators who come poking around looking for things to criticize. While it is perhaps understandable, it can do great harm, just like other forms of denial.

While no one likes complainers and whiners, it is nonetheless necessary to face up to unpleasant truths about deficiencies that weaken and can ruin social structures, like the military, and I have always tried to do that. It is a sure way to make enemies, but I always figured they were the kind of enemies good men should have.

Therefore, the report told it as I found it to be. General White, fine, brave man that he was, listened intently to all that I had to say, and then summoned his senior staff and had me say it all again. He neither offered nor asked for any excuses - he had no time for psychobabble and intricate sociological and intellectually elaborate rationalizations. He told his staff that we had some serious problems, and that it was his - and their - responsibility to try to fix them.

Afterward, he invited me to dinner at his quarters, and said that he wanted me to consider returning to active duty. Would I consider it? I wasn't sure my physical rehabilitation was yet complete, but ultimately agreed that if the medical examiners found me fit to return to duty, I would do so. I was strongly influenced by this man, who along with many that I had encountered during my Pacific Command study impressed me as men of great virtue, great moral courage, and the kind of men our Nation requires for its survival. I wished to be among such men again, and be like them.

Some of them, of course, are real bastards; that happens.

Within a few days, after much poking and prodding, X-rays and lab tests, I was the proud recipient of a clean bill of physical health. Once again the General summoned me to his office and said he had arranged for me to enter the advanced class at the Army Command and General Staff College at Fort Leavenworth, Kansas. He said that since I was certain to become a general in the not too distant future, this course was a must.

Back in Hilo, I bade a tearful farewell to Kay Miyamoto, by now the proud parent of a longed-for newborn girl, her husband Judge Richard, and a host of other truly dear people who had become close, warm friends in the year and a half I had spent on their lovely island. There arose in my heart quite terrible feelings of guilt and remorse that I was abandoning them, but my duty, I believed, lay elsewhere.

What the Army calls the "Regular" course, to distinguish it from a course done through correspondence, at the Command and General Staff College, Fort Leavenworth, Kansas, is a 9-month program of lectures, practical exercises, war games and intensive study. Completion of it is a requirement for advancement to senior officer and especially general rank - one of the "tickets" that must be punched en route - but is no guarantee that one will reach such exalted status.

The College was situated on an historic post that for years supplied the wagon trains headed west to pacify and settle the wilderness that lay beyond it across the Rockies and the Sierra Nevada to California. It was from this Fort that the ill-fated expedition of General Custer set out to meet its doom at Little Big Horn, as well as many lesser excursions into Indian country. The post chapel, a beautiful small Gothic structure of stone, complete with a rose window, has its walls literally covered with plaques memorializing a host of young officers lost "While crossing his command over the Missouri River," "In action against hostile Indians," and similar inscriptions.

The general commanding the school was a small, lean, stern man without humor, who had survived a POW camp during World War II. On my arrival, one day late for the proper reporting date, he summoned me to his office. In a brief, not very friendly interview he noted that General I. D. White had personally arranged for my entry, and that he was aware that I had studied and lectured extensively about POWs in Korea. Despite those facts, I was to understand that there were to be no absences from the College during the year, and that the course of study would demand my uninterrupted attention and my entire energy. He was absolutely right about that.

My class numbered about 600 officers, mostly Army majors and lieutenant colonels. Ten were physicians. A tiny handful were minorities, including a black cavalry officer with whom I struck up a friendship early on and who was to figure importantly in future years in my life, and that of my family. His name was Julius Becton. Unbeknownst to us then, he was destined to reach the high rank of Lieutenant General, command an entire Corps of several divisions in Europe, and through a cruel twist of fate and the perfidy of a sensation-seeking reporter, narrowly miss becoming the Army's first black four-star full general. More about that later.

The course concentrated heavily on standard army doctrine, battlefield tactics and strategic planning and operations. It required intensive study of the multitude of field manuals and training manuals that govern all aspects of Army activity down to the smallest detail. There were fascinating studies of the great battles of history, reaching back to Hannibal, the Roman legions, the American Civil War and all the wars since. Almost never was the subject of casualty care or military medicine even mentioned, reflecting a profound and enduring - and altogether stupid - gap in the preparation of military leaders to assume major leadership roles. That would later become horrifyingly clear to me when I later assumed responsibility, in the Pentagon, for military health care worldwide. The otherwise comprehensive education in command delivered at the college should have prepared me for that shock, but it didn't.

Instead, I was preoccupied with the mass of material that had to be absorbed and retained to keep from disgracing myself and my profession by failure to measure up to my eager fellow students. The language and reasoning and rituals of military thinking were so arcane at times as to make medical school, in retrospect, seem easier.

There were extensive studies on the subject of leadership, a matter of prime importance in military operations. The study material included descriptions and analyses of a number of successful leaders, mostly military. The manuals, however, attempted and nearly succeeded in listing the qualities required of successful leaders, but never quite managed to capture the essence of the subject. It became increasingly clear to me why it was that so many ineffective, really lousy commanders were so bad, in spite of doing all or most of the things the manuals said you had to do, but without actually understanding the persons they were commanding. That was, unhappily, true of many senior medical officers who found themselves in command.

Probably the best short course in leadership that we were given was delivered in about and hour and a half by Harry Truman. What came through was a picture of utter sincerity, conviction, decisiveness, honesty and complete absence of self-deception that had helped this small time Kansas haberdasher-turned-politician become a truly great leader of the Nation in the complex, difficult final days of WWII and the years that followed immediately afterward. Few Americans understand the enormity of his decision to employ the bombs that unquestionably ended the terrible war in the Pacific quickly and mercifully, and saved hundreds of thousands of both American and Japanese lives. No formula-style leader this. He surely never read a manual on how to lead. He just did it, using simple basic principles of honor and decency and awesome determination and courage.

I had always figured that Franklin Roosevelt, ever the supreme manipulator and calculating politician, picked Harry Truman as his last Vice President, knowing his own health was failing and that Harry would succeed him. It was my guess that FDR miscalculated, thinking that Truman's lack of distinction would stand in such bleak contrast to Franklin's imperial grandeur and dominating personality as to ensure the glorification of the great man who came before him. He had, after all, led America out of the depression and to victory in history's greatest war. In truth, Harry Truman may well have been the greater man.

The course took about nine months, but seemed much longer. Although eager to go on to my next duty assignment, I accepted instead an appointment to the special Nuclear Weapons Employment Officer Course and spent several months learning the details of the assembly, targeting, and casualty- and damage-estimating procedures associated with the use of nuclear weapons. Almost no other physicians had ever taken that training, and I undertook it with a certain sense of irony but found it immensely interesting and valuable.

Following that, I was invited to take the special Chemical and Biological Warfare Course, also lasting several months and conducted partly at the College and partly at the Army's proving ground for chem-bio weapons located in Dugway, Utah. That miserable little town was named for the grooves dug into hillsides by settlers headed west in their wagons, who dug trenches for the uphill wheels on the sides of the steep hills, to help the wagons stay on more of an even keel. Just as a monument to the determination and endurance of those early Americans determined to conquer the vast wilderness, I found the long trenches awesome indeed.

Equally awesome, though in a dramatically different way, was what I learned in that place about the devastating power of both chemical weapons and biological devices, both easier and cheaper to build, and infinitely easier to disseminate, than the heavy, bulky nuclear devices. Now, as I write this, the country remains totally unprepared to deal with what must inevitably happen when some hostile small nation or group of terrorists decides to build some such weapons of mass destruction and employ them on our homeland. We know that the Iraqis and the Russians have long had 'chem-bio' weapons, as we ourselves once did, but there is no way to know who else does.

To illustrate the potential of such gadgets, it would be possible for a small, crop-duster airplane, its tanks filled with, say, anthrax spores, to infect hundreds of thousands of people in a city like New York merely by making a single pass three miles distant, upwind of Manhattan. There are almost no systems set up to decontaminate exposed people, and no stockpiles of drugs that could help treat the casualties. First responders would sicken, and both hospitals and ambulances could be rendered useless by contamination.

Similarly, a few pressurized canisters filled with Sarin or VX, gases so poisonous that a tiny drop on the skin can be fatal, set off in a major airport or the subway, and could kill thousands of people. That exact thing was tried in Tokyo, but the agent used was improperly prepared and the dispersion system was inadequate, so only a few people died, although thousands were sickened. The next time, they may do it right, and to us.

Having become, to the best of my knowledge, the only psychiatrist on earth trained to assemble and detonate nuclear devices and calculate the casualties resulting therefrom, and learning how to use deadly chemicals and bacteria to destroy masses of innocent people, I finally finished that 25th year of my formal education, and returned to duty.

The next couple of years were spent once again on the faculty of the Medical Field Service School at Fort Sam Houston, teaching classes on battlefield medicine and traveling occasionally to lecture to civilian audiences. One development at the school proved to be highly absorbing: the development of a special course on the management of mass casualties. We taught this both in the classroom and out at Camp Bullis. With the cooperation of the Air Force, a simulated nuclear explosion was set off after some jet airplanes flew close overhead above the bleachers where the audience sat. After the big bang, complete with a mushroom cloud, we conducted the spectators along a trail lined on both sides with magnificently made-up, simulated casualties.

Some of the 'casualties,' in reality corpsmen in training and happily out of their school for the day, were so realistic that some spectators became ill, fainting or throwing up, becoming themselves patients in need of our expert attention. Everyone loved it.

My next assignment was to the Office of the Surgeon, US Continental Army Command, Fort Monroe, Virginia, where I was to serve as Chief of Professional Services. At that time, the 48 States between the Canadian and Mexican borders were grouped into six districts, numbered one through six, each with a headquarters under the command of a 4-star general. All fighting units, and the multitude of supporting organizations scattered about on various Army posts in that district, or 'Army,' were under his control. The six US-based "continental" armies reported to the command at Fort Monroe, called "CONARC."

In keeping with that scheme, all Army forces in Europe were considered part of the Seventh Army, and all in the Far East, the Eighth.

My new boss was the CONARC Surgeon (all medical officers in command roles are termed 'Surgeon,' which has nothing to do with their medical specialty.) This man, Norman Peatfield, was a senior medical colonel, and until I arrived on the scene, was the only physician on the staff. Long removed from clinical medicine, Norm's seniority derived solely from his many years of service in medical administrative tasks, not his medical skills.

This aging colonel had served in all his assignments with obsessive attention to all the smallest details of procedure and regulations, and he continued to do this in his present job. He was an unnecessarily strict, nit-picking, over-your-shoulder supervisor to all his subordinates: a senior nurse, six or eight Medical Service Corps administrative officers, several master sergeants and a few 'grunts' - low-ranked enlisted soldiers who mainly ran errands, delivered office supplies and swept up. And me.

When I reported in, standing smartly at attention before the Colonel's massive desk, he greeted me formally, did not invite me to stand at ease or to sit down, and proceeded to deliver a short, prepared lecture concerning the immense power and importance of CONARC and the honor of serving on the staff. He said I would immediately assume responsibility for all the professional medical activities in each of the six Armies but did not explain further, evidently assuming I knew what those were. In reality, I didn't have the slightest idea, but of course I did not tell him that.

I did know that each Army had its own command surgeon, all senior to me, who set policy and supervised its execution throughout that Army. In addition, there were any number of large hospitals, medical centers, clinics and the like in each Army, all commanded by experienced senior medical officers. "Norm," as his senior (never his subordinate) officer colleagues elsewhere in the headquarters called him, never did explain to me anything about his concept of the office's mission, or what he expected of me, or what he himself did, other than "advise the Commanding General concerning all medical matters affecting the Continental Armies" and attend staff meetings.

My undefined job, as it turned out, was boring beyond belief. An occasional letter from some member of Congress about the alleged ill-treatment of some sick soldier in one of the Armies occasionally appeared, constituting a major crisis episode demanding immediate response. In reality, what we did was forward the letter to the Command Surgeon in the appropriate Army, demanding an investigation and report. He in turn sent it on to the commander of the hospital involved, who sent it on to his staff for reply and resolution. When the reply was formulated, it came back up the same channels to us. I would prepare a forwarding endorsement to be sent along with the reply to the Surgeon General.

The colonel was never satisfied with my first draft of the endorsement. Nor the second, third, and often even the fourth. His objections were to details so meaningless and irrelevant as to defy all logic, and I despaired of ever producing a satisfactory document, even though these things were always quite brief, routine statements.

Fortunately for me, all this took place before accusations and charges of medical malpractice or mischance became the insanely popular thing they have become today, when the chance to get rich by suing hospitals and doctors is often seen as a much surer way to wealth and leisure than any lottery. Which, unfortunately, it is.

Moreover, local sleazy, greedy lawyers had not yet started advertising in post newspapers for "victims" to seek them out, at no cost unless the lawsuit succeeds, to sue Uncle Sam, along with the Army hospital. They do that today in every community where there is a military health care facility. This practice has become truly a growth industry that does incalculable harm to patients and their relationship to those who treat them, at incalculable cost to the health care industry and, more importantly, to the social fabric.

Thanks to the cleverness of avaricious lawyers, the gullibility of jurors who can readily be led to feelings of pity and sympathy for the sufferings of others, and the growing practice of courts to award outrageous, wholly unjustified financial rewards for the almost always totally subjective "pain and suffering" endured by the 'victim,' the cost of this evil practice will one day outstrip the cost of medical care itself, if it is not stopped.

Some physicians have found themselves to be so vulnerable to financial and professional ruin that they are forced to spend enormous sums to insure their practices. Insurance premiums in excess of $25 thousand or more, annually, are common today, and naturally that cost has to be passed on to all the doctor's other patients.

In addition, it is common now for physicians to order, at great expense to the patient or his health insurance company, a multitude of poorly justified, often completely unnecessary laboratory, radiologic, magnetic imaging and endoscopic examinations ostensibly for diagnostic completeness but actually to protect against claims of inadequate work-ups. The euphemism for this is "defensive medicine." The cost cannot be calculated accurately, but it is huge, and growing daily.

I know of some efforts to cap outrageous court-ordered awards - or, more accurately, REwards - in medical lawsuits, but I am unaware of any concerted or even feeble effort to reign in the costs of defensive medicine. Meanwhile, health care costs, which are often not the costs of the actual care at all, continue to rise, the media revels in its findings and dramatic 'exposure' of a health care 'crisis,' and we move inevitably toward some kind of universally subsidized health care system, whose costs will inevitably continue to rise, while its quality will as inevitably decline.

And all at 'government' (read "taxpayers,'" or better yet, "our") expense!

This has been a century of medical miracles of incalculable benefit to our species, more in number and impact than the combined effect of all progress in medicine in the whole previous history of mankind. The 'free enterprise' system of medical care as it has traditionally been practiced in this country, has advanced the quality, the availability, and the success of medicine in relieving human ills far more than any other health care delivery system, past or present. It is seriously, profoundly in danger of terrible disruption and decay because of the current diabolical marriage of unprincipled lawyers with a population that believes in 'something for nothing,' and 'get rich quick,' and is preoccupied with victimhood, and entitlements, and rights, without much attention to individual responsibility for healthy diets, exercise, and for seeking preventive care.

Years earlier, when I transferred from the Regular Navy to the Regular Army, I was a Lieutenant, Senior Grade. Commissioned officer ranks are designated by numbers, with O-1 being the lowest: Navy Ensign or Army 2nd Lieutenant. O-6 designates a senior Colonel or Naval Captain. Generals and Admirals were O-7 through O-10. My Navy Rank was O-3.

Because the Army and Navy at that time had entirely different promotion systems, my classmates who had entered the Army when I started out in the Navy had been promoted to O-4 several years earlier, which put me in a significantly disadvantageous position. At the time of my inter-service transfer, I asked about rectifying this, and was repeatedly reassured at the highest Army levels that my rank would be adjusted to match. As it turned out, this was never put in writing, and it never happened.

After the break in service, I again requested that the rank inequity be corrected and was again assured that it would be, but once again, nothing happened. At the time of my assignment to CONARC Headquarters, my rank was Lieutenant Colonel, O-5, even though my billet called for a full Colonel, O-6. While this might seem to an outsider to be a trivial problem, it wasn't, both in terms of pay, where the difference was dramatic, and in status, a powerful consideration in the uniformed services. Coupled with the fact that I had over 20 years of active duty and was eligible to retire with a modest pension, this rank and pay handicap persuaded me that I should retire and pursue a new career.

Once again I found an ad in a medical journal seeking a mental health director for the County of Yolo, California. Years before, while in my fellowship at UC San Francisco Medical Center, I had taken and passed the difficult 3-day medical state board examinations for a California license, so the offer sounded ideal. Yolo County lies adjacent to Sacramento, about 75 miles from San Francisco and the same distance from the campgrounds and ski areas around Lake Tahoe, and the job sounded highly attractive.

Accordingly, after accepting an invitation to address the management group at the Kaiser Permanente steel plant east of Los Angeles, I took a brief leave and, resplendent in my uniform, made my way to Sacramento, rented a car at the airport, and dashed over to the Yolo County Courthouse to present myself as their next Director of Mental Health.

The Courthouse turned out to be a grim, gray stone structure looking for all the world like a small penitentiary, situated in a small, drab, rural town, which was hopefully but inaccurately named Woodland. It was early afternoon when I climbed the steps, only to find the building nearly deserted. After some searching, I located the personnel office, where a young woman sat at an old desk idly looking through a magazine.

The personnel director was out, she told me, and might not return for an hour or so, but I could wait, if I wished. I sat for about two hours on an uncomfortable straight chair, and finally the dignitary himself appeared. He was surprised when I told him of my mission, and immediately apologized. They were not really recruiting, he said, but were required to go through the motions and insert the ad because of County regulations. The truth was, they had already decided on the new Director, who was finishing up a year of study in Edinburgh, Scotland, and they were just waiting for him to get back. Sorry! The new man already lived in Yolo County, and was perfect for what they wanted.

I thanked him and left. What to do? Sacramento was not far away so I headed there and drove up the fine mall leading to the Capitol. A building along the mall bore the legend "State Personnel Board," and I decided that was a good place to start, so I parked my rented car and headed inside.

Making my way to the recruitment and hiring office on an upper floor, I presented myself at a long counter and told the woman there, who was clearly impressed by my uniform and rows of ribbons, that I was the Chief of Professional Medical Services for the entire Army in the Continental United States, a fully-trained psychiatrist duly licensed in the Golden State, and was preparing to retire from active duty. I asked her, with no trace of humility whatever, what jobs she had in which I could be "in charge."

She brightened perceptibly at that, and said there were two vacancies for directors of State Hospitals that the State desperately needed to fill. Would I be interested in one of those? No, I definitely would not. My exposure, during my residency and fellowship in psychiatry, to the huge hospitals at Napa and the city of Stockton, had convinced me that they were grim and horrifying. Their superintendents lived in fine houses on the grounds, and were well paid, but I could not picture myself doing that.

I had heard about the exciting development, in California, of a community mental health system in each county, subsidized and supervised by the state, and I would consider running one of those programs. Her face fell a little, but she went bravely on. She explained that the counties hired directly for the local mental health departments, but the state had regional offices that reviewed them and approved their plans and budgets. The regional office for the entire San Francisco Bay Area was in San Francisco, and if I wanted to work in that area I could go see the Regional Director, whom she would call.

There was little more than a day of my leave remaining, so I promptly agreed, and an appointment with the regional chief was set for the next morning, early.

The receptionist in the Regional Office said that the Director was expecting me and to go right in to his office. Entering, I was waived to a seat in front of his desk while, turned away from me, he completed what seemed to be an affectionate, intimate telephone conference, so I had a chance to observe both the man and his surroundings in some detail.

The office was paneled in dark wood and tastefully furnished - especially so for a state facility. I learned later that it was rented space in a small commercial office building. There were attractive prints on the wall, a vase of fresh flowers on a small table, various knickknacks tastefully arranged on the desk and bookshelves, and quite a good, small oriental rug on the floor.

The man himself was strikingly clad in an expensive tweed coat over a fashionably high-collared, gleaming white shirt with a small ascot at the throat. The cuffs of the shirt were adorned with large, elaborate gold cufflinks, and the hands that emerged from them were graceful and perfectly manicured. His hair was carefully groomed and fell into soft waves.

When the last farewells were fed into the telephone, he turned to put it down and let his somehow haughty gaze fall on my handsome military uniform and then full on my face. His eyes widened, and he did not move his hand from the telephone that he had just put down. "Oh, my God!" he exclaimed.

Before me sat Donald, the homosexual Navy psychiatrist that I had seen in my own paneled office in Yokosuka before saving him from disgrace and expulsion for his sexual deviation by evacuating him to the States for treatment of his depression. He jumped from his chair and came around his desk to give me a delighted hug. This was great. This guy owed me. Now he could repay my kindness by finding me a job!

"In charge" psychiatry jobs were hard to get in the San Francisco area, he told me, but there was one, crying out for leadership, in nearby Contra Costa County, northeast of the Bay. There were 'some problems' with it, he admitted with some reluctance, but why didn't I go to the county seat, talk to the hospital director, and decide for myself?

Back in my car, I made my way across the Bay Bridge, through Berkeley, and in an hour found myself in the office of a truly remarkable man. George, the hospital director, was a magnificent physical specimen, startlingly handsome, who was truly a bigger-than-life character in all respects. He was hearty, a bit loquacious, outspoken, ebullient in manner and possessed, seemingly, of boundless energy evident in the way he jumped up to greet me, pumped my hand, and welcomed me to "the finest county hospital in the great state of California!" He obviously meant that.

Our greetings complete, he lapsed into a few moments of silence while he studied my military decorations. He then asked if I were as much of a man as I looked. I mumbled a reply, not too modest nor yet too boastful, and he went on. "The reason I asked," he went on, "is that every psychiatrist I've seen up to this point had ping pong balls for testicles, and you don't look like one of those." I took that to be a compliment.

He went on to describe the most recent mental health director as a complete wimp of a psychoanalyst, hardly a 'real' doctor, who couldn't effectively run any kind of program at all, and there was a great need for a truly 'tough guy' who could 'whip into shape' all these namby-pamby social workers, psychologists and other psychiatrists who labored in the large mental health program. Did I think I could do that?

Unhesitatingly, I assured him that I could, adding that I was a friendly guy on the surface, but a tough, no-nonsense boss who expected and demanded the best of my subordinates and tolerated nothing less. It was the right answer. When could I start? Next month, I told him. Great!

George, it turned out, despised mental health professionals, as was obvious from his comments. Nonetheless, he jumped at the chance to establish a program, once the founding Short-Doyle Community Mental Health Act was passed by the California legislature and he saw the generous state reimbursement scheme that paid 75% of the costs of these programs as a truly golden opportunity to bring substantial money to his hospital. He cared not a whit for mental health, but assumed quite accurately that with a little creative bookkeeping and budgeting, he could make it highly profitable.

Evidence of this lay in the one absolute condition attached to my acceptance of the job. That was, I was to leave all financial planning and management solely to him; all I was to do was run a good program, making certain that I met all the state requirements so as to ensure our full reimbursement, and he would take care of the business end of things.

My years in the military had deeply imbued me with a belief in the honesty and trustworthiness of my professional colleagues. While my fellow officers and I sometimes disagreed on various matters of procedure or tactics, there was never, in my experience, any significant problem of dishonor or lack of trust. Pettiness, selfishness, some shirking of responsibility all occurred from time to time, but were never, in my personal experience, serious.

Consequently, I had no problem with accepting the condition he set, seeing in it no devious or evil intent. Additionally, it was clear that the new mental health laws of California were complex and largely unfamiliar to me, and I had no desire to become a budgeting or accounting expert, only to perform my professional duties in a superior manner.

Our contract was sealed with another vigorous handshake, and I raced back to Sacramento to get my flight back to the lovely, historic, moated fortress of CONARC's headquarters, where my military career would be put forever to rest, after appropriate ceremony and signing of innumerable papers. The Army bestowed one final commendatory medal, as always when a departing comrade in arms retires without being caught at anything undesirable, and within a few weeks I began my westward migration to the Golden State.

There followed a long, difficult journey in a seriously under-powered Volkswagen camper van laden with all my worldly goods and marked by repeated stops for valve grinding caused by an erroneous owner's manual showing incorrect valve settings. Finally, after repairs done by the Rolls Royce garage in Reno, the high Sierra was breached, and I arrived in California to take part in the mental health 'revolution.'

William E. Mayer, M.D.

William E. Mayer, M.D.

CHAPTER 10

REVOLUTIONIZING MENTAL HEALTH

The state of California was an early participant in an international movement that had begun not long before in England, called 'Community Mental Health.' Two prominent British psychiatrists, Thomas Main and Maxwell Jones, independently of one another, began treating a number of psychiatric patients, who would ordinarily have been confined to hospitals, in their homes in the community.

This was yet another step away from earlier practices in which the mentally ill were not only confined in prison-like hospitals but were often chained to the walls of their cells. Main and Jones took the step cautiously. They selected their patients carefully and sent teams of social workers and often a psychiatrist to the patient's home to investigate all aspects of the patient's illness as well as the surroundings and his family to make sure the setting was agreeable and the family members willing and able to participate.

If the patient were deemed acceptable, he or she was admitted to the hospital for careful observation and examination, and started on one of the newly developed drugs, called phenothiazines, that were to mental disease what the antibiotics were to infections. Some years earlier a new group of compounds called "tranquillizers" had appeared on the medical scene, and had proven to have merit in treating some neurotic disorders like obsessions and panic and some depressions. They were quite ineffective in cases of serious mental disease like schizophrenia and manic-depressive disorders.

The phenothiazines, especially a drug called Thorazine, in the proper dosages, made it possible for some seriously psychotic - truly "crazy" - people to return to something like a normal state. These drugs were not without their problems, however. Too little did no good. Too much resulted in a slowed, subdued state often referred to as "Zombie-like." In addition, some cases, prolonged use resulted in a sometimes irreversible disorder called tardive dyskinesia, with strange muscular movements and interferences with speech and coordination.

The patient was returned home after the examinations were complete and a satisfactory level of medication established. The home was visited regularly for counseling of the family and observation of the patient, who was encouraged and assisted to resume at least some customary activities both at home and in the community, like shopping.

Both of the British innovators were friends with a remarkable woman who lived in Berkeley, California, who was a trained psychoanalyst. Her name was Portia Bell Hume. She was the daughter of Alexander Graham Bell, married to a colorful bookseller named Sam Hume. That worthy was the son of a famous Wells-Fargo agent famed for having brought one "Black Bart," himself a renowned nemesis of the Wells-Fargo organization, "to earth," making the stagecoaches safe for travelers and money-chests.

Portia Bell, as she was known far and wide, was the largest single holder of AT&T stock in the world. During the great depression of the 1930s, she undertook to build a medieval castle (with all modern conveniences,) on a Berkeley hillside overlooking San Francisco Bay. She did this both because she really liked medieval castles, and also to provide gainful employment for out-of-work stonecutters, masons, carpenters, upholstery weavers and stained glassmakers, for whom she felt deeply.

The castle was enclosed in a high wall, and contained authentic touches like stone steps circling upward around the wall of a great round tower room, a fireplace big enough to accommodate a small truck, a hand-made clavichord, and in her bedroom, a huge elevated bed with elaborate carved headboard, once owned and used by the emperor and empress of China.

Portia Bell was a fully trained and qualified Freudian psychoanalyst who had known Freud and Jung and Adler and the other greats of early modern psychiatry, who learned her trade both in Vienna and in San Francisco. When I was a resident and fellow at the Langley Porter Clinic there, she was a notable member of the faculty. She was a large, not-very-pretty woman with an imperious manner who held herself and moved as if she were a senior member of a royal family, which in a sense she was.

In those days, when medical-social discipline and practices were strict (nurses stood up when a doctor entered; doctors stood up when a senior doctor entered,) she stood out. No one fooled with Portia Bell. No one ever told a joke in her presence. She could peer down her nose with a gaze that was both penetrating and frightening. We secretly concluded that she was the prototype for the "castrating female" that all males were supposed to fear. It was clear she had no patience for fools, and that she considered most or all male residents to fall into that category. Scary lady!

Shortly after my arrival in Martinez to serve as the Contra Costa County Mental Health Services Program Chief, I was astonished when one day she called to invite me to visit her in her Berkeley office. She served at that time as Director of the State's Institute for Training in Community Psychiatry in that city.

The warmth and enthusiasm with which she greeted me astonished me even further. While it had been more than 15 years since I had last seen her, we had never been what one might call friends. Surprisingly, she recalled my residency days at the University, my close relationship with Karl Bowman, and said she had followed my military career closely.

She was particularly complimentary about some work I had done in the Army helping to set up out-of-hospital treatment programs for emotionally disturbed soldiers and their families, and said I was a godsend to the Community Mental Health program in California. I was astounded. This was not the Portia Bell I had known in San Francisco!

We talked for the entire afternoon, and she said she would be pleased if, thereafter, I would set aside Wednesday afternoons, every week, for meeting with her. Together, she said, we would show the world how community psychiatry was supposed to work! It was the beginning of an altogether wonderful learning experience, for me, that was to pay off grandly.

This relationship was without doubt the most instructive and rewarding professional psychiatric experience of my career in this otherwise dismal field of medicine that still suffers, as this is written, from superstition, bias, fear, cruelty toward the afflicted, and vast public ignorance and abysmal misconceptions. For a year and a half of Wednesday afternoons, almost without fail, I had the enormous privilege of sitting with this great lady, sometimes in her office, sometimes the castle, while we examined the whole history of psychiatry, and how we could, at last, bring it out of the dark ages.

My boss George, who so despised psychiatrists, especially despised Portia Bell. It seems they had attended the University of California together. He once told me she had earned her high grades 'on her back' in professors' offices, whereas she had in reality been a brilliant student while he was a brilliant football player and a worse than mediocre scholar.

Both George and Portia applied to medical school at Cal. She was accepted without question, whereas he was told that his football prowess hardly qualified him for the difficulties of medical education.

Angered by this, George did the unthinkable: he applied at the Stanford University Medical School. Again he was refused, and for the same reason. Determined and persistent, George was finally granted admission to a fine school in Canada, at McGill University, where he finished a year later than his classmates, it was said, because of time spent in a mental hospital!

Both of these two remarkable characters went on into specialty training - hers in psychiatry and his in surgery. George obtained an excellent surgical residency in England, and was on a surgical staff there when WWII broke out. The British government sought George's exemption from the draft from US authorities, and he spent the war working in England.

Upon his return after the war, intending to practice surgery in his home state of California, he sought a state medical license, and was rebuffed, just as he had been, earlier, for admission to the two leading California medical schools. Frustrated and bitterly resentful, he went before the Contra Costa County Board of Supervisors and volunteered to work at their small county hospital for his room and board, no salary, until he could pass the boards, which he eventually did.

He lived in a small room at the hospital, and teamed up with a (then) attractive, energetic, competent young nurse to build the county hospital into a first-class teaching institution that specialized in training young general practitioners to be highly competent surgeons, even though the hospital was not approved for surgical training by the American Board of Surgery since he was not certified by that Board - another source of deep resentment.

The medical community in Contra Costa County disliked George intensely, and he both earned and returned their animosity. His one medical ally was an elderly physician, who, after losing his wife, lived with his daughter in an incestuous relationship that everyone seemed to know about, until he died. Under George's leadership, however, the hospital grew to two hundred or more beds, had a large surgical service, a large mental health service, many general practice residents, a large Tuberculosis ward and a fine rehabilitation service.

The once cute, pert, ambitious nurse grew into a grotesque, obese, dictatorial pariah, barely ambulatory and afflicted with emphysematous wheezing and urinary incontinence. Enshrined as chief nurse on the psychiatric service, she sat, heavy and stinking behind a desk commanding the locked psychiatric ward, whose shades she kept drawn down at all times. She bullied the staff, requiring a young registered nurse to collect her urine-soaked sanitary napkins periodically from under her chair, wrap them up and dispose of them.

Her name was Maxine, and it was clear that she was under the special protection of the hospital director and could do no wrong in his eyes. She had established an iron-clad routine for all patients newly admitted to her ward: they were to be stripped down, showered in the presence of both male and female attendants, and then placed in a small, utterly bare room with an iron bed bolted to the bare concrete floor and held behind a locked steel door until seen by the ward doctor, sometimes two days or more later.

All this took place regardless of the patient's condition or the reason for that person's admission to the ward.

The ward doctor was a perfect match. He was a stout, powerful, darkly Italian man clad invariably in a dark blue double-breasted suit, white shirt and plain dark tie. He avoided eye contact with everyone - staff and patients alike, rarely spoke, at best grunting slightly when greeted, and spent his days shut in his office on the ward, to which he strode purposefully and powerfully each morning, always looking straight ahead. His name was Dan L., and he had been trained in psychiatry at U.C. San Francisco Medical Center, as had I.

From my first day in charge, I told Dr. L. that things must change on his ward. The shades were to be raised. New patients were to be evaluated before being scrubbed down and locked up. I wanted him to lighten the place up, both literally and figuratively, to change the atmosphere. His first reaction was as if I were one of "them," probably a candidate for locking up myself, who obviously just didn't understand. First of all, he told me, Maxine runs the ward; he just works there. Secondly, George supports her; if he pulled up the shades she would simply pull them back down and her cowed subordinates would back her up.

I pointed out that I was now in charge of the entire service, including the nurse Maxine, and that henceforth he was in charge of this ward and I wanted him to act like it.

Returning the next day, I discovered nothing had changed. I went around the day room, opening the shades. I had another talk with Dan. He said the same things as before. The locked, cell-like rooms still held freshly washed, distraught, unhappy people, none of them agitated or apparently in need of that degree of confinement. He reluctantly agreed to talk to Maxine.

Not long after my departure from the ward, down came the blinds again.

In deference to the long-established customs and practices on that locked ward, after several fruitless daily visits I told Dan that he would have a whole week in which to make the simple changes I required, but no more. Every day I came back to J-Ward, as it was called, and found it as it was before. Dr. L. was told to come to my office.

He took the seat I offered him across from me at my desk, and listened, eyes downcast and fixed on his hands, clasped in his lap, while I told him that since he had failed to carry out any of the changes that needed to be made on his dungeon-like, oppressive, unacceptable ward, he could no longer continue to work here, and must leave.

Finally he looked up and peered intently into my eyes for the first time ever. "You know what?" he asked. Without waiting for my reply he went on. "You are a shithead. I knew another retired colonel one time at Atascadero, and he was a shithead too."

"Whatever you might think," I replied, "The fact is, I am your boss and I have concluded we cannot work together and you will have to leave. As of the end of this week, you will no longer be employed here and you will not be paid."

"Do you have any idea," he asked, "What it's like to be brought up by a strict Italian mother? She made me wear a Little Lord Fauntleroy suit and hat to school every single day, and all the other kids made fun of me. She made me wear rubbers if it even looked like rain, and nobody else wore rubbers. I know I may seem a little reserved, but that's why".

"Just give me six months," he added, "And I can do everything on the ward that you've asked."

"Sorry, Dan. You will have to leave the end of this week."

Without a word, he got up and left. He spent the several remaining days contacting every social worker and psychologist on the staff, asking them to sign a request that he had prepared, for his retention. Some did sign it, encouraged by a flyer prepared by two staff psychologists who were active in the Young Communist League at U.C. Berkeley, asserting that I was a reactionary military fascist intent on imposing dictatorial control over the mental health program, all proven by my notorious military record and speeches I had been giving.

He did leave, however, taking along one of our staff social workers and setting up a practice in Oakland, specializing in MediCal patients paid for by state and federal funding. A year later, he was arrested for defrauding the MediCal program, tried, convicted, and sent to a state penitentiary. I had discovered in the interim that each year during his residency, in the annual review, several of the faculty had encouraged that he be excluded from the program because of his obvious psychopathology. He was kept on each time by those who hoped he would get better, which he never did.

The other ex-colonel "shithead" he had referred to was the Superintendent at the California State Hospital for the criminally insane, in Atascadero, who fired him for incompetence, among other things, after less than a year there.

Partly as a result of Dr. L's adventures in psychiatry in the Bay Area, all of us who ran programs in that area formed an unofficial social club named G.A.S.P., the Group for the Advancement of Social Psychiatry, as a witty takeoff on the prestigious G.A.P., the serious Group for the Advancement of Psychiatry. While somewhat light-hearted, our monthly meetings were designed to allow us to compare notes on wandering psychiatrists who might show up at our programs seeking work, to avoid more weird characters whose mothers may have forced them to wear Little Lord Fauntleroy suits and rubbers to school every day.

My own program flourished, even without our recently departed friend. The shades came up and stayed up on J-Ward, the patients were assisted with bathing only by attendants of the same sex, and Maxine started thinking about retirement. A new ward doctor did just fine, for a psychiatrist. He was not one of the many who had obviously chosen that branch of medicine in order to deal with his own emotional and psychological problems, as so many did.

Managing a group of psychiatrists, along with social workers, psychologists and psychiatric nurses, I was to discover, was usually challenging and difficult. Many are fine, often extremely intelligent, effective physicians, but the majority, in my experience, are overly passive, lacking in moral courage, overly empathetic to their patients' failings, needs, and weaknesses, inclined to foster dependency among those they care for, and very often responsible for iatrogenic, which is to say "doctor-caused" disorders and chronicity.

Those who are not like that, and they are relatively few, tend to drift into administration, teaching, psychopharmacology, and some even write books. The current developments in the understanding of brain function, brain chemistry, neurotransmitters, and the interrelationships between physical and mental processes and functions may well attract into the field a new breed of the "real doctors" that Captain Hogan and Karl Bowman, those many years before, had told me were really needed.

There will still be the enormous army, however, of trained and untrained "counselors," pseudo-therapists, psychobabble experts and other forms of modern snake-oil peddlers and out-and-out scam artists ready to pounce. Even the "legitimate" practitioners of psychiatry and psychology are, for whatever reason, contributing increasingly to personal and social dysfunction and abandonment of all concepts of personal responsibility in favor of the philosophy of victimhood, helplessness, and 'entitlement.'

The announcement that enshrines the characterologic decay and threatened collapse as the millennial turning point approaches is that by no less an authority than the Surgeon General himself, backed up by his superiors in the Department of Health and Human Services, fully 20% of all Americans are diagnosably mentally ill, and half of all our citizens will be at some time in their lives.

These are understandable assertions, given that the official nomenclature of mental and emotional disorders keeps steadily expanding to include names and labels for more and more deviations, however small or harmless or transient, from some theoretical perfect state of unachievable "normalcy." (except homosexuality, that is.) If this continues, then before the next century ends, we shall all be diagnosably sick in the head. Then what?

As my Wednesdays with Portia Bell progressed, we found ourselves examining the details of the better community programs around the state, like the excellent one in San Mateo County and a few others, and postulating what would be required in a truly ideal one. There was a certain urgency to this, because the 24 state hospitals for the mentally ill and the retarded continued to be overcrowded, far beyond capacity, and the continuing human tragedy they encompassed was unabated.

Portia Bell, who herself had written the famous Short-Doyle act that launched the community programs in California, visualized this new way of dealing with mental illnesses as serving, ultimately, as a long-overdue replacement for the state hospitals. There was ample evidence that this needed to be done, for a great many reasons.

The state hospital population of mentally disordered persons was growing far more rapidly even than the explosive population growth of the state as a whole. Napa State Hospital, serving an area north of San Francisco along with several other hospitals, held some 6000 patients. It was built to hold 2000. The huge central building had long wards that extended from one end of the building to the other. Those enormous, cavernous spaces had beds side by side - almost touching - the entire length of the building, along both outside walls. Down the middle was a double row of beds, similarly placed side by side but in two rows, with the heads of the beds touching those of the other central row.

While still in the Army and serving at CONARC, bored as I was with little to do except write forwarding endorsements on letters, I began to study the Weekly Morbidity and Mortality Report issued by the Centers for Disease Control in Atlanta. This small document showed the numbers and locations of all cases of "reportable" diseases throughout the United States.

One such reportable disease was Meningococcal Meningitis, a particularly virulent infection, mainly of young people in their teens and very early twenties. Since most soldiers fall into this age group, I began, idly at first, to keep rough tabs on how many such cases there were each week, particularly in states where we had large basic training military posts, and how many deaths resulted therefrom.

Over a period of a few weeks, I noted to my horror that there was a growing incidence of meningococcal infection largely limited to the very states I was interested in, with a shocking number of deaths. Consultation with the command surgeons on each of the posts in the afflicted states, I learned that most of the reported cases were indeed among young soldiers.

At last! Here was a chance to relieve my boredom. What was more, it might really be important, although my boss was reluctant to let me go find out for sure. Some nicely drawn charts and graphs prepared from the raw data reported in the CDC's weekly reports combined with the information collected from the post command surgeons finally convinced him, and I set out with two young preventive medicine officers to visit the suspect posts.

At each post, we reviewed all the cases. There was striking similarity. A young soldier would go out with his buddies for a few beers and a steak in a nearby restaurant, feeling fine when he left his barracks. Sometime during the evening he would begin to feel feverish and sick, and maybe vomit. His friends would at first ignore this, and then, not much later, would become alarmed as the sick soldier collapsed. Rushed back to the post hospital, he could be dead before morning.

We examined the barracks where the youngest, lowest-ranked soldiers were housed. These were long, two-story frame structures built during World War II, largely completely open, with a row of double-deck bunks running down each side. The bunks struck me as being too close together. The standard rule was there must be six feet from the center of any bunk to the center of the next one, the dictum of "six foot centers," established many years before, during the First World War. The rule came from the finding that droplets from coughing and sneezing never sprayed that far.

We found that the bunks were not anywhere near six foot centers! We got an order issued from CONARC Headquarters that instantly, that very day, all bunks were to be separated far enough to meet and exceed the six foot rule, the most seriously affected base was actually closed for a few months (Fort Ord, in California, to the howls of local merchants), extensive fumigation of all barracks was instituted, and the infections dropped to zero.

When I first saw California's state hospitals, with all the beds crowded together, I was horrified at the amount of respiratory infections that resulted from the terrible crowding. While I had heard of no outbreak of meningitis, probably because the state hospital patients were much older than our recruits, on average, it was certain that these were dangerous places.

If you were admitted to such a hospital, and the others were like Napa though smaller, there was a 10% chance that you would die during your first year there. The causes were many, but respiratory diseases played a big part. If you survived, the chances were very great that you would stay there as long as you did live. If you were released, you were never officially discharged, but you were put "on leave." That meant you were under the supervision of a social worker employed by a separate section of the state Department of Mental Hygiene, called the Bureau of Social Work.

Your assigned social worker determined (and could approve or disapprove) your domicile as well as your activities, very much like a parole officer, after whom these worthies were patterned. If the social worker found your living circumstances, activities or associations unacceptable, in his judgment, he could without reference to any other authority have the sheriff return you to the hospital for as long as the staff there wanted to keep you.

While "on leave," and, technically, even if at some later date you were officially discharged, you carried with you more legal 'disabilities' than if you had been in a state penitentiary. You were not permitted to own any kind of weapon (hunting knives included, along with bows and arrows and naturally all varieties of guns,) you could not obtain any kind of license, presumably including marriage, driving, or any business, you could not vote, and you could not convey property.

All of the above applied to anyone admitted to a state hospital, whether voluntarily or by order of a court in a 'sanity hearing,' which officially committed you to the (indefinite) care of the state hospital authorities. A study of the hospitals, many of them quite old, revealed that simply to house the current population properly, it would be necessary to build enough new buildings to double the current available space, and there was no money available in the state budget to build any new hospitals at all.

If a successful community program could be put in place, we believed, we could cut way back on new admissions to state institutions, and eventually reduce their resident populations decisively. It had to be done, and soon.

One Wednesday, Portia was uncharacteristically excited. Normally she was superbly controlled, and rarely given to enthusiasms, but that day she was flushed and a little breathless as she announced, "Our chance has come!" She went on to say that there was soon to be an opening for a mental health director in Humboldt County, on the coast near the northern border of the state. An undistinguished program there was 'going nowhere' with a lady pediatrician-psychiatrist in charge and working half time and half-heartedly because of a reactionary, penurious board of supervisors who were barely dipping into the potential Short-Doyle state subsidy and were simply sending everybody who was "mental" off to the state hospital, 125 miles away.

The county program served both Humboldt and the smaller Del Norte County to the north, at the Oregon border. Together, the two counties had a population of about 100 thousand people - the size group ordinarily used in reporting health statistics. The largest city, Humboldt's county seat, was Eureka. There was a smaller but still substantial college town, Arcata, to the north a few miles, and a smaller one, Fortuna, to the south. Del Norte County's principal town was Crescent City, where a large portion of the county's 15 thousand people lived. There was a large Indian population of uncertain size in both counties. They mainly stayed to themselves.

The region had but two industries of any size: the logging and milling of giant redwoods, and fishing, both of which were largely seasonal. Humboldt State College, in Arcata, was something of a cultural center and had several thousand students. One major north-south highway, alone, connected the area with the San Francisco region, two hundred miles away. A much smaller mountain road ran to the east to the city of Redding. The main north-south highway, US 101, went for hundreds of miles north before encountering any major city, in this case Portland, Oregon.

My letter to the Humboldt County Executive indicating my interest in being considered for the position of Mental Health Director brought a prompt response inviting me to visit the county to meet with him and the Board. I soon made my way through the magnificent redwoods, at times on spectacular mountain roads and along rushing rivers, to the city of Eureka.

It proved to be a most ordinary city with no outstanding characteristics, good or bad. It looked neither very prosperous nor very poor, and consisted of rows of one- and two-story buildings along its single main street. The county courthouse, at four stories, and a fine old hotel, the Eureka Inn, were the two largest structures to be seen. Logging trucks loaded with huge redwood logs and enormous open trucks carrying tons of wood chips roared down the main street with regularity.

The Inn, dating from early in the century, proved to be a comfortable, well-appointed hostelry with a roaring fire in the lobby fireplace and a hospitable, friendly staff. Shortly after my arrival, the part-time mental health director, Mary Ann, showed up to serve as my escort. She was a plump, rather unhappy woman who had several children, an unrewarding marriage, and a strong, barely concealed desire to leave the area. She was friendly, however, and showed me to the County Executive's office but declined to go in with me.

Alex Fletcher, the executive, proved to be a cold, rigid man both posturally and psychologically, who sat behind his large desk, bare except for a small, well-thumbed Bible, and fixed me with a piercing gaze. He asked about my training and qualifications for the job, and my salary requirements. Evidently satisfied with my responses, he then told me that he had been the city manager in Las Vegas, but was forced to leave because of the corruption he encountered there. While not exactly hostile, he was unfriendly in the way I imagined a Puritan father was when examining a stranger in town.

Mr. Fletcher was business-like but not very good at interviewing. I tried to put him at ease, and told him a little about how I thought a mental health program should work. In response, he said, "Tell me, Doctor. Don't you think that if people prayed more, we wouldn't need all this mental health sort of thing?"

I paused, thinking rapidly and shifting some gears; this was not the kind of question I had expected, but it had to be answered.

"Certainly it is true," I replied, "That many emotional problems people suffer from could be relieved, sometimes, by prayer and active participation in their church. Faith can be a great healer. There are, though, seriously mentally ill people like those locked away in the State Hospitals that have profound disorders of the mind that make it truly impossible for them to function normally. It is those people, in particular, that I want to help."

In that connection, I added, in preparation for my meeting with the Board of Supervisors tomorrow, would it be possible for me to see a copy of the County's mental health budget? In addition, it was important that I have a chance to review the medical records of people hospitalized for mental disease, and interview the Sheriff's officers who transported them to Mendocino State Hospital, 150 miles to the south, when the Superior Court committed them there. After some hesitation, he agreed that all that could be arranged.

The interview over, I sought out the Sheriff, two floors below. He told me that his officers transported an average of 125 patients committed each year by the court. This was a problem to his department, he said, because two officers had to accompany the patient, for safety's sake, in a police car, and the process took two days. Worse, if the patient were female, he had to send one of his few women officers along. With that, he took out a document that listed the pay scales of his people, which, added to the cost of operating and maintaining the necessary police car, came to a large cost for each trip.

Finally, he pointed out that the Sanity Hearings were conducted in the basement of the county hospital. That required him to send at least two officers, plus a bailiff, out to the hospital to set up the courtroom and provide security for the judge. The whole process, he concluded, was a pain in the butt, although he admitted that his officers liked the transportation duty.

The acting director invited me to dinner, where I met her kids and her physician husband, who was rather preoccupied and remote. Mary Ann regaled me with tales of the three weird psychiatric social workers who dominated the program and were uncontrollable, and the elderly lady who presided over the outpatient clinic with great severity. The clinic was situated in a remodeled beauty shop a block from the hospital.

The night, much of it at any rate, was spent in the hospital record room, pulling the charts of the 125 people who had been held in one of the two medieval locked cells in the basement, bare except for a thin pad on the cement floor, and then committed to the state hospital at Mendocino.

My plan rested upon the generous subsidy the state paid each county for mental health patients, at that time 75% of the cost. In some counties, like the one I was leaving, costs were often vastly overstated, and when that was combined with some simple budgetary and accounting manipulations, a county could reap a tidy profit from its Short-Doyle program. Many counties were doing just that. A few used the money to good advantage and ran good systems.

Humboldt County officials, suspicious of the whole idea of mental health and equally suspicious of the state, were barely tapping the funds they were entitled to. It was my intention to illustrate this to the Board, whose reception of me the next day resembled that of the county exec.

Armed with an easel, a large pad of paper and some marking pens, I told the Board, as they sat behind an elevated counter at one end of the room looking skeptical from the very outset, that I was there to make them a simple, straightforward business proposition.

They were claiming 75% of the cost of running their little outpatient clinic in the beauty shop they had acquired by condemnation in a plan to build a new street where it stood. When the plan fell through, the building became the mental health clinic. The county was spending only about $50 thousand dollars a year on the operation, and got back 75% of that from the State, feeling quite proud and enlightened at their windfall.

At the same time, they were spending more than $135 thousand a year for the brief incarceration of the seriously mentally ill, the judicial processing, and their transportation to the state hospital where the state government paid for their care, and where they tended to remain for years. Since that process could hardly qualify as a "program," they received no reimbursement for it at all.

My proposal, I told them, was a simple, uncomplicated business proposition. If they would simply put $100 thousand of the $135 thousand for the commitments, plus their $12.5 thousand net cost for the clinic into the budget, I would get them $300 thousand additional from Sacramento. They would save, right off the bat, $35 thousand plus $12.5 thousand, and I would build a 400 thousand dollar mental health program for the county that measured up to all the state-imposed standards.

For that four hundred thousand dollars, of which they would only put up a paltry 25%, I would open and operate an old, unused ward in the county hospital, hire 8 or 10 nurses and aides, employ outstanding students from the college, employ several fully qualified psychiatric social workers and a psychologist, all of who would move here with their families from distant places, adding to the county's tax base and buying houses and all their food and clothing right here!

At first the Supervisors, all older men who owned their own businesses, could not believe it. I ran through it again, read to them from the California Mental Health Law and the reimbursement regulations, added a few flourishes (carefully) about making Humboldt County a leader, not just in the state but in the nation as well, and, incidentally, giving good care to unfortunate souls who needed and deserved it.

All I asked for was one year to prove it to them. And four hundred thousand dollars in my budget, only a fourth of it from their county funds.

After some grumbling and whispering, the chairman pounded his gavel and the room fell silent. Fixing his gaze firmly upon me, his arm extended and finger pointing at me, Sam Mitchell, prototypical blustery, superficially jovial but unmistakably serious-minded and intense small-town lead politician, pronounced, "All right, Son. Show us what you can do. We'll be watching carefully. Come back next year this time and tell us what you did."

Somehow, I had not the slightest doubt that were I to fail, I might well leave town riding on a rail, covered with tar and feathers. It seemed like that kind of community.

Pleased and greatly emboldened by my success with the County leaders, I raced back down the coast to Martinez to end my career under the hospital director, my friend George. He seemed genuinely concerned over my departure, for our program in Contra Costa was thriving, but wished me well. He was disappointed, though, that his plan for me, which was to move up the ladder as an officer in the California Conference of Local Mental Health Directors, in five or six years perhaps reaching the exalted presidency of that body and thus able to influence the State Legislature to give us all more money and power, would not come to fruition. Little did George (or I) dream that I would get that presidency little more than two years later.

When the Short-Doyle Act was signed into law, one of its provisions was that all county mental health directors were to be full members in the Conference, which was to meet three or more times a year to exchange professional information (which it never did) and examine both problems and achievements encountered in implementing the local programs, and also submit a detailed report to the Governor and the Legislature, through the State Director of Mental Hygiene. That report would play an important part in construction of the State budget, and could lead to needed modifications and amendments to the basic law.

By that time I had attended four or five meetings of the Conference, each held in a different California city. Early on it had become clear to me that they were mainly bitching sessions about reimbursements and heavy-handed review and alterations of the voluminous annual plan each county program was required to submit to the Department of Mental Hygiene for approval.

A great deal of time was devoted to attacking the policies and attitudes of the State Director, who was seen to be highly partisan and a captive of the two dozen state hospital superintendents. Those "barons" of mental health greatly feared the erosion of their support as local programs grew, took up more of the state budget, and were having no effect on lowering the exploding state hospital patient loads.

Jim Lowry, the State Director of Mental Hygiene, was also required by the law to attend all meetings of the Conference of Local Mental Health Directors to give them a report on the state of the program as a whole, and presumably to hear about problems and concerns. He faithfully did so, but usually the 'press of important business' allowed him only the briefest of visits to the group, where he gave a short, unhelpful speech, answered a question or at most two, and fled back to his Sacramento office.

Jim was in reality a pleasant, decent man carried over from the previous administration. He was, in actual fact, knowledgeable and somewhat partial to the state hospitals, and neither very interested nor very supportive of the new, community-based system. Jim was a fine golfer and a renowned poker player.

In addition to using the meetings to complain, it was clear that the assembled psychiatrists from the 58 county programs, while possibly good at psychiatry, were obviously poor leaders, for the most part, unskilled at administration, resistant to direction whether giving it or receiving it, argumentative and generally ineffectual. George had attended some of these Conference meetings, always coming away quietly enraged, exasperated, and more than ever convinced about the "ping pong balls" he had mentioned in our first meeting.

A meeting of the Conference was scheduled for the week prior to my reporting date in Humboldt County. It was to be in San Diego, where I had never before been and wanted to see, so I arranged to go, as the law required. The freeway, as it winds around the hills behind La Jolla, entering the city from the north, affords, suddenly, as one rounds a long curve, a splendid view of that magnificent city with its beautiful bay, thousands of sailboats and yachts and an occasional aircraft carrier or huge cargo ship sailing by.

It was an overwhelming, entrancing sight. My first thought, on seeing it on that brilliant, sunny day, was that anyone who could live here and didn't, had to be crazy.

This meeting of the Conference was the annual one devoted to the election of officers. I listened to the tedious nomination speeches and even more tedious, meaningless acceptances, and finally could stand it no longer. I had noticed that one of the country program directors stood out in meetings I had attended, because he tended to be more assertive and outspoken than the others. What was more, I liked some of the things he said.

Without giving it much thought, I got to my feet and delivered an impromptu and rather impassioned speech nominating this man. It was well-received, so I went on to criticize our past performance as a group, name some positions I thought we ought to take and exhorted my colleagues to start acting not only like men, but like true, cutting-edge professionals.

The meeting hall, on the top floor of the hotel where most of us stayed, on the waterfront in Mission Bay, fell silent. I though, "Oh, oh! Now I've really done it!"

Then the applause started, and was sustained. My man was elected president and I found myself elected vice-president. We set out to change the whole meaning and course of future meetings, and began for the first time to have papers presented that were worthy of a professional meeting.

We invited Jim Lowry to spend a little more time with us at the next meeting, and actually said nice things about him, like how much we appreciated his support for this wonderful new development in the treatment of psychiatric patients. He responded warmly, and actually stayed through most of the meeting.

Eager to get on with the new project in Eureka, I stopped briefly to see Portia Bell and seek any last-minute advice (she offered none), spent the night in Martinez and headed out early the next morning to revolutionize the treatment of the mentally ill, starting in Eureka, California. On the way I drove through heaviest rain of the year in the northern part of the state, with the waters of the Russian River nearly inundating the road. I hoped that the downpour was a good omen.

Christmas was approaching, so business was quiet in my new clinic. My friend the accountant and budget expert from the state mental hygiene office volunteered to come all the way up to Eureka, far from his home in Sacramento, and spend the days between Christmas and New Years helping me to construct a formal plan and budget for my new enterprise. We worked from early morning until late at night that week, and came up with what we agreed was a fine scheme that met all the requirements of the law and the regulations, and made use of every penny in our $400 thousand budget.

The Community Mental Health Act required that a county program, in order to qualify for the full 75% state reimbursement, had to follow a plan that provided for a number of well-defined services. These included an inpatient hospital service, an outpatient clinical service, a rehabilitation program, a community education program, and a favorite of sociologists, a 'community organization' effort. Exactly how one was supposed to do that last thing, I was not clear, but I discovered no one else was either.

In many smaller counties, psychiatric patients were scattered around on various wards in the county hospital. That seemed to me undesirable and essentially unworkable, so I approached the Humboldt County Hospital Director with an offer he would have difficulty turning down. There was an empty former ward of the hospital in a wing protruding clumsily out the front of the main building but angling off to the side, which had been empty of patients for years, as other local private hospitals grew and were preferred by most people. County hospitals had long been associated with poor people and others avoided them if they could.

The empty ward, no longer generating any revenue for the hospital at all, even in the form of state and federal reimbursements for the indigent, was being used as an unnecessarily spacious linen room. A number of large, stout, freestanding wooden closet-like structures, with shelves and doors, had been built to hold large quantities of sheets, blankets, towels, and other materials. These were scattered about the long, open space of the ward.

My idea, which he could hardly deny, was that this was a terrible waste of patient-care space. I was prepared to do him the immense favor of converting it back to a rich, revenue-producing, bonafide hospital ward, using patients I would admit.

I would pay him for all the utilities used on my ward, and for the food his hospital kitchen would provide, the linens, the medications ordered from his pharmacy, and necessary laboratory services, all at his exact cost as determined by audit. He would not be required to supply any nursing services nor even customary cleaning and custodial services; I would arrange for all that - (in reality, to be done by my patients.)

In the early days of this country, there was considerable blurring of the boundaries between prisons, jails, workhouses, poor houses, and hospitals for the mentally ill. In truth, all such institutions, then as now, held many people whose principal problem was some form of mental disease. Often enough, it was that which led them into behavior that the community found unacceptable, and in violation of some ordinance or law, so they got locked up. From the beginning of the nation, it was customary and expected that all such 'prisoners,' if they were physically able, but sometimes not, do some kind of work, to help offset the cost of their keep.

While prisons generally occupied their charges with hard labor in quarries, or working on roads, many developed furniture and carpentry shops, and prisoners not so engaged usually labored in the kitchens, laundry and maintenance sections of the place. People confined in mental hospitals were more often put to work on the farms that usually surrounded the hospital, growing vegetables and livestock both to feed the residents but sometimes also to sell. Some helped with laundry, housekeeping, and in the kitchens.

Until well into the 20th century, few if any people entered a mental hospital, usually called 'insane asylums,' voluntarily, and they tended to be the most seriously disordered. Any expectation that they would ever get better, and get out, was unlikely, but some attempt was made to foster improvement, if only to make their management easier. Work was believed to have therapeutic value, and was the only 'treatment' most inmates ever got.

By the time I arrived in Eureka, there were some moderately effective drugs available and, for that reason and others, the majority of hospitalized mental patients were expected to improve enough to leave the hospital, except in the huge, increasingly dehumanized, impersonal state institutions. In those places, patients who could, were put to work in the farms and barns that the hospital maintained, as well as on the hospital grounds and in the buildings.

It had always seemed to me that constructive work was an important part of treatment. It was the reason we had departments of occupational therapy, both for those physically unable to do farm or maintenance work, and also to help people prepare to return to the real world where work was required if one was to eat, be adequately housed, and satisfactorily clothed. It just seemed like common sense.

Even though my new inpatient ward in the county hospital was to be an acute treatment ward, for relatively brief hospitalization of people who for a time were unable to cope with everyday life outside its protective walls, work was going to be part of treatment. Not breaking rocks or building furniture, just the ordinary work of living. That meant all the work of cleaning and maintaining the ward, changing the linens and taking them to be washed, receiving the food in bulk and serving it, washing the windows, and maintaining one's personal hygiene was to be done by patients themselves.

In addition, it was made clear to every patient that the ward, which we now had named "Sempervirens" in honor of the majestic coastal redwoods of our area and the hopefulness that the word imparts: "always living," had some simple but inflexible rules, that must be followed. This was, believe it or not, a dramatic departure from the way psychiatric units were operated almost everywhere, but especially in laid-back California.

It had rapidly developed, in recent years, that psychiatric units should be operated as if they had nothing to do with medical practice. Nurses dressed in slacks and casual clothes. Other professionals, but especially social workers and psychologists, were to be informal in every sense, and many came to resemble their patients' long hair, poor hygiene, sloppy clothes and languid behavior so completely that it was hard to tell them apart. Every effort was made to eliminate any hint of authority or structure, in the evident belief that this was frightening or harmful to poor, helpless patients.

Steeped as I was in the beliefs of our forefathers, I utterly rejected this kind of thing for what it was: a perpetuation of adolescent rebellion and rejection of values and standards, along with the principles and practices of responsible adult behavior. It was at the root of many of the deaths and much of the hardship of the POWs

I had studied long before, and was the way of life of the Hippy culture, and of many of the people who found their way to Sempervirens, unable to cope with the world. But not mentally ill.

So, we had rules. The first was that, after the first day, you could not stay in bed. The second was that you must make yourself absolutely clean and wear decent clothes that fit, and shoes. The third was that you must eat all three meals, every day, sitting at a small table with three others, using knives and forks and spoons properly, and exercising good table manners.

Each new patient was met by the physician and nurse in charge as soon as admitted, unless it happened during the night; then first thing the next morning. In addition to the simple rules, a brief indoctrination talk was delivered. The gist of it was that the new arrival, who was incredibly lucky to have come to this place, could expect to spend five days here. If he or she (Dear Reader, please note: I hate that "he or she," "he/she," "his/her" idiocy that has crept into our language for political or other rectitude, and henceforth I shall avoid it. Unless it is impossible for you to understand that of course I mean "he" if it happens to be male and "she" if female, please allow me to return to the simple use of the pronoun "he," as has been done for generations by learned and wholly acceptable writers of all kinds, secure in the knowledge that of course I am using it in a gender-nonspecific way. If, in any instance in which you are unable to determine whether I am talking solely about a man or solely about a woman, and it seems important and troubling to you, please write me, citing the page and line, and I shall be happy to explain.)

To continue. If he wanted to go to bed this first day, snuggle down and pull the covers over his head (like in the womb?), that was perfectly okay. Today. But only today. Tomorrow he'd have to get up with everybody else, get all cleaned up and shave (if male), sit down and eat breakfast with everybody else, and be there at the morning 'all hands, no exceptions' meeting where he could talk or not - up to him.

He should think of his visit here as being at least as important as going out to shop, going to church, visiting friends or any other event for which one would dress up. If he did not have nice enough clothes for such an event, we would get them for him.

Finally, we would say, as soon as you start feeling better - at most in a day or two - we would expect you to help us welcome new arrivals, and help them to feel at home. Also, at that point, see if there aren't others here, worse off than you, who you could possibly help to feel better, by talking to them, going for a walk, or whatever you felt like. Moreover, you must start planning now for what you are going to do, not more than 5 days from now, when you leave here. We will help you with all of this.

Oh, yes - one more thing. The nurses (the ladies in the white uniforms,) will tell you early tomorrow what we will need your help with: sweeping up, doing the windows, fetching the linens, things like that.

And welcome to Sempervirens. It's going to change your life.

Within days of my arrival, and even before we had arranged the linen lockers and beds so that each patient would have a modicum of privacy but not be shut up in a room, there appeared on the ward a lady who was to be the 'angel' of the mental health service. Gladys Strope, called "Gladdy" by one and all, walked on the ward and announced that she represented the local Mental Health Association, and was ready to do anything we wanted to get things going.

Mental health volunteers are a mixed blessing, and my initial reception of this remarkable lady was probably just a bit tentative, but if so, she ignored that and expressed delight and enthusiasm that we would at last have a "real" mental health program in Humboldt County. We soon discovered that she was the socially prominent wife of the publisher of the newspaper, a fine fellow named Charlie, who helped immeasurably in our efforts by giving space in his paper to announcements and stories about our new program.

The problem with volunteers in mental health, bless their hearts, is that a fair number of them are former or borderline emotionally disturbed people whose impulses to 'help,' while utterly sincere, have more to do with their own problems than with actually helping others. Also, they tend to be less than reliable in their attendance, attention to assigned tasks, and adherence to proper standards of confidentiality, so they frequently require a great deal of training and supervision. One hears things on a psychiatric service that make for simply wonderful tales to tell friends, and gossip about neighbors, especially in a small community, and that can not be permitted.

Gladdy had none of the less desirable characteristics of some volunteers. She had for many years been involved in the state Mental Health Association and was well informed and up to date on the California laws and recent developments in the field. She was attractive, energetic, and best of all possessed with an unflinching optimism and positive outlook. At the same time she was never overly enthusiastic, which can be wearing. She came daily to the ward to help out with the work of setting it up, always willing to take on even the most menial or difficult tasks.

My new head nurse, only 24 years old, showed from the outset a truly remarkable talent for selecting her subordinates and supervising their work. She agreed intuitively with my old-fashioned ideas, like requiring our nurses to wear uniforms and insisting that our patients not look like derelicts. She and Gladdy made an excellent management team, and Sempervirens rapidly took shape as a 'taut ship.' Thanks to frequent items in Charlie's paper, and Gladdy's unceasing efforts, we soon had all the volunteers we could use, and most of the professional staff.

Rather than rely on traditional aides and orderlies, and in order to foster the idea that ours was truly a 'community' activity, we decided to employ carefully selected students from the nearby college, unfettered by preconceptions and misconceptions about mental patients, and train these young people ourselves. This necessitated some sticky work with the County administrator and personnel department, whose immediate reaction was that these kids couldn't meet civil service requirements to be county government employees, which was of course quite true.

We determined to leap over this typical bureaucratic obstacle, never a small task, and did so, finally, by inventing a new civil service category, title, and job description, with a carefully crafted set of required qualifications. To our complete surprise, neither the personnel people nor the county counsel could find any law or regulation preventing this, and the Board of Supervisors reluctantly agreed, so we were in business.

For a student to be employed, he had to be an upper-division (3rd or 4th year, or beyond) full-time student whose major course of study was in a field allied with or related to our mental health program, in good standing and with above-average grades. A faculty member's recommendation was required. The student had to be able to work a full 20 hours each week on a schedule we would tailor to avoid interference with his classes.

We called this new Civil Service classification "Student Professional Worker." We were careful at first to employ people who were nursing students, as well as psychology and social work majors, but after a time we found our definition of "allied" and "related" to be quite elastic, and were able to take on nearly anyone we believed was genuinely interested and motivated.

Contrary to all 'normal' but in reality idiotic, unrealistic civil service prohibitions attached to hiring procedures, like asking about the candidate's family, background, domicile, health, drug and alcohol use, arrest record, ability to read and write, or type, or giving any kind of test except for standardized civil service examinations, we did all of that. We were careful not to make any of our questions or tests, including intelligence and psychological tests frequently used on patients, a "condition" of employment. Instead, we told our applicant students that this was a very special kind of job dealing with unusual kinds of people. The work required special abilities and attitudes on the part of staff, and not everyone could be expected to be sufficiently emotionally mature, stable, and at the same time tolerant and sensitive enough to find the work agreeable.

We had tests that could help us pick the very best people; would they like to take them? In the process, they would learn much about themselves and whether they would fit comfortably into this very special environment. Naturally enough, they each readily agreed, and when accepted, felt that they had joined a truly select, special group of people, which in fact they had. A few were shown by the testing and interviewing to be unsuitable as workers on Sempervirens, and we were able to show them why and help them find something else to do.

Our experience with our Student Professional Workers, over the next few years, was uniformly good. We tailored their work schedules to fit with their classes, and we demanded absolute reliability as to showing up for work, as scheduled and on time, as well as their dress and grooming, (clean fingernails, no gum-chewing, no blue jeans, sweatshirts or ratty shoes) respectful behavior toward patients and other staff, and willingness to follow instruction.

It worked amazingly well. The U.C. Berkeley rebellion against all authority and structure, with its truly obscene language, had not yet arrived in Humboldt County. Our students made enough money at this job to keep them comfortably, if not lavishly. They seemed to enjoy their work and got quite good at it, and finished college respectably. No fewer that six of the students who worked with us between 1966 and 1971 went on to become, themselves, directors of county mental health programs throughout the state in later years.

My message to my fellow citizens of the county was simple. It was that disorders of the mind, like those of the body, were simply illnesses that could be understood and, for the most part, successfully treated. They were not significant causes of violence and crime, and nothing to be ashamed of, for no one was immune, and good character was no guarantee that one could escape such an illness. Sempervirens was designed to bring together the miraculous new drugs that were now available, the understanding and support of the community, and an abandonment of the old ways of locking people away, often for life, and treating them like criminals, which most of them assuredly were not.

Sempervirens had one room equipped with a door. While it could be locked, it could easily have been broken, for it bore a large window in the upper half of the door. There were no bars or locks on the windows, no way to lock the entrance to the ward or the exit from the sunporch. There was a traditional glassed-in nurses' station and small attached medication closet in the center of the ward, and a utility room for mops and buckets in the entry hall, but all of it was unlocked.

When we positioned the large linen cabinets so as to partially screen off the beds from one another, we left a large open space in the center of the ward from the entrance to the nurses' station. In the face of determined and even outraged resistance, we carpeted the entire ward in bright red indoor-outdoor carpeting, and announced that anyone arriving here could expect true "red carpet" treatment.

Thus equipped, we instituted our treatment program. Every morning, as soon as breakfast was over, every patient and staff member was assembled in the open central space for a meeting. This was not an unusual practice on psychiatry wards, where such "community" meetings were often held to make announcements and assign cleaning tasks, and similar things. Our meetings were to be totally different.

To start, our meetings were truly open to the public. While we didn't advertise for curious onlookers who happened to be walking by to just drop in, we did encourage both family members and any patient's friend that the patient wanted, to sit in on the meeting. And talk, if they wanted.

Public officials, including judges, elected officials, attorneys, any medical people, businesspeople, or any adult citizen with a sincere, serious interest in the program or anyone in it, was welcome to join the group as long as they understood and absolutely followed the rules.

The rules were simple. Anyone could talk about anything that seemed important, whether in one's life, or why he was admitted, or what was going on in the unit. No matter what the subject, everyone present must listen respectfully, and anyone who had some comment that might be constructive or helpful, was free to offer it. Participants were free to offer judgments of what was said, but not in a condemning or argumentative way.

Finally, everyone was told, every day, as we started the meeting, there is one absolute, invariable and inviolable rule. It was this. No one, patient or staff or friend or visitor, could ever, under any circumstances, reveal to anyone anything they heard anyone say in this meeting. To do so would be to commit a crime, forbidden by both state and federal law regarding the confidentiality of patient information. If anyone did that, and we would soon and surely find out, I would personally see to it that they were arrested and prosecuted.

Anyone who couldn't agree to abide by this was free to leave, and must do so immediately.

In five years of daily meetings, no one ever broke that rule.

The morning meetings on Sempervirens took on a life of their own, and became an important institution in that little city on California's north coast. The attendees included a steady stream - a trickle at first, but rapidly growing - not only of the families of our patients, and their friends, but of important members of the community and, after a while, visiting psychiatrists and mental health workers from throughout the state's mental health programs and universities.

Two things were most striking about the morning meetings: their content and the role they played, for many people, in their long-term recovery and re-integration into the community. It was truly astounding to listen to the incredible events that people were able to discuss with astonishing openness in the presence of thirty or forty other people, many of them strangers, once the speaker felt safe. It was equally surprising to observe the thoughtful response - by no means necessarily approving or sympathetic - that even some of the most lurid and horrifying revelations brought forth from the group.

The other notable thing was the frequency with which a substantial number of patients continued to attend the meetings for weeks or months after their treatment was ostensibly completed. In addition, some patients continued to show up for a day or two sometimes many months later.

You will recall that every patient was seen, on admission, by the doctor (me, since we had no other) and the head nurse, and that we told them they would only be on the ward five days. We explained, saying, "After all, you can't live here, you know!" but added that, following their discharge, we wanted them back for morning meetings every day for the first week or so. After that, they would be coming three times a week, then twice, then once and after that, whenever they felt the need.

Just as we told our new arrivals that we'd get them decent clothes if they didn't have any, we also said we'd find them a place to live if need be. To be able to do that, we had to seek out and persuade people who customarily rented out rooms to accept our newly-released patients, which they were often reluctant to do, initially. We promised that their rent would definitely always be paid, and on time, and that these people would be spending all or part of every day back at Sempervirens, for as long as was necessary. We would supervise their medication, and would instantly send out one of the staff if any problems arose.

The money for all these things was available through both state and county programs for the poor, and we had been fortunate to attract to our staff some highly skilled social workers who could make use of those systems. In addition, Gladdy and her crew of volunteers helped with this.

Only rarely was a person admitted who was so agitated or disturbed that it was necessary to put him in the one 'private' glass-doored room. Most often, this was someone in the throes of 'DTs'- delirium tremens, the result of severe, long-term alcoholism. Following the disappearance of general paresis, or central nervous system syphilis, from the medical scene, the poor souls with DTs tended to be the most colorful. Their physical discomfort, occasional convulsions, agitation and horrifying hallucinations of dead bodies, monsters, insects or snakes crawling over their bodies, and sometimes terrible self-mutilation, like plucking out an eyeball, required constant attention and segregation from less seriously disturbed patients.

For these people, and occasionally someone in an acutely excited state due to manic-depression or panic, we used the room, but always assigned one of the staff to be at the bedside constantly, giving medication and doing whatever was possible to calm the patient. The lights were never turned off, for such people suffer most acutely in the dark.

It was customary in most hospitals to administer large doses of strong sedatives and hypnotics to patients in DTs, along with huge doses of vitamins and intravenous fluids. Like so many traditional practices in medicine, this routine was made to seem valid not because it worked, but because it is what 'everybody' had always done.

The fact is, the patient in DTs is already over-supplied with a profoundly sedating hypnotic drug, alcohol, and doesn't need any more; also, it could kill him to sedate him too heavily. Secondly, while chronic alcoholics have notoriously poor diets and are probably vitamin-deficient, it has never been scientifically proven that one or several big shots of Vitamin B does any good whatever, for anything. Finally, autopsies of people who die in DTs invariably reveal a hugely swollen brain that literally pops from the skull when the top is sawed off, so the idea of giving them intravenous fluids because the patient's mouth is dry (from heavy, open mouthed breathing!) is dumb, and can be fatal.

Eureka had its share of profoundly sick chronic alcoholics who developed delirium tremens with some regularity. The police would bring them to Sempervirens, and at first we treated them conventionally, and with a conventional lack of success; some stayed wildly crazy for days, and were worse at night. Our whole staff talked it over, and came up with a new idea.

When someone with this serious, life-threatening crisis in the course of a long, unsuccessful devotion to alcohol was brought in to us, usually in handcuffs and sometimes in a strong canvas camisole, the standard "straight jacket," we untied him and took him into our private room with the glass door. One or two of our larger and stronger male student professional workers were posted at bedside, the door was ajar, and the lights bright.

While our young men would talk comfortably to the agitated newcomer, we would give him a fair but not huge injection of one of our then newer drugs, Valium, that was gaining enormous popularity because it had a strong calming effect without the 'knock-out' action of traditional sedatives. No vitamins, no intravenous fluids to puff up the brain.

To offset the inevitable dry mouth and lips, we offered the victim all he could drink of a not unpleasant concoction called Pedialyte. This is a mixture of water and electrolytes, the salts needed by the body to maintain a proper balance of fluid, developed for the treatment of infant diarrhea.

The results of this miracle of modern medicine were dramatic. Patients we had previously admitted with episodes lasting several days and terrible nights under conventional treatment, were over this episode in twelve hours or less, thanks to infant diarrhea medicine and usually only a couple of shots of Valium.

What with this being such a simple, obvious treatment for what the medical profession largely still views as an unpleasant and not very respectable malady among despicable drunken bums, we decided that no prestigious medical journal would be interested in publishing a learned article about it, so we didn't even try. We just kept using our simple little formula of Valium, electrolyte solution and sympathetic attendants, and achieving therapeutic success.

Proof of this came when some of our more 'experienced' severe chronic alcoholics, veterans of many an episode of DTs, began showing up at Sempervirens at the first sign of a new attack, long before it actually took hold, and asked humbly for "the treatment." Some, who hadn't and wouldn't go to an Alcoholics Anonymous meeting, began showing up for our morning group, and even dared to give graphic, tragic descriptions of their sad, downhill course as it took them into a very real kind of insanity.

Most of the people who came to Sempervirens were not, strictly speaking, mentally ill. That is, they were in good contact with reality, were oriented as to time, place and person, knew right from wrong, saw no visions and heard no strange, disturbing voices, and had no unshakeable delusional beliefs. Rather than mental diseases like schizophrenia, manic-depressive disorder, severe paranoia or profound, life-threatening, suicidal depression, they were suffering from emotional disorders that were seriously disrupting their lives.

Many or most such disorders now bear psychiatric labels - diagnoses - and follow more or less predictable patterns of development and progression. Most involve feelings: anger, fear, hatred, resentment, disappointment, bitterness, unhappiness, envy, jealousy and rage, and other feelings that are in themselves 'normal,' and experienced at some time in some degree by all ordinary people. They come - or are sent - for treatment because of the degree or the duration, or both, of such feelings, which have not diminished with the ordinary measures one takes to handle and control them.

It is my belief, after fifty years in psychiatry, but beginning a long time ago, that a great many - perhaps the majority - of these emotional disorders have no psychiatric legitimacy, which is to say they do not constitute illnesses as we generally think of illness, regardless of the cleverness of those who dissect them and label them and qualify them for reimbursed intervention. There is no doubt that they can be painful and deserve or even require some outside intervention for their relief. Just like a headache. Usually that is not an illness either, in any useful sense, and fortunately we have aspirin and ibuprofen and Tylenol.

But beginning at just about the time I was reluctantly beginning in psychiatry, thanks not only to Sigmund Freud but to a whole host of others as well we began to understand something about how emotions develop and are influenced by life's events and interactions with others. The profound, lasting characterologic influence of parents, but especially mothers, and especially in the very first years of life, became increasingly clear. In the attempt to understand the development of unsocial, asocial, and antisocial behavior and other dysfunctional ways of adapting to the world around us, it was perhaps unavoidable that the search for causes became an exercise in assigning blame. It was only a short step to exonerating oneself, and subscribing to a doctrine of victimization, victimhood.

Victims, of course, deserve help; it is an entitlement of victimhood. If one is to maintain that privileged status, one has to become good at blaming, which means assigning responsibility outside of oneself. Then, no matter what, help will come. All will be well.

What we saw, mostly, in Sempervirens, was a parade of victims. Some truly had sad, abusive, deprived childhoods. Some had lost their dairy farms in the floods 9 years ago. Some had had trouble in college, and, their senses dulled by marijuana, had a tough time drifting up Highway 101 from the campus at Berkeley to the foggy bay of Humboldt. Some had married the wrong person, or shouldn't have left high school when they did.

None of them had anything whatever to do with their current unhappy state.

Don't misunderstand my meaning. Some of these people were truly suffering, and needed help. Most were utterly sincere in their belief that they hadn't caused their problems, and couldn't be expected to solve them.

Some truly psychotic people did occasionally show up on Sempervirens. They were started on one or more of the new medicines, and included in all the activities on the ward. We were generally successful in reducing their most troubling symptoms, and after discharge we kept them coming to the ward for morning meetings and often to spend the whole day.

It was my practice to train both the students and the staff continuously, and each newly admitted patient, along with each morning meeting, brought rich, abundant material for that purpose. New patients were never forced or even strongly urged to relate the problems and events that had resulted in admission at their first meeting in the big group, but most were talking freely about these things by the second meeting, at the latest.

With very rare exceptions, one of the students or one of the nurses sat in with me during my initial intake interviews with new patients. We began as we did in the morning group: first a recitation of the ward rules and then a stern insistence that absolute confidentiality was essential if we were to be able to help. If the new arrival couldn't talk freely or objected to the presence of another person, that person left. That almost never happened.

Whoever was to be my companion in one of those most important of all interviews was briefed first. The student or nurse was there strictly to learn, not to help conduct the interview. My 'silent partner' was encouraged to take notes, so we could discuss what went on, later. At that post-interview consultation, we would talk about what kind of a body-language- and facial-expression presentation was made by the patient, how he talked, how I began and pursued the questioning, how the patient reacted to various kinds of questions, and what his emotional status seemed to be.

Then we talked about what the patient seemed to be saying about what brought him in - we sometimes heard it differently - and what each of us thought was the actual, if unstated, reason. We finished with a short discussion of how best to manage this new patient, what to watch for, and what he should be encouraged to do when he was discharged.

These were good experiences, both for me and for whoever was with me that day. We both learned, both connected with that particular patient, at least a little, and the student learned something of interviewing techniques, analysis of what happened in intimate interactions, got a clearer idea of what we were trying to do to help people, and learned a good deal about himself in the process.

Never, in the five years of our work in Sempervirens, did we find it necessary to give or even consider giving electroshock therapy, even though I believed in it then as I do now. For a certain small number of patients, mostly those with deep, incapacitating suicidal depressions that have not responded to any of the several anti-depressant medications that are usually effective, administration of electroconvulsive therapy can be dramatic and life-saving. We simply did not get a patient who needed that treatment.

One day, early in the first year there, the secretary announced that two ladies from Crescent City were there to see me. They were not patients. One of them was to be, like Gladdy, a special angel assigned without doubt by a Higher Power to see to it that our grand, open, truly community-based brand of psychiatry succeeded, if she determined I was worthy of such help.

Her name was Helene Miller, R.N. Her presence was powerful, and her appearance striking. She wore a hat, or so I seem to remember, a tasteful costume, rather a large amount of jewelry on hands, wrists, earlobes and neck, and was carefully coiffed and made up. Her air was nothing short of regal. When we shook hands, I got the impression that I had just now been specifically authorized to do so, but only briefly.

She seated and arranged herself with some deliberation and care, and only then fixed her gaze firmly on my eyes. "So," she said, "You're the new mental health director, are you?" I murmured my assent, and she proceeded to tell me why she was here. She never quite said so, but it was clear she was here to decide if I would be acceptable to her in my new role.

The small northernmost California county of Del Norte lay on the border of Humboldt County, also on the Pacific coast, and extended to the southern boundary of Oregon. Its population was officially 15,000 souls, but the count admittedly failed to include a large number of Indians who resisted being tallied, and kept mostly to themselves. There may have been as many as 1500 or 2000 such additional citizens.

Helene was the senior - and in fact the only - health professional employed by the County in anything like a management position. There was no Health Officer, and no Mental Health Director. Helene commanded the county's only government-supported health facility, a small convalescent hospital near the outskirts of Del Norte's only real town, Crescent City.

From her perch at the 30+ bed convalescent hospital Helene functioned as the de facto health authority in the county. She did annual battle with the Board of Supervisors for funds to run her hospital as well as a bit of mental health service supplied in a contract with Humboldt County, and a variety of medical interventions needed to serve the small but steady stream of hippies and flower children wending their stuporous, laid-back way farther north to Oregon and beyond, having found slim pickings along Hwy 101 as it wended its way up the North Coast.

Crescent City boasted a magnificently situated community hospital on a cliff overlooking the exquisitely beautiful crescentic bay around which the little city grew. There were perhaps ten physicians in town - not many for the population to be served - and while some of them had some additional training in one of the major specialties: surgery, internal medicine, and obstetrics and gynecology, most or all of them conducted a busy general practice. It was not uncommon for any of them to see and treat twenty or thirty patients every day. They were happy - and lucky - to have Helene and her little county 'hospital' around to take care of the Indians, migrants and indigents who showed up needing help, which she did admirably.

Helene was in my office that day to renegotiate the arrangement between the two counties to assure at least a little mental health care in Del Norte, to be supplied by Humboldt. Meaning, in effect, by me. If, and only if, I stood up to her scrutiny and was found acceptable, that was. If I were not, she could, in a pinch, arrange for a psychiatrist from Mendocino State Hospital 200 miles or more to the south, to come by perhaps once a month. She had tried that for a time and found it less than ideal.

Evidently I passed muster during that interview, not appearing to be as 'kooky' as most psychiatrists, she later told me. At that moment I donned a second director's hat, this time for the County of Del Norte. We agreed that I would drive the 85 miles to Crescent City once a week, bringing my head nurse as an assistant, and endow the little county with the special blessings of our new, revolutionary approach to psychiatry. Humboldt County would be reimbursed, modestly, for this.

Thus began one of the most beautiful and meaningful relationships of my life. Over the years my admiration and love for this beautiful, remarkable woman grew steadily, as it does today. As long as thirty years ago, my youngest son, in his innocent recognition of the intense bond that grew between us said, one day, "Daddy, if it wasn't for Heidi, would you marry Helene?"

Her husband, Bun, became equally close and dear to us. He was the only man I had known, before or since, who qualified in my heart and mind as "best friend." We did not spend a lot of time together, were not drinking buddies or fellow sportsmen, although we fished a bit in the bay, hauled in some crabs, and collected a mess of mealy trout (water was too warm that summer) on a lake in Oregon.

Helene and Bun had met and married, I believe, when she was a nurse doing obstetrical work of exceptional, recognized excellence in the San Francisco area. Despite Heidi's intensely inquisitive nature, arising out of her training in psychiatric nursing and association with me as I pursued the social and developmental history of my patients, we never 'took a history' of these two terribly superior, quietly but totally independent-thinking individualists tucked away in a tiny, remote town in the far north of America's largest and richest state. No history was needed; we connected immediately and permanently, understanding and loving one another without reservation.

Bun had done a variety of jobs, many of them more modest, on the surface perhaps, than Helene's, but that mattered not at all to either of them. They loved camping and the outdoors, and early on they moved to Del Norte. For some time Bun fished commercially from his little wooden fishing boat with its one cylinder diesel engine, sailing a hundred miles or more out into the vast Pacific in pursuit of his catch. He went out there alone, quietly and without fanfare exercising a degree of courage incomprehensible to ordinary men. He never dramatized or even commented on his daring in this or any other pursuit, obviously a man satisfied with his lot, suffering from no unrealized goals or ambitions, or unrealized career ambitions.

These qualities were extraordinary in a man of his intelligence and energy, who had a multitude of skills, an active, inquiring mind, a keen grasp of the world nearby and far away alike, and what was going on in it. He was one of those people who could figure out a way to fix anything, from his Lincoln automobile to one of the watches he dearly loved and kept buying.

When I left Northern California and these dear friends for Sacramento, to fix up state government, or at least the part of it that was spending hundreds of millions a year on mental health (Ronald Reagan was handling all the rest, and quite nicely!) Bun gave me a ship's clock from his boat. It was a little dented but ran perfectly and struck the proper number of ship's bells precisely and without fail.

We took and mounted the clock everywhere we lived, moving from Sacramento to San Diego, then to Long Beach and finally to Germany. There, one day, it stopped completely; it would neither chime nor run at all. A cable from Helene the next day announced that her beloved Bun had died the same day the clock stopped. I did not make this up.

We tried off and on for years to get the clock fixed, but no one seemed able to do it. Finally, after we retired for good in this beautiful country just north of where Helene still lives, an ancient clock-maker, indignant at my idea that maybe we could substitute an electronic works for the old mechanical one, said he could fix it, and he did. It as yet doesn't quite keep up with things, just as I don't, and loses a couple of minutes a day, but it still announces the mariners' bells faithfully, every 30 minutes. Eight bells just sounded.

Helene ran her little hospital, despite its age and decrepitude, admirably. Some of her patients were ancient Indians, uncertain of their exact, very advanced age but still able to deliver some of the old chants and drum beats of their distant youth. Others were simply old, chronically ill long-time residents of the North Country, both men and women whose early days in the area were frontier experiences. Every one was given attention and care far superior to the most fancy such places in our big cities…and lived out their lives in relative comfort and contentment in Helene's hands.

My youngest daughter, now a late-30s mother of two, worked for a summer as a ten-year-old candy-striper in Helene's hospital. She recalls it as a beautiful, enriching experience to this day, and came away from it with the absolute determination to find a life's work that had meaning and value for others, which she has fortunately succeeded in doing.

Our weekly trip to Crescent City was a welcome break in an intense routine on Sempervirens that commonly involved twelve-hour workdays, often including Saturdays. The road north wove through glorious forests of giant redwoods and alongside a series of coastal lagoons, and was interrupted mid-way by the tiny old town of Orick. A one-street village resting in a small river-delta valley opening from the mountains along the coast, it had been the scene of an Indian massacre of settlers only 70 years before we first stopped there for breakfast.

The owner-operator of the village's only cafe, a small, drab storefront with a long counter and a half-dozen oilcloth bedecked tables, was without doubt the finest, fastest, most expert short-order cook I have ever encountered. A shy man, he grew used to our weekly visits, early in the morning, and we became friendly. He was one of those surprising people of multiple talents and unsuspected achievements. Not only did he own the only restaurant, but the only motel as well, and worked constantly except for his remarkable big game hunting trips in Alaska and other exotic climes, and deep-sea fishing trips. He built a lovely home on the mountainside, avoided politics, and seemed an altogether satisfied man.

Helene set up a little office for me to use in her hospital, scheduled appointments with people she believed needed them, and regularly hit up the pharmaceutical company representatives who passed through for large quantities of psychotropic drug samples for our poor clientele. She was so good at this that eventually I had a surprisingly well-stocked pharmacy to dispense from, all at no cost.

She always welcomed us with enthusiasm and had lunch for us in the hospital dining room. Occasionally I would see and prescribe for one of her resident patients, or her staff, and then see the mental health cases, which were generally few in number. It was a low-key, low-pressure kind of arrangement, from which everyone benefited.

Often there was time enough to drop by Helene and Bun's house, which was, though small, a splendid showcase of remarkable and often exceedingly valuable art objects, many of them products of the most skilled Indian artisans and craftsmen. Helene had long since achieved distinction as a collector and seller of Indian and other artifacts, and herself became skilled at carving attractive, oriental-looking faces and heads on wooden knots she collected on the forest floor. For a time, she had a shop in the dock area, where tourists often stopped, and Bun set up a fishermen's supply shop nearby, and both shops did well enough but ultimately weren't worth the effort.

It is hard to capture and describe the essence of what made these two people so special, and so dear to my heart. They raised two fine sons, one of them the present mental health director in the vastly expanded Del Norte program and the other a teacher of literature in the high school in Eureka who has been a principal motivator in my writing. Both have long been good friends.

Time spent with Bun and Helene, never with any special preparation or special event, was always stimulating and rewarding. Talk roamed all over the place from politics, which we mostly agreed on, to medical practice, wood-carving, their dogs - poodles like our own, totally spoiled and true kindred spirits - fishing, the damned fools in Sacramento - things just came up and were thoroughly worked over. Both Heidi and Helen are women of strong character, strong opinions freely offered, impatient with incompetence or falseness or artifice, and Bun and I often sat back and let them have at it. Ultimately he or I would offer some typically (being male) wiser and more calm summation of the subject at hand, and off we'd go to another.

Both of these people had an enormous number of friends and acquaintances, not all of whom they liked, and some of whom were not really faithful friends, but they approached and dealt with everyone in a consistently straightforward, respectful way. Helene was particularly sensitive and caring toward her elderly patients, but at the same time businesslike and even a little bossy, like Heidi and all other good supervising nurses. Bun and I loved and admired both of them; they are to this day rare spirits who enriched our old masculine lives.

Bun suffered from severe coronary artery disease, and endured countless episodes of intense pain from angina pectoris. At length it became clear that he must try the newly-developed coronary artery bypass surgery, if there was to be any hope for relief and survival. He asked my opinion about having the operation, and honored me thereby, but in handing me that question he posed for me a serious dilemma. While I knew something about his heart disease and was well aware that it was worsening and at times nearly unbearable, I knew little about bypass surgery.

I begged for time to consider before answering, and undertook a crash course in cardiac surgery, life support during the operation, interruption of normal heart action while the patient is hooked up to a special mechanical pump, and the prognosis for survival, both short and long term. It was just fair.

Fortunately, Bun's local physician in Crescent City was able to arrange a consultation for him in San Francisco with an eminent cardiac surgeon at U.C. Presbyterian Hospital, one of the city's finest and the one that had performed the largest number of bypass operations with minimal mortality. The opinion there was that he could and should consider the operation, and that he was a reasonably good risk.

After listening to the San Francisco specialists, and searching my own still-healthy heart to find the right course to pursue, I concluded that my friend, if he balanced the surgical risk against the likelihood of a shortened life of diminished activity, increasing pain, and a certain, unhappy outcome, should go ahead and do it. After a long talk, he agreed.

The hospital had one of the most elaborate surgical set-ups for cardiac surgery that existed anywhere, and an excellent staff of surgeons and surgical nurses. At Bun's request, the chief surgeon invited me to don mask and gown and stand in during the operation, so I took a position next to the anesthesiologist at Bun's head where I could talk to him until he lost consciousness, and reassure myself as to his condition by touching his gleaming bald pate.

The heart-lung machine was readied to take over the pumping and oxygenation of the patient's blood. The surgeons and nurses gathered around the table, and the moment of nearly unbearable tension and anticipation that surrounds the surgical opening of a living human being was at hand, awaiting the signal of the anesthesiologist that it was time to begin.

In spite of having performed a great deal of surgery myself, opening no fewer than 35 abdomens and several chests during my internship, and far more than that during two years of war in a surgical hospital tent in Korea, and attending and even assisting in the births of each of my children, nothing in my previous experience matched or prepared me for this.

Here, inches from me, a man was making a long, deep incision down my dearest friend's chest, cutting through skin and muscle and cartilage and with his assistants pulling apart the rib cage on both sides to expose the man's beating heart - the core of his physical being. A few feet farther down, others were slicing open his thigh to expose a vein that would be grafted into the wall of the heart itself to give it more blood than his restricted coronary vessels could supply.

With all now in readiness, sterile ice was packed around the heart to slow and eventually stop it, and the major vessels leading in and out of it were clamped off from the heart and connected to the elaborate machine that would keep circulation and life itself going. That done, the delicate task of cutting into the wall of the heart itself began.

There followed a long, tedious period of freeing up the tiny coronary arteries embedded in the heart muscle, and after removing the most seriously restricted sections of them, stitching in segments of healthy vein removed from the leg, to fill in the gaps. The needles and sutures are so fine as to be nearly invisible at any distance. Imagine, if you can, sewing together pieces of tiny garden hose, the size of the lead in a pencil, creating fluid-tight end-to-end connections while preserving the opening inside so it can carry a steady stream of liquid, under pressure! That's what I stood there watching, for all of five hours. Periodically I pressed on Bun's scalp to observe the return of a healthy pink color when I let up, and he seemed to be doing just fine.

At last it was over. The stilled heart was once again allowed to receive and discharge blood, and began once more to beat. The bony rib cage and cut sternum were put back together and held with surgical wire. The great machine, no longer necessary to support life, was turned off, along with the anesthesia machine, and the big guy started to breathe again on his own.

As I watched this friend, who had just been part of a genuine medical and surgical miracle, struggle back up into consciousness, my relief was boundless, and I was struck with a huge sense of humility and awe at what I had observed, certain I could never do anything so stupendous.

Bun recovered well, and within a year was able to re-enter the hospital for a much less dangerous but still major elective operation to replace a hip joint. He largely resumed his normal activities, and went on with life quite matter-of-factly. The cardiac bypass gave him some years of pain-free survival, although the little sharp ends of the wire sutures that stuck out of the skin over his sternum were annoying.

Meanwhile, back at Sempervirens, patients came in steadily for treatment, and we continued to refine our effort to make this truly a community effort that would represent the next major step in caring for mentally and emotionally ill people.

At the end of the first year, true to my promise to the Supervisors to report back, I prepared to describe our progress to them. In place of the average of 125 patients committed every year to the state hospital, we had committed only 3, all of them serious recidivistic criminal offenders who had to go to a facility with sufficient security to protect the public. We did not send these people off to Mendocino State Hospital to help them escape the legal consequences of their crimes, but because they needed intensive treatment, for the present.

None of the three was a "not guilty by reason of insanity" kind of situation. Since psychiatry and the law so often intersect, my half-century in psychiatric medicine exposed me with some frequency to cases of intense interest to both professions. On reflection, I find that I have never urged a jury to find a defendant not guilty because of mental disease. Some of the people I have examined, many times as an independent 'friend of the court' not called by either the prosecutor or the defense, have had serious mental disorders. Sometimes, but very rarely in my experience, the criminal act charged was a direct reflection of the disease. This happens far less often than it is claimed.

Problems arise because while "insanity" is something 'everybody knows,' it is not that easy to define, precisely, particularly in a court. Early in my medical career I was taught, emphatically, that it is not the business of an expert witness to determine or even help determine whether a defendant is guilty or innocent. The expert is called only, in the final analysis, to give an opinion based on the McNaughton Rule - the law's definition of mental adequacy to take responsibility for one's actions.

Most American courts throughout this passing century have tried to use the rule to act faithfully upon the generally accepted belief that an individual should not be punished if he can't help or didn't understand something that he has done. So the rule says that a person is responsible, and therefore punishable 'if he is so far free from mental disease or defect as to be able to distinguish right from wrong, and adhere to the right.' He must also understand the 'nature of the act,' and not be subject to an 'irresistible impulse.'

This can prove to be impossibly difficult to establish to the satisfaction of a judge or a jury, particularly when more than one 'expert witness' testifies and disagrees with the opinion of another. Which to believe?

The second emphasized lesson that I learned early was that committing acts that the man on the street might call "crazy" did not prove someone was legally insane. People regularly commit the most horrifying and bizarre kinds of acts, like eating parts of a murdered victim, without being mentally ill, using psychiatric criteria, or insane, using legal criteria. This can be really hard for a jury to understand.

Over these many years, I have heard and read of cases of paranoid schizophrenia in which the psychotic individual with serious delusions of persecution believes that a stranger approaching him is the Devil, and blows his head off with a shotgun. Never have I examined such a person. I have, however, seen paranoid schizophrenic persons who were seclusive, suspicious, and hostile to strangers and stayed in seclusion most of the time, and then one day stepped out on the front porch and killed neighbor kids playing in the yard, also with a shotgun. Crazy? Sure sounds like it; you'd have to be crazy to do something like that, wouldn't you?

The correct answer to that is, "Not necessarily." The killer of kids certainly had a severe mental disease. Yet he knew right from wrong, and for many years, during his illness, was able to adhere to the right. He was well aware that it was wrong to kill people. He did not have 'irresistible impulses.' Yet he was found not guilty by reason of insanity by a jury. He was sent to a mental hospital, put on medication, behaved satisfactorily, and was released.

He told the staff, convincingly, that he had no hallucinations, and he voiced no clearly delusional ideas, so they had to let him go.

Like so many people with that disease, he distrusted his medication, did not think it was doing him any good, and stopped taking it. Since there is no practicable way to monitor every psychotic person living in a community who should take medicine every single day, no one knew it. One day, a few months after he was released from the hospital as "no longer a danger to himself or others," he stepped out of his front door and fired his shotgun again; fortunately he failed to hit anyone. He was arrested, sent again to the hospital, and once again improved on medication. What happened after that I do not know, but can imagine.

Few people with mental illness are dangerous in the way this man was. Many more people who do not have any classifiable mental disease are far more dangerous, like Jeffrey Dahmer in Milwaukee. He lured young males to his apartment, drugged and then murdered them, dismembered them and stored body parts in his refrigerator alongside the milk and eggs, and ate some of the grisly leftovers from his killings.

His attorney was unable to make a convincing case for the so-called "insanity" defense, in spite of Jeffrey's "crazy" acts, so he went to jail, where other inmates ultimately served their fellow citizens by killing him. The worrisome thing is that in some other court, in another state, with a different attorney, he might well have ended up in a mental hospital until found to be "no longer a danger." Only recently, a man in this state, so released, walked up to a total stranger on a square in Seattle, and killed him.

When we initiated our program in Sempervirens, both psychiatrists and employees of the state's Bureau of Social Work who followed-up patients released on leave from the state hospitals, had an astounding amount of power over the personal freedom of a great many of their fellow citizens. Had we not been determined to change the way psychiatry was practiced, not just in California but nationwide, we could easily have sent at least the usual 125 or more people that annually left our county to enter, involuntarily, the confinement and possible lifetime supervision imposed by the state hospital, instead of the three that the judge ordered to go there.

The reason was not that we agreed with a growing, soft-headed, 'liberal' point of view that seemed to say that any criminal behavior was a form of mental disorder, predetermined by unhappy childhood, poor environments, poverty, bad parenting, or bad genes. Quite the contrary. We took the firm position with all our patients that, regardless of your unhappiness or emotional turmoil, regardless even of those pesky voices you sometimes hear, you and you alone are responsible for your actions. We are sorry that your mean, drunken father beat you as a kid, but that does not force you to beat your wife and kids, and certainly does not justify or excuse your doing so.

Morning meetings on the ward every day frequently addressed issues of this sort. It was often surprising and gratifying to watch that group of twenty or thirty or more people, most of them patients in Sempervirens or recently discharged, some of them important people in the community who were interested and wanted to participate, a few of them toddlers or even infants on the floor in the open space around which sat the patients and staff, and to hear the seriousness and earnestness that people brought to the discussions. This was the real meaning of "community" mental health.

Other programs among the 58 California counties were bringing new attention to mental health matters, and high on the list of issues was the question of involuntary treatment and confinement. As the community part of the state's mental health budget grew, legislative interest grew as well, and discussions not unlike those in Sempervirens were occurring in the Capitol's halls and committee rooms.

The result was a new mental health law, expanding on Short Doyle. It was the creation of one of the original authors, who was joined by a warm, successful legislator and friend of Portia Bell, named Frank Lanterman, and a bluff, hearty Greek-American state Senator, Nick Petris.

Great consternation surrounded the inauguration of the Lanterman Petris Short Act, because it seemed to place excessive paperwork and procedures on our work with patients. No longer could we admit acutely ill people involuntarily unless legal or mental health officials could certify, in writing, that they were dangerous to themselves or others or unable to provide for their own basic needs for food, clothing or shelter. Even then, they could only be held for no more than 72 hours, without certifying to the court that they needed additional time, up to 14 days, for persisting dangerousness.

During that period, the patient could demand to appear before a judge to seek release, and at the end of the 14 days a formal court appearance was required to determine any further action at all. Thanks to the efforts of still another legislator, one known for vigorously advancing 'liberal' (but actually radical) causes of various sorts, patients were able to refuse all medication, no matter how great the need and appropriate the indication.

Finally, patients in the state hospitals even by the commitment order of any court, could demand release at any time and had to be let go unless the hospital was willing and able to mount a court battle to prevent it. Thus began a precipitous decline in the numbers of mentally ill patients in state hospitals and an identical increase in their numbers on the streets and in county jails. There were, naturally, the usual unintended consequences.

Community mental health programs were designed to offer a more humane and ultimately more successful way for society to care for its mentally ill citizens. Some, like ours, did exactly that. Most did not. Instead, like our own social worker-run outpatient clinic, they did not deal with seriously mentally ill people at all, but catered to essentially 'normal' folks who were in the midst of poor marriages, problems with the kids, job conflicts with co-workers and bosses, and things of that sort. Anyone who showed up looking like he had a serious illness was instantly sent over to the inpatient service.

Similarly, at least in our program, people who were treated and released from the hospital went back to Sempervirens as day-care patients; the out-patient staff had no interest in following them up. That was also true in most other county programs, both in our state and across the country.

The majority of community mental health programs, as a result, failed to realize their real potential or fulfill the dreams of people like Portia Bell Hume. They had little or no impact on mentally ill people, becoming instead government-subsidized 'counseling centers' that made, at best, little or no constructive contribution to health or to the communities that supported them. Often they served to perpetuate helplessness, dependency, and the belief in one's victimhood and entitlement to outside help in daily living.

They had no effect at all on the state hospitals' exploding population, for the people they dealt with were rarely if ever sick enough to require hospital care. It is often argued that these low-key 'feel-good' activities actually help dysfunctional people to 'adjust' better, but I know of no valid scientific study that shows this. Even in our own clinic, the staff of three social worker "therapists" and a secretary met with no more than two or three patients a day, each, and kept them coming for 'therapy' at least once a week - often for many months. None of their graduates became outstanding citizens, successful businesspeople, or political leaders.

Another unanticipated consequence of the movement was the spinning off of innumerable largely uneducated, untrained incompetent people who worked for a while in a program, decided "Hell, I can do this!" and set themselves up in private practice as marriage, family, child and adolescent, and sex therapists, since licensing requirements for such 'experts' are often indistinct at best, or non-existent. Their function used to be performed by family members, friends, pastors, priests, and rabbis, and even bartenders. A new "helping profession" has been born, and has flourished, replacing the old traveling medicine-show peddlers of wondrous nostrums, and the infamous snake-oil salesmen of the previous century.

The depopulation of state hospitals that occurred along with the growth of community mental health programs was not, except in rare instances like Humboldt County, with its 98% reduction in commitments, related to those local programs. In stripping away the traditional arbitrary and often unjust power of mental health professionals to confine and treat even profoundly psychotic persons, as long as they were not provably and actively dangerous, the lawmakers exhibited a kind of naive, wholly unjustifiable faith in the local programs to follow up on and care for patients streaming out of the big state institutions and heading for the nearest cities.

The reality was that most of the newly-released did not want to be followed up. The majority threw away their hospital-issued medications, failed to show up for scheduled appointments, and disappeared into the abandoned buildings, sewers and under the viaducts (summer) and over the grates (winter) of cities small and large. They found soup kitchens and food distribution places, stole countless grocery carts to use as mobile repositories for their sad possessions, collected in subways and bus stations, learned to beg and steal to stay alive, and filled up city and county jails. And there they continue to be to this day, while concerned citizens worry and talk about the new 'homelessness' phenomenon in America.

The patient census in the huge, so recently overcrowded state facilities fell so low that many became impossibly expensive to operate for so few patients, and had to be closed. The 'rights' of the mentally diseased were now, gloriously, restored, and a social disaster had occurred. Estimates of the percentage of homeless street people who are mentally ill and in need of treatment range from a low of perhaps 40% to twice that. These people live in unspeakably poor, unhealthy, unbelievably uncomfortable and dangerous circumstances, in many cases.

We seem, as a people, to be essentially content, if mildly concerned, with this situation, and to have decided that life over a grate in the snow of a Washington, D.C. winter street, scrounging for food and wrapping up in filthy discarded plastic, beats life in a large, clean, warm structure where three hot, nutritious meals show up every day, free for everyone, and medicines that really help are handed out regularly.

Our Constitution seems to have made no distinction between people who are mentally healthy and those who are not, even though the "insane" existed and had to be dealt with even in colonial times. Some were simply horse-whipped and driven out of town. Most, if their antics or even words became socially unacceptable, were thrown into gaols, large and small, like a prison ship in San Francisco Bay that was California's first state facility for fools and "loonies" (due to the moon, you see.)

Little more than 150 years after the framers created that hallowed document, however, their legal successors and scholars suddenly realized that the Founding Fathers, in full awareness that crazy people existed and were often a problem, and how they were customarily dealt with in those days, surely "meant" to include such people in all their deliberations, meaning the Bill of Rights, the equal protection clause, and all the rest.

Could this actually be true? How could it? Moreover, if true, how could the law-makers, -enforcers, and judges, for the next 150 years, go on making laws and instituting measures for the forced confinement and abuse of mental patients that were so contradictory to the explicit provisions of the founding documents?

In our dedication to "civil rights" and the most exquisitely detailed conceptions of individual freedom, this great, enlightened Nation seems to have arrived, paralyzed, on the horns of an insoluble dilemma. If we force these terribly impaired, suffering, socially outcast dregs of humanity to accept any care and treatment whatever, we violate their constitutionally-guaranteed civil rights. If we don't help them (like now), we violate everybody else's civil rights in the countless petty crimes and offenses against order, basic hygiene and sanitation, and danger of communicable disease that these people present.

When they do commit offenses against the law that cannot be ignored, we spend large sums of taxpayers' money to apprehend, arrest, try, defend, and convict them, before sending them off to jails and prisons that they overcrowd, to live in totally non-therapeutic environments that rarely provide any treatment at all, also at the taxpaying public's expense.

This makes no sense at all. It is, moreover, an unbelievable situation in a national community so concerned with even implied ethnic or gender-based slights, "assaults" that may consist of a few quietly spoken words, school expulsions for carrying such deadly weapons as nail clippers, and the endless list of presumably God-given, Constitutionally-ensured "Rights" so vigorously asserted and courageously defended on all sides, against all enemies, foreign and domestic.

Surely, in a society of rocket scientists and computer wizards such as ours, solutions can be found for the problem of the millions of untreated or inadequately treated people with mental disease that dwell amongst us, in conditions far worse than most domestic animals and pets.

No one, of course, will admit to playing God, or even remotely wanting to do so. However, to devise a way to help these helpless people, hardly different from deciding, for you, that your appendix needs to come out or your fractured hip needs to be treated, is hardly playing God. It would be, rather, closer to an imitation of Christ to recognize their need, and contrive ways that are firm but gentle, to lead them into safer places and administer the healing salves of our times, the literally miraculous drugs that can dramatically help all but a small fraction of them.

And then, utilize fairly simple, relatively non-intrusive ways to follow along as they progress toward a level of existence that is at least safe and reasonably comfortable, all the while ensuring that they get the chemicals their brains and bodies need. Those substances are no different from the plaster casts, drugs and assistive devices used in other forms of medical treatment, neither more nor less dangerous or respectable. For five years such an approach was shown in the County of Humboldt to be effective, economical, and altogether achievable.

This was the whole idea, originally, behind the concept of "community" mental health services. It is not a perfect solution, as might be expected. Some small but irreducible number of disordered persons, either because of physical damage to the brain or as yet irreversible chemical and hormonal alterations in the body, can not respond to any presently known treatment. Those relative few need the secure, structured environment of a carefully designed and staffed institution, of which many already exist.

Until laws are written to accomplish this, the problems will become ever more severe, and can result in widespread societal disruption with quite possibly terrible consequences. Such laws are long overdue.

My one great regret, as I reflect over the sad disarray of the Nation's brave explorations into new ways of dealing with serious mental illness, is that when I had a chance, a dozen years later, to take some major steps that could possibly have altered the downhill course that has ensued, I did not do so.

When President Reagan appointed me to head the Alcohol, Drug Abuse and Mental Health Administration, the Senate advising and consenting thereto, one of the great national institutes under my control was the National Institute of Mental Health. It was located in Rockville, Maryland and on the campus of the National Institutes of Health in Bethesda.

For some years, NIMH had both conducted and funded some very basic research into mental disorders, but had also made grants to communities around the nation to foster the development of community treatment programs. Coincident with my taking over that job, orders were passed down from our parent cabinet department, Health and Human Services, that the basic research activities were to be given increased emphasis and funds, while other activities would be severely curtailed. It seems that exciting developments in the investigations of brain chemistry and functions were more persuasive in getting money from Congress than were "social" programs out in the boondocks.

This was exactly the wrong thing to do, but I was too new and naive and overpowered by the majesty of Washington to recognize that, and put up a fight. What should have happened was a campaign by NIMH, through its grant program, to get communities to design local programs specifically aimed at cutting State Hospital admissions, following up on discharges, and organizing the community to take an active interest and role in managing patients. A working pattern existed and had been tested and proven; NIMH could have duplicated that pattern around the country by making clear what it was they wanted and would pay for. They didn't, and I didn't have the sense to make them. For that failure I shall always be sorrowful.

William E. Mayer, M.D.

Brainwashing, Drunks & Madness

CHAPTER 11

BIG GOVERNMENT 101 – CALIFORNIA

The years in Eureka and Crescent City convinced me that the ideas advanced by Portia Bell and her British colleagues who dreamed up the idea of "community mental health" were valid and workable, at least in that small city environment. Whether they would work as well in a larger urban setting remained a question. In San Mateo County, south of San Francisco, and to a lesser extent in San Francisco city itself, variations on our program seemed to be successful, but those counties both continued to send fairly large numbers of patients to the state hospitals.

Occasionally, during those years, I would send off a letter to Governor Reagan, presuming on our acquaintance of a few years before, during the making of the POW movie in Hollywood. Generally these notes reported on our success in treating the mentally ill, and complained about what I saw as the continued bias in the state bureaucracy in favor of state hospitals instead of the clearly superior local programs. The result of this correspondence was an invitation to replace Jim Lowry, Director of Mental Hygiene, who was retiring.

The idea of moving to Sacramento did not appeal to me at all, and I recommended that the Governor consider the man who was then running the San Francisco program. He was known as Stub, and I was impressed with him when I became president of the state Conference of Local Mental Health Directors because he enthusiastically supported my efforts to convert that body into an effective professional group that would be listened to in the state capital, and was not one of my former boss's "ping pong ball" types.

Stub was enthusiastic about the prospect, and was ultimately appointed. His first year was not a success. During that year, he frequently talked to me at Conference meetings and in numerous phone calls, complaining about his difficulties with the politicians, his own staff, the local directors, and the families of patients, especially retarded 'children,' (many of whom were physiological adults,) who were becoming increasingly vocal in their criticism of the state institutions for the retarded.

At that time, feeling that I had done what I set out to do in Eureka but fatigued with the long days and concerned about how little time I had to spend with my young son, I accepted a lovely job in Crescent City working half days as the county health officer as well as mental health director. The pay was better than Eureka's in spite of only requiring me to work about 3 hours a day. The rest of the time was spent mostly in the forests and the mountains, fashioning a Walden-like existence with my little boy, who was just then starting in school. Like any young mother, I wept when I left him at the front door of the school that first day, and he half-turned to give me a little wave, hand held at waist level, just before he squared his little shoulders and entered the big front door.

The job was easy, in that there were few mental health patients and only occasional demands in the arena of public health. My office was in Helene Miller's convalescent hospital, where I helped with prescriptions for her patients and infrequent interventions for county indigent patients who came in with lacerations, simple fractures, and the like. The one serious challenge had to do with autopsies. The county coroner, as in many rural California counties, was the sheriff, but of course he couldn't perform autopsies.

The sheriff, normally a fairly relaxed fellow, believed that anyone in the county who died while not under the care of a physician, died suspiciously. Therefore, he reasoned, that person must be autopsied. As the only county-employed physician, it turned out, I was elected to do these. At that point, I became the only psychiatrist in the country, if not the world, who was performing autopsies.

Prior to my arrival, the county had paid a pathologist to travel up from Eureka to do post-mortem examinations - a costly exercise. He did them, I was to discover, on the embalming table in Crescent City's one funeral parlor. I also discovered that he brought his own instruments, since our county had none. My first task, after viewing the little embalming room, was to dig up some instruments. We had scalpels and scissors available, but no special power saw or other device designed to cut through the ribs to remove the sternum so as to reach the heart and lungs.

Stumped, I called the pathologist in Eureka for advice. He was most accommodating, sending me off to the local hardware store for a "good quality" linoleum knife, a wood handle with a short, curved blade at one end. After the main incision down the chest, he said, I could use it to cut through the cartilage that connects the ribs with the sternum. He noted that it would require substantial effort, but would work. He also suggested that I buy a very sharp, long carving knife to make slices of the principal organs to be sent to him for microscopic examination.

His advice was excellent. I was now equipped to do pathology, with my shiny new instruments, a marble slab in the undertaker's embalming room that could be hosed down, and a small tape recorder to talk into.

Just in time. No sooner had I assembled my kit and delved into an old pathology textbook to refresh my memory (the last autopsy I had seen had been nearly 25 years before!) the sheriff called. He had a body that needed "doing." The old textbook did not give any helpful instructions for doing autopsies, and I had never actually done one before, only watched.

Gathering my gear, I made my way to the undertaker's establishment and waited for my first 'operation.' The hearse arrived, and when the rear door was opened, a horrible odor emerged that took me back instantly to a hillside in Korea where a number of bodies of soldiers killed in a battle not long before lay putrefying in a hot sun, waiting to be gathered up.

My first case was an old fellow who had been in the river for many days. My plans for an orderly, systematic post-mortem examination collapsed. He was so badly decomposed that his form barely held together, and no amount of examination could reveal anything useful. My report was short.

Later autopsies, at the rate of about one every few weeks, went better. All were of old people with unremarkable findings except for hardened arteries, mildly fibrous livers, old scars in kidneys, and no evidence of gunshot or stab wounds, or blunt injuries to the head. Never was there evidence of a dramatic event, like serious pneumonia or a major hemorrhage or a bloody, soft area in the heart after a coronary, that resulted in death.

While I could confidently declare that none appeared to have died as a result of violence, I could with only a little bit of confidence declare that these old folks, none of them under a doctor's care, had died of arteriosclerotic cardiovascular disease. They did all have somewhat hardened arteries, and "old age," by itself, is not an acceptable death certificate entry. Nor are such things as "just gave up," or similar diagnostic formulations.

Autopsies are less frequently done today than in earlier times, even on the remains of people who have not been under a doctor's care. Based on that fact, and on my own experiences in the undertaker's shop, I have long harbored serious doubts about widely publicized declarations about the country's mortality rates due to heart disease, cancer, pulmonary disease, and the like. How many, do you suppose, had an autopsy? And how good was the autopsy? We may never know. How is it proven that if someone stops smoking (or drinking, or overeating, or failing to exercise or take vitamins and minerals and supplements) that it will add a year, or ten years, or a day to any given person's life?

We back into such conclusions by counting up the numbers of people who drink or smoke or don't exercise who die at a given age, and compare them to others who don't do those things and live longer. But we do not actually know, given the huge number of other factors that affect people, why they live longer; we just think we do.

My point, perhaps a cynical one, is that we are still so ignorant and devoid of scientifically verifiable facts about what preserves, enhances, extends, shortens and ends life that we in medicine are truly the blind leading the blind. Gross things, like bullets in the head, cyanide, ruptured vessels in the brain or heart muscle, livers hardened to fiber, kidneys scarred to the point they cannot filter, and lungs infiltrated with infectious organisms or tumors, all of that we can pick up. But most deaths are not from those things.

About all one can do, really, is eat right (moderate quantities but lots of fruits and vegetables, whole grains, good proteins), get plenty of rest, avoid poisons insofar as possible in an increasingly polluted environment, and stay alert for signs like pains and lumps and discharges and failures of usual functions, and maybe take your vitamins (although that last one is probably silly.) It may be that the "just gave up" diagnosis is more valid than the law recognizes; that spirit is what is most important after all!

Life in that remote northern corner of California, surrounded by the mountains on one side, with their stupendous redwood forests, and with the beautiful Pacific on the other, had an undeniably idyllic quality. The little metropolis of Crescent City was a microcosm of great cities everywhere; it had all the facilities, factions, problems, politics and developments of every city, albeit on a smaller scale. In addition, the mountains and forests and sea offered endless opportunities for hunting, fishing, exploring, building and adventuring that most people find only in little snatches between long periods of often drab labor needed to be able to afford a few weeks of vacation to enjoy.

When, due to circumstances I could not control, my young son had to leave to live with his sister, whom I desperately missed, in a city 800 miles distant, the idyll ended. There was little real need for the trade I had learned over so many years, and the relative inactivity began to weigh heavily. My friend Stub inadvertently came to the rescue.

He called one day in something of a panic. His chief deputy, a long-time senior civil servant/psychiatrist named Bob Hewitt, was going to retire. Bob had been with the Department of Mental Hygiene for years, and had the experience and the connections to keep things going, but with the old state hospital bias, as opposed to supporting community programs, that had dominated for years under the former director, whom Stub had replaced.

Stub declared that he couldn't run the huge department alone, and desperately needed someone to fill in as chief deputy. He explained that he had left the running of the department up to Bob, and hadn't the vaguest idea how to do it himself. He had functioned as the "outside man," giving speeches, making trips, and signing whatever Bob and the deputy for administration, Andy Robertson, gave him to sign; they were the "inside men." Since I had recommended Stub to the governor, and had therefore "gotten him into this mess," I owed it to him to come bail him out.

Stub knew my kids were in Southern California, and held out some special aspects of the job that he knew would be irresistible. The first was that I could justifiably travel, even weekly, to the Los Angeles area, where our biggest local program, along with several state hospitals, were located. The second was that the state had a telephone network that would enable me to call that area daily, if I wanted, with no cost to anyone.

Since I had been driving that 1600 mile round-trip in my own aging car to see the children, briefly, on weekends, and spending a small fortune calling them every morning, I was easy to persuade. I headed for Sacramento.

My first action, after letting Stub know he would be okay, now, was to seek out Bob Hewitt in his office adjoining the director's, to find out what the job entailed - what I would be doing. I found him to be a rather heavy-set, courtly man with a warm, gracious manner. He was sitting behind his clean desk, gazing out the window at the beautiful golden dome of the state capitol. After he greeted me and I asked him my question about the job he had held for many years, he pondered for a few moments, and then looked at me with a strange, sad expression, and said, "Bud, I haven't the slightest idea."

He explained that since Stub's arrival, he had never been given any hint whatever about what the director wanted him to do. Andy, the administrative chief deputy, took care of all the 'business,' and Stub went to the required meetings in the capitol. That left Bob with little or nothing to require his attention. I sensed a real problem here.

The Department of Mental Hygiene, the largest in the state, held sway over nearly two dozen enormous state hospitals, evenly divided between those for the mentally ill and those for the retarded. All were crowded far beyond their designed capacity. In addition, the department submitted budgets for the 58 county community mental health programs, reviewed their plans and oversaw their operations. It was a monumental undertaking.

The director's office occupied the northeast corner of a new building, one of a pair recently constructed about three blocks from the capitol, on the 12th floor. Flanking the large corner space were two smaller offices, one for the 'professional' chief deputy - my new role - and the other for the also "chief" deputy for administrative matters. The existence of two "chiefs" seemed incongruous only to me.

Andrew Robertson, my administrative counterpart, was a legendary figure in the Department of Mental Hygiene whom I had seen at a distance, briefly, at meetings of the Conference of local directors, usually standing unobtrusively at the back of the hall. We local folks were all aware that he managed the steadily growing budget of the department, and suspected that he actually ran the whole thing, but he carefully avoided attention or interaction with us individually or as a group.

He was a pleasant-seeming fellow, slightly chubby, with a round, red face often wreathed in a smile, sparkling blue eyes, and a carefully arranged shock of beautiful white hair that had earned him the title of "the Silver Fox." Unlike Bob Hewitt, my predecessor, who seemed to me rather subdued and depressed, Andy was upbeat, enthusiastic and evidently genuinely pleased to be welcoming me. I found out later that he had had me carefully investigated, found me to be "blessedly different" (his words) from any of the other psychiatrists - especially Stub, he said - and concluded that he and I could work together and clean up the mess Stub had created.

With no hint of condescension, Andy set out to train me in the ways of Sacramento politics. His credentials were impressive. He had started his career in the department as a low-ranking worker at my favorite state hospital: Mendocino, our newest and one of the smallest of the state's institutions for the mentally ill. It was located in a pretty valley near the town of Ukiah, about a hundred miles north of San Francisco, and served all the northern California counties.

Like most of the hospitals, Mendocino operated a farm, and at one point it had been Andy's job to manage it. He and his crew of schizophrenic and brain-damaged patients became so good at raising hogs at that farm that they regularly took prizes at the State Fair. This was a source of genuine pride to this supremely skillful fiscal and management expert, which he became, to the end of his life. He worked his way up the occupational hierarchy until he reached the top administrative leadership role, second only to the hospital superintendent himself. He later assumed the same role in at least two of the other, larger hospitals, and then moved on to the top administrative job for the entire department, in Sacramento.

Andy was the finest and most skillful manager of budgets, plans, finances and personnel I had ever known - or would ever know, there or later, in Washington. He had little use for physicians, less for psychiatrists as a subspecies, and least of all for Stub, whom he considered a pompous, arrogant, lordly and totally incompetent boob and nincompoop. Despite these feelings, Andy never openly displayed them to Stub or to anyone else except me, and then only after he had satisfied himself that I was completely trustworthy and certain to reach the same conclusions.

Andy had examined every aspect of our program in Humboldt County, and said it made real sense to him, unlike most of the others. He had looked into my report, after the first year, to the Board of Supervisors, when I had appeared before that august body to seek funding for our second year. What had impressed him the most, he said, was the Board Chairman, Sam Mitchell's, loudly proclaimed announcement to me in the courthouse hall after my second budget had been approved.

We had just left the Board's chambers, and Sam, a large man with a loud voice and the grand manner he had cultivated in his exalted position, overtook me as I walked toward the stairs. He put his arm over my shoulders, like a friendly, benevolent grizzly bear, and without preamble said, "Bud, d'you ever wonder why we bought that proposition you made to us when you first came here?" Without pausing for an answer, he went loudly on. "I'll tell you why. It was because you didn't give us a goldarned bleeding heart approach to the poor mental patients. You made us a straight, reasonable business proposition that made sense, so we took it! Keep it up, boy!"

Andy had heard about that, and liked it. He figured I'd be okay, once he educated me.

Over the next few years, in countless hours spent in his office or mine, he did just that. His coaching and explanations and 'practical exercises' in business and financial management drove home every principle I was ever later to learn, on the job or in graduate courses at the business school of the University of Southern California, the Department of Defense or the halls of Congress.

In turn, I undertook to educate Andy, a product of the State Hospital system and the last high-level department official still friendly to the 'barons' who ran them, about the virtues, advantages and potential of community programs as an alternative. The barons, like Andy, could see the handwriting on the wall and the erosion of their great institutions by these new programs and the new laws, and came to Sacramento less and less frequently to advance their withering cause. They always came in a group to see Andy, never bothering with Stub or me: the new enemy.

Andy would invariably take them out for golf on a course whose fairways bordered his fine house, then home to dinner with his extraordinary wife, whom he treated like a great queen. This lady was in her seventies - at least ten years older than he - and had preserved the dress, customs and mannerisms of a giggling debutante, complete with wide eyes and high-pitched, little-girl voice, that were a parody of high society in the early 1900s. She was a tiny little thing (a fact she invariably pointed out at every social encounter) that Andy doted upon, evidently sincerely, to everyone's astonished amusement as they listened to her baby talk and her evident delight at her husband's courtly attentiveness.

Together, we set out to turn the burgeoning community mental health system in the state into an effective, business-like operation. We were not altogether successful in this. An example occurred when I undertook to analyze the cost-effectiveness of a large representative sample of the largest down to the smallest of the county programs. This was easy enough to do, because each program had to submit a detailed monthly report on admissions, discharges, diagnoses, and expenditures.

One of my early discoveries, as I prowled through the corridors, offices and storerooms of our large department, was that these monthly reports, all done on pink, pre-printed forms supplied by headquarters, were collected in stacks six feet high in several storage rooms. No one had ever read them!

There were hundreds of department employees in our fine new building, so I obtained a team of professional and clerical workers from each major branch and put them to work on the tall pink stacks. After selecting our 'representative' sample of about twenty counties out of the total of 58 in the state, the teams were to record the diagnoses of all patients admitted, the number of days they were in the inpatient unit, and whether they were readmitted in the first three months after being discharged. We did not have the information on computer tapes, there being none in the department at that time, and the task was tedious even though only three months had to be looked at, but the teams came through.

What we were looking for was the average number of days that a patient was kept hospitalized, the average daily cost of each patient-day, the total dollar cost of the episode of inpatient treatment, and the number of patients who were readmitted within three months, for how long, and at what cost.

The results of the study were mind-boggling. The shortest average length of stay turned out to be 5 days: Humboldt County. The longest was an adolescent inpatient hospital in Los Angeles: more than 60 days. The lowest cost per day was $30: Humboldt County. The highest was Los Angeles: $120. Thus the average cost of an 'episode' of hospitalization in Humboldt turned out to be $150, while the average cost in Los Angeles was $7,200!

A comparison of the diagnoses showed a similar distribution in all the counties studied. The readmission rate, close to zero in Humboldt, ran 8 to 10% elsewhere.

The findings were so devastating in their implications with respect to the most expensive places, that we did not publish them, but undertook to summon the directors of the highest-cost programs to Sacramento for an intensive educational and threat-making meeting with Andy and me, along with friendly counseling, of course. In addition, we initiated a regular program- and fiscal auditing system that sent unannounced teams into the costliest places to help them along with their improvement program.

I wish I could report that our efforts paid off dramatically. We had a great club to hold over the offenders, since we reviewed and had to approve each county's budget. Naively, I thought we could hold the threat of fiscal penalties over the directors' heads, but that proved to be wrong.

The larger counties, Los Angeles in particular with its 7 million population, proved to have powerful connections in the legislature and the governor's office. They successfully sold the idea that theirs was a 'special case,' requiring special consideration. How frequently I was to hear that! Any reduction in their budget would work unspeakable hardships on untold numbers of innocent patients. That in turn would disrupt important, politically sensitive relationships, reflect badly on the governor, erode support for our legislative friends, and cause a great scandal. It could not, we were told by friend and foe alike, be done.

Nonetheless, using the threat of exposure of the enormous waste of public funds - "taxpayers' money!" - in the more profligate counties, and using Andy's wiles in the management of the budget, we did succeed in lowering costs somewhat and getting people's attention directed toward seeking some genuine economies. This may have been my first powerful lesson in both the uses and the limitations of power.

There were constant reminders in Sacramento that ours was a highly politicized medical activity. Not only were there issues arising from the new laws granting far more freedom and autonomy to mentally ill persons, there was heightened interest in the subject of patient labor, on the grounds and the farms around the big hospitals. A decree from the Labor Department in far-off Washington commanded that any patient doing any work, however trivial, must be paid no less than the federal minimum wage. That was not possible within the budget, and totally unrealistic in view of the low levels of productivity one could reasonably expect of most patients.

That bit of liberal doctrinal wisdom, in a single stroke, wiped out our entire work-therapy program, statewide. The ancient little guy who had raised and lowered the flag in front of Napa State Hospital every morning and evening for more than 20 years could no longer be permitted to do so. He was crushed. Hospital grounds became shaggy and unkempt; new workers had to be employed in food service, the little libraries, and in the housekeeping activities essential to hospital cleanliness.

At the same time, increasing numbers of patients, still sick and on medicines, were leaving for the streets of Los Angeles and San Francisco and many smaller cities because staff could not produce proof that they were dangerous to themselves or others, or 'unable to provide for their own basic needs' for food, clothing and shelter.

The basic idea behind community programs was that mentally disordered people would be referred to them; the local mental health authorities would follow up, provide social services when needed, issue necessary medications and whatever other care these sometimes profoundly impaired people might need. In keeping with that idea, the hospitals sent notes of referral to the county programs where patients said they were going, and even obtained appointments for them.

The reality, it turned out, was that the vast majority of patients never showed up at the local programs, stopped taking their medications, found shelter in flophouses or under viaducts or in abandoned warehouses, and provided for their "own basic needs, etc." by picking through garbage and clothing themselves from trash bins. They endangered themselves by living in filth, eating rotten food and sleeping in the open, and endangered others through the threat of spreading the diseases they picked up, wandering out into traffic, setting cooking fires in old warehouses that spread to other structures, and enraging shopkeepers who often caught them clumsily trying to shoplift, and sometimes fought with them.

There were, you see, no workable definitions about 'danger' and about 'providing for basic needs,' and there still aren't. Even if there were, these issues would have to be examined in the framework of due process, with complaints, warrants, apprehension, preliminary hearings, indictments, pleas, public defenders, judges, possibly juries if demanded, professional expert witnesses, and all the accoutrements of the law. The law courts, already overwhelmed with civil and criminal cases, and the police, already heavily engaged in maintaining order and running down real criminals, can hardly take this on.

Therefore, it was that the patients left the huge, often dehumanizing state institutions, forcing their closure, and ending up on the streets in far more cruel and dehumanizing settings than they had escaped from.

Closing most of the hospitals was hard. Many had been important fixtures in the communities that had grown up around them. Thousands of employees, many of whom had worked at the hospital for decades, were thrown out of work. Businesses closed, and more people lost jobs. A particularly painful and poignant example was the hospital at Mendocino.

That institution, where Andy had been so successful raising prize pigs, had been built in a new style aimed at dismantling the old, grim, prison-like fortress model that had been traditional for over a century. The setting was that of a small college, with modest, gabled, ivy-covered buildings set among trees and bushes, with no evidence of bars or security fences. Many patients earned the freedom of the lovely grounds, and there were few disturbances and only rare 'elopements,' the euphemism for escapes or any other unauthorized departures.

As the patient population dropped, without a comparable drop in the cost of keeping such a campus operating, the cost per patient-day grew to intolerable proportions. In a last-ditch effort to keep the place going, the staff instituted a special treatment program for drug addicts and abusers. They bought into a wholly specious line of reasoning to the effect that only an addict - in some stage of recovery, naturally - could understand another addict and do any effective treatment. Foolishly, the hospital management pretty much turned the addiction program over to the addicts.

Unsurprisingly, the addict-therapists came up with some weird approaches to the problem. One involved the daily use of LSD, until so many spaced-out, seedy characters started disrupting both the hospital and the nearby town that it had to be discontinued. Another approach used the administration by mask of carbon dioxide, with resultant poisoning. After a few months, the program had to be shut down, and so did the hospital. Andy and I both took it rather hard, but it had to be done. Others followed.

Stub seemed unperturbed by what was going on. His weekly staff meetings, dreaded by all senior subordinates but never to be missed, were devoted to what he called "global" issues, like one two-hour session devoted to what he called "the tragedy of Liz and Dick," referring to the impending divorce of Richard Burton by Elizabeth Taylor. Sometimes he noted news items about outbreaks of infectious disease in Africa, or other matters that needed the attention of the World Health Organization. Ultimately, he announced to us all that the Director of the WHO was soon to step down, and he, Stub, was determined to replace him. He was quite serious.

Not long after, using department funds, he flew to Geneva to press his case, believing that it was in the interest of the California Department of Mental Hygiene. His reasons for that belief were never quite clear. During the morning on his scheduled day of departure, Andy and I were sitting in Andy's office planning the things that needed doing in the coming few weeks. Suddenly the door from Stub's office burst open and the director appeared, in an obvious state of excitement and some disorganization, a frown creasing his face. He began to issue a rapid-fire series of instructions about what he wanted done in his absence, none of it very new or surprising.

Thinking to lighten things up a bit, and reduce Stub's high level of excitement, Andy held up his hand. "Stub," he said, smiling, "Just relax. You are running around like a young boy with his dick in his hand, not knowing where to put it. We'll take care of things."

Stub was horrified. His face literally turned purple as he struggled to find an answer to what he clearly saw as a terribly insulting, insubordinate obscenity from a mere underling. He totally missed the obvious fact that this older, wiser, more experienced, rather gentle man was trying, with humor, to help him settle down. Finally, finding no way to respond, he turned on his heel and strode back into his office, slamming the door loudly behind him.

We were not to see him or hear a word from him for two weeks, until he returned, crestfallen, from his fruitless mission to the United Nations. No one ever mentioned it again. It was clear, however, that Stub clearly remembered Andy's insulting offense on the day of his departure, and he never forgot it or forgave him. Within a year, taking advantage of some multi-departmental reorganization plans, Stub made a determined effort to force Andy out of government. I finally had to go all the way to the governor to prevent that truly vicious retributive act from succeeding. More about that little episode later.

Our hospitals for the mentally retarded were not experiencing the drop in patient count that was emptying those for the mentally ill, but there was growing interest in new techniques for raising the functioning level of some retarded 'children' previously thought to be incapable of improvement. This development gave rise to a spreading belief among the families of many of these people who had been in our hospitals for years, that the State was planning to push most of them out, and back into the community. The result was growing agitation.

There was no such plan, and we said so, telling the superintendents of the 'MR' hospitals to spread the word and calm down the families. It didn't work. The parents of the retarded bear a special, unrelenting burden as they try to cope with their special kids. One retarded child in a family of two or three normal children can affect everyone in the family, distort marital relationships, alienate the other kids and cause incredible, unending turmoil.

In my experience with these parents, I found that invariably they bore an almost intolerable burden of guilt, beginning when the youngster began emerging from infancy into toddlerhood, failing to show signs of normal development. Young mothers commonly compare notes with other young mothers about their offspring's progress, and when a new baby fails to start showing signs of expected growth, alarm soon follows. Denial works for a while, along with reassurances from friends and family, but when the child is unmistakably failing to thrive, panic sets in.

Before long, parents - but especially young mothers - in their search for causes and possible remedies, begin focusing on things they did or failed to do during their pregnancy with this child. Since nearly every normal pregnant woman has 'down' days when she wishes she weren't pregnant or even resents the man who got her into this burdensome state, the mother of a retarded kid begins, often, to focus on recalled instances of such negative feelings, however transient they may have been, and suspects they may have played a role in this child's defects. Guilty feelings arise, and grow.

Husbands are frequently not much help with this, and that leads to further problems. As the child grows physically but remains a behavioral infant, the burden on parents and older siblings grows as well. Every holiday or hoped-for vacation has hanging over it the 24-hour demand for care that retarded children impose. When finally the prospect of institutionalizing the child has to be faced, often after years of heroic effort by the whole family to foster and recognize signs of improvement, without much success, the guilt and family conflicts blossom. Placing the youngster, for most families, is a crisis of major proportions.

Many retarded people are physically healthy, even robust, and show no physical signs of their handicap. Often they survive well into adulthood and even old age, continuing to have the intellectual and emotional equipment of a young child. When sexual development occurs, as it often does, the strength and impulsivity of a physically adult, seriously retarded male can pose monstrous problems, as can the casual promiscuity of some retarded adult females.

The rumor that we were going to empty our MR hospitals and dump the patients on their aging parents' front porches, therefore, caused great consternation, fear, and overt hostility. I decided to hold an open, public meeting in the auditorium on the grounds of Sonoma State Hospital, north of San Francisco, to try to defuse the growing turmoil.

The hospital had occupied its site in the lovely Sonoma Valley for many years, and was first called the "Sonoma Colony." It had many buildings, large and small, all quite old, spread in a pleasant, bucolic setting of trees and lawns, that successfully obscured the fact that most of the people who dwelt there were locked up. The

Governor's Secretary of Health and Welfare agreed to come with me to reinforce my reassurances, although he was somewhat reluctant and decided (wisely, as it turned out) that we should have with us a substantial contingent of State Police.

The meeting took place early on a lovely summer evening that literally reverberated with the angry shouts and gesticulations of the masses of troubled parents packed into every seat and every inch of the aisles, corridors, hallways, lobby and even the backstage area of the auditorium. Our police escort became, instantly, hyper-alert as we walked in, fully expecting mob violence of some sort.

The Secretary, Earl Brian, clearly wishing he'd never been tricked into this, made a few comments to the effect that we were not sending our patients out of the hospital, but these went largely unheard in the din. Then it was my turn.

I stood on the stage, essentially motionless, making no attempt to speak or to quiet the agitated audience down, after directing our police guards to leave the stage and in fact the entire building. I did not smile, but allowed a small frown to crease my forehead while I waited patiently for a chance to speak and be heard. Soon enough, loud shouts from around the audience demanded silence, and within a few minutes things quieted.

I thanked them - for coming, for being willing to listen, for caring so deeply about their children as I do about my own (I didn't claim to 'feel their pain,' but said I fully understood their concerns), and for having brought questions for me which I would answer, completely and truthfully.

My first declaration was that my colleagues and I recognized that retardation and mental illness were totally different from one another, and presented entirely different problems and remedies for those problems. Even though both groups were treated in 'State Hospitals,' they were never kept in the same ones (mostly, but not quite true), were not at all alike, were given wholly different medications, treated differently, and subject to completely different laws and regulations.

In response, there was widespread affirmative head-nodding among the audience, facial expressions of great relief, and even a little applause. I had not, until that moment, realized how intensely these people rejected the idea that their children, however seriously retarded, were in any way "crazy." It was easy to understand, when one thought about it. The building of separate institutions for retarded people, when for generations they had simply been thrown together with the insane, was a twentieth century development not even known to most people. The fears of mixing these two vastly different groups struck terror into the hearts of the majority of parents initially facing the awesome, frightening prospect of sending a child off to a remote, prison-like institution to be brutalized by the 'crazies' locked up there.

It was true, I had to admit, that the combination of new laws and new drugs had resulted in a great exodus of patients from our state hospitals for the mentally ill, but this had not and would not happen in the hospitals, like Sonoma, that were operated solely for the retarded. Given what they had been reading in the newspapers, it was easy to understand their confusion, but it was unfounded.

There were few questions. We did not, in fact, have any plans at all to empty out the hospitals for the retarded, so it was easy to be sincere and apparently convincing in my assurances to these terribly troubled parents. As I left the auditorium I chose deliberately to walk up the center aisle, through the audience rather than out a back stage door. On both sides people reached out to touch me as I passed, and I could see exhausted, tear-stained faces all around. It was a profoundly moving experience.

There was no similar concerned constituency in support of the mentally ill patients leaving the hospitals. Their 'liberation' posed, for the doctrinaire liberal population, questions that they didn't even think of. The fact that the mentally ill could exercise 'free choice' about hospitalization and medications was celebrated widely as a great human triumph. The fact that many or most of these 'liberated' slipped into a life of deprivation, danger and misery in back alleys was largely ignored. To a larger extent, it still is, in this new century.

California's population was growing rapidly, and was soon to be the largest in the Nation. Its government and economy had already reached such size as to be the sixth largest in the world. The executive and legislative branches matched or exceeded those of most entire countries elsewhere. Governor Reagan had assembled a number of very superior people in his cabinet and to head larger departments. They included Casper Weinberger, Ed Meese, Michael Deaver and a number of others who were later to play major roles in the Reagan Administration in Washington.

Since the Department of Mental Hygiene was already the largest, in number of employees, and its budget was expanding every year, both Meese, who ran the governor's cabinet, and Cap, who was director of the Department of Finance - the state's most powerful - paid close attention to our activities as hospitals closed and local programs blossomed. I was summoned with some regularity by both of these senior lieutenants, and invariably came away, after explaining some program or event, impressed by their intelligence, energy, and political wisdom. Little did I suspect that I would come to know them far better in coming years, or that each would have a lasting effect on my own career.

Some of the numerous staffers who invariably collect around the centers of power in any government were more troublesome. One in particular, a little guy named McMurray was a passionately conservative fiscal expert who took it upon himself to examine all our expenditures and programs in minute detail. He would call at least weekly, highly incensed about something, however trivial, that he disagreed with, and demanding immediate correction or elaborate, detailed written explanations and justifications.

His harassment grew steadily more intense and emotionally colored, and caused me to go to Meese or Weinberger for relief on a number of occasions. McMurray's phone calls were sometimes so strident, almost to the point of screaming, that I took to recording his outbursts for possible use when it became necessary to take measures to force him into treatment for his manic-depressive disorder. Sadly, for the little wild man, he was struck down with a coronary, saving me a sad and difficult duty, but secretly I rejoiced.

Somewhat surprisingly, the powers that ran our huge government were slow to recognize that health expenditures were rapidly and steadily growing to monstrous proportions. I have learned that their obtuseness is common among political leadership and other power groups, whether in California, the District of Columbia, the Federal Executive Group around the President, or the boards of great corporations.

It seems that people in positions of great power are slow to learn of the steady, sometimes exponential rise in health care costs until long after clear evidence shows up. When finally convinced that there may be a real problem here, power structures are prone to put into place remedial measures that are poorly thought out, oblivious to unintended consequences, and certain to fail in significant ways.

So it was in our great state. Some "thinkers" on the Governor's staff came up with a solution to skyrocketing healthcare costs that they considered simple, brilliant, and certain of success. They would simply combine all health-related departments into one, with supposedly huge savings in budgeting, accounting, procurement and management, under a single, powerful director who could be 'controlled.'

Mental Hygiene, as already noted, had the largest number of employees in our government. A department named Health Care Financing, responsible for funding the state's Medicaid program, named MediCal in California, was the state's largest disburser of money. The State Department of Public Health was the state's oldest and most independent and unmanageable, operating alone in its own buildings in Berkeley, far from government headquarters in Sacramento and proudly ignoring all attempts to supervise it or its budget. None of these three health-related departments, nor the medical social work section of the Department of Welfare, which was to be included in the consolidation, had any relationship at all with any of the others. Nor, in fact, did they ever even communicate with one another.

The concept and rough outlines of the plan were created without ever consulting anyone at all in any of the departments affected - not one medically experienced person was consulted. The order was given, and Stub was taken out of Mental Hygiene to preside over the detailed planning. That move elevated me to State Director of Mental Hygiene, for which I was grateful and along with Andy, relieved. Now we could run things without often troubling interference from the departed director, at least until the new, huge Department of Health was fully in place.

When that happened, we were slated to become simply sub-sections of the new organization, with appropriate loss of power and prestige.

Like Scarlett O'Hara, we decided to deal with that later.

Stub was enormously pleased with his new task, fully expecting to be named as director of the new monstrosity. It wasn't as good as being Director-General of the World Health Organization, but it was pretty good. The fact that he had no idea about how to proceed bothered him not at all. To take care of that, he called forth his most cherished management tool, the "off-site."

Stub's 'off-sites' were notorious. He would arrange for a meeting of the senior departmental staff about once every three months, to take place in a different resort of some kind outside of Sacramento. There were no absences permitted. All participants were required to stay on the premises all day and night, for the two or three day meeting. The twenty-five or so senior staff were expected to take all meals together, spend all day and evening together, were forbidden to receive calls or make any calls, and not allowed to conduct any business whatever.

Stub ran these meetings himself, following an agenda only he knew about, and often dealing with what he saw to be personal failings and conflicts. The whole thing was offensively close to group psychotherapy, especially to those of us far more skillful and experienced at that technique than was our leader.

The idea, we were told, was the resolution of significant conflicts and crises, as Stub saw them, in the operation of our vast department. Once in a while someone would manage to raise a subject of some substance, but more often something quite different took place. It soon became clear to all of us that these meetings were designed to single out a particular official that Stub disliked and wanted to get rid of. As the meetings dragged on, he would concentrate his questions, suggestions, and criticisms on one particular participant. By meeting's end, that person could not fail to realize that his career in the department was over, but this was never said.

Instead, once the meeting had ended, Stub would instruct me, as his Chief Deputy, to arrange for the identified victim to leave. Permanently. He made it quite clear, the very first time - I'd been there three months - that I was to "Get that SOB to go; it didn't matter how. Just go."

One such designated departee was a man I had known for several years. While I liked Bill Beach as a person, it was always evident to me that he knew nothing much about local mental health programs, even though he was the officer in charge of that part of the department. I had no desire to hurt him or his future career, even though the abuse he had endured during the offsite made it clear to all that his presence was no longer acceptable to the boss.

While searching for a way to get Bill to leave after many years in the department, I heard that the state of Pennsylvania was looking for a mental health director to serve under the notoriously tough woman who ran the state department of social services. I called her, and told her of Bill's long experience in California's community mental health movement and strongly urged she consider him. Then I suggested to Bill that the possibility existed for him to move on up in his career field, and try Pennsylvania.

He did, he was accepted, and he did outstandingly. And he thanked me for helping him leap forward and upward in his profession. After several good years in Pennsylvania, he went on to run the excellent, historic mental hospital in Brattleboro, Vermont, with equal distinction and success. He never forgot or failed to mention the immense 'favor' I had done him.

In due time the planning for the new mega-department, such as it was, was complete. Stub was given a new title, Director of Health, and the three and a half departments brought into one became subordinate sections of the new big one. This was done with appropriate fanfare and a suitable media event aimed at proving the administration's creativity and dedication to economy.

As expected, Stub soon called for one of his legendary offsites. Neither he nor anyone else had any idea that this grand get-together, staged in a motel in the charming bay-side town of Tiburon, near Sausalito, would, in wondrously ironic fashion, prove to be the setting for Stub's precipitous fall from glory to the depths of bureaucracy.

It was Stub's grand debut as the single top health official in California, and he played it to the hilt. His opening comments were even more pontifical and pointless than his usual pronouncements. All of us former department heads, now demoted to section chiefs, listened submissively. The great man droned on and on, until interrupted by an obsequious motel manager. That unfortunate creature literally crept into the room, having been told that the sacred gathering was never to be interrupted by phone calls, to announce, *sotto voce*, that there was a call from the governor's office that could not be refused, 'for a Dr. Mayer.'

Obviously irritated, Stub granted me permission to leave to take the call. The caller turned out to be Ed Meese, who seemed uncharacteristically excited. "Bud," he exclaimed. "We just got word from Washington that the president has signed the 'Aging Americans' bill!"

"Oh?" I politely responded, wondering what this could be about.

"This means," he went on, "We can capture a big pile of new federal money, but we will have to beef up our Office of Aging, and we want you to head it up."

The Office of Aging was a tiny (perhaps 16- or 18-person) operation tucked away in an anonymous office in a nondescript building somewhere off to the side of the Capital Mall. No one knew what it did, but obviously it had something to do with old folks.

Thinking quickly, and putting on my best thoughtful and judicious tone, I said to my benefactor, "Ed, I think you are missing a really terrific opportunity here. If the intent is to elevate programs for the aging to great importance, the most powerful message you could send would be to put the very top guy in health, Stub, in that job. (Long pause.) The truth is," I plunged on, "He is simply incapable of running this big department, and he doesn't even know it. The Office of Aging requires no executive skill to run, so he can do that and not screw it up, like he will this.

"I know you are nominating me to be Stub's Chief Deputy in the new Department of Health, but I can serve the governor better as director, and Stub can do just fine in Aging." (Another long pause.) Then, the word that changed all our lives: "Okay. Done."

While I would never tell anyone, at least for several years, about that exchange and the possible appearance it gave of disloyalty and ambition, I felt no misgivings whatever about it. This was not because it resulted in my personal advancement, for that was not my primary concern. Rather it was because Stub was truly incapable of the task, and in running the planning group he had managed to insert a provision that would end Andy's career; this was Stub's retribution for Andy's one overt episode of disrespect. Stub was going to get rid of Andy by simply eliminating the top administrative deputy position. I could not let that happen.

Instead, Stub trudged over to the office of Aging, where he was to assume command. He gathered together his new, small staff, all of whom including the secretaries could fit into his modest office. Stub had been a Navy flier during World War II, and took every opportunity to use naval terms and expressions. He did that now. According to the genuinely shocked reports from members of his new staff, he announced that he was now aboard to set this ship on course. What he said next will live forever in the memory of each of his new shipmates.

I have been, he said, like the Admiral in command of a great fleet. Now, I fear that I have been assigned to command a garbage scow. Whatever he followed that with has blessedly been lost to history. It was an unusual beginning. Nothing was ever heard of the Office of Aging after that.

My elevation to my new position of eminence was not simple, as it turned out. I was designated "Acting" Director of Health when Stub left, a few days later, but my formal nomination as Director was not forwarded to the Senate for confirmation for some weeks. This began to arouse some interest and curiosity when it was revealed that the nomination lay, untouched or acted upon, on the desk of the young, rather brash new Secretary of Health and Welfare, a physician named Earl Brian. Until reorganization, this brilliant Carolinian had made a great name for himself running the former department of Health Financing, and now, at 29, was the youngest member of the governor's cabinet and a power to be reckoned with.

In addition to the fact of his success running the department that handled the huge and growing disbursement of funds to support the state's Medicaid program, Earl initiated a highly imaginative and controversial ancestor and forerunner of the current managed care movement. It was a pre-paid health care plan for indigent citizens eligible under state and federal rules to be treated free under Medicaid, called MediCal in our state.

Under the plan, privately owned health care organizations could bid for contracts to give all medical care that was authorized under the law to eligible recipients who signed up with them agreeing to get whatever treatment was needed only from the organization they signed up with. Organizations who bid, did so offering a complete package of care at a fixed cost per enrolled beneficiary. The more people they signed up, the more money they got - in advance, each month. The organization then had to deliver every needed service, regardless of cost, and could not charge for cost overruns. If they started spending more than the state was paying them, they could try to justify a new bid at a higher per capita rate, but they had to have a pretty convincing case.

One of the inevitable unanticipated consequences of this plan was that it spawned numerous, sometimes shady, highly and on occasion viciously competitive new health care organizations. Some of these sent 'recruiters' of new patients out into slum areas dressed in long white doctor's coats complete with stethoscopes showing in their pockets, to sign up the masses of poor and often ignorant people eager to get in on this wonderful free deal.

There were even a few shootings between competing recruiters, and it wasn't long before some of the organizations showed up to be outright frauds who took their capitation money and ran. Others gave poor care, or turned people away from their storefront 'clinics.' Even though most of the contracting groups were honest and tried hard to deliver what they promised, so much controversy swirled about the project that eventually it had to be abandoned. It had been a good try, and years ahead of its time.

As the weeks dragged by with no action on my nomination, even some of Earl's own staff began to feel all was not right, and they came up with what they hoped would be a stimulus to action. An attractive, well-designed coat of arms was painted by state artists, and presented to me in one of the Secretary's weekly meetings. Across the bottom, on an unfurled scroll, was an elaborate Latin motto. While I forget the exact Latin words, it was announced to all the department heads present that the literal translation of the inscription was:

"What is this 'Acting' Shit?"

Everyone was amused, including Earl, and the next day he summoned me to his presence in the great stone building that housed cabinet members, under that inscription, high above the entrance, that proclaimed, "Give me men to match my mountains!" and that I found particularly appropriate to the occasion.

Earl sat behind a huge desk, leaning back in his chair with his feet up, his coat off, collar loosened, tie pulled down and smoking his customary small, slender cigarillo. He followed his "Hi there, Bud!" with the question, "I guess you're wondering why it's taking so long to get your nomination signed off and sent along to the Senate?"

I admitted that I was wondering, a bit, and he said, "I haven't sent it on because I haven't decided yet whether I can trust you or not." That shocked me a bit, and seeing this, he went on.

"In this business," he continued, "Loyalty is everything. I have to know my people are absolutely loyal, without question. That's what I mean by trust."

"If what you really mean is that you expect me to be blindly obedient to anything you tell me to do, then no, you cannot trust me that way," I said. "If I disagree with you on any important issue, I won't sit back and just take it. I'll argue my case and try to persuade you. If I can't, and it's a matter of important principle, and we cannot agree, then I would have to quit. I will not argue it out in the press or go public with the accusation that you've made a bad decision - in that sense you can trust me. But I won't blindly obey anybody. You will be badly served if you surround yourself only with people who are blindly obedient."

That seemed to end the short conversation. He told me I'd hear in a few days. The next day he sent the nomination on to the Senate, where I made an appearance a few days later, answered a few questions, and became legitimized.

We got along well, with no serious disagreements. I could not help but admire his skill, dealing with the multitude of controversies that always swirl around issues of health and welfare, and with the powerful special interests, in and out of government who had axes to grind. We were in a business of big bucks; health activities of the state government were costing a huge portion of the total state budget. As an example, every 18 months in MediCal alone, we were spending as much as it had cost to build the entire Central Valley Project - the largest irrigation and reclamation project in the history of the world.

That project had transformed the Central Valley of California into the most productive agricultural area on earth, benefiting untold millions of people not only in our state and country, but throughout the world. In contrast, while the MediCal program unquestionably relieved some suffering and possibly even saved some lives, its existence had had no measurable effect, using standard public health criteria, on the overall health status of the citizens of California! That always seemed to me an interesting comparison.

Long-term care for the elderly and infirm in skilled nursing facilities - 'convalescent hospitals'- still a problem in the current days of the new century, was a serious drain on our resources. While such care is far less expensive than general hospital treatment, its costs rapidly deplete the savings and even the property of most who need it. Thus it was that the majority of those patients' care was paid for by the state, under MediCal.

The standard reimbursement for skilled nursing services under MediCal at that time, in the early 1970s, was sixteen dollars a day, to cover the patient's room, food, linens, nursing care and medications. At that same time, the sleaziest, most run-down motels and 'motor courts' in Sacramento were charging 25 to 30 dollars a night just for the room! The nursing home operators were in dire straits and increasingly agitated, but they could do nothing.

Even as Director of Health, and although this was clearly a health matter of some importance, I had no authority to alter those rates. At least weekly, I implored the Secretary's staff to allow an increase, even a few dollars, to stave off what I saw as certain financial disaster for many of the facilities, and serious erosions in quality of care leading up to that. All to no avail.

We had reorganized the health departments into one giant one, you will recall, as an economy measure. Great savings were supposed to accrue as functions were consolidated, and staffs cut and work lessened. That did not happen, but even if it had, savings in one government pocket can ordinarily not be put into another pocket. Savings from budget customarily are turned back into the state's general fund, and somehow disappear there, but in any case we were not creating new savings.

The ideologues and political planners who had gathered around the governor were busily planning his presidential campaign, although no one ever said so. As an important part of that, economies were to be achieved in every activity, no matter, it seemed, who got hurt. In this case, the nursing home patients were getting hurt. Surely, I would argue, that could not help the image of our governor! My pleas fell on deaf ears.

It had long been my practice, as a manager, to hold a daily meeting that was compulsory for all my senior lieutenants. I held these at 7:30 each morning, hardly a popular hour, but the time was deliberately set and not a subject for discussion. The reason for the hour was that I had long recognized that there seems, in large organizations, to be a direct correlation between how high the rank and how late the arrival of the executive.

The early start did several things that were beneficial. It got people's brains working before half the day had slipped away. It more or less assured that participants didn't get involved in other things first, so they could concentrate on the meeting. It took place before the telephone started to ring and the personnel problems started to arrive. Moreover, it gave people something to bitch about.

The larger purpose behind the meeting lay in the old military axiom that declares 'there are always 10% who don't get the word.' It was to obviate that favorite dodge: "I never heard about that," and "nobody ever told me," and "why wasn't I consulted?" and other banners held high by bureaucrats and 'organization man' types. While my meetings were usually short, every person present was required to speak - his or her choice of topic - but speak so everyone knew all were awake and listening. Usually we were off to our respective businesses by 8 o'clock, but in crisis times the meeting could go on much longer. And everybody got the word.

A deeper purpose still for such an exercise is the need to assess one's major helpers. Any top executive who was unable to participate regularly, with some vigor and intelligence, in those meetings, could not long remain in the senior executive group. While I may be a little smarter than average, and (when younger) a little more energetic, I am no organizational genius or spectacularly inspirational leader, yet I have succeeded to the very highest levels of my profession as a physician-executive because of one outstanding skill: I pick really good deputies and assistants. The morning meetings have always helped me do that.

Klausewitz, the great military philosopher, wrote at length about the sorting and selection of one's lieutenants. They fell, he said, into a few distinct groups. First were the stupid and lazy. Give them simple tasks - somebody has to sweep up - and don't expect much from them. Then there are the brilliant and lazy. They don't do much work but they can be good planners. Next are the stupid and energetic. They are dangerous; watch them carefully, impose limits on what they do and be on guard with them. Finally there are the brilliant and energetic. Nourish them. Cultivate them. Place demands on them. Encourage them. These are the guys who will one day get your job; they are precious. Take excellent care of them, for you need them.

While this may sound unduly cynical, it is my conviction that the vast majority of people in big organizations fall into the first three groups. To succeed, one has to find those few in the final group. Just sharing in their ideas and efforts guarantees that you will succeed. I certainly did.

We had had inklings of these leadership principles back in Eureka, with our student professional workers. A few clearly stood out, in ways that were not always easy to define. We tried to cultivate and encourage those few, and as earlier reported, no fewer than six of them that we worked with over the five years we were there went on to themselves become directors of county mental health programs around the state.

In Sacramento, I worked out a scheme for identifying and cultivating not only the best among my senior helpers, but younger, lower-ranked people from farther down in the organization as well. When one of these young people, by speaking up or delivering a specially good product, came to my attention, and with some endorsement by his immediate superiors of his potential, I would attach him to my immediate staff, on a kind of temporary duty. He would sit in on morning meetings and others as well that would ordinarily not include him. He would spend some time privately with me or with Andy, or both of us together, and would be included in our discussions as if he were already a senior member of the staff.

At least three of the youngsters treated thus rose to top leadership positions in the department, in subsequent years, and did well. One in particular, Carl Rauser, became one of the most valuable and valued professional colleagues I ever had in fifty years of work, and a warm, close friend as well, along with his wonderful, dear wife, Bernie. Carl's premature passing a few years ago was one of the most shocking, tragic losses of my life.

At long last, during one of my morning meetings, a call from the Secretary announced a decision at the highest levels of the government permitting us to raise the nursing home reimbursement rate. While the raise was modest, it staved off the failure of numerous struggling facilities, and we all rejoiced. That happy moment, however, was to come back to haunt me as well as others several years later.

It happened in Germany, in about 1979. Old enemies of Governor Reagan and Earl Brian, apparently in anticipation of the governor's likely candidacy for president ahead, managed to launch an investigation into every action taken during his administration in Sacramento. One of the issues turned out to be the timing of the decision to raise nursing home rates. The FBI was put to work. Since those agents could not function in Europe, the CIA was given the job of interviewing suspects there. Evidently I was one of them.

The young agent appeared one day in our Alcohol Treatment Facility at the Army hospital near Stuttgart. He was very serious, very officious, and very mysterious. After displaying his credentials and demanding a private office, and without telling me what it was about, he asked me to recall all the details of a staff meeting I had held on a specific date at least three years earlier. I told him that was ridiculous, and asked if he could tell me exactly what he did and said that morning. Of course he could not.

Pressing on, he asked if I could remember a morning meeting during which Dr. Earl Brian called me. In a general way, I could, this being a rare occurrence, especially when the secret government agent said that the conversation was about nursing home reimbursement rates. I finally said that I remembered the call because it was a happy day for us. That was about all there was to this dramatic encounter. As far as I was ever able to determine, nothing ever came of this, but I suspected someone was trying to prove that the governor or Earl had traded the increased rate for some kind of political favor. So much for partisan politics.

The first task I assigned to myself as the new director of a massive department that consumed nearly a third of the total budget of the largest and richest state in the union was to visit the headquarters of the three departments just consolidated into one, and as many as I could of the regional offices each had in place around the state. My goal was to try, somehow, to develop a sense of relatedness, if not unity. I hoped as well to diminish the pervasive anxiety about draconian budget cuts and massive layoffs.

That experience was a taste of what I would later experience in Washington, when I worked toward similar goals first with the separate institutes of mental health, drug abuse and alcoholism, each further divided into clinical and research groups who barely communicated. That in turn barely prepared me for the separateness, competitiveness, suspiciousness and hostility that I was later to find among the military services in the Pentagon.

Both in California and later in Washington it soon became clear that the most intense resistance to efforts to foster interaction and cooperation among the formerly separate elements of the overall health enterprise invariably came from a small group of people at the top of each element. This reaches its pinnacle and finest expression in the Pentagon, where it assumes the proportions of warring religious groups like crusaders versus infidels, Irish Catholics against Protestants, and Muslims against Jews. This is not an exaggeration.

Since first Stub, and then I, had been named to head the huge new health department, it was a foregone conclusion that somehow the whole thing was a mental hygiene plot. The leader of the health financing element, Jerry Green, who succeeded Earl Brian in that department, determinedly resisted any effort to participate in the merger, acting instead as if his money-heavy enterprise was a world of its own. He missed most meetings of the senior staff, was often gone from the building, and referred all complaints about his avoidant behavior to Dr. Brian, who seemed disinterested at best.

The leader of the Department of Public Health fortified himself in his Berkeley office and was also rarely if ever available. It became clear that he considered himself, his people, and all their activities to be a sacrosanct, divinely-inspired and -mandated, most important of all health functions, that were not to be trifled with by mere psychiatrists and their political masters.

He came to attention when I announced a tentative plan to move his entire little private empire to Sacramento, where it "properly belonged" near the seat of government like the rest of us.

The public health crowd were true Berkeley-ites, steeped in the peculiar cultural and political mores of that wildly radical, violently anti-authority city. They were happy providing venereal disease treatment for the U.C. students, communing with fellow scientists on the campus, and immersing themselves in the artistic and social treasures of the great, storied Baghdad-by-the-Bay across the bridge. The prospect of moving to the dreary wastelands of Sacramento, where dwelled only barbarians and criminals, energized that group of disease-preventers and preservers of human life as nothing else possibly could.

Having captured their attention, the public healthers began showing up for meetings and, while never showing proper evidence of true obeisance to their new masters, did prove to be intelligent and valuable contributors to our infrequent meetings and our overall efforts.

The finance people were harder. The opportunity arose, however, when in response to a question from the governor's staff about abortions around the state supposedly being paid for by MediCal, I had to gather some facts. The health care financing people had, for some time, been gathering paid-claims data on huge, noisy computers of the early design that employed magnetic tapes that ran on large spools contained in glass cabinets taller than a man.

Operated under contract by Ross Perot's company - under a contract of which the staff (and Mr. Perot) were inordinately proud - the computers recorded the age, sex, and residence of every patient treated under the MediCal program, the diagnosis and the date and kind of treatment received. Selecting four counties of different size so as to reflect the total state population in the 58 counties, I asked the computer people to examine the claims for the four counties during one month from each quarter of the preceding year.

My question, it seemed to me, was a perfectly simple, straightforward one. Simply tell me how many females between the ages of 18 and 30 had a diagnosis of pregnancy during those four months in each of the four counties, and how many had an abortion. Extrapolating those figures to a full year, statewide, should answer my question from on high.

Several days passed with no report from data processing. When asked about this, they reported that it would take at least four days of constant computer running time, at outrageous cost, the loss of four full days of claims-processing time, and the result could have an error rate of as much as 30%.

With that, I gained the distinction of being possibly the only person ever to have fired Ross Perot and his whole company. I instructed the staff to seek another data processor immediately, gave them a deadline for replacing the system currently in use, and got their full attention. Not their wholehearted cooperation, of course, but they too began coming to executive meetings.

The next step was to visit the regional offices, in each of which there would be an all-hands meeting where employees would be reassured about their job security, informed of the great things that could result from this consolidation, encouraged to visit and get to know the people in other regional offices that had been operated by the former departments, and find out how they could help one another.

As it turned out, there were more than 60 regional offices scattered around the state! It was, I discovered, a very big state. Everywhere I discovered that offices of the old department of mental hygiene were at best only vaguely aware of nearby offices of public health, sometimes a block away, and vice versa. Neither knew where the MediCal office was, in town. They didn't even know each others' telephone numbers, let alone what they did.

Interestingly enough, there was little evidence of resistance in the field. The people seemed genuinely interested in their counterparts in what formerly were different departments, willing and even eager to learn if they were overlapping and duplicating one another in their activities and how they might help one another, and they seemed downright happy to have a new group of friends. How I longed for those attitudes to spread to Sacramento!

They did, as time went on, but never as easily and fully as had occurred out in the boondocks. Exactly the same thing was true among the Armed Forces, where headquarters resistance to inter-service cooperation and operational collaboration diminished in direct proportion to the distance from the Pentagon, and actually started a few feet from the parking lot.

What was happening to me during these adventures was something Freud called "the degradation of the love object." What he was talking about was the growing realization, among normally maturing sons of loving mothers, that dearest Mom, the little boy's "best girl" who married dear old dad and whose exact image must be sought for future mating is, after all a human being of conventional proportions, and not some sort of goddess who is without sin, without serious blemish, and certainly never has sex.

My 'love object' had been my wonderful profession of healing. Physicians were, above all else, ethical, moral, honorable and bound to one another in a precious, inviolable loyalty. They were intelligent, caring, thoughtful, and ever able to join together for the common good, toward which they always strove. They were unflinchingly honest, and hardly even had sex.

To a great extent, the good people who helped us: nurses, lab techs, aides, orderlies, health administrators, social workers, audiologists, opticians and the whole army of helping professionals partook of the same qualities.

What I was finding, without exactly thinking it through, was that all that nonsense was exactly that. We are all just people, none without blemish or sin, not gods and goddesses bursting with goodness and light. Some among us have better qualities, but no professional training guarantees that in anyone. What a shock! This wasn't exactly a new revelation, of course. There had been a few despicable characters alongside me as we graduated from medical school. I had encountered some physicians whose character was seriously wanting, and some 'helpers' who were bums and criminals.

But in the main, in my previous experience in the Navy and the Army, it was my impression that we in medicine did listen to a different drum, shared a sense of a higher calling, and could count on one another rather more surely than I was finding to be the case in civilian society. What surprised me was the fact that the people I worked with were all career public servants in addition to being trained in the helping professions, and while most were honest and well-intentioned, a significant number were not. What's more, evidence of perfidy seemed to increase as people rose to higher and higher levels in the government bureaucracy.

Even this failed to prepare me for the experiences I was later to have, when dealing with the most senior military physicians of all: the Surgeons General and their immediate staffs.

We did make progress, putting together the new, reorganized and consolidated Department of Health. The good guys, in true American tradition, steadily prevailed over the bad guys, and by the time the Reagan administration had ended, things were going well.

Our new governor "Moonbeam," however, presented a radical departure in leadership from that of Ronald Reagan. For eight years we (even the democrats) knew that a firm, decisive hand was on the controls of state. Reagan, a tall man, was physically and socially supremely graceful. When he made a physical or mental misstep, he instantly recovered his poise and usually made a small joke, with himself the butt of it, that put everyone at ease. More, he was obviously a man of principle and strong convictions.

Governor Reagan had the rare gift of projecting absolute sincerity. In all the years I knew him, before and during his terms in California and later during his presidency, I never once saw him 'fake' anything, or attempt to deceive. He was more open and honest than any political person I ever watched - and I watched a great many of them intently. While he never played dumb, and he was assuredly not even a little dumb, he could, when the occasion demanded, as in the midst of hostile, even outrageous media questions, appear to be a little confused or uncertain in a response, but he invariably moved on to firmly-held ground, and left his attackers feeling bested.

It is well-known that he had a sparkling, unquenchable sense of humor. He loved jokes and worked them into nearly every conversation; if the subject were a serious matter, his jokes were fewer and more clearly illustrative of a point he wanted to make. He never, in my hearing, told sexual or scatological jokes, and I often marveled that there even existed so many jokes that were not 'dirty,' and wondered where he got them and how he could remember them.

His memory, contrary to some reports, was truly phenomenal. When I first saw him in Sacramento (I was in a group and had not been introduced), it was fully eight years since our previous talks on the movie set in Hollywood, yet he strode directly up to me, spoke my name with evident pleasure, and said he had never forgotten our conversations about POWs and America. That made me an instant celebrity, of course. His memory was not just a politician's tool. Whenever I briefed him on an issue of importance to my department, I came away certain that he had understood exactly what I was saying, and would recall it accurately much later on. This is a priceless quality in a boss, and all too rare.

Reagan appeared - and was - remarkably at ease, regardless of the setting and even in the midst of crisis situations. This trait, like some others, was misleading and disarming to those who did not know him well. Some self-appointed experts mistakenly took it to mean he didn't understand the problem, or didn't take problems seriously enough. That was dead wrong.

He genuinely liked most people, and was a true and faithful friend. He picked his closest associates and principal deputies based on a mass of intuitive feelings that in turn arose from his keen eye and sharp ear, attuned to inflection and innuendo that escaped most others. Once bestowed, his friendship and loyalty were unshakeable, sometimes in the face of damning evidence that in a given case they shouldn't be. Mostly, however, his close associates strove constantly to merit his continued regard and trust.

At least partly as a reflection of his strong feelings for those whom he liked and trusted, he had the courage to delegate authority. He did this in a way that indicated not only his trust in you as a person, but his trust in your judgment as well. One came away from such acts of delegation absolutely determined to do the best that could be done, not to fail, and to be totally responsible for the task and the outcome.

When, for example, eight more years after his California term ended and he had become the Commander-in-Chief, I went with Cap Weinberger to the White House to report my findings about the horrifying inadequacy of our medical readiness, he thought for a while and then said, "Bud, fix it." Then, turning to Weinberger he said, "Cap, give him whatever he needs. And my thanks to you both."

What he had actually said, in these terse pronouncements, was that he understood, he believed what I had reported, he believed I knew what to do to correct it, and he trusted my judgment as to how to do it. He was telling Cap that no matter how expensive it would be, it had to be done and he would share in the responsibility for seeing to it that it was done.

He did not set a deadline, ask what steps I would take, demand progress reports, make suggestions or in any way micromanage. This in spite of the fact that hundreds of millions of dollars would be needed, the entire current emphasis of the military medical departments re-directed, and failure could lead to a national scandal and a political crisis. Brave man.

Never in my life had I been sent forth, so clearly yet succinctly, to literally do, or die, feeling that it was the highest possible honor and privilege to do exactly and literally that.

When the new governor of California, Jerry Brown, took office there was a convulsive change. The very day of the inauguration, as soon as the ceremony ended, a small army of state police and other law enforcement people entered every office in Sacramento occupied by a senior official. The men who came to our building, two of whom entered my office without knocking, announced that we would have 30 minutes to clear our desks of all personal items and leave the premises. We were forbidden to remove any official documents. We were to wait at home, resignations prepared and in hand, until summoned. We would then be told our fate.

The clear implication was that we would soon know if we were to remain, to resign, or to be arrested. Upset and disgusted, we all obeyed.

My call came the next morning. I was directed to the new governor's office in the capitol, and told nothing else, so there was no way to anticipate what was going to happen.

When I entered, noticing at once that all decorations and ornaments had been stripped from the shelves, table surfaces and walls, the several men and women already in the office, none of whom I recognized, immediately left. The new governor of California, son of the governor who served just before Reagan, was a dismayingly young-looking, slightly harassed-seeming, handsome fellow of slight build, with an engaging smile.

"Doctor," he exclaimed, extending his hand. "Thanks for coming! I wanted to ask you," he went on, "If you'd be willing to stay on in your present job. Things seem to be going on pretty well over there, and since you are most familiar with all the ins and outs, I was hoping you'd stick around for a while. I'd appreciate it."

There being no burning reason to refuse, and with his assurance that I needn't give him a final answer for a few weeks, I agreed, and began a wondrous journey in an unreal world.

It was not many weeks before the magnitude of the change in the capitol became fully evident. The governor called me to his office with some regularity to discuss issues that had arisen involving health services and budget matters in particular. In spite of his superficial friendliness, Jerry Brown invariably struck me as a rather tense, uncertain man who had strong convictions that were not carefully thought through. He showed, for a man whose father had been governor for two terms, and who was well educated, an astonishing ignorance of how government worked.

On more than one occasion, when he questioned something we were doing in MediCal or Mental Hygiene, I would explain that we did whatever it was because the law required it. His response was something like, "Well, then, I'll just change the law." The first time I suggested that he couldn't 'just' do that, he demanded, "Why not? I'm the governor, aren't I?"

There is something surreal about standing with the chief executive of the largest state in America, in his office in the Capitol, and discovering that he actually did not understand the limits on his power. When I asked if he had a sponsor for a bill that would have to pass both houses and come to him for signature in order to enact a law revoking one already on the books, he seemed exasperated, and turned away grumbling about paperwork.

Matters came to a head when a legislative hearing of the Assembly Ways and Means committee, that controlled all state funds, was scheduled to take up the renewal of our historic contract with the state Dental Association to provide care for MediCal patients. I could not help but reflect on my own dentist-mother's unceasing efforts, so many years before, to persuade the city fathers of Cincinnati to let her provide care for the poor children of that city, and what a wonderful thing it turned out to be.

The previous year, after months of tough negotiation, I had persuaded the dentists to take the deal I offered, at a far lower reimbursement rate than they were requesting. I had to agree that they might lose money, although not a huge amount, but assured them that it was a worthwhile investment. For the very first time, it would put into place a needed service heretofore absolutely unavailable to the poor, and they could argue price when the contract came up for renewal in a year. That time had come, and the dentists had come forth with a new price, and were able to show that they were losing money.

The day before the hearing, a tall, lanky, dark-skinned Latino man wearing cowboy boots, a work shirt and jeans, and crowned with a flat, broad-brimmed, stiff leather hat walked past my secretaries without pausing or taking his long crooked cigar from his mouth, pulled up a chair in front of my desk, and, leaning back, put his feet on my desk.

After having been expelled from my office by hard-eyed investigators on inauguration day, and having met Mario Obledo, the scowling, impatient, disorganized man who now occupied the grand office of Secretary of Health and Welfare, which he had literally filled with stacks of paper all over the floor, I was not totally surprised. The desk, however, was a small but very beautiful, leather topped piece of furniture I had procured personally. Its small size was a subtle power statement proclaiming that I did not need the typically huge thing all other state executives seemed to need to prove their power, and that there was no space here for weighty and important documents awaiting my important attention.

I told the man that the desk was not state property, but my own, and I wanted him to take his boots off of it. We stared at each other for a moment, just like genuine Mexican bandilleros about to draw our pistols. Then he smirked, shrugged, and dropped his feet heavily to the floor.

"Doc," he said, (bad beginning) "Mario (Obledo, presumably) sent me over to fill you in on tomorrow. When the dental business comes up, you won't be testifying. We'll take care of it." I assumed he meant Obledo's staff, which turned out to be right. With that, he got up, adjusted his hat brim, and stalked out.

Sure enough, when I went to the hearing the next day to listen from a back row seat, my visitor of the previous day, but without his leather hat, took his place in the witness chair and was identified as an attorney (never admitted to the California Bar because of inability to pass the bar exam) who was there to represent Secretary Obledo. He opened his testimony by declaring that the Secretary had studied the dentists' excessive reimbursement demands and did not accept them. Instead, he was going to propose a reduction in the contract that would save both the state and the dentists' significant amounts of money.

How, he was asked, was that possible?

With a small, modest note of triumph in his voice, he said that they had studied the services provided, and found that a major cost item was the provision of dentures for the numerous old, indigent MediCal patients who had no teeth. That would no longer be allowed. It its place, and at far less cost, the state would issue to each toothless person an electric blender, thus solving their problems.

There was a moment of stunned silence. Looks of disbelief appeared on the faces of the powerful members of this most powerful of committees, and finally the chairman, shaking his head, said something like, "You are kidding, of course?" When this was not confirmed, he struck his gavel once, with great force, and declared the meeting adjourned. The dentists got the increased reimbursement they had requested, dentures continued to be constructed and fitted, and so far as I could find out, the state never bought a single blender.

Shortly after that I was pleased and honored by an unexpected visit from the former Director of Mental Hygiene, Jim Lowry. Always the affable Irishman, Jim admired my small desk and instantly recognized it for what it was, a kind of reverse status symbol, and laughed appreciatively. He said he had been "in the neighborhood" and just decided to drop by. Jim never 'just dropped by,' and I told him to stop kidding. What was on his mind?

He seemed to like that. Then, pretending to be off-handedly making conversation, he asked if Jerry had asked me to stay on, yet. When I said that he had, my visitor seemed lost in thought for a moment, and then he began to reminisce. He told me how he had been appointed to head the department by Jerry Brown's father, a powerful democrat and very skillful political operator, back in the days when all we had was a collection of huge state hospitals, and no local programs.

The big hospitals provided important, long-duration employment opportunities to their host communities, and through the wages they paid and the goods and services they bought locally, became economic and, inevitably, political powers in their localities. The elder Brown had fully appreciated this, and enjoyed an excellent relationship with Dr. Lowry, who was politically savvy and well able to play the game. As a result, Jim had had a successful tenure as director, improved the hospitals significantly, hired many good people, and enjoyed his tenure thoroughly

When Mr. Reagan was elected and his staff reviewed Jim's record as the manager of the state's mental hospitals, he was invited to stay on in the new administration, and Jim did.

"That," he told me, "Was the worst mistake I ever made." He went on to say he had no idea how differently the new administration looked at things, and how complicated it got when community mental health programs, with generous state subsidies, started popping up 'all over the map.' He declared that he soon realized he shouldn't have stayed past the change in administrations, but that he was in so deep and the problems were so complex that it took him several years before he could "safely" (his word) extricate himself.

He said he thought he should share that with me, before I made any promises, and that I should think about it.

With that he rose, offered me his hand and a smile, and left.

I did think about it, and had been for some weeks. Jim's tale didn't make the decision for me, but it helped. A few days later, my letter to the governor, reluctantly announcing my decision to leave, was delivered. Although I had set a date two weeks hence, they stopped my salary the day I signed the letter, so I bade goodbye to old dear friends and left. I did so with a distinct sense of relief, of having escaped God knew what dreadful events.

The San Diego County mental health program director at that time was a man named Bill Stadel. A bit of a curmudgeon in his public persona, he was actually, beneath that facade, a warm, rather sensitive man, somewhat set in his ways (he drove to Mexico weekly for Mexican rolls and Oso Negro gin and cheap gas for his ancient car). He had hinted to me that he felt he was growing too old for the job and would consider retiring soon, so I resolved to visit and see if he were serious.

A new condominium development in the tiny, posh community of Coronado, just across the bay from downtown San Diego, had advertised in one of the airline magazines I happened to see that if one was interested in buying one of the units, the management would put them up overnight in a model. I called, and when they found out that I was a public figure of such importance, urged me to come down and occupy one of their studios or one bedroom apartments for a few days to see how I liked it.

Equipped with a free room reservation and an appointment to see Bill Stadel, I drove to San Diego, once again marveling at the sunshine, the beautiful bay, the sailboats and aircraft carriers at anchor, and the general air of a subtropical paradise. Coronado Shores turned out to be a new creation of a half dozen 12- or 14-floor towers standing between Glorietta Bay, a lovely yacht harbor near the foot of the soaring Coronado Bridge, and the ocean.

My complimentary suite overlooked the grounds and gardens of the picturesque Hotel de Coronado next door, the largest wooden commercial structure in North America and the first hotel to boast electric lights, whose installation was personally supervised by Thomas Edison. With its gleaming white walls and pointed, red-roofed tops on its towers, it was every bit as pretty as it had been when "Some Like it Hot" was being filmed there as a vehicle for Marilyn Monroe.

Adjoining the hotel to the north lay the immaculately groomed village of Coronado, a 'Navy town' whose inhabitants included no fewer than 54 retired admirals, with houses and front yards as neat and clean as any quarterdeck. The business section lay along a single street decorated with flowering hanging baskets in the grassy center strip, with small shops and eating places at each side. There were no 'fast-food' chain restaurants; no garish neon signs to violate the tranquility, and the small bandstand in the park was clean and freshly painted.

Just north of the town itself, little more than a mile away, if that, lay the imaginatively named "North Island" Naval Air Station, occupying, as might be expected, the northern tip of the 'island,' actually the emergent tip of a long sandy spit reaching up the western edge of San Diego Bay from just above the Mexican border, where it connected to the mainland at the foot of the bay proper.

In short order, and with my friend Dr. Stadel's help, I had submitted my application to succeed him, and made a down payment on a lovely corner condominium at The Shores about five stories above the ground overlooking Glorietta Bay and the Coronado Bridge, with the gleaming skyscrapers of the city of San Diego in the background.

The wheels of the county civil service system ground exceeding slow. After about six weeks I was called for an interview. It turned out to be a not altogether friendly interrogation before a panel of six or eight civil service citizen-commissioners who sat grimly behind a long table, while I fidgeted uncomfortably on a straight chair fifteen feet in front of them.

The proceeding was conducted with no sign whatever of human warmth, kindness, humor or anything but the severest business matters. No indication, pro or con, was forthcoming, and I had to stifle a smile as I imagined that suddenly, and in unison, these deadly serious protectors of the public weal would thrust their thumbs up or down, and my fate would be sealed. Finally it was over, and I was dismissed.

Having so recently left such an exalted but similar position in a much higher and more important level of government, I was forced to conclude that the Lord, in his wisdom, had designed this little exercise as a much-needed lesson in humility. And it worked.

More weeks went by, and not a word was forthcoming from the county of San Diego, so my hopes dimmed. Meanwhile, there had been repeated invitations from the University of California at Irvine School of Medicine, and the Veterans Administration Hospital, Long Beach, which were affiliated, to accept a joint appointment to the faculty and the hospital.

It had now been six weeks since I left Sacramento - my longest period of inactivity and unemployment since I finished the seventh grade. I decided to take the job in Long Beach, and gave notice of my decision to the people in charge. The next day I drove up to the VA hospital, nearly a hundred miles north of Coronado.

Ironically, the very next day a postcard arrived from San Diego County, informing me that I had been accepted for the job applied for! I felt that I could not honorably call the people at the VA and the University and say I had changed my mind, so I reluctantly had to decline the offer of the job so long sought in San Diego.

With no further delay, I became an associate professor of psychiatry on the faculty at U.C. Irvine Medical School, and simultaneously Associate Chief of Staff for Education at the Veterans Hospital. The arrangement was a product of a plan put into place a few years earlier, when the VA set out to improve the quality of care and of post-graduate education in their major hospitals by affiliating them with nearby medical schools, sharing faculty and sharing salaries. This enabled the VA to recruit physicians at a substantially higher rate of pay than would have been possible if the physician were employed solely by the Veteran's Administration, since they could not pay as much as major medical schools.

The hospital at Long Beach was the largest of the 168 hospitals then being operated by the VA. It housed over a thousand patients in buildings that formerly served as a Naval Hospital, but had been sold by the Navy to the VA not long after World War II. It was situated in a pleasant residential area of the city not far from the major north-south freeway, Interstate 405, so my trip from Coronado was a straight shot on the freeway, but not necessarily a quick one.

In addition to the many wards and buildings filled with patients of every variety, since this was a general medical and surgical facility, there were at all times more than a thousand people in various training programs in different departments and sections of the institution. In addition to young physicians pursuing specialty training in the many branches of medicine and surgery departments, we were engaged in training nurses, lab technicians, radiology techs, audiologists, speech pathologists, medical equipment repair technicians, prosthetic device makers, and many others.

It was to be my job to organize this massive educational effort into some sort of orderly system with principles and procedures that cut across the lines of the many disciplines involved. Needed were such things as regularized proficiency testing, and clearly defined areas of responsibility, and identification of exactly who was accountable for the conduct and the outcome of the many training efforts. Surprisingly, this had never been done before, and training in that place was a mass of confusion. In addition, I would help in the training of psychiatry residents and fill in for other faculty members from time to time.

It was a pleasant job, among friendly people, but not very challenging or rewarding once the system was put into reasonable shape. Once in a while the Chief of Staff was away, and I would function in his place. We were given a surprisingly nice apartment in a former barracks building, right on the edge of the hospital's 9-hole golf course, so it was possible to play almost daily. Mostly I attended the countless staff meetings that are required to keep a major teaching hospital operating, and the quality up. As the months went by, I became aware that the academic medical life was not my most rewarding career, and I began to look around, but with no urgency.

An opportunity presented itself unexpectedly, as is so often the case. I was attending the annual state medical convention in nearby Anaheim, and found that a particular presentation I wanted to hear was so packed with attendees that it was impossible to get in. Nothing else at that hour sounded worth listening to, so I made my way into the large exhibition area where the drug and equipment companies demonstrated their wares.

Back during my medical school days, we all went eagerly to the great medical conventions held in Chicago. Not only did it make us feel like real doctors, but also there were generous samples of medications and devices that were free for the taking. Best of all, there were always copious quantities of cigarettes - Camels, to be exact - being handed out by very pretty, scantily-clad hostesses, and we loaded up.

No one noticed at the time, but right after such events, there was always an advertising campaign asserting - and who could argue - that more doctors smoked Camel cigarettes than any other brand. Later they stopped that, because someone complained, but the advertisers then switched to nuclear physicists, implying that they were even smarter.

One of the display booths held only brochures, pamphlets, and a discouraged seeming Army warrant officer, trying to interest physicians in a life of service to their country. Heidi was with me and we stopped to chat. On impulse, I asked if he knew of anything in Europe for an old retired Army doctor-psychiatrist. He brightened up immediately, and said he'd heard they were looking for someone to work in a new alcohol treatment center in Germany. Would I like that? We decided to explore the idea.

It turned out that I could go as a civilian employee of the Army, at a rather low civil service level, but they would transport me and my family - and a car - to Europe, and help with housing costs in return for a three-year commitment. It meant a 50% cut in our combined pay, but it presented the prospect of a great European adventure, so after some serious consideration of our present jobs, and my long twice-weekly commute to San Diego, we decided to do it. Thus began a whole new phase in our lives, both personally and professionally.

Brainwashing, Drunks & Madness

William E. Mayer, M.D.

CHAPTER 12

REVELATIONS IN ALCOHOLISM

Our workplace in Germany was to be in Bad Cannstadt, a suburb of the city of Stuttgart, in the Southeast of the country near the Black Forest. Located there was the Army's 5th General Hospital, where it was planned to open a special residential treatment center for alcoholism.

The 5th General was an old civilian hospital built in the late 1800s and converted to German Army use during WWII. It was a typical concrete and stucco facility of multiple buildings, all with high ceilings and old tile floors. The larger buildings consisted of three floors above a cavernous cellar, and tunnels connected one to another. Rickety elevators served the buildings with more than two floors, and heat was supplied by steam radiators served from a large, ominous boiler whose pipes underlay the entire compound.

One of the buildings had been designated for use as the alcoholism treatment unit, and had been refurbished so as to accommodate 80 patients. A former barracks, it also contained a number of rooms that could be used for group therapy, offices for the staff, and a lounge large enough to permit all the patients and staff, and a few visitors, to assemble for general meetings.

The unit was brand new, and not yet named. Several officers were already assigned: a physician, a clinical psychologist, and a social worker, all commissioned officers, a civilian nurse, and a warrant officer administrator. The physician, Norbert, was a brand-new lieutenant colonel just recently recruited from civilian life; this was his first assignment. He was familiar to me, inasmuch as he had been a local mental health director in Santa Barbara County who had left there abruptly after some difficulty with the Board of Supervisors.

The psychologist was a product of the free speech era at Berkeley, and was married to a sweet lady who had never given up the dress, unnaturally soft speech and gentle manners of her flower-child youth. Jim was an energetic, verbal man whose younger brother was exploring the Eastern religions somewhere in the Indian subcontinent, periodically supplying our eager psychologist, we later found out, with marijuana.

Our social work officer, who had a doctorate degree in something called "counseling psychology" in addition to his training in psychiatric social work, was a warm, outgoing, good-natured and good-looking fellow who had a bright, sunny outlook and who took nothing too seriously. Cal Neptune had been a military police officer who served in combat during the war in Korea, an experienced soldier with an excellent record who was to go far in coming years. He was married to a lovely woman who was a teacher of music, and had three healthy, altogether normal and very bright children.

The new lieutenant colonel, Norbert, was a movie star-handsome man who had in an earlier life been a driver of formula one race cars. He had married a highly intelligent, spirited woman who was the widow of a fellow race car driver who was killed in competition, and who somehow tolerated her new husband's obtuseness and somewhat obsessive personality.

The Army, at that time, was having great difficulty recruiting physicians and had signed Norbert up 'off the street' without paying much if any attention to his personality problems and difficulties in his former job, giving him his unusually high initial rank because of his years in medical practice. They did not give him any formal training, but supplied him with a set of all current Army regulations and a copy of the Uniform Code of Military Justice, all of which material he diligently studied, committing a remarkable amount of it to memory. That fact proved to be a mixed blessing.

Patients were recruited for what we soon named the USAREUR (meaning U.S. Army, Europe) Alcohol Treatment Facility, or ATF, through official Army notices throughout the European continent that encouraged commanding officers to identify subordinates who had problems with their use of alcohol, on or off duty, and send them to us. If our evaluation verified the soldier's alcoholism, he (or less often she) would be entered into our intensive six-week inpatient program. Upon 'graduation,' the soldier would be returned to duty, a full report made to the commander, and any further alcohol-related problems were to be dealt with administratively or through the military justice system.

All officers and senior non-commissioned officers arriving in Europe to command units spent their initial two weeks of duty there in a special training unit. It was set up near a famed, historic invasion route used repeatedly by the German army when it attacked France and the Low Countries in every modern war in Europe.

Called the Fulda Gap, it was on the German-Czechoslovak border, near the small medieval city of Vilseck. Our army had established a huge armored (tanks) training base there, as had the Germans in pre-WWII and pre-WWI days, and part of that was used to train newly-arriving officers and non-coms about the current military realities in Europe. That seemed like a good place to deliver our message about alcohol problems among the troops, and the importance of sending problem soldiers for treatment, as a responsibility of command.

William E. Mayer, M.D.

The EUSAREUR Command Surgeon, a major general, had been a classmate at the Command and General Staff College some years before, so I traded on that relationship to suggest to him that we be allowed to indoctrinate all the new commanders about the growing problem of alcoholism when they were getting the rest of their training at Vilseck. He in turn took the idea to the overall commander, a 4-star general, who agreed. He was to become a stout supporter of our program, which consequently flourished.

My many years of treating alcoholic patients, starting long before in my little private office on Mt. Parnassas in San Francisco when most of the patients referred by the faculty turned out to have serious alcohol problems, had long since disabused me of all the notions I had been taught about the disorder.

The first thing that became apparent, those many years before, was that my psychiatric patients who also drank steadily and too much, did not respond to any form of conventional psychiatric treatment that I had been taught to perform. While they often had 'psychiatric' symptoms: depression, obsessive thoughts, marital disruptions with serious interpersonal problems, sexual dysfunction, and emotional outbursts, they did not seem to fit usual psychiatric diagnostic categories. And they didn't get better.

By the time I reached Eureka, some years later, it was clear to me that serious alcoholics had a definite illness - a disease of some sort. We had always been taught that they had a character disorder, were 'psychopathic' personalities or possessed antisocial traits that made it impossible for them to learn from experience, to consider the effect of their acts on others, or to anticipate the consequences of their actions. It was generally agreed among most psychiatrists that people with such character disorders could not be treated successfully, and they were rarely accepted in treatment.

We physicians were also taught that the inevitable result of the over-use of alcohol was irreversible damage to the liver, first of all, and later to the brain and kidneys and all the body's vital systems. We saw that on autopsy. How sad that bad, weak character led to decay and death! Since we couldn't treat these poor souls, we sent them to their ministers and priests. They had no success either.

One fact that had long troubled me was my discovery that many patients who were clearly addicted to alcohol, or profoundly dependent on it, did not show convincing evidence of having serious character disorders, except after they began steady, heavy drinking, and sometimes not even then. Like most people, in and out of the medical profession, I had been led to believe that alcoholics were generally drunken bums. Everyone has seen them, in the alleys of large cities, lounging groggily in the parks, panhandling for change.

People who are not bums, when being seen by a physician, are rarely asked except in the most superficial terms, about their drinking. People with alcohol problems in a society like ours that has long condemned them in moralistic, judgmental terms, rarely if ever volunteer information about those problems, if indeed they recognize them themselves. Hardly anyone ever tells anyone, including his doctor, that he drinks too much. The result is that the great majority of physicians understand almost nothing about alcoholism.

Since only about 10% of serious alcoholics look or act like bums, the vast majority are not recognized until their disease is far advanced. Families often recognize there is a problem, but resist the idea that someone in the immediate family is an alcoholic; there are no bums or drunks around here!

Fellow workers may notice 'problems,' but in alcoholism, the job is usually the last thing to go, and jobs can be changed more readily than families.

Over my years in medicine, then, almost without thinking it through, I had arrived at a conclusion that put me at odds with almost all my fellow physicians and psychiatrists. That was that alcoholism was truly, in and of itself, a disease. It was not caused by bad character or liver problems. It was not a moral issue, although moral issues often resulted. It was not an emotional problem being solved by self-medication, but it led to emotional problems. It caused marriage and job problems but was not the result of wives' and bosses' mean behavior.

It was, in short, not what I and every other physician had been taught. What was more, it was treatable - manageable - like any other chronic disease. Not curable, but manageable. So are diabetes and hypertension.

The 5th General Hospital was the smallest of the major Army hospitals in Europe and was primarily devoted to the care of internal medicine and psychiatry patients, with little major surgery. It was commanded by a hulking medical colonel, Peter Schroeder, who had followed me by several years at the Command and General Staff College, and whose strict sense of seniority and protocol led him to deal with me as if I were, if not senior to him, at least his equal. He treated his staff quite differently.

Peter was a native of Germany, and had been a member of the Hitler Jungend as an adolescent. When the war ended, he moved with his family to the US where he went to college and medical school before entering the Army. He had readily adapted to Army life, and progressed steadily to his present high rank and responsible role as a hospital commander. His unit was little more than 200 beds, much smaller than the huge installations at Landstuhl and Frankfurt, but was expected to expand rapidly to several times its size were a war to erupt in Europe.

The colonel, who was well over six feet tall and rather bulky, held himself in a rigid military posture at all times, even when seated at his desk. He marched, rather than walked, as he moved about the compound, and strictly observed military customs and formal modes of address. He became quite noticeably on high alert whenever an officer of higher rank came on the post, and his tense attentiveness secretly amused all onlookers. In a not unkind way, he was seen by his subordinates to be a combination of Colonel Klink and Sergeant Schultz of TV fame, partly because of his somewhat blustery manner and his pronounced German accent.

After we had been there for nearly a year, I walked into his office one day - he always jumped to his feet and greeted me in a formal but friendly way - and invited him and his wife, whom he called "Mama," to join us for dinner in our little condominium apartment not far away. He actually flushed and seemed flustered at this.

"Vell," he said in some consternation, "Mama und I nefer accept invitations von my staff. You understand. Vere vould it shtop? Everyone vould vant us to come! However," he continued after a moment of intense reflection, "You und I haf a spetsial connextion, No? Ve are the only two Leavenworth graduates here, hein? Zo, I vill ask Mama."

With that he rose, bade me a cordial farewell, and off I went to await Mama's decision. A call the next day accepted my invitation "Mit great pleasure!" and the date was set.

We prepared a fine, traditional American dinner, and waited eagerly, all in the family scrubbed and in neat, fresh clothes on the evening of the big event, certain that Peter and Mama would arrive exactly at the appointed time, not a second before or after the time set. Sure enough, at the very instant our guests were due, the doorbell rang.

In keeping with German custom, I opened the door, with my twelve year old son standing stiffly at attention by my side. The colonel, in a fresh, well-tailored uniform complete with all his decorations, towered in the doorway, nearly filling it. His wife, also true to German custom, stood behind him. I shook his hand and welcomed him, as he stood there. When that handshake, two decisive, abrupt up and down movements, was completed, Peter leaned down from his great height to grasp my son's rigidly extended hand.

"Und zis is little Bud!" he pronounced in stentorian tones. "Vell, Little Bud, I'll tell you vat I'm going to do. I'm going to let you call me by my favorite nickname!" Long pause, then, "Colonel!"

With that, the great man strode into our small apartment, followed by Mama, who spoke almost no English and seemed tiny indeed, at about 2 inches under five feet, as she trotted along behind and settled herself next to him on our sofa. We were a little surprised at how pleasantly the evening unfolded. True to military tradition, we did not discuss potentially controversial subjects like politics, religion, or specific women, but stuck with reflections about our education, our days at Ft. Leavenworth, and the logistics of running a US Army hospital overseas. They stayed later than we expected, and left evidently happy and certainly well fed.

Our unit, now officially named the Alcohol Treatment Facility and known throughout the European Command as "The ATF at 5th G," was soon full of patients and remained so for the next several years. It proved to be an enormous success, thanks in large part to the Commanding General's express support and the fact that we ran it like a strict military installation.

All new patients, the great bulk of them senior non-commissioned officers, but some commissioned officers as well, were subjected to a not-unfriendly but rather severe indoctrination that left no doubt as to what they were getting into, and how important and serious it was.

First, they were congratulated on their great good fortune in being here, and in having had a commander who had cared enough about them to send them to us. We acknowledged that they were obviously competent soldiers who had been successful and had distinct value to the Army, but who were now in serious danger of ruining both their careers and what remained of their lives.

We touched on the commonly held attitudes about alcoholics, that they were drunks, bums, unreliable, untrustworthy, undependable and, worst of all, a danger to their buddies when the going got rough. At the ATF, we did not agree with those stereotypes, and they were going to help us prove they were wrong.

They would, therefore, from this moment onward, demonstrate that they were exemplary soldiers. Their uniforms, carriage, observance of military courtesies and general attitude and behavior would equal or exceed what is expected and demanded in the finest military academies, whose rules, in any case, were not as strict as ours. Their rooms would be inspected daily. They would participate in calisthenics and jogging, in formation, every day, giving evidence at all times of the highest levels of morale and discipline.

Finally, they were told, they would go back to the same job, exactly, that they had left to come here; that was a condition of their admission. All commanders who referred anyone here had to guarantee that. Those officers would also be instructed (by the Commanding General) not only to expect the ATF graduate to perform his duties in exemplary manner but also to expect close observation for any sign of recurrence. Should that occur, the soldier would be separated from the Service as undesirable. No exceptions. If these conditions were too tough, tell us; that would prove, up front, that they were not fit to be soldiers in this Army.

Each day began, for the patient, with 'policing up' his room and outfitting himself in exercise clothes for calisthenics. Then breakfast. The rest of the day was spent in 'Class A' uniform - no pajamas or sweats or fatigue uniforms worn in the field.

There was at least one formal class held each morning, dealing with the subject of alcoholism as a disease and a series of six detailed health and medical lectures, each dealing with a separate bodily system: circulatory, respiratory, digestive, reproductive, bone and joint, and neurological. These were designed to cover important, basic knowledge of the body that well-informed laymen should have, as well as the effect of alcohol on each.

The most important daily event was 'the group.' Every new arrival was assigned to a separate group of approximately ten people, all in different weeks of treatment. Each group had two leaders, one a recovering alcoholic well past his drinking days, and the other a trained mental health professional. Every member of the group was expected to participate actively in the group's discussions, which were guided but not prescribed by the leaders.

Group discussions always included descriptions of each participant's alcohol history, which was almost always revised in the direction of reality as the weeks went by. Each group member was free to comment or question what was being talked about, and strongly encouraged to do so. The leaders kept the discussions focused and moving along, prevented open conflicts, and often summed up, making appropriate observations and interpretations. Patients in their 5th and 6th weeks in the program invariably proved to be of tremendous value to the newer arrivals, and the groups were the most potent therapeutic tool in the program.

Every Friday a graduation ceremony, called "Big Step," was held to send forth those who had finished six weeks - back to duty, back to the 'real world,' and back to the careers they had well under way before alcohol had threatened to destroy them. Each graduate received a token to carry, both to commemorate his triumph and to remind him of the gravity of the disease he had gotten under control. Most graduates described their ATF experience as the most meaningful of their lives, and continued to believe that for many years thereafter, and so reported to members of the staff.

The most important idea that we tried to explain and implant in each soldier's mind was that alcoholism was a genuine disease like diabetes (often found in the families of alcoholics,) hypertension, cardiovascular disease, and many others that we could not cure, but could manage and control. Like those other chronic diseases, all with genetic and familial factors, and all with recognizable and generally irreversible physical changes, it was not a reflection of defective character or psychoneurosis, and could not be managed, ordinarily, by will-power alone. Strength of character and willpower are of undeniable help as one struggles to manage any chronic disease, but more is required.

Alcoholism, almost alone among the common chronic illnesses, is distinguished by having as one of its causative factors a single agent, alcohol, that the affected person can actually "control" by never allowing it to enter his body. It matters not why he is one of the perhaps 10% of all people whose body, and especially the tissues of his brain, cannot cope with this particular protoplasmic poison. What is important is his recognition and acceptance of the fact that he is in that 10%, that he cannot wish that away, and he is not there because he had a tough childhood, mean boss, bitchy wife, or a run of bad luck. Those things don't cause diabetes or high blood pressure, either.

Then what the alcoholic needs is an honest recognition of what alcohol causes him to do or fail to do, once it enters his body, and how impotent is his willpower or strong character to do anything about it when it is there. The trick, of course, is to keep the alcohol from getting into the body. A program like ours, with no alcohol available, can be the first step, but without real understanding of the disease, and without help from others, it is unlikely to be enough.

The only consistently successful way to enlarge upon the understanding that can be gained in a good program like that at the ATF, and to produce the greatest likelihood of long-term control of the disease of alcoholism that I have found, dealing with many hundreds - perhaps thousands - of alcoholics over this half century, is to participate in Alcoholics Anonymous: AA.

The daily group therapy sessions held at the ATF sometimes, in some ways, resembled AA meetings, but the latter are not at all the same. AA does not pretend to do therapy. It embodies and attends to twelve 'steps,' that are essentially restatements of some simple, basic precepts of mental health along with attention to the concept of a 'higher power.' That concept is not explicitly religious, as is sometimes thought, but acknowledges a spiritual component to human beings that is generally entirely absent from mental health work and practices, if not in theory as well.

Alcoholics Anonymous meetings were held regularly at the ATF and were an important part of the program. All patients were strongly urged to seek out an AA group as soon as they returned to duty, and to stick with it.

We also administered the drug Antabuse to all patients, and sent them back to duty with a six-week supply. All were carefully educated about this drug. As is well known, it can be a help in keeping the newly 'dry' alcoholic, now re-entering an environment where alcohol is widely used and easily available, from slipping back to using it. Reinforced in his 'recovery' by the knowledge that if he drinks, with Antabuse in his system, he will become sick, the ability to be with friends who are drinking, while sticking to soda water or soft drinks, hard at first, becomes easier and more natural with practice.

The success of the program at Bad Cannstadt was phenomenal. The nature of military organizational structure enabled us to keep track of the performance of our graduates long after they left, and we found that over 90% of our soldiers maintained their sobriety and avoided any further trouble related to alcohol usage for more than two years. That level of success was unmatched anywhere.

Even more important to us who worked there, however, was seeing our graduates return for the annual 'reunion,' usually looking so much healthier as to be almost unrecognizable, and coming with their families and with tales of how their lives had changed, thanking us all for having literally saved their lives and those families.

What was perhaps most striking about the ATF experience was the nature and quality of the men and women who took part in the program, both as patients and as staff - some of whom were in fact former patients themselves.

Some, like the colonel who was in command of a nuclear artillery unit and the helicopter pilot assigned to ferry generals and diplomats around the theater of operations, and the officer in charge of all major repair of the Army's new tanks, held positions of enormous responsibility. They had been performing their duties for months or even years, drunk the whole time! Most drank not only daily, but during the entire workday, carrying around a coke can actually filled with vodka, and went for long periods without attracting any undue attention or overtly failing in their duties, but they were, in fact, impaired. This revealed a great truth about alcoholics: most are not recognizable 'drunks,' and few are bums, or look like bums.

A unique and immensely effective element in the ATF program made possible by the military setting was our requirement that the wife or husband of every participant, if present in Europe, must be admitted to the unit for the final two weeks of the patient's six-week stay. The referring command had to arrange transportation as well as child care for any small children in the family. Adolescent children were strongly urged, though not required, to come and would be admitted along with the spouse.

Not only was this spousal requirement met without objection, but on more than one occasion arrangements were made by the referring command to bring a spouse who was still in the States all the way to Germany to take part. Husbands and wives shared a room, but were never put together in the same morning group. Some special couples' groups were conducted in the afternoons, and a small but surprising number of wives asked to remain for a full six-week course for their own alcohol problems.

The success of the program was unmatched in any other that we were able to assess. There were other good military programs, back in the US, that did not manage to get as good results, possibly because they did not have the same kind of high-level command support, or didn't routinely include wives and children, or were not as determinedly military in their conduct as we were. Unfortunately, no exhaustive analysis was possible of the reasons for our patients' success in returning to duty and eventually even being promoted.

But both during our three years of working in this program, and in the many years since, I have reflected about what was happening to the hundreds of men and women whose lives were changed there. The last twenty years and more in this country have been a period of apparently declining concern with what, earlier in the 20th Century, were widely accepted values and moral and ethical principles.

As this has happened, coming to a climax with the failings of the nation's supreme leader to adhere to standards of decency, honesty, and personal integrity, or even simple adherence to the law, the absence of any general public outrage or apparent concern has been striking. In the group sessions and discussions at the ATF that would not have been possible. Those men and women were in the process of revitalizing certain simple, basic values that the Army considers fundamental to military operations, and their lives.

Those values, in today's atmosphere, are rarely mentioned, and sound to many to be unsophisticated, 'corny,' unfashionable - and worse: unimportant. Recently our senior military leaders, after deep, probing deliberation and discussion, agreed that they were the following:

Duty
Honor
Integrity
Loyalty
Courage
Respect
Selfless Service.

Without them, these senior, experienced, wise leaders said, no military force could function effectively.

We believed that, in our old remodeled German barracks filled with people battling a tough chronic disease. In every aspect of what we taught and what we demanded of each soldier, those values came through, and were often talked about. I believe it was that, more than anything else, that helped those men and women resume command of themselves and their future lives.

While this country is not a military force, in the main, it has been a militant force for freedom and individual liberty during most of its first 200 years. It is quite possibly true that those things cannot survive without general acceptance of those same seven values the Army rests upon, and the use of them to guide social and political behavior.

At this moment no powerful foreign enemy threatens at our gates. However, there may be an internal enemy that could in the long run prove more devastating, as it has in countless societies before ours: complacency in the face of widespread retreat from values that guide men's lives. The signs abound: the acceptance of cheating in schools; the influence of money on the political process; the explosion of gambling as a reflection of the 'something for nothing - no work necessary' philosophy; the growing erosion of the family; the insistence on the rights of deviant groups of people; the eager embrace of victimhood; the explosion of litigation to assign blame and reap rewards.

All this, and more, in a world that is still dangerous. Terrorists will surely strike again, and yet again. Infectious diseases are far from eradication. No spot on earth is immune to natural disaster. Weapons of mass destruction far more effective than the simple, crude devices that demolished Hiroshima and Nagasaki are increasingly available to groups and nations who believe us - and our free, capitalist system - to be evil. Any significant blow to our tranquility can demand that we function, as a people, in ways that are based upon those simple, fundamental values, if we are to endure.

The experience at the ATF was, in many ways, the most gratifying clinical activity of my half-century in medicine. There was much to like and admire about most of the patients, who were in serious trouble but were not losers. To see them improve, progress and grow, and know we had something to do with that was singularly rewarding. Any physician who is honest knows that most of his patients get better regardless of what he does to them, except for simple things like removing a tumor or a hot appendix, administering an antibiotic that does the work for him, or relieves pain with drugs and splints.

Most patients need none of the above. Moreover, even when the physician has the honor and good fortune to serve as the agent of other men's genius and discoveries - Pasteur, Fleming, the Curies, Osler, and an army of others - and succeeds in helping someone heal or even survive, he mainly deals with the crisis of here and now. He has rarely done anything that significantly changes the future course of his patient's life.

Not so at the ATF. These people were undergoing a major life change. Most would live longer and better as a result of their efforts there. Most were escaping an inexorable process of deterioration both physical and mental, that had already begun and would ultimately kill them, if not others as well. They could feel the changes taking place in them, and we could see those changes occurring. It was immensely gratifying, and a great privilege.

Those three years were a major learning experience, for me, about the nature and the potential of people of all kinds, all social classes, and all levels of education. The cost of their progressive illness and eventual loss to the organization could have been horrendous; as it was, the cost of their stay at the ATF was minuscule, and the reward on that investment incalculable, both for them and for the Army and nation as well. Nothing I had ever before done in medicine had a comparable payoff.

Our three years in Germany, living in our tiny apartment and working near an historic city whose surrounding vineyards had been planted by the armies of Julius Caesar, came to an end in the fall of 1980, and we arrived back in California just in time to vote for my old friend, Ronald Reagan, who was running for president.

We settled into our lovely condominium on Glorietta Bay in Coronado, and I managed to make my way through the San Diego County bureaucracy and went to work in county headquarters preparing at last to take over Doctor Stadel's role as head physician. He had finally retired, at long last after many false starts, and I happily took over the job I had wanted for at least five years. We had a happy, sunny Christmas.

Then, one characteristically bright, glistening San Diego morning, "the call" came.

My young son rushed excitedly from the kitchen after answering the phone there exclaiming, "Dad! It's the President's Office!" Sure enough. It was short. Would I be willing to come back to Washington to head up the Alcohol, Drug Abuse and Mental Health Administration, ADAMHA, the counterpart for those problem areas to the National Institutes of Health? I'd have to talk it over with my family.

We assembled immediately to discuss the idea. I had just gotten the job of my life with essentially lifetime tenure. We were living in beautiful surroundings in one of America's premier cities. The job in Washington, a political appointment, had an uncertain future. God knows where we would live. It was even more expensive there. We would have to sell the condominium. Heidi would have to quit her good new job. My son would have to enter a new high school. I would have to endure confirmation hearings in the Senate.

Finally my young son decided the matter. "Dad," he said, "When the President of the United States asks you to do something, you can't not do it." We all agreed that was obvious, and began the psychological and emotional preparations for this momentous move. We had no inkling of just how momentous it would prove to be.

The acting administrator of ADAMHA, one of the finest and most skillful, competent and dedicated federal civil servants I was ever to meet, called the next day to confirm my acceptance. He volunteered to fly out to our place in San Diego and brief me about the job, and I readily accepted his offer.

He arrived in a few days, and we spent three full days together while he tried to teach me everything I ever wanted to know, and much more than any mere mortal could absorb, about what I was getting into. An attorney by training, Robert Trachtenberg had been in the government for many years and had achieved the highest rating possible in federal civil service as well as numerous awards and commendations for outstanding work. He had an encyclopedic knowledge of ADAMHA, its history and the political currents that had swirled around it, and all the players, past and present.

The Alcohol, Drug Abuse and Mental Health Administration consisted of the National Institute on Alcohol Abuse and Alcoholism, called NIAAA or more commonly "N-I-triple A"; the National Institute on Drug Abuse, called "NIDA"; and the National Institute of Mental Health, or "NIMH." These three organizations, each with research and services elements, had been separated into one "Administration," smaller but coequal with the National Institutes of Health, composed of research organizations dealing with specific physical diseases like cancer, heart disease and stroke, digestive disorders, allergy, and others.

The exact reasons for keeping these three institutes separate from all the others, under their own Administrator, which was to be me, were not altogether clear. They had to do with the quite different nature of these three areas of human disorder, their close relationship to one another, and the need to foster and develop programs of services, in addition to both conducting and sponsoring research in each.

What no one ever admitted was that these disorders all carried a degree of stigma that did not attach to more respectable things like cancer and venereal diseases, and true to historic tradition, many people felt they should be kept apart so as to avoid contaminating those more respectable ailments.

ADAMHA and its three institutes, except for their research laboratories, were situated in their own building in Rockville, MD, the Parklawn, about a mile away from the main campus of the National Institutes of Health in Bethesda. The building also housed the headquarters of the U.S. Public Health Service, of which both ADAMHA and NIH were a part. The building was a grim, pseudo-modern giant with narrow halls and hundreds of rabbit warren offices, built by three physicians on speculation and leased to the Department of Health and Human Services, making the three rich.

Brainwashing, Drunks & Madness

William E. Mayer, M.D.

CHAPTER 13

ALCOHOL, DRUGS, AND INSANITY

My appointment by President Reagan to be Administrator of the Alcohol, Drug Abuse and Mental Health Administration, I discovered on my arrival in Washington, was the result of that quality of "loyalty" that Earl Brian, then Secretary of Health and Welfare in California, had questioned me about as I awaited formal appointment to head the Department of Health. It was Earl, acting as part of the transition team for the new administration, who - now confident of my loyalty to Ronald Reagan and his ideas - had acted to secure my new federal job. It carried with it the rank of Rear Admiral in the Public Health Service, and designation as Assistant Surgeon General.

Assumption of a relatively high-level presidential appointment job in the federal government is a fascinating process. After the initial telephone call signifying selection, the appointee is invited to Washington to meet the most important players in the hierarchy, essentially to gain their approval or at least acquiescence. The only such characters who would be directly above me in the pecking order were the Secretary of Health and Human Services, Richard Schweiker, and the Assistant Secretary for Health, Doctor Edward Brandt.

The two men were about as different as possible. Dick Schweiker, formerly a senator from Pennsylvania, had all the qualities of a successful politician. He was taller than average, very friendly and warm but with a certain theatrical quality, exuberant in his welcome, and superficial in his questions about my background, interest in the job, and any goals I might have in carrying it out. I could tell he had simply found my name in a specific, limited time-slot in his calendar one day, had been handed a brief summary of my experience and political connections, and then followed a fairly standard set of comments and questions typed out on a sheet of paper placed before him on his desk. It wasn't insincere, exactly, but rather mechanical. Nonetheless, I liked him and was comfortable with him. He obviously knew nothing at all about ADAMHA.

Ed Brandt was warm, friendly, rather intense, and better prepared. An eminent physician, he had been appointed for his obvious medical professional skills and management experience rather than for his political connections, which I wistfully hoped was also the case with me. His questions were good ones, revealing an understanding both of physicians who had political and administrative experience, and also of the nature of the special institutes I was to operate and the maladies they addressed. I liked this Texan immensely, immediately, and our friendship endured for the several years we served together, and beyond. He expressed satisfaction with my answers to his questions, and, it seemed to me, quickly concluded that I was not one of the often strange if not bizarre creatures that people in the field of psychiatry sometimes seem to be.

Dr. Brandt was quite candid about "HHS," as our Cabinet-level department was known. It was huge and historically had proven to be largely unmanageable as well as a fiscal albatross around the neck of every administration. The 'health' part of it, which he and I agreed was by far the most important to the well-being of our citizens, was vastly overshadowed in its budget and political support and attention by the 'human services' elements.

Ever since Franklin Roosevelt signed the Social Security Act into law in 1935, the welfare advocates had attracted to government an army of left-wing 'liberal' intellectuals who now formed a huge, entrenched body of career civil servants dedicated to 'giving away' the public's treasure to the poor, the unproductive, the losers and social parasites whose numbers increased daily like the growth of an exuberant virus.

The grants of money and supporting programs for these people increased as their numbers increased, and were termed "entitlements." That meant the Congress and every administration were essentially powerless to restrain the growing quantities of money it took to keep the programs going. Every year a larger fraction of the total federal budget had to go to these welfare functions, reducing the amounts available for everything else.

This situation was not popular among elected politicians. Welfare recipients generally do not form any effective voting block, but can generally be counted on to support the Democrat party, who enacted the original entitlements and periodically enlarged upon them, but often resented the welfare drain on the treasury.

Republicans, as a rule, have been skeptical about the value of welfare spending, and often scornful of those who are dependent upon tax dollars instead of working for a living, unless they are clearly incapacitated.

Members of the executive branch, regardless of party, are often horrified at the vast sums poured out for the poor, and the effect that has on public funds that might otherwise be used for pet projects and politically popular actions that reinforce their standing with the electorate.

What all this means, ultimately, is that the Department of Health and Human Services has few friends and supporters. It is often seen as a necessary evil, but one that has grown to monstrous proportions, and desperately in need of a giant-killer. The new administration had hoped that Secretary Schweiker, known as a "liberal"

Republican, might be able to bring the monster under some more effective fiscal control but still satisfy other 'liberals' because he would do this compassionately. That turned out to be a serious miscalculation.

The man chosen to be Surgeon General and head of the Public Health Service was also from Pennsylvania, but there the resemblance to Dick Schweiker ended. C. Everett ("Chick") Koop, M.D., was something of a legend in his own time. If any single man could be considered the founder of the entire field of pediatric surgery, it was he. His ground-breaking work doing surgical repair of seriously malformed infants was both unprecedented and highly courageous, and he was one of the first ever to successfully separate a pair of conjoined "Siamese" twins.

Dr. Koop was a large man with a strong, commanding voice and great presence. He held his majestic head high, and sported a neat but outstanding beard on his chin, which jutted prominently forward. When I first called on him, following my meeting with Ed Brandt, I found the great man sitting disconsolately at a desk in a small office, actually twirling a pencil. When he stood up to shake my hand, I found the image of a nineteenth century prophet inescapable. He looked ready to deliver a hell-fire and damnation sermon on the spot.

He didn't, but his first words were of condemnation toward the bureaucracy and the 'idiots' in Congress, who couldn't get together on the subject of his confirmation. "The word" around the capital was that Koop was some kind of right-wing religious extremist who wouldn't fit in with the sophisticated Washington crowd and could prove embarrassing; after all, he did look like an old-time evangelist - almost Old Testament-Biblical. Also, hadn't he written some kind of religious book? Actually, he had written a book after the death of a beloved son while mountaineering, and there were references to God and faith in that book.

The delays that ensued in his confirmation process, with his nomination languishing in the offices of political "experts" in the administration who gravely debated the possible fallout from letting him represent the government, went on for months. I took to visiting him weekly, down in the little office he was given in the Hubert H. Humphrey building, to keep his spirits up and teach him about military things: uniforms, ribbons, chain of command, traditions, awards, ceremonies, and structure. Of these things he knew absolutely nothing, which he frankly admitted, yet he might soon become a Vice Admiral in charge of one of the oldest uniformed services. He was a quick study, and when he was finally legitimized, did the job well.

Over the years that followed, we came to know Dr. Koop well, and twice he performed a new spinal procedure on Heidi's back, which had become seriously affected by a congenital bony malformation. The procedure was highly effective. Koop's wife, Betty, became a friend as well, and we all were often in attendance together at social functions. While I was one of several assistant surgeons general, I did not report to him but instead came directly under Dr. Brandt, and later, in my job in the Pentagon with authority over all military surgeons general, Chick showed up in my office for our meetings.

Dr. Koop was an intense, dedicated, totally sincere man. His opinions were strongly held, but carefully constructed. For many years he carried on a crusade to stop the common medical practice of giving up on newborns who were horribly deformed and would likely not survive infancy anyway. He insisted, and proved, over and over again, that many of them could not only be saved, but could be sufficiently restored that they could enjoy much of what intact people take for granted. I have heard a number of his 'children,' grown to adulthood despite serious, often multiple, handicaps, declare fervently their gratitude to this great, good man for helping them cling to a life, whose quality they considered blessed and good, even wonderful.

In the nearly ten years we served together, never was I to hear Dr. Koop advance any 'right wing' attitudes or philosophy. He lectured to us all about how we cared for this magnificent, impossibly complex organism we are given to carry us through life. He railed against those, like some of the tobacco executives, who deliberately lied and tried to mislead the people about the scientifically proven danger of their products. He tried with all his might to be the nation's family doctor, and succeeded far better than anyone could have foreseen.

No sooner had I returned to San Diego after my Washington trip and visits with the important players in HHS than I was introduced to the next step in the vetting process, albeit an 'informal' one. A call came from the medical director of the American Psychiatric Association, Dr. Mel Sabshin, asking if I could possibly meet him in Los Angeles, to discuss my appointment to ADAMHA. I wasn't sure exactly what this meeting would involve, but assumed that this powerful professional organization would have something to say about my acceptability, and would be listened to.

Dr. Sabshin turned out to be a gracious, friendly man of late middle age. For many years he had provided the professional oversight guiding the Association and the continuity of its actions and official positions. Each year a prominent and successful psychiatrist was elected president of the group, but Mel worked closely beside these men and managed the organization.

We met in the lobby of a beautiful new, very grand Los Angeles hotel. Somehow he recognized me on sight, and we settled at a table in the bar where we could pursue our discussions in relative privacy. The good doctor was very gentle with me, I thought, as we talked about recent developments in our field, and about government's ideal function with respect to it. I found it easy to be open and frank with this fine, experienced man, as he probed, without seeming to pry, into my attitudes and opinions, which I freely gave.

While Doctor Sabshin was a trained psychoanalyst and thus a member of an in-group to which I never wished to belong, I felt safe in expressing to him my disapproval of traditional psychoanalytic practice. Even though most of my teachers had been dedicated analysts, my own experience convinced me that theirs was an approach I could not comfortably adopt. I believed, moreover, that the classical analytic technique involving daily 50-minute sessions extending for a period of anywhere from 3 to 7 years was a wholly unacceptable waste of a long medical education.

Encouraged by my examiner's evidently calm acceptance of my Freudian heresy, I went on to say that, what was more, I had yet to see any solid evidence that those long therapeutic relationships did much of anything worthwhile, aside from possibly making the patient a little more comfortable with himself. Therefore, I declared, I would oppose any use of public funds to support such treatment, even though it was considered a legitimate form of therapy. Well aware that I might be risking the disapproval, if not the outright wrath, of many of my colleagues, I plunged ahead.

My own professional experience, other than with alcoholics whom I no longer believed were basically psychiatrically disordered, was mainly with two groups of people. First, and most numerous, were the troubled souls who sought help in public mental health programs. The vast majority of them had no diagnosable mental or emotional disorder. They were usually involved in some kind of life crisis that was beyond their ability to handle, but their turmoil rarely reflected an underlying neurosis that required protracted treatment.

We had dealt with such people, using a modification of the well-proven techniques developed during war that rapidly helped soldiers work through the terrible emotional upheavals that we called combat exhaustion or combat fatigue. It was those techniques of brief intervention involving a short period of total withdrawal and escape from conflict followed by thorough 'ventilation' of feelings and encouragement to help those more acutely disturbed, that had worked so well in our community program in northern California.

We had demonstrated that the great majority of the patients coming to our community programs needed no more than five days in the hospital, little or no medication and a relatively short period of partial-day participation in the program to get back to a reasonable level of functioning. That, I told Dr. Sabshin, was a proper use of public funds.

The other group who in my experience both needed and deserved public support were the much smaller group, though still very large, who suffered from major mental illness: the schizophrenics, manic depressives, severe paranoids and the profoundly, suicidally depressed. I even ventured to advance the ideas planted in my head so many years before by great men like Adolph Meyer and Karl Bowman, to the effect that those major psychotic disorders would one day be shown to reflect observable, measurable disorders of the brain itself. Government should support the research that was needed to illustrate this, and discover remedies that worked.

Thanks at least in part to Dr. Sabshin's courtly attention as I waxed eloquent about my favorite biases, it wasn't long before I was sure I had talked too much (not unusual in my youth), and maybe had destroyed any prospect of assuming a high-level, powerful position in the federal government. Nothing that the man said hinted at that, but I drove back to San Diego figuring that I had surely alienated the world's most powerful society of psychiatrists, who would be certain to blackball me and oppose my appointment.

Instead, thanks to Mel Sabshin, the American Psychiatric Association enthusiastically endorsed me for the ADAMHA job. Within a few days I found myself driving to Washington in Heidi's little French car, our cockatiel hanging upside down in his cage, terrified, on the seat beside me.

We made it from San Diego in three days, arriving during an unseasonable spell of intense heat in mid-May.

My office turned out to be a large, airy corner suite on the twelfth floor of the infamous Parklawn Building in Rockville, Maryland. While it was only a dozen miles from the seat of the most powerful government on earth, it was, like all organizations anywhere outside the precise center of power, another world altogether, utterly lacking in the grandeur and splendor of the historic buildings surrounding the capital mall. The building was drab, with narrow corridors, tiny offices, and few amenities save for a huge cafeteria in the basement. Our digs in Sacramento had been far more glorious.

The staff was warmly welcoming, though I detected a certain tentative quality in everyone at first. The reason was soon clear: my predecessor, while a famed professor and researcher, had been noted for his severe, unfriendly, rather unfortunate personality. He had evidently personally offended nearly everyone in the huge building. Even the competent, highly experienced, attractive secretary I inherited with the office later confessed that she had stayed on as long as she had solely out of loyalty to the organization, and that in her mind I was strictly in a probationary status until I had proved myself 'human.'

In actual fact, it is a great advantage to follow a man like the one who had been there before me. Even the slightest indication on my part that I cared about other people's feelings was taken to be a blessing from heaven. My need to be liked and accepted fitted perfectly with the staff's needs to have someone at the top who was kind and considerate, and I was soon being hailed as the savior of what had been a pretty unhappy place.

The honeymoon, however, was brief. Within a few weeks the word came down from on high - the Secretary himself - that it would be necessary for me to effect a 25% reduction in the staff within less than three months.

The government calls this a "RIF," or reduction in force. It is the most dreaded, most shocking, and seemingly the most cruel and inhuman act that the federal government can commit. The several hundred as yet unnamed victims of the RIF were all federal civil servants. Everyone subscribed, it seemed, to the firm belief that 'permanent' civil servants were exactly that: permanent. Lifelong. Can't be fired unless convicted of a felony - and sometimes not even then. Forever secure.

Now along comes Dr. Mayer, supposedly Mr. Reagan's personal friend and selection for the job, and hundreds of dedicated, hard-working, deserving, selfless civil servants were going to get fired. Fired! Unheard of in the federal service. Monstrous!

The union to which most employees belonged came charging into the fray. Mass meetings were held. I was invited, to serve as the stand-in target for my heartless superiors, and expected to offer wholly insupportable and in any event unacceptable excuses and rationalizations for this terrible travesty of justice and violation of all that is sacred in federal service. As it worked out, it was impossible to talk at all to the excited masses, for no single voice could be heard over the excited din.

It was reminiscent of the wild confrontation with the parents of the retarded 'children' institutionalized in California state hospitals who expected their seriously handicapped offspring to be forced out into the streets, except that this time there were no state police around to ensure my safety.

In a federal RIF there are elaborate "bumping" rights, whereby people whose jobs have been eliminated can bump employees of lesser rank or seniority in other jobs that have been preserved. What this does is ensure that many such more senior people end up in jobs for which they have absolutely no qualifications except seniority. Real turmoil - even chaos - ensues. Morale plummets. Terrible tales of family hardship and tragedy spread like wildfire. Everyone hates the people in charge, even more than usual.

The system does have some provisions for lessening the tragedy. A number of people who have stayed around long past their eligible retirement dates decide that they will, after all, go ahead and retire. Some 'early retirement' schemes are offered, but don't help many. Assistance with finding jobs in other departments is organized, but this is of little help when the RIF is government-wide, as it was then. Finally, some portion of the employee force that has been considering seeking a fortune elsewhere, in the private sector, is encouraged to do so.

Somehow, in a few months, we got through it. Very few people ended up completely out of work, but gone forever was the sublime belief of bygone days that once you got a permanent civil service job in Washington, you were set for life. People settled into their new, often smaller offices doing jobs they hadn't dreamed they'd be doing, and life went on. I was never again as popular as I had been at the beginning, but the open hostility of the mass union meetings eventually went away.

An incident that helped with my redemption occurred not long after the RIF upheavals. Early one morning, while people were still arriving for work, the unmistakable sound of gunfire could be heard in the parking lot next door to the building. Looking out the window of my office, high above the lot, we could see a woman lying on the ground, bleeding profusely, while a man rushed to a nearby car and drove off. For a moment, everyone was stunned.

My new administrative assistant, an English major from Gettysburg College and daughter of a member of the Marine Band, said something like, "She's bleeding! She needs someone to help her!" Turning to me she said, "You're a doctor, aren't you?"

It was enough. Without waiting for the elevator, I raced down the twelve flights of stairs and out into the parking lot. The woman lying there had been shot more than once in the face, and was moaning piteously. Calling upon my recollections of distant days in a tent in Korea, I cleared the blood from her mouth to assure she had an airway, took off my coat and pressed it against the wounds to stop the bleeding and shouted for someone to call an ambulance. The woman was conscious, and I leaned close to her to assure her that she would be okay, and that we'd have her in the hospital in just a few minutes.

By the time the ambulance arrived, a crowd had gathered in the parking lot, and every window on that side of the Parklawn Building was filled with faces peering out at the drama being enacted below, with the new ADAMHA administrator saving the life of a poor woman bleeding from gunshot wounds just inflicted, as it turned out, by her husband. That man, it later developed, had driven his car off, not to some hideout, but to his regular job in a nearby office building, where he was soon apprehended.

The towering Parklawn Building housed scores of physicians, but not a single one showed up in the parking lot to help. The result was that a huge, largely undeserved amount of credit and admiration was bestowed on me, and my post-RIF redemption was pretty much assured. There was a "real" doctor in charge! People actually greeted me in friendly fashion in the narrow corridors of our building.

Our organization was part of the United States Public Health Service, one of the oldest of the uniformed services. In time of war, it becomes part of the Navy, whose uniforms its officers wear and whose regulations it follows. Its most important services to the American people have been performed in peacetime, in its efforts to prevent disease, abort epidemics, promote the universal immunization of infants and children against infections, gather intelligence about disease worldwide, and conduct and promote research into every variety of human ills and the means to prevent and control them.

The Public Health Service is of incalculable value to our citizens, and yet is one of the least well understood elements of government. It includes the Food and Drug Administration (FDA); the National Institutes of Health (NIH); the Alcohol, Drug Abuse and Mental Health Administration; the Centers for Disease Control and

Prevention (CDC); the Medical Service of the Coast Guard; the Indian Health Service; and the Medical Service for the U.S. Department of Corrections, among other things.

Certain elements of the PHS are well known: the National Cancer Institute, for example, but it is only one of many comparable research institutes on the NIH campus in Bethesda. Equally well-known is the FDA, frequently criticized by special interest groups for not approving new drugs fast enough, but responsible for the unparalleled safety and efficacy of the miraculous drugs now available in this country.

The CDC is always called, world-wide, when disasters occur like the chemical deaths in Bhopal, India, or the release of poison gas in the subways of Tokyo. Its agents have played a major role in tracking the spread of diseases like AIDS and the Influenza that killed as many as 30 million people around the globe in 1918. Most of the senior officers in both the FDA and the CDC are commissioned officers in the Public Health Service, as are most of those in ADAMHA.

A surprise to many, even in medicine, is the fact that both the National Institute of Mental Health and the National Institute on Alcohol Abuse and Alcoholism, NIMH and NIAAA, both parts of my new administration, conduct most of the entire world's scientific research in their areas of interest.

The research arm of NIMH, physically located on the NIH campus in Bethesda, had for many years conducted studies of schizophrenia and bi-polar disease, as well as considerable research into learning theory and other elements of psychology. One of the other institutes at NIH had done extensive work with the new CAT scan - the computerized X-Ray device that had dramatically increased the visibility of body structures - and had begun working with a new gadget, called the PET scan.

PET scanning - positron emission tomography - involved administering a harmless radioactive isotope that behaved in the body like glucose or some other "marker" substance, and then scanning the body or part of it with a huge, sensitive camera that revolved around it and photographed the emissions from that isotope. While the CAT scan was superb for revealing structure, the PET scan could observe tissue function.

The brain uses the simple sugar, glucose, as fuel. When a radioactive form of glucose is administered, the brain 'takes up' the radioactive material in varying amounts, depending on what part of the brain is active or inactive at any given time. The greater the activity in any area of the brain, the more glucose is taken up for use as cellular fuel, and a brighter image is photographed as a result.

Some NIMH researchers were eager to see what the PET technology might reveal about brain function, and were given very limited access to the other institute's machine. I was excited about the prospects, and decided that NIMH deserved to have its own PET scan capability, so I was able to arrange funding for them to get one.

One of the first things they discovered, when the machine was in place, was that certain areas in the brains of people with schizophrenia functioned differently from those same areas in normal brains!

For the first time in history, we could actually observe brain functions taking place, and here was evidence that there is an observable distortion in the brain's function in this most common of the serious mental diseases. At long last, the beliefs of my old teachers and their forbears in psychobiology were vindicated. Until the PET scan, our instruments and techniques were, as those teachers had said to me, too gross, too crude and clumsy to show what we knew must be true: there is a profound fault in the brain itself that causes schizophrenia. Now, 40 years after I learned from those teachers, came the great privilege of playing a small part in demonstrating this great truth.

The further use of this technology will without any doubt lead to the development of specific drugs or genetic manipulations that can actually render this terrible disease a thing of the past. A true miracle.

Great discoveries were also afoot in the Alcoholism Institute. A brilliant young researcher at the University of California, San Diego was producing stunning evidence as to the genetic and familial aspects of alcoholism that demonstrated the high incidence of the disease in the offspring of alcoholic fathers, particularly. Clinicians who took careful family histories had long believed this, but the research strongly supported that belief.

The directors of my three new institutes were special characters. Doctor Herbert Pardes, head of the National Institute of Mental Health, was an enormously competent psychiatrist-administrator who proved to be a good friend and strong supporter. He later left government service to become dean of the medical school at Columbia, where he continued his outstanding work.

The NIDA director was an older man, also a physician highly regarded within his field, who was nearing the end of a long government career but was willing to stay around long enough to lend support to my efforts to give some new life to our Administration.

The director of the National Institute on Alcohol Abuse and Alcoholism, who was not a physician and seemed not to be interested in the important medical aspects of the disease, turned out to be something of a problem. He rarely attended meetings of my senior staff, an important part of my management system, and I discovered that he was usually 'away' at some meeting in a distant city that usually had some connection to alcohol problems but hardly seemed to be of much value to the operation of his institute. I decided to check it out.

What soon emerged from an examination of his travel reimbursement claims was the fact that he regularly took along an 'assistant' in the form of an outside-government consultant hired specifically for each trip. The paid consultant turned out to be an attractive, single female with no professional qualifications whatever in the field. It further developed that the director, a married man with several children, spent most of his evenings with the same young woman when they were in town. Consulting, of course.

Asked about this, he offered a rather vague explanation about the young lady being of value to his thinking as he reflected on the many meetings' scientific papers and discussions. His recitation was halting, and his voice tended to drift off at times, probably because his 'consultant' was not there to help with his thinking. I let him talk for perhaps 7 or 8 minutes, while I stared at him intently but not unkindly and said nary a word. Finally he lapsed into an uncomfortable silence lasting fully two or three more minutes.

When he looked like he was about to bolt from his chair and run for the safety of the corridor outside, I said quietly to him, "Let's not kid. I am no moralist, but I know, and you know, that what you are doing is not right. There are people around here, in fact, who would say it is illegal. Your young lady is no consultant. I don't think you can stay in this job."

With that, he stood up, shook his head sadly, and without a word made for the door. An hour later his secretary delivered his resignation, effective immediately. The next morning, a memorandum was delivered to all the offices noting John's departure and announcing that "the Administrator" (I) would, until further notice, also serve as acting director of that Institute.

It turned out to be fun. NIMH required nothing much of me as their overall boss; Herb Pardes was more than adequate to the task. NIDA needed help, not because of any inadequacy on the part of the director, although his wife's health did distract him considerably. That Institute had no constituency like the National Mental Health Association, with a long history, distinguished supporters and a splendid annual meeting. Even Alcoholism, long (and to some degree still) looked upon by many as an affliction of 'bad' and 'weak' characters, was starting to achieve some respectability as prominent people began to come forward to confess ethanol-tainted pasts and their struggles to conquer the old demon.

Drug abuse and drug addiction remained inextricably tied to criminality and the continuing futile efforts to stamp it out through law officers. A fair number of mental health professionals asserted that there was, in both alcoholism and drug addiction, an underlying 'addictive' personality. I considered that pure baloney.

That theory was an attempt to assert that, since the underlying psychological cause was the same, so was the treatment. This was such a transparent attempt to bolster admissions to both alcoholism and drug programs, promoted vigorously by snake oil salesmen intent on making a buck, that it never got very far, but remnants of such thinking remain.

Many alcoholics and some drug addicts show strong obsessive-compulsive tendencies in their thinking and their behavior, but then so do lots of other people who never develop alcohol or drug problems. The fact is, it is desirable and even necessary to be somewhat compulsive in order to succeed in education, business, and every profession. Successful people in all those activities must be self-directed, motivated to succeed even in the face of obstacles and set-backs, methodical and orderly in the conduct of their affairs, and more reflective concerning the causes of both failure and success than the average person is.

Those same qualities, if they become too absorbing and occupy too much of an individual's attention, become incapacitating, and the correct diagnosis is obsessive-compulsive psychoneurosis. I have had patients so obsessively preoccupied with cleanliness that they not only washed their hands dozens or even hundreds of times a day, they took hours to take a bath because they believed anything they touched climbing out of the tub contaminated them and required the entire bath to be repeated. Recall, if you will, my obsessive squab rancher who had to count every letter in every sign he drove by. It took him hours to drive a few miles, and he was a traffic menace.

Most of us are a bit obsessive as children. We may count pickets in a fence, going back if we lose count, or avoid stepping on all cracks in the sidewalk or count floors in tall buildings. However, we soon tire of that. Instead we dwell on little sayings from Ralph Waldo Emerson or the Bible or a catchy commercial on the radio, and eventually that gives way to 'normal' rituals of personal hygiene, filing our taxes on time, taking out the garbage, and all the countless activities that make daily life tolerable and relatively orderly.

Only rarely have I encountered an alcoholic who was seriously obsessive-compulsive. Some of them, struggling to throw off the burden of daily serious drinking, take up daily serious eating, at least at first. Usually they get over even that. Those who have been successful in their life work before alcohol became too important, and who are therefore somewhat more compulsive than average anyway, throw themselves more obsessively than ever into that work.

Except for their drug use, especially of morphine, heroin, opium, cocaine and barbiturates, addicts do not behave obsessively. They do so when "hooked" on drugs because their bodies have made massive adjustments to the drug, and when it is not supplied, they suffer withdrawal: very real, often extremely unpleasant physical reactions as their 'readjusted' physiology no longer has its chemical to adjust to. Their desire for more drugs is really their desire to avoid the physical agonies that ensue when it is not there. Many long-term addicts have told me they have long since given up any hope of achieving some kind of 'high' from their drug; they simply want to be in a state of comfort approaching normalcy.

Some serious alcoholics who daily ingest substantial quantities of alcohol and are abruptly denied any at all, as when they have been admitted to a hospital for some other problem, have a reaction that superficially - but only superficially - looks like some kind of withdrawal. This has caused the erroneous belief that it is like the discomfort drug addicts endure. It is not.

Instead, it is an organic psychosis - a real, if temporary, insanity - with a complex physical basis primarily involving swelling of the brain. Encased in its hard shell, the skull, the brain has no place to go when it swells, and as pressure within it builds up, it acts crazy.

We call this delirium tremens: "DTs." People die from it. When they do, the wet, soggy brain literally pops up out of the skull when released on autopsy as the crown of the skull is lifted off. With typical medical eloquence, we call this "wet brain." Other organs and systems in the body play a part. The liver is generally severely damaged long before DTs is first experienced. Likewise the kidneys are disrupted and the ability to properly balance fluids and salts - electrolytes - is impaired.

Addicts do not have anything like the florid insanity that bedevils the poor soul in DTs, who sees horrifying visions, feels bugs and snakes crawling all over his body, has periods of indescribable terror that may cause him to do violent things to himself and others. I have seen such a patient pluck out his own eyeball and cast it aside, and others slash themselves with razor blades.

Thus it was that by the time I took on overall control of the three institutes: mental health, alcoholism, and drug abuse, I had spent thirty-four years dealing with all three kinds of disorders in hundreds of people, and had developed fairly strong opinions about each of them.

About mental illness I had mixed feelings. A reluctant psychiatrist at the beginning, the year spent at Fort Worth gave me abundant daily proof of the gravity and enormity of the major psychoses - schizophrenia, manic-depressive disease, global paranoia, psychotic depression and organic brain disease in particular. For most of human history, such diseases were essentially untreatable and untreated, thought to be 'possession' by the Devil himself or unnamed evil spirits. Victims were always expelled from society, often cruelly abused, beaten, chained, even tortured, not infrequently in the name of some religion, including my own.

What I soon learned was that the overwhelming majority of psychiatrists wanted nothing whatever to do with those diseases, and the people who had them.

Instead, attention was almost solely focused on those who were not 'crazy,' except for the group called "psychopaths," whose antisocial, asocial and otherwise conscienceless deviations from acceptable behavior had been labeled "moral" insanity to distinguish them from the truly insane. Even after sometimes effective drugs, like Thorazine, started showing promise in the treatment of many psychoses, most psychiatrists and other physicians wanted nothing to do with them.

Initially, with few exceptions, the object of American psychiatry's devoted attention began with the administration of various forms of psychotherapy to people with anxiety neuroses, phobias, hysteria and conversion reactions, mild to moderate depressions, and non-incapacitating obsessive-compulsive neuroses. The determining quality in each case was the patient's ability to remain out of the hospital - to come in to the psychiatrist's office on his/her own, and to pay.

The poor got their psychotherapy, so to speak, from family, friends, pastors and bartenders. If they became incapacitated, they were shipped off to public hospitals. When the paying patients needed a spell of 24-hour care, they were escorted to private 'sanitariums,' 'rest homes,' 'retreats,' and other euphemistically designated, much smaller facilities, usually situated in some pleasant rural setting well out of town, for a rest.

Almost no privately practicing psychiatrists treated anyone at all, poor or rich, who was in a hospital, no matter what it was called. The physicians in mental hospitals were usually employees of the institution, were generally not very well paid, did not see outpatients, and ranged in quality from sleazy borderline practitioners of questionable background all the way up to the truly inspired, like the Menningers of Kansas, who were rare.

The result of this self-selected division of labor was that the seriously ill were often poorly treated, if at all, and their stigmatization continued. The ambulatory, less ill, paying population of potential patients failed to increase as rapidly as the psychiatrist population did, and as psychiatry became more respectable, increasing numbers of relatively normal people began seeking assistance with their emotional problems from psychiatrists, and a truly "funny thing happened on the way to the office."

What happened was that more and more attention began to be paid to less and less important disruptions in the emotional lives of a population that had increasingly left the small towns and farms where families, friends and the churches were close by and available to help. People moved to cities where they were frequently lonely, anonymous, uneasy and without traditional social supports for the inevitable crises of everyday life.

Psychiatrists, along with a whole new army of 'counselors' and various kinds of psychologists that were springing up like dandelions in an untended lawn, stepped into the breech. Names were found for more and more deviations from some hypothetical mental health norm, after solemn deliberations of eminent psychiatrists, ultimately reaching a level of absurdity unmatched in the history of medical nomenclature.

Each new name became a diagnosis with its own many-digit numerical designator, and was collected in an "official" volume bearing the imprimatur of the entire profession of psychiatry. Its "treatment" thus became eligible for reimbursement by insurance companies, managed care organizations, and, most importantly of all, the government.

It is now possible, no matter how mentally healthy, mature, well-adjusted, productive, happy and successful you may think you are, for me or any other psychiatrist, armed with the official nomenclature of mental disorders, to bestow upon you an official, reimbursable diagnosis that some '3rd party payor' will happily reimburse me for treating. There are, incidentally, few really clear rules about what constitutes "treatment."

It is true that everyone experiences some periods of emotional distress, and it is also true that many people in our urbanized, migratory, increasingly uncommitted (note the marriage vs. 'living together' figures, and the divorce statistics and the retreat from church membership) social system lack any very effective social and emotional support systems. Thus the case can be made for ever-larger numbers of 'helping' professionals with at least some training, who can lend a hand. Whether or not this requires psychiatrically trained physicians with 24 years of education is doubtful. Whether or not bartenders or self-appointed untrained family 'counselors' can do it well is also doubtful. In any event, we have yet to come to terms realistically with the problems of emotional distress and who should do what about it, while we move steadily toward a psychiatric diagnosis for everybody.

Then does the government start handing out Prozac and its imitators to everybody? George Orwell, here we come!

Add to this the possibilities of interactive television and drugs over the internet, and we have almost made it to 1984.

Meanwhile, on a brighter note, there has been some stunning research into the causes and remedies for the profound, serious psychotic disorders, especially since the PET-scan showed up and the genes are being identified. Unfortunately, no one seems interested in addressing the problem of giving treatment, no matter how good, to the great bulk of mentally ill people who do not want it. As their numbers grow and the institutions that could protect them shrink and close down, and the 'big brother' problems of 'involuntary' care and treatment remain unresolved, big trouble lies ahead.

No one has yet come up with a solution, but my experience at ADAMHA led me to believe that there is at least a partial one. It grew in my imagination as I confronted the worst mental health situation in the country, which happens to exist in our nation's capital, and tried, unsuccessfully, to solve it.

Just across the Anacostia River from downtown Washington, D.C. is a lovely, grassy hill where Abraham Lincoln sometimes sat as he contemplated the capital city and agonized over the terrible war that raged between the northern and southern parts of his country. It is on the grounds of historic Saint Elizabeth's Hospital, housing as it did then many of the wounded from that war.

St. E's, as it has long been known, then housed large numbers of battle casualties, but it is technically the federal hospital for the mentally ill, falling under the purview of the National Institute on Mental Health and thus of my 'command,' the Alcohol, Drug Abuse and Mental Health Administration. At the time I assumed responsibility for it, the hospital housed around two thousand patients and gave employment to many more than that number of nurses, physicians, aides, orderlies, groundskeepers, firemen, security officers, laundrymen, carpenters, plumbers, roofers, food preparers, sweepers, housekeepers, supply clerks, procurement agents, personnel managers and clerks, medical records technicians, telephone repairmen, maintenance and repair people and many others. All were federal civil service employees with assured lifetime jobs. No RIFs here!

This little city of more than four thousand people, complete unto itself, is contained in dozens of buildings situated in the midst of one of the most appalling, filthy, run-down, dangerous black ghettos in America. Officially part of the District of Columbia, it is in theory governed, though barely and poorly, by the District government, then enjoying a glorious period of self-government under the reigning monarch, Marion Barry, a convicted felon about to be imprisoned for drug violations, and later re-elected to 'govern' this disastrous social experiment.

The hospital contained almost no "federal" patients, save for a handful of Cuban criminals from the Mariel invasion launched by Fidel Castro and an even smaller handful of ancient holdovers from earlier days. All the other patients were products of the city of Washington, population about 600 thousand people. A short lesson in arithmetic is instructive here.

The 2000 occupied patient beds at St. E's amounted to one psychiatric bed for every 300 residents of the city.

In contrast, there were fewer than 2000 beds in the California State hospitals for the mentally ill, serving a population in excess of twenty million citizens of that large state, which included some pretty unhealthy places, like much of Los Angeles - itself with more than ten times the population of DC.

In contrast to DC's 1 to 300 ratio of beds to citizens, the state of California's ratio was 1 to 10 *thousand*! The contrast was striking, to say the least.

It was not because there was no community mental health program in the District. There was, in fact, an extensive one with at least ten separate clinic sites, each fully staffed, on paper, with psychiatrists, psychologists, psychiatric social workers, psychiatric nurses and assistants. To match that, California would have needed about 333 fully staffed clinics. Instead, there were fewer than 60.

Something was seriously amiss here. For one thing, when I sent agents out to inspect the clinics, there were rarely more than one or two staff members present during clinic hours. The others were nowhere to be found, but all were drawing full salaries. A records review showed that little work was being done, other than calling for the police to come pick up some disturbed person who had walked in, and deliver him to St. E's.

The hospital was thrust into my consciousness, along with that of everyone else, when the would-be assassin of Ronald Reagan was placed in its maximum security unit, designed and operated much like a prison. The shocking assault on the President, as he emerged in mid-day from a large Washington hotel, occurred shortly after I took my place in the Parklawn Building, and required that I make a rapid assessment of the hospital.

All public mental hospitals had security sections similar to St. E's. Housed therein are those people who have been found to be unable to stand trial because of mental disorder, are unable to understand the nature of the charges against them or unable to participate in their own defense. In addition, people who have committed a crime but who have been found not guilty by reason of insanity are held in such units. These places are locked up and have many more guards than the rest of the hospital.

Young Hinckley was held in St. Elizabeth's pending his trial, and kept there after the court found him not guilty by reason of insanity. The policy in such cases generally calls for confinement until the hospital staff declares that he has recovered sufficiently from his mental disorder to make it safe for him to return to the community, however long that takes.

The problem with that medicolegal reasoning, which began long before there were any effective drugs to combat psychosis, was that most serious mental disorders tend to recur at unpredictable times. When no drugs were yet available for treatment, up to two thirds of patients with schizophrenia never did get more than marginally better, and those who did improve could slip back at any time.

To make matters worse, the prediction of future behavior is at best a risky exercise in clinical judgment. The mentally ill are generally less likely to commit crimes of violence than are people who are not mentally ill. In both groups, a single such act is not necessarily predictive of any more. In every instance, moreover, one such act is the individual's first one and does not have the same predictive value as a string of them.

The advent of effective anti-psychotic medications has, paradoxically, made the situation even more difficult than before. Many patients, including severely ill, dangerous cases of paranoid schizophrenia, respond rapidly and well to appropriate drugs, and seem to return to normalcy. They may remain entirely so for many years, as long as they are adequately medicated. After a while, as little as a few weeks, the patient decides for himself that he is now normal, and stops taking his medication. He may get along fine for some time, or he may revert to his psychosis very quickly.

Recognizing this, people with serious mental disorders who have been put in hospitals and improved on medication are monitored closely after being discharged to encourage them to keep taking their drugs, and to detect any signs of regression. This takes considerable trained manpower, and ideally a well-run local mental health system, but even then, there is no sure way to keep the patient from disappearing elsewhere in town or running off to Detroit or El Paso to be 'left alone.' Along with such flights, the patient usually throws away his medicine, and can soon become crazy again.

When someone like Hinckley, who has committed murder or attempted murder, comes up for consideration for release, psychiatric staffs become understandably skittish. Many meetings are held. Many tests are repeated. Interviews are done over. Copious notes are made. Votes are taken.

Ultimately, when the individual has appeared free of symptoms long enough, and usually only when the staff unanimously agrees he is no longer a danger, and may safely be released, and so recommends to the court, who must also agree, he is discharged. The medical staff must also recommend the conditions to be met after discharge - how often he should be seen for medication checks, how often he must be re-evaluated by a mental health professional - and the court again must agree and may set further requirements.

Generally this process works reasonably well, but in the occasional instance when it does not, and a former patient commits another offense, there is usually florid media attention directed to the case, and the public outcry and outrage wells up and makes later release decisions even harder. Thus it is that today, over twenty years since Hinckley's assault on Ronald Reagan, there is heated debate over whether the would-be assassin can be allowed so much as a brief unsupervised visit with his family.

My visits to St. E's were eye-openers. First, of course, was the wholly indefensible, almost medieval atmosphere created by the enormous numbers of patients, most of them chronic, long-term residents of African ancestry. The buildings, while relatively clean and in fairly good repair, were mainly old brick structures typical of 19th Century institutional design. The numbers of staff, few exhibiting little more energy than most of the patients, were astonishing. A fully-staffed fire department, rarely called upon, was a somnolent collection of mostly old fire engines and mostly old firemen.

The laundry, a huge concrete structure that may well be the free world's largest wash house, lay completely idle, laundry now being shipped out to a laundry contractor who does it both faster and more cheaply. A huge, ancient powerhouse puffs away constantly, and just as constantly requires major maintenance and repair.

On one visit, I discovered that in addition to its large campus in Anacostia, the hospital owned property a few miles to the south, along the Potomac River on the north side of the Woodrow Wilson Bridge. That property included a complete farm, with house, barns, outbuildings of various kinds, old farm implements and out-dated machinery, and expansive fields. It had been turned into a kind of public park, where school children could be brought to learn about how farming used to be done when this was a country of small family spreads. The setting, despite its proximity to the city of Washington, was peaceful and bucolic, suggestive of an idyllic, rural style of life.

The contrast between this tranquil, clean, undisturbed pastoral setting, so close to the city but so utterly removed from it, and the filth, squalor, decay and rampant crime of the immediate vicinity of the hospital, was striking. More, it was an invitation to start addressing several long-neglected problems, including the vastly excessive size of St. E's inpatient population, the obsolescence of the facility, the incredible waste of highly-paid federal civil service manpower, and the progressive decay of the surrounding neighborhood, which cried out for some form of urban renewal that was at least 50 years overdue.

For many years, federal officials in the old Department of Health, Education and Welfare, now called Health and Human Services, had made half-hearted attempts to turn St. E's, or most of it, over to the D.C. government, since the place was essentially a 'state hospital' for the District. No one was at all interested, neither the DC Committee of the Congress, when they ran it, nor the District government under 'self-rule,' when that marvelous experiment in democracy was instituted.

The bureaucracy presided over by Mayor Marion Barry was notoriously inefficient and disorganized. What we had found in the lavishly funded mental health clinics where few people showed up for work, was not at all unusual. There were pockets of moderate competency, but they were the exception, and the poorly led, fumbling District Health Department could not even imagine taking any responsibility for Saint Elizabeth's. Additionally, of course, this might jeopardize the federal civil service status of several thousand happy, long-term employees.

What I believed, in my naiveté, was that I could make the District officials an offer so good, and so potentially rewarding, that they could not refuse. At the same time, a new kind of 21st Century public mental health facility could rise on the banks of the Potomac and shine forth as a brilliant model for the whole nation, of what an enlightened, humane, civilized therapeutic community for the mentally ill should be. My old, beloved mentor and super-capitalist castle-dweller herself, Portia Bell Hume, would have been proud.

And we - the taxpayers, citizens of the District, and the DC government - could make enough money in the process that it would essentially pay for itself, and be an income- and profit-generator for years to come.

My proposal, in its simplest form, was to move the St. E's patients to a newly constructed, dispersed cottage-style installation at the 'farm,' which we already owned. That done, most of the old buildings on the current grounds that lacked true historic significance warranting their preservation, should be torn down. In their place, atop this magnificent hill with its breathtaking vistas of the Capital City with its gleaming buildings and lovely rivers, build a group of modern high-rise towers.

The lower levels of the towers could accommodate a multitude of retail stores of all sizes. Just above them, the mid-level floors would make for superb office spaces. The floors above those would be residential in nature, with hotels and apartments ranging from modest to magnificent.

The construction, later maintenance and multitudinous services called for as the space was leased, rented or sold, would both pay off the initial investment and provide a steady revenue source in the future, particularly since the priceless ground on which the development stood, was already owned by the District.

The new site of the old St.E's would serve then as a powerful driving force for the renewal of the entire blighted district. Small businesses would move in to serve the new population, housing for employees of the shops and service organizations that would be attracted would be good investments, and the whole character of the decayed, crime-ridden area would change.

Meanwhile, down on the farm next to the Wilson Bridge, a new kind of therapeutic mental health community would operate. It would consist of a central core structure for the small fraction of mental patients who needed to be held in secure surroundings. Around it would be structures housing much smaller numbers of patients still needing daily attention, medications and perhaps unobtrusive perimeter grounds security, but not locked buildings.

Still farther out but still surrounding the central core area, patients would be housed in small (6 to 8 or 10-person) home-like structures, and beyond those would lie a multitude of still smaller structures for occupancy of two or three, or even just one, person.

Interspersed among these buildings would be small shops selling food and personal items, along with modest park-like areas for recreation and here and there something resembling community centers. Staff, most concentrated in the central core area, would in addition move about the 'community' to conduct both individual and group therapy sessions, and patients would move farther out from the central core area as they improved, in preparation for return to the 'real' community outside.

An architectural engineering firm was employed to draw up a preliminary plan for the undertaking. Several of the designers became so excited and enthusiastic about the proposal that on their own time and expense, they actually built a model of the new hilltop site where the old one used to be, and volunteered to come along when I presented the plan to the DC people.

Those dignitaries could not have been less interested. They were bored-seeming about the whole thing, had no desire to renew Anacostia, and couldn't care less about the huge patient population, in reality a purely local problem and responsibility, being paid for by the whole US taxpaying population. So much for self-rule.

Some years afterward, once Marion Barry had gone to prison and then been reelected to the mayor's office, the Congress pretty much revoked the myth of self-government, the District having proven itself wholly incapable thereof, and somehow maneuvered the DC government, back again under federal management, to become somewhat more involved in St.E's, but little has changed.

The months passed swiftly. My job as Administrator was not really very demanding, but had its lively moments. One came when an exquisitely groomed, exceedingly attractive blonde lady showed up in my office one day to solicit my help dealing with my dear friend, C. Everett Koop. She was about forty, and had until recently had a distinguished career in pediatric renal pathology research at the University of California Medical Center.

She had shared a laboratory with her husband, a fellow research scientist. The couple had one child, and had been increasingly at odds with one another, culminating in a wild, equipment-bashing battle in their lab as they laid claim to items of equipment they each wished to keep following their acrimonious divorce. The court had awarded the divorce and shared custody of their young daughter, along with a strict order that this woman was not to leave California taking along her daughter.

She sat in my office, facing me with her handsome legs crossed and her skirt pulled up just enough to provide an abundant view of them just short of overt indecency. Every hair of her elaborate coiffure was exactly in place. She was made up with professional skill, though not excessively, even to the faintly darker lip-lining border around her lipstick, her carefully applied eye shadow and mascara, and her perfectly manicured nails. Her clothes were expensive and designed to reveal and flatter her outstanding figure.

Her violation of the divorce court's order, bringing as she did her young daughter to her parents' home in New England and then heading for Washington, was driven by her desire to join with Dr. Koop to initiate a new, nation-wide health program which she was certain he would support with vigor and enthusiasm.

As she began to describe her program, she leaned forward a little, fixed me with a penetrating gaze, and moved her shoulders about in a way that commanded attention while just avoiding overtly seductive behavior. It was impossible to ignore this woman, who was clearly inspired and determined.

She had a plan that would require each patient admitted to every hospital throughout the country to be given a complete, thorough "spiritual work-up" along with the regular work-up consisting of a medical history, physical examination, and appropriate laboratory studies. This would be mandated by federal law and enforced by federal examiners.

The purpose of this spiritual work-up was to ascertain the exact nature of the patient's relationship with God, so that defects could be corrected. As long as this was not being done, all medical care was incomplete.

My attractive visitor was certain that Dr. Koop, who was known to be a highly religious man of great spiritual dimensions, would join with her, enthusiastically, to make sure that this would become the law of the land.

My training in psychiatry, along with some common sense, mandated that I listen to her politely and attentively, manifesting neither surprise nor disapproval of her revolutionary proposal, let alone argue with any of her points or express particular support for them. Therefore, I did my best to listen, with interest, while searching for some indication of what this person's special aberration, if any, might be.

She had not just thought this up. She'd been working on the idea for many months, and had advanced it to any number of colleagues and superiors at the university. Their reaction, she said, had been one of great interest, and they had all encouraged her to seek out high officials of government for their reaction. I could just visualize those meetings. Was this just a terribly earnest, dedicated Christian? A fanatic? She didn't look wild-eyed, and talked very rationally, seemed to be in good contact with reality, and had no other 'far-out' ideas to advance, but this was, to say the least, unusual.

There was a certain grandiosity in this woman's ideas. It was coupled with evidence of obsessive-compulsive qualities, but also with hysteric traits - an unusual combination. Nothing she said was clearly delusional, although when she said she believed God intended for her to work with, and in time even to marry, Dr. Koop (his dear wife, Betty, would have been surprised), I did look carefully at the possibility of a carefully hidden psychosis. There were, however, no other obviously crazy ideas.

I did, therefore, what all her California colleagues had done: told her it was an interesting idea, and sent her off to see Dr. Koop. But at least I called him first, and related the entire encounter so that he would not be taken by surprise.

He wasn't, but he called me, nevertheless, the minute she left his office. His message was: Help! He insisted that since I was a trained psychiatrist, I must know how to handle this sort of thing, so please do so. Please! After all, what are friends for? I agreed to see her again, but without enthusiasm.

On the next interview, a few days later, I took the initiative. She must understand, I said, that Dr. Koop could not institute a new law, and that she must consider that another approach might be better. In any case, he could not properly establish a working relationship with her while she was in clear, deliberate violation of a court order in California, and he would never marry anyone but Betty. She must go home and work things out in her personal life. That done, she must re-think her proposal, put it down in writing, and (shamelessly invoking the traditional bureaucratic dodge) submit it through proper channels to the Department of Health and Human Services, whose staff, I felt sure, would give it careful consideration.

She was not totally happy with this, but seemed to accept it. I wondered what she might do next, and hoped Betty Koop was safe.

After three or four unsuccessful attempts in the following week to gain an audience with the new Surgeon General, she disappeared and was not to be heard from again. Chick thought I was a genius.

The most rewarding time during my stay at ADAMHA came during my self-appointed term as director of the alcoholism institute. Many of the ideas gained over the decades of treating alcoholics were, it seemed to me, being validated steadily in our laboratories and those of several great universities. I decided that it was a moral obligation to embark on an effort to spread the idea that I had found most helpful to me in treating alcoholics, and most helpful to them when they accepted it. It was one of those ideas that I arrived at independently, though I was not the first to do so and could not claim credit for.

The concept of greatest value and importance, I had come to believe, was that alcoholism was neither a psychiatric disorder nor a defect of character; it was a disease. It had measurable dimensions, distinct characteristics, a predictable course, involved genetic elements, and included physiologic and metabolic distortions. Alcohol must be metabolized - digested, if you will - in a process that changes its basic chemical structure through a series of steps that produce different chemicals altogether, some of them quite toxic, until finally the original atoms of ethyl alcohol are converted, completely, into carbon dioxide and water. About 90% of people do this in an orderly way and without a problem, as long as they don't take in too much too fast.

About ten percent of all people cannot do this in normal fashion. Alcohol, a protoplasmic (tissue) poison itself, breaks down into acetone - also toxic - and acetaldehyde, a relative of embalming fluid and even more toxic, on its way to water and CO_2. The brain is especially vulnerable to all three of these toxins, and they linger in different amounts in different times in the brains of alcoholics, interfering with that organ's functioning. This is alcoholism.

Once this notion of alcoholism as a 'respectable,' chronic, progressive disease is accepted, traditional attitudes toward it can be abandoned, both by the alcoholic himself and by medical people, who have ignored it shamelessly. The sad truth is that the disease is rarely diagnosed until it has progressed dangerously. Most physicians have been curiously shy about asking patients about their drinking history, evidently fearing to offend 'nice' people who would resent the implied accusation of being a drunk.

Medical students are routinely taught to include questions about the patient's history of drug and alcohol use, but these generally take the form of benign inquiries, gently and almost apologetically offered and not pursued in any detail. Since the patient, even if a serious alcoholic, is not seeing the doctor because of alcohol problems, and since most alcoholics do not think they drink much, or that it is a problem, that ends it. The heartburn, constipation, arthritis or headache becomes the focus of attention, and the alcoholism remains a secret.

What further complicates the discovery of the disease is the fact that most - by far the great majority - of true alcoholics don't look like alcoholics are supposed to look. They are businessmen, young mothers, priests, other physicians, and others who are conducting their affairs in seemingly normal fashion, unlike the 10% of alcoholics who are obvious drunken bums.

The result of this doctor-patient conspiracy to leave the whole subject alone is that this progressive disease insidiously damages the liver, a remarkable organ that can function fairly well when 80% of it is gone, the kidneys, the brain, the digestive system and other important parts of humans. There can be extensive damage long before the first DWI arrest (can happen to anyone) or serious family disruption comes to light. Meanwhile, the alcoholic continues to work, for the job is the last thing to go.

Most alcoholics share the rest of society's disapproval and condemnation of habitual drunkenness, and go to great lengths to deny to themselves that any problem exists with their drinking. In consequence, they do nothing about it except rationalize their behavior, and steadily become sicker without realizing it. They develop a serious, ultimately life-threatening disorder that is, so far, incurable. But then so are diabetes, rheumatoid arthritis, chronic cardiovascular disease and a host of other chronic disorders.

This is not to say that they cannot be treated. Every one of them can be managed so as to prolong life and preserve its quality. An example is diabetes, which has a curious relationship with alcoholism.

Two years before I was born, during this century of medical miracles, two physicians named Banting and Best discovered that insulin, a naturally occurring hormone that affects how the body uses sugar, was of paramount importance in diabetes. They showed how it was produced in the pancreas gland, and could be extracted from those glands of pigs and cows, purified and used to control the raging excess of blood glucose that throughout history has killed diabetics, blinded them, and, aside from warfare, caused most amputations needed to control gangrene.

Those two Canadian gentlemen saved my life, not to mention my eyesight and my feet, along with millions of others. They did not cure my diabetes, but they helped me manage it. An army of nutritionists and dietitians also helped, and countless endocrinologists continue to work to improve the management of this chronic, progressive, ultimately fatal disease. God bless them all.

There is as yet no 'insulin' or other hormone or chemical to aid in the treatment of the disease of alcoholism. The drug Antabuse, which causes a nearly intolerable physical reaction of sweating, palpitation, flushing of the skin, coughing and shortness of breath, is a helpful short-term management tool to keep one from drinking alcohol, but is not a long-term aid like insulin and dietary control in diabetes.

There is, however, one infallible measure that stops the disease of alcoholism from progressing, and permits some actual organ repair, and it is free. That is abstinence - total abstinence. It cannot be imposed by a physician or, as we have seen, by laws and lawmakers. Not even Carrie Nation with her ax, breaking up saloons, or the Women's Christian Temperance Union, both seemingly quaint and faintly absurd reflections of the Prohibitionism of a century ago, or the vigorous actions of policemen and the courts, can impose abstinence on society, let alone on alcoholics. Only the alcoholic himself can do that. And it's hard.

This is especially true of a particular variety of alcoholic patient who has essentially come face to face with his alcoholism, but who has concluded that it is impossible for him to live, even for a day, without drinking. These people come to resemble those who have become addicted to certain drugs. They continue to drink because they honestly believe they cannot stop, and are often dismayed and frightened by that belief.

While it may help such people to understand that alcoholism is a disease, although they are likely not to care a whole lot about that, they must come a step farther, and accept the fact that it is controllable - that there is the real possibility of escape. In these cases, the influence of fellow alcoholics who are in the process of recovery is generally more effective than the arguments and exhortations of professionals.

It is in these instances that participation in Alcoholics Anonymous may accomplish what the medical professional cannot, through the example of others who have felt the same way initially, yet have been able to resume control of their drinking, and their lives.

Throughout most Western nations - much less so in Asia - alcohol is such an integral part of celebrations, wakes, stressful settings, weddings, parties, and episodes of unhappiness that most adults and many younger people are more or less constantly encouraged or urged to drink. Without extraordinary determination not to do so, it is difficult for anyone to avoid all alcohol, and many times harder for an alcoholic, but it can be done, and it works. No other human act, perhaps excepting sexual abstinence to prevent pregnancy and venereal disease, has such a certain effect.

From time to time there have been advocates of "controlled drinking," which can supposedly be taught to alcoholics. Even the august Rand Corporation published an endorsement of this technique. Along with millions of alcoholics and thousands of those who have treated them, I am absolutely, utterly convinced that is wrong.

A word about Alcoholics Anonymous. In the first few years after a man named Bill Wilson, along with a physician friend, organized AA, most of us in the medical profession thought it was little more than a 'nice' but likely ineffectual, cultist way of addressing the problem. It was erroneously dismissed as an exercise in religiosity combined with bragging sessions about how much one drank and how "bad" he got, like college boys after a beer bust.

Over the last half of the 20th Century, however, a far different picture has emerged. While the '12 steps' of AA do address matters of faith - non-sectarian - and involve a certain kind of confession along with recognition of a 'higher power' called God only if that pleases you, it is neither a matter of religiosity nor is it a collection of drunks bragging about how bad they are. It is not a prohibitionist or any other kind of advocacy group, does not recruit members, does not pass judgment, and only requires that participants have a sincere desire to stop drinking, behave properly in meetings, and above all, preserve the confidentiality of each person in attendance.

Alcoholics Anonymous works for almost everyone who faithfully takes part in meetings and makes a real effort to apply what he learns there - not from some professional or paid staff, but from others who share his affliction. It is the only known instrument that has proven successful in the long-term management of this progressive chronic disease with its inevitable downhill course.

Because of its success, AA has spawned a growing group of imitators addressing drug abuse and drug addiction, marital problems, grief management, stress reduction and other problems, and is the ancestor of the wild proliferation of "support groups" to help with every conceivable real or imagined suffering. Possibly, as people become further separated from social support systems that existed in a more relaxed, less mobile culture in the distant past, that was less preoccupied with social advancement, material acquisition, "stress" and victimhood, the advent of the support group is necessary and maybe even useful. But I wonder.

Over the years, as I tried to treat my alcoholic patients, most of whom had come for help for something else, the concept of alcoholism as a 'legitimate' disease was the single most effective way I ever found to get them to accept the fact of their illness, and seriously consider ways to get it under control. It also helped dispel the deep-seated biases that medical colleagues and community leaders held about 'drunks,' and began a process, still far from complete, that allows for a rational approach to the whole problem. Moreover, Carrie Nation and the WCTU were right, it *is* a problem - one of the most serious facing medicine today.

The year and a half I spent at ADAMHA and the Alcoholism Institute were instructive in that they illustrated a good deal about the Washington scene with its enormous numbers of often self-anointed powerful and supremely important people, the machinations of the political appointees as they maneuvered to solidify and enhance their status and power, the strained relationship between the civil servants in high positions and the appointees they nominally worked for, and the truth of the saying ascribed to a former president that if you wanted a true, faithful friend in government service, get a dog!

A glimpse of what I'm talking about attended the recognition by high-level White House staff, though probably not President Reagan, that the man selected to run the always problematic Department of Health and Human Services had been, politically speaking, a bad choice. Dick Schweiker, former Pennsylvania Senator and long-time Republican, turned out to be far more liberal than expected. HHS, home of welfare programs as well as health, had long been the albatross around every administration's neck.

Not only was the thing huge, far-flung, and steadily growing, but so was its cost. Worse yet, the programs it ran were mainly 'entitlements' firmly established in statute and tied to population growth as well as growth in the numbers of people eligible for some kind of taxpayer-supported aid. It had proven to be impossible to find enough people in Congress with the courage to eliminate or even reduce small parts of these humanitarian-seeming programs, so they grew and grew, taking up more and more of the federal budget and steadily diminishing discretionary spending ability.

Dick Schweiker, by nature a kind, generous and caring man, was of no help in keeping this monstrous department under good management control, let alone reining it in. This made him a disappointment to the many social and fiscal conservatives who had helped elect the President and obtained jobs in the White House. Somehow, in the 'policy discussions' among these people, it was decided that Schweiker had to go. I was selected to play an important role in his departure from office, unbeknownst to me.

My selection for the Judas-like role rested upon my good relationship with the HHS Secretary, my well-known long association with Reagan, and the decision to make a health issue the instrument of Schweiker's political destruction.

Ronald Reagan was noted for his loyalty to his principal lieutenants and senior staff. Once he decided to place his trust in you, he was unwavering and unimpressed by rumors and allegations that fly among envious competitors for favor and position in Washington. He tolerated disagreement, listened to arguments for policies he initially did not favor, and was gracious in explaining his decisions when you lost your case. He fully, if sometimes naively, expected his loyalties to be fully returned, and was slow to act on allegations of inadequacy or malfeasance on the part of those he trusted.

There was, however, one thing he would not tolerate: a threat.

The scheme, I realized too late to avoid participating in it, was to get Dick Schweiker, who was basically loyal to his boss, to threaten him. The issue was the establishment of an Undersecretary for Health in HHS. It was, on the surface, an entirely reasonable step in recognition of the deep division between health programs and welfare programs, and the exploding importance, cost and political impact of health care. There was, of course, an Assistant Secretary for Health, and no undersecretaries of anything, and the social services community was violently opposed to the elevation of health to a higher-seeming position in the HHS structure.

Thus, curiously largely unbeknownst to the HHS Secretary, there had been extensive, hotly-debated arguments among policy staff in the White House about elevating anyone in health to such an exalted position, and the decision of the senior political staff around the President was that it would be exceedingly unwise and politically destructive to do this. The President evidently had accepted this judgment. Discussion closed.

Based upon my experience at ADAMHA and earlier, as Director of Health in California, I favored the Undersecretary idea. This country has no real health policy, or health agenda. Despite the heroic efforts of the American Medical Association, and the burgeoning involvement of federal, state and local government in health care, there is in my judgment no effective national leadership in this crucial area. Health costs have skyrocketed, the advent of 'managed care' has given financial managers, speculators, and business people with scant knowledge of medical issues an inordinate voice in crucial health care delivery systems, health insurance rates go up faster than inflation, and an industry among the largest on earth is floundering around waiting for some messianic character to come make it all well.

I thought, personally, that there should be a federal Department of Health, with real expertise and real power, as exists in a number of other modern industrialized Western nations. Short of that, establishing an undersecretary in HHS would be a solid first step in the right direction. I never actively campaigned or lobbied for such a change, but never made a secret of my beliefs, either, though they were certain to be denounced as medical chauvinism or personal power seeking.

Parenthetically, I should say a word about the Surgeon General - at that time the distinguished, idealistic, totally dedicated C. Everett Koop: "Chick." Originally, those doctrinaire political ideologues who surrounded and tried to steer Ronald Reagan in the White House, delayed Koop's confirmation in that job out of fear that he was too 'right wing,' too conservative, too fundamentalist religious.

Later, Chick was to scare those same ideologically pure conservatives by daring to speak out, without their permission, on politically 'sensitive' issues like cigarette smoking and AIDS. He wanted to be, and nearly succeeded in being, the country's family doctor. He identified medical issues and spoke his mind about them - politicians be damned! - to the benefit of us all.

Koop was arguably the most influential (and beneficial) medical public servant ever to hold that office. The sad fact, however, is that the Surgeon General of the United States has no power whatsoever, either to make policy or to enforce it. Koop turned the position into a "bully pulpit" that Teddy Roosevelt would no doubt have approved. He had an impact, at least for a while; people listened to him, and heard him. He did make a difference.

However, he was not listened to by anyone, especially in government, about health policy for the nation, management of the exploding health care system, or any coherent plan for its future direction and configuration.

The plot to get rid of Schweiker involved getting him to fall on his sword over the issue of an undersecretary for health. Bud Mayer, dedicated to the idea, was to convince the Secretary that he should go directly to the Boss, and insist that it needed to be done, which it did. I was told to convince him that he should pull out all stops, and threaten to resign if he didn't prevail in this.

He did exactly that. The President listened, conferred with his staff, and the following day signed a letter thanking the Secretary for his services and directing him to find another job. The White House, he was assured, would help him with his job search, but wanted a former congresswoman, Margaret Heckler, to take over at HHS. I never knew if Mr. Schweiker ever found about the conspiracy to have him depose himself with his threat, or about my unintentional part in it, but he remained cordial to me for years afterward. He was given a highly-paid job in an insurance conglomerate, and seemed to do well in it.

I found the whole episode distasteful. Moreover, I felt I had been duped, and my sincere convictions exploited by mostly young, smart-aleck political manipulators who listened to an entirely different drum. In comparison to the crowd surrounding Bill Clinton, however, those people were paragons of virtue. They risked my going to the President to complain, but of course I did not since it would not help poor Schweiker and they counted on my, at best, reserved support for him in that position.

"Maggie" Heckler was, if anything, less able to manage the department than Schweiker had been. That seemed to be fine with the White House bunch; she did what she was told and was no fervent advocate of anything.

One last tragic-comedic ADAMHA episode, and I shall leave my scant description of that fascinating place. It was there that I began to realize that high rank in the DC hierarchy, and especially personal acquaintance with the President, was widely perceived to carry with it enormous power and influence. A steady stream of applicants seeking senior management jobs in my agency appeared in my office. The majority were women. All claimed long, devoted membership in the Republican Party. Many had, or so they said, actively campaigned for Mr. Reagan. What struck me most forcefully was how often these people seemed to assume I could grant them Dukedoms without regard for their qualifications. Every one insisted that my success in office rested upon their joining me at the highest levels.

Not a single one got hired.

The three institutes: Mental Health, Alcohol, and Drugs, all had dual missions: research in their respective fields, and development of clinical programs for treatment of sufferers. The researchers were rather detached, both physically and psychologically, from the heretofore more highly touted and better-supported community programs. Those programs, especially in mental health (alcohol and drug being far less chic), involved grants to set up clinics and parts of hospitals, supposedly adhering to standards for treatment, staffing, facility, 'community organization' efforts, public education, and an ill-defined 'rehabilitation' effort.

Roughly similar, but far more puny, efforts were made to address problems of alcohol and drug abuse.

In all the institutes, there was little or no communication or any evident relationship between the researchers in the labs over in Bethesda on the campus of the National Institutes of Health, where the other researchers into more legitimate ailments like cancer, heart disease, allergies and venereal diseases largely ignored them, and the workers in the field actually treating patients. In spite of John F. Kennedy's National Mental Health Act, and the heroic efforts of the National Association for Mental Health, it hadn't really caught on very much when I first got to ADAMHA.

Worse, from the federal establishment's viewpoint, the victims of these ailments didn't vote, were social outcasts, and worst of all, were tended to by mushy-headed left wing pseudo-intellectuals who were noted for being anti-authority, anti-government nuts who somehow identified with these "losers" who populated our mental hospitals and drunk-tanks and pot parlors - all at huge expense to the government and to 'decent' citizens.

I was told by the White House recruiters when they gave me my marching orders after I arrived on a day in early May, temperature in the 90s and humidity near 100%, that I was to have the privilege and honor of serving as the U.S. Government Administrator of Mental Health, Alcoholism and Drug Abuse Institutes and all their activities nationwide, parallel to the Director of the National Institutes of Health, because the President had said I was the only psychiatrist he knew, that he trusted!

This meant, they explained, that I would truly represent and advocate for the President - not for the employees and special interests at ADAMHA - would make the programs rational, cost-effective, and not given to public attacks on the Administration. While they were sure I knew how to do this (which of course I didn't), and was free to take whatever steps I felt were needed to quell the wild-eyed, bushy-haired radicals without interference from on high, there would be one direct order that I must follow at once.

That was that order to reduce the staff of the entire organization by 25%. It didn't matter how - just do it. The salary savings would be outstanding.

Somehow, both ADAMHA and I had survived the turmoil of that early "RIF" and in a surprisingly short time the goal was accomplished, helped by accelerated attrition as employees decided this wasn't such a good place to work and sought jobs in more stable agencies or even in private industry. Meanwhile, the entire organization was scrutinized and streamlined, job descriptions were rewritten to conform more closely to reality, and life went on. The mass meetings had dwindled to small groups, giving me a chance to talk quietly and rationally about our goals, my plans for the agency, the great honor and privilege of public service, the coming revolution in the understanding of mental disorders and alcoholism, and how to deal with these enormous human problems.

You will note I did not mention drug abuse and addiction. There were reasons for this. First, I did have vast experience in mental health, and was an acknowledged 'expert' in community programs, deinstitutionalization of the mentally ill - having emptied most of the huge California state hospitals and closed them as local mental health programs grew and flourished in that state, and in the use of the new and literally miraculous chemicals that had begun to flood the market and at least partially liberate the 'insane.' The ADAMHA staff learned that I was in fact one of them: I could speak their language, understood their problems, and was not Attila the Republican Hun, as they had initially feared.

Similarly, my experience of many years dealing with alcoholics, after having to unlearn the glib, popular psychiatric misconceptions about their bad character, antisocial and psychopathic traits, and untreatability, was altogether unique in the upper levels of federal government. Thus I was soon perceived as a friend rather than an enemy. Encouraged, I ultimately took over active direction of the National Institute on Alcohol Abuse and Alcoholism - "NI-triple-A," launched the nationwide campaign to reduce teenage drunk driving fatalities through the use of designated drivers, especially at Prom time, and led the charge to establish alcohol programs as legitimate medical attacks on a manageable chronic disease. At that time, this was a revolutionary idea: both that it was a legitimate disease, and that it could be managed, like diabetes or other chronic diseases, even if they couldn't be "cured."

My feelings about drug abuse and addiction were different, and far less sanguine. Unlike the case in alcoholism, drug problems involve a wide array of totally different chemicals with differing effects. In "the old days" when I was a resident physician in a federal narcotics hospital, the great majority of patients were addicted to opium derivatives: morphine, heroin (far and away the drug of choice), opium itself, codeine (infrequently), and paregoric. All of those rapidly caused users to become psychologically as well as physically dependent on them, tolerant to larger and larger doses - sometimes enough to literally kill a horse - and truly severe physical and emotional symptoms and suffering when they were withheld.

That more simple time provided abundant evidence that people so addicted rarely escaped from it; some said never. We never saw cocaine "addicts." Cocaine was an 'upper,' while the opium derivatives are clearly 'downers,' and people never, we thought, got truly hooked on it.

By the time I got to Washington, all that had changed. The widespread use of opiates in the Viet Nam War did not generally lead to long-term, traditional addiction. No one knows why. Moreover, cocaine was becoming popular and even fashionable in certain circles, and people did seem to be developing a destructive compulsion to use it, unlike the mythical Sherlock Holmes and very real Sigmund Freud, who allegedly used it for years without serious ill effects.

To complicate matters, a host of new compounds burst upon the scene, led by LSD, advocated enthusiastically by an asinine professor named Timothy Leary and an army of spaced-out disciples. That substance seriously disrupts brain function, causing hallucinations and delusions along with gross and bizarre distortions of reality, and can usher in a full-blown, permanent psychosis, following 'flashbacks' and suicidal impulses. Various amphetamines, beginning with benzedrine first used by truck drivers to stay awake in the 40s and 50s, emerged as dangerous, disorienting stimulant drugs that appeal to young people, in particular, and can play a part in violent and criminal behavior. There are many others, often called "designer drugs," and to this day there have been no - repeat NO - generally effective methods developed to deal with the problem.

However, our researchers (bless their hearts!) in both mental health and alcoholism have made monumental contributions to our understanding of those problems and ways to deal with them far more successfully than in the whole previous history of the human race. It dawned on me that if I were to "make a difference" in my (inadvertently) chosen professional field, now was my chance to do so. I had neither the imagination, the background in pure science, nor the impulse to search for esoteric truths that were necessary to conduct research.

Nevertheless, I did have the ability to recognize great researchers, to understand and appreciate what drove them and what they were trying to do, and to translate much of that into plain English. Most researchers, interestingly, cannot do that very well, and often don't even try. I began to see my 'leadership' role as, in reality, a translating-communicating project. I was head of a number of disparate groups who didn't, and perhaps couldn't, communicate effectively with one another: researchers and clinicians. Still other groups who needed to be communicated with included the administrators and financiers hovering over both research and clinical organizations, and who were often truly ignorant of what the professionals were actually doing.

Then, within the federal government like in the states and counties, there were managers, officials and accountants still further removed from the action and often only peripherally interested in it, at best, but who had a powerful effect on programs. Some of these were entrenched career civil servants, many dedicated to preserving the status quo (their obscene mantra invariably being "if it ain't broke, don't fix it!")

Still higher in the pecking order were the elected officials and their appointees, struggling for ascendancy over the more experienced, entrenched career civil servants and for public acclaim, if not votes and political glory and advancement. Their influence can be profound in any publicly supported professional endeavor, and too frequently has no relationship whatever to the merit - or the dangers - of what is being done by the professionals.

Instead of playing to the voting public directly, senior government officers are very commonly excessively concerned with their relationship with the media, who can be helpful and supportive but are able to turn into bloodthirsty predators almost without warning. The media, then, are another group to be communicated with - carefully.

Finally, one must send and receive communications from the ubiquitous special interest groups that form around every activity of government. In our case, these included advocacy groups for the mentally ill, the retarded, the elderly, children, the poor, the homeless, and the helpless cast-offs of the mental hospital system, aimlessly wandering the streets, among others. Hard on their heels came the pharmaceutical people, the professional groups of physicians, psychologists, nurses, social workers, aides and orderlies and the exploding armies of 'counselors.'

All these groups have an agenda, and special concerns. All want to be heard at the very top. Each speaks a different language, in a sense, that has to be learned and used with them, or trouble ensues. When a surgeon loses too many patients, or we find the Army shooting pigs and goats for wound research, or someone on a tranquilizer shoots up his neighborhood, or a lab gives morphine to a group of monkeys, or a kid dies from drinking his addict mother's methadone-laced orange juice, or we aren't buying some astronomically expensive medicine that wipes out schizophrenia, some of these special groups pound on the doors of the almighty in Washington, demanding resolution of the problem.

The first internal challenge is communicating with the researchers. They become enraged if they think you are trying to tell them what to research. Like all of us, they need to feel appreciated - even loved. Their successes must be broadcast. Their findings need to be explained to clinical people eager to apply them, and whose clinical needs must be told to the research people so they can help solve the problems. They do not generally understand one another. This is where 'leadership as communicator' comes in to play.

Beyond that, the splendid and usually expensive work of both the researchers and the clinicians has to be explained, understandably, to the upper echelons of management and budget in the Department of Health and Human Services, who are generally abysmally ignorant of mental health and alcohol issues and not much interested. Selected members of the congress serving on relevant committees, and their all-important and often imperious, arrogant staffers need to be filled in, and their support enlisted.

Having done all that communicating, it is still necessary to talk to the appropriate special interest groups and the media - carefully. Always carefully. You never know exactly how it will come out until you read it or hear it on the evening news.

Recognizing these realities of high-level government service, I came firmly to my second basic operating principal. Beyond the first - picking and then firmly supporting excellent, loyal, trusted senior lieutenants - came learning, and learning to accept, that what you principally were was a communications link between disparate groups who talked in different special languages, had to be listened to carefully and respectfully (no matter how outrageous their desires or revolting their behavior,) and then talked with in their own special patois.

Application of these principals did not guarantee success, but failure to apply them was extremely risky, and sure to make life hard. They were to prove at least as important, if not more so, when I moved to an even more exalted and genuinely powerful position in the Pentagon rather abruptly and wholly unexpectedly, in coming weeks.

One last anecdote concerning my adventures at ADAMHA bears retelling, for it taught me something about the utilization of employees, the U.S. State Department, and the intricacies of federal budgeting.

One of our senior employees in the National Institute of Mental Health had 'bumped' into the role of director of the Office of International Affairs in the agency. He was a former Methodist minister, I was told, who moved from pastoral counseling into the more organized mental health field. He was a plump, pleasant man with glowing, puffy cheeks, a startling (for a male in his 50s) cupid's-bow shaped mouth, curved perpetually into a beatific semi-smile that signified absolutely nothing, no knowledge whatever of international affairs and apparently no interest in it. He was, as far as I could determine, utterly useless, but of course could not be fired.

We had been visited by high-level foreign government mental health officials on a number of occasions, and many of them insisted that I visit their countries, learn about their programs, and offer suggestions based upon our own rather advanced system. When my own agency was running smoothly enough that I felt comfortable about leaving for a couple of weeks, I put my man with the beatific smile to work setting up an itinerary and schedule for a trip that was to take me around the world. He finally presented it to me, after much prodding, and suggested that he go a week ahead of me, as my advance man, to firm up arrangements locally in each country. I agreed, and off he went.

It happened that another employee, a Pakistani by birth, was at the same time on 'official business' in Karachi. Since he and my man were old friends, they would meet in Pakistan and jointly work on arrangements for my visit there. Sounded great. I was later to learn that the Pakistani was expert at dreaming up wholly imaginary "official" business two or three times every year, enabling him to visit his family in the old country, where he did absolutely nothing else, all at U.S. taxpayers' expense.

About a week before I was to leave on my grand tour, I was awakened at home at about 4 in the morning by an urgent call from the duty officer at the State Department. After identifying me as the ADAMHA chief, the young male caller, greatly indignant, related that he had had great trouble finding out whom to call and demanding to know why I did not have a full-time duty officer present at all times in my agency to deal with emergencies. After I told him we didn't have emergencies, ordinarily, he announced triumphantly that we did now!

The 'emergency,' in this case, was that my ex-preacher envoy had walked into the lobby of the American Embassy in Karachi and dropped dead, so the State Department had an urgent need to know what I was going to do about it. Actually, I hadn't planned to do anything. What did he have in mind?

Exasperated, the young Harvard graduate (he had to be!) told me I would absolutely have to do something about the body. It was my responsibility.

Equally exasperated (not being at my most gracious at 4 AM when jolted from a sound sleep) I told him - I think I called him "Sonny," that he was wrong; it was his problem. To illustrate, I pointed out that the corpse was than of a senior U.S. Government official on U.S. Government business who died on U.S. Government property in Pakistan. The Embassy, therefore, should ship the body, post haste, home to the United States.

After a few moments of shocked silence, my attacker said that they could not do that without a fund citation. "Fund Citation!" I thundered in my most authoritative tones, "You must be crazy." Agency heads, I explained, do not issue fund citations (where had he learned about how government operates?) and certainly not at four o'clock on Sunday mornings. I told him to just arrange to have the body flown back here and appropriate money people could handle the financing later.

The distraught young diplomat told me that American tourists regularly drop dead in Pakistan, though not at the Embassy proper, and that State Department policy forbade Embassies to get involved in 'that sort of thing.' In addition, he said, time was of the essence. Pakistan is a warm country, and there are no undertakers there. Every dead body must be cremated or buried within, at most, three days, for obvious reasons, since there is no way to embalm dead bodies and - "You know..." I could just imagine him gagging at the thought.

Whatever. I told him there was no way even to ask for a fund citation until sometime the next day (too late, apparently), so I wished him and his department well as they solved their - not my - problem.

The following day I put my accounting people to work contacting their counterparts at State, and went on to other things. Nothing more was heard for several days, whereupon we were notified that a large package was arriving by airfreight and should be picked up. The package turned out to be a conventional household refrigerator, turned to its lowest temperature level and with its interior cleared of shelves and groceries to be replaced by my man, neatly tucked in, deeply chilled, and ready for the mortician.

The poor dedicated civil servant's widow was outraged and announced that she would be suing the government and me personally for working the poor fellow literally to death and treating his remains in so disrespectful a manner, but evidently she abandoned that idea. No member of the ADAMA staff was invited to the funeral.

That trip took me to Britain, where I paid tribute to the great men who had started the Community Mental Health movement; to Germany, where Adolph Hitler solved the problem by gassing mental hospital patients and retarded citizens; Sweden and Denmark with typically well-run, humane systems; the World Health Organization headquarters in Geneva, where Mental Health was run by a charming, urbane, devout US-hating Communist from Romania with the wonderful anatomical name of "Sartorius," the name of the long muscle lying diagonally across the front of the thigh; and then Pakistan. My reception there was cool, at the embassy, but quite friendly elsewhere in the country.

The most exciting and instructive part of that trip was my week in India. At that time, and possibly still, Indian currency could not be converted into US dollars, and the embassy in New Delhi regularly accepted Rupees for various debts owed to the U.S., as a diplomatic gesture. I think they had whole rooms full of rupees that were useless elsewhere, and when any American official visited on government business, he was given an enormous pile of Indian paper money to use as he wished for all expenses while in country.

The schedule called for staff conferences at several large general hospitals and a couple of university medical centers where I gave speeches. The most interesting of the institutions was the medical university in Bangalore, far to the south on the Indian subcontinent. The crowded amphitheater-style lecture hall was impossibly hot and humid, but the eager, smiling faces of the students and their rapt attention more than made up for it. Following the lecture I was taken to a huge, sprawling mental hospital holding thousands of largely unsupervised psychotic people who milled about aimlessly among the many bungalows scattered over the extensive, lush tropical grounds adorned with innumerable small temples and shrines to some of the multitudes of gods and religions that are so much a part of life there.

It was an Asian version of St. Mary's of Bethlehem - "Bedlam," in the cockney tongue - of 17th Century London, and seemed to have about the same therapy program that must have existed there. In spite of pockets of primitive populations, aching poverty, dirt, sad little villages that used a single pond both for drinking water and waste disposal, and 'hospitals' like that massive campus with its crowd of wandering psychotics, the country so entranced me that a few years later, after leaving government, I took my adventuresome wife along and spent several weeks there. No free rupees that time, but the same crowds hanging on trains and buses, the same immolation areas where the dead were cremated on piles of wood, under a small canopy, and the same snake charmers and monkeys and elephants.

William E. Mayer, M.D.

William E. Mayer, M.D.

CHAPTER 14

THE PENTAGON: CITADEL OF POWER

Unbeknownst to me, while I happily labored in the fields of alcoholism, attending meetings of increasingly excited alcohol researchers and clinicians, and trying to interpret their findings and hopes to my surprised superiors in the federal bureaucracy and the purse-string holders on Capitol Hill, along with the public at large, a massive change was about to take place in my life. It was called The Pentagon.

Everyone knows, of course, that the Pentagon is a huge, 5-sided building along the Potomac River, where America's military leaders are gathered while they design and direct the most powerful, most awesome, most complex and surely most expensive offensive and defensive military structure in the history of the world. It houses more than 20 thousand full time employees, in and out of uniform, and at one time held 60 thousand. When it was built, in the early days of World War II, it was the world's largest building. It was designed for eventual use, at war's successful end, as a veteran's hospital, but somehow that never materialized.

The building itself is a marvel of design and engineering. Its five sides surround a central courtyard. Its five floors are laid out in concentric rings transected at regular intervals by ten corridors radiating outward from the smallest, central ring. The rings are designated by letters from A to E, with the outermost being the E-Ring. The intersecting corridors are numbered from one to ten. Each office is numbered according to the floor number, followed by the letter-designated ring, followed by a three-digit number beginning with the lower numbered corridor of the two that bordered the office on each end of that ring's segment. Clear? Actually, the scheme is relatively straightforward and simple, but since there are 17 miles of corridors it was possible to get hopelessly lost. Rumor had it that people had starved to death trying to find the cafeteria. Floors were connected by stairways, a few elevators, and long ramps originally intended for wheelchair traverse. Several parts of several floors and wings were totally sealed off and heavily guarded, which complicated trips from one part of the mammoth structure to another.

The higher rank one was, the farther out from the center was his office. Everyone in the topmost echelons had an office on the "E-Ring" and thus had the priceless privilege of windows to the outside world. Nearly everyone else dwelt in concrete caves, at best only peeking out at the next ring.

Only two major entrances exist, although some small minor ones can be found and are usually locked. The most important entrance, for the most important civilian officials: the Secretary, his deputy, and his Assistant Secretaries, was called the River Entrance. The other main entry was for the highest-ranked military: the Chiefs of Staff and the organization of the Joint Chiefs, who were the uniformed heads of each service. All these dignitaries were arrayed along the E-Ring, which was about a mile in total length.

It would be pointless as well as hopelessly confusing to describe the organization that functions within those five walls. To grasp the basics, however, one must understand that the overall boss is the Secretary of Defense, a civilian who answers only to the President. His personal staff consists of a deputy and a number of assistant secretaries, each in charge of some specific function, like health affairs, personnel, reserve affairs, procurement, strategic planning, public affairs, budget, congressional relations and the like.

Similarly, each military department, or service, has its own civilian secretary, also appointed by the President but subordinate to the Secretary of Defense. Thus the building also houses a Secretary of the Army, Secretary of the Navy (which includes the Marine Corps), and a Secretary of the Air Force. They work closely with the military Chief in each service, but also with SecDef.

All the way across the building, exactly opposite to the SecDef's office and about a half-mile distant from it, was the second largest office in the entire structure. It had been designed to accommodate the Office of Civil Defense, when that had been a major concern of the nation at war.

When Civil Defense ceased to seem so important, and the war ended, the idea of an over-all Department of Defense took hold. In a couple of years that structure was created. The individual service secretaries, their staffs, the military chiefs and their staffs were all arranged along the E-Ring as close as possible to the Secretary of Defense. The office of Civil Defense was banished to the basement, and its grand big office and suite were turned over by "Doc" Cook, the powerful building manager, to Health Affairs.

It is well known, but frequently forgotten, that the 'birth' of the Department of Defense was not exactly a joyful event. The military services were unanimous in their disdain and dislike for the whole idea. They accepted the constitutional concept of civilian control of the military, but only reluctantly at best. The idea of a 'super' secretary, even higher up than their individual service secretaries, was shocking to most career military people.

To make matters worse, the administration and the congress had (foolishly, most Army and Navy and Marine Corps people believed) fallen prey to the outrageous propaganda of the "fly-boys," whose position seemed to be that aviators, by themselves, had conquered Germany and Japan. As a result, they had created a whole new service, called the Air Force, complete with its own secretary, chief of staff, and worst of all, budget.

Then, to make matters still worse, if that were possible, these people decked themselves out in pale blue uniforms, for all the world like postal workers, and made heroic efforts to distance themselves and their regulations and practices, from the other services. This was outrageous.

The first Secretary of Defense, James Forrestal, killed himself by jumping out of a window at Bethesda Naval Hospital. One of his successors, a fellow named MacNamara, who had arrived from Ford Motor Company, had announced that he admittedly knew nothing of military organizations, but as a top-flight manager, he could manage anything; the principles were the same. During the war in Viet Nam, he proved how wrong this was. These two men, more than any others, firmed up and ensured the hostility of the uniformed leadership toward the despised Department of Defense.

By the time Ronald Reagan and Caspar Weinberger arrived on the national scene, military morale was at its lowest, congressional complaints about the Pentagon's budget were growing, and articles were appearing with increasing frequency in the press, even including the Reader's Digest, asserting that military medicine was poor at best, dangerous to patients, and poorly managed.

The acting Assistant Secretary of Defense, a bright, too-young former Air Force short-term doc whose only military experience had been at Andrews Air Force Base in Washington, tending to the crew of Air Force One, seemed incapable of dealing with the problem. Partly, this was a reflection, in a way, of his Chief Deputy's open contempt for military physicians. I was to get to know that deputy well.

It was little more than fifteen months after my arrival at ADAMHA that the invitation came to meet with Caspar Weinberger, Secretary of Defense, in his Pentagon office to discuss an appointment on his senior staff, as Assistant Secretary of Defense (Health Affairs.) I hastened to accept the invitation, already feeling that I had done all I wanted in my current job, and excited over the prospect of higher rank, greater power and opportunity to do something really constructive in a military environment I knew well.

"Cap," whom I had known in California when he headed the all-powerful Department of Finance and I the hugely expensive Department of Health, greeted me warmly and enthusiastically. He was invariably, toward friend and foe and hostile press alike, gracious, attentive, rather intensely focused, and obviously totally dedicated to his job. He had an air of formality that I found admirable and that called forth a kind of decorum and dignity from everyone he dealt with. I was to come to regard him one of the truly great men - the very few such - that I had ever had the privilege of meeting or working with.

He wasted no time and few words outlining the situation in Health Affairs. The last official occupant of the Assistant Secretary position, Dr. John Moxley, was a distinguished academician and administrator who had left after turning up seemingly insurmountable problems in military medicine. The position had been offered to several equally prestigious physicians who declined the job, and Cap indicated that the only reason they had not asked me sooner was that I was doing such a great job in the Department of Health and Human Services. However, he said, the need was greater in Defense. I wasn't at all sure I believed his compliment, but I accepted it - modestly, of course.

The annual worldwide defense exercise conducted on the massive computers in the Pentagon and involving all the military services, their intelligence elements, the CIA, the Federal Emergency Management Agency, and selected allied military leaders, would begin shortly. It was following last year's exercise that Moxley had uncovered disastrous shortcomings in military medical readiness for war that were potentially disastrous. This was said to be a factor in his decision to leave.

The young man in the "acting" role of Assistant Secretary was not a possible candidate for the job because of his youth and inexperience. That man left gratefully, when I accepted Cap's offer, to take a teaching position at a local medical school. Even though he had liked his moment of glory in office, even if only "acting," his wife had had a lovely time decorating the spacious room with draperies and carpeting of pale baby blue, unwittingly confirming the widespread in-house vision of Health Affairs as something less than fittingly masculine and fully equipped as such.

I played no games with Cap but accepted the offer at once. He cautioned me that I would instantly encounter deeply troubling problems. The first was the medical readiness issue. The second was an emerging series of articles in the press and over the airwaves denouncing military health care as shoddy and of poor quality. Finally, there was the perennial conflict over whether the military medical departments should be combined into one, in a fanciful purple-colored uniform. This was the "purple suit" controversy. It started during Eisenhower's presidency, when he called the existence of three separate medical departments idiotic. A recent long study by eminent medical scholars and administrators, mostly retired military, said the same thing. I would have to study this, and advise him what should be done. The Services and their Surgeons General violently opposed any change.

In a matter of days, word came down from Secretary Heckler's office that I was to move to the Pentagon. My departure from ADAMHA involved a series of farewell gatherings with staff in headquarters as well as in each of the Institutes, all surprisingly warm and friendly and full of well wishes but accompanied by seemingly sincere regrets at my leaving. My understanding and acceptance of my proper role as chief communications link had evidently paid great dividends and I was gratified to find that even though I was the official representative of the enemy, which is to say the Republicans, the ADAMHA staff thought of me as 'one of them,' a friend and effective advocate.

Making my way across the Potomac I was deluged with wonder over my new status - one step below Weinberger and only one more from the President - and with reflections on my whole life until then, what events and people had gotten me there, what I was bringing to this job of monumental importance.

Inevitably, as I always did when I started any new job, I wondered seriously if I were smart enough and competent enough to do it successfully, and harbored serious doubts about this. Maybe people's expectations of me and my abilities were inflated and unrealistic. In my heart I knew I wasn't as good at almost anything as people thought I was, because, I always thought, I had so successfully cultivated an air of confidence and an apparent grasp of the task at hand - while carefully avoiding a show of arrogance - that most others thought far more of my abilities than I myself dared believe was true.

As long as I could remember, feelings of intense anxiety had played an enormous role in everything I did, but it was supremely important to me to hide that from everyone. I would never admit this to anyone.

Memories of my mother, surely the most powerful characterological influence in my life, came readily to mind. I realized that she had instilled in me many old concepts of virtue, honor, loyalty, duty and responsibility that years before on a movie set in Hollywood, Ronald Reagan and I had rather fervently agreed upon and which had assured our friendship. Such ideas were even less current and 'popular' when he took office, and I arrived at the Pentagon, than they had been in mid-Century and before.

Actually, such concepts were considered by many people to be out-dated, old-fashioned, and a bit quaint. This was less true in the military, however, and I had long recognized that was what I had most liked about being part of that community, and I was happy to be joining it again. It helped moderate the intense anxiety and uncertainty that surrounded me as I walked up the broad steps to the River Entrance of the huge building.

As I tried to conduct an objective assessment of myself as a person, and identify who had most effectively steered me to this place as probably the single most powerful physician in the free world, I found myself looking back at literally an army of people who had touched my life, helped me along, tried to teach me what was truly important, for whatever reasons, and I had great difficulty picking out those who had had the most impact.

Some of my teachers at the old Todd School for Boys had had a significant influence on my path in life, but the only one who really stood out was Mr. Lindall, who was only there for three of my highschool years. He took a special interest in me, sent my theme papers to colleagues at the University of Chicago, and told me in the 9th grade I was fully prepared to enter college right then. He always required that I stand at attention while he lectured to me in his dormitory room, admonishing me severely to avoid being "cheeky" toward the other boys, but at the same time declaring that I had without doubt the "finest mind" (his words) that he had ever encountered.

Mr. Lindall, like my mother, insisted that I could take no credit for this. Indeed, such a gift imposed upon me far greater responsibilities than my peers even dreamed of, and I would be absolutely required in my life to live up to those responsibilities, avoiding distracting frivolities and useless pursuits, constantly working to improve myself and become, ultimately, the truly great man that God intended I should be.

It was never altogether clear to me what all that meant, and no grandiose schemes or life plans emerged to reveal what lay ahead, but I never forgot Mr. Lindall or his earnest exhortations. They so emphatically echoed what my mother had told me, not once but more or less repeatedly, that they profoundly influenced certain of my attitudes and behavior.

It seemed quite evident to me that I was 'smarter' than any of the other kids, even much older ones, and I was impatient with their plodding attempts to master ideas and subjects that seemed abundantly clear to me. That had, without doubt, contributed to my total lack of desire for close friendships, and I realized that while I did like many people, and wanted them to like me, I had no desire to be close to anyone, to have a 'best friend,' or buddy. This quality in me had established a kind of isolation, an aloneness that has persisted throughout life. It created both the appearance and the reality of a certain level of self-reliance and self-confidence, but those were always secretly accompanied by significant anxiety, carefully hidden from view.

College was much the same, in that I had no close friends, and saw my fraternity brothers as silly in their preoccupation with beer, sexual conquests, rebelling - mostly harmlessly - again authority, and hazing their inferiors by paddling their posteriors and otherwise tormenting them during hell week.

The college professors, who in those gentler days mainly did their own teaching rather than give it over to graduate student assistants, included some impressive people, but in the main validated the assertion of one of their members that when one reflected on the whole educational experience, through graduate school, it would become clear that you could count the really great teachers you had ever had, on the fingers of one hand.

There were a few exceptions. One, in particular, the tall, lank, white-haired grand old man of the chemistry faculty named Dehn, affected me deeply. He let me join a small post-graduate seminar in organic chemistry, that involved two informal meetings a week in his office during which there were no assignments except to consider, between meetings, what he had shared with us six or eight students, of his giant intellect, and come back prepared to talk about it next time. Everybody in the class got a final grade of 'A.'

One session addressed Bakelite, a hard material discovered by accident in a lab when two liquids were accidentally mixed. It was coming into wide use for knobs on radios. Dr. Dehn declared that this was the first of what would be an endless series of compounds derived from organic chemicals that would be called "plastics." He said they would change the world, and directly affect every one of us in countless applications in industry and in everyday life. This wonderful man played a part in my being awarded a full scholarship to medical school, but I didn't learn that until years later.

One other college professor also affected my future in a short, elective class I took in philology. I have forgotten his name, and never talked with him personally, but he brought to life the whole history of language from primitive Indo-European to modern American slang. He was an obese, disheveled man who had fled from Nazi Germany, but he was clearly entranced with language. It was he who steered us to a new book by a Japanese-American semanticist, S. I. (Sam) Hayakawa, called "Language in Action," whose every chapter was, to me, a brilliant revelation of the uses of language and the selection of words and phrases to influence thought in others. Ever after that I was conscious of this man's ideas, and made a conscious attempt to employ them in my every public utterance, to good effect.

Nearly forty years later I was to meet Sam Hayakawa, who had distinguished himself in the interim as a college president in San Francisco during the tumultuous student days in the 60's when he stood atop a car and quelled a student riot by his marvelous semantic skills, and was then elected to the U. S. Senate at an advanced age, and slept through most sessions.

We met at a glittering Washington reception that he attended, as usual, with a flashy, sexy young female - a different one, I was to learn, at each such event - clinging delightedly to the ancient man's arm. I thanked him for the beneficial influence he had had on my career through his writings. Neither he nor his nubile companion seemed to have any idea of what I was talking about.

My years in the military services had acquainted me with a large number of really fine men and a substantial number of mediocre (or worse) ones. A few were outstanding, and left their mark. Bartholomew W. Hogan, Captain, Medical Corps, U. S. Navy was one such. "Bart" (no one ever called him that in his presence) ran the Naval Hospital in Philadelphia where I interned for 12 months after medical school and who decided I was not born to be one of the world's outstanding surgeons. He was a remote, cold, imperious officer of the 'old school,' who wore his flowing, scarlet lined cape with a flourish, while his old-style, narrow-brimmed World War I - vintage hat sat perfectly straight, no tilt, on his massive head.

It was Bart Hogan, later to become the Navy's first Roman Catholic and first psychiatrist to be Surgeon General, who decided I would be trained in psychiatry and neurology - no discussion. Despite my shock and dismay at his seemingly arbitrary, autocratic decision about my entire professional life, I was impressed by him and learned from him. He was every inch in charge: the absolute, unquestionable commander. His curled, wax-tipped mustache and ramrod posture, even when sitting down, could have made him seem ridiculous, but they did not.

In my daily formal encounters with that remarkable man, following his examination of my diagnostic and therapeutic actions in behalf of every new patient admitted to my psychiatric 'observation' ward, he not only taught me a great deal about mental disease but also implanted those ideas about the organic - physical - basis for such diseases. While unproven at that time in medical history, I had been able years later in ADAMHA to provide our researchers with the technology that validated his theories. That was a great triumph and tremendously gratifying to me.

In the years right after World War II, a certain number of military doctors who had entered service at the war's outset or just before, and had not been very successful in civilian practice, found themselves at fairly high rank and elected to stay on duty. Since almost everyone else was frantic to get out and go home, that put those who remained in service, almost by default, into high-level positions, often commanding hospitals, where they proved they were wholly unfit and incompetent to do the job. I had at least two such commanders - one at Naval Hospital Mare Island, in California, and one other in the Naval Hospital Yokosuka, Japan.

The latter was a martinet who knew little medicine and little of the real Navy. He and his wife occupied lavish quarters on the naval base, entertained continuously, and along with his unattractive wife paraded their exalted status and privilege shamelessly, causing all his subordinates to detest them. The fellow at Mare Island, ensconced on a hill overlooking San Francisco Bay, held weekly formal dinners in his quarters' grand dining room, complete with crystal chandelier and mess boys in attendance. He customarily kept his infant son in a high chair next to his own, and was given to disciplining the child when he became noisy by reaching over, pulling down his diaper, and striking him sharply on the penis, to the absolute horror of all the dinner guests. Great disciplinarian, he.

Both of these men taught me everything anyone needs to know about how not to be a commander. Both were intensely preoccupied with their own personal importance. Both were given to outspoken 'dressings down' of subordinates in the presence of others. Both made "pronouncements" and did not consult or discuss issues before doing so. Both made a great show of what they perceived to be naval customs and traditions, and in so doing, diminished them. Both were sickeningly obsequious toward superiors.

Still another such inept commander, like the others a full Navy Captain, was the officer in charge of the Navy element located within the U.S. Public Health Service Hospital in Fort Worth, scene of my first residency among the raging psychotics and homicidal maniacs that could not be managed elsewhere.

Still another Navy captain, the medical officer commanding the U.S. Naval Hospital aboard the U.S.S. Repose, supporting our forces in Korea during the war there, welcomed me aboard with similar graciousness. He told me he had heard something about my being 'involved' with some woman at the Naval Base in Yokosuka, and wanted me to know that no such misbehavior (!) would be tolerated aboard his ship and I was to watch my step. I soon learned that this worthy gentleman was believed by his crew to be carrying on a florid, sexual affair with the chief O.R. nurse that began two days out from port when the ship sailed from San Francisco.

As supposedly was every other senior officer with every one of the other 23 nurses aboard the ship except for one - the older, strikingly unattractive (but great good sport) nurse on my psychiatric service, who, unlike all the others, failed to become daily more desirable with each passing mile from the continental United States. These pairings, believed in by every one of the five hundred enlisted sailors aboard ship, all with raging libidinous impulses that were rarely allowed exercise save in infrequent port calls, had an increasingly disruptive effect on the crew's morale. I finally wrote a letter through official channels - which included the captain - to the Chief of Naval Operations in Washington. Citing my psychiatric training and expertise, I set forth a treatise proving beyond any question that having 24 female nurses cooped up in a ship overseas in the midst of 500 sex-starved young males was a needless, poorly conceived, destructive arrangement that should be denounced and abolished forthwith for the sake of our men's mental health, if not their actual sanity. I named no names, of course.

"Official Channels," I was to learn, can be very lengthy and labyrinthine indeed. I never got an answer. The Captain glared at me whenever we met. In only a few months, I was to find myself near the Yalu River in North Korea with the Marine Division as it 'attacked to the rear' to escape annihilation by the surrounding Chinese Army, many times its size. So much for outstanding military leadership and mental health.

My tent mate at first in Korea, Commander Dick Lawrence, of Lawrence, Massachusetts, came about as close as anyone ever did to becoming my friend. A wild man at heart, he was a former smuggler of Chinese rebels; arrested by the Kuomintang and released from prison only with the help of a family friend who happened to be the US Ambassador, Joseph Grew; former amateur boxer; first person ever to take a black woman to dinner at the Copley Plaza in Boston; an internist and a genuine hero from the war in the Pacific during WW II.

Dick was in the habit of springing to his feet and assuming the position of a boxer just before he woke up, at or before dawn. He would then come to my bunk, hit me in the stomach and announce, "Time to get up, Willy!" He was the only person who ever called me Willy. He commanded the medical battalion; I was his executive officer. We shared martinis every night, even under fire, and it was he who placed me in command of four different combat field hospitals over the next two years. He was a great soldier, a fine Marine, and an intuitively successful leader of men. I tried to be like him in many ways, and found that this helped me greatly in commands of my own.

What I tried to imitate, at least in part, was his outward fearlessness, his confidence, his decisiveness, his detailed knowledge of his men and obvious concern for them, his demand for obedience, enthusiasm, and skill at one's job. His men worshipped him. Good model, I decided.

Those 'leadership' examples, and a large number of other people I had encountered in my multi-faceted military career, occupied much of my thinking as I approached my new office on the E-Ring to take up my new duties. My placement in the job of Assistant Secretary of Defense, responsible for all policy and its execution throughout the military medical departments was a dramatic departure from the past. I was still an officer in the Public Health Service with the rank of rear admiral. Assumption of my new position conferred upon me, for the duration of the assignment, the rank of full admiral (or 4-star general). Not only were all my predecessors in that position not uniformed officers still on active duty, but almost none had had any substantial military experience and none had ever experienced combat.

Secretary Weinberger had emphasized to me that I was the medical professional superior to all three of the Surgeons General, adding that they had never before had any very effective leadership. He expected that to change. I did not wear a uniform while in office, since senior DoD officials were required to be civilians, and while the Public Health Service commissioned officers served as active members of the armed forces only during wartime, I would occupy a unique position as a quasi-civilian while in office, but with the rank and authority of a military officer out-ranked only by the Chairman of the Joint Chiefs of Staff.

This arrangement was so complex and unprecedented that it required study and ultimate approval by the DoD legal office as well as the Congress, but it was finally found to be legal, if a touch unusual, and I duly began the usual pre-confirmation interviews with members of the Senate Armed Services Committee. Meetings ensued with Teddy Kennedy, Strom Thurmond, Pete Wilson, and other Senators who had expressed an interest in who was to run military health affairs.

To my surprise, I was summoned to the office of a junior congressman from Texas named Loeffler. He was an artificially friendly, bluff, hearty man - a typical Texan - who let me know that while the House did not 'advise and consent' to presidential appointments, he had powerful friends in the Senate and could assure my confirmation or, he emphasized it, my failure to pass muster.

His interest in my assumption of office, he said, had to do with an Army hospital in San Antonio - Brooke Army Medical Center - I knew it well. It was housed in an aging, faintly Spanish-styled building with ancient plumbing, no air conditioning, inadequate electrical wiring and decaying walls and tiled roof, the whole thing crying out for replacement. His close friends in the Army and his political allies in San Antonio were absolutely determined that a new hospital be built to replace it, which probably should have been done many years ago.

The problem, for those many years, had been the cost. The government's cost for building a complex modern medical center, at that time, was about double what the civilian community spent, per bed, for such a facility. The reason for the difference was that the military included large out-patient and ambulatory treatment areas not normally incorporated in a standard hospital as well as extensive warehousing, supply systems and expansion capabilities not usually needed in a civilian hospital. It all came to about one million dollars per bed. (As this is written, that cost has nearly doubled.)

The Army wanted a 1000-bed hospital: one billion dollars!

The existing hospital was having some difficulty filling approximately two hundred beds, and regularly arranged for patients from other Army hospitals to be transferred in for no discernible reason other than to keep the census up. There were good reasons for this. First of all, the Air Force had a hospital of 1000 beds on the other side of town, named Wilford Hall, on Lackland Air Force Base, which was vastly under-utilized. Moreover, there were no Army forces of any appreciable size anywhere near Fort Sam Houston. The Sixth Army Headquarters was located there, as was the Army Medical Field Service School and a corpsman training facility, neither of which had large numbers of troops.

The nearest major Army post was Fort Hood, more than a hundred miles to the north, a training center for armored forces with thousands of soldiers stationed there, and with its own hospital. Army medical planners had kept that hospital smaller than was reasonable, so that it could shunt patients to San Antonio, to keep Brooke "alive." The Army's desire for a billion dollar, thousand bed medical center was purely an exercise in inter-service competition and prestige that was absolutely, outrageously unreasonable.

Congressman Loeffler was very direct. He wanted my absolute assurance that I would approve the new hospital. My confirmation in office depended upon it - of that I could be sure. When I told him I could make no promises about this until I studied the situation carefully, he became overtly threatening. He told me to tell the president that unless he and his friends in Texas got their new hospital, he could forget getting any support for the new missile defense program or any number of other 'big-ticket items' in the administration's budget. I suggested, rather gently I thought, that a new hospital in San Antonio had nothing to do with weapons systems. He told me, haughtily, that I was dead wrong about that, as I would soon see.

At my Senate confirmation hearing, all went smoothly despite the Congressman's threats. The subject of a replacement hospital for Brooke did in fact come up, but my assertion that I could not yet approve the spending of one billion dollars of the taxpayers' money for something I had not yet carefully studied, seemed to satisfy the members and I was confirmed.

Mr. Loeffler, bereft of his hoped-for guarantee of a shiny new pile of pork for his San Antonio constituents, among other things, failed of reelection and left Congress after his single two-year term. I was relieved, and as yet unaware that his bullying tactics would one day be adopted by another Texan, Senator Phil Gramm, who would one day dedicate himself to my dismissal over the same issue. That is another story.

In preparation for my confirmation hearings and preliminary interviews, I was introduced to a traditional Washington exercise called the "murder board." I was to go through many such events in preparation for particularly contentious hearings before committees of both the house and the senate and the sometimes bloody battles each summer in meetings of what was called the Defense Resources Board, where final budget decisions were made in dead-serious deliberations of senior DoD officials and the chiefs of the respective military services.

A murder board was an assembly of people from within the department who had special knowledge of the issue at hand, and the principal - me - who would have to face the committee. The board members were expected to find out, by whatever means, what questions were likely to be asked by members of the congressional committee holding the hearing, and what were the most difficult issues likely to be raised. In preparation, I would be briefed at length on the subject, and to have conducted my own inquiries and research, and then the performance would begin.

Always gingerly at first, but increasingly pointedly and sometimes quite acrimoniously, the murder board members would ask me questions about the issue, often adding gratuitous remarks and little speeches like the committee members were wont to do, always probing for soft spots in my testimony or politically explosive points that opposition members were eager to grasp and exploit for the TV cameras and press members that sometimes crowded the hearing rooms.

These little dramatic performances, which could become quite cantankerous when my staff got comfortable enough with the new boss to risk that, often went on for an hour or two, and sometimes much longer. They were not designed to be fun, and usually were not. They were designed to help me make my case, avoid unnecessarily antagonizing the 'members,' and keep me from suffering damage in the process. The hearings before Congress are probably the most complex, most personally risky and most difficult tasks given to any senior government official, as I was soon to learn.

Hearings were held in small rooms to large, depending on the committee or subcommittee conducting them, the importance of the issue being discussed, the expected size of the audience, and the anticipated media attention to the topic. All were a special variety of theater - often of the absurd - conducted for effect. They are, more often than not, conducted for reasons other than what the published agenda would seem to indicate, though related to that, and always to illustrate the majesty and most importantly the power of the legislative branch and its dominance over the executive branch, with whom custom and practice seem to require a constant state of conflict if not open warfare.

Officers of the executive, therefore, can count on having nearly or more than half the members, depending on which party is in the majority, in some degree of opposition, regardless of the matter being discussed. Commonly the opposing - and sometimes the supporting - members are far more interested in making points of their own, performing for the television cameras, pontificating importantly on sometimes wholly unrelated subjects, and paying little or no attention to what the hapless soul sitting at their feet, almost literally, is trying to say.

The rules of conduct for such hearings are arcane, and provide the witness little or nothing in the way of protection from what can sometimes be the most flagrant and outrageous distortions of historical or current truth, or deliberate misinterpretations and obvious corruptions of what the witness is saying, or trying to say. The posturing of many members and their obvious pandering to their constituents, their contributors and the more predatory members of the media are all evidence of a simple, obvious, yet to innocent and sincere observers and witnesses dismaying fact.

That is the fact that hearings are not held to decide anything, and generally not conducted by the people who actually make decisions. Those people, the staffers who surround each member, are often present, running in and out of the hearing room, whispering in their members' ears when those worthies are not talking on the telephone while the witness is desperately trying to make his presentation, bringing papers to be signed, or calling the member out of the room for more important matters of national importance like the survival of the Free World.

The witness, no matter how expert, how distinguished, how powerful and highly regarded outside these chambers, is expected and required to render to each member, no matter how sleazy and despicable that person's actions may be, a measure of almost worshipful deference, respect, polite attention and obsequy once reserved solely for crowned heads of state. I am not making this up.

The staffers fall mainly into two groups. The smaller, and far the most effective and important group, consists of people so long in place and so politically adept as to make them more powerful than the senators and congressmen they ostensibly serve, and sometimes harder to gain access to. These people do not seek attention, and generally follow a personal, undeclared agenda that may differ markedly from that of the member, but never openly.

The larger group, mainly much younger people, are often fervent ideologues who have worked in the congress member's campaigns with zeal and conviction that broaches no dispute from political appointees in high office, who are likely to be considered mindless toadies of the chief executive, appointed to pay back favors and large contributions, and therefore a variety of political prostitute unworthy of serious consideration.

It is these staffers who largely run the affairs of Congress. Some of the senior staffers, particularly of senators who have served several terms, are highly principled, dedicated men and women who have contributed mightily to the welfare of the Nation. They are the true political aristocracy, if there is such a thing, expert in negotiation, able to see the big picture, and superb at guiding the behavior and enhancing the image of their member so as to assure success in the polling place and a statesmanlike perception in the press. These guys are good. You never hear their names.

One such, a truly splendid public servant of great skill and wisdom who was, astonishingly, abandoned by Dick Schweiker when that man deposed himself as Secretary of Health and Human Services, was later, to my great benefit, to become my principal deputy. He was responsible for much of my success during six years in the Pentagon's tough, unforgiving environment. He had been Schweiker's chief of staff when that man was a senator from Pennsylvania, went with him and served him well in the department of HHS, and was hung out to dry when his principal left. Very unusual indeed, but very beneficial to me and to military health care. His name was David Newhall. More - much more - about him later in this tale.

Upon assuming a new command, or a new job in civilian life, it had always been my practice to avoid drastic changes, clean sweeps, or dramatic changes of direction. It seemed important to me that I leave everyone of importance in his or her existing position, so as to decide for myself whether I could work with them, whether they were actually competent to do the jobs they were there to do, and, selfishly, what I could learn from them that would be to my advantage as I took charge.

Thus it was that my first principal deputy was inherited from not just one but several of my predecessors. Like David Newhall, who eventually replaced him, Vernon MacKenzie was a skilled, career civil servant who had not only served more than twenty years in high level positions in DoD's Health Affairs organization, but had before that served as long on active duty in the Army Medical Department.

Vern was a robust, immaculately groomed, rosy-cheeked gentleman in his sixties who reminded me some of Andy Robertson, my deputy director of Mental Hygiene and then Health years before in California State government. Both men were absolute experts at what they did, and were highly discriminating judges of competence and reliability in their subordinates. Both had a certain disdain for physicians, based upon long exposure to that species and repeated disappointments at their failures, especially as managers, but were unfailingly courteous - if not exactly warm and friendly - in their dealings with them.

There were, however, significant differences between these two very senior public officials. Andy, who had risen from hospital orderly to hospital superintendent to chief administrative officer of the state's largest   department, was always eager to learn, even after fervent devotion to his hard-earned convictions when they no longer seemed valid, and through it all preserved a twinkling sense of humor. He was an avid golfer, an amused observer of the ridiculousness of the human condition, and openly, jovially contemptuous of pomposity and self-importance in people like our old boss, a very serious man indeed. He had a wonderful, sparkling sense of humor.

Vern, on the other hand, had little evident sense of humor. He was very much a solitary man with only one known friend in all of DoD, who happened, unfortunately, to be the deputy Inspector General. That fellow was an ambitious, somewhat hyperactive little guy who caused us, in Health Affairs, to receive an inordinate amount of attention, often unfavorable, from the I.G.'s office. It took me a while to figure this out, and when I did, it made me sad.

Mr. MacKenzie lived quite far out in the Virginia countryside, commuting regardless of sometimes bad weather in his little Mazda RX-7 sports car, which seemed strangely inconsistent with his reserved, dignified manner. No one on the staff had ever seen his house; he neither entertained nor accepted social invitations. He ate alone in his office, or with the I.G. in his.

Vernon set up the murder boards, which proved helpful to me in hearings on the hill, and performed his duties flawlessly. Papers never lingered on his desk. He informed me of personnel and budget problems when he thought they were important enough, but never volunteered information that I might have found valuable from his vast knowledge of the history and the internal politics of the Defense Department. That was disappointing. I always had the feeling that he was watching me carefully, which was a little unnerving at first, but eventually I was able to ignore that.

Eventually it became clear to me that he could not fulfill the role I expected and needed from my principal deputy. I told him this, while admitting I could not criticize his duty performance, and he accepted it solemnly. A few days later, he quietly announced that he would be retiring - it was time - and he quietly disappeared, declining all farewell parties and recognition. I was surprised to discover that many of my staff expressed relief at his departure, and the three service Surgeons General and their staffs were effusive in their ebullient expressions of gratitude that I had finally 'gotten rid of' the one person in DoD they considered to be their antagonist and enemy.

It was only then that I discovered Vern had been a highly successful medical administrative officer who reached the rank of full colonel. After years of resistance to the idea, the physician-generals who ran Army medicine had finally agreed that there could be one general in the Medical Service Corps, and he would be limited to the rank of Brigadier: one star. Vern was the expected first in his corps to achieve that pinnacle, but was passed over for a lesser character. He promptly retired, and was said never to have been able to forgive the medical corps generals who did him this injustice. I was finally able to understand his soft-spoken but very real contempt for the military medical leadership, his steady criticism of it to his friend in the Inspector General's office, and the problems we had as a result.

In the beginning, I undertook to learn all I could both about the Health Affairs organization that had become my responsibility, and about the elaborate, complex structure and culture of the Pentagon as a whole. In addition, Cap Weinberger had charged me at the outset to examine and analyze the 'Purple Suit' proposal that the recent special commission had proposed for military medicine. I soon learned that there had been at the least three or four similar studies of that matter, all generally agreeing that some consolidation should be made. They harked back to the days when Dwight Eisenhower, even before becoming president, had damned the existing fragmented structure, which had remained unchanged ever since.

Health Affairs had a number of sections. Heading each was a Deputy Assistant Secretary. Of greatest immediate importance were sections for medical readiness, professional affairs, administrative affairs, public affairs, administration, and legal affairs, the latter being the smallest since DoD had a major Legal Office that handled all-important legal issues. My own personal staff consisted of the principal deputy, my executive assistant, a uniformed military assistant, a senior secretary who has already been described, and a junior secretary and scheduler, also a uniformed person, a non-commissioned officer from one of the services.

Of all of these, the deputies for medical readiness and for professional affairs were to prove the most important - and the most problematic. An Air Force Medical Department colonel ran the readiness section. From the outset, he appeared to feel distinctly antagonistic toward me and even a bit disdainful. He appeared to operate entirely on his own, and it was clear he was unable or unwilling to accept my direction. He revealed this in small ways that reminded me of some of the passive-aggressive and passively resistant junior enlisted people I had encountered over the years. My instructions were often misunderstood; his briefings left me bewildered and the man never met the deadlines I set. He had to go.

It seemed to me that my principal deputy, Vern MacKenzie, was ideally suited to solve this first major personnel problem. I told him to notify the Air Force that we appreciated the colonel's service, but would be happy if they could find him another assignment. Vern took care of that handsomely, and the colonel departed for command of one of the myriad of small Air Force hospitals spread around the country.

The guy from Professional Affairs, who let it be known from the outset that he was to be addressed as "Doctor" J, was a civilian with a degree in 'counseling psychology,' considered somewhat déclassé by both clinical and research psychologists. He had spent many years in the Army Reserve, much of it attached to an officer who became a reserve major general and soon arranged for J. to be promoted to Brigadier when he retired. He was inordinately proud of both his PhD and his retired one-star rank.

Within not many days of my arrival in office, Dr. J. arrived in my office by appointment, first complaining about how difficult it had been to gain access to me. I had made it abundantly clear in initial meetings with all the senior (and many junior) staffers that they could see me at any time, as long as I was not seeing Secretary Weinberger or some other dignitary. No appointment was ever necessary. J. however, insisted upon being given a time-certain, one-hour appointment, and the office staff had found that difficult to arrange to his satisfaction.

He carried with him a bulky document that he handed to me, saying that this was something he and his associates throughout the Pentagon (that was a surprise) had labored over for some months. All had completely agreed on its contents, which were of paramount importance, and he would appreciate it if I would present it to Secretary Weinberger.

The label revealed that the massive manuscript was a proposed Department of Defense Directive, which has the force of law throughout all the military services, establishing a new regulation. On the first page, as is customary, there was a statement of purpose that said something like: "This regulation, which applies to all members of the uniformed services and their families, is established to ensure the mental, physical, and spiritual health of all members of the military services of the United States."

After reading that remarkable assertion, twice, just to be sure, I said to this intense, deadly serious man that already I had several questions. The first was whether he had shown this to the other deputies and my legal officer. No. The second was where he had come up with measures that would "ensure" such things as mental health and physical health, since I was unaware of any valid scientific research in either of those fields, both of which were my own professional business, that described such measures. Could he cite such research? No.

However, he hastened to assure me, he and his psychologist associates both within and outside the Pentagon had agreed that what they proposed would do just that. Everyone had agreed.

Finally, I asked him, just what was "spiritual health?"

He launched into a discussion of such things as one's relationship to God and belief in, and adherence to, Christian principles.

After listening to a few minutes of this, I asked him if it were his belief, then, that 'spiritual health,' however that might be defined, was properly the business of a major element of the government, namely the medical departments of the armed forces of the United States.

Growing irritated, he insisted that spiritual health was an integral part of all mental and physical health - surely I had to agree!

Whether or not I agreed, I told him, I did not agree that it was something that medical people or anyone else knew how to 'ensure,' with or without a new regulation, that it was presumptuous to assert that it was, and no matter what he and his psychologist 'associates' had agreed upon, I believed it both arrogant and unconstitutional to propose such a thing. I would not examine his proposed directive; reading its statement of purpose was more than enough.

Furthermore, I added, as he, unbidden, got up to leave, it seemed to me that he and I had vastly different conceptions of the functions of the deputy assistant secretariat of health affairs in the Department of Defense, and I believed he should seek some other organization in which to serve. With that I handed him his document and watched him leave. He stalked from my room with no effort to conceal his anger and indignant contempt for my stupidity.

In future fleeting encounters, he indicated that he had no intention of leaving his position, and when, several weeks later, I gently suggested that he might consider going back to his former job at the Industrial College of the Armed Forces, he haughtily announced that he was not interested in my "career counseling." That did it.

Once again I turned to Vern. J. was a member of the SES - Senior Executive Service - the highest rank in the Civil Service structure. As such, he could not be fired, but was required to accept any appropriate job assignment given to him, wherever it was and regardless of personal inconvenience, or mandatorily resign. MacKenzie agreed we could assign him to OCHAMPUS, the office of Civilian Health and Medical Programs of the Uniformed Services. It was located in the long unused TB wards at Fitzsimmons Army Hospital, in Denver.

Dr. J. did not want to go to Denver. He resigned and managed to get his old job back at the College, where he spent the next five years telling anyone who would listen about what an awful, incompetent person I was.

That, along with the disgruntled passive-aggressive Air Force colonel, made two dedicated enemies right off the bat, but at least they were no longer in the Pentagon. There would be others, including a startlingly hostile, openly antagonistic and obviously incompetent woman in charge of the administrative office, and later, another retired officer who ostensibly ran CHAMPUS but in reality delegated everything to others and traveled a great deal, uselessly, at government expense.

William E. Mayer, M.D.

Brainwashing, Drunks & Madness

William E. Mayer, M.D.

CHAPTER 15

BATTLEPLAN

My investigations of how the Pentagon worked soon revealed that there was a long-ensconced civilian official who wielded enormous influence and power, but did so quietly and without fanfare. That, which was his plan, led many in the building, to their sorrow, to disregard him. His name was David O. ("Doc") Cooke. Doc ran an administrative office attached directly to and part of the office of the SecDef - Weinberger, as he had for many years and many previous Secretaries of Defense.

Doc's staff included a team of management analysts who were regularly employed by the Secretary, usually in response to some inquiry from the Congress or one of the deputariats, to assess the staffing or operations of some part of the organization. Rather than make revisions in the Health Affairs structure, I decided to ask these people to conduct a detailed audit of performance, staffing, assignments and job descriptions within my new staff element, listen to their recommendations for improvement, and then take such steps as appealed to me, to make it both better, and my own. Thus began a cordial, supporting relationship with Doc, who became a faithful friend and advocate with the boss, and a great help with many management (read "personnel") issues that arose from time to time.

Shortly after my arrival, the Army Surgeon General asked me to travel to Honduras to examine and evaluate a new field medical unit that had been placed there both to test the facility and to serve as a training area for Army active and reserve medics. I flew on military aircraft to Florida, where I stopped for briefing by Central Command headquarters staff and the Commanding General, whose responsibilities included Central America operations as well as those in much of the Middle East.

Flying on to Honduras, I was informed by the pilot that word had just been received, by CNN even before it came through official channels, that U.S. forces had just invaded the tiny island nation of Grenada. The announced intention was to save a group of students at the island's medical school, mostly Americans, from a communist uprising that had taken place. That military operation, involving all the services supposedly working in concert with one another, was to prove highly instructive. Interservice communication proved to be so faulty that a ground commander, at one point, used a commercial telephone to call his headquarters in the U.S. to arrange naval support from vessels that he could actually see from where his people were engaged.

On at least one occasion, a medical evacuation helicopter carrying casualties was forbidden to land on a vessel just offshore because the pilot had not been 'checked out' for a shipboard landing by the Navy, even though he was very experienced and wholly competent to do so. The after-action reports on that operation, never completely shared with the press or the public, revealed many difficulties, mainly of an inter-service variety, in that small undertaking. If nothing else, they revealed an incredible inability - or was it unwillingness? - of the services' medical departments to work together.

This fact both surprised and disturbed me. I had always believed that American casualties lost their service identity when they needed medical care, particularly in combat, and that American medical people treated all who needed them regardless of the color of the casualty's uniform. All the medical brass insisted that was the case, of course, but in practice it did not work smoothly at all.

This was to become even more evident, when shortly after the Grenada affair a suicide bomber blew up the Marine Barracks in Lebanon killing a large number of Marines in their beds. U.S. military authorities in the area had failed to establish adequate security around the barracks; the Marines were strictly forbidden to make any show of even conventional preparedness for any kind of attack, and our emasculated intelligence apparatus apparently never dreamed it could happen.

When it did happen, the Marines' parent organization, the Navy, sent some junior medical officers to the site from ships offshore, who performed heroically tending to the relatively few Marines who had escaped death in the blast.

The Air Force, in keeping with its major mission of medical evacuation, showed up fairly promptly, and initially planned to take the casualties to Israel, a few minutes north, for hospital care. Someone in authority, however, got the word that our airplanes did not have the necessary pre-arranged flight clearance to land in Israel and would be fired upon if they approached. So much for our $3 billion a year loyal ally in the Mideast!

Meanwhile, our old friends the British, who operated a large, modern, well-equipped general hospital in Cyprus, a few minutes farther away, offered the whole of their medical capability there to take care of our wounded. They discharged all but the sickest patients from their hospital, called in every doctor and nurse on the island, even including some who were civilians, and made ready to treat our people.

They were ignored. The Air Force had no plan for landing in Cyprus!

Instead, all the casualties were flown to Frankfort, Germany, many hours away. That was the 'regular' medical evacuation route from the Middle East, and an Air Force brigadier who assumed command of the evacuation insisted that there they would go.

At Frankfort things got even worse. A relatively junior Air Force officer with official technical responsibility for patient distribution, after a heated battle with an Army evacuation officer who showed up, dispatched all the wounded to the Air Force's principal hospital in Germany, at Wiesbaden, some miles from Frankfort. That hospital was the pride of its proprietors and had received considerable favorable press attention for receiving and treating several high-profile cases, although the hospital itself was small and by no means fully up to treating any substantial number of serious cases.

Even closer to Frankfort stood the Army Hospital at Landstuhl, by far the largest, best staffed and best equipped military hospital anywhere in the world outside the continental United States. The Army medical administrative officer on the tarmac at Frankfort argued vehemently, but to no avail, with the Air Force officer, that Landstuhl was the only logical place for these wounded people, which was absolutely true. The Air Force Brigadier who had taken personal charge of the entire evacuation prevailed, and off the hapless Marines went to Wiesbaden.

Miraculously, and surely through the grace of a benevolent God, none of the injured Marines died during - and as a result of - this debacle. They were spared as well through the efforts of the splendid nurses and crew of the Air Force 'medevac' airplanes, who managed them through many hours of delay and prolonged, unnecessary flight, but many could well have died.

Grenada and Lebanon, then, early on in my tenure at the highest levels of our beloved nation's military structure revealed a kind of sickness within that structure that persists to the day this is written, and places untold numbers of our finest young people in unnecessary and wholly unjustified jeopardy.

We find our country's political (and some of its military!) leadership so committed to avoiding casualties when we send people in harm's way, that it has not yet become apparent to the American people that the danger exists and is as great as it actually is. So far we've been lucky in the extreme. We have avoided casualties in the Balkans in two "wars," avoided even getting involved in more dangerous places like Rwanda and Congo, and as a result have accomplished next to nothing. This in spite of highly suspect and even disproved assertions of the effectiveness and effect of high altitude bombing and promises of severe consequences to terrible people like Sadaam and Milosevic, who continue to thrive, and to offend against humanity.

The day must surely come, however, when we engage somewhere - perhaps even here at home when some crazy manages to send a missile through our non-existent defenses with a nuclear or chemical or biological device on board that wipes out Manhattan or Seattle - or in some distant place like Korea, and we take lots of casualties. Unless there are major revisions to the eternal greedy battles among the services for money and power and prestige, we will find ourselves without the ability to take adequate care of our own.

And so it was less than twenty years ago, when it became my problem. The first world-wide exercise to test our military capability that took place shortly after my arrival in the Pentagon confirmed what my predecessor had turned up: even in a conventional war - no nukes, no chemicals, no germs - we were able at best to give medical care to no more than one out of every ten casualties. The death rate following injury or wounding on the battlefield could well be the highest in our history.

While I was able in my six years in office, with the firm support of Secretaries Weinberger and Carlucci and the President himself, to very largely correct that situation (by 1989 we could adequately care for about 9 out of ten,) it has already deteriorated again, and for the same reasons.

Those reasons involve the entrenched, unshakeable resistance of the three surgeons general and their senior aides to active collaboration with each other. This applies to such basic issues as supply, communications, specialty and continuing education, financial matters, and most of all, unified command and control in crisis situations.

Each group perpetuates the myth that patients can only be treated by people wearing the same uniform, that the medical needs of patients with identical medical problems are different in the air forces than they are in ground or sea forces, and that each service's medical problems are unique to that service. Often cited are the special problems of high altitude or the deep sea, which are undeniable. The fact is, however, the overwhelming majority of people in pale blue uniforms never operate at high altitude, and the ones in dark blue suits almost never work in the deep seas - unless their ship sinks.

The ground forces, meanwhile, be they Army troops or Marines, believe that the other services fail to understand their special vulnerability and special operations, which is why they take the most casualties (this is true,) and that the others' insatiable appetite for ever more costly weapons and other gadgets drains away the resources needed to take care of man: the ultimate weapon.

When these things are coupled, as they were in the 1990's, with national leadership whose disdain and distaste for the military is evident to the lowliest soldier, sailor or airman, it is little wonder that the public has little or no clue as to the internal dangers that magnify those from outside our borders. Medical response inadequacy is but one of them.

Back home from Honduras, where I examined an inflatable field hospital whose generators made so much noise they could never be kept safe from enemy ears, I also saw a touching, remarkable demonstration of the power of health care to capture the minds and hearts of people everywhere.

The Army regularly sent teams of physicians, nurses, dentists and all their supporting corpsmen and technicians into primitive areas, to treat villagers. Without exception, these visits were not only superb training experiences for our own people, opening their eyes to what much if not most of the world is like, but they were also seen by the natives as among the most blessed gifts of their lives. Such activities can be far more effective than military assistance and diplomatic gestures, however grand, but we do pathetically little of it. Castro, among others, knows this well, and does much more of it than we do in Central America and Africa, to his great benefit.

Back home in my grand office overlooking the parking lot (but at least on the E-ring with windows to the outside) another kind of a battle had erupted. So far it was taking place largely in the press and the broadcast media, but that was enough. The early morning meeting each day in the Secretary's office usually involved a quick perusal of something called the "Early Bird." This was a daily publication produced by the Office of Public Affairs, gathering articles from newspapers around the nation and the world, and media transcripts from the major networks, dealing with military and DoD matters.

With increasing frequency, articles had been appearing describing medical misadventures and alleged malpractice and patient disasters in the military hospitals and clinics around the country. Both Weinberger and the President had become greatly concerned about the incidents and the editorial judgments that military medicine was substandard, asserted by some to be uniformly of poor quality and even dangerous to helpless patients. At that juncture, the armed forces medical services were responsible for the care of about ten million of our citizens: uniformed people, their dependents, and retired members. Growing doubts about the quality of that care, if valid, required immediate corrective actions. Take care of it, Doctor!

The many years I had spent working in both large and small hospitals run by the Navy and the Army had left me with the firm belief that the quality of the care delivered in them was good - solidly so. In those periods when I was out of service, my observations of civilian hospitals, even including some of the major teaching hospitals associated with leading medical schools, had convinced me long before my arrival at the Pentagon that the quality was far better, consistently, in the military facilities.

There were lots of reasons for this. In the civilian institutions, whether they were non-profit or charitable hospitals or the so-called 'for profit' ones, governance of the hospitals was far more diffuse and far less decisive than it was under a military commander whose authority was clearly defined, whose accountability was unquestionable, and whose direct power to affect operations was far greater, more immediate, and more effective than the pronouncements of a largely non-medical board of directors or even the medical staff organization. The rules governing the operation of military units were clearly outlined in regulations with the force of law.

This combination of rules and unity of command, an ancient and proven principle of all military activities, was a powerful deterrent to sloppy performance and dereliction of duty, be that medical duty or military.

The physicians in military hospitals were, in essence, the direct employees and subordinates of the commander - the boss, if you will - of the hospital, in addition to being sworn officers of the government of the United States, commissioned by the President and approved by the Senate. The process they had gone through to achieve that status involved far more than simply getting through medical school and internship, and passing their exams. It was far more rigorous and demanding, generally, than what was required to join the staff of the overwhelming majority of civilian hospitals.

The military authority system, moreover, does not stop with the hospital commander. Each service or department within the uniformed services hospital has a designated chief who is, in effect, the subordinate hospital commander for all the personnel and activities on that service. He has far more power, and with it far more accountability, for the actions of the physicians, nurses, aides and orderlies under his supervision than does the chief of surgery, or medicine, or obstetrics in any civilian hospital, and generally has daily supervisory contact with all of them.

All of these factors, and more, lead to far greater scrutiny of everything that is done for and to patients in military health care organizations, including what is done in the outpatient clinics before and after patients are admitted to inpatient care. That, in turn, safeguards the patient in ways that are simply not possible in community hospitals anywhere.

Finally, the military hospital is a public, open institution. It is next to impossible to hide what happens there. While most civilian hospitals voluntarily subject themselves to periodic scrutiny by an organization created by the medical profession, the Joint Commission on the Accreditation of Healthcare Organizations, this is not generally required by law. It is required by law for all military hospitals.

Beyond all that, both the offices of the Surgeons General and the military departments' Inspector Generals are required to examine and periodically to review the operations of military facilities, and to review any and all complaints about what is done there, regardless of the source.

Knowing all this first hand, I was confident that the anecdotal horror stories appearing in the media and eagerly pounced upon by a small but noisy, sleazy element within the legal profession, did not accurately depict the quality of military health care. My dander was raised. My righteous indignation was driven to new heights. I had a crusade to embark upon with all the fervor of my crusader ancestors. I liked that.

The first thing that had to be done was to select my lieutenants. The great military philosopher, Clausewitz, and that undeniably expert leader, Napoleon Bonaparte, had both devoted considerable thought to the subject of lieutenants, along

along with Robert E. Lee, Grant, Pershing and others of their ilk, and I had listened to them all.

The philosopher had put lieutenants into several categories. The first he called the 'stupid and lazy.' These could be used, but should be limited to simple, dull jobs that had to be done but no one wanted to do.

The next were the 'stupid and energetic.' These were dangerous and to be gotten rid of if at all possible, and soon. One way that I had found, you will recall, was to order their transfer to Denver. They were invariably troublesome and should never be given significant responsibility and authority. Some in this category had gotten very high up in Civil Service!

The category Clausewitz had labeled 'brilliant and lazy' presented another special challenge. These people, he said, had bright ideas and could formulate problems and solutions, but were not motivated to actually do much of anything. It seemed to me that my inherited principal deputy fit, at least loosely, into this category. Vernon was not exactly lazy, but he was not energetic either. He was bright, if not altogether brilliant, but very experienced and knowledgeable, and while he could answer nearly any question I put to him, volunteered almost nothing, to me at least, in the way of ideas or proposals or plans, leaving all such things to me. He had served for several months, several times, as the 'acting' Assistant Secretary, in between terms of official appointees, and had done an adequate job.

His lack of regard for physicians generally, however, and his first-hand observation of more than one of my predecessors, not all of whom had been shining examples of managerial excellence, made me think he was not a man I could count on to help constructively in my crusade. In truth, his long friendship with the deputy inspector general, his luncheon buddy, was widely believed to have been at the root of the burgeoning public criticism of the quality of military medicine. He would, I believed, bring to any project aimed at increasing the assurance of medical quality, a negative bias that would not be helpful. His active involvement would have guaranteed open hostility and resistance from the uniformed medical leadership.

In any large bureaucracy like the Department of Defense, but especially there within the Pentagon, such resistance could prove fatal to any undertaking. A prime example was the massive resistance mounted by the service Surgeons General and their staffs to the 'purple suit' idea, or indeed any suggestion at all that the services actively interact and collaborate. We needed a uniform medical quality assurance program that operated the same way in every one of the military departments and involved cross-fertilization of ideas and a willingness to tolerate examination of one another's practices and outcomes.

Such a program was certain to be a very hard sell to my distinguished senior military medical colleagues. It proved to be that and more. Their resistance to the imposition of 'rules' of any kind by the cordially despised *civilians* in the Defense

Department was monumental. It was in connection with my ideas for establishing a model quality assurance program for military medicine that I first became fully aware of the seriousness and destructiveness of the Services' deep-seated resentment and antagonism toward DoD, fully 36 years since its creation - about nine generations in the culture of the building. Each service dealt with its negativism toward the whole concept of a Defense Department with authority over all of the uniformed services, which had only existed since 1947, in different ways.

The Navy cherished the ancient idea that once a ship put to sea, the Captain of the vessel was its absolute master. Since early Colonial times, Naval officers commanding ships of war far from our shores were authorized to interpret their orders broadly, and in confrontations from the Shores of Tripoli and battles against the Barbary pirates to encounters in Manila Bay, Tokyo Bay, Cuba and elsewhere made decisions and took actions *that* are today the province of the President himself, or his Secretary of State or, not long ago, the Secretary of War.

As a result there were many senior officers in the Navy, including the Surgeon General at that time, Admiral Rickover's protégé, who couldn't quite accept or even believe in the actual existence or authority of the Department of Defense. They seemed to view it as a temporary aberration that flew in the face of hallowed naval tradition, and would surely, some day, go away. For the present, therefore, it could largely be ignored, which the Navy leadership frequently did.

The Army took a different tack. Borrowing from a classical military tactic harking back to ancient (Trojan) times and successfully employed by the Soviets with their 'volunteers' in the Spanish Civil War and Hitler's 'Fifth Column' inserted into every country he planned to conquer, the Army happily sought positions for their officers in every office of the Defense Department. All the services were encouraged to supply some of the staff for each element of the DoD. Officers detailed to those jobs were there to help in whatever way the respective Assistant SecDef desired.

My office had a number of Army officers, the most important of which was my Deputy Assistant Secretary for Medical Readiness. He was a Major General in the Army Medical Corps, and like most of the others supplied at my request by the Army, was a fine soldier, a bit of a maverick within his own Corps, and thus temporarily expendable. He had a strong sense of duty, was absolutely loyal to his boss (now me), able to function without special ties to his own military department, and altogether an excellent lieutenant.

My senior military assistant, however, was quite different. He was a senior major in the Army Medical Service Corps, not a physician but a medical administrative officer. He was about to be promoted to Lieutenant Colonel. He was a friendly, outgoing, almost boyish, always jovial fellow who collected teddy bears and filled his office with them. Sometimes, after arriving at the office - he was always early - he slipped into a pair of fluffy pink slippers with little bunny faces and floppy ears at the toes. He evidently wanted desperately for everyone to love him.

The truth was, he was a spy. While they would never admit it, the Surgeon General's staff had assigned him to my office to observe, record, and report on any and all actions and decisions that could have any impact at all on the Army's medical organization and functions. He followed my every movement like a shadow, quietly and unobtrusively inserting himself into a far corner of my office for all meetings, conferences, interviews, and planning sessions.

It soon became apparent to me that he was not functioning solely or even mainly as my military aide; he stayed too close and was too curious. It also soon struck me that the Army people seemed to know what we were about almost as soon as my own immediate staff knew it. Finally, one late evening when my civilian executive assistant went back to the office for some notes needed the next morning, she found him going through my desk and collecting important papers that he evidently intended to duplicate. She immediately asked him to surrender his office keys, which he did, and to remain at home until I called the next day, which he also did.

He was told that next day to report for duty at the office of his military superiors. His departure was easy, since I had, weeks before, told him to clear his office of all his teddy bears and furry slippers, and he had already done so.

In his place, the Army loaned me a Brigadier General, also a Medical Service Corps officer, who was not getting along well in the Surgeon General's office and was clearly not a spy. We became warm friends, and he worked well in a more distant section of my organization than the executive suite proper.

The Air Force dealt with its antipathy toward the Defense Department mainly by pleading special circumstances. They made it clear in a myriad of small ways that their widespread activities around the globe create wholly unique problems of supply, communications, personnel management and medical support. The rules that apply to the other services, therefore, are not feasible to impose in their far-flung, special settings and special activities.

While this is true to a considerable extent, Air Force managers have become expert at extending the special circumstance philosophy to many places and activities where it does not logically fit. For example, they insist that they must have their own general hospitals, however small the capacity and the military population served, in "remote" locations like Fargo, North Dakota.

While Fargo may seem pretty remote when one is driving down Pennsylvania Avenue in the District of Columbia, it is hardly a Third World location. There are excellent hospitals in Fargo, but the Air Force absolutely must have one of its own, at great expense, on the base to serve the relatively small population there, rather than treating them at the high quality civilian hospital just outside the gate.

All three services have developed another powerful weapon with which to do battle with the despised DoD. Over the years, initially for the purpose of enlisting

Congressional fiscal support, each service has cultivated members of the House and Senate to function as their own powerful advocates. Such members as have military bases and civilian military suppliers in their States or Districts are often easy recruits for such a role. Those who serve on the various committees dealing with military procurement and other military affairs are particularly cherished.

Whenever there is movement detected at DoD level that one or all of the military departments find not to their liking, they run to their respective Congressional advocates. Those worthies, in turn, send blizzards of official Congressional inquiries to those offices in the Pentagon involved in some issue that one or the other of the Services opposes. Replies to the inquiries must be formulated, reviewed, extensively coordinated with other offices in the vast building, and obediently sent off in a relatively short time. A study of this phenomenon revealed that it took up fully thirty percent of the working time of my entire staff.

The issue of medical quality seemed certain to be my first major test of strength in my dealings with the services' surgeons general. For this battle it was absolutely critical that my primary lieutenant fit into Clausewitz' top category: brilliant and energetic. In addition, he (or she) needed to meet those criteria that over the years had appeared to me to be essential elements of character and personality in anyone entrusted with great tasks.

First among these, just as Earl Brian had asserted to me many years before, was the quality of loyalty - not blind obedience to the boss's every whim but willingness to consider whatever was asked in a thoughtful way and start to search immediately for ways to do it. Many sincere and loyal associates tend to look first for obstacles and dangers, and identify reasons why whatever is proposed cannot be done, often because it has not been done before or is not specifically authorized in statute. Most government lawyers I had dealt with were like that, probably out of a desire to protect me (and themselves as my legal advisors) from the consequences of my crazy ideas.

One notable exception to that had been a deputy state Attorney General I had once recruited away - stolen, actually - from the AG's staff to serve first as my chief counsel in the California Department of Health and then as my Chief Deputy Director of the Department. This man, who became a fast friend over the years, was distinguished by his 'can do' attitude, a quality I had come to cherish when I commanded field hospitals in the Marine Corps in Korea. Tom Warriner was brilliant and energetic, and never once reacted to my proposals negatively at the outset, but always sought ways to get done what I thought should be done, while at the same time keeping me out of jail.

After I left California government, Tom went on to become the Under Secretary of Health and Welfare, did well, and later became a judge in his home county of Yolo, across the river from the capital in Sacramento. I wished that I could steal him away again to help me in the Pentagon, but he was understandably unwilling to vacate the bench.

Another potential lieutenant of the highest order, also from California, was a young man named Carl Rauser. I had spotted him as a valuable player when he was quite young and new in state government, and took him on as one of my informal management-intern assistants first in the Department of Mental Hygiene and then the state Department of Health. As such, he accompanied me in everything that I did - conferences, hearings, interviews, planning sessions, inspection trips, hirings and firings - every action necessary to function as director of the state's largest department. It was my practice to rotate those assignments among young people on the staff who showed real talent and promise, and each of them had gone on to positions of much greater importance and authority in steadily higher offices.

Carl had been the best of the lot. He later rose to become director of the Department of Mental Health, and then left government to work successfully in the private sector of the health care industry in his own consulting firm. He too had a can-do attitude, great energy and enthusiasm, and a certain special kind of courage that enabled him to ignore the status quo and the traditional ways of doing things in bureaucracies. He would have been a splendid collaborator in my Pentagon adventures and crusades.

I tried to entice Carl and his wonderful wife, Bernie, to join us in our new life in the Nation's Capital, pulling out all the stops concerning duty to one's country, the glamour of Washington, the vast challenges and potential for doing something really valuable and important, and the fun we could have doing this huge job.

At one point I felt he was seriously tempted, but his good sense prevailed. He and Bernie opted to remain in their home territory, where their families were and where their outstanding kids, a beautiful girl who took part in a championship rowing crew and became a professor of art history, and a son who developed into an exceptionally talented architect, were completing their professional development.

That proved just as well for that fine family. Only ten years later and while still a vigorous young man who had just had a physical exam and been given a complete bill of good health, Carl suffered a massive coronary while making morning coffee in the newly, beautifully redone kitchen he and Bernie had just completed, and died instantly. So much for medical prognostication.

Fortunately for me and my upcoming crusade to establish that the quality of military medicine was exceptionally good, in reality, despite all the bad press, there was an ideal leader/lieutenant close at hand, and I set about to recruit him for what might be a bloody battle. Jarrett Clinton was a physician serving as a senior commissioned officer in the Public Health Service, who had rejoined the Commissioned Corps at my urging, when I recruited him to work with me in the Alcohol, Drug Abuse and Mental Health Administration.

Jarrett had, earlier in his medical career, served in the PHS, but had left and had had a colorful career as senior physician for the Peace Corps and work in Asia before becoming the Senior Medical Officer for the Agency for International Development, AID, an element of the Department of State but separate from it. My wife worked as his executive assistant, and regularly came home in the evening with glowing descriptions of his intelligence, dedication, and skill. It was her testimonials that led me to try to persuade this truly superior physician to rejoin the Commissioned Corps of the Public Health Service and come work with me.

He did just that, and fully lived up to his billing. When I moved over to the job in the Pentagon, he agreed to come along, and took over the office of Professional Activities, whose designation had been enlarged to include "and Quality Assurance," as Deputy Assistant Secretary of Defense, Health Affairs. He replaced John, of spiritual health fame.

Together, we plotted the Renaissance of Military Medicine, and its reputation. My job was to proclaim to all who would listen, in the press and the Congress, at receptions and meetings and conferences, what I knew to be true about the quality of care that I knew existed in our military hospitals. Treading a very fine line indeed, lest I offend or even enrage my civilian colleagues, I asserted with increasing fervor that quality was better in our uniformed medical facilities than it was 'outside,' and declared that we could prove it.

I wasn't altogether positive we could prove that, but since I believed in my heart that it was true, decided to take that position and say so without any equivocation. After all, very few people in medicine had spent as much time, especially in managerial roles, in the military medical services of the Army, the Navy, the Marine Corps, the Public Health Service, and the Veterans Administration, along with substantial periods of time in civilian hospitals, both public and private. That gave my assertions some credibility.

Meanwhile, Jarrett went to work, drawing on the burgeoning literature of quality assurance and the experience of the better teaching hospitals around the country, including our own, designing a regular process of retrospective review of randomly selected cases on every service in every one of our hospitals, with systematic analysis of shortcomings and regular reports to hospital commanders and those higher up in the chain of command all the way to the Surgeons General.

While much of this was already being done, we would issue regulations with the force of law within the military departments, making sure it was being done regularly, and done right. We would publicize in the press, the broadcast media, and the professional literature the fact that we were doing this.

The next thing we determined to address was the great American get-rich-quick bonanza called "medical malpractice" lawsuits. The number of these, and the number of huge monetary awards, especially for "pain and suffering" had been increasing exponentially for a decade. This was a peculiarly American phenomenon, curious in a country with the magnificent medical capability of the U.S. It worked like this:

Go to a doctor. Note carefully everything that he does for your complaint. Find something - anything - that didn't work out as planned or seems to indicate something was left undone. In our society, where the National Enquirer is present at every supermarket check-out counter and is filled with medical and quasi-medical and spurious scientific health information, and where medical miracles receive so much attention that people's expectations often far exceed actual medical capabilities, it has gotten easier and easier to claim the doctor's care was inadequate, or wrong, or downright harmful, all of which is sometimes true.

Having identified such a failure or mischance, find a 'malpractice attorney' willing to take such cases "on contingency." That means he will not get paid unless you win your case against the doctor. Attorneys who specialize in this kind of law used to be called ambulance chasers. Now they simply advertise in newspapers and magazines, so they are easy to find.

The attorney writes a letter to the doctor, describing your medical misadventure in dramatic, even heart-rending, detail and announcing that you intend to file suit for an outrageous sum ("pain and suffering" has become absolutely priceless.)

If the doctor carries malpractice insurance, which many or most do, sometimes at a cost of $30 thousand a year or more, he turns the letter over to his insurance company. The company then negotiates with the lawyer, usually settling for far less than first demanded. In the great majority of cases, settlement is reached, often for outrageous amounts of money, the lawyer takes his cut of one third or even more, and the whole thing is over.

There is no accessible public record of such settlements, or at least there wasn't then, because no suit has actually been filed in any court. Insurance companies keep records, naturally, but they are loath to reveal anything at all about how much they pay out.

In a military hospital, every complaint about medical care instantly becomes a matter of public record, by law and regulation. No matter how trivial or unfounded a complaint by a patient or family may seem to be, it must be made a matter of written record, must be investigated, and the results also recorded.

There is a law that forbids uniformed personnel on active duty to sue the government for personal harm, but nothing to prevent a soldier or sailor from complaining to the hospital commander and the inspector general, and every such complaint must also be permanently recorded. There is also nothing to prevent a civilian dependant of a military person, or a retired person or his family from bringing suit. All such complaints and suits, being recorded, can be counted.

We decided to count all such events. We would also count all civilian medical malpractice suits that actually got filed and therefore became matters of public record, knowing full well we could not count the much larger numbers of threats that ended in settlements with no case ever being filed or recorded. We would then compare the numbers. When we announced that we intended to do this, the Surgeons General went, as they say, ballistic.

That plan proved to be a good one. The number of complaints in military hospitals, per thousand admissions, proved to be no more than a small fraction of the number of actual filed malpractice suits in the civilian hospital community. This in spite of the fact that most allegations of malpractice in civilian hospitals never became matters of record but are settled; these, of course, could not even be counted.

While being careful not to cast aspersions on our civilian colleagues and their hospitals, we disseminated our findings widely. After all, we didn't cause the explosion of malpractice claims!

A second front in our battle for respectability arose from the outraged cries of some media figures who discovered that not all physicians in uniform were actually licensed. While any doctor entering one of the services had to present valid credentials showing that he had actually earned his M.D. degree in an accredited U.S. medical school and had successfully completed an internship, he did not have to obtain a state license if he came directly on active duty following his training. "UNLICENSED DOCTORS SERVING IN THE ARMED FORCES," shouted a number of inflammatory articles in various publications. Congress and the White House noticed, alarmed.

No amount of explanation was adequate to calm the disturbed waters. The fact that many of our new physicians had passed the National Medical Board examinations, which many states accepted as the basis for obtaining a license, but had not applied for that license, meant nothing to sensationalist members of the Fourth Estate.

The implication of the outraged complaints was that we were employing unqualified - therefore incompetent and illegal - non-"real" - doctors to treat our fine young citizens in uniform, who deserved the best. This was not true in any sense at all, but we had to deal with this misconception decisively and at once.

We decided to issue regulations that required every physician in uniform to possess, and keep current, a valid medical license, in any state desired. While this sounds simple and an easy solution, it was far from that. It meant that every uniformed doctor had to travel to some state, perhaps far from his duty station, pay a sometimes very high fee, take that state's medical licensure examinations successfully, pay another fee, and bring back a license.

Worse, some of our physicians had served for as much as twenty years since graduating from medical school, had become specialists in what could be a narrowly defined area of medicine, and therefore could face enormous difficulties trying to come up to speed in the entire broad array of medical subjects which they had learned many years before and were now to be examined about in great detail. We ended up having to allow up to three years for licenses to be obtained, but eventually it got done.

Like most people, I do not like meetings. At every step in our campaign to rehabilitate military medicine's reputation, there had to be all kinds of meetings: weekly with the surgeons general, oftener with people from the media, irregularly with staffers from the Hill, the young hotshots employed by Senators and Congresspeople mainly, it seemed, to harass officials in the executive branch, occasionally with advocacy groups like 'Citizens Against Military Injustice,' and many others.

The toughest, in many ways, were the weekly meetings with the Surgeons General. Early on, it had become apparent that they were all mutually antipathetic toward one another and their respective organizations, each of which had larger staffs, by far, than did I, their putative leader and professional boss. They barely knew one another and dealt with their counterparts with a thinly disguised, cool contempt and evident distaste. One thing they shared: their resentment of DoD and its Health Affairs Office.

It had long been my practice, ever since commanding combat field hospitals with the Marine Division in Korea, to assemble all my principal deputies every morning, first thing. Each was called upon to report to all present exactly what was going on in his part of the unit, problems encountered and solutions attempted. Each was encouraged to make comments and suggestions at the end of each report. Shouldering aside a vague uneasiness about the similarity of these daily gatherings to the Communists' infamous "self-criticism" meetings, I used them to make sure everyone 'got the word,' stayed focused on the mission, knew what was expected of them, and the consequences of failure along with the rewards for success.

This had worked well in combat, and also in subsequent jobs for county and state government, in the Alcohol, Drug, and Mental Health Administration, and its validity as a process was strongly bolstered by Cap Weinberger's daily meetings, first thing every morning, with his senior staff. Therefore, with no hesitation, I set up the same sort of thing in my own Pentagon office, insofar as was possible.

The "S.G.s," as we habitually referred to them, were not exactly my own staff in any sense, so I could hardly assemble them daily to get the word and get their orders. They were not under my command, so to speak, although they were technically obligated to support my policy decisions and make certain their personnel obediently and faithfully executed all directives and regulations we issued. This did not mean they couldn't argue.

A weekly, non-optional meeting of the S.G.s was set up in my office. They proved to be a fascinating group. Like so many senior officers in very high positions, each was highly competent in a medical field, experienced in a wide variety of settings within their respective military departments, graduates of the Command

and General Staff College, the various War Colleges, and others. They had to have served at sea or in the various kinds of field units, both in this country and abroad.

Most importantly of all, they could never have offended anyone in a position of authority, never advanced an original or possibly controversial idea, and spent much time over the course of their careers socializing with their superiors. What this produced was a kind of supreme mediocrity. What they lacked included decisive leadership skills, imagination, the courage to do battle for what was right, the willingness to take risks, and the unwillingness to offend.

There were many fine officers in the medical corps who did rock the boat, go to bat for changes that needed to be made, didn't give much of a damn about who liked them or didn't, and were willing to risk all for the sake of doing what they believed was the right thing to do. A few of them - only a few - eventually made 'flag rank,' becoming generals and admirals. However, they never became Surgeon General. They were often controversial, always with good reason, but the appearance of that "C-word" in the individual's personnel record was the kiss of death.

So it was with the group waiting to do battle with 'the new guy' in the Health Affairs office. They were somewhat taken aback when they found that I wasn't really a civilian (those people just don't understand), had served in four uniformed services, with two years of actual combat experience, had been director of health in our largest and richest state (California's is the sixth largest government on earth!) and could not be influenced by any kind of special military bullshit.

All this had been dug up by the 'researchers' each SG employed to 'scope out' the new situation in Health Affairs. One more thing they discovered, and this was worse, I had been a personal friend of the President for more than twenty years, of the SecDef nearly as long, and had immediate and direct access to them both.

Needless to say, all this left the S.G.s and their staff in a state of somewhat apprehensive disarray, not knowing what to expect, especially since my personnel records, dug up by each service, repeatedly included the word "Controversial." Even "highly controversial." But never court-martialed.

Each one of my principal (but unlabelled) medical deputies, the distinguished Surgeons General, faithfully showed up each week for our private meeting. They were an interesting bunch. They learned right away that they could not send a substitute - any substitute - and could not bring along any staff.

One was an extremely bright, haughty man, an ophthalmologist whose devotion to the Navy bordered on religious fanaticism. It was he who had asserted publicly that the authority of the CNO (Chief of Naval Operations) exceeded that of the Secretary of Defense. He barely concealed his contempt for the other services, and the stupidity of their failure to recognize the supremacy of naval forces over all others. He had found favor with Hyman Rickover, no small achievement, and had served as medical officer aboard a nuclear submarine that made the first ever underwater and under-ice voyage to the North Pole.

It was ironic, and somewhat sad, that it was he that was almost court-martialed and was denied the 'senior officers' so-called 'Good Conduct medal,' the Legion of Merit, when he retired. More about him later on in this narrative.

The second of the three S.G.s at my weekly meetings had been a flight surgeon. He subscribed fervently to the myth that air forces, almost single-handedly, had won World War II and were capable of winning any and all wars that might occur. Just like they would be doing in Viet Nam were it not for the interference of the goddamned civilians in DoD. And of course the way they did later in Africa, Bosnia and Kosovo.

This man, outwardly friendly, even jolly, was in fact a shrewd, manipulative man whose attitudes showed clearly when, in a meeting with the leadership of the American Medical Association, he declared that only the Air Force had a respectable, truly excellent medical service. He explained that they had to be superior, because Air Force personnel were superior in every way to members of the other services. Also, of course, they were needed to win our wars.

The Army, he further declared publicly, considered their soldiers little more than cannon fodder, and their medical care was merely a token. The Navy, according to this military medical expert, wasted its medical resources and indeed its very medical substance by stationing its physicians aboard ships at sea for prolonged periods of little beyond treating "runny noses and runny dicks" instead of real medical problems.

The third member of this supreme military medical triumvirate was an old acquaintance, a urologist who had risen steadily through Army ranks until he commanded Walter Reed Army Medical Center and was picked as the Surgeon General. He was, of the three, the most friendly and reasonable. We had met in Germany, when he visited our alcohol treatment facility in Stuttgart and had reacted violently when he sat in my office and found himself next to a stuffed cobra my family had just given me as a Christmas present. Thoroughly flustered, he explained that he had spent his childhood in Dutch Guiana as the son of missionaries, and learned early on to avoid large snakes.

The three Surgeons General, I soon discovered, hardly knew one another. The weekly meetings in my office were their first regular encounters, and tended at first to be somewhat formal. Using my best group therapy techniques, surreptitiously of course! I set about to overcome the atmosphere of wariness that overlaid our first encounters. Each of these officers was accustomed to being the senior medical person present at whatever meetings they had attended in the building, up until now, so they approached these gatherings gingerly.

What brought them together most effectively, however, was not my group therapy skill, but my announcement that we were launching the most extensive review, ever, of the quality of military medical care, and the establishment of a powerful, uniform medical quality assurance program. This instantly brought forth indignant protestations from each of them to the effect that they already had great 'QA' programs and that the quality of care in each of their services was just fine.

I let them vent their pride and indignation for a while, and then, knowing this was to be my first real test of just who was in charge, showed them. First, I laid out on the conference table a half dozen of the most recent press attacks. Whatever they knew, or thought they knew, about how good their medical care was, this was what the press - and therefore the public - was saying about it, and believing. Worse, both the President and the SecDef had seen this stuff, weren't sure what to believe, and wanted me to do something about it. So we would. Jarrett Clinton would be in charge of designing and implementing the process, and would update us all in our weekly meetings.

Protocol with respect to meetings in the Pentagon was strict and everyone was expected to know the rules of conduct. Those rules, while never written down, were based on ancient, hallowed military traditions and customs, and were largely inviolable. First among these rules was the one requiring that every officer commissioned by the President obey the orders of those appointed over him. That included senior staff of the Department of Defense, regardless of the resentment harbored by many military people, especially since the McNamara years.

These eminent medical officers, all with three star rank, had been accustomed to listening politely to my predecessors in our four-star status, but often interposing objections, delays and all kinds of bureaucratic obstacles to the expressed wishes of the mere civilians 'appointed over them.' This, I was determined to demonstrate, was about to change, at least with respect to medical services.

We four senior physicians of the military services engaged in lively but respectful arguments about my plans for ensuring and publicizing our actions to ensure the highest possible quality of medical care in all of our facilities, but no one openly opposed them. That they saved for an official of lesser rank, in this case my friend and colleague Jarrett Clinton, my deputy for Quality Assurance.

As the weeks went by, with Jarrett appearing at each weekly meeting with the S.G.s to report on QA plans and progress, the attacks upon him by the three service medical leaders grew steadily more strident and antagonistic. It was never necessary for me to intervene directly, even though their attacks on him were in reality attacks on me.

It was clear from the outset that Jarrett needed no help from me, even in the face of sometimes outrageous, impassioned arguments and accusations leveled at him by the Surgeons General. He always listened courteously, answering their concerns logically and reasonably, and never for a moment appearing flustered or defensive or - justifiably - offended and angry. His performance during these weekly inquisitions was exemplary.

The most intense objections to our program occurred when we announced that we were going to form a panel of eminent civilian physicians who had no connection to the Armed Forces, to evaluate the quality of health care in military hospitals and clinics worldwide. They were to be given free and complete access to all our facilities, our medical records, our staffs and our patients, and report their findings back to me and Secretary Weinberger.

The three S.G.s were apoplectic in their rage. Rising from their seats at my conference table (itself a grievous violation of protocol), they all began exclaiming loudly that this would surely do devastating damage to military medicine. Not only would this action prove we didn't trust our own people to evaluate the system, but these (ugh!) civilians, who had no loyalty toward us, would seek out every possible failing and fault, denounce it, leak their findings to the press, and do us irreparable harm.

Neither Jarrett nor I reacted to this outburst. After the three gentlemen settled down a bit, I told them that I could not understand their obvious lack of confidence in their own people, and their equally obvious certainty that there were abundant defects to be unearthed. Moreover, their lack of confidence in their fellow physicians, civilian or not, was astounding. They clearly believed these distinguished medical people were our enemies, incapable of understanding our special problems and dealing with us fairly.

In any case, we were going to do it. If they wanted to put their objections in writing, I would personally deliver them to the Secretary of Defense, but I was determined to proceed unless he or the President ordered me not to. Visibly shaken, the three Surgeons General fled from my office when the meeting ended, no doubt rushing to their staffs to announce this latest horrifying indignity imposed from on high, and alert all hands to the awful threat this posed to the status quo.

As it turned out, the eminent physicians selected for us by the governing board of the American Medical Association, later reported after a thorough look at many of our military medical facilities that they were of consistently superior quality, compared favorably to the finest civilian hospitals, and had an admirable quality assurance program fully in place and functioning. The press gave this little notice, but the horror stories ceased to appear.

William E. Mayer, M.D.

CHAPTER 16

JOUSTING WITH THE JOINT CHIEFS

While all this was going on, spring turned to summer and with that came the annual meeting of the Defense Resources Board. This annual event was of paramount importance to every element of the Department. It was here that all DoD funds for the following year were allocated. It was held in great secrecy, under conditions of strict security, and the Board's decisions were immutable and not subject to appeal. This was really serious!

The Board was chaired by the Deputy Secretary of Defense, William Howard Taft, IV, descendant of the president who bore the same name but with a lower Latin numeral appendage. Will Taft was a deferential, thoughtful man who showed the assembled top brass the same quiet, grave, attentive respect that Cap, who did not attend these meetings, always did on every occasion.

In attendance were the chiefs of each of the three military departments, the Commandant of the Marine Corps, and the generals who commanded the major 'armies' or theaters of operation around the world, who were always referred to as the "CINCs," designating their assignments as Commanders in Chief of the major commands. Also present was the SecDef's military assistant, a young major general named Colin Powell. He never took an active role in the discussions, but paid close attention, made copious notes, and doubtless kept his boss informed in great detail of what went on.

The civilians who took part in the DRB included the civilian secretaries of the Army, Navy and Air Force, and most of the Assistant Secretaries of Defense, though not all of them, for reasons that were never very clear to me. I took it as my due that I was included, believing as I did that health issues cut across all others. It soon became evident that not all the other participants saw things my way about health care, but it was my intention to change all that!

The daily meetings went on for several weeks. It was absolutely forbidden, and everyone understood this, to discuss with anyone - staff, spouse, girlfriend or especially politician! - anything at all about what was discussed or decided in that heavily guarded, electronically swept (daily) conference room. Once the meetings ended for the year, all decisions were revealed, except for highly classified, sensitive secret matters. At that point the plans and budgets for the entire military establishment worldwide were set for the coming year.

When it came time for me to make my presentation to this overwhelming collection of renowned, bemedalled, terribly impressive and truly powerful men, it seemed that this must be what it is like to confront the supreme powers of the universe, Saint Peter presiding, when one applies for admission to Paradise. Or maybe what it was like to make an appearance before the Sanhedrin during the Inquisition.

My preparation for this moment had been as exhaustive as my staff could make it, and my head was stuffed with facts, arguments, statistics, some history, and the plans that needed to be 'sold' to this august body. No previous experience, even addressing audiences of several thousand people assembled in theaters, field houses and state legislatures, had adequately prepared me for this. I was about to start a campaign that seemed to me more important than anything in my life before this, and in some mystical way was the reason for everything that had gone on before. These people gathered here, none of them with more than a superficial knowledge of modern medicine with all its miracles and its skyrocketing costs, had the power to advance my cause or shoot it down instantly.

Uppermost in my mind were my experiences in Japan and Korea. To this very day the memories are still vivid of actually doing surgery on my knees on the corridor floors of the Naval Hospital, Yokosuka, on young Marines riddled with shell fragments (did any of them get inside a body cavity?) while we ran out of antiseptics, antibiotics and even simple bandages and local anesthetics within hours of their arrival. Here we were, a handful of junior officers - obstetrician, general surgeon, internist, and (of all things!) psychiatrist - shuffling about from one stretcher to another, cutting and probing and swabbing and occasionally sticking a rubber tube in some poor kid who yesterday was having a beer with his friends.

Those memories had recently been renewed when a new generation of the same young Marines were crushed and lacerated in their beds in the Beirut barracks, cared for by young medical officers off ships nearby and then flown for hours - needlessly - for outrageous distances to a hospital in Germany before getting proper care.

Then had come the revelations of the 'world wide exercise' when our computers showed we would only be able to give care to one out of ten of our wounded on a "conventional" battlefield.

Unless I could make my case to the DRB, whose generals and admirals and high-ranking civilians were far more interested in air-to-air missiles and nuclear submarines and smart bombs, all of them horribly expensive and not all that effective, we'd be right back, medically, not only to Beirut and Korea, but to the Civil War. That was what these people had to be convinced of. I was at least as nervous as a pregnant teenage bride.

It doesn't really help to have psychiatric training in a situation like the DRB. These people were not sick, contrary to some liberal intellectual convictions about the 'military mind,' and the 'military-industrial complex' ruled by Dr. Strangelove types. They were a special breed, without question, mature, highly educated, widely experienced, professionally at the top of their trade and certainly not without certain biases and convictions that would not, today, be considered politically correct, or very 'liberal.'

They were also, generally, realists. Numerous people were more or less constantly trying to sell them something, be it schemes or hardware, and they were skeptical if not cynical about new or unfamiliar ideas. Each of these men commanded not only the activities and potentially the very lives of thousands of subordinates, but also unimaginably large sums of money provided by the citizens and directed by politicians and lobbyists who were not always principled nor even very intelligent.

What they were, in the main, were idealists, tempered by stress of great magnitude and intensity, acutely aware of their real importance but rarely carried away with this, unlike most members of Congress and many high level government and business executives. Every one had experienced war, the ultimate violence, and while conscious that they owed much of their exalted status to that most insane of mankind's activities, most of them were truly dedicated haters of war.

While this may sound like a rather naive, idealized, hero-worshipful and perhaps unrealistic assessment of the leaders of a dismal profession, it was my impression increasingly during the six years I spent deeply immersed in the culture and practices of the great five-sided building. It does not mean that these people were a fun bunch. Nor were they invariably right in what they believed, or without human foibles. Some, like Bernie Rogers who commanded all our forces in Europe, grew imperious, distant, and arrogant. Some abused their power, in mostly small ways, but none, in my experience, was corrupted by it.

And so it was that confronting these men, all at one time in one place, was a sobering, humbling experience that no training course adequately prepares anyone for. I listened carefully to the presentation that preceded my own, trying to ascertain what the guidelines were, and what seemed to work and to be acceptable to the group. Presenters generally came equipped with masses of statistics and financial data, were very direct and succinct in their delivery, and followed certain rules. The first commandment, and it was absolute, was that it was never permitted even to hint at trade-offs with anyone else's materiel or resources, including manpower. It was nearly irresistible, for example, to point out that a single test-firing of a single exotic missile, cost more money than an entire field hospital! Surely that medical field unit was more valuable than that single missile shot, but I couldn't say that, or even think it.

It was also unacceptable to be dramatic or emotional in one's presentation. Hyperbole must be avoided. Cost-effectiveness was to be emphasized. All assertions must be accompanied by proof. Repetition was frowned upon. I was reminded, however ridiculous it may sound, of my first presentation to the Humboldt County Board of Supervisors when I was seeking their approval of me as their new mental health director and what seemed like a huge budget increase.

On that memorable occasion, I had begun by first paying homage to the undeniable splendor of the county, the vigor of its population and its colleges, and the efforts of the tiny mental health clinic housed in a former beauty shop condemned by the county for a new road (that never got built.)

Then they were treated to the actual facts on the number of people they annually, through expensive court proceedings and costly expenditure of money and sheriff's staff, sent away to the State Hospital far to the south, from whence few ever returned. And exactly how much that cost.

Finally, I told them what I proposed to do, how many people would be newly hired, how they could get money from the state (congress?) to pay for all this, how much it would save them in the long run, how it would benefit the overall health of the county and, almost as a seeming afterthought, how it would benefit individuals and their families.

That convinced the Board members, some of whom clearly thought of themselves as being at least as powerful and important as the Joint Chiefs of Staff back there in Washington. They hired me and revised their budget. A year later the Chairman of the Board, a wonderfully ebullient and skillful local politician, meeting me in a courthouse corridor, pounded me on the back and declared in his usual stentorian tones that he was pound of me.

He went on to let me in on the 'real' reason they had bought my proposal. It was, he said, because I didn't give them that goddam bleeding heart, tear-jerking approach to mental health care. Just told them what the problem was, what I was going to do about it, and how much it would cost.

I decided to try the same general approach with the Defense Resources Board. It had worked in Humboldt County. Why not here?

So I started by telling the assembled brass, military and civilian, what an honor it was to be here and part of this body. Describing the recent scurrilous attacks in the media on the quality of military health care, I told them we had proved them wrong, established the best medical Quality Assurance Program in existence, and our fine doctors and nurses and corpsmen continued to get better. They were also reminded that U. S. military medical care in wartime had achieved the highest rate of survival following wounding on the battlefield in the whole history of the world. Finally, I told them we had the finest modern military hospitals in existence, and the highest percentage of fully qualified specialists in any hospitals, military or civilian. All this was true and we had the figures to prove it.

Next, the problem. My distinguished predecessors in and out of uniform, in their dedication to excellence and determination to keep abreast of the latest and best - and incredibly costly - scientific advances in medical technology, had been spending all available healthcare resources on our splendid hospitals like Walter Reed, San Diego Naval Hospital, Wilford Hall Air Force Hospital, and many others. This had left little for field medicine; after all, while we had many thousands of troops 'in the field' overseas in Korea and Germany, no one was getting shot at. We had come to depend on the splendid trans-oceanic evacuation capability of the Air Force, so we could bring serious cases back home to our magnificent medical centers.

The problem with that was that first priority for airlift in case of war is not field hospitals; it is men and ammunition and equipment. If a man is seriously wounded in battle, and if he is not given substantial medical attention in the first six to eight hours, he is likely to die. He will die from bleeding, from shock, and from overwhelming infection. Right now we can only give care to one out of ten wounded men. No longer can our troops expect the 97% survival rate from wounds that obtained in the late stages of World War II or Korea.

What I was proposing was to 'cure' our medical readiness problem. It would be far too late once any shooting started. Instead of further investments in our already superb stateside hospitals, we needed to increase our supplies of field medical equipment, field hospitals, medical ground transport, and prepositioned fluids, drugs, surgical instruments and field diagnostic devices like X-Rays.

We need to take this message to Congress, and ask for the relatively modest amount of additional money over and above what is needed to keep our forces combat ready, to provide these things.

It didn't go over quite as well as my pitch to the Humboldt County Board of Supervisors, but it went okay. Colin Powell told me later that I had taken a little too long making my pitch, and I promised to do better next year. However, I told him this was more important a matter than anything else I'd heard in the interminable deliberations of the DRB, and he seemed to accept that, though he walked away shaking his head gently from side to side.

The result of those meetings was probably all I could have hoped for. The Joint Chiefs and CINCs were directed by the Board to instruct their Surgeons General and medical staffs to devote more effort and funding to increasing medical readiness and field training. This might set the tone for what was to come, but would hardly correct what I saw as potentially a terrible disaster if we got involved in even a small war anywhere at all, with innumerable preventable casualties and deaths, and a national scandal.

Secretary Weinberger was quick to pick up on this. He called me in for exhaustive explanations of what I had said briefly at the DRB, and one day without any warning informed me after the morning meeting in his office that he and I were going to see the President.

We proceeded in the Secretary's limousine to the White House where we were waved through Security instantly. A senior secretary and Secret Service agent met us just inside the door and led us directly to the Oval Office. I'd seen it before, on a tour, but this was the first official meeting in what I considered to be hallowed surroundings.

The President was alone behind his desk, and arose immediately, hand outstretched to greet us warmly and enthusiastically, as was his custom. He recalled our days together in Sacramento, including some details I could not believe he would have remembered and were surely not in his daily briefing book. He also reflected briefly on our talks years before in a movie studio in Hollywood, where he discovered I fervently shared his convictions about old-fashioned ideas of honor, loyalty, duty, personal responsibility and courage, and his surprise at finding a psychiatrist who believed in such things.

In this encounter, as in a myriad others in previous years and many more to come before he left office, I found Ronald Reagan to be a warm, totally sincere, twinkling man of enormous personal grace and charm. More, he exuded without any effort or pretense an aura of force and power that was not dissipated even slightly, except perhaps to stupid and unperceptive people, by his unshakeable good humor, occasional jocularity, and wonderful jokes and sense of humor.

No matter how distressing a situation or political setback, I never heard him utter even the mildest profanity. When he criticized his critics or his openly declared enemies, it was invariably done with an overtone of good humor and never a disparaging or vicious expression of any kind. This sometimes exasperated his staff and advisors, who wanted him at such times to cut loose and cuss out the bastards.

Like Caspar Weinberger, a warm friend and trusted comrade, Reagan had the ability to focus instantly and intently on the matter at hand, and to recall prodigious amounts of relevant information and history bearing on the topic. His ability to concentrate, reflect and respond appropriately even in the face of complex, troubling situations, while seeming to be completely at ease and at times even inappropriately undisturbed, was disarming to his adversaries and sometimes dismaying to his staff.

While he had been an actor in years gone by, a memory he rather enjoyed, this was no act. He utterly personified the biblical admonition to 'love your enemies,' not as some kind of technique but innately and spontaneously. My dear dead mother would have adored him.

Reagan had some rather simple, clear-cut beliefs about the perfectibility of human beings, and about the importance of dedication to what he saw as the governing beliefs of the Nation's founding fathers, particularly their reliance on God and their belief in the assertions of the Declaration of Independence and the Constitution and Bill of Rights. This too was no pretense, or act. His approach to government and governing derived directly from his strong conviction that at the heart of our political and economic system lay the concepts of personal freedom and personal responsibility.

On this occasion one bright morning as we sat with this truly remarkable, almost innocent-seeming, wholly good man, Cap gave him a succinct, detailed, highly accurate resume of what I had said at the DRB and in more detail to him. For a few moments the President seemed lost in thought, his brow creased but otherwise seemingly relaxed. Finally he looked directly at me and said, "Bud, can you fix this?" I told him I thought so, but it might take time. "Do it," he said, adding that the American people and he personally would be forever grateful.

Characteristically, he offered no detailed instructions and no pep talk. What he clearly implied when giving this kind of order was that he believed I could do what was necessary, would do it right, and that he absolutely trusted me and would support my efforts.

To sit in this room at the center of the greatest power on earth, with the single individual who presided over that power and was directing me to perform a truly major duty, was an experience like no other could be.

It is no wonder at all that people like me who had the great good fortune to be given a mission and expression of confidence in this historic room by a truly good, earnest man who wanted nothing less than the very best for the fortunate citizens of this great, exalted Nation, seemed to me a privilege and an honor of incalculable importance. I would do what this man asked no matter what the cost or effort, and I left the room determined to succeed exactly as he would wish.

It is also no wonder that those of us who shared such experiences have been devastated by the disgusting, immoral, unprincipled and wholly degrading and depraved behavior that has occurred in those sacred, historic precincts during their occupation by a clearly sociopathic opportunist for the last years of the twentieth century.

My task was to take nearly five years. There were profound systemic problems that created serious impediments to any real progress. The first of these was the fact that, in flagrant disregard of one of the first principles of military operations, called "unity of command," there was in fact no one in charge. Even the individual surgeons general in each service were not really 'in charge' of health care budgeting and operations. Operations were directed by so-called 'medical commands' composed of elaborate staff who functioned largely as committees. The S.G.s had no direct control over these groups, each of which was headed by a lesser general or admiral who fully expected one day to get the S.G.'s job and often didn't care much for the incumbent.

Major training and research elements in each service were also quite separate and distant both from the S.G.'s office and the 'Med Command' leadership, both geographically and psychologically. In addition as noted earlier, there was little meaningful interaction between the medical departments in the different services. The main reason for the intense opposition of the Surgeons General to our Quality Assurance campaign was, in reality, their fear that the other services would be able to look into their own, and were certain to identify invidious comparisons.

No previous occupant of my office, technically the highest medical authority over all the military services, had made much of an attempt, if any, to assume operational leadership of military medicine. Any attempt would have been largely fruitless anyway, because of the second systemic problem.

That problem was that there was no medical budget. Despite the expenditure each year for medicine that was greater than that for the Nation's entire foreign aid program worldwide, there was no plan for that $13+ billion dollars. Accounting for medical spending was fragmented and downright sloppy, no single element or person controlled the process and no one was accountable for it!

As every CEO or business manager knows, if you don't control the money you don't control anything. That's got to be the first lesson in Management 101, and seems to me just common sense.

The way things actually worked, the medical commands sought estimates from all their hospital commanders about their next year's dollar needs, listed in priority order. These were reviewed, along with rationales and 'defenses' for amounts and priorities, by the folks in the medical command headquarters, who might modify them significantly. They were then consolidated and presented at budget planning sessions within that service.

Additionally, separate commands, research laboratories, medical air and ground transport units, supply depots and the like submitted their own wish lists, also reviewed by Med Command and added to hospital and clinic costs. Medical units 'organic' to combat units like divisions deployed to Korea, cranked their budget needs into the division's or brigade's budget, and were often barely identifiable as medical costs. Finally, warehousing and maintaining inactive, stored, or mothballed medical units' costs were often buried in some budget line hidden elsewhere in the Army or Navy budget seemingly unrelated to conventional medical expenditures.

It was a real mess.

It seemed to me that correcting our glaring medical readiness deficiencies required correction of these two major problems up front. First, I had to establish my authority for the overall direction of all military medical activities. While this idea was about as popular as a raging dose of some horrible venereal disease, there was an obvious way.

I was not authorized, on my own, to issue a Department of Defense Regulation, which, having the force of law within all military departments could only be done by the Secretary of Defense himself. However, I could write up a DoD Regulation, and if I could get the Secretary to sign it, that was it. I made it clear to my entire staff and the senior staffs of all the Surgeons General and MedCommand commanders that I saw and talked with the Secretary of Defense every day, and occasionally, with him, the Commander in Chief as well.

It rapidly got around that the three of us were actually old friends who had worked together for years. The word rapidly spread, though it was not quite entirely true, that Cap would do anything that I asked him to do with respect to military medical care. People in the building would casually ask me how often I saw the President and Nancy, what they were like privately, how often we dined together, and so on. I always made it a point, quite accurately, to say that we rarely saw them or Ed Meese or Michael Deaver socially, which only served to reinforce the idea that we were together a lot, and I was just being coy about it. I was, after all, a bonafide, charter member of the 'California Mafia,' as it was often called. Worse, the word got out that Nancy Reagan's stepfather had been my professor of surgery during medical school! The truth was, I didn't like him much at all.

The Pentagon, if nothing else (and there is much else) is a culture that unabashedly worships power. Every uniform bears on its front side a clear indication of rank, which is to say status, along with a recognizable sign of authority, seniority and particular professional specialty, as well as a history, as it were, of the wearer's experience in both war and peace; where that took place; was there actual combat involved; were wounds received; and were actions in both war and peace rewarded with medals acknowledging great bravery, uncommon excellence or achievement, or even simple good conduct in bygone years as an enlisted person.

All of this has to do with power. The most powerful in that culture are generally men in their fifties with four stars on their shoulders, numerous other symbolic items of military jewelry earned in specific ways, and many rows of colorful ribbons depicting a colorful and often highly meritorious set of experiences in harm's way, defending our way of life.

The rewards of power include some material comforts like one's own car and driver, aides, a private bathroom next to your office, admission to small private dining rooms, time off whenever you want it, inclusion in a host of glittering military and civilian social functions, and reserved parking spaces in front of the PX and the Commissary, as well as near the main entrances to the building.

The principal and most sought-after rewards, however, are less tangible but very real. They include overt exhibitions of deference and respect, sometimes even awe. The greater the status and thus the power, the more quickly your calls are answered, access to the mighty is both easier and faster, people listen more carefully to what you say and respond with more alacrity to your expressed wishes and instructions. People open doors for you, both literally and figuratively, stand up when you enter a room and fall silent, never interrupt, and are invariably polite. Even your peers - at least in the presence of others.

It would be next to impossible for anyone to experience all this without gaining some feeling that he has some importance. It he revels in it, he is generally despised by all. Usually he soon realizes that much of what he experiences has very little to do with him as a person, much of it has resulted from sheer happenstance and luck, and it doesn't really prove anything about his real value as a human being. He also discovers that most of it disappears instantly when he leaves the scene. Permanently, when he retires, in most cases. Sic transit gloria mundi, as the saying goes.

The 'rewards' of power, at least the external ones, never appealed to me very much, although I would have liked to have my own bathroom. As the word spread that there was a long-term close relationship between me and the Secretary and The Boss, however, it was vaguely pleasing and mostly rather amusing to find myself deferred to and attended to in various ways. This was especially notable during foreign trips, of which there were many. All of the troublesome details of arranging travel were done for me. Schedules were devised, submitted for my approval, and then prepared in writing, daily, to assure everything went smoothly.

During the actual travel, which was always done in Business Class or First Class or on small executive jets, there were always aides to carry the luggage, supply written briefings and background material for every meeting, accomplish the customs and immigration requirements, check into hotels, arrange all meals, set up all transportation and generally make life as simple and pleasant as it could possibly be. It was immediately evident to me that only the supremely rich and powerful in our society ever got to travel like this. There was nothing to do but relax and enjoy it, so I did just that.

While all my journeys had specific goals and often involved sensitive and difficult interactions with senior military and medical officials as well as government dignitaries and our own State Department people in our embassies abroad, they were a welcome break from the struggles in the Pentagon, for the most part. Those struggles continued, in the effort to establish a consistent, effective quality assurance program, correct the appalling deficiencies in our medical readiness to support whatever combat situation might arise, establish some sense of command and control in the medical system, and take over supervision of medical finances.

In my first and all subsequent performances in the annual Defense Resources Board meetings, these were my principal themes. There was, during the 1980s, growing attention to 'joint' operations within the armed forces. It wasn't as if this was an entirely novel idea. After all, the historic assaults on Japanese strongholds across the Pacific, as well as the invasions of the Nazi fortress of Europe, were classics of joint actions. They always began with Naval and Air Force bombardment of target areas, the insertion of special Marine Corps and Army amphibious landing forces and air-dropped troops and supplies, the setting up of massive re-supply systems for all of these, and finally the actual occupation of land masses to ensure their control.

With the coming of peace, however, the individual Services invariably drew back into themselves to regroup, resupply, refurbish and retrain. This makes some sense insofar as each has unique functions and capabilities. It makes less sense, as many military experts and philosophers have long asserted, in the case of medical care, which accounts for the perennial attention paid to the "purple suit" medical department idea.

As a possibly acceptable alternative to putting all medics in one pot, as had been done in some other countries' military structures, it seemed to me that many of the benefits of unification, including better use of money, manpower and other resources, greater breadth and depth of available services and medical specialists, and an enhanced rapid response capability, could all be achieved, or at least brought closer, in another way.

That way involved collaborative centralized planning, with operational execution of plans remaining decentralized. All that would be needed was a clear idea of how much money and manpower was currently being spent by each service, and for what. Then, the leaders of each service's medical department and their planners would assemble together, discuss their ideas of what the priorities were and what needless duplications were taking place, and come up with an overall plan for the medical support of the whole military enterprise: who would do what, and where they would do it.

To keep things simple, those medical elements that were 'organic' - an integral part - of operational units like Army and Marine Battalions, Air Force and Navy Air Wings, and the like, would remain as is. The huge medical infrastructure, however, the more than a hundred military hospitals scattered throughout the Continental United States and overseas in Europe and Asia would become, in effect 'unified' medical commands. They would serve the healthcare needs of all uniformed people and their families in their vicinity. They would be staffed by medical people from all branches of the service as dictated by medical need.

No 'purple suits.' Just white coats like in every hospital. The color of their trousers wouldn't really matter. Their patients, being largely undressed anyway, would look like patients always look.

The first step in this simple, logical coordination and collaboration of the separate medical departments, all of whom, after all, treat the same species of mammalians, was to find out how much money there was, as of now, how many people were employed in the task, how much equipment was needed, and how much medical supply it took.

That little task took about two years.

So too, did the preliminary planning.

It was incredible to me that the large and small groups of intelligent, competent, supposedly well-motivated and well-intended people that we assembled could spend so much time doing so little! The ability to look busy while accomplishing not much is widespread in all great bureaucracies, such as the armed forces. It is finely honed in numerous individuals, and the advent of the computer has been a godsend to such people. But long before the computer, there was the committee, and it flourishes in large organizations.

We worship today, more than ever before, before the altar of inclusiveness, letting everyone have his say, dignifying every point of view however illogical or even outrageous. We try mightily to accommodate all opinions, consider everyone's feelings, avoid anything remotely offensive or allegedly deviant from some hypothetical 'norm,' and try to crank it all into the committee's final product.

What often results is far off the original mark, but above all things, it is benign. It cannot be blamed on anyone. No one is responsible. And very little gets accomplished.

So it was with the groups of accountants and analysts charged with identifying all medical expenditures, all assets, all anticipated costs - in other words, the overall medical 'budget.' So it was equally with the 'planners,' who labored long and mightily and finally came up with a peanut. It was, unsurprisingly, in the form of a modest test run, a sort of clinical trial. We would select one small area, and set up a medical "joint command" that involved two or more military departments. This would prove whether it could be done.

At least, I hoped, it would be better than having to use a commercial phone in Grenada to call a ship just offshore, a battle on the tarmac in Lebanon to decide where patients would be sent and another battle on the tarmac in Frankfurt to decide on which hospital to head for, or waiting for a small shipment of medicine for an Army hospital in Germany to come from the warehouse in New Jersey when there was plenty of it a few miles away in an Air Force hospital also in Germany! Back to that first, glorious, "Joint Medical Command" later.

William E. Mayer, M.D.

Brainwashing, Drunks & Madness

William E. Mayer, M.D.

CHAPTER 17

CRISIS RESPONSE

While this cumbersome process with implications for future warfare, deployments to far-off battlefields, casualty care, and strategic plans was plodding along, we were making great strides on a more local battleground: the struggle to 'ensure' the highest possible quality of medical care to the nearly ten million active duty and retired military people and their families around the world. As is true in all battles, however, this one was not without its rough spots.

One such involved the splendid old flagship of Navy medicine, the National Naval Medical Center in Bethesda, Maryland, less than ten miles out on Wisconsin Avenue from the White House.

It came to be known far and wide as "The Billig Case," so-named in honor of the main character, who was serving as Chief of Cardio-Thoracic Surgery at that hospital. Both junior medical staff and nurses called attention to the fact that the mortality rate in that department far exceeded expectations. Alarmed, the Navy leadership invited a cardiac surgeon from the Walter Reed Army Medical Center a few miles away in Silver Spring, Maryland, to come have a look.

Russ Zajtchuk, a feisty, dedicated, outspoken and highly competent surgeon did the looking. He was selected because of his skill and experience, and possibly because his rank of Lieutenant Colonel was identical to Billig's Naval Rank of Commander. He 'scrubbed in' on a number of cases with the Commander and was shocked by what he found. He immediately reported to the Navy Admiral in charge of the place that their cardiac surgeon had the skills of a first year resident, at best, and was blind in one eye to boot. He should never, he opined, be allowed to operate alone, if at all!

"The Word,' as they say, leaked out promptly. Naval investigators were called in and ended up charging the commander with manslaughter, finding that his behavior far exceeded simple medical mischance or even malpractice. While Billig managed to avoid criminal penalties in the trial that followed, he was forced to resign. Worse, the Vice Admiral Commanding the Naval Medical Command was found to have failed to perform his duties properly with respect to Billig and was held to be ultimately responsible, was officially censured and his long and distinguished career was ruined.

This tragic set of events and ruined lives and careers lighted up two other cases of senior officers, not long before that, that ended up giving our efforts in Quality Assurance a great boost, tough as they were on those involved.

The boost to our QA efforts was two-fold. First, it dramatized to our physician-commanders at every level that the project was really important. Not only was patient welfare involved, but so also was their own personal welfare, and the survival of their careers unless they paid closer attention to what their staffs were doing.

Second, it brought to our tiny staff under Jarrett Clinton, who were totally engaged in the monumental task of creating what would become the world's finest medical quality assurance program, a new recruit. Somehow - I was never quite sure how, but it was connected with the Billig case - Bert Brown, M.D., burst upon the Health Affairs scene, to our great good fortune.

Nearly fifteen years before, I had had the honor of glimpsing and briefly conversing with this shining star of psychiatry when he was director of the National Institute on Mental Health in his office in Rockville, Maryland. While I was always good at not showing things like this, I stood in some awe of this storied character who was not even as old as I was, yet headed the nation's premier institution for research and program development in mental health, following John Kennedy's signing of a national Mental Health Act and the early days of community mental health programs.

Bert was a handsome, completely self-assured, debonair man who looked even younger than he was. He exuded vigor, enthusiasm, certainty about the importance of our shared field and the institute he headed, and he said nice things about our efforts in California, where at that time I was but a lowly County Mental Health Director.

You will recall that my entry into the field of psychiatry was less than enthusiastic and wholly involuntary. I had found it fascinating and badly in need of emphasis on the truly mentally ill and the physiologic and even physical components of serious mental disease, but I never liked it very much until I discovered community mental health.

Traditional, especially psychoanalytic, psychiatry with its emphasis on intense self-preoccupation, interminable courses of treatment, not altogether convincing formulations of psychopathology and almost masturbatory examination of fantasies and obsession with sexual impulses and thoughts had never really captured my attentive devotion. Almost every psychiatrist I had gotten to know, moreover, struck me as really odd, largely in ways that made me a little uncomfortable.

There were exceptions, of course, like Bart Hogan and Karl Bowman and Commander Griswold, who used to cuss out the martinet Navy Captain at Mare Island as he walked by the locked ward, but they were all definite "characters" that I could relate to. And now, here was Bert Brown. He wasn't like any of the rest. Definitely a character: fast-talking, full of ideas and enthusiasms, very quick, a doer, and a manipulator like me - only better at it. Good guy.

After leaving the National Institute on Mental Health, I had heard that he became Dean of the well-respected Hahneman Medical School in Philadelphia and later became a consultant of some sort, but the details were obscure. In any event, he was here to help us with our QA efforts, and plunged into the task with great energy and enthusiasm.

It wasn't until about fifteen years later that Bert told me that he was first drawn to involvement in our QA efforts at least partly because our famous Dr. Billig was a graduate of Hahneman! But I digress.

The first boost to our QA efforts - getting the commanders' attention, had to do with a 3-star (highest possible rank for a physician) Air Force General named Myers. As a two-star major general, he had commanded the Air Force's premier hospital, Wilford Hall at Lackland Air Force Base in San Antonio. While there, he had been informed of a similarly inept - but not blind in either eye - cardiac surgeon who was, to put it bluntly, killing patients. At the time, the general was campaigning hard for appointment as Surgeon General of the Air Force, and in fact was ultimately successful in being awarded that supreme medical honor.

It was later alleged, and apparently well established, that rather than risk the public outcry and possible censure that could have resulted from media attention to the problem in cardiac surgery at his hospital, which could ruin his chances for elevation to Surgeon General, Myers simply arranged a rather contrived "training assignment" to a civilian hospital in Wisconsin and got the poorly performing heart surgeon off the premises - far off.

Were it not for a terribly sad incident that followed, the solution might have worked, the inept surgeon might have gotten better at his craft, and all might ultimately have been forgotten. Instead, while at the Wisconsin hospital and assigned during a routine surgical case to hook up and attend to the heart-lung machine, the doctor-exile from Lackland hooked up the machine backward, destroying the brain of the young mother on the O.R. table.

During the investigation that followed, accompanied by considerable press attention, the doctor's history of malfeasance in the Air Force hospital and his convenient diversion to Wisconsin for 'training' even though he was ostensibly fully trained already, was pounced upon by the local reporters, picked up by the wire services, and read by members of the Senate Armed Services Committee.

Our general, meanwhile, was enjoying his exalted status as Surgeon General of the Air Force, until time came for him to retire. At that point, as required by law, the Senate was asked to confirm his retirement in 3-star rank.

They refused to do so, citing his mishandling of the cardiac surgeon.

The general left office as S.G., reverted to his former 2-star rank, and was ordered to duty at Walter Reed with no defined duties where he languished while his Air Force superiors lobbied mightily for a full year before finally getting the Senate's reluctant approval for him to retire, quietly and without public notice, in three-star rank.

Next came the Mittemeyer case, filling out the Navy-Air Force-Army spectrum of high-level problems relating to medical mischance or malfeasance. While commanding Walter Reed Army Medical Center, Major General Mittemeyer had on his staff as chief of Anesthesiology a colonel named Watson.

The colonel, a respected specialist in his field, was said to have owned a substantial share in a medical supply firm that sold, among other things, a plastic airway used to support respiration in serious cases. He persuaded the Army medical procurement people, based on his eminence in the field, to buy large quantities of this new airway, without hinting at his investment in the company that sold it. The airway proved defective, harmed several patients severely, and was withdrawn. An investigation followed, indicating the colonel's involvement. The FBI was called in, and agents visited the hospital commander, General Mittemeyer, to inform him of the suspicions about the anesthesiologist but instructing him to stay completely out of it until they finished their work. He complied.

When the case finally came to public attention and trial, Mittemeyer was criticized for not intervening sooner than he did, despite the FBI's instructions not to do anything at the time. This came up when Bernie was ready to retire, and once again the Senate refused his 3-star rank, based on this. Distraught, the General came to me for help. I went to Sam Nunn, a Senate expert on military affairs and a fine southern gentleman, and with his help, Bernie got the retirement he deserved.

And so it was that Billig, Myers, Watson and Mittemeyer all, without intending or wishing to do so, gave impetus at command level to the importance of Command attention to the serious issues of maintaining the highest possible levels of medical competence and propriety - lessons that have endured to this day.

Consternation over the casualty care fiasco when the Marine barracks was bombed in Lebanon, and the poor inter-service coordination off Grenada during our medical student rescue mission there, both in the early months of my tenure in DoD, had convinced me that the time was ripe to initiate a serious, searching investigation of military medical planning and operations, particularly in Europe, but also in the Far East. I chose to look at Europe first, where we had major hospitals in Germany and Italy, and a couple of hundred thousand troops and their families.

On one of my early 'familiarization' trips, this one to the huge naval establishment in and around Norfolk, Virginia, I had met a vigorous, sharp, medical admiral known for his outspoken manner and decisiveness. He was James Zimble, Chief Surgeon of the Atlantic Fleet. Known for his independent thinking and occasional controversial stance on various issues, he had nonetheless risen high in Navy ranks. It seemed to me that he was an ideal senior medical person to conduct the investigation that was needed.

Admiral Zimble readily agreed to take on the task, if the Chief of Naval Operations would permit him to do so, and I promptly sought out the CNO and got that permission. It was a personally risky thing for Zimble to do; the European Command was a powerful, entrenched entity, almost an army of its own, and both the line and the medical officers there would not look kindly on having their affairs pried into by one from 'outside,' and a different branch of service to boot.

More than twenty years before, General I. D. White, CINCPAC - Commander in Chief, Pacific - had issued me a set of orders in Hawaii sending me all over the Pacific theater to examine into problems in morale and discipline throughout the ranks in that area. The orders were clear and simple: travel anywhere I chose in the entire area, talk privately and in great detail with all ranks from Private to General, Seaman to Admiral, as the CINC's personal representative, and promise, in his name, absolute confidentiality and protection from any possible reprisal.

The orders we prepared for Jim Zimble were essentially the same, and this set was signed by Caspar Weinberger himself. Zimble would report everything to me, and I would pass it to the Secretary, along with my recommendations for action.

Just as we expected, the Admiral was not exactly welcomed with enthusiasm by the senior Army people in Europe. He pursued his task with great energy, however, usually selecting his subjects for interview personally to avoid the invariable tendency of unit commanders to select the 'best' subjects for such investigatory probes, and collected an enormous amount of useful information.

Using what he dug up, it was possible to go directly to Cap Weinberger and make an unshakeable case for a single, senior military physician in overall charge of all medical activities in the theater of operations. He would be the medical 'CINC' for Europe, able to call upon people and resources from any and all services located there, with the authority to order people, equipment and medical supplies anywhere that he or the overall Europe Commander determined they were needed.

This was a huge leap forward. The CINCs had always had a 'Surgeon' on their immediate staffs, but those staff officers had only indistinct knowledge of all the medical resources available throughout the command, and no authority whatever to order them around. In crisis situations, they could try to persuade the CINC to take certain measures, but without a supporting staff of medical logisticians and planners they were largely impotent.

"Unity of Command" had finally arrived in military medicine, or at least in this one major part of it.

One major problem with doing this sort of thing has to do with the fact that each branch of the military is confined by law to a specific, limited number of general or 'flag rank' officers: those with stars. In the Army, Marines and Air Force these are one-star (Brigadier), 2 star (Major), 3 star (Lieutenant), and 4-star (Full) Generals. The Navy calls these ranks Rear (Lower half and Upper half), Vice, and full Admirals. Each service can decide which of its branches - medical, dental, engineer, ordnance, supply, etc. - can have how many of each, with the bulk reserved for the "line," that is the people who command combat forces.

When a new position is established that calls for a general or flag officer, such as the Command Surgeon for all of Europe that we had just invented, the general "slot" has to come from within the existing limit. This means that some existing organization, commanded by a general, has to give up its general's slot and settle for being run by a Colonel - the next step down. There is enormous resistance to doing this.

If, moreover, the new position for a general or admiral is to be rotated among the services, it produces some turmoil in each of them when it comes their turn. In any rigidly structured hierarchy, be it military or civilian, such "temporary" assignments are thought to disrupt the orderly upward progression of senior staff, and meet with determined resistance.

The Air Force, in this case, evidently saw some advantage to be gained in this assignment of one of their own, and hastened to volunteer one of its generals for the honor. His name was Greendyke, a major general who turned out to be a terrible, embarrassing mistake.

Shortly before we established the Command Surgeon post in Europe, the Secretary had announced that the office of Health Affairs had come up with a major plan to improve CHAMPUS - the Civilian Health and Medical Program of the Uniformed Services. Costs of the program had been escalating wildly and had reached billions of dollars. Many civilian physicians were declining to treat patients under the program, which served dependants and retired military people mainly, because of unsatisfactory payment rates and frequent reimbursement delays.

Even worse, the beneficiaries of this scheme, originally expected to be a modest supplement to care in military hospitals and clinics, were increasingly unhappy with the program and complained loudly about it.

Under the splendid and careful stewardship and creativity of my principal Deputy, David Newhall, and a brilliant young civilian who had formerly worked in the Office of Management and Budget in the White House and was now our consultant, Don Moran, we had created a variation on what later came to be called 'managed care' and resembled some aspects of Health Maintenance Organizations - HMOs. We called it the "Champus Reform Initiative," or "CRI."

Although he knew very little about it, General Greendyke, who had a distinct tendency to intellectual arrogance, immediately decided that this was a bad idea. He began touring his new European 'command,' giving talks to military audiences, declaring that this new CHAMPUS thing was going to ruin their health care benefits.

In addition, he damned the Department of Defense and its health office for saying we couldn't take care of all of our casualties in case of war, and insisted we could readily take care of all of them. Evidently carried away with his own eloquence and the highly emotional response it evoked, especially among the troops' family members, he then committed an unforgivable mistake - a felony, actually.

Both in his speeches and in print, in an interview with reporters for the leading free 'hand-out' magazine distributed in all the military PXs and commissaries, he advised that soldiers and their families lobby their representatives in Congress to reverse the SecDef's decision.

It is forbidden for a serving officer in the Armed Forces to advocate to his subordinates or to the public that they take action (like writing letters) to get Congress to impose something on the military. He had, as they say, 'stepped on it.'

All this lecturing and advocating in direct opposition to a published decision of his superiors took place during the first 25 days of Greendyke's assumption of his new post of Command Surgeon, U.S. Forces, Europe. After his first week on the job, reports from Europe showed that there was major turmoil among our people there, so I flew over to see what I could do to offset it.

On my arrival, I met with Greendyke and the senior Army and Navy medical generals, and tried to explain Champus Reform to them. Then I arranged for an exhausting series of public meetings at our bases all over Europe, to assure the people we wouldn't be going out to contract for the cheapest, "lowest bidder" variety of medical care and would, in fact, greatly improve the service and care that they got. They were unconvinced, raucous and rude in their shouted condemnations of DoD and their assertions that their congressmen would soon shoot us down.

On General Greendyke's 25th day in office, while I was in Heidelberg at the Army's European Headquarters, a call came for me from the Pentagon. It was Colin Powell, telling me in confidence - I was not to pass it along to anyone at all - that the Secretary had first asked, and then directed, the mighty Bernie Rogers, Commander in Chief Europe, to relieve Greedyke immediately and send him back to the U.S. - that day.

Evidently General Rogers, jealous of his prerogatives as the almighty boss of all US forces in Europe, at first seemed reluctant to do anything about the rebellious medic just because some civilian in the Pentagon wanted him to. The directive call from Weinberger, which I am certain was conducted in Cap's usual quiet, gracious manner, no doubt clarified the Constitutional chain of command situation for the general.

Colin said everything would become clear the following day, when Greendyke departed for home, at which time Cap would appreciate it if I went to General Rogers' headquarters in Belgium to thank him, mollify him if necessary, and clarify the situation.

Sure enough, the next morning General Greendyke left the premises, and indeed the continent without ceremony. Quite early. The word spread like wildfire that he had been fired. I left for Rogers' headquarters soon after.

Forever after that, the Air Force people (and of course Greedyke himself) believed that I had asked Cap to fire the guy and thus ruined the life and career of this fine officer, but I had done nothing of the sort. I fully intended to when I got home, but never got the chance!

On my arrival it was clear that General Rogers' staff was extremely alert, attentive, very quiet and quite tense in anticipation of what would surely be one of the general's classical explosions. Instead, to my (and his own staff's) surprise and relief, what followed was a cordial, far-ranging and really quite friendly discussion of medical readiness and related matters that went on pleasantly for so long that a second pot of tea was sent for. Relief was written all over the face of the young officer who quickly brought it.

That ended the Greedyke saga. 26 days. I flew home, and we never heard a word from Congress.

William E. Mayer, M.D.

Brainwashing, Drunks & Madness

William E. Mayer, M.D.

CHAPTER 18

MEDICAL EXPEDITIONS ABROAD

Shortly after returning to Washington, I left again for Japan, the Philippines and Korea to see for myself what our medical situation was in the Far East. What it was, was appalling. Our own diplomatic staff and top government officials in all three countries treated my small party and me graciously and even enthusiastically, but what we were to learn was disheartening.

We were lodged in the magnificent old Manila Hotel, where MacArthur had once kept a suite. The lobby and public rooms, all high-ceilinged spaces whose walls and pillars were clad in polished Philippine mahogany, brought back warm memories of the old Sorrento Hotel in Seattle where I had had such a wonderful job during college days, but the Manila was far larger and grander.

Before we even had a chance to check in, however, our embassy officials announced that I was scheduled to meet with the Surgeon General and his senior medical staff at Manila's large military hospital, where we were due momentarily. Having little choice in the matter, I managed to dig a necktie from my carry-on luggage, struggle into a wrinkled jacket while the embassy car lurched into town from the airport, and prepared to be friendly.

On arrival at the hospital grounds, we found assembled at the entrance a small army of about 75 officers all done up in full dress uniforms, and a military band that launched into a variation of ruffles and flourishes followed by our national anthem. A senior officer took my arm firmly as I was alighting from the car, and steered me to a small, elevated, one-man platform facing the troops, all fully armed and standing at attention.

Once the two national anthems, ours and theirs, had been played, the assembled soldiers passed in review. It then became apparent that they expected me to deliver some kind of speech, and somehow I did. All this took place in the late morning, and the atmosphere was hot and humid, like those islands generally experience. While I was exhausted, jet-lagged and soaked with sweat, I could barely imagine the discomfort of those soldiers in their heavy, elaborate dress uniforms straight out of an old operetta.

The ceremony over (I thought,) we were ushered into the main hospital conference room. At a long table stood perhaps two dozen men and women who were chiefs of all the major services in the hospital. They too wore dress uniforms, stifling in the humid heat that was barely lessened by two noisy fans.

We all sat. Each officer was formally introduced, and then delivered a description of his department and its role in the hospital.

About half-way through this interminable set of recitations, it having now reached the noon hour, serving people appeared and set before each of us a cold hamburger, wrapped in paper, and a paper cup of fruit juice. The contrast between this elemental luncheon menu and the elaborate uniforms and formality of the event was striking, and in a way seemed innocent and disarming.

The entire group was then ushered on a tour of the sprawling hospital, the largest in the island nation. Every ward was crowded with patients, mostly on rather simple cots placed much too close together, and collectively they exhibited every conceivable injury and tropical disease.

At one point we were led through the main laboratory. I was unprepared for its small size, and for the fact that there was only a single microscope in the entire lab, which served several thousand patients!

The tour brought the length of the visit to about three hours in all, and finally we were taken back to the front entrance of the hospital. To my horror, I found the entire assembled honor guard and band still in place, where they had stood since we first arrived. To compound my distress at this treatment of the troops, which seemed to me abusive, I was told by the hospital commander, proudly, that the assembled officers were his entire physician and nursing staff. Unbelievable, but true.

Once back at the hotel, a bath and a nap brought me back to life. Seizing every moment that was free of meetings and official duties on all such trips, I ventured as far out into Manila as my feet would carry me. It was a frantically busy, bustling, crowded city with throngs of people and a huge number of rickety, noisy, wildly painted jitneys and busses carrying their human overloads every which way, at breakneck speed.

Visits on subsequent days to Clark Air Force Base and the Naval Base at Subic Bay revealed that while our people were getting good medical care, there was no evidence of planning or preparation to respond to any major demand for service, whether for natural disasters, serious civil unrest or a military uprising. There were Communist guerillas operating in various parts of the islands, but no one seemed very concerned about them.

The medical situation of our forces in Japan, where all three services had bases and some personnel, was similar. I found nothing more than the levels of medical equipment and supply that had existed right up to the outbreak of the war in Korea. Again, no one seemed at all concerned.

Finally, Korea. The city of Seoul was a gleaming metropolis of skyscrapers, automobiles, grand apartment buildings, thriving shops, theaters and large department stores. When I had left there in the early 1950s there had been no single building of two stories or more left intact; all were leveled or seriously damaged from the war. The contrast was dramatic - miraculous.

There were more than thirty thousand American troops stationed in that small country, accompanied by a large number of civilian dependents and civilian employees. The main body of troops was part of the 2nd Infantry Division, a combat-ready force positioned near the 38th parallel separating the north and south, not far from Seoul and the demilitarized zone. The remainder were support units of various kinds, including hospitals and a medical supply warehouse.

It looked to me that the infantry division was in good shape and ready to take an active part, with the Korean divisions, in the defense of South Korea were the forces massed in communist North Korea just above the parallel to attack toward the south once again. What I learned about the enormous amounts of artillery, tanks and soldiers poised only a few miles to the north, however, made it seem certain that the communist forces could largely destroy and probably take Seoul if they chose to advance across the DMZ and through the huge tunnels they had dug beneath it.

Were such a thing to occur, what I discovered, like a medical warehouse with sparse supplies, a MASH hospital with only a skeleton crew, and 'community' hospitals ill-equipped to receive any substantial number of casualties, made me despair. We were horrifyingly unprepared, even in a country poised for thirty years for another invasion and in spite of our single infantry division in place, to give anything like adequate medical care to the wounded who would with certainty show up in large numbers should Kim Il Sung, the north's communist dictator, decide to invade again.

As would almost always prove to be the case when I returned from a trip abroad, I found my part of the Pentagon in some turmoil. This time it was because of the "Friends of Animals," who objected strenuously to the military's use of animals for research and training.

For many years we had used some dogs, cats and monkeys, but more pigs and goats and rats, particularly in carefully managed research projects always conducted with great care to avoid causing the animals to suffer. In addition to conventional forms of medical research, it had proven most valuable to use goats and pigs, especially, for wound research. For this purpose, the animals were anesthetized, and generally shot in the thigh using standard military weapons. Surgery was performed to establish the exact effects of these high-velocity projectiles, and then the wounded animals were used to train surgeons in the most effective methods for treating humans similarly wounded in combat. They were cared for, after surgery, exactly as humans would be, and many survived.

Some of the activists for animal "rights," a concept subject to dispute, found our use of animals barbaric. They insisted that there were abundant alternatives in computer simulations, and the training of our surgeons in civilian emergency rooms in large cities. These alternatives were in fact in use, but they had serious limitations. No computer program was found that could accurately depict the immediate and the distant effects throughout the body after being hit with a high-velocity military weapon.

As for using the emergency rooms, that was found to be useful but also limited. Rarely are high-powered, immensely destructive weapons used in warfare used also in street crimes in our cities. Smaller, lighter handguns, like 'Saturday night specials' are much preferred by our criminal classes. They do damage, and can kill, of course, but the damage is far different.

In addition, there is no common civilian parallel to the multiple penetrating fragment wounds produced by artillery and grenades. Terrorist bombings are, so far at least, blessedly uncommon in this county, and have not provided much opportunity for training combat surgeons.

The "rights" people, unsatisfied with the government's response to their concerns, conducted some abortive demonstrations on the Pentagon steps, and ended up delivering a herd of goats on Weinberger's front lawn early one morning along with placard-bearing demonstrators and invited press.

This did, in fact, get the Secretary's attention, along with that of his wife, a former nurse and now a successful author of children's books. The subject came up at the morning meeting in Cap's office, and in spite of certain humorous aspects to the whole thing, was discussed with great solemnity. It was decided that we would suspend using animals for training purposes or wound research, while we reviewed our policies. That move served to diminish the uproar, for a time. It came up again later, of course.

My next overseas trip was designed to put into place a clear agreement with the government of Israel that would allow us to use their hospitals (and air space to get to them!) in case there were US casualties anywhere in the volatile Middle East.

The Israeli armed forces people welcomed us when our plane landed near Tel Aviv, and whisked us to a fine hotel on the coast. Everywhere we went, in addition to personal escort officers, we were guarded by armored cars full of heavily armed troops, both ahead of and behind our own heavy, armored limousine with its thick bulletproof glass. It was great fun roaring around with the sirens wailing constantly, and the lights flashing.

Israel's medical establishment, a combined and thoroughly integrated military-civilian system, was superb. It had been created and refined continuously since the country was founded, of necessity, driven by the hostility of the surrounding countries and the multitude of armed clashes, small and large, that had occurred and had generated casualties.

Like Switzerland, Israel has nearly universal conscription of all able-bodied males in the country, who are required in late adolescence to serve on active duty long enough to be adequately trained and then to function for some months as members of active units. When that is completed, each man is allowed to return home but he remains in the Reserve. That status requires periodic retraining and drills, and the man can be called up for active duty again at a moment's notice. He remains in that status for some years.

Thus it is that practically every male physician in the country who is not lame, halt, blind or aged is either on active duty or in the active Reserve, ready to be mobilized at any time. Female physicians probably have some military obligation as well, but the exact rules for this are not known to me.

The trip to Israel proved both enlightening and inspirational. This tiny, arid country, the scene of so much of importance to Christians, Jews and Muslims alike over past millennia seemed to me a shining beacon of human potential and effort to realize that potential. It was no less moving and impressive to visit the ancient Hebrew Wailing Wall and the cemeteries, shrines and monuments to the heroes of that faith, than to visit the site where Christ was born, made his last tortured walk, carrying his cross, and the hill on which he died, and to stand at the foot of the hill from which Mohammed, mounted on his great white horse, flew up to heaven.

The Israelis took me and my companions to all those places and more, explaining something of each while we walked ancient streets and paths trod over the ages by so many of the authors of civilization's founding and most important beliefs. While I had not been active in any organized church for some years, nonetheless the exposure to Jerusalem, and other parts of the Holy Land - holy to so much of humanity - led to an unmistakable sort of spiritual awakening that drew me back repeatedly to that site, and has never left me. In some not quite explainable way, it gave added importance and impetus to what I was doing, and would have to do, thousands of miles away along the Potomac.

On that first and several subsequent visits to Israel, I was to encounter an assemblage of truly remarkable people, and inspect their splendid hospital system and much of their military. The Army Chief of Staff, the Prime Minister, Rabin, the military governor of the West Bank, the Surgeon General and a host of others took the time to meet with me, often privately.

Their intelligence gathering system is so expert that they knew everything about me personally: my military career, my 'brainwashing' studies, my long acquaintance with our President and Secretary of Defense, and probably much else that was long forgotten. Naturally I assumed that my ready access to the top power structure was due to their assumption that I would carry back to my own masters the ideas and desires they wished to communicate, rather than because of any intrinsic importance I might have.

To some extent that was true, yet none of the powerful men who talked to me "lobbied" me for specific goals. Instead, they seemed eager that we understand them and identify their struggles with our own, their dedication to our founding political principles with theirs, and their enormous efforts to carve a modern nation out of an ancient, backward desert region with the early days in North America, where settlers and frontiersmen battled great dangers and distances to establish our own new nation. There was never any talk of military assistance or foreign aid.

The subject of my interviews with the almighty always included sometimes extensive references to their healthcare system. The Prime Minister got around to it after a long discussion of hostages in the hands of terrorists. He noted our government's oft-repeated assertion that we would not negotiate for the return of Americans held hostage by hostile groups, and told me that his government could not agree with that. He cited several instances during which his people's negotiations had succeeded, but added that when they did not, his military took very decisive, often violent action. That fact, he assured me, gave their negotiations much more credibility.

Both Rabin and the Surgeon General took some pains to describe their hospital system. It had been designed and refined in response to the relentless hostility of their Arab neighbors in the entire region, many of whom openly continued to declare their determination to wipe out the Jewish state, as they had done since its founding.

Israel's repeated wars had turned the country into a special kind of armed camp. This was evident just walking through Jerusalem especially, but also Tel Aviv and other cities. One commonly saw young Israeli soldiers who were on leave or just day passes from their units. They were always in uniform, fully armed, and always with at least a few other soldiers.

Outside the cities, in the Kibbutz's I visited, there were few soldiers, but always some, and arms rooms were part of the little communities, as were well-dug fortified bomb shelters and emergency medical spaces. No one made much of a point of these things; they were a simple fact of everyday life that everyone took for granted.

Israel's hospitals, distributed carefully throughout the country, were very much like our own. They were clean, well-staffed, and equipped with good quality, modern medical gear. Unlike hospitals in this country, however, every hospital in Israel had a much more extensive emergency suite than the day-to-day run of injuries and acute medical situations called far. Every bed had fluids and medical gasses, instruments in sterile packs, and a variety of splints and bandages at its side. The pride of the mostly young soldiers, many of them adolescent boys and girls, as they showed me these things was palpable, and touching.

In the mid-1980s, most of the world was concerned with the potential for nuclear holocaust, but not much attention was being paid to chemical and bacteriological weapons, at least as any kind of immediate threat. Except for the Israelis. They had long since recognized that chemicals and germs were the 'poor man's nukes.' Much cheaper and easier to produce, and far easier to conceal and deliver upon an enemy, they were believed to be agents that the more fanatic among their surrounding enemies were certain, sooner or later, to crank into their plans for the extermination of Israel.

What's more, with no intention of glamorizing or glorifying the skills of Israel's Mossad, it is probably safe to assume that their agents had already found evidence, in the Arab countries they regularly penetrated, that such weapons were under development and were intended, one day, for them.

Thus it was that every hospital I inspected in that troubled land had, in addition to conventional back-up systems for electrical power and water, as well as waste disposal, and special security posts, a substantial facility and plan for decontamination of large numbers of people smeared with chemicals or bacteria. Such unfortunates cannot, no matter how grievous their injuries, be allowed inside a hospital until they are thoroughly cleaned up, or every patient already there, and the facility itself, are in great danger.

Hospital decontamination stations were generally situated, below ground in a covered trench about 8 feet deep, or above it in long, low structures in the parking lot close to the entrance. They consisted of a series of rooms, first for removing and destroying all clothing, then for massive flushing with water and ordinary soap, then, if necessary, with appropriate special antidotes like Clorox or other appropriate agents, and finally for drying and re-clothing victims. A secure perimeter could be set up around the hospital to make sure that casualties could not get in without being funneled first through the decontamination station. The process could accommodate people on stretchers.

Given that hordes of disorderly, panicked people including both the unhurt and the 'walking wounded' tend to descend on any available hospital or clinic following both natural and man-made disasters, the Israeli-designed decontamination preparations made excellent sense to me, and started me thinking about what we might do at home to prepare for the unspeakable.

Several problems immediately jumped to mind. The first was our own history of Civil Defense preparedness. Shortly after the end of WWII, and especially after the Soviets developed nuclear weapons, a little-known program was begun across the US to prepare public hospitals to deal with casualties that could result from weapons of mass destruction. As far as I know, no one set up decontamination stations, but County hospitals across America were given supplies to be kept in standby status for big trouble.

The supplies, in large wooden crates intended to be tucked away in hospital basements and utility areas, included stretchers, blankets, bandages, splints, airways, other equipment common in medical emergency use, disinfectants, and a small variety of drugs including anesthetics, antibiotics, I.V. fluids, and some narcotics. All perfectly sensible and needed in acute care settings. Should a nuclear bomb or other diabolical device go off anywhere near the hospital, the crates were to be torn open, the precious contents extracted and put to good use treating the wounded citizenry.

All of this enormously costly enterprise was undoubtedly dreamed up in the very office I now occupied in the Pentagon, Civil Defense having been banished to its far more modest spaces in the basement. Some of the stuff was undoubtedly excess military supplies no longer needed, but it all had to be sorted, crated, and delivered.

Among the unintended consequences (rule number one of great government schemes!) were the prompt rifling of the crate contents and theft of the narcotics and anesthetics, the pilfering of much of the rest, particularly blankets and saleable equipment, and sometimes even the crates. Little was heard about that program, and within a few years even most hospital officials did not know it had existed.

Other problems predictably emerged. The 'out-dates' on all the fluids and other supplies expired. Funding for replacement and maintenance was never forthcoming. The vulnerable citizenry lost interest and reopened its swimming pools, formerly roofed over as bomb shelters.

It occurred to me as well that our climate, in much of the US during much of every year, made duplication of the Israeli system impractical. No open, tent-style decontamination shelters could possibly function, even if there were room, in Chicago or Boston or Denver in the cold season. And the political climate, especially after the Cold War was declared over, would never permit it.

In consequence, nowhere in this country, as this new century (of peace?) bursts forth, nowhere in America can we clean up - decontaminate - any substantial number of people. If, therefore, even a simple 'demonstration' event involving chemical or biological agents perpetrated by one of the world's crazies should take place, it will be catastrophic. People will just have to die, without hospitals now contaminated or medical people now also poisoned. Maybe only in Philadelphia. Or New York. Can't possibly happen, can it? How about San Francisco?

That first visit to Israel was certainly instructive. I returned to the Pentagon a bit dismayed by possible catastrophes, but full of hope for the splendor of the human spirit exemplified by many of those I met in that little, troubled land, and more determined than ever to restore combat readiness to our military medical forces.

My superb lieutenants in the Quality Assurance office had done well indeed. Now, in addition to workable retrospective reviews of patients' records taking place in all our hospitals, and efforts to ensure that all military physicians had a license to practice, a growing attention to professional credentials was taking hold. Credentials Committees were formed in all military hospitals, charged with examining and verifying each physician's documentation of his training through medical school, internship and residencies in the specialty areas. In addition, records of service elsewhere before arriving at the current hospital were examined and verified.

This exercise created a huge additional workload on the hospital staff, and set off a blizzard of correspondence to medical schools and hospitals all over the country. Curiously enough, most doctors did not keep a neat, organized file of all their diplomas, certificates, licenses and other pertinent documents up until that time. But they do now. In any event, it allowed us to demonstrate that we had, generally, a higher percentage of fully trained and certified specialists in our military hospitals than existed even in the finest civilian institutions.

One particularly rewarding aspect of my exalted position as a senior DoD official was the recurring opportunity to bestow military decorations on members of my staff. Generally these had been recommended by previous commanders, before the staffer came to work in the Pentagon, and they often resulted from truly outstanding performance. I made it a practice to have impending awards ceremonies publicized well in advance, and made it clear that every member of the staff of nearly a hundred people, including secretaries and interns, was strongly urged to attend.

The military award system, well-known to all, is nothing if not cumbersome and slow. Sometimes the recipient of a medal did not know for certain that the nomination for it was approved 'all the way up the line,' for many months, since many levels of command had to approve it and send it on. Its arrival, then, since it came to me rather than to the person being honored, could be something of a surprise, when that person was instructed to bring his wife and children, and any other available relative or close friend, to a ceremony in my office on a given date. We always made certain that the family was going to be in town, before setting such dates.

On such occasions, my office was literally packed with people from our own staff as well, often, as others who knew the honoree. At the appointed moment, the officer to be decorated was escorted, with his wife and kids, to a specially prepared spot, flanked by flags and with a small podium.

The opportunity to deliver a speech was one I never passed up. It was a special joy to have before me this captive audience of truly superior men and women who had dedicated their adult lives to serving their country. These occasions, singling out one of their number for special recognition and commendation, were an opportunity for me to recognize not just the recipient of the award (which never includes money or extra vacation time, as it often does in industry) but also the group in which he worked. I always described the special contribution they made to our overall mission, how it fit in to what I saw as the 'big picture,' what I understood to be the goals of the President and the SecDef, and what an enormous privilege it was for us to be responsible for this holiest of military acts: the preservation of the lives and limbs of our finest young men and women.

My objectives in all of this were complex. First, it was evident to me that following some years of eroding respect for the armed forces and steadily diminishing financial support for them by both the White House staff and many in the Congress, the President was determined to revitalize the military, building up its strength, its financing, and its recognition as a vital part of the Republic in the minds of the people. He did this in small ways and large, requesting growth in the budget, openly listening to his senior military advisors, and even returning the salutes of his guards when he left his airplane, which a number of us had encouraged him to do.

In addition, without being maudlin or corny, I wanted to stimulate in each of my officers, regardless of the Service they came from, renewed pride in their status and their uniforms. In the years before Reagan, few people in the Pentagon ever even wore their uniforms, which I saw as a kind of denial similar to that of Jimmy Carter, a Naval Academy graduate who acted like he'd never heard of the place!

Weinberger let it be known, when he took office, that uniforms were no longer "out," and in dealings with military people, from the lowliest to the mighty Chiefs, he dealt with them graciously and respectfully, which I doubt any previous Secretary had ever done, never in the slightest way indicating the kind of "we - they" attitudes that had prevailed in the past.

I took my cues from my bosses, and invariably treated all my uniformed people with respect and dignity - even the little Army spy with the bunny rabbit slippers and teddy bears. That unnerved him, I'm sure.

My 'decoration' ceremonies took place about every six weeks, and since we also served refreshments, they became quite popular. In addition, people seemed to like getting the word directly from the boss, hearing that what they were doing was incredibly important and that they were doing it well. Since I really believed this, so did they. Each speech was admirably short - five to ten minutes - and the formalities followed.

The audience was called to attention by my military assistant, who then, as tradition called for, announced, "Attention to Orders!" She then read the official order, starting with the letterhead and date, outlining the circumstances of the award, and ending, generally, with the signature of the Secretary of the Army, or Navy, or Air Force.

Maintaining my best military posture, I would walk up to the person getting the medal, and while never taking my eyes from his - or hers - take the medal handed to me by the aide, pin it on the proper place on the uniform, take a step backward, and extend my hand in a congratulatory handshake. The recipient was invited to say a word, which most did, while avoiding a long list of Academy Award thank you's, whereupon we would give the spouse a bouquet of flowers, and the medal-holder the rest of the day off.

These occasions, even more than my first-thing-in-the-morning meetings every day with my senior staff, while without the give and take of our monthly all-hands staff meetings, still gave most people the feeling that they pretty much knew what was going on, and more importantly, why. One thing I was determined to do was dispel the feeling, once quite prevalent, that assignment to the DoD staff was an impediment to further advancement within one's own branch of service.

Over those years, one of the people I decorated was Jim Zimble, the senior Navy officer who had served us well investigating the Marine Barracks disaster in Lebanon. He was recruited into my office, served well there, and ultimately became the Navy Surgeon General.

Another was an outstanding nurse, Nancy Adams, then a Lieutenant Colonel in the Army. She came highly recommended and soon outperformed her recommendations by far. Later, after leaving us and continuing to excel, she became the first Nurse Corps officer to command the Army's major hospital in El Paso. Today she is a two star general commanding Tripler Army Medical Center in Hawaii - also a first. Tripler was the first military medical center to score a perfect 100% when inspected by the Joint Commission on Accreditation of Health-care Organizations. Nancy did that. People are talking about her for the post of Army Surgeon General - never before held by a non-physician.

Thanks to those people and others who worked with us in Health Affairs, the old worries about a DoD assignment being the 'kiss of death' rapidly disappeared. Jarrett Clinton was a special, spectacularly successful graduate. As a Rear Admiral, he became the officer in charge of the southeastern US sector of the Public Health Service, served for a prolonged period as Surgeon General while the Clinton administration searched for a suitably politically correct minority officer for that now impotent, totally politicized post that Chick Koop so effectively, for a while, made into a bully pulpit. Today, Jarrett serves as Acting Assistant Secretary of Defense, Health Affairs, my old job.

My new Israeli friends and medical colleagues, during my travels there, had been very forthright about the hostility and intransigence displayed by their Arab neighbors, except for the Jordanians. While the two countries had fought a brief but serious war some years before, resulting in the ousting of the Jordanians controlling East Jerusalem and the West Bank, there seemed to be surprisingly little residual antagonism from that clash.

During a long visit with the powerful, impressive, exceedingly bright Israeli Army general who was the military governor of the largely Palestinian West Bank, I was surprised when he told me quite frankly that the public health situation there was poor. He said that he hoped the US could give more financial and military assistance to the Jordanians, who provided most of the health care in the area but needed support from outside to do it properly. His government, he told me, could not afford to pump money into the area for that purpose, and Jordan was itself the poorest country in the region.

He told me with the sometimes surprising candor I had come to expect from senior Israeli military officers, that the pro-Israel lobby in the US mistakenly opposed aid to any Arab country, but Jordan was 'different' from the others and deserved our aid.

My next trip, not long after the visit to Israel, was therefore to Jordan. It was true that Congress had refused to pass legislation to support the President's promise to King Hussein to increase our military assistance, in spite of Hussein's consistent efforts to bring about greater amity between his Arab brethren and the Jewish state, and I wanted to see for myself what the situation was there.

The Jordanians welcomed my little group of medical people with pomp and circumstance befitting the arrival of a crowned head of state, when we stepped off our plane from Europe. We were delivered to Amman's most luxurious hotel by an unusually large military procession of cars filled with heavily armed soldiers, and ceremoniously ushered in to a lavish suite of rooms. Wherever we traveled in that ancient land, we were so escorted, and always met by a formal welcoming party of high-level Jordanian officers.

Some of the staff at the American embassy expressed great, somewhat surprising enthusiasm over our visit, noting that it was often not very easy to maintain friendly relations with the Jordanians when promises of assistance from our President were repeatedly repudiated by our Congress. This was consistent with attitudes I found in many countries, not just in the Middle East, who believed that our head of state, like their own, surely had powers far exceeding those of the legislature, and were often confused about how our government actually worked.

The routine, when visiting hospitals both there and in other Mideast countries, was elaborate. After being met at the door to an institution, we would be led to an enormous reception hall by a pair of huge men who I was certain were eunuchs, outfitted in elaborate vests and billowing pants and carrying large, elaborate silver chalices containing burning incense.

The reception rooms were huge spaces, completely empty except for the largest, most elegant oriental carpets I had ever seen, and a continuous row of upholstered chairs lined up side by side around the entire four sides of the hall. After being seated, we were offered the tiny cups of pungent, spiced hot tea that at first tasted a little like paregoric, a common remedy once but no longer much used in our country for diarrhea control, that was concocted from an alcoholic mixture of opium and camphor. The taste grew on one after repeated such exercises. The tea, of course, was strictly herbal.

What followed was an exchange of largely meaningless pleasantries about the trip, the weather, and the excellent tea, and after a suitable restful pause, an invitation to tour the facility. The Jordanians were actually pretty relaxed about this, but the Saudis, I was to discover later, were far more formal, rigid and ritualistic.

Jordan's Surgeon General proved to be a truly remarkable cardiac surgeon, trained under DeBakey in this country. Lieutenant General Daoud Hanania was a small, ebullient, genuinely warm and friendly man who was the first in the Arab world to perform a heart transplant, and later the first to do so on a child.

Following successful bypass surgery on the Sultan of Oman, that grateful royal patient gave him a gift: a complete, state of the art, fully equipped hospital designed solely to perform every variety of heart surgery. It was built next to the main building of the King Hussein Medical Center, and contained five separate operating amphitheaters, all connected through television monitors to Hanania's office in the building. He customarily began each morning's surgery in each of the five operating rooms in sequence, leaving each to start the next and carry it through far enough that the surgical residents could finish and close up. When he had done the fifth one, he retreated to his office, watched the television monitors to check on progress, and talked briefly with the surgeons still at work.

This great good, courageous man honored me profoundly by becoming, almost instantly, a warm and affectionate friend, whose friendship was to increase steadily over the ensuing five years. I shall never forget standing beside him on a hillside overlooking the Jordan River, where the army of King Hussein actually defeated an Israeli force during their war. With tears coursing down his cheeks, he pointed to a cluster of buildings just visible on the far, western bank of that river, in the valley near Hebron, now Israeli territory, and told me that had been his family's home, where he had been raised.

On that first visit, we commiserated about the resistance among our lawmakers to extending aid to Jordan, evidently in the mistaken belief that this small country was part of the fanatic Arab cabal whose hatred for the Jewish state was unrelenting. In truth, the Jordanians under Hussein, in spite of previous battles in Jerusalem and the Jordan Valley, harbored fewer feelings of antagonism toward the Jews than did any other Arab country, and the King had been a voice of reason and moderation over the years.

Hanania was the King's personal physician and the country's acknowledged medical leader, both for civilians and the military. He traveled with his monarch wherever the king went, frequently to various places in the United States. Both these men harbored genuinely warm, admiring feelings for our country, and attempted to introduce many of our beliefs and practices among their own people. The king's wife was the daughter of the former Administrator of the Federal Aviation Administration, and Daoud had sent his children to this country to college.

I was able to convey to Hanania and through him the King, President Reagan's severe personal disappointment at Congress' refusal to confirm his promises of aid to Jordan, and decided on a scheme that could partially offset this failure.

What I had in mind was a seemingly small thing that we could do without seeking permission from Capital Hill, that would bear with it great symbolic importance and serve as a genuine sign of our concern and regard for Hussein's unflagging efforts to calm the troubled waters - or better, sands - of that tumultuous region.

Well aware of the extent and refinement of medical institutions and programs in the U.S., Daoud had lamented the great gap between the military and civilian medical systems in his country. The Jordanian armed forces were an offshoot of the British Army, formed and trained by the officers trained at Britain's Sandhurst, and the legendary sergeants of British lore, not to mention the Arab Legion and Lawrence of Arabia. This heritage was clearly evident in the appearance, behavior and discipline of the troops and their leaders, and carried over into their army medical department.

In general, the military medical personnel and equipment were far superior to what the struggling civilian health ministry was able to provide for the general population. The public hospitals were closer to Third World standards - crowded, not always clean, understaffed and ill-equipped. This was true in spite of the fact that there were a fair number of private medical practitioners, and most of the country's doctors had been trained in good European and American medical schools.

Quite commonly in medically under-developed countries, one important element of modern medicine is woefully inadequate - witness the single working microscope I could find in the largest military hospital in the Philippines. That missing element is clinical laboratories and trained pathologists and technicians. Even in their splendid new cardiac surgery hospital, the Jordanians struggled along with minimal laboratory and clinical pathology services. The civilian hospitals were even worse.

My scheme, for which I needed no special approval outside the Pentagon, was to select a fairly senior, experienced pathologist-M.D., with an adventurous nature and administrative skills, and a small crew of like-minded pathology lab technician-soldiers, and send them off for a year of special medical training and experience in the Middle East. Many of our existing contingency plans, always under development in the bowels of the big 5-sided building, contemplated deployments to that troubled area of the world, and we needed to know much more than we did about the health problems and hazards that existed there.

We had no trouble at all finding recruits for the mission. Shortly after returning to the States we were able to assemble a fine team that promptly flew off to the King Hussein Medical Center in Jordan, and set to work putting a modern, effective pathology service in place. Since the whole thing only cost a tiny fraction of even the smallest usual kind of military assistance program, it attracted no attention whatever, and paid enormous dividends of good will.

The other part of the scheme to make up for our failed promises was to offer my experiences as former health director in California - a far larger 'country' than

Jordan! - to assist my friend Hanania to develop a more closely blended public health and military health system, to elevate the quality of care generally and even to offset its cost, at least partially, by a tiny levy on all Jordanian citizens. The King soon appointed Daoud to be the overall supervisor of all the country's medical care and services, and the slow, difficult process began. It has always bothered me some that with just a fraction of what we give to Israel every year in aid, we could have advanced the state of medicine in Jordan by a century.

This experience, as well as similar ones in places like Tunisia, Egypt, sub-Saharan Africa, and the tiny third world countries just south of the Rio Grand and into South America taught me what I firmly believe are great truths. Those truths have to do with the universal human longing for a decent level of health - not just health care, but health itself. Also with our own country's tremendous, unrealized potential for satisfying this worldwide longing and desperate need.

Everywhere I traveled during my six years in the Pentagon, to nearly two score countries where I met with the leading medical people in each one, from the most primitive to the most medically sophisticated, it was evident that more than any other professional group, the world's health care workers speak the same language, cherish the same ideals, pursue the same goals. This is not nearly so true among business people, engineers, economists and bean counters, and certainly not among politicians.

What's more, common people in most countries understand poorly if at all the arguments and positions of politicians and economists, but no trouble understanding that health measures keep babies and young mothers and old people alive, keep sick children from wasting away with diarrhea, young adults from dying, still young, from Aids, and whole communities from struggling with the fatal fevers of malaria. Much of the earth's population dies from avoidable and treatable ailments, like cholera and dysentery, even measles and tuberculosis, none of which matters much at all on this soil where we Americans, through mere chance, happen to exist.

It is striking to find that physicians occupy high levels within the power structure in many countries, and invariably do so in most underdeveloped ones. This should be no surprise, I guess, since medical education is costly and not generally available at all in poor nations, so the sons and daughters of the wealthy and powerful travel to Europe and America. While they learn the principles and practices of science abroad, much of what they have learned is not possible to apply when they get home. Nonetheless they go to work, and while they maintain many of their relationships with those who lead their countries' political and economic policies and activities, they can and often do influence the paths their countries take.

It seems obvious, then, that we can do good for suffering humanity by exporting more of our medical know-how, along with our tons of 'outdated' medical equipment and supplies that are still centuries better than what is available over most of the planet. We can also influence the developing nations struggling up from the scientific dark ages, politically, in directions we hold to be dear, and beneficial to mankind, like those ideas set forth in our founding documents.

This probably sounds hopelessly idealistic and utopian. But I am no starry eyed romantic world-level socialist dreaming of sharing the wealth with all of humanity and thus wiping out all of Mary Baker Eddy's 'sin, sickness and death,' all violence and greed and cupidity ensuring freedom from all hardship and war, and some kind of paradise on earth. God alone can do that, in His own good time. Which has yet to be announced.

This country cannot police, or feed, or guarantee the health of the rest of the world. It is, however, in the strongest position of any country in history to influence humanity in the direction of peace and prosperity, and I submit that it is through the judicious export and exploitation of health knowledge, health practices, and health materiel that we could exert the most powerful possible influence in that direction.

Even the communist dictator in Cuba, which has little of material value to export, has assiduously exported health care workers and elementary school teachers to poorer countries to earn their support. We could do the same on a scale ten thousand times as large, for a tiny fraction of what we spend in a single year's presidential campaigns, or the cost of a single nuclear carrier.

William E. Mayer, M.D.

Brainwashing, Drunks & Madness

William E. Mayer, M.D.

CHAPTER 19

FINAL BATTLES

The idea of centralizing medical planning and budgeting in the Office of Health Affairs was slow to catch on. It was to take several years of talking about it with the Surgeons General and other Assistant Secretaries in DoD before matters finally came to a head. There were several 'big ticket' items that cut across Service lines, required huge amounts of money and effort, and became items of serious interest to the Congress, which actually helped me to make the case.

One of these was the development of a standardized computerized data system that could be used in all military hospitals worldwide. Not too many years before, the Navy maintained a unique Health Record for every person in that service. It consisted of a loose-leaf pad of forms measuring about eleven inches long by four inches wide, held together at the top by removable brads that were commonly used to hold perforated pages together. The front and back covers were thin cardboard. Every sailor and officer had his own Health Record, kept for him in the local hospital or clinic and transferred along with him to each new ship or shore assignment.

Every clinic visit or hospitalization was recorded in that pad of long, narrow sheets. Entries regarding the complaint, diagnosis, treatment, medication and disposition were all made chronologically, hand-written, with the most recent on top. Major hospitals kept their own, more detailed records on larger forms, but a summary of the hospital episode was put into the small, portable record that accompanied each man.

This neat little record of a person's medical history, from the first day of active duty to the present, ceased to be useful shortly after WWII. The explosion in medical technology and diagnostic and therapeutic measures made it impossible to put everything down on so small a document. By the time I reached the Pentagon, and actually long before, all the Services were swamped with medical documentation, and the situation cried out for the introduction of electronic data processing.

Back in the early seventies, when MediCare and MediCaid were generating huge amounts of information, mainly for billing and reimbursement purposes, the State of California had contracted with Ross Perot's Electronic Data Systems to do this job for us. We had a huge area on several floors of the Department of Health buildings containing enormous, class-enclosed cabinets with great wheels of magnetic tape spinning inside, on which was recorded every service provided to every eligible recipient of care under those programs, along with the date, place, and provider of care, and the amount of money disbursed to pay for it.

The system, by today's standards, was ponderous and intolerably slow. Users of the data often had to reserve 'time' on the computers for the answers even to rather simple questions ("How many women aged 18 to 24 had delivered babies in San Bernardino County in 1973 that were paid for by MediCal? for example.)

The military was making great strides in data processing, but mostly in connection with major security issues like an air defense system covering the Eastern Seaboard. That computer took up a whole city block. The Veterans Administration, with its 168 hospitals around the country, plunged into computerizing its medical activities, thanks to electronics enthusiasts in several of its hospitals, and came up with a number of respectable systems. Unfortunately, because of the VA's dedication to decentralized, largely independent hospital operations, these systems didn't "speak" effectively to one another and recorded limited amounts of information.

We needed a system for hospitals of 20 beds up to a thousand or more beds, in more than a hundred and fifty settings not just in the US but also around the world. The system had to incorporate complex military information about active duty people, as well as different kinds of information about their dependents, retired military folks, and their dependents as well.

The locations, small and large, had to communicate with one another, using the same computer language (there were several in use at that time) without delay. Important parts of the information had to be accessible, as well, to personnel offices for their records, finance and accounting people, and the air evacuation and sea transport systems.

While any number of civilian hospitals had automated part of their medical information and records, there was no data system in existence that could even begin to handle our needs. Several congressional committees became interested in our problem, and one of them - Veterans Affairs - chaired by a gracious, shrewd southern congressman named Sonny Montgomery, became our gadfly and nemesis.

Sonny had for many years made his career and most of his reputation supporting veterans' causes, and had done some really good things, like developing the G.I.Bill. He was a fervent supporter of the VA's "decentralized" hospital system.

Along with that, he had become convinced that the VA's computer system was the finest, most sophisticated on earth. He could not understand that it was not a system at all, but a collection of programs, some quite good but limited in scope, in a score of different hospitals. He decided that the military should simply "adopt" the VA 'system,' since it was in his judgment ready-made, perfectly adequate for our purposes, and we could save untold amounts of money by using it.

Sonny called numerous hearings to advance his idea, pursuing it with a degree of dedication that became overtly obsessive, attacking me personally for my intransigence when I tried, at first patiently but with increasing irritation over the months, to explain that the VA didn't really have a unified system, that it couldn't be adopted - if for no other reason than that most of the programs they had, had simply grown by trial and error and were not documented so couldn't be replicated. He took this to mean that we believed what was good for veterans was not good enough for soldiers - horrors!

This courtly, silver-haired, prototypical Southern gentleman became, for many months, my personal nightmare. Not only did he hold numerous hearings at which my presence was mandatory so that I could be properly and publicly chastised for my thick-headedness, biases, and willingness to waste 'millions' of the taxpayers' dollars. In addition, he personally called me innumerable times, pleading in his characteristic argumentative but superficially reasonable, good ole' boy southern style as if arguing the price of pork bellies, never listening to the facts of the matter.

Whether or not Sonny had any kind of monetary stake in getting me to adopt his scheme, I did not know, but I believed, based on reports of his contacts with computer firms, that he must. In addition, not content to bask in the glory of having provided our heroic veterans with educational subsidies, he clearly wanted to establish his legacy as the father of automation in the field of health care.

This sort of pressure on the Federal Executive Branch by members of the Congress is a fairly frequent occurrence in Washington. It is always rather shocking to discover that it happens without the slightest regard for facts or the actual merits - or downside - of various proposals, like this one. Had we attempted to adopt the VA's medical information automation system(s), we would have expended untold amounts of public treasure in an enterprise that was demonstrably certain to fail, and delayed by months or years the establishment of a useful system of our own, tailored to our needs.

As it was, it took a million dollars and many months just to fashion the RFP - Request for Proposal - to submit to the computer industry for them to look over, price out, design proposals that would cover the myriad requirements involved, and write up firm bids for the government to consider. It was discovered that the care of a single patient, in a complex modern hospital, could generate over a hundred separate bits of information that should be recorded in a single day. Every day!

When this is added to the problem of multiple users of the system, multiple activity locations, cost accounting and personnel administrative information, research data, and coordination of data amongst numerous departments and sections, the task approaches monumental proportions. The RFP itself was over a hundred pages long.

We held the customary 'bidders' conference' in an amphitheater at the Uniformed Services University of the Health Sciences in Bethesda. Several scores of potential bidders showed up, and there was great excitement, seeing representatives of nearly all the major electronic data firms in the country. The meeting lasted several hours. Many questions were raised. Many of the participants expressed great interest and the confidence typical of computer types that they could do this thing, and finally took their copies of the RFP back to their firms eager to compete. The deal was certain to involve hundreds of millions of dollars before it was done. It did just that.

Over the next few weeks, almost all the potential bidders dropped out of the competition, indicating that they didn't think it was possible to fulfill the requirements set forth in the RFP within the limits of the funds available. Several had devoted weeks of effort and thousands of dollars working on their proposals. We began, ourselves, to wonder if we were after something impossible.

Government is often accused of selecting 'lowest bidders' whose product is inferior. In this case, we accepted not only the lowest bid; we took the only bid that came in. It was from a respected company, SAIC, that has been known on occasion to promise more than it could deliver, but their proposal seemed to make sense, and the work began. It involved millions of dollars and was the largest medical automation project ever undertaken. We called it CHCS: the Composite Health Care System.

Many months later, we were able to accept the final plans and begin to implement the program in several different hospitals of differing sizes, the so-called "Beta Sites." Many problems surfaced and had to be overcome, not the least of which was the requirement that all users had to be able to type. A surprising number of our physicians and nurses could not do that, and had to learn.

A major problem, from the outset, was the Congressional prohibition on including the medical history and physical examination findings in the record. This reflected a concern for privacy and the fear that such personal information could be used to the detriment of the patient, even years later. A medical record without a history and physical may be fine for the bean counters, but is ridiculous as a useful instrument in patient care management. The same thing was applied to progress notes.

For a long time we pointed out that, even the handwritten notes in these crucial areas, or dictated summaries in a secretarial pool, used for many years, were no more sure to maintain privacy than information stored electronically. The semi-magical aura surrounding invisible, detailed memories inside computers was responsible for this, so for a number of years the basic elements of medical records had to be written laboriously by hand.

Many medical people write so poorly that I suppose bad penmanship offered some small privacy protection, but that was unintentional. Today, so many people have access to individual medical records in connection with managed care organizations, insurance companies and medical malpractice law firms that those early worriers' fears were proven realistic, but mostly unrealized. The use of passwords, and the enactment of confidentiality laws, has kept privacy violations under control, mostly.

The comprehensive medical data system has for some years been in place in all military treatment facilities, and works reasonably well. As both medical and computer technology rushes onward, it requires constant 'tweaking,' but without it the problems would be unimaginable. Sonny Montgomery continued to grumble for some time after it got going, but finally wandered off to other matters.

While we were engaged in quality assurance and automated data problems, other conflicts were growing. One had to do with drug testing. Drug use and abuse had been growing rapidly, and since the armed forces are a reflection of the rest of our society, they were involved.

The use of mind-altering substances, starting with alcohol, has long been recognized as increasing the inherent dangerousness of operating automobiles and other machinery. Military machinery is particularly dangerous, even to be around, be it tanks, trucks, artillery, bombs, airplanes, rifles, machine guns or battle ships. Unlike the situation of a solitary drunk behind the wheel of his car, a drunken pilot, sailor or soldier is usually working his machinery in the company of others. His equipment, unlike modern cars, is hardly 'user-friendly,' and quite often capable of exploding or burning violently.

Obviously, then, substance abuse cannot be allowed among military people. The over-use or abuse of alcohol, particularly while on duty, has always been a violation of regulations and is generally punished promptly. Unlike most drugs, alcohol makes its presence easily recognizable by its odor, in spite of mouth sprays and Tic Tacs, and most military supervisors are intolerant of the dangers it presents to the groups they supervise.

Many drugs, however, are far more subtle and deceptive in their effects, and the user may not give off any characteristic odor or other distinct sign that something is altering his central nervous system functioning. This is true of many of the so-called "recreational" drugs. In turn, these drugs are mistakenly thought, especially by young people, to be safe to use and essentially harmless. They can, however, even in small doses, produce problems in judgment, spatial orientation, coordination and concentration that can be deadly when operating almost every kind of military equipment.

Based on these simple, common sense kinds of ideas, we concluded that we should take advantage of the wide variety of reliable tests revealing the use of drugs, and start testing all military people. That way, potentially dangerous people could be identified promptly and removed from situations where the safety of their comrades was jeopardized. We could also start them into programs of treatment, to minimize future problems.

Invasion of privacy! Violation of Constitutional guarantees of due process and assumption of guilt! Unwarranted intrusion into personal life! The accusations went on and on. Particularly outspoken were the marijuana advocates, who pointed out that traces of the active ingredient could show up for days or weeks after last use. However, there were others. Including those who insisted that small doses of cocaine actually improved performance, so should be tolerated.

In spite of all the uproar, we instituted random urinalysis of personnel, beginning with those in hazardous settings, but eventually extending to everyone. As expected, the outcry died down, and the military's program rapidly spread throughout industry, especially in transportation.

Related to this anti-drug use campaign, but separate and distinct from it, we decided to adopt a rule raising the legal drinking age for soldiers to 21, as had been done in a growing number of states. Over the years before I came to this powerful medical job with health policy responsibilities for a million or more young Americans, I had been firmly on both sides of this question.

During the first months of the war in Korea, we were not permitted to make beer available to our combat troops, and in the Marine Division this fact was the source of much complaining and discontent. The thinking behind this policy was said to be the fact that so many of our Marines were from 17 to 19 years old and therefore too young to drink.

I shared some of the general contempt for this do-gooder kind of reasoning, and was myself indulging most evenings with a cherished, straight gin 'martini' with my leader, Commander Dick Lawrence. Well aware of the relaxing, brief escape from the stress and horrors of warfare, I was strongly in favor of letting the troops have a little such therapy. Along with just about everyone else, I was indignant that these kids were considered old enough to get killed in battle but too young to drink a bottle of beer. It seemed so unfair!

Accordingly, I joined in the general rejoicing when the first 'beer ration' was announced. Everybody was issued three or four bottles of beer, and one of those unintended consequences instantly showed up. As it turned out, there were many youngsters who didn't want their beer, and found it to be a great trading item for souvenirs or even cash or cigarettes. The Division became a great, happy trading bazaar for a few memorable days. It was during this great celebratory morale-boosting event that one of our amphibious tractors, called 'Ducks,' turned up missing along with its 3-man crew. These three certified heroes were the famed entrepreneur-adventurers who managed, through judicious trading and stealing, to load their Duck with cases of beer and extra diesel, aimed their vehicle-vessel due east, and proceeded to drink themselves into oblivion. All this in mid-winter on the Sea of Japan.

They awoke to find themselves on the sparsely settled western shore of Japan, somewhat short of their original goal of California but far preferable to the Korean peninsula. They explored the frozen beach until they came upon a tiny, remote fishing village whose occupants had never before seen a Caucasian. There they were welcomed, treated almost as visiting royalty, and were fed and housed for many weeks before word of their presence filtered out of the village and investigators arrived to 'rescue' them. The Japanese authorities, marveling over their feat, nonetheless returned them to Korea.

The story soon came out, and eighteen thousand Marines immediately adopted these intrepid explorers as their heroes. Everyone stuck on that miserable, hostile, frozen peninsula felt a grand sense of vicarious victory and glee over the escape, however temporary, of a few of their buddies. They were court-martialed, of course, but given modest punishment. And forbidden to drink any more beer as long as they stayed in Korea.

In subsequent years, I learned a lot about alcohol. By the time I had arrived in Washington and had become director of the National Institute on Alcohol Abuse and Alcoholism, dear old 'N.I.-Triple A,' I had concluded that the brain tissue in young people, which does not reach full cellular maturity until about the early 20s, was particularly vulnerable to all toxins. Alcohol, a protoplasmic (tissue) poison toxic to brain cells, was particularly capable of disrupting brain function in young people, and the 21-year old drinking age rules actually made physiological and medical sense.

Coupled with the growing number of alcohol-related traffic fatalities among teenagers, the physiologic facts of alcohol's effect on young neurons led me to undertake a nationwide crusade to reduce drunk driving among teens. Our statistical analyses showed that the great bulk of such tragedies occurred every spring, at the exact same time as the junior and senior proms.

A number of high schools, often after a drunk-driving death or deaths among students, had designed and instituted student-led programs to minimize or eliminate drinking and driving. Many involved skits dramatizing social situations, poster displays, personal testimonials and contests of various kinds. The kids had created their own version of MADD - Mothers Against Drunk Driving, calling it SADD - Students Against Driving Drunk.

We approached every state's education leaders, encouraging them to initiate a statewide competition among all their high schools to identify the most creative and effective student program to combat student drunk driving. We would underwrite the cost of six or eight students who could put on their school's program, along with two faculty member-chaperones, to travel to Washington. Each of the fifty state teams would make their presentation to all the others, be given tours of the capitol and main monuments and museums, and meet dignitaries like Elizabeth

Dole and the Secretary of the Department of Health & Human Services, Margaret Heckler, and other famous Washington people before returned home in triumph.

We had had fifty takers - one team from every state. We gathered them in a campus-like group of buildings owned by the 4-H Clubs of America, and the kids had a highly emotionally charged, totally wonderful experience. From that 'convention' of bright young people, came a genuine movement across America that has continued to diminish the numbers of teenage drunk driving accidents and fatalities that used to be associated with prom week. It was from that event that the idea of having a 'designated (non-drinking) driver' emerged and grew.

Watching those several hundred eager, bright youngsters, earnestly trying to solve a horrendous problem, convinced me permanently that kids shouldn't drink, and our military kids as well.

When we announced our policy of a 21-year minimum age limit for drinking alcohol, the Service leadership nearly unraveled. All the old arguments re-emerged. Emotional tirades were directed at Health Affairs and its crazy leader. We would kill soldiers by making them leave the post, sometimes driving long distances, just to get a beer. It was unenforceable. It was un-American and unimaginable.

And it became the law. Drunk driving deaths among soldiers dropped, immediately.

Not all my battles in the big building that I had moved to came out nearly as well as the huge new medical data processing system, or the raising of the drinking age. A good example was the battle over the "Jackson Amendment" hospitals. This involved perhaps a half-dozen hospitals, some of them quite large that had been built for the Public Health Service. They harked back to the days when the PHS was responsible for the care of merchant seamen, who had for many years been so important to the nation's growing foreign trade, and had played a major role in the massive sea transportation required to support our troops in Europe and the Pacific during WWII.

Seamen coming to our ports from distant lands also, from time to time, posed the threat of bringing serious infectious and parasitic diseases to our shores. The Public Health Service had long served as a protection against that threat, and the famed Centers for Disease Control in Atlanta had part of its origins in that function. Several large hospitals had been built, particularly in port cities like San Francisco, Seattle and New Orleans as our foreign trade expanded, and the federal government undertook to treat merchant seamen in them. By about 1980, alternative systems developed by shipping companies, and the expansion of other federal medical programs rendered these hospitals redundant, and Congress in its wisdom ordered them closed.

The senior senator from Washington State, Henry "Scoop" Jackson, whose nickname reflected his earlier career as a newspaperman, introduced legislation, which came to be known as the Jackson Amendment since it was tacked on to some other bill. Designed to save those hospitals. It provided that each one could be turned over, at no cost, to any medical group that would keep them operating, be that a group of doctors, or in at least one case the Sisters of Something or Other, who ran other hospitals.

In order to ensure a steady flow of patients and income and legitimize the government's actions in giving away these multi-million dollar institutions, the law also declared that any person in the uniformed services, active or retired, or their families, could elect to go to these hospitals for care, just as they otherwise would go to a military hospital, and the Department of Defense would pay all costs. This was great for military retirees who lived in places where there was no active military hospital, like Seattle, or Houston, and no large numbers of troops to justify building one.

People eligible to get care at the military's expense were already entitled to get it from civilian sources under the CHAMPUS program, but that involved co-payments and deductibles. These new facilities, now called "USTFs" meaning Uniformed Services Treatment Facilities, were essentially free. They proved to be remarkably popular, as reflected by the cost to DoD, which escalated from $24 million the first year to $172 million each year - and rising, after less than five years.

Alarmed by this wholly unforeseen explosion in cost, far beyond even the dramatic inflation of medical expenditures under the CHAMPUS program and in the country generally, we sought to discontinue the program, as provided for in the original legislation.

The reaction was instantaneous and indignant. Hearings were set up in both houses of congress to examine this flagrant violation of the commandment that says once a federal giveaway program is started, it may not be stopped. Senators and congressmen from every state where one of these places was operating demanded that we retreat. Expenses be damned! The medical directors and CEOs of every one of the hospitals assembled at the hearings to denounce our heartlessness and praise their own service to mankind.

The target of the entire outcry was, of course, me. My explanations that the costs were unreasonable and rising, that the huge expenditures contributed nothing of substance to national defense, that they eroded our ability to restore our medical readiness for war, and that they were a wholly unjustified waste of taxpayers' money went unheard and unheeded. The hospitals were "saved," and continue to this day. My one small victory in that otherwise disastrous battle was permission, reluctantly granted, to establish for each of the hospitals a cap on our total reimbursement that would be no larger, each year, than an increase in the official cost of living.

A similar battle, also carried to the hearing rooms in congress but with a somewhat better outcome, involved testing for the AIDS virus. Like all other elements of society in this country and elsewhere, we had been finding cases among military personnel and their families. The disease, surely the most serious, deadly threat to human health emerging in the twentieth century, still not curable nor preventable by any medical measure yet known to science, poses a special kind of threat among soldiers and sailors and airmen.

In even the calmest of peacetimes, the men and women of all the world's armies work with dangerous machinery and equipment, and do so in close proximity, usually, to others. Cuts, scrapes and all manner of injuries, small and large, are a common part of everyday military life, and now posed a threat beyond any that existed before this new infectious agent emerged on the scene. During active operations, be they actual war or the training exercises that must precede it, injuries and wounds increase exponentially in number and seriousness.

By the mid-1980s it was already well established that the disease progressed rapidly when there was an exchange of bodily fluids, but most especially blood. It was also well established that the disease was enjoying explosive distribution among homosexual males and was clearly related to their singular sexual practices. For the most part, there have never been large numbers of active homosexuals busily exchanging bodily fluids within military ranks. Exposure to someone else's blood, however, is not at all uncommon as people work together in a charging tank or a pitching destroyer or aboard an aircraft in turbulent skies.

Much of that kind of bloodletting is relatively minor, in peacetime, but common indeed in armed conflict. Even tiny exchanges of blood from barked knuckles are sufficient to transfer the virus, and when seriously wounded men in battle are being transported and cared for by their comrades or field medics, the chance of exposure to blood is great. It is, therefore, highly desirable to have people doing that kind of thing whose blood does not contain any virus at all, but particularly the deadly one that causes AIDS.

It follows, then, that we should try to eliminate from the ranks anyone who carries the infection, no matter how healthy he seems at the moment, so as to minimize the risk to anyone else. How? Test everybody, obviously. It is true that a negative test one day can change to a positive one soon after, but that is no reason not to do it, not just once but regularly. As is so often true in life, this is no absolute guarantee, but it is the best defense available at this point in history, and we decided we had no choice.

The minute the idea was announced, all hell broke loose. The newly vocal, newly assertive homosexuals (you'll notice I never use the silly term "gay" for these folks; I never met a "merry, lively" homosexual) denounced the military for what they called a sneaky, dishonest campaign to identify, persecute and root out homosexuals in uniform. Their homophilic friends and families, and others, saw the idea of testing as an invasion of privacy, violation of the constitution, bigotry and wholly unjustified.

Despite their earnest attempts to enlist congressional support for their position, no one on the Hill caused us any serious problems about the decision to test, and we began a program. The controversy, however, is typical of what has happened since HIV infection and AIDS burst upon the scene in this country. Despite a long history of advances in public health with enormous benefits to our society, we were suddenly bullied into abandoning some of the simplest basic concepts in infection control in response to a strident minority group whose personal behavior deviates dramatically from the norm. This has endangered the American public.

There is not, and never has been, a coherent national health policy in this great country. Throughout the century, however, there has been broad social and medical acceptance of the fact that there are serious, easily spread communicable diseases: smallpox, typhoid fever, cholera, tuberculosis, syphilis, and what were once considered relatively benign childhood diseases like measles, mumps and chicken pox.

Some of these, notably tuberculosis and syphilis, were long considered so serious as to require segregation or legally mandated, compulsory treatment under threat of arrest and imprisonment. None of these great scourges carried with it the certainty of death, as does AIDS, yet in the absence of effective national medical leadership, no steps have been taken that even approach those taken in the past for such comparatively benign ailments as mumps!

Part of the reason lies in our absurd national reluctance to discuss much of anything about sex, particularly things like the often-flagrant promiscuity of many - perhaps most - adult male homosexuals. This has long been an obstacle to many attempts to reduce other sexually transmitted venereal diseases. Part of the problem has to do with 'political correctness;' it is still considered bad taste to call AIDS a venereal disease, the rationale being that there are other ways, besides copulation, to get it. Using that standard, we would have to call gonorrhea an unintentional, accidental bacteria-induced urinary tract inflammation or some other nonsensical euphemism.

In all other venereal (and some non-venereal) communicable infectious diseases, it has long been conventional medical practice to attempt to identify and warn or treat "contacts" of the infected person, to protect them and impede further spread of the infection. Not so with AIDS. For some bizarre reason, absolute secrecy about cases, regardless of how many others they may infect, is the practice, flying in the face of common sense.

Even the staid, proper national treasure called the Red Cross, which in reality is the world's biggest and most profitable purveyor of human blood - its principal enterprise, far outstripping its highly (self-) praised humanitarian activities like bringing coffee to our fighting men abroad - has willingly taken part in this extraordinary departure from basic public health and preventive medicine. It occasioned one of my most serious battles.

The American Red Cross has for many years relied heavily on blood donation drives on military installations. The young people serving in uniform have given far more blood than has come back for their benefit, and what does come back, we pay for, more than it would cost to collect it ourselves. The pressure on young soldiers to give blood, like the pressure to contribute to 'voluntary' charity drives, is sometimes quite coercive, if only unofficially so.

When AIDS became a recognized problem, and transfusions had been identified as the causative agent in some patients, especially hemophiliacs, the Red Cross started testing the blood it was collecting. When they found a donated unit to be infected with HIV they threw it out, and told no one. At first, they didn't even tell the infected donor! This remarkable departure from common medical practice and simple decency, was explained as protection against eroding their blood donor base if the word got out that sometimes they inadvertently collected infected blood.

My responsibility as a physician was to every individual soldier under my care, which was all of them whatever color suits they wore. It was my belief that if any one of these youngsters was found to have a fatal, incurable communicable disease, he - and we, his medical support people - needed to know that, and promptly. Only then could we assure him of proper medical care, and assure that his comrades were not jeopardized.

I so informed the leadership of the great blood-collecting and -selling organization, whose answer was a flat "No way!" They told me they couldn't possibly violate their strict confidentiality rules, or it could ruin their program (read "business.")

After 24 hours of pondering this incredible, supposedly non-negotiable refusal to conform to basic public health and preventive medicine principles and practices, I returned to the Red Cross offices, without an appointment! Upon my arrival, I offered them an alternative. In return for their immediate notification of the preventive medicine officer on every post of the name and unit of any military blood donor testing positive for HIV infection, we would grant them continued access to our installations for their blood drives, which otherwise ended now.

They did not even need 24 hours to ponder, but more like a half hour. They then agreed to my proposal. Blood drives continued, and some early HIV cases were identified for treatment, well before symptoms appeared to indicate an advanced infectious state.

All this took place long before my friend Elizabeth Dole, who had helped me some years before in my project to reduce teenage drunk driving, had taken charge of the Red Cross, and no doubt she was never told of our little battle. Losers in such disputes have a remarkable inability to recall them at all.

When situations like the battle with the Red Cross arose, I mentioned them at Secretary Weinberger's daily morning meeting, especially if there were any possibility at all that some reference to them might (or already had) appeared in the press and shown up in the 'Early Bird' media summary for that day. After carefully observing the behavior of all who attended those meetings, it became clear to me that there were certain unspoken but very definite rules that had to be followed. First, the subject one brought up had to be really important enough for that high-powered group to be made to listen to. There was no small talk. Second, one had to be brief, clear, and factual and get quickly to the point. Finally, if there was a problem, one had to have one or more solutions to propose.

Cap Weinberger was remarkable in his ability to focus in on whatever subject came up. He was invariably attentive, extremely quick to grasp the essence of sometimes extraordinarily complex issues, and while he was always thoughtful and rather formal and polite when addressing any of us directly, he was very decisive. In five years of daily meetings involving, often, weighty matters of defense policy, international affairs and sometimes bloody confrontations with the Congress, he never appeared to be flustered, uncertain, or emotionally reactive in any way. He could be quite unmistakably angry about some situation, but he didn't dramatize his feelings or sound off.

In this, he resembled his boss, the President, except that, unlike Ronald Reagan, he was not given to making small jokes or telling humorous anecdotes to illustrate or reinforce a point. Reagan did that more masterfully than any major public figure before or since his time, and to great effect. It put some people off, infuriated his adversaries, disarmed many who had intended to be antagonistic, and charmed most others. His great good humor and good-natured approach to life generally, while seated in the most powerful position on earth, had the effect of needling the aura of self-importance that so permeates Washington.

Cap's approach was not without humor, but he possessed a kind of dignified gravity that was striking, and his authority and powerful sense of purpose and mission were unmistakable. After seeing him function in a multitude of difficult, challenging situations over my five years as his assistant, I came away aware that I had been in the presence of a truly great man. Would that there were more like him in the crucial top jobs in our government!

After sizing up my role in the daily coming together of the most powerful officials in the country's defense establishment, and learning the 'rules of engagement' that prevailed in those meetings, I began to conduct my campaign to improve the antiquated, fragmented, internally antagonistic and dysfunctional health care system of the US Armed Forces. Grandiose? Perhaps. But if not me, who? If not now, when?

As it turned out, my goals were not fully achievable, but I knew that going in. Some improvement was possible, and was accomplished, but many of the problems I faced persist to this day.

It was in those daily morning meetings with Cap and the senior staff that my main objectives were pursued. The first was the campaign to centralize planning and budgeting for military medicine in my office. Because the services "hid" many medical budget items in other parts of their individual budgets, it necessitated digging up all those hidden expenditures, like the huge costs of warehousing and transporting major medical elements, and including them in what would ultimately become a total DoD medical budget.

The Services' budgeteers and planners were highly resistant to this, since it meant pulling parts of their logistical budgets out, with a possible loss of some important stashes of money. The only way to get them to do this, it seemed to me, was to convince the Service Secretaries, all of whom attended the early morning meetings, that they had to order their military subordinates to comply. This in turn meant convincing the SecDef that it was the right thing to do, so he in turn would declare that it should be done. It took me at least three years of morning meetings to put that system in place, but at last it was done, and the DoD Directive ordering it was published.

It was about this time that Admiral William Crowe, a brilliant officer who collected military headgear that was arrayed over an entire wall of his office when he was CNO - Chief of Naval Operations - head of the Navy, summoned me to his office for a 'friendly chat.' He called me by my first name and invited me to call him Bill, and we first exchanged small talk while coffee was served.

Then he got down to the real reason for the visit. In essence, what he said was that the power structure in the Pentagon, mainly the Joint Chiefs and the Service Secretaries, had gotten the impression that Cap Weinberger would do anything, concerning the military medical system, that I asked him to do. That, in turn, threatened some other, serious Service priorities, like the 600-ship Navy, for example. He simply wanted, he said, to caution me about the antagonism this could arouse among "the leadership."

I gave him my little sermon about man, not machinery, being the 'ultimate weapon,' more elaborate, complex, delicate and irreplaceable than even the smartest weapon or big bomb. That most effective (and priceless) weapon needed continuous, costly, exquisitely refined maintenance, and it had been sadly and unconscionably - and stupidly - neglected for many years and many budget cycles.

But, I hastened to assure him, I really did appreciate his good advice, and would exercise extreme care in the future to avoid any appearance of being a special pet of the Secretary, and cultivate an air of humility. He smiled at that, and we parted in wholly friendly fashion.

Meanwhile, we developed a fairly realistic 'medical budget,' and the truth of the old saying to the effect that unless you controlled the money, you didn't really control anything, soon proved to be true. It came about after the launching of the great ship "Mercy," the largest, most splendid hospital ship the world had ever seen.

The USNS Mercy began life as an enormous oil tanker, by only a few feet in girth the second largest supertanker ever built. Longer than three football fields placed end to end, it was just able to traverse the Panama Canal with only inches to spare on each side when going through the locks. It had the conventional double hull of great tankers, with the space between the inner and outer hull a watertight compartment that could be filled with seawater to serve as ballast when the main space was empty of oil.

A far cry from my old ship, the Repose, this one was twice as long, much wider, faster, and had a thousand beds, more than a hundred of them comparable to those in a modern emergency suite and equipped for doing extensive surgical procedures. It had, in addition, twelve state of the art surgical operating rooms equipped at least as well as those in any of the country's finest metropolitan hospitals. The laboratory and X-Ray spaces were comparably equipped, and the latest CAT-Scan was included.

The earliest hospital ships were designed and thought of as sea-going ambulances, for the most part. As they evolved through the Second World War, several operating rooms and enlarged emergency treatment spaces were added, but there had never before been anything like the Mercy. The Repose, for example, had nearly 900 beds crammed into less than half the space, many of them in narrow triple-deck bunks with barely enough room between the tiers to allow a nurse (no fat ones) to walk by and try to give care. There were double deck bunks for some of the crew on the Mercy, and for less serious patients, but plenty of room for nursing care.

A relatively spacious helicopter landing platform was built atop the main deck, and a large port was cut through the hulls near the water line to allow relatively easy access to small boats bearing the wounded.

In all respects, the new sea-going hospitals (one more was built) were designed to be thoroughly modern medical facilities unsurpassed by even the newest academic medical centers anywhere, and far better equipped to deal with large numbers of acute, serious cases. Their mission had changed as well. In no sense were they intended to be transport vehicles. They were, instead, to take up a position close to areas of conflict and settle in, to provide tertiary - definitive - care of the kind and quality previously available only within the continental United States.

The opportunity to demonstrate this soon appeared.

The Philippines had shed its corrupt Marcos government and Mrs. Aquino had been elected. She had come to visit President Reagan, who had pledged all possible aid to her needy country, and the Mercy perfectly fit the bill for the task. The President, urged on by Secretary Weinberger, promised that the great ship's first mission would be to extend the miracle of modern medicine to remote, deprived areas of her country. It became my job to make that happen.

The ship had finished its sea trials, and was ready to go. There was, however, no medical staff. Since the mission would not be, exactly, a naval 'operation,' it seemed to me a golden opportunity to advance my belief in joint military operations, by drawing equally from among the military departments to construct the medical, nursing, and support staffs. The Navy objected strenuously; this was a NAVY mission they insisted!

I fully agreed: moving the great ship to the Philippines was indeed an operation only the Navy could accomplish. It would also be terribly costly; the expenses of such a major voyage were not contemplated at budget time and would come out of their hide. Were they to pull doctors, nurses and corpsmen sufficient to man the hospital from their shore bases, it would cost them a fortune in funds for temporary help for the two months or more that their own people would be afloat. I would be happy to solve that financial problem, by providing soldiers, airmen, and Public Health Service people to fill out the hospital staff on the ship.

The Navy finance people took only a short time to see the wisdom in this scheme, and convinced the Navy line, thus ensuring the establishment of the military's first major, truly joint, medical enterprise.

Mercy's medical staff treated some 63,000 ailing Filipinos during their two months in and around islands remote from Manila. Countless orthopedic miracles were performed on club feet, thousands of diseased teeth were treated or removed, hundreds of cleft palates and lips were repaired, numerous older people regained their sight when their cataracts were removed, and scores of women lost fibroid and other tumors to our surgeons' scalpels. Many or most of the people treated would otherwise never have been freed from what would have been lifelong incapacity and ostracism because of their deformities and disabilities. It was a huge medical success.

More, it was a personally exalting experience for the young medics who staffed the ship, and a triumph of joint military operation. Scores of letters arrived in my office soon after the ship returned to our shores, asserting that the medical experience had been the most inspiring and rewarding of the writers' lives, and that the fellowship among them, regardless of which service they came from, had been heartwarming and fun. All it had taken was a little budgetary manipulation - and a multimillion-dollar ship!

Warmed and encouraged by this abundant evidence of inter-service cooperation and goodwill, and the total dismantling of traditional inter-service rivalry, I pressed on with another maneuver designed to get the services to work together. It can be called the "Joint Military Medical Command" maneuver. Brilliant in its conception, it failed to contemplate the deep-seated, implacable, interservice antagonism that exists, mainly, in the offices of the respective Surgeons General and their staffs. Unlike the young people who enthusiastically worked together on the Mercy, and free from years of ancient, traditional rivalries among older senior officers, the older generation were adamantly opposed to cooperating with each other.

From what I have learned recently, they still are, 15 years later.

Erroneously concluding from the truly splendid collaboration among the medical personnel from all the services aboard the Mercy that the time was ripe for further exploration of "jointness," I decided to try it in one of the several places in the country that literally cried out for collaboration among the military departments.

Four such places, in particular, were outstanding examples of needless duplication, senseless competition, inefficient utilization of resources and lack of communication or even rudimentary cooperation. These were Washington, D.C., San Antonio, the San Francisco Bay area, and the Delaware Valley. Each had redundant medical facilities, duplicative supply and maintenance systems, and little or no interaction. All of them, moreover, had no substantial military populations, except retirees, from which to draw patients.

We decided on San Antonio. The Army, with no troops to speak of anywhere nearby, was lobbying for a billion dollar, thousand bed hospital to replace aging Brooke Army Medical Center. Across town, the Air Force was operating a 1000-bed, recently refurbished (at $300 million) hospital with hundreds of empty beds. The University of Texas had recently built a splendid new teaching hospital in town. Two independent surveys proved the city had far more available beds than it could use, and recommended closing Brooke altogether.

The situation, we decided, was pregnant for a joint command. We decided to set one up, commanded by a 2-star Air Force physician, with a 1-star Army general as his deputy, and plans to rotate command between services. These medical generals, supported by their headquarters in Washington, were to design a system that made the best use of the best parts of the two hospitals, replace part of Brooke if necessary, combine their logistical support systems, consolidate their staffs, produce a combined budget and increase efficiency and economy of operations and training.

The newly appointed Army brigadier, soon after taking office as the deputy commander, promptly attacked the whole idea, but just carefully enough to avoid being fired. He conducted an extensive campaign of speeches and public meetings to illustrate the difficulties and obstacles he foresaw to the successful operation of the joint command.

The Air Force two-star general, now the joint commander, did nothing effective to counteract his deputy's efforts to discredit the command. After I had left office, after two years of stumbling, halting, unenthusiastic efforts to make it work, the project was abandoned.

Similar joint efforts in the Bay Area and the Delaware Valley were more successful and not as openly sabotaged as the San Antonio fiasco, at least partly because powerful officers, mostly retired Air Force, in an insurance company in San Antonio who wanted a new Brooke Medical Center to serve their new major retirement center had no interest in the other places. Following the demise of the San Antonio command, however, they too were ultimately abandoned in favor of the older, more inefficient, more expensive independent arrangements. So much for the best use of public funds.

Today, a dozen years later, the effort to get the military medical services to work more closely together continues, as does the vast, institutionalized, mindless resistance on the part of the senior members of the respective medical establishments. Today's effort arises from the need to control the costs of what was originally called the CHAMPUS program.

That program, you will recall, was designed to allow military dependents and retirees to obtain needed health care from civilian physicians and other providers of care, largely subsidized by military funds. It required that patients contribute a substantial amount of the charges, and the costs to the government skyrocketed along with the escalation of civilian medical expenditures.

In response, largely through the efforts of David Newhall, my principal deputy, Donald Moran, a consultant, and a host of others, we instituted a modified managed care program that we initially called CRI - the CHAMPUS Reform Initiative. This introduced contracted care from civilian 'preferred providers' and HMOs, and slowed down the rising costs of care but didn't wholly solve the burgeoning problems. Just as it had with the Medicare and MediCaid programs, the government vastly underestimated what was happening (and continues to happen) in health care costs, and a new system was devised. It was called TriCare.

Under this new scheme, eligible beneficiaries of military medical care have more options, and the government contracts with multiple providers in large, circumscribed geographic areas. Each region, in this system, is at least partly under the fiscal management of a "Lead Agent," a senior officer from one of the Services who is there to oversee contractors' performance and at least partially manage resources for all military medical facilities in the region, working with the installation commanders.

Giving the Lead Agent in a region of the country more control over the resources available to each hospital in his region, and closer supervision of the civilian contractors treating military beneficiaries in the area is hardly a major move toward joint operations, but it inches forward in that direction. What is astonishing is that this is taking place fully fifteen years after we started pushing for it!

As this is written, at the start of the new century, the powers that be in the Pentagon have ordered a 'pilot project' in the very region I live in, giving the local lead agent more authority over resource allocation, along with the challenge to increase productivity in the five military hospitals, see more patients in the clinics, improve patient satisfaction and help contractors to better deliver services. All without increased personnel or money! It's hard to see how this is possible, but that's the charge.

When the pilot project fails, as it surely must without substantial additional people and money, the stage will be set for major reorganization of military medicine. This could involve designation of a 'supreme' military medical commander, or a Defense Medical Agency something like the Defense Logistics Agency that is designed to consolidate and streamline all the activities of the Services' medical departments. Like the other such agencies, however, it is likely to succeed mainly in creating a new, added bureaucracy costing more money and accomplishing little of its goals.

For many years, the bean counters and political ideologues who descend on the big building with each new political administration, have included many who instinctively view the problems of military medicine and their solution in terms of "out-sourcing," or simply buying the needed services on the competitive - and therefore supposedly cheaper - open market.

These simplistic - and I would add, simple-minded - economic philosophers know little of medical economics, which is far different from other branches of that dismal science. They also do not know, or they ignore, the lessons of the past: the wild escalation of costs in the Jackson Amendment hospitals in an incredibly short period of time, or the withdrawal of all but one single bidder for the original contract to reform CHAMPUS when the other twenty or so potential bidders figured out how much was needed, and how much it would undoubtedly cost.

If, as is likely, the uniformed services' efforts to become yet more productive as their budgets and personnel are cut, and fail they surely must, and those who worship at the outsourcing altar have their way, a magnificent system unmatched in history for saving the lives and limbs of those men and women who defend this nation will first languish, then descend into ineffective chaos and end up utterly destroyed.

This will be the case no matter what form future armed conflict may take. The ponderous machinery of warfare is slow to change, and tends to reflect on battles long past, under conditions that have altered unimaginably. Just now our leaders are gingerly exploring ways to achieve greater mobility than just being able to move a single tank at a time in the largest airplanes on earth, or a single field hospital in several score such airplanes. They are also trying to figure out how best to use incredibly destructive weapons in the hands of a mere handful of men facing others, similarly equipped, facing them.

But whatever form 'modern' warfare takes, and wherever it occurs, human beings will be damaged and need immediate attention if they are to survive. Some such victims may well appear in our own cities, but more are likely in distant jungles and deserts and icy mountains. How will we get help to them? Certainly not with paid mercenary doctors - hired on the open, "competitive" market and willing to drop everything and rush off to exotic foreign climes to save lives and stamp out disease!

There is not today, nor has there ever been, even the sketchiest outline of a plan for what to do when the military health care system is dismantled. The civilian health establishment could readily care for the entire military medical beneficiary population physically present in the continental United States, but at vastly increased cost, and only so long as no terrorist sets off a single weapon of mass destruction on our shores.

That splendid establishment, however, could not - would not - be of an iota of use in a repetition of Somalia, or Kuwait, or Bosnia. And there will surely be more of those. A certain disaster looms for our 'greatest military power on earth,' so widely proclaimed, if military medicine is not healed and rescued from its present precarious state. And no one is working on that.

Nevertheless, I digress. This was intended to be a recitation of what happened to me in this long medical life, not a Jeremiad about the future.

On reflection, I find that the challenges facing me in my years in the headquarters of that 'greatest military power on earth' were really quite simple. No one thought much about weapons of mass destruction; we had only one that got much attention and that one - fission and fusion devices - was mainly dealt with by using denial. What we did think about was more conventional forms of warfare popular in the recent past: Viet Nam, Korea, Germany and Okinawa.

Even in those horrific battlegrounds we would have been, by the early 1980s, desperately hard put to care for more than a tiny fraction of the people who were certain to need massive amounts of expert medical and surgical attention. In just a few short years since our last serious meetings with hostile adversaries, our ability to deliver battlefield treatment had been allowed to erode almost to the vanishing point, while our stateside military hospitals had been expanded and improved. It was time to change direction and emphasis.

It seemed clear to me that my main effort should be to increase our medical readiness - our ability to deliver care on and near the battlefield. At every opportunity during the morning meetings with the secretary and senior staff, and during the ponderous, drawn-out summer meetings of the Defense Resources Board I made the point that, whatever our general state of readiness for armed conflict, our medical readiness was a disaster waiting to happen, and a devastating reflection on all of us who were in charge.

After doing this steadily during my first two years, solutions had to be proposed in terms that the assembled generals and admirals used and understood: personnel, training, equipment and supplies. Accordingly, I proposed expanding the numbers of combat medics - the heroic corpsmen who tended the wounded where they fell; increased annual field exercise training for all hospital-based medical people, including physicians of all specialties, nurses, technicians, even chaplains; procurement of the latest evolution of DEPMEDS - Deployable Medical Systems or field hospital units; and training of all medical personnel in their use.

All of these things were costly, but a real bargain when compared to an intercontinental - or even an air-to-air - missile, a small ship, an F-15 fighter plane, or many other "conventional" accoutrements of war. One last thing: it was my plan to pre-position the DEPMEDS and many of the supplies needed to operate and move them, including their trucks, water purification equipment, generators - everything needed to operate the thing. That, I explained, would avoid using up critically needed air transport, during emergencies, so that they could be used to transport troops, ammunition and food.

There was some urgency to all of this, mainly because of the ponderous character of federal budgeting, congressional hearings, and procurement complexities. From the time a decision is made to institute a new program such as this, it can be nearly two years before it actually starts up. In the case of the DEPMEDS, moreover, it took nearly two years from the time it was ordered (from a large assortment of equipment makers) to get it all together and packaged for deployment.

Training programs could be set up or enlarged a little faster, but not very much. They too required new equipment, sometimes new locations, and the assignment and transfer of personnel to do the training. Hospital schedules had to be modified, and Reserve Forces' assignments tailored to keep the hospitals going while the staff was out in the field getting trained.

And so it was that it took nearly four years to raise our medical readiness to an acceptable level. Nearly everyone except the newest soldier- and sailor-medics had had field training, and there were medical systems deployed in Europe, Asia, and the Middle East - ready to be moved further if needed, and turned on quickly. Some have subsequently been used, and others continue to be in place where they may be needed. However warfare and armed conflict may change in the foreseeable future, these prepositioned units can prove to be priceless.

As I reflected on those long-ago days digging shell fragments out of wounded Marines lying on stretchers in hallways in Japan and running out of antiseptics, fluids, antibiotics and even bandages within hours, and treating wounded and dying troops in tents in midwinter in the mountains of Korea, it seemed to me that what I was doing in the Pentagon was far and away the most important task of my entire life as a physician. It would not have been possible without the direct, active encouragement of Caspar Weinberger and Ronald Reagan, and was worth all the effort and all the hassle. This is what my whole past life was designed, by some higher power, to prepare me to do.

Now, a decade after my departure from the Pentagon, it is hard to know with much certainty whether the progress we made in restoring the medical readiness of our forces has been sustained. What is certain, however, is that we succeeded only in improving our medics' ability to deal with the kind of warfare that may be a thing of the past. Until a clearer picture emerges of the shape and nature of future hostile encounters, the military leadership will be hard put to design a force to confront them. Until that happens, it will be impossible to design an appropriate medical support structure for the new force.

The basics, of course, remain unchanged: rapid medical intervention for the wounded, rapid removal to safe areas, ready access to sophisticated equipment and supplies required by modern medicine. Some of this our people can do quite well, but much depends on where it has to be done. Some of it will have to be done under much more difficult conditions, as when an adversary uses chemical and biological weapons.

For those situations, in spite of heroic efforts by military research people, we remain woefully unprepared. If, as seems likely, rogue nations or terrorist groups manage to inflict such weapons on even a single target in the United States, the damage may be unimaginable. We have as yet no simple, sure ways even to identify the agents that might have been used. We have no installations or even plans for them in the myriad locations where they might be needed, for the decontamination of large numbers of poisoned or infected people to keep them from inadvertently poisoning or infecting those who would help them.

If those charged with defending the nation are devoting serious thought and effort to these issues, I never heard them discussed in the Pentagon, and I doubt that has changed. It may well be that until something really bad happens, that will continue to be true. Perhaps the security of the nation is not as fragile as I suspect it may be. However, we continue to be bogged down in the strategic and tactical thinking of centuries past, wars long over, and systems that are obsolete.

This is not to say that working in the Pentagon, focal point of the greatest military power in the history of mankind, was a dark and dismal struggle solely for power, conducted largely by Dr. Strangelove types each pursuing individual agendas and pet projects and self-aggrandizement. Quite the contrary. My six years in the building exposed me to a host of truly fine Americans, acutely conscious of their responsibilities and duties to protect and defend this magnificent nation. I probably came as close or closer than anyone on the senior staff to being seen as a single-minded zealot, if not a fanatic, pursuing my own parochial interests in medicine, but I think I avoided that, however narrowly.

And I prevailed in some things, while failing substantially in others. Hopefully, we awakened in at least some of the warfighters a new awareness of the critical importance of medical care for our young troops, which all readily subscribed to but few understood. There has been some sliding back from this. While troop strength was being drastically reduced during the Clinton years, demands on those who remained increased. Health care was degraded by removing it a step further below the level of the Secretary of Defense, placing it under the control of a decent but incompetent woman with no appropriate background or skills and who reported to a bureaucrat equally unqualified to make medical system decisions.

Thus it was that the huge, complex, costly medical program of the US armed forces was emasculated, shorn of any real voice in the deliberations of the Defense Resources Board during the summer competitions for budget, and rendered unable to access the ultimate decision-makers. Well-meaning bureaucrats and accountants, clinging to the economic misperceptions and myths about the way medicine works, have hollowed out the health care system far more than the overall armed forces strength reduction justifies.

Now they call, in their arrogant naiveté and ignorance, for "increased productivity" and lowered costs in an already undermanned and underfunded overstressed system that is under steadily increasing demands.

Who, you ask, are "they?" Who is doing this? It is not, I am certain, the senior Army, Navy, Air Force and Marine officers, "busting their butts," as they say in more private moments, to do their respective jobs, keep their troops trained, decently housed, well led, superbly armed and motivated to 're-up,' to stay the course, stay on their underpaid duty, and cling to the idea that their obscure and unfamiliar missions somehow serve the interests of this great nation, and of security and peace in the world.

The Pentagon probably contains the world's largest collection of war-haters and peace-mongers in existence. Their opposition to war as an instrument of national political policy is a direct correlate of their exposure to it. Over my years in the building I was forcefully impressed with the strength of character and sense of honor and dedication evident in the splendid senior military leaders I encountered there. Exceptions were rare. With some I disagreed and even fought, but never did I encounter even one whose motives were questionable or petty. Some had less senior advisors and lieutenants who were more impulsive or biased or self-seeking, but such people rarely lasted long and never prevailed.

Some of these senior people are, inevitably, simply wrong in their judgments and opinions as to how best to perform their duties and accomplish their missions. While I have been critical of most of the Surgeons General for their lack of vision and their parochialism, for example, and blame them for much of what ails the military health system because they have failed to grasp how it needed to come together and jointly meet the challenges of modern warfare, modern bureaucracy, and even modern medical technology in some cases, my criticism has not been of their personal character.

Each has been, on careful examination, a man dedicated to his twin professions in the military and in medicine. Each one followed a course he truly believed was in the best interests of those he served, and served with. Most were not skilled at picking lieutenants, and were sometimes unable to distinguish good from bad advice. Few of them saw themselves as leaders, and even fewer were willing to take strong stands or rock the boat.

A big part of the problem, even at high levels in the Pentagon, has to do with the distinction between 'staff' and 'line.' Staff officers advise commanders. The Surgeon General in each service is the senior staff advisor for medical affairs to the commander in chief of that service. Thus it was, early on in my years there, that when I confronted the Navy Surgeon General about a horrifying medical situation involving a cardiac surgeon at the National Naval Medical Center that had come to the President's attention, and said to him that he had a serious problem to deal with, he said to me, "I don't have a problem, Sir. I'm not in command of anything. Navy Med-Com does that."

Dumbstruck, I told him that since he was the senior doctor in the entire US Navy, it was indeed his problem, along with everything else that Navy medicine did or failed to do. This officer was a truly fine, totally loyal, by-the-book naval officer. He was trained in more than one specialty in medicine. He sailed aboard the first submarine to transit the North Pole beneath the ice. He had reached the most exalted position in his corps in the Navy, yet he so blindly subscribed to the 'line-staff' dichotomy that he truly believed he had no operational responsibility, except to give medical advice to the Chief of Naval Operations.

That, I found, was not unusual at all. In some ways it is a cop-out, the common "It's not my job - not my problem - not my responsibility" idea that let men die in POW huts in North Korea and a young woman be killed while screaming for help on a public street in New York. Nevertheless, coupled with the parochialism of each service's medical establishment and the interservice competition for funds, it has served to isolate each one from the others and rendered impossible any meaningful collaboration to better use resources and people to serve the patient population. Further, it prevents forming any effective, joint resistance to the erosive schemes of high-level technicians and entrepreneurs within and outside the Pentagon who would solve medical problems they don't understand with 'management' measures that will not work.

After more than six years in 'the building,' I felt some ebbing of my enthusiasm to rebuild and rectify the magnificent system I had been assigned to put in order. There were some late-term successes. I had started a nationwide recruiting drive to entice civilian physicians and nurses into the Reserve elements of each service. That was so successful that even my own dear wife, unbeknownst to me, signed up, to become the first junior grade lieutenant in the Navy to be sworn in the presence of the Secretary of Defense, the Surgeons General, and the respective Chiefs of Military Nursing. And was later called up for full-time active duty during Desert Storm.

Another successful battle was waged, at least for a time, to prevent a psychologist on one of the Senator's staff, from pushing through a law giving non-physician psychologists the right to prescribe controlled drugs, which they were not trained to do.

The presidential elections brought a new, good man, George Bush. He used me to help him decide about a new White House physician, and while we were well acquainted and quite friendly, it was clear I would have nothing like my relationship with Ronald Reagan, with his successor. Or with the new Secretary of Defense, Dick Cheney, who seemed little interested in such trivial issues as health care. Thus when his staffers let it be known that he wanted 'his own team' as his assistants, I took the hint and put in for my retirement.

Inasmuch as my entire life, from boarding school to entering California on a freight train as a homeless person, through college and the 'initiation process' that was medical education in the 1940s, the years in the Navy and Marine Corps and the Army, the POW studies, the revolution in psychiatry, the revelations about alcoholism, and the top medical job in California, had all, in highly specific-seeming ways, been a preparation for my six years in the Pentagon, I found myself wishing that some great, profound and useful truths might have been revealed to me that I could share with you.

But I find that I cannot. Suffice it to say that it has been a long and wondrous journey through a time of miracles, during which I have been the beneficiary of incredible good fortune, countless gifts of the love and companionship of hosts of people, a chance to see and know some of the world's leaders, and opportunities to do some actual good - even, possibly to make a little difference, to pay back, at least partially, the good fortune of having been born in this place, at this time. Rejoice with me.

Brainwashing, Drunks & Madness

Postscript

In spite of the length of this thing, I have, as you will agree, left out a lot. Some day, if I last long enough, I shall try to chronicle the really most important things about a life in the twentieth century, all of which I have neglected, deliberately, in this tale. Those things have to do with people.

The reason I have neglected them is my own sense of inadequacy to do them the justice they deserve. An endless procession of people, from the least to the most mighty, have had an influence on what I have done, and what I have failed to do. Along with them and over it all has hovered a Higher Power of some sort, that has seen fit to bestow great good fortunes, not of my doing, that often arrived disguised as one or another of the people in that procession. Some in that 'innumerable caravan' bear far more credit for my successes and victories, whatever they may be, than do I, but I alone get the credit for failures and defeats. They have all been self-imposed.

Also I have left out my post-*gloria mundi* days in the National Academy of Sciences' Institute of Medicine trying to lead an International Forum on AIDS Research to produce something of value, and my exploration of the great Satan of 'managed care' until my coronaries put a stop to that, or the year in Sacramento trying to direct the languishing Department of Mental Health.

And then there is actual (finally!) retirement in our glorious Pacific Northwest, the final great gift of that beneficent Higher Power. It is such a blessing, now that we have actual friends that we see regularly - unique for us - that I worry I have more payback due. But you must tire of my story-telling.

Brainwashing, Drunks & Madness

Printed in the United States
43476LVS00002B/4-9